ABC-CLIO LITERARY COMPANION

Encyclopedia of
Satirical
Literature

ABC-CLIO LITERARY COMPANION

Encyclopedia of
Satirical
Literature

Mary Ellen Snodgrass

ABC-CLIO
Santa Barbara, California
Denver, Colorado
Oxford, England

Library of Congress Cataloging-in-Publication Data

Snodgrass, Mary Ellen
    Encyclopedia of satirical literature   /   Mary Ellen Snodgrass.
       p.   cm.—(ABC-CLIO literary companion)
    Includes bibliographical references and index.
     1. Satire—Encyclopedias.   2. Satire—History and criticism.
  I. Title.   II. Series
  PN6149.S2S56   1996   809.7′003—dc21   96-47329

ISBN 0-87436-856-1 (alk. paper)

02 01 00 99 98 97 96   10 9 8 7 6 5 4 3 2 1

ABC-CLIO, Inc.
130 Cremona Drive, P.O. Box 1911
Santa Barbara, California 93116-1911

This book is printed on acid-free paper ∞.
Manufactured in the United States of America

Sigh no more, ladies, sigh no more,
Men were deceivers ever,
One foot in sea and one on shore,
To one thing constant never.
Then sigh not so, but let them go,
And be you blithe and bonny,
Converting all your sounds of woe
Into Hey nonny, nonny.

(Much Ado about Nothing, II, iii, 61-68)

CONTENTS

PREFACE

The plan of the *Encyclopedia of Satirical Literature* is to present essential rhetorical devices and modes, literary periods, writers, titles, and characters as a method of defining and exemplifying the vast trove of literature that depends on satire for its strength and uniqueness. Entries listed alphabetically provide pronunciations of difficult terms, textual commentary, definitions, and generous citations. In cases where the original language offers verisimilitude of rhythm and alliteration, e.g., in Juvenal's epigrams, Rabelais's doggerel, Molière's *Tartuffe*, and Colette's *Gigi*, the lines appear above English translations. Under some rhetorical devices, miniature time lines systematize the development of a method, for instance, major examples of burlesque or parody; under other devices, key models demonstrate individual styles, as with the varied examples of repartee, from the familiar *Life with Father*, by Howard Lindsay and Russell Crouse, to the lesser-known story "My Melancholy Face," by Heinrich Böll. Significant to the motivation of the satirist are extensive biographies of important contributors to the genre:

- the prejudice that forced poet and dramatist John Dryden to pay double taxes after he converted from Anglicanism to Catholicism

- the political intrigue that cost playwright and spy Aphra Behn a stint in debtor's prison and years of penury

- the religious maelstrom that spun Jonathan Swift into scatological spewings and madness

- the bitter recriminations of Oscar Wilde that dried up his wit and replaced it with melancholy, regret, and outrage

- the curiosity about black history and feminism that drove Terry McMillan to study human nature and replicate her findings in the masterpiece novel *Waiting to Exhale*.

Beneath each entry are cross-references, primary sources, and bibliography offering additional commentary, for example, articles and analysis of camp humor and rap, sources of Restoration plays, or a return to the essay on satire as a refresher on the encyclopedia's focus.

PREFACE

As an adjunct to reading, lesson planning, research, or self-directed study of satire as a genre or of individual periods, titles, and authors, this volume appends self-explanatory study aids:

- a timeline of satire, naming in chronological order works dating from the eighth century B.C. to current times and demonstrating periods dominated by the giants of satire, for example, Terence, Molière, John Dryden, and John Gay

- a listing of primary sources either in single issue or compendia that feature footnotes, commentary, and glossary, for instance, *The Riverside Shakespeare, The Complete Oscar Wilde,* and *The Florence King Reader*

- a bibliography of overviews, collections, compendia, commentary, and other reference works, especially studies of literary terms, e.g., Hugh Holman and William Harmon's *A Handbook to Literature,* Ron Padgett's *The Teachers and Writers Handbook of Poetic Terms,* and Laurie Henry's *The Fiction Dictionary*

- a comprehensive index of titles, authors, periods, literary styles and devices, characters, themes, and settings, e.g., *Brighton Beach Memoirs,* Beth Henley, Restoration drama, kabuki, mock-heroic, Mother Bunches, homosexuality, Becky Sharp, and Tralfamadore

The flow of information and contrasting modes of satire turns up surprising versions of classic works, insights into literary careers, and an impetus to multicultural readings, as with China's classic novel *The Dream of the Red Chamber,* Thomas Berger's *Little Big Man,* and Amy Tan's *The Hundred Secret Senses.* A casual perusal of the *Encyclopedia of Satire* offers the researcher, reader, writer, and teacher a compelling reason to sample, contemplate, and chuckle at the vast store of human effort that has gone into the creation of satire.

ACKNOWLEDGMENTS

Gary Carey
writer and editor
Lincoln, Nebraska

Burl McCuiston
Lenoir-Rhyne College Library
Hickory, North Carolina

Lynne Bolick Reid
Catawba County Library
Newton, North Carolina

Wanda Rozzelle
Catawba County Library
Newton, North Carolina

Frances Hilton
Chapter One Books
Hickory, North Carolina

Cindy Sears
Elbert Ivey Library
Hickory, North Carolina

Laura Kelleher
Elbert Ivey Library
Hickory, North Carolina

Jeanne Wells
rare book researcher
Powell's Books
Portland, Oregon

Special thanks go to my secretary, Andrea Pittman, for sorting mail, filing, and juggling *Books in Print*, reference works, telephone calls, faxes, and photocopiers with lights a-flash.

INTRODUCTION

Satire is a victim of bad press. Casual observers equate the term with ill-tempered outbursts, petty carping, discourteous reviews, and snide remarks. When analysts apply satire's traits and aims to literary history, they tend to ignore a wealth of possibilities and mention a handful of touchstones in a limited number of eras:

- Aristophanes and Plautus's comedies from ancient Greece and Republican Rome

- epigrams derived from Juvenal and Martial and Horace's odes from the Roman Civil War and incipient Empire

- stock figures and situations from the *commedia dell'arte*

- plays of Molière and the Restoration stage

- *The Tatler* and *The Spectator,* forerunners of the modern newspaper

- Jonathan Swift's *Gulliver's Travels* and "A Modest Proposal"

- George Orwell's *Animal Farm*

- Mark Twain's one-liners

- Dorothy Parker's putdowns

- Neil Simon's Broadway hits

This meager litany circumscribes satire in a whittled-down arena and proposes an incomplete overview by accepting too narrow a set of expectations. In so confined a space, there exists no room for most women, nonwhites, biographers, creators of children's literature, or modern poets, dramatists, screenwriters, and fiction writers, particularly Marsha Norman, Calder Willingham, Marge Piercy, T. Coraghessan Boyle, Florence King, Hugh Leonard, and Margaret Atwood.

Beyond this narrow point of reference lies a truth that deserves a champion: satire thrives throughout the humanities as a natural outgrowth of the human need to examine self and milieu in a perpetual act of betterment. At the core of satire's relegation to so few titles and genres lies the failure of critics to

INTRODUCTION

differentiate between satire as a genre and incidental satire as a useful literary device and a ubiquitous glimmer or shading in every form of expression. In art, dance, film, sermon, comic monologue, editorial, review, television series, joke, and song, the ridicule of substandard morals, shaky ethics, questionable relationships, and mere foolery is nonstop. The universality of satire lauds enterprising creativity and fosters a genuine interest in worldly, mundane matters, from the ostentatious neighbor to the scheming con artist and inept political candidate.

There can be no Richter scale for satire, for the term stretches beyond a two-dimensional printout that would rank it by decibels, from mild titters to cacophonous denunciation. However hard they are shoved into line, Catullus's poems and the *Spectator* papers refuse to stand in queue on a continuum listing *Pride and Prejudice*, Huck Finn, Uncle Remus stories, Ogden Nash's ditties, *A Visit to a Small Planet*, and the political columns of Molly Ivins and Ellen Goodman. Comparatives pall in an unlikely match-up of Virginia Hamilton's *The People Could Fly* with Gilbert and Sullivan's *The Pirates of Penzance* or Charles Dickens's Mr. Micawber with Pearl Bailey's or Dick Gregory's autobiographical self-analysis. Studies of Geoffrey Chaucer's command of satire bear little resemblance to a critique of theater of the absurd, "Mad Dogs and Englishmen," or tellings of Inuit trickster lore and stories of Old Man Coyote. However the reader evaluates satire, each work must stand apart from rigid fences that limit myriad invitations to muse on the human situation.

Significant to a study of satire is an understanding of related terms that define style and tone and isolate modes of diction, purpose, and methods. Within the wide shelf of pure satire reside variants, nuances, and contributing factors:

- Fabliau, the moralistic folk tale common to the Middle Ages and developed in Boccaccio's *Decameron* and Geoffrey Chaucer's *Canterbury Tales.*

- Epigram covers an expanse of brief outtakes that capture in little the gist of wit or comedy, for example, the clever wording of a line from Benjamin Franklin's *Poor Richard's Almanack.*

- Invective names the harsh side of satire that escapes the bounds of laughter for correction's sake, a nasty habit in set-tos between robot and scientist in Karel Capek's *R.U.R.*

- Whimsy, the unpredictable rabbit from the hat, designates a literary mode that allows the imagination to wander and find meaning in a young girl scamping down a hole to Wonderland or in Candide's journey to Eldorado, where gemstones dot the footpath.

- Bathos defines an overflow of emotion that carries sympathy to extremes, producing derision for the author's ineptness and lack of control, a failing in Edwin Arlington Robinson's poem "Mr. Flood's Party."

- The black humor that engulfs repartee between townspeople and Claire in Friedrich Dürrenmatt's *The Visit* and fuels their murder of a citizen to propitiate a vengeful benefactor.

INTRODUCTION

Tucked in near satire proper is the ubiquitous writer's tool kit compartmentalized to accommodate pun, wit, burlesque, mock epic, beast lore, and parody. Caricature, a *sine qua non* of satire, populates literary scenarios with Punch and Judy, Don Quixote and squire Sancho Panza, Sir Fopling Flutter, Yahoos and Houyhnhnms, Gargantua, Dame and Rip Van Winkle, Br'er Rabbit, Yum-Yum, Hawkeye Pierce—a spectrum of scapegraces and *picaros* who bring to life the satirist's plaint. Scripture, mystery plays, *commedia dell'arte,* adventure lore, and didactic exempla pour into the canon of humor a wealth of misers, old maids, chatterers, fashion plates, politicians, klutzes, straying spouses, and self-appointed pedants. Without these stock types and their ever-fresh redressings, satire would wither from lack of the ichor that assures its immortality.

Because satire sprouts a branch on *Homo sapiens's* family tree, the history of satire is as rich as the events of the day. During eras of political distress—Athens after the Peloponnesian War, Rome under the dementia and excesses of its worst emperors, England during the abstemious Puritan Commonwealth, the United States in the Vietnam War era—satire punches up straightforward complaint with verbal barbs and brickbats:

- Aristophanes makes his case against political chicanery by dressing up actors in bird suits and having them build a rampart around a perfect sky-world

- Seneca spoofs defied emperors in a ceremony known as pumpkinification

- George Bernard Shaw tweaks the *nouveau riche* by turning the mythic Pygmalion into a British voice coach who transforms a violet seller into a lady

- Joseph Heller vivifies battlefield carnage by reflecting on his career as a bombardier during World War II, played out in the shenanigans of Aarfy, Major Major, and Captain John Yossarian.

Public life for these and other truth-tellers has varied to extremes: in recompense for their candor, Lucan was forced to commit suicide, Alexander Pope fattened his purse, Jane Austen became a cult figure, H. L. Mencken made enemies, Sinclair Lewis became the first American to win a Nobel Prize for literature, and Neil Simon had a theater named after him. In some instances, the work outshines the creator. A handful of people recognize Richard Hooker as the impetus to the MASH frenzy in film and television reruns; only a scholarly few know that Pierre Beaumarchais created Figaro, the trickster servant who prefigured the rise of the working class during the French Revolution; and movie buffs fail to connect the screen success of *The Madness of King George, Driving Miss Daisy, Torch Song Trilogy,* and *Mrs. Doubtfire* with authors Alan Bennett, Alfred Uhry, Harvey Fierstein, and Anne Fine.

Whether the writer is toasted, defamed, or unacknowledged, literature achieves some of its finest moments in the writings of the satirist. Without the medium that provokes laughter at human foibles, there would be no *Carmina*

Burana, "Miller's Tale," *Much Ado about Nothing*, *Barber of Seville*, *Threepenny Opera*, "The Open Window," limericks, *Harvey*, *Animal Farm*, *The King and I*, *Waiting for Godot*, *Gimpel the Fool*, *Catch-22*, *Grendel*, or *A Funny Thing Happened on the Way to the Forum*. The absence or suppression of satire—whether subtle or overpowering, novel-length or a one-liner—is unimaginable. In the mirror of witty or cutting lines, humankind laughs at others and overtly or covertly winces or gasps at itself. The sustaining force of satire keeps readers honest and forces them to accept reality at the same time that it accommodates the urge for perfection. The self-revelation of satire's jest sugar-coats the necessary pill that heals—at least for the moment—the habits, animosities, and prejudices that keep individuals earthbound among contemporaries who are just as bad or worse.

Encyclopedia of
Satirical
Literature

ADDISON, JOSEPH

One of England's most revered essayists, Joseph Addison, a man of impeccable character and a friend and colleague of Richard Steele, allied himself with the coffeehouse wits and joined in the publication of *The Tatler* and *The Spectator*, harmlessly satiric journals and forerunners of the modern newspaper. Addison wrote 42 out of 271 issues of *The Tatler*; for the second publication, he composed nearly half of the 555 papers, often attacking the unprincipled crudeness of the Restoration age and extolling courtesy, humanism, and a return to reason in matters of public behavior, wooing, and worship. His most quotable epigrams, both didactic and witty, include these:

- Reading is to the mind what exercise is to the body.

- 'Tis pride, rank pride, and haughtiness of soul;
  I think the Romans call it stoicism.

- Beauty soon grows familiar to the lover,
  Fades in his eyes, and palls upon the sense.

- I shall endeavor to enliven morality with wit,
  and to temper wit with morality.

- There is not a more unhappy being than a superannuated idol.

- Our disputants put me in mind of the skuttle fish, that when
  he is unable to extricate himself, blackens all the water about
  him, till he becomes invisible.

- The fraternity of the henpecked.

In his estimation of an appropriate eulogy, Addison wrote, "I shall be ambitious to have it said of me, that I have brought philosophy out of closets and libraries, schools and colleges, to dwell in clubs and assemblies, at tea-tables and coffeehouses."

Born May 1, 1672, in Milston, Wiltshire, the eldest son of Jane Gulston and Archdeacon Lancelot Addison (a rector, political writer, and dean of Lichfield), Joseph Addison studied at Amesbury, Salisbury, and Lichfield Grammar School before enrolling at Charterhouse in London. At Queen's College, Oxford, he made a fortuitous alliance with friend and colleague Richard Steele, with whom he collaborated in journalistic experimentation. For distinguished scholarship in the classics, Addison was made fellow at Magdalen College, where he taught for a decade in preparation for a career as scholar and lecturer. He translated the fourth book of Virgil's *Georgics* and the second book of Ovid's *Metamorphoses*, and he published *An Account of the Greatest English Poets* (1693), an unassuming overview of the age of Shakespeare.

Opinions vary as to why Addison shifted horizons to government in the next period of his life. Most observers incline to believe that he met with good fortune, but others insist that he anticipated political patronage offered a bright future. For whatever reason, he set out on a four-year European tour, in the course of which he met major literary figures and published *A Poem to His Majesty* (1695), which caught the attention of the staff of William III. Tastefully understated in mannerisms and dress, Addison cut an appropriately decorous figure among some of the Restoration era's most flamboyant fops, dandies, and wits.

The choice to create complimentary verse in exchange for a haphazard living proved difficult for a shy man like Addison. As an ambassador for the crown, he maintained a busy schedule of foreign correspondence and lived on a pension of £500 until 1702, when William III's death ended Addison's ties with men of influence. In an era of sparkling conversation, he was terrified of public speaking and chose private composition as a means of drawing attention to his brilliance. Thus he composed *The Campaign* (1704), an insipid but popular verse paean to the Duke of Marlborough's heroism at the Battle of Blenheim. That same year, he acquired a position as tax collector for the excise commission, which he maintained until his death on June 17, 1719. For months, he lived and collaborated with Steele on his comedy *The Tender Husband* (1705). Addison's attempt to write opera led to the fiasco of *Rosamond*, a dismal Drury Lane offering that closed on March 7, 1707, its third night.

Election to Parliament from Lostwithiel, Cornwall, in 1708 centered Addison's life in London. As chief secretary to Lord Wharton, he lived in Dublin from 1709 to 1710 and achieved a meaningful role in establishing British policy toward the Irish. Simultaneously, he wrote for *The Tatler* on sojourns in London, where he fraternized with his literary cronies at the Kit Kat Club and caught up on events of the day. Again turned out of office, Addison joined Steele in restructuring their second journal, *The Spectator*, which they inaugurated March 1, 1711, and kept in circulation until December 6, 1712. The use of masked identities—Sir Roger de Coverley, Mr. Spectator, Captain Sentry, Sir Andrew Freeport, Will Honeycomb—enlivened the varied fare, which ranged from local tittle-tattle to serious criticism, delighting 3,000 subscribers daily Monday through Saturday. In a period of intense Toryism, the pro-Whig sentiment of Addison's Senecan tragedy, *Cato* (1713), brought him instant fame and the release of his work in French, Italian, and Latin.

Because of nettlesome disputes and bad choices, Addison's last years drastically altered his contentment. *The Drummer* (1715), his first and only prose comedy, failed because it deviated from his metier of periodical essays and

English essayist Joseph Addison, 1672–1792

gentle Horatian satire. He revived his journalistic career with *The Freeholder,* a Whig biweekly that ran for 55 issues, but the next year brought additional disappointments: advancing invalidism from asthma and congestive heart disease and his dismal marriage to Charlotte, Countess of Warwick, with whom he retired to Holland House, Kensington, to rear their daughter, Charlotte. An unexpected disagreement with Steele over restrictions on the peerage ended a lifelong friendship. Eulogized by John Dryden and Jonathan Swift, the literary lions of the era, Addison was interred in Westminster Abbey. His popularity spread to America and influenced Washington Irving's creation of *Salmagundi,* a journal imitative of *The Spectator.* A critique by Samuel Johnson has become Addison's lasting memorial: "Whoever write to attain an English style, familiar but not coarse, and elegant but not ostentatious, must give his days and nights to the volumes of Addison." (Addison 1952, 1973; Baugh 1948; Drabble 1985; Hornstein 1973; Inglis 1952; Magill 1958; McArthur 1992; Sheedy 1972)

See also "The Coquette's Heart"; didacticism; Dryden, John; epigram; Irving, Washington; Restoration drama; satire; *The Spectator;* Steele, Sir Richard; Swift, Jonathan; *The Tatler.*

ADELPHI

Terence's *Adelphi (The Brothers),* a treasure of controlled comic irony written for the funeral games honoring the famed consul Lucius Aemilius Paulus, represents the last plateau of the playwright's evolution as a writer and adapter of Greek drama. Produced in 160 B.C. only months before Terence died suddenly on a journey to Greece, the play pays homage to Menander, the father of Greece's new comedy. Like the "well-made play" of Restoration England, the work demonstrates the playwright's dedication to tight plot construction, focused dialogue, and mature theme development. Terence's prologue announces its own innovation:

> Do not expect a summary of the plot:
> The old men who appear first will begin
> To clarify the action, and the rest
> Moves with the play. Keeping an open mind,
> You'll give the poet further heart for writing.

Following this enigmatic introit, the play opens in the two-dimensional style Terence inherited from the Greek stage—directly on a street in Athens where the homes of Sostrata and the aged Micio adjoin. Micio frets that his adopted nephew, Aeschinus, has been out all night without informing his uncle. Micio boasts of his liberal child-rearing philosophy:

> I support him, don't often punish, try not to nag,
> And as a result, while others are pulling the wool
> Over their fathers' eyes, he's honest with me.
> That's simply the way that I've managed to bring him up.

By comparison, Demea, Micio's brother, wields a stronger hand with Aeschinus's brother Ctesipho and slips in a dig at Micio's lenience. Unshaken in his trust in Aeschinus, Micio maintains that honesty bolsters the family.

Terence makes the most of two pairs of brothers, a generation apart, forming two sets of literary foils. Uncle Demea, who is pleased to prove Micio wrong, broadcasts catastrophic news: Aeschinus has turned delinquent. After breaking and entering, he beat a man and kidnapped his daughter. Meanwhile, the paragon Ctesipho labors diligently in the country. Micio conceals alarm while muttering a frenzied soliloquy:

> He's fallen in love with a dozen prostitutes
> And paid them well, then, tired of them all,
> Claimed he was all for settling down to marriage.
> That made me hopeful that his blood was cooling;
> Fine, I thought, fine!—Till it all began again.
> I need the facts.

The pace quickens. While Micio shuffles toward the forum, Aeschinus and a floozy enter from the other direction. A grousing pimp starts a shoving match; Aeschinus wins. Before the pimp can grab the girl, Aeschinus hides her in Micio's house. A revelation vindicates Micio: Ctesipho, a mealy-mouthed goody-goody, congratulates Aeschinus for rescuing the girl, whom Ctesipho loves. He acknowledges that Aeschinus has deliberately assumed both the blame and ignominy. Aeschinus rushes away to pay off Sannio, the slave seller; Ctesipho hurries to comfort his girl. A bit of dramatic irony: the audience knows more than the older brothers, who haven't gotten to the bottom of their quandary or learned that each misreads the parenthood of the other.

The playwright produces a fair-weather friend, Sostrata, the plot complication, who clucks over Aeschinus's naughtiness. Gradually, she reveals her gripe with his embarrassing escapade: he has jeopardized his engagement with her daughter. Demea returns and confers with Syrus, Aeschinus's manservant, who pretends to flatter the old man for rearing Ctesipho. Hegio, the stereotypical Roman meddler, commiserates with the family's upheaval. He adds a choice tidbit—Pamphila is about to give birth to Aeschinus's child. Demea can't wait to gloat and dashes off to regale Micio with more bad news. To prolong the trip, Syrus uses an age-old stage ploy, the comic patter of indecipherable directions:

Syrus:	You know the colonnade by the butcher's?
Demea:	Yes.
Syrus:	Go past that up the street until you find
	The hill in front of you; go down that; then
	There's a chapel on this side, and next to it an alley.
Demea:	Which side of the street?
Syrus:	The one with the big wild fig tree.
Demea:	I know.
Syrus:	Go down there.
Demea:	That's a dead-end.
Syrus:	You're right.

The directions continue—go past, turn, straight, right, across from the mill. With Demea out of the way, Syrus concentrates on his usual aim—a pleasant dinner and quiet drink.

While Micio gathers information about the new wrinkle in the family scandal, Aeschinus paces and talks to himself. The climactic moment, built up with Terence's skill at suspense, brings father and son together. After a bit of dishonest badinage, Aeschinus weeps. Micio, moved by his son's emotion, admits that he knows all and that, whatever happens, Aeschinus deserves his father's love. He promises that Aeschinus may marry his girl. Demea, fatigued from following Syrus's bogus directions, imposes his self-applause on the tender scene:

> To lead a life like that—immoral! mad!
> Bride with no dowry, lute-girl settled in;
> Household he can't afford; son spoiled past saving;
> Father a fool.

Syrus, by now drunk to the gills, sways into view. The game is up when the truth reaches Demea that Aeschinus stole the girl to please his lustful brother.

The falling action comes down with a thump. Micio at last has a chance to needle his sneering brother. Because of his innate courtesy, he handles the situation with tact. In the focal speech, Demea marvels that the turn of events has shaken his faith in himself and his philosophy of child-rearing. In graceful Latin, he contends with self:

> Numquam ita quisquam bene subducta ratione ad vitam fuit
> quin res, aetas, usus semper aliquid adportet novi, aliquid
> moneat: ut illa quae te scisse credas nescias, et quae tibi
> putaris prima, in experiundo ut repudies.
> [No one ever has life all planned out; indeed, circumstance,
> age, custom—there's always something new to contend with.
> Be warned that those things you're convinced are clear are
> unknown and, through experience, what you originally thought
> you later discard.]

The play ends with Terence's characteristic generosity—Demea's plans for an immediate wedding. In his joy that the matter can be settled amicably and scandal avoided, the tough-mouthed Micio lets himself be talked into marrying the midwife and into manumitting Syrus and his wife. The conclusion, a model of Terence's departure from Plautus's raucous, countrified horseplay, demonstrates the gentrification of the Roman comedy and his desire for less slapstick and more realism. (Feder 1986; Hadas 1954; Hammond and Scullard 1992; Hornstein 1973; Howatson 1989; Mantinband 1956; Plautus 1900; Radice 1973; Terence 1910, 1974)

See also comedy; irony; Menander; Plautus; slapstick; Terence.

THE ADVENTURES OF HUCKLEBERRY FINN

The touchstone novel that freed U.S. writers from the tyranny of British literati, Mark Twain's *The Adventures of Huckleberry Finn* (1884), a universal classic in many respects, rivals his other satires for invention, humor, and vision. Laced with local color, river lore, dialect, suspense, and rich low comedy, the novel has triumphed as a children's adventure tale and as an allegory of America's pre–Civil War conscience. The central action—Huck Finn's assistance in the escape of a Missouri slave—unites boy and man in a complex relationship that is part father-son, part mentor-student. Companions in equality, the two navigate a river that separates slave and free states. A satire of uneven quality and intensity, the novel incorporates scenes that ridicule social status, public dueling, con games, funeral etiquette, and frontier justice.

Told through the experiences of 13-year-old Huck, the plot details how the abused and neglected son of the town drunk eludes his father, sets up a fake murder scene in the woods to cover his own escape, and embarks down the Mississippi River on the most flexible form of transportation available—a ramshackle raft. After holing up on Jackson Island, Huck encounters Jim, Miss Watson's slave, and decides to travel to a free state, even if aiding a runaway makes Huck a "low-down Abolitionist" and dispatches him to hell, an ominously real locale in his mind and a genuine source of worry.

A frequent ploy of Twain's satire is Huck's perpetual need to rationalize. In chapter 12, Huck indicates what he has learned from his father's larcenous example:

> Every night now I used to slip ashore toward ten o'clock at some little village, and buy ten or fifteen cents' worth of meal or bacon or other stuff to eat; and sometimes I lifted a chicken that warn't roosting comfortable, and took him along. Pap always said, take a chicken when you get a chance, because if you don't want him yourself you can easy find somebody that does, and a good deed ain't ever forgot.

By lying to himself, Huck maintains a comfortable compromise with his morals, which, counter to public belief, are alive and well throughout the process of rescuing Jim from sale "down to Orleans."

During one of Jim and Huck's frequent separations, the boy finds himself in a shooting war between feuding Arkansas families. Twain's satire of country gentility among the murderous Shepherdsons and Grangerfords places Huck in a home that contrasts Pap Finn's old cabin with a glittering display of frontier *objets d'art*—a gaudy pair of chalk parrots, a crockery dog, turkey wing fans, a basket of fake fruit, an oilcloth painted with an eagle, a coffeetable Bible and a copy of *Pilgrim's Progress,* wall hangings, and a scrapbook of sentimental verse. Huck's naiveté lends humor to his notion of an upscale home. The emphasis on respectability temporarily overlays the shoot-out that results in multiple deaths; at the end of the episode, however, grimness prevails: Huck weeps for his dead friend Buck and, abandoning the temporary alias of George Jackson, is again on the run. After enjoying a working-class meal of greens, pork, corn dodgers, cabbage, and buttermilk, he gladly parts with backwoods gentility, just as Jim delights in leaving a snake-infested swamp.

A dominant episode draws Jim and Huck into the power of the King and Duke, hucksters who would willingly turn them in for the reward. This lengthy segment displays Twain's considerable experience with riverboats and grifters fleeing the law. Together, the King and Duke have run the gamut of fraud, from phrenology and temperance revivals to teeth whitening, patent medicine, mesmerism, singing-geography school, faith healing, camp meetings, missionarying, and acting. Twain's implication that acting plays a part in all of these scams precedes the King's higgledy-piggledy pseudo-Shakespearean soliloquy that concludes:

> . . . And thus the native hue of resolution, like the poor cat i' the adage,
> Is sicklied o'er with care,
> And all the clouds that lowered o'er our housetops,
> With this regard their currents turn awry,
> And lose the name of action.
> 'Tis a consummation devoutly to be wished. But soft you, the fair Ophelia:
> Ope not thy ponderous and marble jaws,
> But get thee to a nunnery—go!

The King's rehearsal of this marvel of bastardized rhetoric precedes arrival in an unpromising Arkansas burg, where Huck leaves the raft and scouts the ragtag thoroughfare, filled with trash, loafers, a suckling hog, and the brief diversion of a dogfight.

The slack street scene turns ominous when Boggs, the local taunt, calls out Sherburn with scurrilous accusations and air-fed bluster. When Boggs returns at the appointed hour to challenge Sherburn to a gunfight, he summons up an emblem of the Old South—Colonel Sherburn cloaked in righteous outrage and perched on the end of patience. Two shots stop Boggs's tirades. Rescuers, who only moments before were absorbing the tense moments like addicts feeding on laudanum, carry Boggs to a drugstore:

> They laid him on the floor and put one large Bible under his head, and opened another one and spread it on his breast; but they tore open his shirt first, and I seen where one of the bullets went in. He made about a dozen long gasps, his breast lifting the Bible up when he drawed in his breath, and letting it down again when he breathed it out—and after that he laid still; he was dead.

In these two unrelated episodes, Huck observes violent deaths and precipitates a third event—the lynch mob that comes for Sherburn. The voice of Twain speaks through the Sherburn mask in scorn of southern vigilantism: "Because you're brave enough to tar and feather poor friendless cast-out women that come along here, did that make you think you had grit enough to lay your hands on a man?" In a nervous chatter, Huck turns tail with the others and heads for a circus that, ironically, stages mock violence as a crowd pleaser.

Huck's breaking point comes in Chapters 24–30, in which the Duke and King attempt to rob Mary Jane, Susan, and Joanna Wilks of an inheritance of $3,000 by pretending to be their uncles, Harvey and William Wilks, and by placing their inheritance with the girls' gold pieces in a straw tick. Before Huck foils the phony uncles' plot, the con men sell the land and divide the slaves, sending the mother to Orleans and her sons to Memphis. Huck, reduced to melodrama, mourns, "I can't ever get it out of my memory, the sight of them poor miserable girls and niggers hanging around each other's necks and crying." Huck's confession to Mary Jane unites them in love and trust. She promises to pray for him; he quips in a voice that recalls Twain's comments about his straitlaced wife Olivia, "Pray for me! I reckoned if she knowed me she'd take a job that was more nearer her size."

The irregularity of plot and tone indicates the author's duress during the eight-year composition of *The Adventures of Huckleberry Finn.* Twain began this sequel to *The Adventures of Tom Sawyer* (1876) immediately after finishing the first book and worked erratically while completing the autobiographical *Life on the Mississippi.* The 1991 discovery of a handwritten segment of the original manuscript resulted in a court battle over rights. When the issue was settled, a new edition cleared up errors and lapses in the initial versions. A parallel development of the story in multiple stage, cartoon, and film versions has offered viewers numerous interpretations of Twain's satire. (Budd 1983; Hoffman 1988; Kesterson 1979; Rasmussen 1995; Twain 1962a)

See also comedy; *A Connecticut Yankee in King Arthur's Court;* diatribe; didacticism; Finn, Huck; irony; Morgan, Hank; satire; Twain, Mark.

AESOP

The most accessible moral satirist of the ancient world, Aesop (ca. 620–560 B.C.), a Thracian—or possibly Lydian—slave and founder of the iambic beast fable, was honored by a statue in Athens for his miscellany of 350 satiric beast satires that lampoon the standard human failings of pride, arrogance, greed, and foolishness. According to Herodotus's *Histories* (fifth century B.C.), Aesop lived on the isle of Samos in the household of Idamon until his manumission. Legend describes his comic fables in the same mode as the clever dialect adaptations of African lore written by Joel Chandler Harris—a blend of original beast fables and collected moral stories, which Aesop frequently stripped of human characters and recast with anthropomorphic animals. In others, such as "The Old Woman and the Wine-Jar" and "The Ass and His Purchaser," humans interact with animals, often coming up short in comparison by displaying poor judgment, venality, or weak character. A pragmatic ethicist, Aesop salted these brief stories with realistic confrontations, for example, the plop of frogs into a pond in terror of approaching rabbits, and concluded each tale with a clearly stated universal moral.

Of questionable authority is the conception of Aesop the gadabout, who may have accepted a diplomatic mission from King Croesus of Lydia to Delphi. Locals are said to have hurled Aesop from the Delphian crags after plotters hid a treasured wine bowl in his luggage, then pretended to search for it and find him guilty of theft. Although no motivation exists for this savagery beyond envy of a former slave, the story gains credence by including Iadmon's grandson, who purportedly demanded payoffs in recompense for the senseless killing. Another version claims that a Delphian carried bags of gold to Samos to offer Iadmon's household because the city suffered a plague and the collective guilty conscience forced citizens to atone for the old man's murder.

At least 250 years after Aesop flourished, Demetrius of Phalereum systematized the oral canon of folklore, myths, aphorisms, trickster motifs, and animal yarns into a written manuscript. Refined into four manuscripts by freedman Gaius Julius Phaedrus (ca. A.D. 15–50) during Tiberius's reign and adapted by Valerius Babrius (second century A.D.) and by Avianus Flavius (ca. A.D. 400), the Romanized stories deviate from the original source but continue to reflect a honing of wit and a didactic intent suitable for use as a text for young children. Educated people in the Mediterranean world were familiar with Aesop's simple, personalized advice:

- Avoid complaining because there is always someone worse off than you.
- Watch out for familiarity, which breeds contempt.
- Join with others to create strength in union.
- Don't consort with evil companions.
- Don't tempt trouble: if you're only a kid, stay on the roof.
- Don't value outward appearances: fine feathers don't make fine birds.
- Pride often precedes destruction.
- Necessity is the mother of invention.
- Look before you leap.
- Expect times when the small triumph over the weak.
- Keep an eye toward the place from which you least expect danger.
- Don't try to run from adversity because changing place does not change your nature.
- Ignore tiresome yappers who bark rather than be ignored.
- Speak up when you want attention because the squeaking wheel gets noticed.
- Slow and steady wins the race.
- Don't undervalue the ordinary things that you depend on.
- Remember the goose that laid the golden eggs by holding on to a sure thing.

Legend credits Socrates with setting the raw material to meter in response to a dream in which God proposed the exercise as a means of whiling away his days in prison. Aristophanes claims that the verses were favorite dinner recitations as well as sources of allusions—the fox and the grapes, the ostentatious peacock, the foolish pup, the one-eyed doe, the proud lion—which permeated Greek comedy.

ESOPVS

Satirist Aesop, circa 620–560 B.C., created fables populated by animals. His portrait, included in *Vita et Fabulae*, a German collection of his works, was published about 1476.

Restated by Jean de La Fontaine (1621–1695), the stories ("Le Loup et le Chien," "Le Vieux Chat et la Jeune Souris," "Les Deux Pigeons" [The Wolf and the Dog, The Old Cat and the Young Mouse, The Two Pigeons]), published in 1694, retain their witty twist and their virtuous morals, which French school children still memorize. In a generous gesture of goodwill to his source, the fables of Phaedrus, La Fontaine declares himself incapable of imitating the elegance and brevity of Latin. He adds that, to compensate, "j'ai cru qu'il fallait en recompense égayer l'ouvrage plus qu'il n'a fait" [I believed that I should at least liven up the work more than he did]. (*Aesop's Fables* 1986; Feder 1986; Flaceliere 1962; Hammond and Scullard 1992; Howatson 1989; Mantinband 1956; Phaedrus 1992; Radice 1973; Snodgrass 1988)

See also epigram; Harris, Joel Chandler; mock epic; mock-heroic; Phaedrus; satire; trickster.

AFRICAN-AMERICAN SATIRE

The black writer is no stranger to satire, both as genre and incidental rhetorical device. At times black satire strains to the far negative extremes of dramatic irony, invective, didacticism, and diatribe, as revealed in the writings of Richard Wright, Frederick Douglass, Ralph Ellison, Toni Cade Bambara, Nikki Giovanni, and Toni Morrison. The reason is implicit in history: the repression of blacks through discrimination and repudiation overrides light humor and forces the harsher form to the surface. On the other end of the scale stand the capricious fiction of Terry McMillan and the autobiographies and verse of Maya Angelou, which bristle with sharp, witty darts honed to a keen point and hurled at bigotry.

Characterized by the sardonic stand-up monologues of Moms Mabley, Richard Pryor, Pearl Bailey, Whoopi Goldberg, and Bill Cosby, the humorous strand of black fiction is woven of a variety of shades and studded with rhetorical gems. Black satire suffuses the strongest fabric of cultural expression— the black musical cloak of many colors—reggae, rap, soul, R&B, spiritual, black country, and rock. In *Pearl's Kitchen* (1973), singer Pearl Bailey's lively black female voice salts her *pot au feu* with such stingers as "Hungry people cannot be good at learning or producing anything, except perhaps violence." In a lighter vein, one of her favorite live performance one-liners offers tongue-in-cheek advice on couture: "Basic black and pearls go anywhere." The blend becomes her *modus vivendi:* like the sturdiest survivor, Bailey recognizes the value of wisdom layered with humor, but lightly tipped with carbon steel.

Less a musician than a one-woman literary marvel, Angelou, a powerhouse writer, teacher, speaker, and actress, has earned stardom by packing multiple autobiographies and speeches with the widest span of satire. In *I Know Why the Caged Bird Sings* (1970), Angelou reaches the zenith of comedy by soaring over the peaks and valleys of her life's story. In a brisk dismissal of the classroom version of racial history, she snorts:

> A pyramid of flesh with the whitefolks on the bottom, as the broad base, then the Indians with their silly tomahawks and teepees and wigwams and treaties, the Negroes with their mops and recipes and cotton sacks and spirituals sticking out of their mouths.

Intuitive at an early age, she observed her grandmother, a local store owner and unusually successful entrepreneur during the Depression. In retrospect, Angelou recognized the heart-stopping fears of the black parent: "The Black woman in the South who raises son, grandsons and nephews had her heartstrings tied to a hanging noose." Angelou, who is sensitive to Momma Henderson's tenuous hold on a mercurial grandson, Bailey, Jr., honors her grandmother's guile in preserving his life during treacherous times when a black teen could be garroted and dropped in a ditch for looking at a white woman. In a darker mood, Angelou typifies the pervasive racism that made the American South into a Klan haven: "Stamps, Arkansas, was Chitlin' Switch, Georgia; Hang 'Em High, Alabama; Don't Let the Sun Set on You Here, Nigger, Mississippi; or any other name just as descriptive."

Determined not to be overwhelmed by the stereotypical black fundamentalism, with its acceptance of the status quo in hope of a race-blind heaven, Angelou directed some of her drollest passages at the church. She was unwilling to accept Momma Henderson's rigid Bible-based values system and comments on the differences in class depictions of a deity:

> I find it interesting that the meanest life, the poorest existence, is attributed to God's will, but as human beings become more affluent, as their living standard and style begin to ascend the material scale, God descends the scale of responsibility at a commensurate speed.

At times, Angelou glories in the mild sin of pulling a fast one on the white world. Headed to a real job, that is, not the make-do maid's work that black women accepted in defeat, she coolly describes her artifice:

> Sitting at a side table my mind and I wove a cat's ladder of near truths and total lies. I kept my face blank (an old art) and wrote quickly the fable of Marguerite Johnson, age 19, former companion and driver for Mrs. Annie Henderson (a White Lady) in Stamps, Arkansas.

The bold deception—on a par with her lively badinage with the receptionist—lands her the job of streetcar conductor.

The black male writers of the twentieth century have stuck closely to harsh truths and the rare glitter of humor, often directed at self for being so foolish as to expect justice in a white-dominated world. In his tortured memoirs, *Black Boy* (1937), Richard Wright relives in minute detail the insecurity, hunger, religious fanaticism, and racism of his boyhood in Mississippi. Shuttled among relatives after his father deserted the family and his mother suffered a stroke, Wright learned early the difficulty of presenting the correct face and behavior to potential white employers. In Chapter 6, he describes his inquiry about a job washing dishes, chopping wood, and scrubbing floors for a white woman. Their interview is as close as the tight-jawed narrative comes to humor:

newspaper and theater district. During the 1920s and 1930s, the hotel regularly hosted a group of ten to thirty musicians, artists, writers, newsgatherers, and critics, who decamped from Heywood Hale Broun's flat in search of more room for word games and lunch (more the former than the latter). Assembling at Tony's speakeasy by night and gathering by day in the Oak Room, then, later, at the strait-laced Round Table in the Rose Room, for celery and popovers, the "Algonks" tippled and smart-mouthed their way through Prohibition and the Depression years with therapeutic one-liners, sarcasm, puns, and in-crowd gossip. The club owed its longevity to the style-conscious dining-room manager, Frank Case, and the Algonquin Club's founders: humorists Robert Benchley and Dorothy Parker, and playwright Robert Sherwood, Pulitzer Prize-winner for *Idiot's Delight* (1936), *Abe Lincoln in Illinois* (1939), and *There Shall Be No Night* (1941). The three founders, all writers and critics for *Vanity Fair,* whose offices were located on the same street, welcomed a bright gathering of wits:

- Selwyn publicist Ruth Hale and husband Heywood Campbell Broun, a liberal columnist for the *New York Tribune*

- columnist and creator of the radio quiz show "Information Please," Franklin Pierce Adams

- banker Henry Wise Miller

- musician Jascha Heifetz

- comic Arthur "Harpo" Marx

- *New Yorker* editor, columnist for "Talk of the Town," and essayist Elwyn Brooks (E. B.) White, author of children's classics *Charlotte's Web* and *Stuart Little*

- Frank Capra, film director of *It's a Wonderful Life*

- Edmund Wilson, critic and reviewer for the *New Yorker, New Republic,* and *Vanity Fair*

- newsman George Backer

- Irving Berlin, composer of "White Christmas"

- editors Herbert Bayard Swope and Harold Ross, the latter the founder of *Vanity Fair*

- actors Alfred Lunt, Lynn Fontanne, Helen Hayes, Lady Gregory, Tallulah Bankhead, Peggy Wood, Paul Robeson, Douglas Fairbanks, and Joyce Barbour

- novelist Alice Duer Miller

- producer Crosby Gaige

- satirist and playwright Noel Coward, author of *Private Lives* and *Blithe Spirit*

- socialite Gerald Brooks

- publisher and baking heir Raoul Fleischmann

- manufacturer Paul Hyde Bonner

- essayist and anthologist Alexander "Aleck" Woollcott, who helped J. P. Marquand dramatize the Pulitzer Prize–winning novel *The Late George Apley* (1938)

- novelist and playwright Edna Ferber, who wrote the saga novel *Giant*, the romantic novel *Show Boat*, the satiric play *Dinner at Eight* (written with George S. Kaufman), and the Pulitzer Prize-winning novel *So Big* (1924)

- Marcus Cook Connelly, satirist and playwright who won a Pulitzer Prize for *The Green Pastures* (1930)

- Russel Crouse, collaborator on *Life with Father* (1930), a domestic comedy; *State of the Union*, a 1946 Pulitzer Prize winner; and a perennial stage favorite, *Arsenic and Old Lace* (1941)

- George S. Kaufman, co-author of the Pulitzer Prize–winning musical *Of Thee, I Sing* (1932) and the popular comedy *You Can't Take It with You* (1936)

On Saturday afternoons, the male club regulars reconvened after lunch in an upstairs room at the Thanatopsis Pleasure and Inside Straight Club for more jesting over poker. With women kept at a distance as handmaidens and kibitzers, the men stepped up their round of jests and illicit boozing, which sometimes lasted all weekend.

By 1927, the Algonquin Club had renamed itself the Vicious Circle. Anita Loos's *But Gentlemen Marry Brunettes* (1927) ridiculed the group as exhibitionists who

> are always trying to say something readable on purpose, like a match game of amusing tiddlywinks, or charades at one another's parties, or some laughable croquet championship in Central Park where you can draw quite a crowd with almost anything.

Adding and losing members, the wisecracking group—caricatured in a sketch by Al Hirschfeld, which hangs on the lobby wall—became a tourist attraction among readers of columnists Parker, Adams, and Benchley, whose flashy table repartee formed the nucleus of the nostalgic movie *Mrs. Parker and the Vicious Circle* (1991), starring Jennifer Jason Leigh as a whimsical, sad-mouthed Dorothy Parker. The film leans heavily on an implied platonic relationship between Benchley, a devoted family man, and Parker, who is devastated after her friend's death and never satisfied with subsequent suitors, however sexy or charming.

Legends arose from the Algonks' uncharted discourse, which sparkled with the grace and bon mots common to irony and satire, but which sometimes sank to the less elegant levels of snide invective—as in Dorothy Parker's description of Verlaine as "always chasing Rimbauds" and her response to President Calvin Coolidge's death, "How can you tell?" The group eventually separated and left New York. Parker removed to an illustrious expatriate enclave on the French Riviera and later to Hollywood, where she wrote forgettable screenplays. Two books detail the growth and behavior of the Algonquin Club: hotel manager Frank Case's *Tales of a Wayward Inn* (1938) and his daughter Margaret Case Harriman's *The Vicious Circle* (1951). In 1987, the beaux arts building, home of the East Coast's wittiest public salon, became an official landmark and is undergoing restoration. (Benchley 1940; Broun 1989, 1991; Buck 1992; Davidson 1995; Ehrlich 1982; Frewin 1986; Hart 1983; Holman 1992; Katz 1982; Keats 1970; Maggio 1992; Meade 1987; Parker 1994, 1976; Perkins 1991; Time-Life Books 1969)

See also Coward, Noel; epigram; invective; irony; Kaufman, George S.; Parker, Dorothy; pun; repartee; sarcasm; satire; *You Can't Take It with You.*

ALICE IN WONDERLAND

A complicated nonsense tale composed by Lewis Carroll as an afternoon's entertainment for three daughters of the dean of Christ Church, Oxford, *Alice in Wonderland* (1865) contains Britain's richest montage of children's verse, riddles, puns, allegory, doggerel, and satire. The dream sequence that forms the plot begins with Alice sinking into a doze about the time that a white rabbit studying a large pocket watch hurries past and plunges down a hole. The satire on time, proportion, and order follows a naively curious Alice down that same opening and into an unaccountably slow-motion tumble to a small door. To enter, Alice follows instructions on a bottle and drinks an unidentified potion without pondering the consequence. The suggestibility of children is one of Carroll's focuses as he explores Alice's immature reasoning. A major component of growing up is the perpetual search for identity, which Alice exhibits in her frequent alterations of size and her inability to recognize nature's cues to normalcy, such as gravity, proportion, and order. The pun on the name Liddell allies naturally with the story's action, which depicts Alice as alternately little and big.

Carroll sharpens the vigor of his satire by ridiculing the rote learning that passed for education in the Victorian era and defeats the development of logic in the young. Before giving an impromptu recitation, Alice comments to herself, "this was not a very good opportunity for showing off her knowledge, as there was no one to listen to her, still it was good practice to say it over." She has learned arithmetic and the difference between longitude and latitude, but she still lacks a pragmatic logic that will help her cope with the impermanent, unnatural laws of Wonderland. Understatements emphasize Carroll's black humor as Alice reminds herself that hot pokers burn if held too long, a deep cut usually bleeds, and drinking from poison "is almost certain to disagree with you, sooner or later." Typically childish in her thinking, Alice assumes that the bottle is safe to sample because it isn't marked poison.

In a scene filled with anthropomorphic characters, Carroll broadens the cast. Weeping copiously, Alice generates enough tears to flood the scene and swims alongside a mouse, duck, dodo, lory, and eaglet. On the way, toward land, she pointlessly declines in a Latinate grammar exercise, "A mouse-of a mouse-to a mouse-a mouse-O mouse." To dry the creatures, she turns the English history of William the Conqueror into a dry tale, a pun that ridicules classroom texts comprised of long, laborious words and phrases that bore children. The Dodo—a self-mocking sound Carroll associates with his own stuttering pronunciation of Dodgson—invites the others to a caucus race, a meaningless competition for which each wins a prize. The White Rabbit returns and, without justifying his command, insists that Alice bring his gloves and fan. Like all well-bred Victorian children, Alice has been brought up to obey authority without question and subjugates herself to the imperious rabbit.

An episode with a caterpillar lampoons courtesy. The Caterpillar ignores the conventions of polite conversation, asks personal questions, and, in a rude, haughty manner, orders Alice to recite a poem. She encounters the nasty-tempered Duchess, a baby who turns into a piglet, and an infinite tea party hosted by the Mad Hatter and the March Hare. A spoof on manners and logic, Carroll's tea party is one of his most successful satires. Alice, continuing to display compliance and sweetness to appease deranged creatures, observes the animals talking over the Dormouse's head, ignores uncivil remarks ("Your hair wants cutting") and attempts to understand a time frame that never leaves six o'clock. The drowsy dormouse—a pun on the Latin *dormire,* or sleep—muddles through a table recitation of "Twinkle, Twinkle Little Star," which he turns into the parody "Twinkle, Twinkle Little Bat."

The final episode finds Alice arriving by trial and error at the White Rabbit's destination—the queen's garden, where card values determine the satire: royal face cards play croquet in a garden of white roses, which are painted red by lower-class workers dressed as spades; clubs serve as honor guards; diamonds indicate courtiers; and the ten royal children are the lesser hearts. The authoritative Queen of Hearts tries to terrorize Alice by forcing her to join the game, but Alice sensibly realizes that "they're only a pack of cards," which, by lying on their faces, conceal arbitrary social stations by turning up a universal pattern on their backs. The story concludes with a melange of madness: the Mock Turtle sings his melancholy song about a bankrupt educational system, and the Knave of Hearts appears at a trial that Alice interrupts by telescoping rapidly upward into a giant size. She awakens on the green, reorients herself to the sounds around her, and returns home, where Dinah, the cat, is sure to have missed her.

Sprinkled throughout the whimsical tale are numerous morbid jokes. Illogically, as Alice falls down the hole, she attempts to place an empty marmalade jar on a shelf "for fear of killing somebody underneath" if she drops it. She congratulates herself for maintaining her control during the fall and adds,

"I shall think nothing of tumbling down stairs! How brave they'll all think me at home! Why, I wouldn't say anything about it, even if I fell off the very top of the house!" (which was very likely true).

A recitation of a shaped poem concludes with "I'll try the whole cause, and condemn you to death," a foreshadowing of the concluding life-or-death scene in the courtroom, where instant growth saves Alice from mob violence. Stooping while growing saves her from breaking her neck; a dash from the Duchess saves the child/pig from murder. Carroll's emphasis on survival implies a real psychological nightmare—that dangers to children haunt their dreams and fantasies.

The unifying element in Wonderland lies in its interpretation of sanity. Alice attempts to adjust her logic to that of animals that behave bizarrely, including the Mad Hatter, who represents a workplace hazard for hatters, who must mold felt in a solution of mercury, which causes delusional behavior. On confronting the Cheshire Cat, Alice hears her first sane commentary on Wonderland: "Oh, you can't help that . . . we're all mad here. I'm mad. You're mad." The gradual disappearance of the cat down to its grin creates an afterimage, a phenomenon that a photographer like Carroll would understand, but that Alice writes off as "curious." The connection between head and body recurs in the courtroom scene when the axe-obsessed queen demands the sentence before the court has rendered its verdict. After Alice shakes herself awake and reacquaints herself with the real world, she recounts her story to her sister, who matches sounds and stimuli with actual happenings in the meadow around them. Thus, a gentle storyteller sets his audience safely back on home turf, out of the welter of images aswirl in his obtuse, ambiguous Wonderland. (Carroll 1960, 1994; Drabble 1985; Hornstein 1973; Muir 1954)

See also allegory; black humor; Carroll, Lewis; doggerel; lampoon; limerick; parody; pun; whimsy.

 # ALLEGORY

Allegory is an art form—story, poem, song, painting, tapestry, statue, dance— that implies a meaning or set of meanings beyond its literal interpretation. With the deft creation of metaphors and symbols, allegory leads to one of two ends: to a sincere morality or didacticism or to satire. An example of the former, "Little Red Ridinghood," derives from folk tales and represents two abstractions, innocence and curiosity, both human frailties, that confront menace in the form of a wolf, symbol of the uncivilized, willful predator. The heroine— with the help of a deus ex machina, the woodsman—bests the wolf; thus the allegory depicts a triumph of good over evil. Herman Melville's earnest novella *Billy Budd* (1924) furnishes a similar example. Melville's multilayered allegory depicts the struggle of the inarticulate, unsuspecting sailor against evil, here represented by impressment, a brutal form of recruitment that forces sailors into service aboard battleships.

Things are not what they appear in the allegorical folk tale *Little Red Ridinghood.* Here, Little Red Ridinghood believes the disguised wolf to be her grandmother. Gustave Doré illustrated Charles Perrault's collection of fairy tales *Les Contes de Perrault* in 1862.

Allegory need not be ponderous or grim. A humorous version of allegory occurs in the action and names of the central characters of Saki's classic short story "The Open Window" (1930). Compact and pointed in its revelation of a devious prank, this classic tale features a creative liar named Vera Sappleton (from the Latin for "true"), who terrorizes Framton Nuttel, a neurasthenic Caspar Milquetoast. Framton abruptly flees the scene after Vera makes him believe he has seen a party of ghosts, leaving her aunt nonplussed at his unexplained departure.

A self-limiting, complicated rhetorical device, allegory is often preferred by didactic thinkers, such as the stoics and medieval Christians. To turn such abstractions as patriotism, seduction, courage, justice, selfishness, and virtue into concrete characters, the allegorist uses metaphor or personification, an embodiment of the intangible in a visual form. A method of reader control, allegory directs interpretation beyond the sphere of the work to particular aspects of history, religion, or the world at large, for example, Horace's prototypical "Ship of State" ode (first century B.C.). Medieval Christian apologists attempted to impose simplistic allegory on Virgil's *Aeneid* to render it preChristian prophecy. Their inept application provoked strong questions about overeager critical methods and motivation. As a tool of the Reformation era sermonizer or church school teacher, allegory extended symbolism to an alternate, more significant set of meanings. A notable example in British literature, John Bunyan's *Pilgrim's Progress* (1678), allegorizes the gamut of pitfalls and enticements (seduction, duplicity, and coercion) that lure the Christian soul from its heavenward goal. Bunyan presents his allegory as the arduous voyage of a journeyman (Christian), who faces nearly insurmountable physical roadblocks. Because of the duality of surface and submerged meanings, Bunyan's allegory depends on an even correspondence between the literal events of Christian's odyssey among double-dealers and brigands and their spiritual interpretation.

Derived from the Greek term for "speaking otherwise," allegory manages diction, tone, and theme, organizing meanings into a complex of denotative and connotative applications. Like the beast fable, emblem or shaped poem, exemplum, or parable, allegory fuses a primary meaning with one or more implications, often with satiric or didactic intent, to create parallelism or similitude. Thus do the resourceful rabbits of Richard Adams's *Watership Down* (1972) represent the contemplative everyman fighting off bullies, tyrants, and potential enslavers. Judicious use of figurative language permits the writer to imbue characters, actions, and settings with an overlay of abstract meanings that may derive from politics, religion, ethics, or morality. The reader has the option of focusing on the simplest concrete or denotative level—the odyssey of Richard Adams's rabbits—or of delving into subtle, quaint, or piquant criticisms of human nature, religion, government, or society as a whole.

Because of its confining superstructure, allegory has enjoyed isolated periods of popularity and success, notably in these classic works:

- *Aesop's Fables* (sixth century B.C.)
- Dante Alighieri, *Divina Commedia* (1321)
- William Langland, *Piers the Plowman* (fourteenth century)
- *Everyman* (sixteenth century)
- John Milton, *Paradise Lost* (1667)
- John Dryden's *Absalom and Achitophel* (1681)
- Joel Chandler Harris, *Uncle Remus* series (late nineteenth century)
- James Thurber, *Fables for Our Time* (1940)
- Virginia Woolf, *Between the Acts* (1941)

The best-known uses of allegory as a mode of satire are Dryden's satiric verse and George Orwell's *Animal Farm* (1945), a dystopic beast fable ridiculing the excesses of World War II dictators in the strut of pigs that totter on hind legs while grasping their frail batons in their front trotters. To parallel political purpose, Dryden's *MacFlecknoe* (1684) derides the weaknesses of Whigs caught in a plot against the English king; to justify his shift from Protestantism to Roman

Catholicism, Dryden composed *The Hind and the Panther* (1687), a detailed study of religious forces, each taking on an animal shape and set of behaviors. Jonathan Swift, often labeled as Britain's most gifted satirist, crafted similar political and religious allegories by interlacing complex strata of meaning in *A Tale of a Tub* (1704) and *Gulliver's Travels* (1726).

Not all allegory is easily interpreted in the one-for-one style of Adams, Dryden, or Dante. Lewis Carroll's *Alice in Wonderland* (1865), the classic children's fantasy novel, follows an episodic trek through Wonderland, a Disneyesque name for the perplexing landscape of Victorian England as seen through the eyes of a lost girl who lacks a clear perception of events. She even loses control of her size, which alternately mushrooms and shrinks, confusing her relationships with amusing, whimsical, sometimes terrifying animals. The satire turns dark near the end of Alice's dreamscape when she approaches the royal enclave and meets the Queen of Hearts, a virulent monarch devoid of statecraft but abundantly endowed with malice. Cowed by royal edicts to slice off heads for minute peccadilloes and slips of court etiquette, Alice and the menagerie of Wonderland assemble for the grand finale—a court trial of the Knave of Hearts and a rout that ends both tyranny and the nightmare. The code restores Alice to childhood, but not to her former innocence.

The American allegorist L. Frank Baum occupies a spot alongside Carroll as one of the most enigmatic narrators of children's lore. In 1900, Baum, a tableware salesman-turned-raconteur, produced his best-selling adventure tale, *The Wizard of Oz*, which spooled out into a long-lived series of illustrated adventures in Oz. In the initial volume, the Cowardly Lion, Tin Man, and Scarecrow—the three followers who trust heroine Dorothy to lead them to the Wizard's palace—long to trade fear, bestiality, and witlessness for courage, heart, and brains. The whimsical, episodic adventure, which is more didactic than satiric, concludes with Dorothy and her entourage looking within to reevaluate their natural abilities. (Abrams 1971; Adams 1972; Baldick 1990; Barnet, Berman, and Burto 1960; Baum 1983; Bunyan 1986; Carroll 1960; Cuddon 1976; Drabble 1985; Encarta 1994; Feinberg 1967; Gassner and Quinn 1969; Gray 1992; Hammond and Scullard 1992; Henry 1995; Holman 1980; Hornstein 1973; Howatson 1989; Lovett 1932; Mantinband 1956; McArthur 1992; Saki 1958)

See also *Alice in Wonderland*; *Animal Farm*; beast lore; Carroll, Lewis; didacticism; parody; satire; whimsy.

ANDROCLES AND THE LION

Derived from a story in Aulus Gellius's *Noctes Atticae* (*Attic Nights*) (second century A.D.), George Bernard Shaw's whimsical 1913 two-act beast tale, subtitled "A Fable Play," pretends to amuse playgoers but actually presents an astringent satire on martyrdom, cruelty, religious hypocrisy, and fanaticism. As a sideline, the play demonstrates Shaw's predilection for getting rid of internal punctuation, one of the playwright's lifetime goals. In his hefty preface,

George Bernard Shaw based his two-act play *Androcles and the Lion* on a work by Aulus Gellius, a second-century Roman writer. In the 1946 production of the play, the tailor Androcles (Ernest Truex) pulls a thorn from the lion's paw as a Christian act of faith and trust.

appended December 1915 at twice the length of the play, Shaw clarifies his affinity for Christian principles and his distaste for orthodoxy:

> Jesus certainly did not consider the overthrow of the Roman empire or the substitution of a new ecclesiastical organization for the Jewish Church or for the priesthood of the Roman gods as part of his program. He said that God was better than Mammon; but he never said that Tweedledum was better than Tweedledee.

Insisting that religious sects carry their private agendas to un-Christian lengths, the playwright claims that the divine right of kings is one example of the priestly caste wandering astray. Shaw hesitates at this point in his polemics by admitting that the British (for whom the play is written) can't differentiate among sectarian views "without bringing the empire down with a crash on their heads."

Opening on the familiar caricature of Androcles, the spindly limbed, watery-eyed, overburdened tailor, and his buxom wife Megaera, Shaw begins with a sight gag—the puny, frau-ruled husband who, in deference to social custom, lets his pampered wife travel unencumbered while he stumbles along with their packs. The bickering and complaining set a stereotypical scene of the downtrodden mate condemned to a life of placating a scold. At the first sign of the lion, Androcles, a Christian in faith and actions, offers to risk his life while "Meggy" flees. The silly infantilism of "Andy" asserts itself in his parental love for the lion, which he treats like a wounded child:

> Did um get an awful thorn into um's tootsums wootsums? Has it made um too sick to eat a nice little Christian man for um's breakfast? Oh, a nice little Christian man will get um's thorn out for um; and then um shall eat the nice Christian man and the nice Christian man's nice big tender wifey pifey.

The extended pantomime between tailor and lion ends with a rapturous waltz, to which Meggy grouses, "you havnt danced with me for years."

The play proper begins after this comic *ménage à trois.* On the outskirts of Rome, a military column marches Christian prisoners to the emperor. Shaw takes a quick poke at Christian hymns, which the Romans forbid, except for "Onward Christian Soldiers," a martial melody popularized by warriors eager to reach the Crusades. A second butt of satire is the captain's rejection of the term "persecution" to describe acts of the emperor, whom he honors as "Defender of the Faith." Rationalizing gladiatorial brutalities, the captain notes, "In throwing you to the lions he will be upholding the interests of religion in Rome. If you were to throw [the Emperor] to the lions, that would no doubt be persecution." In a further demonstration of opportunism, the captain, an officious bootlicker, cozies up to Lavinia, a comely female prisoner, and urges her to offer incense on the pagan altar "as a matter of good taste, to avoid shocking the religious convictions of your fellow citizens."

Shaw's seriocomic depiction of faith put to the test eventually encompasses the full list of dramatis personae. Contemplating his fate in the arena, Spintho keeps up a running commentary with himself, shoring up his gutless faith with the thought that "all martyrs go to heaven, no matter what they have done." To the grisly prospect of providing nourishment to the imperial menagerie the prisoners respond by choosing roles to play on the menu: olives and anchovies, fish, and roast boar, a pun on "bore" that the self-important Ferrovius, the Christian strongman, acknowledges. This sardonic overview of the Roman diet, which pushed the limits of bingeing and purging, concludes with Androcles as the mince pie and Spintho, cowardly and dragging his feet, as the emetic. Spintho whimpers, "I'm not fit to die"; ironically, he strays into an open hallway filled with lions and dies before showtime.

Shaw's skill with death jokes laces colosseum scenes with fearful comedy. Overseeing the show, Caesar advises Secutor to fight fair because "the audience likes to see a dead man in all his beauty and splendor." While Ferrovius prolongs a melodramatic departure, his brethren in faith urge him on with bromides about "divine love" and promises that "nothing can hurt you." Meanwhile, the captain, stricken with love for Lavinia, again tempts her to drop incense before Roman idols and be saved. An uproar in the arena follows Ferrovius's victory over six gladiators. The emperor is so impressed that he declares, "If Christians can fight like this, I shall have none but Christians to fight for me." He frees all but one Christian, who will serve as food for the lion.

The menagerie keeper chooses Androcles, the Greek weakling, because he is known as a sorcerer and not as a Christian.

The farce ends in low comic posturing: the emperor cowers while Androcles tames the lion. To prove to the lion that Rome's ruler is a friend, Androcles shakes the emperor's hand. Freed momentarily from fear, he growls, "I'll have you burnt alive for daring to touch the divine person of the Emperor." Ferrovius marvels that he, who fears no man, quivers before the lion:

> In my youth I worshipped Mars, the God of War. I turned from him to serve the Christian god; but today the Christian god forsook me; and Mars overcame me and took back his own. The Christian god is not yet. He will come when Mars and I are dust; but meanwhile I must serve the gods that are, not the God that will be.

In the meantime, Ferrovius opts for an earthly position in the Praetorian Guard. The play concludes with a conundrum: the emperor makes Androcles the slave of anyone brave enough to lay hands on him. Androcles concludes to his pet lion, "Whilst we stand together, no cave for you: no slavery for me."

Shaw's satiric comedy ridicules a variety of character types: people who enjoy flouting custom and rule by being part of a cult, people who think themselves above others because of rank or power, and people who set themselves up for failure by aiming for perfection. A deeper layer of satire emerges from the play's study of a period of history when Rome valued might over virtue, when the imperial hierarchy made a magnanimous gesture to placate a savage mob. Beyond this second level of satire, Shaw develops Androcles as a character who learns that strength and power come from unusual sources and that manipulation of the source, in this case, friendship with a lion, can sway lesser people. Although he composed his play before the term "black comedy" existed, Shaw toys with a terrorizing scene in the antechamber of the Roman arena, where human martyrs tremble at the roar of animals their remains will soon feed. Anticipating the twentieth century's preference for a blend of horror and satire, the playwright surprises the audience by evoking their laughter at the devaluation of life. (Bermel 1982; Brockett 1968; Gassner and Quinn 1969; Hill 1978; Hornstein 1973; Johnson 1968; Magill 1958; Negley and Patrick 1952; Shaw 1967, 1952)

See also beast lore; black humor; caricature; comedy; farce; pun; Shaw, George Bernard; satire; whimsy.

ANIMAL FARM

George Orwell's classic dystopic beast fable, *Animal Farm* (1945), mirrors the post–World War II political scene in which Marxists abandon their ideals and tyrannize the workers they had sworn to rescue from hereditary fiefdoms. Central to the mordant humor is Orwell's skillful caricature and his sympathy for the paralysis and vulnerability that gradually returns the rebellious underlings to their former servitude. Set on Manor Farm, the fable parodies the propagandists, tyrants, and authoritarian governments that deceive unsuspecting victims. The allegory vivifies the methods by which Hitler, Mussolini, and Stalin created nazism, fascism, and hard-line communism. The theme of this disarming idyll is an egalitarian struggle against exploitation, which flourishes typically in an unsteady peace. Rich with irony and satire, the story depicts beasts who unseat Farmer Jones, a decadent, careless human despot, and find themselves entrenched in a dismal animal police state supervised by a porcine Praetorian guard.

Like William Shakespeare's *Julius Caesar* and *Macbeth*, Orwell's slim novel expands on a touch of superstition: the prophetic dream of a prize Middle White boar named Old Major, who calls a meeting of barnyard denizens— sheep, horses, cows, pigs, dogs, ducklings, plus a goat, crow, and donkey. With altruistic fervor and polished oratory, the speaker—originally named Willingdon Beauty—summarizes the misery of slavery, for which he blames man. Old Major exhorts his listeners to follow nature and rebel against Mr. Jones, their profligate master, by creating an animal society to be engineered and run by themselves. Ironically, like Karl Marx's sweeping generalizations about the utopian communist state, Old Major's conclusion—"All animals are comrades"—proves faulty. The farm rally ends in a rout. With a blast of number six shot, Jones disrupts the comrades' singing of "Beasts of England," a worthy anthem comprising seven noble verses set to a "stirring tune, something between *Clementine* and *La Cucaracha.*" Three days later, the venerable boar dies of old age and is interred in the orchard.

Orwell predicts the type of demagogues who will rush to fill the vacuum. Old Major's protegés—three opportunistic pigs named Snowball, Napoleon, and Squealer—set up deceptively simple principles under which Animal Farm will function: they call their manifesto the Seven Commandments of Animalism:

1. Whatever goes upon two legs is an enemy.

2. Whatever goes upon four legs, or has wings, is a friend.

3. No animal shall wear clothes.

4. No animal shall sleep in a bed.

5. No animal shall drink alcohol.

6. No animal shall kill any other animal.

7. All animals are equal.

On Midsummer's Eve, Mr. Jones, like the recalcitrant Tsar Nicholas II of Russia, angers the animals by drinking to excess and forgetting to tend the stock. In retaliation, the animals emulate the Russian proletariat and oust him and his family and workers from the premises. Under new management, the pigs, eager to create the perfect farm, make a public display of burning whips, blinkers, nosebags, reins, and halters, all evidence of human oppression. In a bathetic act of piety, they give a ritual burial to Jones's hams. Having taught themselves to read and write, they supervise labor, challenge the animals to surpass productivity under human management, and retain for themselves the fruits of the harvest. Eventually, Snowball reduces the seven animal commandments to a single precept: "Four legs good, two legs bad"; meanwhile, by keeping the other animals overworked and in a perpetual state of tension and anticipation, the three pigs conceal their duplicity while plotting the next stage of the power play.

Orwell switches his attention to the villagers at this point, matching animals and humans in an unlikely battle of wits. In mid-October, the experimental farm suffers an unforeseen setback after Mr. Jones organizes a party of neighbors at the taproom of the Red Lion pub in Willingdon, including the gentleman farmer Mr. Pilkington, who actually spends his time hunting and fishing. The mob fuels a countermove to rout the animal rebels. Orwell heightens the satire of the melodramatic *coup d'état* by reporting neighborhood rumors of animal torture, cannibalism, and free love. At the glorious Battle of the Cowshed, Napoleon, a Stalinesque despot, and Snowball, a student of Julius Caesar's battlefield strategies, lead Manor Farm's pigs to victory. At the high point of the engagement, Boxer the cart horse inadvertently kills a stable boy with a blow to the skull and regrets that fighting leads to death. Snowball disagrees, offering inflammatory truisms: "War is war. The only good human being is a dead one." For his bravery, Boxer receives a medal; the animals reward themselves with the evolving legends of the Rebellion and the Battle of the Cowshed.

Orwell stresses the role of revolution in creating a "snowballing" chain of violent and dismaying events. Peace at Animal Farm is shortlived; Snowball and Napoleon, who are contenders for supreme command, fight over an emblematic goal—the building of a labor-saving windmill. When the matter comes to a vote, Napoleon vanquishes Snowball with a surprise tactic, summoning nine savage brass-adorned dogs, the equivalent of Germany's SS. Snowball scampers away. No longer compromised by a rival, Napoleon oppresses the animals by enforcing obedience, overworking them, and reducing rations. To heighten the emotional impact of the flagpole, he digs up Major's skull to serve as a graphic totem to unity.

Like Russia's numerous work plans, the scheduled accomplishments of Animal Farm fail to materialize. The dimwitted Boxer pushes himself to serve his overlord even more slavishly than before. After the animals labor 60 hours per week, plus Sunday afternoons, to complete the windmill, it is mysteriously destroyed; Napoleon accuses the absent Snowball of lurking nearby and of sabotaging the mill and causing subsequent flaws in farm plans. The pigs, more firmly in power, hire Mr. Whymper as intermediary. They negotiate with humans in Willingdon and move into the farmhouse, rephrasing the Seven Commandments to accommodate luxuries for the ruling party.

At this point in his narrative, Orwell exposes the false goals in the grandiose plan for Animal Farm. Following rationing, starvation, and an unprecedented number of confessions and executions, the poet Minimus (Latin for smallest) composes a hymn to Napoleon, "Friend of fatherless! Fountain of happiness!" A second foray, led by Farmer Frederick the next fall, results in a setback for the animals, for part of Animal Farm falls to human adversaries. Frederick's forces blow up the windmill, but the animals defeat them. Squealer, propagandist for the pigs, rallies the workers to embrace their victory and re-dedicate themselves to completing the mill. In Animal Farm's fourth spring, the overachieving Boxer, who wears himself out with physical labor, longs to retire. Pretending to send him to a hospital in Wellingdon, the pigs have him removed to the slaughterhouse. Squealer revises history—one of Orwell's chief themes in *1984*—by reporting that Boxer died in the hospital and that his last words confirmed Napoleon as leader.

Orwell emphasizes how the immediacy of oppression pales before the day-to-day fight for subsistence. Years pass in scandal, trickery, and deceit; the rebel animals die off, leaving a younger generation who have no memory of Manor Farm, Old Major, or idealism. Because of their sketchy knowledge of history, Napoleon manages to deceive the animals with a new credo: "All animals are equal but some animals are more equal than others." With the assistance of his human cohort, Mr. Pilkington, Napoleon strengthens his control over the land, which he renames Manor Farm. The pigs, in imitation of Jones, walk on their hind legs. The worker animals, still in Napoleon's power, notice that the tyrannic pigs resemble human beings. Orwell concludes, "The creatures outside looked from pig to man, and from man to pig, and from pig to man again; but already it was impossible to say which was which."

To manage the willy-nilly disorder of the rebellious animals, Orwell creates in Napoleon a satiric despot. Napoleon is a fierce, secretive, taciturn Berkshire boar of 24 stone (336 pounds) who allows ambition to overrule principle. Cunning and self-serving, he deceives his rival, the ingenuous Snowball, and trains nine puppies into a jackbooted hit squad that assures control. He scuttles the Sunday morning meetings as examples of wasted time and instead sets up a puppet committee of pigs, headed by himself. Although he has no concrete plans for Animal Farm, Napoleon manages to achieve his political aims by subverting Snowball's plan to construct a windmill and by seizing psychological control through militant posturing, intimidation, and brainwashing.

The satire explores the elements that precede fascist takeover. The animals, cowed by Napoleon's audacity, ask no questions; Boxer, an influential sycophant, overrides dissension with the claim that "Napoleon is always right." Napoleon's presumption impels him toward greater atrocities. In Chapter 7, he kills three disobedient hens and slaughters sheep for minor offenses. In despotic style,

> They were all slain on the spot. And so the tale of confessions and executions went on, until there was a pile of corpses lying before Napoleon's feet and the air was heavy with the smell of blood, which had been unknown there since the expulsion of Jones.

This silent conspiracy fuels Napoleon's bold bids for power and bloody public purges. As the old generation dies off and new animals take their place, the young, who have never known any other system, accept Napoleon's savagery as the norm.

In the end, Napoleon prevails by applying blitzkrieg tactics against the failed Snowball, by blaming all setbacks on his former rival, and by allying the pigs with Pilkington, a human neighbor who helps resurrect Manor Farm, the name by which Animal Farm was once known. Luxuriating in the farmhouse and partaking of whisky, human beds and clothing, and the best farm produce, Napoleon subverts the Seven Commandments to his own ends. He appears in full strutting glory in Chapter 10, "majestically upright, casting haughty glances from side to side, and with his dogs gambolling round him. He carried a whip in his trotter." A formidable, greedy overlord, he overworks and underfeeds the farm hirelings, who succumb to exploitation because they lack his savvy.

A witty yet poignant literary tour de force, Orwell's engaging animal fable combines powerful elements: the revelation of intolerable farm conditions; Old Major's dream of an animal utopia; rebellion and subsequent counter-rebellion; the undermining of the master plan to make Manor Farm into a haven run for and by animals; the regressive internal strife of animals against animals; and the coercion of lesser animals by members of a tyrannic superstructure whose behavior replicates that of Mr. Jones, the farm's human tyrant. A brilliant and cohesive satire composed for the enlightenment and edification of the postwar generation, *Animal Farm* exposes the ease with which conniving and traitorous manipulators can employ jingoism. By shifting blame, the pig cabal deceives a gullible, poorly educated nation into accepting subjugation as a substitute for their dream world. Just as the generations following the initial overthrow of Mr. Jones have no direct knowledge of former animals' struggles, the children born after World War II, Orwell implies, will lack a clear and honest picture of the dangers of totalitarianism and fascism, the destructive forces that ignited world leaders into global war against Hitler, Mussolini, and Tojo. (Alok 1989; Calder 1987; Connelly 1986; Oldsey and Browne 1986; Orwell 1946; Snodgrass 1991)

See also allegory; bathos; caricature; irony; Orwell, George; satire.

ARCHILOCHUS

One of early satire's angry young men, Archilochus, born on Paros and reared in a Greek colony on Thasos in the mid-seventh century B.C., exhibits the change in Greek sentiments and literary taste in the generations following Homer and Hesiod. Lacking the high moral tone of Hesiod and the romantic genius and glories of godhood that Homer immortalized, the gritty commoner Archilochus anchored his career on temporal values. Although it incited accusations of slander, and though Sparta banned the verse of Archilochus in textbooks, the canon of this Greek soldier-poet caught the eyes of Aristotle and the odist Pindar and influenced Quintilian and Horace.

As a result of his illegitimate parentage—he was born to the slave Enipo and the aristocrat Telesicles, leader of the Greek colony on Thasos—Archilochus enjoyed virtually no prestige or recognition in his lifetime. A questionable legend claims that Telesicles traveled to Delphi to consult the Pythia about his offspring. He received a straightforward reply from the Pythia, teller of fortunes: the son who first greeted his father on his return home would achieve a lasting name. The Pythia correctly foretold Archilochus's reputation for innovative, colloquial elegies recited to a single flute and for a formal paean to victory sung at Olympia.

An alternate legend adds a touch of magic to the poet's lore. Confined to his life as an oxherd, Archilochus is said to have chafed at his bleak prospects until he was visited by deities. While leading an ox to market, he stopped to flirt with a group of girls who changed into the Muses. The cow vanished; in its place, the Muses gave him a lyre and urged him to do what Hesiod the farmer had done—seek his fortune in verse and song. He used his newfound outlet to comment on the deadly balance of nature. In Aesopic style, he smirks, "The fox knows many things, but the hedgehog knows one great thing," a tribute to the prickly courage that helps the small survive a tricky adversary.

Archilochus gained fame as a Greek troubadour, a soldier for hire who was skilled in gruff, down-and-dirty iambic couplets, which he appended to odes. Pouring his immediate reactions into rhyme, he seemed eager to explore emotions and reactions aloud, as in this candid two-line commentary on the death of his brother-in-law, who drowned in a shipwreck:

> Since weeping will not cure my grief,
> Pleasure and feasting cannot make it worse.

The cynical tone of Archilochus's lines suggests why he suits a different audience from the lovers of the more elegant, polished verse of Homer and Sappho. A realist, Archilochus uses his terse satiric couplets to sublimate his inner angst and to vent the spirit of the moment, whether angry, confused, pensive, or lusty.

The extant fragments of Archilochus's first-person rhyme manifest a somewhat harsh personality driven to snatch moments of joy from the tedium of farm life and the horrors of battle. In rough jest at a prostitute sneeringly called Pasiphile or "Loved by All," he tweaks her for promiscuity:

> Fig tree of the rocks, where many rooks delight to feed,
> How sweetly, Pasiphile, you make your guests at home.

More blatantly carnal, the thought of Neoboule, his lover, brings out the soldier's longing for full breasts, scented tresses, and a quick coupling to ease his unfulfilled sexual drive:

> Wretched am I, unable to breathe, overwhelmed with desire, and the gods stabbing me with bone-deep pangs. . . . Now am I tamed by the longing that turns my bones to water: no longer do I ease hunger or strum my instrument. . . . Oh how I long to grasp my Neoboule, tumble to the ground on my sweaty wine-skin to grind belly to belly and thigh to thigh.

Reports of Archilochus's success with Neoboule suggest a source of his bitter verse. Once the noble Parian Lycambes learned that his future son-in-law was illegitimate, he humiliated Archilochus by reneging on the promised match. The conclusion to the failed romance is one of satire's darkest tributes. Stung by Lycambes's rejection, Archilochus launched a retaliatory verse cycle on the fox and the eagle, a thinly disguised diatribe against his former love and her father. To grieve Lycambes, Archilochus wrote a love confession of an afternoon spent in a lush meadow in the willing arms of Neoboule's younger sister. To spite Neoboule, he taunted her on her fading youth and exulted that "the plough of old age is digging its furrows there." The victims of his verse are said to have hanged themselves.

Smarting from the ego bashing he had suffered during courtship, Archilochus opted for compromise: he married a courtesan and settled for a life as a mercenary in the Ionian isles and Thrace. Content for the moment with his decision, he wrote a hymn to Herakles:

> To thee, lord Herakles, famed conqueror, hail,
>   and to thee, Iolaos,
>   both valiant warriors!
>
> To thee, famed conqueror, Herakles,
>   all hail!

Archilochus, no longer obsessed with personal enemies, turned his verse against his foes and against boastful military brass and used it to honor his comrade Glaucus. Like Robin Hood championing his bow, Archilochus vaunts:

> On my lance I depend
>   for my ration of black bread
>   and my skin of Ismarian wine,
>
> And on my lance I lean while I drink.

These sentiments, echoed by his admirers, became popular couplets among Greek soldiers. Sinking deeper into cynicism as carnage became his lifestyle, he renounced war as a way of life. A forerunner to William Shakespeare's Sir John Falstaff, Archilochus settled his fame in one boldly honest, pragmatic admission:

> Now my shield is Seian's pride. Whatever my intent, the quicker I locate a stretch of underbrush, the quicker I withdraw from this noble force. You see, I want to live. I have no worry over parting with this shield. Let it pass: I will buy another one no worse.

Ambivalent toward war as a way of life, the poet died in battle against the warrior Calondas around 604 B.C. in the conflict between Thasos and Naxos. (Feder 1986; Flaceliere 1962; Hadas 1954; Hammond and Scullard 1992; Hornstein 1973; Howatson 1989; Magill 1958; Mantinband 1956; Radice 1973; Snodgrass 1989)

See also Aesop; diatribe; Falstaff, Sir John; Horace; invective; satire; Shakespeare, William; trickster.

ARISTOPHANES

Greek dramatist of the late fifth century B.C., and the most revered writer of old comedy, Aristophanes suffers from the lack of a comparison, for most of the canon of ancient comedy has not survived. A workaholic, he excelled at energetic, fast-paced skits and topical humor that remained in vogue well into the Roman era. Scraps of biographical data blend with misinformation and legend. Born to Philippus and Zenodora around 450 B.C. in the Athenian deme of Cydathenaeon, he grew up south of Piraeus harbor on the nearby island of Aegina. He began composing the first of his 55 comic dramas around 432 B.C. and in his late teens bested experienced playwrights at the spring drama festival by capturing five medals, displaying a precocity that astounded his elders.

Unusually open with his opinions and frustrations, Aristophanes used the parabasis, or prologue, as an open letter to the Greek world, which, to his dismay, changed beyond his expectations. Freely employing satire and parody rather than nostalgia, he fought the decadence that followed the Peloponnesian War and lampooned moralists. In general, Aristophanes repudiated corruption, immorality, elitism, violence, and war. His joy in the *bon mot* was an appropriate weapon against Attic decline; he spared no one and no opinion, targeting even the sacrosanct Socrates and Plato, as well as clannish aristocrats and notorious pub crawlers. One of his victims, Cleon, a pompous demagogue, appears to have suffered a public skewer for prosecuting the playwright for violating immigration laws forbidding aliens to hold public office.

As a landowner and city magistrate, Aristophanes maintained the dual role of poet-in-residence and civil servant. He sired three sons, Philippos, Araros, and Nikostratos, who became comic playwrights. In 387 B.C., two years before his death, Aristophanes saw his sons win a competition. At his passing, Aristophanes left rollicking slapstick, allegory, and pointed invective in his *Daitaleis [The Banqueters]* (427 B.C.), *Babylonians* (426 B.C.), *Acharnians* (425 B.C.), *Knights* (424 B.C.), *Clouds* (423 B.C.), *Wasps* (422 B.C.), *Peace* (421 B.C.), *Amphiaraus* (414 B.C.), and his most notorious side-splitter, *Lysistrata* (411 B.C.), the chronicle of antiwar women whose voluntary abstinence from sex conquers their randy mates. His other works include *Thesmophoriazusae [Women Celebrating the Thesmophoria]* (411 B.C.), *Plutus [Wealth]* (408 B.C.), *Frogs* (405 B.C.), *Ecclesiazusae [The Assemblywomen]* (392 B.C.), and a second *Plutus* (388 B.C.). Of his canon, only 11 of his works remain. His favorite play, *The Birds* (414 B.C.), an escapist lark, searches for a better world. To uplift his countrymen, Aristophanes encourages the postwar era to abandon compromise, democracy, and the sophists' new morality and return to simplicity and tradition.

Witty beyond any other voice in the ancient world, Aristophanes bears comparison with James Joyce for his delight in allusion, alliteration, jingle, and puns and with Monty Python for his exuberant execution of whimsy, burlesque, buffoonery, caricature, doggerel, farce, and contrived dialogue. Although Socrates disliked the cruel caricature of himself Aristophanes included in *Clouds*, Plato, Socrates's spokesman, buried the grudge and made Aristophanes a participant in the *Symposium*. The humor of Aristotle's scene, which depicts the

Athenian playwright Aristophanes, circa 450–399 B.C.

playwright battling hiccups, compares with similar jests in Aristophanes's plays. In critical passages, Aristotle lambastes the comic for failure to control his comic excess—mockery, scatology, and sexual innuendo—and accuses him of flaunting any indignity for a laugh. Aristophanes makes no reply to the charge of blatant vulgarity. His son, Araros, apparently shared his father's bumptuous good nature, which he displayed in productions of Aristophanes's last plays, *Aiolosikon* and *Cocalus*, and, after 375 B.C., in originals that echo his father's taste in comedy. (Aristophanes 1962; Bermel 1982; Feder 1986; Hadas 1954; Hammond and Scullard 1992; Hornstein 1973; Howatson 1989; Lord 1963; Magill 1958; Mantinband 1956; Radice 1973; Snodgrass 1989; Spatz 1978)

See also *The Birds*; burlesque; caricature; comedy; doggerel; invective; parody; Plato; Plautus; satire; scatology; whimsy.

ATWOOD, MARGARET

The most prominent feminist author of the late twentieth century and a champion of contemporary Canadian literature, Margaret Atwood is an internationally acclaimed poet, critic, essayist, and short fiction writer. Skilled at irony, symbolism, pun, allegory, sarcasm, and internal monologue, she has utilized the full range of literary devices to produce an impressive array of works. Her bestselling speculative fiction, *The Handmaid's Tale* (1986), resides among the classic models of satiric dystopia and broke centuries of stereotyping of the satirist and dystopist as essentially male. Under her controlled examination of a post–atomic disaster society, the image of woman as an expendable being reduced to functioning womb grows into a monstrous dystopian perversion and features Offred, the era's enduringly feminist, survivalist heroine. The unidentified Handmaid clutches at sanity, release, and love in a fundamentalist theocracy that threatens dissidents with hanging and condemns Unwomen— those who are infertile or too old to conceive—to permanent clean-up work in a sterile land killed by toxic radiation.

The second of the three children of Margaret Dorothy Killam and forest entomologist Carl Edmund Atwood, Margaret Eleanor Atwood was born on November 18, 1939, in Ottawa, Ontario, a setting that has deeply influenced her literary allegiance. In childhood, she read widely and patterned her writing on Grimm's *Fairy Tales* and George Orwell's *Animal Farm*, both of which established dark, problematic prototypes of victim and victimizer. She enjoyed camping in the north Quebec outback, where her father conducted insect research. When she was seven, her family moved to northern Ontario. She came of age and attended high school in Toronto, a city that she frequently uses as an urban model.

In Atwood's humorous, self-effacing speech to the American Booksellers Association Convention in 1993, she said that her parents had wanted her to be a botanist. Obeying an urge that began in childhood, she chose instead to study literature and completed a B.A. from Victoria College at the University of

Toronto, an M.A. from Radcliffe, and graduate studies at Harvard from 1962 to 1963 and 1965 to 1967. During her formative years, she encountered critic Northrop Frye and found a mentor in Jay MacPherson, who helped shape Atwood's philosophies of literature and feminism. In her undergraduate years, she composed pithy, tightly constructed verse that she contributed to *Acta Victoriana* and *The Strand*, publications of Victoria College. After graduation, she served as lecturer and writer-in-residence at various Canadian, American, and Australian universities while pursuing a prolific schedule of writing. Her most famous novels—*The Edible Woman* (1969), *Surfacing* (1972), *Life Before Man* (1979), *Cat's Eye* (1989), and *The Robber Bride* (1993)—focus on themes of exploitation and victimization and feature protagonists who counter both challenges with native wit.

Atwood's *Handmaid's Tale* stands chief among her studies of people—mainly women—rejecting passivity in the face of menace. The book won her the *Los Angeles Times* Book Award and the title of Woman of the Year from *Ms.* magazine. Subsequent honors include the Arthur C. Clarke Award, the Commonwealth Literature Prize, and *Chatelaine* magazine's Woman of the Year. In 1990, *The Handmaid's Tale* was filmed by Cinecom Entertainment Group. Scripted by Harold Pinter, the movie starred Natasha Richardson as Offred and Robert Duvall and Faye Dunaway as the infertile ruling-class couple for whom the Handmaid is expected to produce a child.

In recent years, Atwood has continued to lecture and give public readings. In 1992, she published *Good Bones,* a collection of verse, essays, and short fiction; in 1993, her darkly comic novel *The Robber Bride,* a wicked, teasing trickster tale, was a best-seller. While introducing the novel at the ABA convention, she summarized her intent in writing the book: "Where have all the Lady Macbeths gone? Gone to Ophelias, every one, leaving the devilish tour-de-force parts to be played by bass-baritones." The witty womanist fable redeems the neglected role of villainess by depicting the fall of Zenia, a supposed-dead schoolmate whom Atwood pits against an intense coterie meeting at The Toxique, a Toronto restaurant. In league against the lethal homewrecker are an unlikely trio—Charis, a hippy; Roz, an energetic yuppie; and Tony, a specialist in military history who sets up a sandtable and reenacts European battles with soldiers made of spices: "cloves for the Germanic tribes, red peppercorns for the Vikings, green peppercorns for the Saracens, white ones for the Slavs." Currently residing outside Alliston, Ontario, Atwood lives with her daughter Jess and her husband, writer Graeme Gibson. She remains active in women's issues and literary circles, particularly the Canadian Authors Association. (Atwood 1972, 1993; *Contemporary Authors* 1994; *Contemporary Authors New Revision Series* 1989; *Contemporary Literary Criticism* 1987; Davidson 1986; *Discovering Authors* 1993; Dreifus 1992; Hammer 1990; Ingersoll 1991; *Major Twentieth-Century Writers* 1990; "Margaret Atwood: Interview" 1983; McCombs 1988; Talese 1993; Van Spanckeren and Castro 1988; Wilson 1993)

See also allegory; *Animal Farm;* black humor; *The Handmaid's Tale;* irony; Orwell, George; pun; sarcasm; satire; trickster; wit.

AUSTEN, JANE

One of the early nineteenth century's most inventive, self-restrained writers of comedy of manners, Jane Austen has always drawn a wide and enthusiastic audience of readers. Her sagacious wit and keen observation of human foibles prove as great a draw today as in her own time and shortly after her death. Most recently, Austen's sophisticated satire has permeated twentieth-century film, with Emma Thompson and Hugh Grant's performances in *Sense and Sensibility* (1995); a version of *Persuasion* (1995) starring Amanda Root and Ciaran Hinds; and a BBC made-for-television duo—*Emma*, starring Gwyneth Paltrow and Toni Collette, and *Pride and Prejudice*, starring Jennifer Ehle and Colin Firth. An irony that Austen would not fail to turn into jest is the fact that she earned less than £700 in her entire career from the publication of six novels.

A native of Steventon in south-central England, Austen was born to Cassandra Leigh and the Reverend George Austen on December 16, 1775, at the roomy, seven-bedroom rectory. Next to the last of eight children—six brothers, James, George (who was deaf and retarded), Edward, Henry, Frank, and Charles, and a fond sister, Cassandra—Jane enjoyed a full but unremarkable childhood. Her education was a mix of home schooling under her father, who also taught boarding students, and brief attendance at the Abbey School at Reading, where, by age 11, she had learned more about embroidery and the composition of thank-you notes than about math or language.

On her return to the rectory, Jane took up residence in a third-floor suite, which she shared with Cassandra. Like the Brontës, the Austen girls entertained themselves with recitations, rainy-day plays in the barn, make-believe and charades, reading aloud, and visits to neighbors. Throughout her life, she read widely and kept up a lively correspondence with friends and family, including her brothers Frank and Charles, who became navy admirals, and James, who entered the ministry. After Jane's death, Cassandra—who married the Reverend Samuel Cooke, Jane's godfather—edited personal commentary from her sister's letters, but left plenty of proof of Jane's affability.

Austen began writing parody in childhood and developed her juvenilia into full-blown fiction. She received three proposals of marriage: the first ended in the death of her suitor, a young clergyman; the second came from old friend Harris Bigg-Wither, whom she didn't love; and the third issued from the Reverend Edward Bridges, who didn't appeal to her. Intent on her career, she completed three novels before her twenty-third year: *Sense and Sensibility* (originally entitled *Elinor and Marianne*) (1811); *Pride and Prejudice* (originally *First Impressions*) (1813), her masterpiece satire of courtship and social maneuvering; and *Northanger Abbey* (originally *Catharine, or the Bower*) (1818), her most didactic novel, which she sold for £10. The order of her publications deviates from the time of writing; a work-in-progress, *The Watsons*, she abandoned in 1805.

When Austen was 27 years old, she and her family moved to Bath, an odious move for Jane, but a more sophisticated setting filled with seasonal visitors to the famous Roman spa, where her father retired to take the sulfur waters.

English novelist Jane Austen, 1775–1817

In 1809, she and her widowed mother settled at brother Edward Austen's country house at Chawton, where she used the parlor as a work station. After Edward's adoption by his aunt and uncle, Edward and Elizabeth Knight, he inherited Rowling House, where Jane enjoyed house parties and led dances. During the next five years, she completed *Mansfield Park* (originally *Lady Susan*) (1814), *Emma* (1816), and *Persuasion* (1818). In her professional correspondence, she referred to herself as Mrs. Ashton Dennis, and she published her first novel anonymously. She dedicated *Emma* to Edward, the Prince of Wales. After her father's death, she and her mother returned to rural Hampshire. In 1816, Austen left her work on *Sanditon* untouched as her health worsened and back pain from arthritis impeded concentration. Despite treatment during the last ten months at Winchester for Addison's disease, a tubercular condition of the adrenal gland, she sickened and declined in spirits. She spent her final hours with her head on Cassandra's lap and died on July 18, 1817. At a private service, Austen was buried under a black marble slab in Winchester Cathedral. Subsequent publication of her juvenilia and private papers has added little to her canon. (Austen 1961; Baugh 1948; Buck 1992; Chapman 1948; Drabble 1985; Hainer 1995; Halperin 1984; Hornstein 1973; Lovett 1932; O'Neill 1970; Schickel 1995)

See also comedy; *Pride and Prejudice;* satire; wit.

 ## *BACK TO METHUSELAH*

George Bernard Shaw's bitterly dystopian five-part play, *Back to Methuselah* (1921), is a laborious, prophetic closet drama meant to be read rather than staged. An unusual approach to stage satire, *Back to Methuselah*, which requires a marathon performance, offers an unusual opportunity for the playwright to analyze, reject, and replace humankind with a thoughtful, fleshless race. More suited to the cerebral human creature Shaw preferred, the play amplified his private thoughts on creation and his heartiest wish to deprive humanity of body so that he could glorify the mind. In the playwright's words, "The progress of the world depends on the people who refuse to accept facts and insist on the satisfaction of their instincts." The play failed with most readers and viewers because of its extreme negativism and its capricious conclusion. Even Shaw found it tedious when he read it aloud to his wife and friends.

Subtitled "A Metabiological Pentateuch," the satire, heavy with symbolism and didacticism, leaps over a chasm of time from creation to 30,000 years in the future. Named for Methuselah, an Old Testament patriarch who lived 969 years, the text projects a new religion based on myth overlaid with biological concepts of adaptation to environment. Shaw's use of the term "pentateuch" connects the play with the Torah, the first five books of Moses—Genesis, Exodus, Leviticus, Numbers, and Deuteronomy—which contain the most fundamental Hebrew myths, laws, and cultural traditions. Shaw's mordant humor, which he aims at repetitive wrongs that have become a human pattern, freights the play with pessimism and cynicism, two qualities that defeat the purpose of illustrative ridicule.

In a satire on the mythic first couple, the first act returns to Eden, where the death of a fawn signals a change in Paradise and the coming demise of innocence. Adam and Eve contemplate the ugliness of a corpse; the serpent, a beguiling, lovely creature who interrupts their private conversation, surmises that the fawn's death is balanced by the beauty of birth, an unknown concept in Eden, which was created by God's hand. To Eve's queries about reproduction, the serpent replies enigmatically, "You see things; and you say 'Why?' But I dream things that never were; and I say 'Why not?'" As the couple listens to the serpent's wily sophistry, the glib snake inspires Adam with a new emotion and names it jealousy. Adam broods that the future is uncertain and, like a petulant child, threatens to kill the serpent if he refuses to restore faith. Like the stereotypical dirty old man, the snake moves aside to whisper to Eve the secret of procreation.

Act Two, the next domestic segment, typifies the now familiar dysfunctional family and displays Shaw's didacticism at its weightiest. The first couple face their vengeful son Cain, the prototypical *miles gloriosus*, the merciless spoiler of Plautine comedy and Italian *commedia dell'arte*, who boasts of the murder of his weaker brother Abel. Cain's argumentative, blasphemous strutting causes Eve to chastise her vain son and disdain his theory of hero and superman. Although Cain has already slain Abel, the gentle farmer, Eve retains hope for her remaining sons, Enoch and Tubal, neither of whom resembles their quarrelsome elder brother. At Cain's snide departing words, Adam damns him. Eve, unfamiliar with damnation, asks for a definition. Shaw composes for Adam a reply with a mythic ring: "The state of them that love death more than life."

The rapid change of scene that opens Part 2 resets the play on Hampstead Heath outside London. In Shaw's incisive satire, a gathering of gentlemen discuss World War I, an outgrowth of the first murder. Franklyn Barnabas, an ex-cleric, comments to Lubin on the enigma of perpetual life in Paradise:

> Adam and Eve were hung up between two frightful possibilities. One was the extinction of mankind by their accidental death. The other was the prospect of living for ever. They could bear neither.

The other conversants ponder alternate views of longevity. The Barnabas brothers conclude that pure creativity is limited because human beings die too soon to develop their talents. The third tableau of the play, its weakest segment, moves ahead to A.D. 2170 to examine the theme of lengthened life. By Part 4, Shaw has moved 830 years ahead to A.D. 3000, a time when England is famous for its long-lived populace.

In Part 5 of this convoluted study of the appropriate length for human life, Shaw introduces a surreal summer idyll in the year A.D. 31,920. Similar to H. G. Wells's *The Time Machine* (1895) in its classic setting, the scene opens on a temple, grove, and melodies played on the flute. Young men and women dance in Grecian attire. This stage of evolution finds human life springing from eggs, but the emerging embryo has already matured to the late teens. People pass rapidly into full adulthood, advancing at age three or four from trivialities to a contemplation of abstract math and philosophy. For 700 to 800 years, these Ancients survive in their idyllic state until an accident kills them.

Pygmalion interrupts the dancing couples to proclaim that he has created a human male and female who function in the old way, by eating and digesting food and by reproducing sexually. The man and woman appear as automata—he portraying Ozymandias, King of Kings, and she in the guise of Semiramis-Cleopatra. The pair exhibit what Shaw considers the worst of human vices, that is, vanity, egotism, selfishness, violence, passion, cowardice, and fear of death. So depraved is the woman that she bites Pygmalion and kills him. Contemplating this savagery, the Ancients conclude that human unhappiness stems from enslavement to the body.

Against the backdrop of a renewed dance, Lilith, the Earth-Mother in Hebrew lore who has more in common with Guinevere or Aphrodite than with the ingenuous Eve, appears to muse on creation. She laments that human beings have lost the use of breast and bowels and is dismayed at their audacity. Her complaint dominates Shaw's conclusion to this mammoth work:

> I had patience with them for many ages: they tried me very sorely. They did terrible things: they embraced death, and said that eternal life was a fable. I stood amazed at the malice and destructiveness of the things I had made: Mars blushed as he looked down on the shame of his sister planet: cruelty and hypocrisy became so hideous that the face of the earth was pitted with the graves of little children among which living skeletons crawled in search of horrible food.

Still willing to see what human life will spawn, Lilith ponders woman's greatest gift, curiosity, a parallel to Pandora and to the goddess's own interest in future developments.

Lilith concludes that stagnation is the greatest sin. She notes in her parting soliloquy: "And now I shall see the slave set free and the enemy reconciled, the whirlpool become all life and no matter." She promises to have patience with humankind, even though they waste their longevity. The moment that humanity ceases to thrive and begins to kill hope and faith, she intends to end its stay on earth by annihilating all people. For the moment, she looks ahead into the endless cosmos and focuses on "its million starry mansions," many of which are empty or unbuilt. Before she vanishes from the stage, she longs for the day when her offspring shall master creation and concludes, "It is enough that there is a beyond." (Hill 1978; Holroyd 1989; Hornstein 1973; Johnson 1968; Magill 1958; Negley and Patrick 1952; Shaw 1988)

See also caricature; *commedia dell'arte;* didacticism; irony; Plautus; Shaw, George Bernard; satire.

LE BARBIER DE SÉVILLE

Published in 1774 by Pierre-Augustin Caron de Beaumarchais, a dabbler in foreign diplomacy, gun running, printing, theatrical production, and the Spanish slave market, *Le Barbier de Séville [The Barber of Seville]* represents only a fragment of the combined energies and talents of one of the least understood men of the revolutionary period. Labeled a farce for its witty improvisation, topical lampoons, disguises, mix-ups, and exaggerations, the work displays the playwright's considerable skill in transforming polemical thought and personal vituperation against his enemies into a light, entertaining drama punctuated by both original and traditional Spanish music and dance. An example of Beaumarchais's wit is the inventive character names: he assigns L'Éveillé (Wakeful) to a dull-witted serving boy and La Jeunesse (Youthful) to an aged staff member. Adapted from a play by Scarron and Molière's *École des femmes,* the vivid, fast-paced romantic comedy is set in eighteenth-century Seville and follows the plot of a Spanish grandee, Count Almaviva, to free his love, Rosine, from her lecherous foster father, Dr. Bartholo.

To please an audience expecting romance, Beaumarchais observes the conventions of convoluted love plots. In the rising action, Almaviva, disguised as the soldier Lindor, conveys a love note to Rosine. Bartholo orders her to hand over the note; she substitutes a letter from a cousin. Almaviva tries a second disguise—the scholar Alonzo, a substitute music teacher and supposed accomplice in Bartholo's plot to force Rosine to marry him. The music lesson goes awry when the real teacher arrives. Figaro, a local meddler who busily orchestrates the comic ins and outs of Almaviva's ruses, evicts the teacher, but not before Bartholo realizes that Figaro and Almaviva are up to something. To assure marriage to Rosine, Bartholo sends for the notary and convinces Rosine that Almaviva intends to abduct her.

In high comedic style, the action rises to chaotic proportions. Before the authorities arrive, Figaro and Almaviva climb through Rosine's window. Almaviva discloses his real identity; Rosine, overcome by the involved stratagem, collapses. Bartholo interrupts Figaro's plot to win Rosine for the Count. Bartholo, who lacks the wit to catch Figaro in the act of rebellion, initiates a series of comic complaints:

Bartholo:	Damnation! It's infuriating! That Scoundrelly thief of a Figaro! You can't leave the place for a moment but when you get back . . . you can be certain that . . .
Rosine:	Has someone been annoying you, Sir?
Bartholo:	It's that confounded barber. He's just put the whole household out of action at one swoop. He's given Wakeful a sleeping draught, Youthful a sneezing powder, and he's bled Marceline in her big toe: even my mule—he's put a poultice on the eyes of the poor blind creature.

Before Bartholo can have Almaviva arrested, Figaro, the wily commoner, bribes the music teacher to serve as witness and convinces the notary to wed Almaviva and Rosine.

Bartholo interrupts the postnuptial scene and challenges the Count in a duel of love songs:

Wilt thou have me
Rosinette?
A prince of husbands
You would get.
'Tis true I am no beauty
But I know a husband's duty
And this much I can say—
And this much I can say
Though I may not look much catch by day
In the dark all cats are gray!

Bartholo orders the judge to stop the newlyweds' departure. At a climactic moment, the Count delivers one of the damning satiric gibes at upper-class privilege:

> The lady is fair and of noble birth. I am a man of rank, young and rich. She is my wife. Does anyone presume to dispute a title which confers honor on both of us? . . . The gentleman whom you yourself brought here will protect her from the violence you threaten her with. True magistrates are ever the defenders of the oppressed.

The judge agrees and, suspicious of Bartholo's dealings, presses for an audit of Rosine's inheritance. Bartholo realizes that his conniving has found him out. With regret, he signs the marriage certificate. Figaro commiserates with the curmudgeonly doctor and adds that old age is no match for young people in love. The dynamo that turns the plot is Figaro, the tricky slave, a carryover from the smart-mouthed servants of Plautus's Roman comedies and from Scappino, a stock figure of the *commedia dell'arte*. In his involvement in the Count's suit for Rosine, Figaro describes Bartholo as

> a stoutish, shortish, oldish, greyish, cunning, smarmy, posing, nosing, peeping, prying, creeping, whining, snivelling sort of man . . . coarse, mean, infatuated with his ward, jealous beyond all measure where she's concerned, and she hates him like poison.

In rapid repartee with Almaviva, the scene continues:

The Count: And his likeable qualities?

Figaro: He hasn't any!

The Count: So much the better. Is he honest?

Figaro: Just enough to avoid being hanged.

A thinly veiled duplicate of Beaumarchais himself, Figaro successfully insults his master and subverts authority under the noses of the privileged ruling class. After his introduction to the French stage, he became a hero to the growing underclass, whose anger was manifesting itself in revolt, expulsion of unscrupulous aristocrats, and regicide. Beaumarchais reprised the role in two comedies, the popular *La Folle journée ou le mariage de Figaro [The Foolish Day's Work, or The Marriage of Figaro]* (1784) and *La Mère coupable [The Guilty Mother]* (1796), the third in the Figaro trilogy. Made more famous by translations all over Europe, the artful figure, brimming with irreverence toward his master, appeared in operas by Paisiello, Rossini, and Mozart and in numerous prose versions. (Beaumarchais 1964; Bermel 1982; Cross 1947; Magill 1958; Magnusson 1990)

   See also comedy; *commedia dell'arte*; farce; *La Folle journée ou le mariage de Figaro;* Plautus; repartee; satire; trickster.

 # BATHOS

A pejorative critical term, bathos, a form of overstatement, characterizes an inept literary style that accentuates a sad or tragic set of circumstances or sequence of losses to the point of creating humor or melodrama. Often the inadvertent loss of tone control by a neophyte or clumsy author, bathetic literature—richly ridiculed for the first time by name in Alexander Pope's "Martinus Scriblerus" and *Peri Bathous, or the Art of Sinking in Poetry* (1727)—rarely heads anybody's must-read list. Derived from the Greek for depth, the term refers to a failed assault on sublimity or elevation with three potentially disastrous outcomes: sentimentality, anticlimax, and predictability.

Bathos is not limited to the worst of authors, and indeed it occurs in several regrettable passages from great authors. Two notable examples come from the verse of Percy Bysshe Shelley and Gerard Manley Hopkins, both facile authors and critics. In "Ode to the West Wind," Shelley wails, "I fall upon the thorns of life. I bleed!"; similarly distressing is the unfortunate internal rhyme in Hopkins's "The Windhover: To Christ Our Lord," in which the speaker declares, "My heart in hiding stirred for a bird." In neither case does the poet appear to anticipate the bathetic results of a gush of emotion, which in both cases defeats the dignity of the effort. In a gleeful celebration of these literary bloopers, Wyndham Lewis and Charles Lee compiled a collection of bathetic poems in *The Stuffed Owl: An Anthology of Bad Verse* (1948).

At home in prose as well as poetry, bathos extends to prose in speech, essay, short story, drama, and novel. Novelist Charles Dickens, a master of caricature and sentimentality, slid into weepy prose with the overdone image of a dying golden-haired child, Lucie and Charles's unnamed son in *A Tale of Two Cities*:

> Thus, the rustling of an Angel's wings got blended with the other echoes, and they were not wholly of earth, but had in them that breath of Heaven. Sighs of the winds that blew over a little garden-tomb were mingled with them also, and both were audible to Lucie, in a hushed murmur—like the breathing of a summer sea asleep upon a sandy shore.

A violation of audience expectations by modern standards, outpourings of sighing winds and gushing tears were part of the Victorian era's literary heritage and occur on the stage as well as throughout Dickens's prose, as in the death of Paul Dombey in *Dombey and Son*, of Little Dick in *Oliver Twist*, and of Little Nell in *The Old Curiosity Shop*. American literature contains its own version of Dickensian bathos, the prime example being the death of Little Eva in Harriet Beecher Stowe's *Uncle Tom's Cabin* (1852).

Bathos is not irrevocably attached to inept novels, ballads, and melodrama. One of Woody Guthrie's beloved anti-management union laments, "The 1913 Massacre" (1961), scrolls out ten verses of morbid details about the "copper boss thugs" of Calumet, Michigan, who yell "There's a fire!" and cause a group of Christmas celebrants to die at a blocked exit. The juxtaposition of innocent women and children against smirking villains overwhelms the poem with sentiment: over a hundred victims lie on the floor while the tricksters yuck-yuck at a "murderous joke." However heartfelt Guthrie's intent in the composition of his ballad, the result is an overlong didactic meditation on cruelty and concludes with a weighty moral on the excesses of greed.

The tragic death of Little Eva, depicted in the 1927 movie adaptation of Harriet Beecher Stowe's *Uncle Tom's Cabin*, is an example of bathos, or tragedy so overstated that it becomes funny.

Even a Pulitzer Prize-winning poet is capable of bathos. In his tenderly poetic sketch of a town souse, Edwin Arlington Robinson depicts Eben Flood, the main character of "Mr. Flood's Party" from *The Three Taverns* (1920), as a resident of Tilbury Town out on a binge under a double moon. With motherly care, the mellow tippler sets his jug on the ground with shaky hands and recalls "that most things break," a sentimental reference to Eben's fractured relationships. A parody of vaudeville's stereotyped drunk scenes, Eben wishes himself well "for auld lang syne" and ponders the end of a life that offers nothing to return to and less to hope for.

Similarly intent on image, Isabel Allende makes skillful use of the sentimental version of bathos in *In Love and Shadows* (1987) by setting up her main character, journalist Irene Beltran, for a coming to knowledge of the human rights violations of the Argentinian dictatorship to which her fiancé dedicates his life. Normally capable of tolerating all manner of on-the-scene assignments, Irene observes the daily convulsion of 15-year-old Evangelina Ranquileo, the child of country folk whose neighbors have turned her predictable spasm into a religious phenomenon. The first episode concludes with the dramatic arrival of soldiers who seek to alarm the girl and her followers to prevent future contortions, which locals take as a prophecy.

On a second visit to the Ranquileo residence, Irene and her photographer anticipate a joyous pig roast. The distress on the human faces mirrors the plight of the main course as the grossly obese hog is dragged in. He has been rid of tapeworms by an expert who thrust his fist down the animal's gullet to withdraw any offending parasite. Feasting on grains and vegetables while the other pigs subsisted on scraps, the sacrificial animal had no inkling of doom:

> Isolated, captive, and immobilized, the animal had awaited its fate, adding fat to fat, its hams growing juicy and tender. Today was the first time the beast had traveled the two hundred meters separating its pen from the sacrificial altar, stumbling along on its hopelessly short legs, blinded in the light, deaf with terror.

Allende plays out the "pig pity" motif in detail: the stunning blow, bone-handled knife, and two-handed stroke when the butcher plunges the weapon "like an Aztec priest." The hog howls its pain as blood exudes from the wound, dribbling abundant gore for the dogs to lap from a puddle. Punctuating this extended image is Irene's unforeseen collapse, an uncharacteristic loss of her usual poise and aplomb.

The skillful use of bathos in Allende's novel deceives the reader into expecting something comic or at least amusing from Irene's fainting spell. Instead, the author sets up a vast apotheosis—the search for Evangelina, who has been "disappeared" Argentine style and whose parents hold no hope of her return, either alive or dead. Like the savagely victimized pig who is no longer capable of blinking innocent eyes on the crowd who have come to watch it die, Evangelina's remains apparently lie among the slaughtered, whom Irene views in unceremonious piles in a fetid makeshift mortuary, or among the "desaparacidos" at the bottom of a mountain ravine or seaside cliff. Thus, the bathetic pig massacre not only parallels Evangelina's abduction, but also the sudden and violent devastation of Irene's naiveté. No longer can she love her soldier fiancé or face escalating militarism and mayhem. (Abrams 1971; Allende 1987; Baldick 1990; Barnet, Berman, and Burto 1960; Cuddon 1976; Dickens 1960; Drabble 1985; Gray 1992; Henry 1995; Holman and Harmon 1992; Hopkins 1970; Padgett 1987; Robinson 1976; Shelley 1948)

See also didacticism; hyperbole; Pope, Alexander.

THE BATTLE OF THE BOOKS

One of Jonathan Swift's most humorous scholarly satires, *The Battle of the Books* (1704) depicts the ongoing squabble between classicists and moderns, each staking out literature as a fiefdom to be guarded against encroachment by the opposing party. In response to Sir William Temple's essay "Ancient and Modern Learning," Swift turns the controversy into a mock-heroic battle during which the books themselves face off to settle the matter. In a simple preface, Swift defines his métier:

> Satyr is a sort of Glass, wherein Beholders do generally discover everybody's face but their Own, which is the chief Reason for the kind of Reception it meets in the World, and that so very few are offended with it.

The actual skirmish, which the narrator dates to the previous Friday, arises over territorial disputes concerning Parnassus, the classical residence of wisdom and erudition. Swift smirks, "In this Quarrel, whole Rivulets of Ink have been exhausted, and the Virulence of both Parties enormously augmented." The narrator, who had previously proposed a blending of ancient and modern works, insists that his friends have pressed him to give the details of the fight.

During the battle, the narrator inserts an element of beast lore: a bee lands in a spider's web, which, like modern literature, exudes from the spider's inner vileness. The spider, swollen with his diet of insects, swears at the bee for wrecking the spider's domain. In self-defense, the bee, a symbol of the liberal arts, claims to visit "all the Flowers and Blossoms of the Field and the Garden, but whatever I collect from thence, enriches my self, without the least Injury to their Beauty, their Smell, or their Taste." In contrast to the generous sampling of nature's best, the spider possesses "a good plentiful Store of Dirt and Poison in [its] Breast" and functions "by a lazy Contemplation of four Inches round; by an overweening Pride, which feeding and engendering on it self, turns all into Excrement and Venom; producing nothing at last, but Fly-bane and a Cobweb." The bee claims that his method of enlarging his range to all the flowers "with long Search, much Study, true Judgment, and Distinction of Things, brings home Honey and Wax." Swift's heavy-handed satire demonstrates his didacticism, through which he illustrates the moderns' self-limiting methods.

To add a word from the ancients, Swift introduces Aesop to break the silence of the combatants, which have paused to observe the spider and bee. The noted fablist concludes that the insects should be known by their products: the spider by his "Wrangling and Satyr" and the bee by hives filled "with Honey and Wax, thus furnishing Mankind with the two Noblest of Things, which are Sweetness and Light." The opposing sides ignore Aesop and launch a shooting war, with Homer, Plato, Euclid, Aristotle, Herodotus, Livy, and Hippocrates on the side of the ancients and Dryden, Wither, Cowley, Hobbes, Harvey, and Descartes in the vanguard of the moderns. Swift gets in a rabbit punch at his personal foes: Glimpses of participants show Criticism distended from gobbling books; her husband, Ignorance, is too blind with age to read.

Parodying Homer's epic battle scenes from the *Iliad*, Swift has Bentley hurl a spear that Pallas, goddess of war, blunts by replacing its point with lead. The soft-tipped weapon falls harmlessly away from the first shield it strikes. A single shot trusses Bentley and Wotton together like a brace of woodcocks. The bodies are so neatly pinioned that Charon, the deity who ferries the dead over the river Styx, believes them only one passenger and charges one fare instead of two. The silly battle ends in midsentence, as if the text were defective. Swift, having served his purpose of ridiculing the fatuous moderns, leaves unfinished the eternal confrontation between ancients and moderns. (Drabble 1985;

Harrison 1967; Hornstein 1973; Magill 1958; Manguel and Guadalupi 1987; Pollard 1970; Swift 1958; Woods 1947)

See also Aesop; allegory; beast lore; burlesque; didactic; mock-heroic; parody; satire; Swift, Jonathan.

BEAST LORE

A unique form of allegorical satire, the beast epic or beast fable maintains the style, tone, and diction of classical epic or episode while substituting pastures, forests, barnyards, and wild or domesticated animals for elevated settings and dignified human characters. Employing a pseudo-serious approach to base or ludicrous situations, European beast lore derives from the animal lore of the Greek Aesop (sixth century B.C.), originator of such epigrammatic morals as "sour grapes," "dog in the manger," and "the goose that laid the golden egg." Aesop's Roman imitator, Phaedrus, achieves humor through parody of the high-flown style of the serious poet and through personification of great persons as rabbits, foxes, pigs, cows, and fowl. Expanded and stereotyped by the Romans, the genre evolved its own conventions—lurking predator, lack-logic deterrents to deadly stalkers, vaunting pride, pragmatic themes, and the stereotypical names of Chaunticleer the Rooster, Noble the Lion, Old Man Coyote, Br'er Bear, and Reynard the Fox.

Beast lore satires compare with burlesque and caricature in their targeting of elitist nobles, rulers, and churchmen. This limited genre champions the underdog, who, like the peasant, is usually powerless but clever. The beast epic form reflects the influence of parody. Rich in human conversation, the discourse of animal characters reveals common prejudices and vices. A typical pairing of the vulnerable with the exploitive comes from this exchange at the high point of Jean de La Fontaine's "Le loup et l'agneau" ("The Wolf and the Lamb"):

> —Je ne puis troubler sa boisson.
> —Tu la troubles, reprit cette bête cruelle;
> et je sais que de moi tu médis l'an passé.
> —Comment l'aurais-je fait si je n'étais pas né?
> Reprit l'Agneau, je tette encor ma mère.
> —Si ce n'est toi, c'est donc ton frère.
> ["I can't be bothering your drink."
> "You do trouble it," replied the cruel beast;
> "And I know that you have slandered me during the past year."
> "How have I done such a thing if I wasn't even born?"
> Replied the lamb, "I was still suckling from my mother."
> "If it wasn't you, it must have been your brother."]

The cynicism and foreboding illuminate bestiary style: the author exaggerates innocence and potential harm by pairing unlike conversants: lamb with wolf, rabbit with fox, monkey with lion, and so on.

Beast lore, an allegorical satire developed by Greek author Aesop, uses animals as caricatures of humans. English illustrator Arthur Rackham's frontispiece of a 1912 edition of *Aesop's Fables* includes the Tortoise with a nattily dressed Hare and Fox.

Beast lore allows the author to lampoon the mighty by clothing them in animal hides and exposing their human foibles. The genre is common not only in European but in Asian, Middle Eastern, and African literature, as well.

- A laughable tale from the Asian Indian *Panchatantra* (ca. 200 B.C.), "Numskull and the Rabbit," pits a foolish but proud lion against a cunning trickster rabbit, who shows the strutting lion his own reflection down a well. The lion, roaring as if confronting an enemy, is bowled over by the echo, leaps into the well after his foe, and drowns.

- One of Britain's most entertaining beast epics, Geoffrey Chaucer's *Nun's Priest's Tale* (1385), lauds the exalted cock, Chaunticleer, a strutting male among adoring hens.

- France produced *Le Roman de Renard*, a 30,000-line beast epic cycle evolving from the twelfth to the mid-thirteenth centuries, as well as the late seventeenth-century fables of Jean de La Fontaine, who adapted themes from Aesop, Phaedrus, and the Hindu Bidpaï.

- Johann Goethe's *Reinhart Fuchs* (1780) anticipates the deadly serious corruption of power underlying Joel Chandler Harris's Uncle Remus stories (1848–1908), the logic of Rudyard Kipling's "Rikki Tikki Tavi" and *Just So Stories* (1912), and the warren lore of Richard Adams's *Watership Down* (1972). Whereas Goethe centers his wit on the excesses of rebels during the French Revolution, Harris lampoons the resourceful slave who uses a forest dweller's wisdom to outwit the master.

A parallel development of beast epic and beast fable appears in the numerous animal series in world literature, notably in the trickster motif of Native American lore. "Old Man Coyote and Buffalo Power," related by Shoshone storyteller Arthur Big Turnip, pictures Old Man Coyote, a typical dupe, bemoaning his age. Buffalo strikes him and transforms him into a calf. Coyote, intoxicated by the power and might of youth, dashes off without questioning the source of his power. When he encounters a tired old coyote similar to his former self, the former coyote strikes his victim as he was once struck. Instead of reviving youth in the old coyote, the striker loses his youth and turns himself into the dotard he had been. The moral—a feature of beast epic—reminds hearers of this Shoshone myth: "Don't start anything unless you know you can finish it." (Baldick 1990; Barnet, Berman, and Burto 1960; Cuddon 1976; Feinberg 1967; Harris 1952; Henry 1995; Holman and Harmon 1992; Hornstein 1973; Kipling 1974; La Fontaine 1965; McArthur 1992; *Panchatantra in Literature: World Masterpieces* 1991; *Plains Indian Mythology* 1975)

See also Aesop; *Animal Farm;* burlesque; caricature; Chaucer, Geoffrey; Chaunticleer; didacticism; epigram; Horace; Orwell, George; parody; Phaedrus; Reynard the Fox; trickster.

BEAUMARCHAIS, PIERRE-AUGUSTIN CARON DE

A master of French comedy, as well as financier, spy, and major gun dealer for American revolutionaries, Pierre Beaumarchais earned a reputation for rebellion with the creation of his innovative Figaro, the devious valet of *The Barber of Seville* (1774), which historians credit as inciting the anti-monarchists who led the French Revolution. The handsome, graceful son of watchmaker André Caron, Beaumarchais was born January 24, 1732, in Paris and was apprenticed with his father. A lawsuit over his invention of a timepiece escapement device brought him notoriety that caught the eye of King Louis XV. Beaumarchais entered Versailles, the royal household, as harpmaster to the king's daughters. At the age of 24, Beaumarchais married Madeleine Francquet de Beaumarchais, one of his father's clients and the widow of one of the king's advisers, and gained the title by which he is known.

The friendship of Joseph Duverney provided Beaumarchais enough investment savvy to capitalize on the Spanish slave trade and tobacco market based in Louisiana, which he schemed to monopolize. In 1761, he bought a royal office, through which he exerted increasing influence among courtiers. He sought a position as *Grand Maître des Eaux et Forêts* [Grand Master of Streams and Forests] but compromised for a lesser post as associate deputy of the royal warren, a sinecure that assured him a steady income and pension for two decades. After his wife's death, his growing capital, enhanced by his subsequent marriage to a wealthy widow, provided him a comfortable living, noble status, and leisure to pursue his interest in drama; however, his domestic happiness ended suddenly with the deaths of both his wife and young son. Scandals of the era suggest that Beaumarchais enjoyed gambling at high stakes in shipping and contracting, inveigling reputable women in questionable business deals, and applying his guile and chicanery to amassing a fortune. Among his failed plots was an attempt to place a French courtesan in the Spanish inner court as a pro-Gallic influence. He was no stranger to the law courts and had mixed success in defending his reputation and that of his sister, Marie Louise Caron, whom the Spanish writer Clavijo had dishonored.

Beaumarchais published two didactic works sympathetic to the oppressed working class: a mediocre sentimental comedy, *Eugénie* (1767), which the Comédie Française produced, and *Les Deux amis ou le négociant de Lyon [Two Friends or The Trader of Lyon]* (1770). His formal challenge, *Genre dramatique sérieux [The Genre of Serious Drama]*, called for an end to the use of nobility and courtiers as the subjects of art. Following the death of his partner Duverney, Beaumarchais battled Count de la Blache, Duverney's heir, in ten years of court suits over contracts, payments, and outstanding debts. Beaumarchais's public behavior and humble background earned him the respect of commoners; from the king, he accepted a discreet role in international intrigue, a spy operation that Louis XVI orchestrated in London, Vienna, and Germany. Swept up in the zeitgeist that pitted corrupt courtiers against the working class, Beaumarchais composed the stingingly satiric polemics *Mémoires du Sieur Beaumarchais par lui-même [Beaumarchais's Autobiographical Memoirs]* (1774–1778), which directed sympathies toward his case and cemented his growing friendship with the libertarian philosopher Voltaire but won Beaumarchais no favors with Court Justice Goëzman, whom his work pilloried as corrupt.

In the same irreverent vein, Beaumarchais published his most famous satiric comedies, *Le Barbier de Séville* and *La Folle journée ou le mariage de Figaro [The Foolish Day's Work, or The Marriage of Figaro]* (1784), for which he came under the severe censorship of the Comédie Française. Court minions delayed production; Beaumarchais served a brief jail term in Fort l'Évêque for slandering the aristocracy. At length, in 1784, Louis XVI himself agreed to a public performance in the Theatre Français in Paris. The crush of eager ticket-holders produced a panic among guards, scalpers, and performers. The play, elongated by frequent applause, ran from 5:30 to 10:00 P.M. Overall, the first 68 performances netted 347,000 livres, an unprecedented box-office take for the eighteenth century. To reestablish his good name, Beaumarchais publicly donated his share to charity. Texts were soon pirated, translated, and performed in London's Theatre Royal the next February.

The tale of a scheming servant defaming his aristocratic master was the expression of mounting discontent with the privileged overclass, some of whom Beaumarchais makes no effort to disguise. For one line, "to dare lions and tigers," the playwright served a five-day sentence in St. Lazare, a detention hall for juvenile delinquents. Overwhelming success made Beaumarchais's work a frequent choice for translation and revival on European stages; three musical settings account for a parallel strand of operatic performances:

- Giovanni Paisiello and Cesare Sterbini's *Il Barbiere di Siviglia* (1782)

- Wolfgang Amadeus Mozart's *Le Nozze di Figaro* (1786)

- Gioacchino Rossini's *Il Barbiere di Siviglia* (1816)

During this heady period, Beaumarchais organized a writer's guild, La Société des Auteurs Dramatiques, and, under its protection, published political pamphlets.

Beaumarchais's sudden rise to fame followed an up-and-down course to a permanent nadir. A failed court appeal against de la Blache forced Beaumarchais to sell his property to pay a sizeable fine; the decline of his prospects lured creditors and demanding relatives out of dim corners. Public airings of old business deals in Spain brought out his resourcefulness in court, where he spoke his version of the truth to a hostile audience of aristocrats and won the public's acclamation for his boldness and persistence. In retaliation, Goëzman labeled him a forger and cheat. During this period, Beaumarchais managed a third marriage, this time to his mistress, Mademoiselle Willermawlas, the mother of his nine-year-old daughter Eugénie. The strength of the marriage enabled him to survive greater challenges, build a grand home, and write the libretto for *Tarare* (1780), an opera for which Salieri composed the music.

Despite Beaumarchais's questionable reputation, Louis XVI dispatched him to Austria on a secret mission and commissioned him to organize a fleet to ferry arms and equipment to the desperate American colonists, whom Beaumarchais proclaimed "invincible." Because of his brilliant coup, he earned the suspicion of restless French workers who despised all entrepreneurs. During the French Revolution, he was classed with wealthy emigrés and lost his investments; he received no recompense from the American colonists for arming them against the British, for which he had taken out a loan of a million livres to underwrite a private fleet.

Implication in the illegal arms sale forced him into hiding before he could realize a profit on his publication of a 70-volume collection of Voltaire's works. Ironically, in 1792, Beaumarchais, his wife, daughter, and sister were jailed in the Bastille along with other monarchists for his role in organizing a sale of Dutch muskets to French revolutionaries. He obtained the family's release and lived incognito in Holland, England, and Germany. In 1796, he returned to Paris to reclaim his property and attend the performance of his final work, *La Mère coupable [The Guilty Mother]*, sometimes labeled the third in the Figaro trilogy. Once more the toast of Paris, he died of a stroke on May 18, 1799. (Beaumarchais 1964; Cross 1947; Magill 1958; Magnusson 1990)

See also Le Barbier de Séville; comedy; didacticism; *La Folle journée ou le mariage de Figaro*; Restoration drama; trickster; Voltaire, François.

BECKETT, SAMUEL

One of the practitioners of black humor and a major figure in theater of the absurd, expatriate Irishman Samuel Barclay Beckett distinguished himself by his scholarly studies of James Joyce and Marcel Proust and by his brilliant drama, *En Attendant Godot (Waiting for Godot)* (1952). Beckett's most devoted disciples consider him the father of the absurdist movement and class him among his followers, Tom Stoppard, Harold Pinter, and Edward Albee, with the best of the absurdist playwrights. A disgruntled Dubliner born in Foxrock on May 15, 1906, Beckett, the son of surveyor William Frank and Mary Roe Beckett, an interpreter for the Irish Red Cross, tolerated bourgeois attitudes and a church-dominated parochial education at Portora Royal School. After his completion of a degree in modern languages from Trinity College in 1927 and two years teaching in Belfast, he fled to L'École Normale Supérieure in Paris and earned a graduate degree in Italian and French. He taught French at his alma mater while helping James Joyce—who was nearly blind—transcribe his novel *Finnegan's Wake*.

Feeling inadequate as a teacher, Beckett began a full-time writing career and produced a prodigious number of plays and novels, most in the ambiguous, tragicomic vein. After he returned for good to the Continent because of the severity of Catholic censorship, he chose Paris as home base, traveled extensively, and produced the avant-garde plays that have defined and strengthened the experimental drama of the mid-twentieth century. The Nazi infiltration of France forced him out of Paris to Roussillon in the Vaucluse region, where

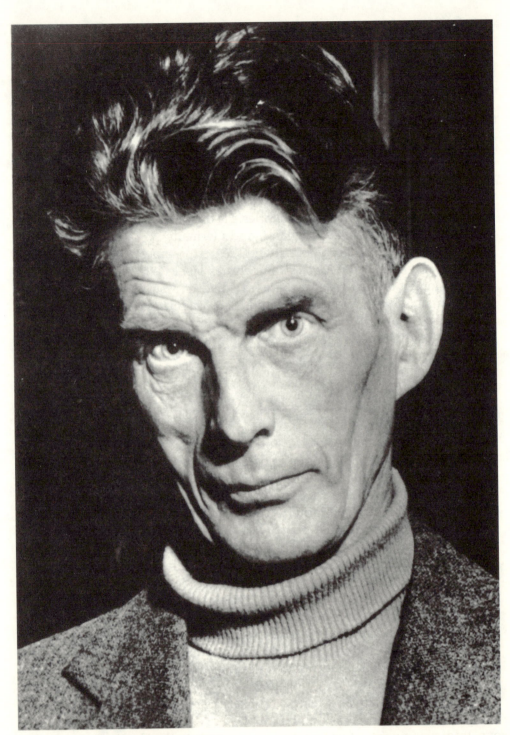
Irish playwright Samuel Beckett in 1964

he hid from authorities while posing as a farmhand and supporting the French Resistance. After the war, he distinguished himself as an interpreter for the Irish Red Cross Hospital at St. Lo. In 1961, he married a Frenchwoman, pianist Suzanne Deschevaux-Dumesnil, and spent the remainder of his life either in Paris or in seclusion at the couple's country estate. Writing stage, radio, and television plays and novels in French and translating them into English, he expressed the dismay that colored literary thought in post–World War II Europe.

As a spokesperson for a disaffected modern audience, Beckett rose rapidly in the public's estimation with *Endgame* (1958), *How It Is* (1964), *Krapp's Last Tape* (1959), and *Not I* (1973). His energized mix of snappy patter, surreal setting, clowning and mugging, denuded style, and plotless situations earned him an Obie, an Hours Press Award, the Italia prize, an honorary doctorate from Trinity College, the International Publishers prize (shared with Jorge Luis Borges), and the 1969 Nobel Prize, which he refused to accept in person at the annual Stockholm ceremony. At his death from respiratory failure on December 22, 1989, Beckett commanded the respect of a farflung literary audience of readers, writers, critics, and philosophers. (Abbott 1973; Beckett 1954; Ben-Zvi 1986; Esslin 1965)

See also black humor; theater of the absurd; *Waiting for Godot.*

BEERBOHM, MAX

A charming in-crowd essayist, bon vivant, cartoonist, and wit whom George Bernard Shaw dubbed "the incomparable Max," Sir Henry Maximilian Beerbohm was a compact, dapper Britisher known for crisp tweeds, silk foulard, and a wicked twinkle in his blue eyes. A Jewish Londoner educated at Charterhouse School and Merton College, Oxford, Beerbohm crafted satires and caricatures with a refined discretion, forgiving tone, and unerring sense of the ironic bull's-eye. Admired by George Bernard Shaw, Rebecca West, Algernon Swinburne, Aubrey Beardsley, and Christopher Morley, Beerbohm formed the hub of a perpetually active social set who frequently attuned their opinions and laughter to his dictates. He characterized his readers as delighting in suffering and contemptuous of the unfamiliar; his major victims were popular author Rudyard Kipling and John Bull, the caricature of English gung-ho imperialism. In characterizing himself, Beerbohm brushed aside an honorary doctorate from Edinburgh University and modestly summarized: "My gifts are small, I've used them very well and discreetly, never straining them, and the result is that I've made a charming little reputation."

Born August 24, 1872, in Kensington, the last of the nine children of Lithuanian grain merchant Julius E. E. and Eliza Draper Beerbohm, Max Beerbohm focused on convivial socializing in school and left the university before finishing a degree. He returned to his parents' home at Marylebone and remained there for three decades, devoting his energies to *fin-de-siècle* observation and commentary. Under the pose of insouciant aesthete border- ing on impertinent snob, he worked steadily at his career and nurtured a spiffy man-about-town image, which he emphasized to avoid the ostracism that of- ten plagued Jews. He married an American, actress Florence Kahn, in 1910, and retired to Villino Chiaro near Rapallo, Italy, where he hosted semi-perma- nent houseguest Ezra Pound.

Beerbohm's return to England in 1936 to broadcast from the Langham Hotel, a temporary home of wartime BBC radio, came after a radical excision of England's former gaiety. Reacquaintance with his native land depressed him when he realized that the Gay Nineties and Edwardian era had given place to a vulgar commercialism and persistent, unsettling clangor. Critics accused him of refusing to compete with budding female wits who challenged his former status as premier satirist. The gnawing doubt that he had nothing in common with his homeland extinguished his familiar sparkle. Knighted in 1939, he took little pleasure in appended honors. The ebullient Max lost even more zest after his wife's death in 1951. He married his secretary, Elizabeth Jungman, in April 1956 and died in his Italian home four weeks later on May 20.

Beerbohm spoofed the fusty atmosphere of Oxford in his only novel, a whimsical romantic satire, *Zuleika Dobson* (1911), which features a self-absorbed, prom-trotting heartbreaker who leads Oxfordmen to vows of suicide. In an absurd debacle, every male at the university—except one with a sprained ankle—drowns himself, leaving Zuleika to seek new prospects at Cambridge. Obsessed with the clay feet of socialites, politicians, and writers, Beerbohm wrote dramatic critiques for the *Saturday Review* and published a stream of satiric essays, caricatures, and parodies collected in *The Works of Max Beerbohm* (1896), *Caricatures of Twenty-Five Gentlemen* (1896), *More* (1899), *The Poet's Cor- ner* (1904), *Yet Again* (1909), *A Christmas Garland* (1912), *And Even Now* (1920), *Rossetti and His Circle* (1922), and *The Dreadful Dragon of Hay Hill* (1928). (Beerbohm 1967; Drabble 1985; Eagle and Stephens 1992; Grigson 1963; Kunitz 1942; Magill 1958; McArthur 1992)

See also caricature; political satire; satire; Shaw, George Bernard; whimsy.

THE BEGGAR'S OPERA

John Gay's masterwork blends low comedy, drollery, double entendre, and political satire of the corrupt Whig regime of election-riggers under Prime Min- ister Sir Robert Walpole. *The Beggar's Opera* has remained one of the most popu- lar stage works of the eighteenth century. After its opening on January 29, 1728, it ran for 62 performances, a record at the Lincoln's Inn Fields Theatre, and earned Gay £1,000. Its original 69 songs, supplied by composer John C. Pepusch, became popular ballads. The vitality and music survive in Bertolt Brecht and Kurt Weill's musical *The Threepenny Opera* (1928) and in the 1952 film version, adapted for screen by Christopher Fry and starring Laurence Olivier. Bobby Darin reprised the focal ballad "Mack the Knife" in 1954 and spun the single to the top of the pop charts; Ella Fitzgerald had similar fortune with the tune in 1960, as did Frank Sinatra in 1986.

The negligible plot, set in London's underworld, concerns a lovable scape-grace, Macheath, the leader of bandits Jemmy Twitcher, Crook-Fingered Jack, Wat Dreary, Robin of Bagshot, Nimming Ned, Harry Paddington, Matt of the Mint, and Ben Budge. The introductory tune sets the satiric tone, which mocks white-collar crime:

> All professions be-rogue one another.
> The priest calls the lawyer a cheat,
>> The lawyer be-knaves the divine;
> And the statesman, because he's so great,
>> Thinks his trade as honest as mine.

At the play's opening, Macheath has married Polly Peachum, daughter of the fence for a theft ring. The senior Peachum plays the sexist male and de-mands that Polly become a devoted wife; Mrs. Peachum disagrees and de-scribes the plight of a wife, who,

> . . . like a guinea in gold,
>> stamp'd with the name of her spouse;
> Now here, now there; is bought, or is sold;
>> And is current in every house.

Mrs. Peachum blames playbooks for giving Polly the notion of falling in love like gentlefolk, marrying Macheath, and remaining faithful to him. To rid daugh-ter Polly of her bad influences, the parents conspire to have Macheath arrested so Polly can be rid of his bad influence. Afflicted with a "bleeding heart," Polly helps Macheath elude authorities, but he foolishly has the gang summon his many "free-hearted" women friends—Mrs. Coaxer, Dolly Trull, Mrs. Vixen, Betty Doxy, Jenny Diver, Mrs. Slammekin, Suky Tawdry, and Molly Brazen—so he can bid them a proper farewell. Jenny Diver and Suky Tawdry steal his pistols and hold his neck; Jenny signals to the constables. Peachum hands him over; Lockit, jailer of Newgate Prison, leaves Macheath to his "meditations."

The melodramatic scene at the jail offers no out for Macky. Lockit's daugh-ter Lucy, one of Macheath's many heartthrobs, attacks him for being dishonor-able. He denies that he has married Polly and vows that, as soon as he walks free, he will marry Lucy. To corroborate the story, he charges Polly with vanity and conceit. Lucy's father mocks her tears and urges her to "make yourself as easy as you can by getting all you can from him"; Macky's two warring rivals sing a bitter duet pitting flirt against jade. Polly pleads, "How can you see me made the scoff of such a gypsy?" Against Lockit's advice, Lucy helps Macheath flee in exchange for a promise of marriage. Lockit heaps scorn on his daughter, calling her a slut, hussy, and wanton strumpet.

Venality becomes an object of satire, as well, when Macheath meets his buddies at a roadhouse and derides "the modes of the court," where money buys a way out of trouble. At large only briefly, he falls into Lockit's hands and, against an outcry from the rabble to set him free, is condemned to the gallows for jailbreaking. Lucy and Polly recognize that the tyranny of fathers makes them sisters; Macheath urges them to try their luck in the West Indies. A bit of stage trickery retrieves the play from "downright tragedy"; Macheath goes free and reunites with Polly. The beggar pronounces the didactic epilogue: that "the lower sort of people have their vices in a degree as well as the rich; and that they are punished for them." Macheath leads a dance of the many women who have claimed him. (Baugh 1948; Bermel 1982; Brockett 1968; Burdick 1974; Drabble 1985; Feinberg 1967; Fowler 1989; Gay 1952; Magill 1958; Pollard 1970; Roberts 1962; Woods 1947)

See also Brecht, Bertolt; burlesque; comedy; *double entendre;* Gay, John.

BEHN, APHRA

England's first professional female author, Aphra Behn received critical commentary as early as 1695 in a collection of the poems of Anne, Countess of Winchilsea:

> He lamented for Behn, o'er that place of her birth,
> And said amongst Women there was not on the earth,
> Her superior in fancy, in language, or witt,
> Yet own'd that a little too loosely she writt.

Behn was born early in July 1640 in Harbledown, west of Canterbury, Kent. At the baptism of Behn and her brother Peter on December 14 at St. Michael's Church, the family registered her first name as Eaffry; later sources list it as Ayfara, Afra, Aphara, Apharra, Aphaw, or Astrea; the latter became her pen name. In girlhood, she read French heroic romances, which colored her later writings with the grandeur of elevated fiction. Her family set out for Surinam, or Dutch Guiana, in the West Indies, where her father, tentatively identified as either John Amis or Amies of Wye (and sometimes falsely named as James Johnson, a Canterbury barber), anticipated being sworn in as lieutenant governor under the patronage of Francis Lord Willoughby of Parham, the island administrator. Before the ship docked, he died, proving a reflective epigram from Behn's *The Lucky Chance* (1686), "Faith Sir, we are here today, and gone tomorrow."

Mother Amy, son, and daughter settled on foreign soil and lived at St. John's Hill, where Behn read widely in historical fiction and grew into a winsome, attractive, affable woman. In her youth, she attempted her own version of the story of King Alcamène, *The Young King.* Adept at observation and local color, she later incorporated into her romantic novel *Oroonoko, or The Royal Slave* (1688) the story of a slave revolt against British colonialists that became the source of Thomas Southerne's play in 1695. Algernon Swinburne lauded her denunciation of slavery, proclaiming: "This improper woman of genius was the first literary abolitionist—the first champion of the slave in the history of fiction."

Behn's fortunes were tenuous. Living in Surinam as mistress of William Scott, son of the king-killer Thomas Scott, she adopted the pastoral name of

Astrea and referred to Scott as Celadon. On her return to London in 1662, she married a Dutch vendor named Behn. During her marriage, she met and charmed Charles II. After her husband died of plague in 1665, Behn was left penniless. On the recommendation of Thomas Killigrew, she chose a life of intrigue and, drawing on her ties with the Dutch, served in Antwerp from summer to midwinter 1666 as a spy for the crown, gleaning useful details from Scott's observations at his office at The Hague. (Some accounts claim that her sole purpose in selling information was a reprieve for her lover, whose father took an active role in the beheading of Charles I and was executed October 17, 1660.) Because of the secret nature of her employment, Behn had no recourse to the usual channels of seeking pay. On her return to England in January 1667, she served a term in debtors' prison. Before surrendering, she wrote a willful note to her contact at court, Tom Killigrew:

> I will send my mother to the king with a Pitition for I see every body are words; & I will not perish in a Prison from whence he swears I shall not stirr till the uttmost farthing be payd: & oh god, who considers my misery & charge too, this is my reward for all my great primises, & my indeavers. Sr if I have not the money to night you must send me som thing to keepe me in Prison for I will not starve.

As determined as the fictional Scarlett O'Hara to keep herself from starvation, Behn survived prison and her resulting disillusion with her failed career in espionage.

Behn depended on support of friends John Dryden, George Etherege, George Buckingham, Edmund Waller, and Thomas Otway. She actively pursued a literary career by studying French masters and by publishing verse, histories, translations, and comedy written in the style and tone of the age. She utilized European models to write a tragicomedy, *The Forced Marriage, or The Jealous Bridegroom* (1670), produced at the Duke's Theater; *The Amorous Prince* (1671), an intrigue plot set in Florence, Italy; and *The Dutch Lover* (1673), a romance set in Madrid, Spain. Amply supplied with the contemporary wit and scurrilous humor of the Restoration era, she salted her plays with segments of works preceding the time period. Among her lengthy borrowings, she copied wholesale from the anonymous *Lust's Dominion* (1600) to create *Abdelazer* (1676) and *Sir Patient Fancy* (1678), which she adapted from Molière's *Le Malade imaginaire*. In a note to Emily Price, Behn acknowledges her debt to Otway and promises:

> When I shall let the World know, whenefer I take the Pains next to appear in Print, of the mighty Theft I have been guilty of; But however for your own Satisfaction, I have sent you the Garden from whence I gather'd, and I hope you will not think me vain, if I say, I have weeded and improv'd it.

The boast hints at the bold, resourceful woman who navigated a man's world with skill and a measure of success, despite the carping of critics.

Because of her skill at intrigue, Behn succeeded with *The Rover, or The Banish'd Cavaliers* (1677–1680), produced at the Duke's House, Dorset Gardens. An imaginative two-part tale of English royalists carousing at Naples in carnival season during the English Commonwealth, the story centers on love matches, disguises, thwarted matings, and a satisfactory resolution. She loosely based the hero, Willmore, an amorous rowdy, on the life of satirist John Wilmot, Earl of Rochester. Richard Steele's commentary in *The Spectator*, April 28, 1711, relishes the scene in Act IV in which Behn describes Blunt as "rarely cheated of all but his Shirt and Drawers." To compound the humiliation, the whore who cozens him "turn'd him out before Consummation, so that traversing the Streets at Midnight, the Watch found him in this Fresco, and conducted him home." The roistering grows bolder in Blunt's comment:

> A Pox of all poor Cavaliers, a Man can never keep a spare Suit for 'em; and I shall have these Rogues come in and find me naked; and then I'm undone; but I'm resolv'd to arm my self—the Rascals shall not insult over me too much.

Less clever than other satires of the period, the play achieves its aims with simple buffoonery conducted during a night traditionally given to pranks, drinking, and devil-may-care. In the end, Willmore is won over to his "brave girl," whom he admires for her love and courage, a trace of the Aphra of early days who dared work as a spy and live as she pleased.

Near the final curtain, Behn pushes satire to a dangerous extreme. The epilogue compounds anti-Cavalier jokes with a direct assault on the crown:

> But tell me, pray,
> What has the House of Commons done to day?
> Then shews his Politicks, to let you see
> Of State Affairs he'll judge as notably,
> As he can do of Wit and Poetry.
> The younger Sparks, who hither do resort
> Cry—Pox o' you gentle things, give us more Sport;
> —Damn me, I'm sure 'twill never please the Court.

The outspoken anti-royalist fervor glows throughout the play, reducing the Cavaliers from rovers to witless clowns whom women easily deceive and manipulate.

Behn remained brash in her next three works, lampooning royalists in *The Rover, Part 2* (1680), *The Roundheads* (1682), and *The City Heiress* (1682), one of her most scathing satires. Bold words and merry jests cost Behn her support from Whigs, whom she ridiculed unmercifully for being bumbling fools. One critic lashed out at "the Lewd Widow . . . with Brazen Face." Less jovial was the official writ of August 12, 1682, calling for Behn's arrest for having

> committed severall Misdemeanors and made abusive reflections upon persons of Quality, and have written and spoken scandalous speeches without any License or Approbation of those that ought to peruse and authorize the same.

The outcome of the suit is unknown; shortly afterward, John Dryden, a literary lion, committed a similar satiric outrage with impunity. Given this disparity, literary critics infer that Behn was the victim of sexism. Perhaps she grew more canny of the double standard. In deference to royalty, she took the occasion of

Charles II's death on February 6, 1685, to offer a memorial verse in his honor, as did numerous court favorites. She was careful to follow her elegy with a welcoming "Poem on the Happy Coronation of His Sacred Majesty" when James II took the throne.

The threads of Behn's life are severely frayed in her later years, partly by fate and ill health, which appears to have been triggered by overwork and an attack of gout. Behn's reputation does not rest on her last works—*The Adventures of the Black Lady* (1683), *Love Letters between a Nobleman and His Sister* (1684), *The Lucky Chance* (1686), *The Fair Jilt* (1688), *Agnes de Castro* (1688), *The History of the Nun, or The Fair Vow-Breaker* (1689), and the posthumous *The Unfortunate Happy Lady: A True History* (1696)—frivolous novels that follow the late seventeenth-century trend of de-emphasizing the upper class and returning to common folk for inspiration. She is remembered instead for *Oroonoko* and the stirring depiction of a black regent striving against the debasement of the slave trade. After her death on April 16, 1689, she was buried in Westminster Abbey's east cloisters, a tribute to the first Englishwoman to earn a living from writing, translation, and theatrical production.

For most of literary history, critics have treated Behn as a raffish, often ludicrous female bohemian rather than a contributor to the wit and drollery of Restoration drama. Her epigrams include reflective, often sardonic observations:

- Love's a thin diet, nor will keep out cold.

- He that knew all that ever learning writ,
  Knew only this—that he knew nothing yet.

- Money speaks sense in a language all nations understand.

- Variety is the soul of pleasure.

- Dear me no dears, Sir.

Her plots resemble the typical conflicts of Shakespeare's romances: star-crossed romance, secret trysts, novices fleeing from convents, and the kidnapping of hapless maidens. In Behn's own day, John Dryden, for example, found her characters too one-sided to achieve life.

In later critiques preceding the rise of feminism, Behn is passed over as feminine fluff, not worth serious consideration. Some of the blame for the convoluted facts of her literary success belongs to Charles Gildon, who published a biography, *The History of the Life and Memoirs of Mrs. Behn, Written by One of the Fair Sex* (1696), which muddled the facts of Behn's life with interpolated segments of her fiction. Another source of faulty biography is the tendency of male contemporaries to expect stay-at-home womanliness from a writer who chose to exercise her talents and sell her works for profit. Championed by Vita Sackville-West, Virginia Woolf, and the wider feminist movement, Behn's canon experienced a resurgence and her talents received more objective study. (Baugh 1948; Behn 1915; Brockett 1968; Burdick 1974; Drabble 1985; Eagle and Stephens 1992; Lovett and Hughesl 1932; McMillin 1973; Norman 1995; Roberts 1962; Wilson 1965)

THE BIRDS

A whimsical dystopian farce resulting from Attic malaise following the Peloponnesian War, Aristophanes's *Ornithes* or *The Birds* (414 B.C.) skewers the rampant power grab that imperiled Athens, the author's hometown. The political satire centers on multiple targets: civic arrogance, outworn religious rites, and human faults. Because Athenians had voted to spend tax dollars on an expedition to colonize the southern and eastern shores of Sicily, Aristophanes invented a civic boondoggle—Cloudcuckooland—a black hole capable of swallowing up the city-state's meager treasury and exposing it further to threats from Sparta, which lay in wait and let the city destroy itself. On a personal level, Aristophanes chose local parasites, boobs, lobbyists, loonies, and dreamers as minor personae to illustrate how quickly opportunists cluster around loafer's paradise, a do-nothing utopia.

Ridiculing the dreary political squabbles of the playwright's milieu, Aristophanes introduces two of his most perfect satiric characters: Euelpides ("Hopefulson" in Greek) and Pisthetairos ("Friend-Persuader"), two elderly citizens who flee urban unrest by buying a jackdaw and a crow from Philocrates, a bird seller who promises that the birds will carry them upward to Hoopoe, Epops's haven in the sky. The duo's anticipations crumble when they land in a rocky, gorse-dotted wasteland. Undaunted, they question Philocrates's advice about "greener grass" beyond Athens. They knock at the entrance; a fierce, beak-nosed butler answers. They beg an appointment with the Hoopoe bird.

Aristophanes heightens the satiric thrust by connecting the denizens of heaven with human sin. In the foyer, the visitors meet Epops, a naive sovereign once known on earth as Tereus, a mythic villain whom the gods punished for seducing Philomela, his sister-in-law, and for running up debts. Transformed into a scruffy bird-ruler, Epops draws on experience and observations of the faults and missteps of earthlings to guide his decisions. The malcontents petition Epops to find them a restful nook where friendships are genuine. Still burdened with human appetites, the two also require women who will meet their sexual demands without expecting commitment or legal rights. Aristophanes may have devised this satiric turn of events as a direct commentary on local scandal or a sweeping condemnation of casual liaisons that degraded both parties and weakened the state of matrimony.

After the duo makes its demands, the haggling begins. To establish his openmindedness, Epops claims that his kingdom welcomes sports fans, gourmands, and idlers. He selects for the two seekers a city near the Red Sea where citizens have no need for money, but Euelpides and Pisthetairos reject a place by the shore. They inquire about aviaries and improvise *Nephelococcugia* or Cloudcuckooland, a town in the clouds, far above mortal imbroglios and blessed with serenity. A potential power broker, Pisthetairos exults at the notion of holding sway over the lands below. Epops and his wife Procne, a mythic night-ingale, approve the plan, but Pisthetairos must acquire consensus from the birds before committing the plan to a builder.

Aristophanes's jerry-built utopia abounds in idiosyncratic pitfalls. At a session with the bird delegation, the outsiders thrill to the massing of birds, which Aristophanes describes with a mock-heroic touch:

> Jay and turtle, lark and sedgebird, thyme finch, ring-dove
>   first, and then
> Rock-dove, stock-dove, cuckoo, falcon, fiery-crest, and
>   willow wren,
> Lammergeyer, porphyrion, kestrel, waxwing, nuthatch,
>   water-hen.

Koryphaios, the head fowl, chides the Hoopoe chief for encouraging human habitation in their humanless abode. The birds churn up enough dissension to terrorize the interlopers with "death by dissection" and threaten to shred the meat from Euelpides and Pisthetairos's bones, a parallel of the Spartan wish to trounce Athens so thoroughly that only a skeleton will remain. Epops calms the council and declares a temporary truce and a sheathing of talons so the Athenians can present their request.

Diffident in the face of a steely-eyed council, Euelpides and Pisthetairos, like Athens's oily politicians, compromise themselves with meaningless inducements. Pisthetairos elevates the birds, who lived before human creation and therefore must outrank the gods themselves. He concludes that, as emblems of sovereignty, muscle, and wisdom, birds deserve to govern humankind. He concocts a construction project: "I propose that the air ye enclose, and the space 'twixt earth and sky." If humans object, sparrows would gobble all grain and scratch out the eyes of livestock; if humans allow the wall to go up, the birds, in a valuable conciliatory gesture, would eradicate the insect population. As Pisthetairos winds down his persuasive oratory, he challenges the birds to rise above servility. This ornate speech, echoing an empty gesture of nobility, epitomizes the milieu in which Aristophanes lived and the extent to which politicians connived to mesmerize voters.

As the idea takes shape, Pisthetairos drafts plans for a brick bastion as strong as ancient Babylon. Upon completing the wall, the birds should reclaim ancient powers by confiscating Zeus's scepter. If he repudiates their claim to the throne, the birds will launch an avian jihad against Mount Olympus and deprive lustful divinities of opportunities to couple with human mates, a common motif in anthropomorphic religion. After the gods capitulate to their new masters, the birds will strengthen their rule by forcing humans to sacrifice on their altars, from which deposed gods could snatch the scraps, a direct hit on the Athenian political situation—a once-great city reduced to beggar status.

Aristophanes ridicules the boneheadedness of committees by describing how the birds iron out the remaining details. How will they control money, which men appear to worship like a god? Pisthetairos suggests that the birds lead earth's gold-diggers to hidden caches. To assure a chummy alliance with humankind, birds could deliver weather reports and save the shipping industry from losing fleets and cargo to storms. As the bird council warms to the plan, Pisthetairos plays his ace-in-the-hole, as he compliments the birds for living simply by scorning the faults of Greek religion:

> No need for their sakes to erect and adorn
> Great temples of marble with portals of gold.
> Enough for the birds on the brake and the thorn
> And the evergreen oak their receptions to hold.
> Or if any are noble, and courtly, and fine,
> The tree of the olive will serve for their shrine.
> No need, when a blessing we seek, to repair
> To Delphi or Ammon, and sacrifice there.

Aristophanes closes this masterful putdown of Greek religion with Pisthetairos's locker-room harangue. The birds applaud enthusiastically and, professing nationalistic zeal, vow to overturn the gods.

With Epops in the lead, the two Athenians quickly implement their plan. Epops offers them a magic herb that grows wings on their bodies. Meanwhile, the birds rehash their ancient lineage, which predates humankind and gods. Flaunting their natural wind-resistant shape, they glory in streamlined frames that soar above humans, who must keep their feet on the ground. At the end of an extravagant pro-bird rally, the Athenians, in full feather and tricked out in beaks and wings, return to the stage to model their metamorphosis. Undoubtedly one of Aristophanes's most colorful sight gags, the awkward birdmen are the high spot of the play's satire.

As Cloudcuckooland rises brick on brick, Aristophanes enlarges the satire at a pace equal to the builder's ego. Seizing the momentum, Pisthetairos grandly superintends bricklayers and oversees priestly ritual. The playwright tweaks state versifiers with a meddling poet who wants to compose a paean to Cloudcuckooland. Useless to the workers, the poet gets shoved out of the way. An oracle-reader merits a similarly unceremonious heave-ho. A third meddler—Meton, the surveyor—is also ejected. Pisthetairos proclaims a necessary ordinance—confidence games will earn the faker a public lashing. Recognizing himself in the description, Meton quickly locates the stage exit. Additional self-appointed nuisances interrupt Pisthetairos and his crew. He rewards an officious Athenian building inspector with a smack on the jaw and manhandles a venal wardheeler eager to peddle legal influence. These final two prove more persistent and retreat only after a thorough trouncing. Alone with his work, Pisthetairos returns to walling in heaven. The chorus trills a hymn to birddom and implores the judges to award Aristophanes a blue ribbon.

At this point in the conflict, Aristophanes introduces potential violence and tragedy. When the wall rises to six hundred feet, the birds boast of their achievement. A messenger raises the alarm: a god has eluded security; Pisthetairos sets the birds on him. Iris, the rainbow goddess, surfaces in polychromatic splendor. Pisthetairos demands her arrest. She dares any feathered upstart to challenge a deity and flaunts the omnipotent "Father of mankind." Pisthetairos blasphemes "Zeus-born gods" with his claim that birds now outrank Olympus's divinities. Iris warns that Zeus won't back down, but the Athenian compounds sacrilege with threats of death to Zeus and "outrage" for Iris if she should dare the patience of a short-tempered old man.

The next runner, who returns from earth with an outpouring of worship and a jeweled coronet, brightens the tense moment. Pisthetairos has so over-turned the old way of doing things that humankind now spurns gods and bows before anything with feathers. Birds are hailed at religious gatherings, in popular melodies, as names, and as tourist attractions. With thousands of humans headed for Cloudcuckooland, Pisthetairos feels the stress of success. He plunges into frenzied preparations, ordering Manes to fetch an emergency stock of

> . . . musical wings,
> And the sings of the seers, and the sings of the sea,
>   that as each one appears,
> The wings that he wants you can get.

A parade of emigrants passes through. The birds first welcome the sire-striker, a youth fleeing laws against patricide. Crestfallen to learn that he must honor his parent, he blames Pisthetairos for forcing him to return to his father's house to support him through his dotage. Pisthetairos compromises by turning the would-be father-killer into a black-winged orphan, supplying him armaments, and dispatching him to a war in Thrace. The parade of incompetent boobs continues. After sire-striker come Kinesias the dithyrambist and a spy. Pisthetairos takes pity on the poetaster by outfitting him with wings and as-signing him the job of bird chorister to rid him of tedium. Next, the spy, a law-perverter, requests wings to streamline his hunt for likely clients. Pisthetairos intercedes with his cat-o'-nine-tails, drives out the seedy informer, and hauls a store of wings back to the closet.

Aristophanes, grown bold in the falling action, satirizes Zeus. Muffled in a disguise, Prometheus, the renowned Zeus-defier, alerts Pisthetairos of rum-blings in the divine camp. Timidly peering out from a sheltering umbrella, Prometheus lauds the extinction of Zeus's tyranny and announces that the former lord of heaven plans to extend an olive branch. Prometheus advises Pisthetairos to hold out for a total surrender and to demand the hand of Basileia, Zeus's chargé d'affaires. His counsel delivered, Prometheus slithers back to Mount Olympus.

At last comes the peace commission, composed of Herakles, Poseidon, and Triballus, a barbarian deity muttering in doggerel Greek, "Me gulna charmi grati Sovranau Birdito stori." Poseidon acts as peacekeeper and tethers Herakles, who is accustomed to settling matters with a one-two punch. Pisthetairos counters the trio by ignoring them and, in a bored tone, interrupts his meal with a call for oil. After deigning to notice the salivating embassy, he demands sovereignty over heaven and sweet-talks the three negotiators (but does not offer even a morsel from his table).

At length, Poseidon agrees that the birds deserve the royal scepter. Pisthetairos follows the concession with a demand for Miss Sovereignty, a trophy wife who betokens the truce. At first, Poseidon hedges, then, with Herakles's concurrence, agrees. The play closes with the procession of King Pisthetairos and his lovely consort, Basileia. Birds throng to the scene and cavort about the newlyweds. The closing chorus gloats that

> All that was Zeus's of old now is our hero's alone;
> Sovereignty, fair to behold,
> Partner of Zeus on his throne,
> Now is forever his own.

This jolly, bumptious comedy, Aristophanes's best and most timely parody, retains its freshness, wit, and creative nonsense, even though it dates to 414 B.C. Second-place winner in the local contest, *The Birds* lauds irreverence: the creation of a cloud sanctuary where Pisthetairos, through connivance, blasphemy, and audacity, subsumes Zeus's place. As diatribe, the play depicts the playwright's distaste for authoritarian meddling in citizens' lives, civic malfeasance, and the free-floating unease that saps Attic society. In contrast, the insane fantasy of Cloudcuckooland, which fends off hucksters, special interests, pandering, and violence, offers an ethereal utopia and a retreat from earthly vice. (Aristophanes 1955, 1962, 1993; Feder 1986; Hadas 1954; Hammond and Scullard 1992; Hornstein 1973; Howatson 1989; Lord 1963; Magill 1958; Mantinband 1956; Radice 1973; Snodgrass 1989; Spatz 1978)

See also Aristophanes; comedy; diatribe; doggerel; mock-heroic; parody; satire.

BLACK HUMOR

A sinister, unsettling segment of comedy, black humor exaggerates fun into the surreal tragicomedy and theater of the absurd that has come to dominate much of the twentieth century's fiction and drama. A negative, bitter nihilism born of existentialism, black comedy feeds on disillusion, despair, and cynicism to produce grotesqueness and horror. A frank exploration of incongruity with a sardonic twist, black comedy sets its sights on death, war, madness, and disease and peoples its landscapes with inarticulate bunglers who flounder in meaningless crises. The antiheroes grasp at wisps of any credo that can account for futility or pernicious cruelty and inhumanity. God, the author of the absurd, remains silent and allows events to proceed willy-nilly. The weak laughter of fate's victims echoes bleakly against a stark landscape littered with the victims who have gone before.

Although black humor is currently popular in jokes, television cartoons, and theater, it has always lurked at the periphery of comedy. Dark humor permeates some of William Shakespeare's comedy, notably *The Winter's Tale* (ca. 1610–1611), *The Merchant of Venice* (ca. 1596), *Measure for Measure* (ca. 1604), and *All's Well That Ends Well* (ca. 1604). The title of *Much Ado about Nothing* (ca.

1598) precedes scenes of condemnation of Hero, a virtuous bride-to-be, whose pretended death brings to light an evil slander against her maidenhood. The "nothing" of the title suggests the playwright's bemusement at society's insistence on a double standard in a sexist world where sullied noblewomen might as well be dead. Rich with double meaning is the epitaph read aloud by Claudio, the duped groom:

> Done to death by slanderous tongues
>> Was the Hero that here lies.
> Death, in guerdon of her wrongs,
>> Gives her fame which never dies.
> So the life that died with shame
>> Lives in death with glorious fame.

The lively resolution of Shakespeare's near-disastrous comedy merely winks at the black humor that marks the crisis, flirting with the verbal stoning of a shamed woman branded as a common jade. Dancing replaces lamentations; a double wedding compounds joy in matrimony. In the final scene, where characters smooth over the monstrous plot to ruin a defenseless girl, there is little left to suggest the death-in-life that would have been the lot of Hero if she had failed to prove her maidenhood.

Gallows humor, a subgenre of black humor, satirizes fearful, eerie situations and dread of death with bald jest, such as "Death is nature's way of telling us to slow down" and "Rearranging the deck chairs on the Titanic." An amusing cartoon brings the viewer closer to what Stephen Crane calls "the great death" by picturing a wife hovering by her dying husband and whispering, "One last word, Irving, please. How do you program the VCR?" The humor takes the edge off fears all people share and mocks their efforts to dispel the inborn doom that marks humanity for the grave. By trivializing a wife's final words with her husband, the joke-teller holds at bay a personal confrontation with mortality by pretending to be vigorous and quick-witted enough to outsmart death in a single punchline.

One of the most vivid displays of death jokes occurs in William Shakespeare's *Romeo and Juliet* (ca. 1593), a town's tragedy that reflects the debilitating effects of quarrels between the houses of Lancaster and York during the Wars of the Roses. In the duel scene of Act III, Mercutio, who is pro-Capulet, stumbles from a lethal blow by a pro-Montague gangster, blearily passes it off as a scratch, and continues his sarcastic banter without indicating that he is dying. Sustaining his usual wry badinage, he faces Romeo, whose interference prefaced the fatal stab:

Romeo:	The hurt cannot be much.
Mercutio:	No, 'tis not so deep as a well, nor so wide as a church door; but 'tis enough, 'twill serve. Ask for me tomorrow, and you shall find me a grave man. . . .
Romeo:	I thought all for the best.
Mercutio:	Help me into some house, Benvolio, Or I shall faint. A plague o' both your houses! They have made worms' meat of me.

The poignant puns on well, church door, and grave suit the farfetched images that the gang comes to expect of their babbling poet. The embodiment of youthful trifling with death, Mercutio, the repository of quicksilver wit and poetic grace, epitomizes deadly gang warfare in Verona. The flip side of these funereal jests is the price yet to be paid—the deaths of Romeo and Juliet.

Classified as a phenomenon of the 1950s, black humor—sometimes termed *l'humour noir* in a nod to André Breton's *Anthologie de l'humour noir* (1939)—is too comprehensive a point of view to be limited to such a short period. Senselessness is endemic in black comedy, which is often laced with laughter, but, at heart, is as confounding as the perplexities that the modern era misclaims as its unique invention. An uproarious example of quirky, sick humor, Larry Larson, Levi Lee, and Rebecca Wackler's *Tent Meeting* (1987) depicts the caricatures of a tent revivalist, Reverend Ed, and his dysfunctional family: Darrell, an immature son incapable of serving honorably in the military; Becky, a daughter who hums and stuffs her ears with cotton to keep her mind off the birth of a profoundly handicapped child sired by Ed; and the unseen child, an apparent male infant born without genitals whom its mother insists on naming Arlene Marie. Introduced to its Uncle Darrell, the infant prompts a remark that the dog wouldn't play with the baby if the family hung a pork chop about the baby's neck—if they had a dog and, by implication, if Arlene Marie had a neck. The buildup of explosive tensions in the family's confining trailer home results in a riotous baptism scene during which Darrell plunges the swaddled figure into the font. Both Darrell and his father learn too late that the mother has anticipated the plot and left an eggplant in place of the deformed child. The pseudo-madonna and child depart by taxi to the tune of a nonsense lullaby.

Dependent on such morbid, death-centered repartee, absurdity, and grotesquerie, black comedy suits much modern drama and fiction:

- Franz Kafka, *Metamorphosis* (1915), *The Trial* (1925), *The Castle* (1926)

- Nathanael West, *A Cool Million* (1934)

- Jean Anouilh, *Voyageur sans bagage* (1936), *La Sauvage* (1938), *La Valse des toréadors* (1952), and *Pauvre Bitost* (1956)

- Jean Genet, *Les Bonnes* (1947), *Les Nègres* (1959)

- Eugene Ionesco, *The Chairs* (1951)

- Samuel Beckett, *Waiting for Godot* (1953)

- Albert Camus, *Myth of Sisyphus* (1955)

- Günter Grass, *The Tin Drum* (1959)

- Edward Albee, *Who's Afraid of Virginia Woolf* (1962) and *Tiny Alice* (1965)

- Thomas Pynchon, *V* (1963) and *The Crying of Lot 49* (1964)

- Kurt Vonnegut, *Cat's Cradle* (1963) and *Slaughterhouse-Five* (1969)

- Harold Pinter, *The Homecoming* (1965)

Beatrice (Emma Thompson) and Benedick (Kenneth Branagh) take a momentary break from their romantic bickering in Branagh's 1993 film adaptation of *Much Ado About Nothing*. Black humor plays a major role in Shakespeare's 1598 play, which mocks society's condemnation of a noblewoman falsely accused of unchastity.

- Joe Orton, *Loot* (1966)

- Mordecai Richler, *Sir Urban's Horseman* (1966)

- Beth Henley, *Crimes of the Heart* (1979)

- Marsha Norman, *'Night Mother* (1982)

Chief among the black humor novelists are Margaret Atwood and Joseph Heller. Perhaps the masterpiece of mid-twentieth-century black humor, Joseph Heller's *Catch-22* (1961) succeeds as novel and movie that lampoons both the warmonger and the entrepreneur, both supporters of a cataclysm that feeds their perverse ambitions. The dire comedy of Yossarian, a World War II pilot, tries to make sense of circular logic: the catch that allows, even encourages the trapped flier to admit insanity, then refuses to ground him on the basis of his request, which military antilogic classifies as proof of sanity. Paddling a lifeboat from the Mediterranean war zone toward the safety of Scandinavia, Yossarian has next to no chance of eluding the fate of the doomed warrior. Heller's work, like the Renaissance romps of Shakespeare, contains the classic elements of dark humor—laughable incongruities set against the real possibility of catastrophe.

Atwood's dystopian novel *The Handmaid's Tale* (1985) initiates with its wry, witty title—a pun on tale/tail—the central theme of female invalidation save for the single purpose of procreation. Atwood pictures the chilling fundamentalist society of Gilead, a futuristic military compound outside Boston. The nameless narrator is called Offred to designate the servitude that makes her the woman "of Fred," the walking womb intended to provide the sterile Commander Frederick Waterford and his aging wife Serena with a child. In her private thoughts, Offred hears the plaintive cry of Rachel, Jacob's barren favorite in the book of Genesis: "Give me children, or else I die." Rachel's predicted death is the silent withering of a childless wife. Offred makes repeated sick jokes about dying or proving unfit to conceive of a viable fetus. Should the latter occur, Offred would face real disaster: transfer to the colonies, an equally barren locale polluted with the detritus of atomic war that inevitably rids the world of useless "unwomen." (Atwood 1972; Baldick 1990; Beckson and Ganz 1989; Cuddon 1984; Gray 1992; Heller 1961; Henry 1995; Holman and Harmon 1992; Hornstein 1973; Larson, Lee, and Wackler 1987; Shakespeare 1959, 1980; Vonnegut 1990)

See also *Androcles and the Lion;* Atwood, Margaret; caricature; *Catch-22;* Falstaff, Sir John; *The Handmaid's Tale;* Heller, Joseph; Henley, Beth; Norman, Marsha; pun; Shakespeare, William; *Slaughterhouse-Five;* theater of the absurd; Vonnegut, Kurt.

LE BOURGEOIS GENTILHOMME

Molière's comic ballet, *Le Bourgeois gentilhomme*—sometimes translated *The Burgher, a Gentleman,* or *The Would-Be Gentleman*—was the concept of Louis XIV, whose costume encrusted with a fortune in diamonds received no notice from a Turkish ambassador. For a hunting party and feast held October 4, 1670, at Chambord, Molière produced the late evening diversion with himself in the role of the burgher and mummers playing the bargaining Turks, who seek a wife for the Grand Turk's son. Jean-Baptiste Lully, who set the play to music, also played the Mufti, the foolish character of the parvenu takes shape in the first two acts. The neglected plot emerges in Act III, when the burgher insists that his daughter marry up in society. Act IV, a spoof on an envoy of Turks, precedes the grand ballet that concludes the final act, in which the burgher fails to realize that he has been bamboozled. The genius of Molière's play is that he presented the work to social parasites just as obsequious and ingratiating as Jourdain, the butt of his satire.

The gist of the story depicts Monsieur Jourdain, a wealthy merchant's son, who adopts an aristocratic pose as a means of bettering himself. His notions of ornate dressing gowns and hovering lackeys are as ridiculous as his lessons in fencing, singing, philosophy, and dancing. In the background, his wife and her maid Nicole ridicule his social climbing. In deadpan mock alarm, Madame Jourdain observes her husband on his way into town to impress people and challenges him:

> Ah! ah! voici une nouvelle histoire. Qu'est-ce que c'est donc, mon mari, que ce équipage-là? Vous moquez-vous du monde de vous être fait enharnacher de la sort? et avez-vous envie qu'on se raille partout de vous? [Aha!, here's a new twist. What is this, then, my husband, this getup? Are you ridiculing yourself by going out in public in this absurdity? Do you want everybody to point and hoot at you?]

Madame Jourdain fears that their home is turning into a carnival of ballet masters, fencing masters, and tutors of all sorts going and coming. Jourdain assures his wife that efforts to impress the count advance the family's position in society, even though the count seems interested only in borrowing money.

In his characteristic twinning of love plots, the playwright portrays Jourdain as failing in his pursuit of the Marquise Dorimène while being duped into allowing his daughter Lucile to marry her love, Cléonte. Determined that she marry a gentleman, Jourdain disdains his wife's good sense. To Madame Jourdain, the alliance of families of differing social stations portends troubled relationships, but her husband admires a fake Turkish entourage and longs to accept the proposal of a foreign lord for Lucile. There is a ridiculous scene similar to the word duels of the *commedia dell'arte* in which Cléonte plays at being a Turk and makes up a pastiche of gibberish:

Le Mufti:	Dice, Turque, qui star quista? Anabatista? Anabatista? [Tell me, Turks, who is this? An Anabaptist?]
Les Turcs:	Ioc. [No.]
Le Mufti:	Zuinglista? [A Zwinglist?]
Les Turcs:	Ioc.
Le Mufti:	Coffita? [A Copt?]
Les Turcs:	Ioc.
Le Mufti:	Hussita? Morista? Fronista? [A Hussite? (Two garbled words.)]

Les Turcs:	Ioc, ioc, ioc.
Le Mufti:	Ioc, ioc, ioc. Star pagana? [Is he pagan?]
Les Turcs:	Ioc.
Le Mufti:	Luterana? [A Lutheran?]
Les Turcs:	Ioc.
Le Mufti:	Puritana? [A Puritan?]
Les Turcs:	Ioc.
Le Mufti:	Bramina? Moffina? Zurtina? [A Brahmin? (Two garbled words.)]
Les Turcs:	Ioc, ioc, ioc.
Le Mufti:	Ioc, ioc, ioc. Mahametana? Mahametana? [Mohammedan?]
Les Turcs:	Hi Valla! Hi Valla! [Yes, by Allah!]
Le Mufti:	Como chamara? Como chamara! [What is his name?]
Les Turcs:	Giourdina, Giourdina. [Jourdain.]

With the aid of his future mother-in-law, Cléonte fools the phony Jourdain and the bargain is struck. At last raised to nobility, the posturing, socially ambitious Jourdain believes himself the future in-law of the Grand Turk. Molière's double jest—at the expense of Jourdain and the audience—turns brilliant repartee into grand farce and a disguise motif into spectacle. Without realizing they are themselves mocked, the audience howls with delight. (Baugh 1948; Bermel 1982; Brockett 1968; Burdick 1974; Gassner and Quinn 1969; Guicharnaud 1967; Molière 1965; Roberts 1962)

See also caricature; *commedia dell'arte;* farce; incongruity; Molière; repartee; satire.

BOYLE, T. CORAGHESSAN

One of the most facile, entertaining jesters and purveyors of literary exotica of the late twentieth century, T. Coraghessan "T. C." Boyle has produced a steady output of Kafkaesque short fiction and novels. A ribald example is his caricature of Dr. John Harvey Kellogg, inventor of corn flakes, in Boyle's fifth novel, *The Road to Wellville* (1993), the vehicle for a moderately successful film starring Anthony Hopkins as Kellogg and Matthew Broderick as Lightbody, whose wife, played by Bridget Fonda, is enamored of the atmosphere of Kellogg's health spa. A master of scatology, zany humor, and cliff-hanging suspense, Boyle demonstrated virtuoso wit in boyhood. Born in 1948 in Peekskill, New York, he changed his middle name from John to Coraghessan at the age of 17. Obviously well read, he graduated from State University of New York and received a Ph.D. from Iowa University in 1977. He had an unremarkable career as a high school English teacher at Lakeland High School, Shrub Oak, New York, and as assistant professor of English at the University of Southern California before striking a responsive chord in readers with "Heart of a Champion," published in *Esquire* in 1975. He followed this success with submissions to *Harper's, Utne Reader, Playboy, Paris Review,* and *Atlantic Monthly.* Rich with incongruity, dizzying biological metaphor, and a Mephistophelian imagination, Boyle orchestrated a quick succession of short story collections and novels and garnered a cult following at the University of Southern California.

Alternately scorned and revered for his cornucopia of extravagant imagery, shallow throwaway lines, and ardent mismating of eccentrics, Boyle continues to tease and dismay with fiction that intrigues, repulses, and mesmerizes readers. His verbal legerdemain illuminates a host of Dickensian phantasms in *Water Music* (1982), a novel in which chapters alternate between the fictional picaresque coterie that accompanies Mungo Park on his tracing of the source of the Niger River and the ragtag adventurers encountered by huckster Ned Rise, vendor of phony caviar. The comic death of Mungo's companion, Johnson, a Mandingo tribesman and former slave, pits a spindly human hero against an 18-foot crocodile. The mock-heroic details leave little of Johnson's dignity intact:

> The explorer flies through the water like a hurdler, self-sacrifice pounding at his ribcage, but it's too late, too late, and [Mungo] watches, helpless, as Johnson's eyes cry out to him and the grim Mesozoic beast sinks into the ooze.

Boyle's success at black humor and surreal fiction won him the St. Lawrence Prize in 1980, the Aga Khan Prize the following year, and the 1987 PEN/Faulkner Award for Fiction.

Boyle's whimsical mix of incongruities delights readers of *East Is East* (1990), a satiric romp that pits Hiro Tanaka, a harmless Japanese-American sailor, against the vituperative backbiters posing as writers at a Georgia retreat. The rumor that a crazed Oriental stalks local backyards sends an unsuspecting Immigration and Naturalization Service agent to Savannah on a rainy night in search of an appropriate partner to help corner and subdue the illegal alien. At this point in Hiro's mottled record, he has

> cursed a bunch of people at the local grocery, filched three pairs of ladies' undergarments from a clothesline at the artists' colony and made off with a tin dish of dogfood the sheriff himself had set out on his back porch.

The blend of cultures brings the INS agent face to face with a local redneck who offers assistance in locating Tran Van Duc's store. The yokel truck driver points and mumbles, "Rye chair." To the imported Yankee, the southern-accented idiom means nothing until the truck driver points and repeats "Rye chair," indicating the agent's destination.

The deliciously gossipy, competitive artist's colony teems with its own stock figures: the wannabe novelist, the effete critic, and the intrusive femme fatale. The novelist, Ruth Dershowitz, studies her quarry, Sax, a ripe-smelling outdoorsy type:

> He hadn't had a chance to clean up—his hands stank of perch and darter and of the rich fecal muck of the Okefenokee, and the thighs and backside of his jeans were stiff with the residue of his fish-handling—and Ruth took him by surprise.

Dressed for the cocktail hour, Ruth surrenders to his embrace, "hot already, hot instantly, a gas grill gone from pilot to high at the merest touch."

Not given to clownish humor for its own sake, Boyle coaxes his plots along toward an explosive resolution. In *East Is East*, the AWOL Japanese sailor internalizes samurai training, flees human habitation, but falls into the clumsy clutch of the authorities. Incarcerated in a hospital, he eviscerates himself with the sharpened handle of a spoon, marveling at "giving birth, his own pale intestines bulging at the hole he'd torn in himself." Typical of Boyle's fascination with all phases of biology, particularly anatomy, the ending releases Hiro to death, which he envisions as a Nirvana, a "City of Brotherly Love" where he can rest from his rigorous evasion of people who misunderstand him.

More spectacular still is the final scene of *The Road to Wellville* (1993), in which the mountebank, Dr. Harvey Kellogg, meets a stock character from literature, the ingrate foster son. Threatening to burn to the ground Kellogg's hokey health farm, George, whom Kellogg adopted in childhood but failed to socialize, challenges the source of Kellogg's nutritional cant and the wellspring of Boyle's humor—Kellogg's fascination with feces. George, a peculiar mix of avenging nemesis and naughty boy, menaces:

> "I'm here to give you a history lesson, Dr. Anus, that's what I'm here for—I'm here to make your life the cesspool you've made mine, here to cram all your zwieback and your enemas and all the rest of it down your throat once and for all."

In a comic set-to, George dashes up and down corridors setting fires before Dr. Kellogg tackles him and soaks up "a roiling miasma of body odor, of filth and grease and the stink of unwashed underclothes and fungus-infested feet." But the capture comes too late to halt George's release of Kellogg's prize stool samples, which he has evaluated by shape, color, odor, and texture. The inevitable annihilation of George occurs in a vat of macadamia butter, where Kellogg, ruing a failed social experiment, holds the frail aberration under the yellow muck until the man-boy drowns.

A manipulator of comic hyperbole, Boyle is at his best in short takes, the chance encounters around which he builds brief satiric fiction. One of his best, "Modern Love," adorns *If the River Was Whiskey* (1989) and prompted *Utne Reader* to reprise the pivotal scene. The pun-laced story is a failed love match between an ardent male and a fastidious, demure young woman from Croton, who lives "on the ground floor of a restored Victorian." Obsessed with germs and disease, she smells of "Noxzema and pHisoHex." On the culminating date when the pursuer intends to bed his love, she withdraws coyly to prepare herself for intercourse. He loses his appetite for sex when she returns wearing a Swedish full-body condom.

Boyle's skill is the shrewd interweaving of satire, caricature, puns, and darkly repugnant humor into multiple strands of an enthralling plot peopled with freaks and gothic anomalies. A craftsman at word lore gleaned from zoology and human anatomy, he textures his descriptive passages with the kinkily comic, the insanely laughable. Raw, graphic, at times nauseatingly precise in his explication of body effluvia and disease, Boyle's ribbing of contemporary scenes lies in his grasp of the absurd, the unexpected, the cruelly ill-fated. His satire unmasks the poseur, the ignoramus, the con artist, and the flake. In his wide sweep, Boyle—a promising offshoot of Petronius Arbiter, Dickens, and Shaw—spares no segment of society. (Boyle 1983, 1985, 1989, 1990, 1993; *Contemporary Authors* 1994; *Contemporary Literary Criticism* 1986; *New York Times Book Review* 1993)

See also black humor; caricature; hyperbole; mock-heroic; picaresque; scatology; Shaw, George Bernard; whimsy.

BRECHT, BERTOLT

Germany's most forcefully didactic writer for the twentieth-century stage and a student of George Bernard Shaw, Eugen Bertolt Friedrich Brecht achieved an enviable position among European dramatists. Inverting Aristotle's theater paradigm, Brecht preferred epic spectacle, an open display of stage machinery to convince the viewer that the play is an expression of the players' art and that pretense and imaginative involvement are not as necessary as laughter and learning. A native of Augsburg, Germany, Brecht, born February 10, 1898, was the son of a paper manufacturer. While studying at the local Realgymnasium, he published immature verse in the local newspaper under the pseudonym Berthold Eugen. During World War I, his unpopular opinions on pacifism put him in jeopardy with local authorities. In 1918, he worked as a ward medic for the army in Augsburg while writing *Baal*, his first play.

The end of the war freed Brecht to study and develop his talents. He enrolled in medical courses at Munich and Berlin, then rebelled against bourgeois tastes and abandoned science in favor of poetry, translation, scripts, scenarios, and plays. He reviewed productions for the Augsburger Volkswille and studied mime and irony under comic Karl Valentin before embracing Marxism and allying with Berlin's radical artists and film companies. His early successes were *Drums in the Night* (1922), *In the City's Thickets* (1922), *A Man's a Man* (1924), and *One Is Another* (1927), all distorted by heightened hyperboles, incongruities, and experimental expressionism. The height of Brecht's early career came shortly after his twenty-fifth birthday, when he became literary consultant to Munich's Kammerspiele.

The next year, Brecht made a break with straight drama and collaborated with Kurt Weill on the popular musical *Threepenny Opera* (1928), a resetting of John Gay's *The Beggar's Opera* (1928) featuring the picaresque Mack the Knife, one of musical theater's most enduring rakes. The play ran for five years in New York. Subsequent experimental pieces languished. At the failure of a youthful marriage, he divorced his first wife and married actor Helene Weigel, who starred in some of his greatest works. Their strong leftist message permeated plays and films, especially *Kuhle Wampe*, which was banned in Berlin and became a *cause célèbre* to German Communists. The police began dogging his places of work, burning his published plays and reviews, and spying on his colleagues.

German playwright Bertolt Brecht in 1926

Brecht's liberal political opinions made him a natural enemy of Hitler's Third Reich. In February 1933, to escape the Nazis, he, Helen, one of their children, and other supporters exiled themselves to Switzerland. Brecht moved about in France and Austria, settled in Denmark, collaborated with composers Paul Hindemith and Arnold Schonberg, then wrote and sold works in England before moving to Russia, Finland, Norway, Sweden, and New York, constantly organizing groups according to his precepts and producing drama and poetry for stage, radio, and public recitation. A forceful, intellectual moralist, Brecht produced work that emphasized the vitality of the proletariat: *Mother Courage* (1937), *Galileo* (1939), *The Good Woman of Setzuan* (1940), *Herr Puntila* (1941), *The Resistible Rise of Arturo Ui* (1941), and *The Caucasian Chalk Circle* (1945), a comic parable interspersed with black humor. The latter, set in feudal Georgia on Easter, echoes the legendary mothers' battle at the throne of Solomon. Opening on an overstated satire of doctors' squabbles meant to impress the aristocratic Abashwili family with their concern for Governor Georgi Abashwili's ailing baby Michael, the play grows out of a series of contrasts:

> *First Doctor:*   May I remind you, Niko Mikadze, that I was against the lukewarm bath? There's been a little error over warming the bath water, Your Grace.
>
> *Second Doctor:*   Mika Loladze, I'm afraid I can't agree with you. The temperature of the bath water was exactly what our great, beloved Mishiko Oboladze prescribed.

In private, the second doctor quarrels with his colleague over who must take a turn "in this accursed house on that little brat's account."

In an earlier scene, beggars plead for lower taxes, aid for an amputee, justice, the return of an only son conscripted into the military, and relief from the corrupt water inspector. Meanwhile, Grusha Vashnadze, a country girl dressed for church, must miss services so that she can search for the best goose to prepare for her employers for dinner. After the governor's family departs, a revolution sends soldiers scurrying. Grusha promises to wait for her love, Simon, one of a mobilized brigade. In the uproar, Natella Abashwili abandons her son and flees from the advancing Ironshirts, who have departed their barracks. Miraculously, an adult voice calls to Grusha from the child's body. She remains to aid him, then, near dawn, grabs the child and departs toward safety.

Grusha's decision to take the abandoned Michael and flee to the mountains on a seven-day crossing of the glacier calls for personal sacrifice in a land where hearts are as stony and cold as the ice under her feet. She finds a likely husband—one on his deathbed. Before Grusha's marriage to Jussup, his mother, already scrimping on hiring a priest for the funeral, objects to the shame of an illegitimate grandchild. At the end of the nuptial ceremony, the monk asks, "How about extreme unction?" The mother-in-law brushes him off with the cost of feeding six hundred people at the reception. Her darkly comic muttering diminishes her further: "If he doesn't die today, I'll have to bake some more tomorrow!" To Grusha's surprise, not only has she quickly become a mother, but, when the war ends and there is no more need for soldiers, Jussup revives and makes her a wife, an ironic switch on the usual order of marriage and family.

Two years after Michael's abduction, soldiers take Grusha into custody and reclaim the boy for his mother Natella. Azdak, the buffoon of a judge, conducts a hearing by asking Grusha if the infant had refined features. She replies, "He had a nose on his face" and complains that the judge pays no heed to petitioners from the peasantry. The corrupt Azdak admits that he believes Grusha wants justice, but tempts her to better Michael's lot:

> You'd only have to say he wasn't yours, and he'd have a palace and many horses in his stable and many beggars on his doorstep and many soldiers in his service and many petitioners in his courtyard, wouldn't he? What do you say—don't you want him to be rich?

Because Grusha refuses to give up her foster son, Azdak concludes that the child must be won by placing him in a chalk circle, where the two women will tug until one pulls him over the line. The scene ends in tidy parable fashion with Azdak awarding custody to Grusha and mistakenly okaying her divorce from Jussup. Natella, a caricatured aristocrat accustomed to favoritism for the elite, collapses and is carried out of the courtroom. The play ends with a song that reflects scripture and befits a working-class idyll:

> Children to the motherly, that they prosper,
> Carts to good drivers, that they be driven well,
> The valley to the waterers, that it yield fruit.

Brecht's influence shaped the theater of the mid-twentieth century. His pacifism caused a stir in 1944 with the publication of *The Private Life of the Master Race*, an episodic, anti-Nazi piece picturing scene after scene of atrocities. In the post–World War II era, he called the atomic bomb a mechanical schism between humanity and science. Although he never found the financial backing to achieve his heady dreams, his incisive plays brought audiences back to the theaters. He exemplified the relaxed mode by rejecting black tie and tails and dressing in rumpled sweater and tweeds and neglecting to shave or comb for public appearances.

Politics dominated Brecht's final years. After testifying against the House Un-American Activities Committee during the McCarthy era, Brecht and his wife returned to East Berlin via Switzerland in 1949 and assembled the Berliner Ensemble, Europe's notable experimental repertory company, which performed at the East Berlin Deutsche Theater. However, Russian censors did not always agree with his style and philosophy, particularly in *The Trial of Lucullus* (1934) and in his adaptations of Sophocles's *Antigone* (1947), William Shakespeare's *Coriolanus* (1953), Molière's *Don Juan* (1952), and George Farquhar's *The Recruiting Officer* (1955). Still working out the details of a worker alliance, he died of heart disease in Berlin on August 17, 1956, and was buried near his Berlin home. (Anderson 1971; Brecht 1967, 1981; Brockett 1968; Gassner and Quinn 1969; Roberts 1962)

See also *The Beggar's Opera*; black humor; caricature; didacticism; Gay, John; hyperbole; incongruity; irony; picaresque; Shaw, George Bernard.

BURLESQUE

A mocking imitation, ridicule, or exaggeration, burlesque— whether in painting, architecture, sculpture, drama, dance, or song—derives its satiric energy from the elements of caricature, distortion, and vulgar buffoonery aimed at serious artistic expression. To achieve humor, burlesque must create a disparity by carrying the distortion of behaviors to the extreme opposite of expectation, whether in high burlesque, a form of mock-serious exaltation, or low burlesque, obvious deflation. An outgrowth of the Italian *burlesco*, meaning "drollery" or "jest," theatrical burlesque blends outlandish parody, tit-for-tat persiflage, mock-angry raillery, and undignified farce that is usually of short duration, as with the comic interludes and satiric masques or antimasques of the Middle Ages and the minstrel shows of the nineteenth-century American stage.

Classic Western literature proves that no author of stature is safe from ridicule. Perhaps as a left-handed tribute to Homer's epic verse, an anonymous funster penned a mock serious burlesque, *The Battle of the Frogs and Mice* (sixth century B.C.). In Greek theater, rudimentary burlesque graces the comedies of Aristophanes and the satyr plays that provided comic relief from formal tragic trilogies of the Classical era. Plautus, Rome's most influential and prolific funnyman, wrote extensive burlesque into his comedies, the best known being *Menaechmi* (second century B.C.). The Middle Ages, Renaissance, Restoration, Neoclassic, and Romantic eras produced a varied and sparkling list of burlesque:

- Geoffrey Chaucer, *Sir Thopas* (1387) and *The Nun's Priest's Tale* (1387)

- Miguel de Cervantes, *Don Quixote* (1615)

- Francis Beaumont, *The Knight of the Burning Pestle* (ca. 1607)

- Samuel Butler, *Hudibras* (1662)

- George Villiers, *The Rehearsal* (1671)

- John Dryden, *The Hind and the Panther* (1687)

- Jonathan Swift, *Baucis and Philemon* (1709)

- Alexander Pope, *The Rape of the Lock* (1714) and *The Dunciad* (1728)

- John Gay, *The What D'ye Call It* (1715) and *Three Hours after Marriage* (1717), a collaboration with John Arbuthnot and Alexander Pope

- Henry Fielding, *Tom Thumb* (1730), *The Covent Garden Tragedy* (1732), *The Historical Register for the Year* (1736), *Shamela* (1741), and *Joseph Andrews* (1742)

- Henry Carey, *Chrononhotonthologos* (1734) and *The Dragon of Wantley* (1734)

- Richard Sheridan, *The Critic* (1779)

- George Byron, *Don Juan* (1824)

A high point for the genre of burlesque is John Gay's *The Beggar's Opera* (1728), a raucous comedy that features Mack the Knife and assorted thugs and prostitutes in a spoof of Italian opera. Recent times have continued the tradition with these:

- William Gilbert and Arthur Sullivan, *Patience* (1881)

- Jane Austen, *Northanger Abbey* (1818)

- Stephen Leacock, *Nonsense Novels* (1911)

- Max Beerbohm, *A Christmas Garland* (1912) and *Savonarola Brown* (1919)

The last half of the twentieth century has seen the advent of the mock-heroic knockabout irreverence of Monty Python and his Flying Circus, among others.

One of the most frequently revived burlesques is the delightful play-within-a-play at the end of William Shakespeare's *A Midsummer Night's Dream* (ca. 1593). As the three newly married couples while away the time before bed, Theseus, the host, introduces a local amateur production of "Pyramus and Thisby," which Bottom and his fellow "rude mechanicals" practice in earlier scenes of comic relief. A nonsense version of a tale of suicide and unrequited love, the height of the burlesque occurs as Pyramus (played by Bottom) stabs himself with a sword and expires:

> Now am I fled;
> My soul is in the sky.
> Tongue, lose thy light;
> Moon, take thy flight.
> Now die, die, die, die, die!

In a sotto voce to the audience, Theseus, who is annoyed by the inept performance, comments, "With the help of a surgeon he might yet recover and yet prove an ass." With the brief parallel suicide scene and speech by Thisby, the burlesque comes to a merciful end. Lest the moral drag on, Theseus quickly demurs, "No epilogue; I pray you, for your play needs no excuse."

A similar show of exaggerated mummery marks the Native American *koshare*, also called *koyala* or *kacale*. A Pueblo clown society that mocked death, the *koshare* coated themselves with black paint topped with white stripes to mimic a skeleton. The *koshare* interrupted serious ritual with mock acts of vandalism, cross-dressing, begging for handouts, stealing food from plates, and drinking from priests' cups. At dramatic moments in traditional ceremonies, the *koshare*, like the Cherokee boogers, interacted with the audience, grabbing celebrants in fake terror and lapsing into faints at the solemnity of the service. During a break in the religious festival, the *koshare* competed for a prize of food by climbing greased poles and performing pratfalls and phony slides. In similar mummery, the Zuñi mudheads depicted the first humans, who pushed through primeval muck like infants emerging from a birth canal. Dressed in black kilts, neckerchiefs, and mud masks formed into lumps at top and sides, the mudheads lampooned holy men by eating dirt, mincing, and performing silly made-up rituals.

Burlesque contains elements of disparity, distortion, and buffoonery. Comedienne Fanny Brice, a member of the 1911 *Ziegfeld Follies,* was a popular burlesque performer.

In the early twentieth century, burlesque abandoned theatrical conventions and adapted the disreputable contrivances of *commedia dell'arte* to please a noisy, catcalling audience, a phenomenon of the post–World War I era. Vaudeville— a melange of juggling, clowning and slapstick, gymnastics, instrumental acts, and song and dance—reduced the level of entertainment to gutter humor, audience interaction, bosomy ingenues, and pie-throwing. Implicit in the Parisian version of burlesque was the can-can, a vigorous leg show that aligned dancers along the apron of the stage for synchronized kicks, brief glimpses of fishnet hose and lacy briefs, and, in the seamiest versions, bare-arsed bumps and grinds. The antithesis of the brutal, misogynistic *apache danse* (a popular *pas de deux* that acts out a relationship between a suppliant female and a domineering male), can-can concluded abruptly with gleeful chaos: police whistles, dashes for cover, and mock arrests and arraignments.

Further distanced from the drolleries of earlier eras, the least respectable form—called "Burly-Q"—featured scenes with little more action than striptease, the métier of stars Lydia Thompson, Little Egypt, and Gypsy Rose Lee. Often appended to swings and carousels lowered from the ceiling, the performer engaged in audience give-and-take while gradually removing clothing. A regular high spot of an evening's entertainment required the stripper to remove a garter and toss it to a spectator.

A few high-quality comics—Bert Lahr, Edgar Bergen and Charlie McCarthy, Red Skelton, George Burns and Gracie Allen, Jack Benny, and Fanny Brice— developed comic monologue and repartee to a new level of respectability by evolving radio personae, such as Fanny Brice's child voice, Red Skelton's Klem Kadiddlehopper, and Jackie Gleason's bartender. The verbal equivalents of Charlie Chaplin's tramp and Buster Keaton's sad sack from the silent "flickers," talkies and television offered a new avenue of burlesque to a burst of comic talent, including Carol Burnett, Phil Silvers, Arte Johnson, and Lucille Ball. (Abrams 1971; Baldick 1990; Barnet, Berman, and Burto 1960; Cuddon 1984; Drabble 1985; Feinberg 1967; Gassner and Quinn 1969; Gray 1992; Holman and Harmon 1992; Hornstein 1973; McArthur 1992; Patterson and Snodgrass 1994; Pollard 1970; Shakespeare 1958)

See also Aristophanes; *The Beggar's Opera;* comedy; farce; Gay, John; masque; mock epic; parody; Plautus; repartee; satyr play; Shakespeare, William; slapstick.

 CAMP

Camp is a stylized, affected, cultish form of satire. With an insider's cynical, world-weary eye, camp marginalizes certain architecture, furnishings, decor, clothing, behavior, film, novels, songs, dance, and drama. It raises its eyebrows at examples of mediocrity that others take seriously—a velvet painting of Elvis, the thriller film *The Attack of the Killer Tomatoes* (1978), or a print displaying a pale Christ with pitiful, uplifted eyes and exposed, oversized bleeding heart. Whether theatrical or naive in its origins, camp deliberately skirts the edges of snobbery, elitism, vulgarity, and bigotry, especially toward the WASP's perceptions of Jews or the straight world's notions of homosexuality. Often associated with androgynous or homosexual behaviors or stereotypes, camp relies on audience sophistication, for its esoteric humor depends on a familiarity with codes and mannerisms recognized and accepted by those in the know, often a self-limiting substratum of the populace. Without complicity between writer and reader, camp's extravagance and artifice would swamp humor and replace satire with invective or ridicule. A model of the staccato exchanges, rapid-fire one-upmanship, and verbal precocity common to camp is Mart Crowley's screenplay *The Boys in the Band* (1970), which relies on the aficionado's knowledge of Broadway minutiae, gay bar shtick, and protracted mocking repartee.

The use of camp as a synonym for outrageously exaggerated mannerisms, anachronisms, and self-conscious gimmickry dates to the first decade of the twentieth century, for example, smirky, suggestive nightclub acts that spoof the meeting of the nerdy male and the vamp or the innocent virgin and the roué. A predictable opening scene that sets the mock-humorous tone of Harvey Fierstein's electric screenplay *Torch Song Trilogy* (1979) is the glitzy transvestite nightclub show that precedes more serious study of Arnold. He is a lonely, unfulfilled stage singer whose desire for "motherhood" results in the mixed blessing of a sixteen-year-old gay foster son almost simultaneously with Arnold's unforeseen "widowhood." In the Broadway version and the 1988 film, Arnold spoofs the smoky boîtes and skeletal, overtly enticing chanteuses of mid-twentieth-century France. On the marquee, he bills himself as Virginia Ham, a throaty vamp sporting sequins and feathers and playfully cruising the audience while filling the lyrics of "her" torchy ballad, "Love for Sale," with double entendre and mildly flirtatious interaction with club patrons.

A perennial reprise during the post-AIDS guilt-relieving openness of the straight world toward gays, camp scenes adorn popular novels, television sitcoms and soaps, and movies, notably Anne Fine's young adult satire *Alias Madame Doubtfire* (1988), the prototype for the 1993 cross-dressing film smash *Mrs. Doubtfire*, a bittersweet study of a father's attempt to watch over his children by donning drag and applying for the job of babysitter. In pre-nanny scenes, scripted by Randi Singer and Leslie Dixon, actor Robin Williams calls on his brother, a makeup artist, who initiates a drawn-out scene of makeovers that wind down to an acceptable image—a stout British governess "of a certain age." The limp-wrist mannerisms, fey posturing, and bitchy repartee between the gay artist and his mate undergird the intense but lighthearted focus on helping the artist's brother, an out-of-work actor and down-on-his-luck father, by transforming him into a suitably sedate applicant for afterschool governess.

According to Jack Babuscio's essay "Camp and the Gay Sensibility," the term "camp" implies four elements: irony, aestheticism, theatricality, and humor. Comic incongruity, the basis of an artistic work that questions the sexual orientation of the viewer or reader, tends to pull images toward ambiguous ground. Because the relationship of same-sex partners causes straight society to question motives and morals, the irony of books such as Virginia Woolf's *Orlando* (1928) and movies such as *Victor/Victoria* (1982) becomes the author's focus, as demonstrated by Woolf's comment on Orlando:

> She had a great variety of selves to call upon, far more than we have been able to find room for, since a biography is considered complete if it merely accounts for six or seven selves, whereas a person may well have as many thousand.

Essential to the creation of irony is the aesthetic sense, the way in which art reflects existence. Camp is a form of humor that protests rigid morality. It provides an unorthodox, antipuritanical mode that frees expression and response, whether in style of dress, exaggerated poses, or androgynous behaviors and sensibilities—for example, the mannish actions and macho facial expressions displayed by Barbara Stanwyck, a butch role model in western films and television roles.

As far back as the phallic dances of ancient Greece, ribald European morris dance, and the posturings of early kabuki theater, camp has stimulated and refreshed performances. A protest against prejudice and exclusion and an avenue of widening experience, camp encourages hearty audience response to theatricality and humor, which is the life's blood of a Halloween costume competition, masquerade ball, Mardi Gras scenario, or Caribbean carnaval dance. The rich effusion of a parade motif, masque, or spectacle draws on a natural curiosity toward traded roles—male for female, old for young, or human for animal or the supernatural. More than mere freak show voyeurism, enjoyment of camp allows the theatergoer to laugh at the three hairy-legged football players carrying off the part of the witches in a college production of William Shakespeare's *Macbeth* or to admire Sandy Duncan flying through the air in a theater version of Peter Pan.

The reader experiences a similar respite from realism in Charlotte Brontë's *Jane Eyre* (1847), in which the dour, authoritarian Edward Rochester dresses in drag to portray the fortune-teller, Mother Bunches, who dismays Miss Ingram, a potential fiancée and rival of the title character, until she becomes dark-faced, dissatisfied, and sour in her disappointment. When Jane takes her turn with the seer, Edward, vamping his part as female gypsy, elicits her opinion of him, then, at her insistence, pretends to tell her future:

> I see no enemy to a fortunate issue but in the brow; and that brow professes to say—"I can live alone, if self-respect and circumstances require me so to do. I need not sell my soul to buy bliss. I have an inward treasure born with me, which can keep me alive if all extraneous delights should be withheld, or offered only at a price I cannot afford to give."

At the end of Edward's charade, he drops the mask that allows him more effrontery than proper society condones between employer and employee. At this point, the light touch vanishes; Jane questions whether she is awake or dreaming. Edward's hand stretches toward her, revealing a familiar ring that establishes Jane's departure from the metaphysical and her unceremonious jolt into a world where governesses don't cultivate lasting intimate relationships with their employers. (Babuscio 1993; Bronte 1981; Fine 1988; Henry 1995; Long 1989; Roman 1992; Sontag 1966; Woolf 1928)

See also double entendre; irony; kabuki; repartee.

CANDIDE

Voltaire's didactic fantasy, *Candide* (1759), subtitled "Optimism," survived the Age of Voltaire as its classic satire. The work earned praise for its lean, incisive wit and virulent satire against the church, the Inquisition, tyranny, greed, and the rest of the deadly sins that plague humankind. The caustic story of the wanderer Candide manages to parody adventure romances like Miguel de Cervantes's *Don Quixote* (1615) while lampooning the most predatory of society's parasites: monarchy, corrupt municipal officers, lechers, grifters, apostates, picaros, and a host of nondescript thugs and brigands. The theme of irrepressible, irrational optimism results in a guarded humor at the expense of the antihero, a bumbling, generous lack-wit whom Voltaire ridicules for his exuberant search for "the best of all possible worlds" against a dreary procession of natural disasters, cruelty, slavery, oppression, torture, prejudice, venality, violence, and treachery.

The story begins without suspense: "Comment Candide fut élevé dans un beau château, et comment il fut chassé d'icelui" [How Candide was brought up in a lovely castle, and how he was banished from it]. Candide, a likable but naive bumpkin whom the author hints is the baron's illegitimate nephew, lives in the Westphalian castle of the Baron of Thunder-ten-tronckh and studies with Doctor Pangloss, a caricature of the ivory tower instructor in metaphysico-theologo-cosmolo-nigology, a bit of doggerel that reflects his crackpot theory of optimism. A fictional Gottfried Leibnitz, the mathematician who believed that all earthly events are planned by God, Pangloss impresses on Candide in daily recitation that evil and good are both parts of the same whole and that all events work to a necessary and fitting end. Candide's residency with the baron ends after he commits a coltish indiscretion—going behind a screen to kiss the hand of Cunégonde, his host's daughter, whom Voltaire describes as "extremely pretty." Candide takes a boot in the rear and departs his enraged former host to roam the world.

Voltaire's first target is the military, which he satirizes for abusing recruits. Traveling by foot to the nearby village of Valdberghoff-trabk-dikdorff, Candide meets a pair of uniformed officers who admire his physique and enlist him in the royal army. Candide learns to march and drill with ramrod to shoulder, then, as a result of the sadistic caprice common to the army, is inexplicably beaten with sixty whacks of the baton and tossed into the stockade. With equal disregard for his dignity and rights, the king of the Bulgarians extricates Candide so that he can war against the Abarians. Despite his height and robust youth, the rookie proves unworthy for battle because he detests war.

Candide, whom Voltaire depicts as unbelievably altruistic, escapes to Holland, which is at peace, and expects the Christian Dutch to extend welcome. Only James, an Anabaptist, treats him humanely. By coincidence, Candide reunites with Pangloss, now fallen into extreme poverty and suffering from venereal disease, which he contracted from his paramour, Pacquette. Candide discovers that Bulgarian invaders have killed Cunégonde and the rest of the Baron's family. At word of Cunégonde's death, Candide faints. On reviving he cries, "Ah! meilleur des mondes; où êtes-vous? [Ah, best of worlds, where are you?]" With his benefactor's assistance, he and Pangloss sail to Lisbon, offshore of which their ship disintegrates. Added to their misfortunes are the drowning of their friend James and an earthquake that devastates the Portuguese. While Candide and Pangloss attend survivors, Portuguese scholars capture, flog, and condemn both men by auto-da-fé to burn at the stake for violating church morality. Shortly after authorities hang Pangloss, a second earthquake ends the executions. Already deep into misery and injustice, the story is just beginning to vent Voltaire's indignation at earthly woes.

Voltaire pursues his insightful plot from the foregoing cliffhanger to a series of episodes worthy of Jonathan Swift's picaresque *Gulliver's Travels* or of the *Indiana Jones* films. During the confusion, an old woman rescues Candide, salves his wounds, feeds him, then leads him to Cunégonde, who survived the Bulgarian attack on the castle and the dismemberment of her family:

> Je repris mes sens, je criai, je me débattis, je mordis, j'égratignai, je voulais arracher les yeux à ce grand Bulgare [I recovered my senses, I wept, I struck myself, I bit, I scratched, I wanted to claw out the big Bulgarian's eyes].

Candide learns that for six months Cunégonde has shared a residence with the grand inquisitor and a Jew, Don Issachar. Candide slaughters both men, then gallops away with Cunégonde and the old woman to elude capture. While listening to the extensive misadventures of the old woman, who claims to be the daughter of Pope Urban X, the trio press on west toward the Sierra Morenas, then seaward to Cadiz, where Candide joins a party sailing southwest across the Atlantic to Paraguay to suppress a Jesuit cabal.

Voltaire easily transfers his meandering tale from Europe to the New World. In Buenos Aires, Candide loses his fiancée to the lustful, conceited Don Fernando d'Ibarra, whom the author ridicules as "y Figueora, y Mascarenes, y Lampourdos, y Souza," the many-titled governor of the province. A Portuguese posse pursues Candide for killing the inquisitor. Cacambo, Candide's faithful Spanish-Argentine valet, urges his master to flee to the Jesuit compound, where they meet the colonel and chief oppressor of natives. To Candide's surprise, the man turns out to be the baron's son, a second unforeseen survivor of the brutal Bulgarian assault on Westphalia, a bit of hyperbole that Voltaire expands with later astounding rescues and incredible events.

The ups and downs of Voltaire's comic fiction continue as Candide enjoys a fraternal reunion until he mentions that he, a commoner, intends to marry Cunégonde, a baron's daughter. Instantly, a fight breaks out. Locked in mortal combat, Candide plunges his sword into the colonel's abdomen and disguises himself in Jesuit robe and headpiece. He and Cacambo escape the compound. Along the way, they encounter the Oreillons (the Big Ears), man-eaters who detest all Jesuits. Cacambo's quick action saves the duo from the cannibals, who assume that priestly vestments indicate enemies. The pair continue their trek through South America until their horses die. They board an abandoned canoe and paddle toward Cayenne, a French settlement.

Here, Voltaire allows himself liberty with a utopian convention based on European hopes of instant wealth, a delusion dating to Christopher Columbus and the *conquistadores*. High in the mountains, Candide and his servant arrive at Eldorado, a fabled utopia so far removed from civilization that its people live in contented innocence of their wealth. Candide marvels at the blissful society, which Incas founded. A retired courtier explains the customs of the Eldoradan court and of their religion. Quite simply put, the Eldoradans worship God from morning till night:

> Nous sommes tous prêtres; le roi et tous les chefs de famille chantent des cantiques d'actions de grâces solennellement tous les matins; et cinq ou six mille musiciens les accompagnent [We are all priests; the king and all heads of families sing hymns of thanksgiving solemnly each morning; and five or six thousand musicians accompany them].

After a month of peaceful recuperation among the gold-rich Eldoradans, Candide grows restless for his lady. He ignores the king's warnings and sets out for Paraguay, carrying sheep laden with gold and jewels. Lifted by crane over the crags, Candide, Cacambo, and their beasts return to the eastward trail.

Voltaire, a dissenter from doctrinaire theological texts, centers on atrocities committed in the name of religion. Near Surinam, Candide meets a black sugar-mill slave whose foot and hand a Dutch Christian has lopped off. For the first time doubting that all things happen for the best, Candide concludes that life in Surinam parallels the evils he has witnessed on other parts of his journey. In the harbor, Candide pays a Spanish captain for passage back to Europe—away from religious fanaticism, bigotry, and persecution. While Cacambo returns to Buenos Aires to fetch the Lady Cunégonde, Candide sails east for Italy. Before embarking, a pirate chief steals Candide's sheep, and an unscrupulous judge refuses to help Candide recover his property.

Simulating the organization of Geoffrey Chaucer's *Canterbury Tales* (1387), Voltaire inserts a story line based on individual tales. Candide sails first to Bordeaux aboard a French ship. Characteristic of Voltaire's style, coincidence reunites Candide with his Eldoradan sheep. After leaving Paraguay, he observes the sinking of a Dutch vessel, which bears the pirate captain who stole his treasure. In the cataclysm, Candide reclaims only one sheep, which he later donates to science. He enlists fellow escapees from Surinam to narrate adventures and promises to pay passage for the victim who tells the most pathetic story. Candide selects Martin, an impoverished intellectual who debates philosophy with him.

A thin disguise for Voltaire and his anti-French, antichurch opinions, Martin warms to the affable Candide and informs him of Parisian decadence. The warning goes unheeded after a scheming abbé from Périgord mesmerizes Candide. As a result of the connivance of a greedy actress and the Marchioness of Doublestakesworthy, Candide loses at the gaming tables and is seduced and tricked out of two diamonds. The abbé presents a forged letter panting with Cunégonde's passion:

> Le gouverneur de Buenos-Aires a tout pris, mais il me reste votre coeur. Venez, votre présence me rendra la vie, ou me fera mourir de plaisir [The governor of Buenos Aires has taken all, but I still have your heart. Come, your arrival will restore my life or cause me to die of pleasure].

Willy-nilly, Candide falls for the bait and hurries to his love. The frauds conceal a fake Cunégonde behind a curtain as a means of cheating Candide of more wealth. He and Martin are arrested. They gain their release and depart north immediately. Voltaire emphasizes that Candide, the idealist, searches in vain for safe harbor. In Portsmouth, England, the winsome antihero witnesses the killing of Admiral Bynd, then moves south to Venice, where he converses with a carnival of dethroned kings.

Candide remains hopeful of reuniting with "la belle Cunégonde," who, like Don Quixote's idealized Dulcinea, represents all that is good. He looks for Cacambo, who planned to join him in Europe after rescuing the girl. Instead, Candide encounters Pacquette, the prostitute who was once Pangloss's mistress, and Giroflée, a malcontented monk. Candide offers money to the seedy pair. Next, Candide and Martin visit Count Pococurante ("Count Care-Little"), a literate Venetian sybarite who claims to live for pleasure. Candide anticipates meeting a model Epicure, but finds the count to be a world-weary cynic incapable of enjoying theater, books, even the divine Milton. Martin comments that, for Pococurante, "qu'il y a du plaisir de n'avoir pas de plaisir [it is a pleasure not to experience pleasure]." By this point, Voltaire replaces Candide's dependence on Pangloss with the young man's appreciation for Martin's wise commentary. Thus Candide begins his transformation from easy answers to true wisdom.

When Cacambo at length appears, he urges Candide to journey to Constantinople to find the baron's daughter, who is enslaved with the old woman and is washing dishes on the Sea of Marmora (modern-day Turkey). Cacambo warns that the idealized beauty, through severe hardship and neglect, has lost her youthful dewiness. At the Bosporus, Candide encounters a droll coincidence in a lengthy cavalcade of happenstance: he locates Pangloss and Cunégonde's brother, who labor as galley slaves. Both men recount fantastic scrapes with death: Pangloss escaped hanging because of a severe storm and was removed alive to a doctor's lab to be dissected; the baron's son recovered from the sword thrust to the belly.

At Propontis, Voltaire begins to rein in his fantastic plot at the same time that Candide matures. Candide ransoms Cunégonde and her faithful companion. Despite his beloved's wrinkled, decrepit condition, he sticks to his plans for marriage. Because his money is gone and his dreams unrealized, he dispatches Cunégonde's brother to Rome and settles in Turkey with his bride, Doctor Pangloss, the old woman, and his valet, Martin, on a small vegetable farm. Pacquette and Giroflée return, causing Candide to reflect on the nature of vice and ill luck. From a neighboring Muslim, Candide learns how to cope with adversity—to stop traveling helter-skelter, to stay home and tend his garden, a microcosm Candide is more capable of managing. Together, the group apply their talents to everyday survival.

Stemming from public dismay over the brutal Seven Years War, Voltaire's *Candide,* a clever but vitriolic attack on war, denigrated violence and excoriated the falseness of government, ecclesiastical vice, unbridled crime, corruption of the young, and authoritarianism. To the tyranny that overran France, the author raised his famous outcry, "Ecrasez l'infâme [Crush the infamous]." An altruist by nature, Voltaire wrote his satiric fable to demonstrate how close he came to capitulating to disillusionment in his bitter diatribe against violence, folly, wickedness, and greed.

The peripatetic protagonist of Voltaire's caustic diatribe observes the wickedness and depravity of France, Germany, Holland, England, Portugal, Italy, Paraguay, and Turkey through youthful, innocent eyes. His name suggests an ingenuous character too green and untried to anticipate corruption, suffering, loneliness, torment, danger, and despair in his efforts to reunite with his idealized maiden. Schooled in the Leibnitzian theory that events turn out to the good, whatever their apparent evil, Candide idolizes his philosophy teacher and raptly absorbs his unrealistic teachings. Subsequent misadventures dim Candide's optimism but fail to dampen his love for Cunégonde.

In the early segments of his odyssey, Candide remains openminded to a wide range of behaviors and beliefs. In serene contemplation of the peaceable Eldorado, he listens to the 172-year-old son of the king's equerry describe a spontaneous religious system by which all people worship one god and sing their hymns in unison. The grateful citizens recognize that their lives are touched by God's providence and exert themselves in perpetual thank offerings. In contrast, Voltaire creates a rogues' gallery of Judeo-Christian scamps, no-goods, despoilers, and leeches who violate the meaning of their vestments by taking advantage of trusting souls like Candide, who is slow to reject users and abusers until his life is in peril.

Motivated by youthful infatuation, Candide recovers from brief periods of depression and disillusion, abandons the utopian world of Eldorado to rejoin his lost love, and loses along the way the wealth his benefactors have given him. On his route east, he euphorically inscribes trees with the name Cunégonde. Like the epic hero Don Quixote, who adores the fair Dulcinea, or Hank Morgan in Mark Twain's *A Connecticut Yankee in King Arthur's Court* (1889), who worships the original Hello-Central thirteen centuries away in Hartford, Candide grows more worldly wise yet remains true to his beloved even after she loses her looks and becomes a kitchen drudge for a Turkish slavemaster.

Voltaire narrows Candide's expectations by offering him an attainable horizon more in keeping with one man's worth. Trusting to the profound truth of love, Candide weathers disillusion and marries his Westphalian sweetheart. His aim achieved, he undergoes a coming to knowledge from an unlikely source—a neighboring Muslim suggests that contentment lies in his meager household, where Cunégonde cooks excellent pastry, an old servant washes his linen, and Pacquette, a reformed prostitute, embroiders. At the neighbor's suggestion, Candide overcomes disillusion by abandoning an untenable optimism and contenting himself with domestic blessings. Voltaire's satiric dismissal of the transcendent utopia lauds the corner of his hero's soul that abjures the greed and bloody intrigue of the worldly as well as the complacency of the magical Eldorado. For Candide, a small retreat dedicated to gardening and a circle of loved ones who share his philosophy suffices against whatever crises he may endure. Long past the age of roseate dreams, Candide the gardener propagates an appreciation of reality. (Andrews 1981; Ayer 1986; Gassner and Quinn 1969; Gay 1988; Mason 1981; Richter and Ricardo 1980; Voltaire 1961, 1965)

See also *Canterbury Tales;* caricature; Cervantes Saavedra, Miguel de; Chaucer, Geoffrey; *A Connecticut Yankee in King Arthur's Court;* diatribe; didacticism; doggerel; *Don Quixote;* epigram; farce; picaresque; satire; Swift, Jonathan; Twain, Mark; Voltaire, François.

CANTERBURY TALES

Geoffrey Chaucer's *Canterbury Tales* (1387), the most significant work of the Middle English period, is enjoyed and praised for its humor, wisdom, and intriguing view of medieval society. On April 17, according to the Prologue, a motley party of 29 pilgrims of varying social levels assembles at the Tabard Inn in Southwark outside London on the south bank of the Thames to launch a 60-

mile religious journey the next morning at dawn. Their destination is Canter-bury, one of the period's religious centers, where the shrine of martyr Thomas à Becket (1118–1170), whom Chaucer calls "the holy blisful martyr," is said to cure the sick. With both subtle and overt digs at his characters, Chaucer en-hances caricature with small observations and ironies that later grow into ma-jor flaws:

- The squire who serves the knight is a snappy dresser who wears a short gown "all embroideered like a mead," a pun on "maid," which implies that the self-important horseman is as vain as a girl.

- Madam Eglantine, a proud female who leaves the aristocracy to enter a religious calling, sings the mass through her nose and prides herself on her comely posture and her ornate French, which she speaks with "an accent queer." A contrast of religious and worldly details, she wears both a rosary and a locket proclaiming "Amor vincit omnia [Love con-quers all]."

- The monk, a bold violator of cloister rules, loves to hunt, decks his mount in harness edged with bells, and appears to eat well. Chaucer implies that he pays lip service to vows of poverty and ignores the dangers of gluttony, one of the Seven Deadly Sins.

- A fiddle player and poseur, Hubert the friar is well known in taverns and among local women, whom he bribes with trinkets. He despises the sick and poor.

- The merchant expects the military to guard his North Sea interests and brags about being a self-made entrepreneur.

- The lawyer is "a learned man, at least he sounded so." Chaucer con-cludes that the lawyer makes a false show of being busy.

- The franklin, a good host, expects his table well set and berates his cook if the food is late or poorly prepared.

- The five guildsmen adorn themselves with silver daggers and take plea-sure in trophy wives, who flaunt their attire at religious gatherings.

- While remarking on the cook's tasty blancmange, Chaucer implies that a man with a running ulcer on his shin may spread contagion in his dishes.

- The shipman has been seaman, smuggler, and pirate; as captain of the *Madeline*, he has made men walk the plank.

- The physician uses astrology to determine the cause of ailments and appears to be in collusion with a pharmacist. Chaucer harshly lambastes the doctor for neglecting his Bible and for profiting during the plague.

- One of the least savory characters, Robin, the miller, robs his custom-ers, tells uncouth jokes, and is known to drink, lie, and carouse.

- The manciple, according to Chaucer's sly jest, fools everyone by demanding fat commissions from the provisioners he patronizes.

- Not much different from the manciple, the reeve also enriches himself at his lord's expense, then lends back to the master from stolen loot.

- A clownish fool, the summoner knows Latin court jargon but understands none of it. Because he is red-faced and reeks of garlic and onions, he terrifies children with his appearance.

- An obvious mountebank, the pardoner sells indulgences and purveys fake religious trinkets. In church, he sings the offertory and encourages parishioners to fill the collection plate; on the pilgrimage, he appears to sing a love tune to the summoner.

In short, the group ranges from mildly vain and obnoxious to lecherous, unclean, sacrilegious, rapacious, and reprehensible, perhaps Chaucer's view of humankind as a whole.

The author sets up a useful framework that will supply him with a variety of social points of view and literary styles. Harry Bailly, the Tabard's jovial host, proposes that each traveler entertain and instruct the gathering by telling two tales on the way to Canterbury and two on the return. The winner of the competition would receive supper paid for by the other participants. After drawing straws to determine the first speaker, the knight, a calloused veteran of the holy wars, launches the narrative series with his rather predictable chivalric tale about Theban cousins, Palamon and Arcite, both unjustly imprisoned in Theseus's dungeon and both in love with Emily, whom they admire in the street below their cell. The story ends with the exile of Arcite. Palamon, still incarcerated, gains no reprieve, but still has a clear view of Emily. The knight asks who is more fortunate, the exiled knight or the knight who is daily within sight of his love.

From the straightforward moral tale, Chaucer introduces Robin, the miller, teller of a bawdy story about Nicholas, a student who loves Alison, the young wife of John, an old carpenter and Nicholas's landlord. Trickery deceives John into believing that a flood threatens his farm. He falls and breaks his arm; the neighbors ridicule him. When the miller completes the tale, Oswald, a reeve (estate manager), complains that the story ridicules the elderly; to retaliate, he begins a ridiculous folk satire about a miller married to a vain social climber. The upshot of the story is the chicanery of John and Alan, two university students whom the miller wrongs. To get even, Alan beds Molly, the miller's daughter. John's plot is more involved: he moves the baby's crib closer to his bed so the miller's wife will become confused and climb in beside him:

> John waited for a while, then gave a leap
> And thrust himself upon this worthy wife.
> It was the merriest fit in all her life,
> For John went deep and thrust away like mad.

Roger the cook approves the bawdy vengeance tale and promises to tell the third story in the series, a true event from his village concerning Perkin Reveler, who robs his master by dicing, wenching, and carousing on money stolen from the owner's till. Chaucer abandons the story after three paragraphs.

The troop spends the night at Dartford and gets a late start on their pilgrimage. Bailly, who tries to keep the plan of storytelling in motion, appoints the man of law as the next narrator. His three-stage legend describes Constance, a Christian whom the Syrian sultan, Aella, marries by renouncing Islam. The couple part and are reunited in England, where they live in felicity until Aella dies. Bailly calls on the parson to outdo the man of law. A bit of grumbling precedes the turn of the captain of the *Madeline*, who insists on taking the next turn rather than listen to the churchman. He tells an amoral story about Dan John, a merchant who falls prey to a deceptive wife and a lecherous monk. Upon dunning the monk for a loan, the merchant learns that the monk has repaid the merchant's wife by "double entry." The bawdy double entendre escapes the merchant, but not the wife, who claims to have spent the money on finery. The story ends with a carnal fillip: "And now my story's done, and may God send us/Plenty of entries until death shall end us!"

Bailly, a mask for Chaucer, roars with approval and warns the others to guard against such knavery. Next, Harry calls on the prioress, Madame Eglantine, a prissy, self-absorbed woman who tells a stock anti-Semitic miracle story: how Jews slit the throat of a Christian youth. The bizarre story ends with the maimed corpse singing *O Alma* to the Virgin Mary. To clear the air after the grisly tale, Bailly turns to Chaucer. The author, selecting the chivalric mode, bores the group with the aimless, trite tale of Sir Thopas, or Topaz, in search of an elf queen. The rhyming doggerel, too trivial to deserve an audience, displeases Bailly. Chaucer complies with Bailly's request for better storytelling with the limp, meaningless allegory of Melibeus, whose enemies ravage his wife Prudence and their daughter. While approaching the town of Rochester, the halfway mark of the trek, Bailly, glad that his own spouse was not present to hear the story, instructs the monk to tell a happier story, but the monk follows with tragic incidents from the lives of Adam, Samson, Hercules, Nebuchadnezzar, Belshazzar, Zenobia, Nero, and others.

The knight halts the morbid tale and calls for a cheery story. Sir John, the nun's priest, promises to entertain and begins Chaucer's most popular story, the beast fable of Chaunticleer the rooster. Following a series of prophetic dreams, the rooster falls for the fox's flattery by singing a solo. Before Sir Russel Fox can nab him, Chaucer mourns in mock epic style:

> O destiny that may not be evaded
> Alas that Chaunticleer had so paraded!
> Alas that he had flown down from the beams!

After the fox carries him from the barnyard, Chaunticleer's wife Partlet and the other hens summon the widow and her daughters by raising a loud shriek. The fox, taken in by the sly fowl, takes his advice to sneer at the screeching peasant family. Once he spreads his mouth, the rooster leaps free and takes refuge in a tree.

At the high point of Chaucer's medley, Alice, the worldly wife of Bath, a buxom widow and gaudy dresser who has survived five husbands, begins a lengthy diatribe on women's liberation and the significance of sex to human procreation:

> Had God commanded maidenhood to all
> Marriage would be condemned beyond recall,
> And certainly if seed were never sown,
> How ever could virginity be grown?

After a lengthy, seamy build-up, she begins a story of a knight from Arthurian lore who extricates himself from a death sentence by consulting with a wise old crone to help him name the thing that women most love. The knight's relief in freedom from death withers to dread when he faces the price of the consultation—marriage to the old sage. Obliged by the code of honor, he keeps his word and marries the unattractive woman. On their wedding night, a single kiss turns her into a beauty.

Chaucer satirizes jealousy as the group nears Sittingbourne by having Friar Hubert and the summoner speak next, each telling an unflattering tale about the other. By now at the edge of Southwark, the group listens to the lengthy story of the Oxford clerk, a shy man who tells of the obedient Griselda, wife of Walter, who tests his long-suffering spouse by taking away their daughter. The six-part tale so impresses the host that he wishes that his wife had been listening. In contrast to this story of a faithful wife, the merchant recites one of the most comic in Chaucer's marriage group—the story of January, the aged husband of May. Afflicted by blindness, January correctly suspects that May uses the opportunity to meet a lover, Damian. While May and Damian hide in a pear tree, the god Pluto restores January's vision. The jealous husband accuses his wife of adultery, but she convinces him that his newly restored sight has produced a coarse picture of her, smock pulled over her head while she copulates with Damian. With the deep sigh of the unappreciated mate, the wife complains, " 'That's all I get for helping you to see / Alas,' she said, 'that ever I was so kind!' "

The squire's incomplete story of Gawain, a knight of Arthur's court, introduces the romantic tale of four magic gifts. The merry, white-haired franklin balances the story with a second romantic tale about Arveragus and Dorigen, a happily mated pair whom Aurelius threatens to disjoin. Because Dorigen proves faithful to Arveragus, the story concludes with an upbeat reunion. Immediately, the physician launches into the story of Virginius, who slaughters his young daughter rather than give her to Appius, a lustful judge. Appius seems so real to Bailly that he rails at the villain. The pardoner eases Bailly's outrage by telling of his own career, which involves bilking worshippers by exhibiting phony relics. A debased prelate, he mocks Christian teachings with cynicism:

> I preach for nothing but avarice; therefore, my theme is now and always was: Radix malorum est cupiditas. [Greed is the root of evil.] Yet, though I am guilty of that sin myself, I can still make other folk turn away from it and bitterly repent.

The pardoner's morality tale is a chilling allegory about three young carousers who plot against each other. The second nun's tale of St. Cecilia's martyrdom returns the theme from debauchery to faith and devotion.

Bailly's neat plan of orchestrating stories to entertain and enlighten alters at Boughton-under-Blean, five miles from a regular stopping place near Ospring, where a canon and his yeoman join the travelers. The yeoman humiliates the canon by telling a two-part story about a canon who deceives a gullible priest by pretending to transform mercury into silver. A tool of Chaucer's warmly humorous style, the priest, who falls easily into the canon's trap, begs, "For the love of God, who died for us all, how much does this formula cost, if I deserve it from you? Tell me now!" A brief to-do over Roger, the drunken cook, precedes the manciple's Aesopic beast fable about Phoebus, whose meddling white crow divulges that Phoebus has been cuckolded. The crow, snatched featherless for his pains, is forever decked in black feathers. The narrator laments:

> A moral: pray take heed of what I'm saying.
> Never tell anyone in all your life
> That any other has enjoyed his wife,
> For he will hate you mortally, believe it.

At four o'clock, as dark falls, Bailly suggests that the parson tell a quick story. The boring sermon on the seven deadly sins ends Chaucer's incomplete story cycle with another jab at organized religion. The sting of Chaucer's bold satire may have troubled him in his declining years. When the author neared death, he appended the final paragraph, in which he recants his original intent and prays for forgiveness. (Chaucer 1957, 1966, 1969, 1992, 1993; Chute 1946; Gardner 1977; Keates and Hornak 1994; Robinson 1957; Scott 1974)

See also Aesop; allegory; beast lore; caricature; Chaucer, Geoffrey; Chaunticleer; diatribe; doggerel; double entendre; fabliau; "The Miller's Tale"; trickster; the Wife of Bath.

CARICATURE

Caricature takes its cue from hyperbole by stretching faces and behaviors into easily recognizable comic features. In political cartoons, caricature leans toward the snide, cruel mug shot suited to invective. In the genial, forgiving spirit of burlesque and parody, caricature imbues characters with exaggerated names and features and ludicrous idiosyncrasies, turning them into hard-edged, clownish portraits. Lacking the nuances and polish of high-end literary satire, caricature thrives in set pieces: the comedic stock figures act out domestic scenes as old as the Greek satyr play, Plautus's comedies, the Italian *commedia dell'arte*, and the universal trickster tale and as new as camp theater and the comic page of the morning newspaper.

Caricature is a reliable rhetorical and motivational device: used in moderation, it always gets a laugh, often as a bit of comic relief from more serious fare. An expected spot of humor on the classical stage and its offshoot, the *commedia dell'arte,* caricature over-rouges the spots of color on the ingenue's cheeks, enlarges the nose of the avaricious landlord, lightens the falsetto of the effeminate grammar teacher, intensifies the bloodlust of the soulless avenger, and lengthens the sword and the macho strut of *miles gloriosus,* the boastful soldier. The broadening of gesture and intensification of physical and moral flaws during the Italian Renaissance produced the stereotypes that evolved into the languishing maidens, sinister manipulators, and vainglorious heroes of opera, operetta, and music hall skits.

The Elizabethan age reveled in masterly caricatures for the stage. In Shakespeare's plays, the absurdity of names such as Dogberry, Sir Toby Belch, Sir Andrew Aguecheck, and Bottom cue the playgoer to acknowledge that the author has suspended reality. Thus, the audience expects a humorous, overplayed, or grotesque figure. On the English Renaissance stage, characters still in touch with the stereotypes of their forebears exhibit enough of their former overdrawn traits to retain the enlivening spirit of caricature: thus, for example, William Shakespeare's lovable cowardly boaster, Sir John Falstaff, introduced in *The Merry Wives of Windsor* (ca. 1597); the beastly Caliban in *The Tempest* (ca. 1610); and a common pair, the vicious schemer Shylock and the selfless maiden Portia in *The Merchant of Venice* (ca. 1596).

Indeed, Shylock embodies the Elizabethan religious tensions that pit Protestant against Catholic and both against the Jew, their common enemy. Portraying the stereotypical self-pitying pinchpenny, Shylock, a Jewish moneylender, thunders against Antonio,

> He hath disgrac'd me, and hind'red me half a million, laugh'd
> at my losses, mock'd at my gains, scorn'd my nation, thwarted
> my bargains, cool'd my friends, heated mine enemies; and what's
> his reason? I am a Jew.

For all his reason in decrying anti-Semitism, Shylock is wicked, vindictive, and spiteful; his traits drain him of the humanity that would gain him the audience's sympathy. He is Shakespeare's sop tossed to an audience well versed in religious outrage, factions, and hypocrisy.

The sweet-natured orphan Portia offers a counterweight to Shylock's hypersensitivity and willfulness. She offers this bittersweet lament concerning the convoluted terms of her betrothal:

> But this reasoning is not the fashion to choose me a husband.
> O me, the word choose! I may neither choose who I would, nor
> refuse who I dislike; so is the will of a living daughter curb'd
> by the will of a dead father. (I, ii, 21–25)

Portia is still tethered to generations of maidens who languished for love because patriarchy refused them free choice. Indeed, her initial loss of autonomy allies her with one of literature's most honored victims, the luckless virgin who has no say in selection of a mate. Shakespeare's use of Portia as the voice of justice is an inspired portrayal of a female character who springs from English religious entanglements, yet professes a humanity far beyond the grasp of the average citizen.

On the other extreme of casting, Falstaff jollies the audience with his winsome, amoral plots. As boozer and good-timer in *The Merry Wives of Windsor*, he toys with words and postures about the stage in a style recognizable as the flamboyant loverboy *miles gloriosus*, slightly less menacing than the arm-plated warrior of previous centuries:

> Indeed I am in the waist two yards about; but I am now about
> no waste; I am about thrift. Briefly—I do mean to make love to
> Ford's wife. I spy entertainment in her. She discourses, she
> carves, she gives the leer of invitation.

In each example, Shakespeare demonstrates his familiarity with caricature and its effect on the audience. His skill lies in removing the character far enough from predictability to create a lasting portrait: developing Shylock from mere miserly grouse to a potential torturer, advancing Portia from the role of handwringing maiden to gallant and bold artificer, and redeeming Falstaff from an off-duty, carousing barfly to an inspiringly honest and boisterously energetic friend and courtier, a role the playwright enlarges in *Henry IV, Part 2* (ca. 1597).

A master at the quick sketch of overblown cartoon figures, Charles Dickens introduces the ill-bred, caddish Mr. Bounderby in *Hard Times* (1854):

> He was a rich man: banker, merchant, manufacturer, and what not. A big, loud
> man, with a stare, and a metallic laugh. A man made out of a coarse material,
> which seemed to have been stretched to make so much of him. A man with a
> great puffed head and forehead, swelled veins in his temples, and such a
> strained skin to his face that it seemed to hold his eyes open, and lift his eyebrows up. A man with a pervading appearance on him of being inflated like a
> balloon, and ready to start. A man who could never sufficiently vaunt himself
> a self-made man. A man who was always proclaiming, through that brassy
> speaking-trumpet of a voice of his, his old ignorance and his old poverty. A
> man who was the bully of humility.

Dickens's bravura parallel structure and overworked comic exaggeration achieves his satiric intent: to reform the worst in English society. So many of his portraits have immortalized abominable personal habits and attitudes that the mock-serious names on their own trigger a guffaw or grimace, as expected from Waxford Squeers, Noggs, Mr. Bounderby, Mrs. Sowerberry, Uriah Heep, Mrs. Havisham, Mr. Gradgrind, Jerry Cruncher, Mercy Pecksniff, Mr. Thwackum, and, of course, Ebenezer Scrooge.

Because of its straight shot to the heart of ridicule, caricature has found a home in serious British and U.S. satire: in the anti-Victorian Ernest Pontifex of Samuel Butler's *The Way of All Flesh* (1903), in the arch and urbane characters of Oscar Wilde's *The Importance of Being Earnest* (1895), in the stilted and grotesque snobs of E. M. Forster's *A Passage to India* (1924), and in the regionalisms of William Faulkner's Snopes clan (Mink, Eck, Ike, Flem, Wallstreet Panic, and Montgomery Ward Snopes), the semi-literate redneck cast of his major short fiction and of the trilogy that includes *The Hamlet* (1940), *The Town* (1957), and *The Mansion* (1960). The use of "Snopes" as a synonym for "cracker" or agricultural-class dolt epitomizes the image of the rural southern

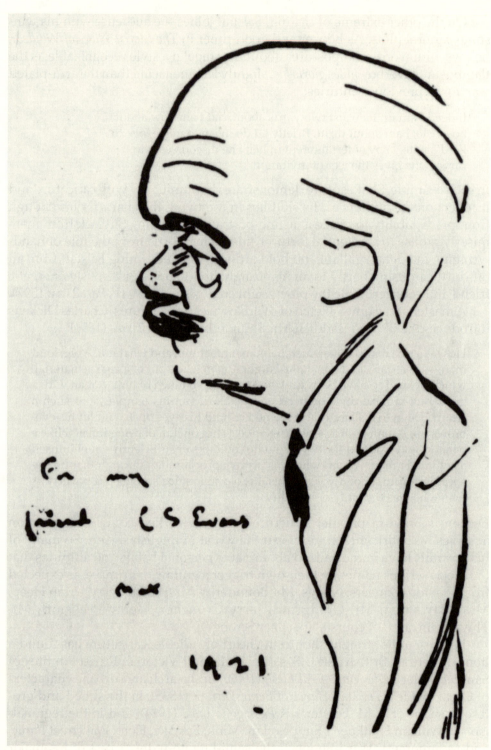

Similar to literary caricature, artistic caricature parodies and exaggerates an individual's features and traits. English critic and cartoonist Max Beerbohm drew a caricature of himself in 1921.

know-nothing, a stereotype that invigorates Eudora Welty's short stories and Clyde Edgerton's novels. In more current fiction, the comedic convention of humorous descriptive names continues with the resurrected Plautine names of Lycus, Pseudolus, Tintinabula, Panacea, Vibrata, Gymnasia, Erronius, and Miles Gloriosus in Burt Shevelove, Larry Gelbart, and Stephen Sondheim's *A Funny Thing Happened on the Way to the Forum* (1963); Radar O'Reilly, Hawkeye Pierce, and Hot Lips Hoolihan in Richard Hooker's *MASH* (1968); Nurse Duckett, Major Major, General Peckem, and Lt. Scheisskopf in Joseph Heller's *Catch-22* (1961); and Anne Fine's heroine of *Alias Madame Doubtfire* (1988).

Less obvious than the caricatures of early drama, modern literature uses the caricature as a springboard to enrich characterization and comedy. A favorite butt of Ruth Prawer Jhabvala's satire in *Heat and Dust* (1975), Chidinanda, the wannabe Hindu who makes a display of wisdom, piety, and obedience to higher laws, opens himself to ridicule by sneaking and spying on his lover and by freeloading on a vulnerable female. Before the anonymous speaker tosses him out, she tries to appreciate his study of body, energy centers, physical contortions, and oddities of diet, dress, and hygiene. At length she offers her summary:

> I get very bored with all this. It seems to me that Chid has picked up scraps of spiritual and religious lore here and there, and as he is neither an intelligent nor very educated boy, it has all sort of fermented inside him and makes him sound a bit mad at times. Perhaps he is a bit mad.

The ironic coming-to-knowledge that ends the speaker's fascination with the English ascetic precedes her denunciation of a perennial parasite. After ranging freely over her quarters, he develops liver and kidney problems during a retreat to the hill country. Grown intolerant of the odor and filth of common Indians, he departs for England on airfare supplied by his parents.

In a current stage satire—*Tent Meeting* (1985), by Larry Larson, Levi Lee, and Rebecca Wackler—the playwrights overdo the audacity of Reverend Ed, an overbearing revivalist and child abuser, to create a figure known to followers of twentieth-century scandals among indiscreet televangelists, sonorous street preachers, and religious charlatans. A failed father and devious huckster, Reverend Ed avoids truth by raving, "God's on his highway and all is right with the world." By implication, he leads his dimwitted son Darrell to attempt to drown the freakish infant whom Reverend Ed sired on his daughter Becky Ann. Act III, a stage re-creation of a fundamentalist baptism, depicts the frenzied sin-bashing, breath-sucking style of the pulpit:

> Sweet Jesus . . . you have shown us that . . . even in death . . . there is resurrection. And let it be known . . . that . . . in the second coming of our Lord . . . sweet Jesus became a man.

The chaotic yet predictable spiel jerks on in disconnected cadence toward a lengthy, supercharged emotional jolt, "and was resurrected . . . as an eggplant." The skill of Reverend Ed to move people with his rambling, emotive sermon contributes to rising hilarity. Unwitting viewers get caught up in the hypnotic images and find themselves snookered by a disreputable, jake-leg Bible-thumper. The character, by nature deserving of ridicule, seems to stand in front of a tomato-hurling mob with defiant nose uplifted in delicious anticipation of his just deserts. In this pose, caricature suits satire as a broad stroke of candor encircling the figure in the spotlight for the world's delight and edification. (Barnet, Berman, and Burto 1960; Butler 1960; Cuddon 1976; Dickens 1986; Faulkner 1967, 1977; Feinberg 1967; Fine 1990; Forster 1984; Gray 1992; Heller 1961; Henry 1995; Holman 1980; Hooker 1969; Jhabvala 1975; Larson, Lee, and Wackler 1987; McArthur 1992; Philip and Gadd 1928; Pollard 1970; Shakespeare 1957, 1974; Shevelove and Gelbart 1991)

See also burlesque; camp; *commedia dell'arte;* hyperbole; invective; parody; political satire; satire; Shakespeare, William; trickster; Wilde, Oscar.

CARMINA BURANA

A vigorous, joyously decadent thirteenth-century secular verse cycle composed of randomly written verses and six ecclesiastical plays accredited to wandering students, itinerant prelates, minstrels, and troubadours, the *Carmina Burana*—literally, "Songs of Beuron"—remained unread and unappreciated until the cycle's resurrection in 1803 from Benediktbeuren, a Bavarian abbey in southern Germany. Literary historians attribute the varied odes, paeans, parodies, dances, pastoral idylls, love lyrics, wooing songs, satires on church doctrine, and doggerel to Goliards (gluttons), the vagabonds who sampled liberal arts coursework in a variety of major universities and begged or entertained for their supper like Anglo-Saxon scops or present-day street or mall buskers. The incongruity of Latin lyrics as a part of the Goliards' polyglot verse contributes to the saucy humor of lines in medieval German and French, for Latin was the ecclesiastical language.

Exuberant stanzas burst with youth's hormonal urges brought to an intemperate boil in spring. Sexual innuendo compares bursts of energy with a throbbing penis ("All that Venus bids me do,/Do I with erection"). To justify the resounding "Yes," the rhymester falls back on rationalizing:

> I have uttered openly
>> All I knew that shamed me,
> And have spewed the poison forth
>> That so long defamed me;
> Of my old ways I repent,
>> New life hath reclaimed me;
> God beholds the heart—'twas man
>> Viewed the face and blamed me.

The satiric comparison between going to confession and achieving sexual climax frames the theme of youth bound by orthodoxy. After a long, loveless winter, young people chafe to gad about and relieve their social and physical tensions.

A factor in the collection's appeal is its irregular pairings of amorous, sweet, and lecherous verses. "In trutino [On the Scales]," a verbal and spiritual sparring between virginity and sensuality, appears alongside "Ego sum abbas [I Am the Abbot]," a song about a medieval game of strip poker, and "Olim lacus colueram [Once I Dwelt on the Lake]," the mournful plaint of a spitted swan cooking to a turn to be served on a platter. The debate of the "In trutino," which rapidly shoves aside modesty for a brief farewell to ladylike behavior, concludes with the polite, but unwavering "suave, suave transeo [sweetly, sweetly I cross over]." In the roast swan and the gambling verses, both the abbot who succeeds at gaming and the cygnet that regrets its fate on the rotisserie denote an acrimonious satire centered on the hypocrisy of amoral students attending coursework that will ready them for monastic lives and for the Christian church's demands for poverty, chastity, and stewardship. The satiric complaint of the swan prefigures the poet's visions of hell, where he will find himself the main course, roasted in recompense for his youth-driven carnality.

Much of the *Carmina Burana* parallels the twentieth-century "spring fling," the annual debauch of college students who are shedding parental control and campus authority. In 1937, Carl Orff chose to feature in a cantata 25 of the 200 poems that comprise the verse cycle; after its premiere at the Frankfurt Opera, the work became a standard choral litany. Beginning with a typically classical prologue set to vigorous percussion and compellingly pessimistic harmonies, the cantata rejects the Christian notion of God's will and embraces the pagan concept of fate, which the poet depicts as the arbitrary rotation of a wheel, the waxing and waning of the inconstant moon. From this cynical depiction of reality, the poem turns to its three collections: "Primo vere [In Spring]," "Uf dem Anger [In the Tavern]," and "Cour d'amour [The Court of Love]."

"In the Tavern" heightens the conflict between sacred and secular conscience and flesh. Bitterly, the anonymous poet mourns in "Estuans Interius [Seething Inside]," and "In Taberna Quando Sumus [When We Are in the Tavern]," the sweaty drinkers and dicers form a cross-cultural blend as varied as Chaucer's pilgrims:

> We drink for Pope and King alike, and then we drink, we drink!
> . . . the mistress drinks, the master drinks, the soldier and the
> clergyman, this man, that woman, the servant,
> the maid, the industrious, the lazy, the whiteman, the black, the localman,
> the vagabond, the ignorant, the learned, the poor, the rich, the
> sick, the exiled, the unknown, the youngster, the oldster, the
> Bishop and the Deacon, the sister, the brother, the old woman,
> the mother . . . Women drink and men drink by the hundreds and
> the thousands . . . It takes a lot of money for this aimless and
> intemperate drinking
> . . . And though our drink is always gay,
> there are always those who nag us. A toast! May they who nag
> at us be confounded, and never be inscribed amoung the just!

The rapacity of the *Carmina*'s wit anticipates the flowering of the Renaissance, a time when a Vatican-dominated populace found itself less cowed by churchmen and less resistant to the draw of humanism. The motet ends with an epilogue that returns us to its starting point—the fate of the spring frolic, the enticements of gambling and drink, and the longings of the flesh for sexual fulfillment, all of which require that Venus bless their efforts, or not, depending on the whim of fate.

The genius of the *Carmina Burana* lies in its use of form and meaning to satirize lack of order at the same time that it celebrates diversity and individuality. Just as Europe was rebelling against the strictures of classicism and ecclesiastical authority, young people were overthrowing parental and civic regulations, demanding a greater choice of subjects, and achieving a harried truce with the townspeople who fed and housed them. An energetic round number five aligns 18 five-line verses in strict parallel. The eighth verse captures the spirit and flow of the piece:

> Ordo languet
> Pudicitia sordescit
> Pietas refugit
> Doctrina rarescit
> Sophia hebescit.

The chanting of the lines gives the noun subjects to one group and the verbs to the antiphonal group. The translation forms a vivid give and take as the two groups compete:

First:	Order
Second:	languishes.
First:	Modesty
Second:	is sullied.
First:	Piety
Second:	flees.
First:	Knowledge
Second:	grows rare.
First:	Wisdom
Second:	dims.

Paradoxically, number 145 counters the cynicism of number 5 with a joy in the muse, which arrives in verse. The poet urges the singers to join in unison to the "greening of meadow, countryside, and grove." The lime trees spread limbs, branches, and foliage; wild thyme thrusts spruce-colored flowerheads under the trees, where all can dance in a circle. With nature lying open for human enjoyment, the poem welcomes all to a festive place where winds whisper spring's ripeness. (Bryant 1967; *Carmina Burana* 1974; "Goliardic Verse" 1994)

See also doggerel; satire.

CARROLL, LEWIS

A nonsense fancier in the same era that produced limerick specialist Edward Lear, Lewis Carroll, pseudonym of Charles Lutwidge Dodgson, was a meticulous bookman who refused to release his whimsical manuscript for print until the art, layout, and cover suited the overall purpose of his two masterworks, the "Alice" books. Carroll was born to Francis Jane Lutwidge, an endearing lover of children, and the puritanical Reverend Charles Dodgson on January 27, 1832, in a grimly proper, secluded rectory in the rural village of Daresbury, Cheshire. A shy, diffident lad, Carroll was the third of 11 children and the eldest son. The Carrolls were a prim Victorian family with ties to northern gentry of longstanding honor. Pressed to excel from early childhood, Carroll adapted to partial deafness and a misshapen spine and accepted his parents' decision that he must forego left-handedness and rely on his right hand. His peers recall that, on presentation to his elders, he stammered severely but grew calm as the distance between himself and adults increased. This distancing from intimidation and disapproval may have produced Britain's most beloved spinner of satiric yarns and verse parodies, which he disguised as children's literature.

A natural loner and homebody, Carroll loved word games, wire puzzles, ciphers, anagrams, shaped poems, symbolism, and number rebuses. Many of his puns and jests rely on a stereo-opposite or mirror image, the most famous being *Through the Looking-Glass and What Alice Found There* (1872). His family placed him in charge of seven sisters, among whom he felt at home. His use of games, sleight of hand, and narrative as a babysitting technique evolved into a method of talking to young girls, who became his most treasured companions. After the family moved to Croft Rectory, Yorkshire, where father Dodgson advanced to the archdeaconry and canonship of Ripon Cathedral, Carroll, aged eleven, entered Richmond Grammar School. He developed a skill with puppetry and wrote his own stage material, which he published in juvenile magazines—*Rectory Magazine, Rectory Umbrella, Mischmash*—that hint at the talent he would one day polish for international audiences. In 1846, Carroll entered Rugby and suffered the drubbings that bullies commonly dispense to nonathletic, scholarly types. Once enrolled at Christ Church, Oxford, in 1851, he excelled in literature and math and remained happily at home in academia for the rest of his life.

A math tutor, hall master, librarian, and deacon, Carroll was a so-so teacher but a stickler for logic. His penchant for parody and satire required him to dissociate himself from classroom duties. Dodgson achieved the distance by renaming himself—first B. B., then Dares, and finally Lewis Carroll. The need for a mellifluous pen name plentifully sprinkled with r's and l's was occasioned by Dodgson's speech impediment; his middle name was wickedly difficult for a stammerer like him. While teaching himself the details of writing, Carroll also published humorous pamphlets. He developed a love of photography, an emerging craft in his day, and applied his talent to provocative shots of children. He left an account of his opinions and activities in a hefty correspondence, another method of speaking without stuttering; his photographs, however, were destroyed at his death.

Critics and literary historians make much of Carroll's failure with adult heterosexual relationships and his intense friendships with little girls, especially Alice Liddell, the prototype of his masterpiece, *Alice in Wonderland*

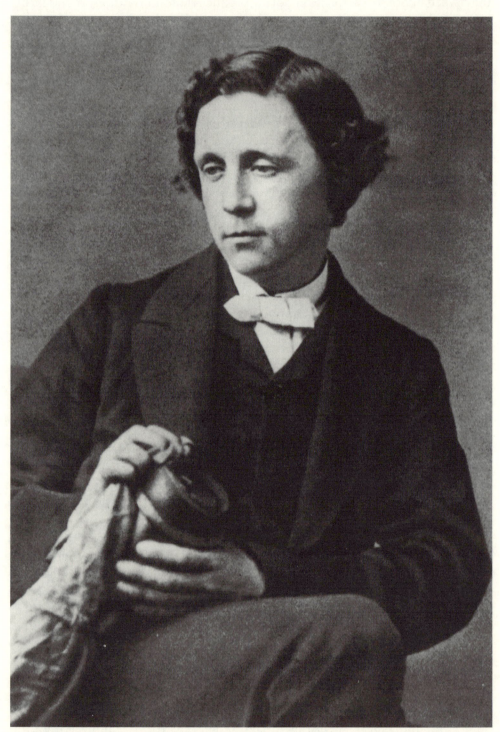

English writer Charles Lutwidge Dodgson, better known as Lewis Carroll, in 1863

(1865). Evidence from letters and diaries offers no hint of impropriety or even repressed sexual urges. Rather, psychological analysis suggests that Carroll felt relieved of flirtation and wife-hunting when he was among prepubescent girls like Alice, who was the daughter of Henry George Liddell, dean of the college. Moreover, the fact of his friendship with actress Ellen Terry defeats the notion that he had no adult female friends.

Pleasant afternoons chaperoned by a nanny named Miss Prickett placed Carroll in the midst of the three Liddell girls on the sofa of his residence. He told new and refurbished classic fantasies while drawing pictures in pencil and ink. A holiday at the family retreat at Llandudno, Gwynedd, included Carroll, who narrated original stories to entertain the girls. A boat trip on July 4, 1862, took Carroll, Alice Liddell, her older and younger sisters Lorina and Edith, and Reverend Robinson Duckworth up the Thames to Godstow. Carroll filled the day with the narrated adventures of Alice, which he promised to write in finished form "to please a child," he claims in his diary (Carroll 1960, p. 22). Completed February 10, 1863, the poem had doubled in length and appeared in print with the drawings of John Tenniel, a cartoonist for *Punch* magazine whom Carroll hired as illustrator. By 1865, the book was an unprecedented success in Britain and the United States and remains a classic. Carroll published numerous other titles—*The Hunting of the Snark* (1876), *A Tangled Tale* (1885), *Sylvie and Bruno* (1889), *Curiosa Mathematica* (1893), and *Sylvie and Bruno Concluded* (1893)—that did not survive the era. He died on January 14, 1898, at his sisters' home in Guildford, Surrey. (Carroll 1960, 1994; Eagle 1992; Muir 1954)

See also *Alice in Wonderland*; doggerel; limerick; parody; whimsy.

 # CATCH-22

One of the most influential satires of the twentieth century, Joseph Heller's *Catch-22* (1961), a cult classic to the 1960s antidraft protesters of the Vietnam War, has stirred heated debate about the author's purpose and motive for writing a novel about a wartime deserter. The novel is a complex network of clustering episodes and flashbacks and juxtaposed recurrent motifs that heighten satiric elements. Set on Pianosa, an island off Italy, during World War II, the plot centers on the wartime service of Captain John Yossarian, a quirky, instrospective 28-year-old bombardier to the 256th Air Force squadron who signed up for flight school in the mistaken hope that the war would end before he would see action.

Heller creates a controlling image of death: Yossarian boxed into a bombardier's compartment in the Plexiglas nose of the B-25 like a corpse in a coffin. Vulnerable against exploding ack-ack fire, he has good reason for verbally harassing McWatt, the pilot, as they seek their target. To perform the bombardier's role, Yossarian must select the I. P.—casual military jargon for Impact Point—on which to drop bombs. Losing his nerve on a flight over

Avignon, France, he battles haunting flashbacks to the death of Snowden, a moribund replacement gunner on whose thigh wound Yossarian applies a tourniquet. Unable to locate morphine, he shoves two aspirins between the blue lips. In response to Snowden's trembling and request for cover, Yossarian spreads over him a wispy length of parachute silk, an ironic symbol of rescue and safety. The movement discloses a lethal shrapnel wound on Snowden's torso. Yossarian compares the gaping hole to a football, Heller's dark joke on the soldier's importance to air force brass. The horror of a "soggy pile" of Snowden's organs protruding from the wound sticks in Yossarian's mind, which ponders an English/French pun, "Où sont les Neigdens d'antan?," a silly "Snowden" version of François Villon's "Where are the snows of yesteryear?"

War's craziness grows more oppressive. Gently treated for trauma by Doc, Yossarian recovers and rates a reward for his attempt to save Snowden. After being awarded the Distinguished Flying Cross, however, he rebels against military hypocrisy, a pseudopatriotic scam that could kill him. To make his point that war decorations are a mockery of service, Yossarian attends the presentation ceremony naked; General Dreedle supports his decision and cows Colonel Cathcart, who reverses position to bleat submissively, "Those are my sentiments exactly, sir!" The chaplain counsels Yossarian about his bareness. Sick of the carnage that uniforms symbolize, the antiheroic bombardier considers giving up military clothing as a form of rebellion. The shedding of clothes elevates him to an everyman, timorous and fragile. The swirling madness of war sweeps around Yossarian, leaving him the only sane man amid rampant lunacy: Captain Black launches a Glorious Loyalty Oath Crusade, a rotating propeller dismembers Kid Sampson, the medical corps discovers that a bandaged victim is really a corpse, and the chaplain, an Anabaptist, torments himself with questions about God's existence. Within the confines of Pianosa's air base, the war becomes the only reality.

In subsequent scenes, Yossarian suffers an overhanging gloom that the escalating numbers of required bomb runs increase his chance of dying in war. Spinning out of control, his terrorized brain envisions potential violence from a 50-caliber machine gun that could grasp and fire

> savagely against all the demons tyrannizing him: at the smoky black puffs of the flak itself; at the German anti-aircraft gunners below whom he could not even see and could not possibly harm with his machine gun even if he ever did take the time to open fire.

His ridiculous methods of avoiding future assignments—cultivating liver disease from a bad diet, displacing a boundary on a map of enemy territory, and yanking out his communication lines—become ever more desperate. Doc Daneeka, the pilot's only salvation, introduces the satiric premise of the novel, a slang term that has become a part of the English language: Yossarian can invoke Catch-22, which states that pleading insane is a sign of sanity and proof that the complainant is sane and should continue service to the military.

The absurdity of paperwork develops into a humanistic theme by ridiculing the value of neatly signed pages over the lives of the people they affect.

Driven to babbling, Yossarian petitions Major Major, a loony squadron commander promoted in error. The major leaps from his office to avoid making decisions and signs documents with the name Washington Irving, an act that causes the Criminal Investigation Department to search for internal fraud. Yossarian, fighting his own paper war, cannot convince authorities to remove a dead man from his billet because the man was never properly registered. Grating on his nerves is roommate Orr, a tedious piddler who perpetually assembles and tears down the minute parts of the heater valve, a symbol of the small roles played by individual soldiers in supplying "heat" to the enemy. In the background, Yossarian hears the wails of Hungry Joe, who suffers nightmares that eventually kill him.

Heller contrasts the fliers' concerns with the trivialities emphasized by the brass. General Peckem expects tight flying formations during bomb runs over Sicily, Italy, and France. Colonel Cathcart continues upping the number of bomb runs required before a soldier completes a tour of duty. The rhythms of camp suggest the frenzied lives of stir-crazy caged rats who fight, drink, exercise, and conduct amours with local Italian prostitutes to keep themselves occupied between air strikes. Aarfy goes insane and rapes a maid, then hurls her out a window. Paralleling the cynicism of war is the insanity of mess officer Milo Minderbinder, who jeopardizes the men's morale and lives by bargaining on the black market with food, parachutes, morphine, and other matériel necessary to the war effort. In Milo's warped view:

> We're people, aren't we? So we might just as well keep the money and eliminate the middleman. Frankly, I'd like to see the government get out of war altogether, and leave the whole field to private industry. (Heller 1961, p. 266)

The cynicism of his misapplication of free trade suits the wartime madness of milk runs and bombing patterns, paperwork and chaplains praying for victory.

Heller twists the capitalistic ethic into a lethal climax. When Milo overstocks Egyptian cotton, he makes up for his miscalculation by contracting with the Germans to bomb the Pianosa airfield with all the planes he had amassed for the M & M syndicate. In one of the most insane scenes of black humor, Milo strikes heartlessly:

> the airfield, bomb dump and repair hangars as well, and all the survivors were outside hacking cavernous shelters into the solid ground and roofing them over with sheets of armor plate stolen from the repair sheds at the field and with tattered squares of waterproof canvas stolen from the side flaps of each other's tents.

In a moment of illogical camaraderie, Milo carefully avoids the mess hall and airfield so that the men can land and get a hot meal before going to bed. His cool control enrages Cathcart who, for the first time, knows the feeling of imminent death.

Heller stokes up the black humor as the escalating pressures of war drive Yossarian over the brink. Nately and Dobbs die; Nately's whore, whom Colonels Cathcart and Korn consider a Nazi assassin, blames Yossarian for Nately's death. Dressed in military green, she becomes one with the enemy—a female version of the Grim Reaper—and stalks Yossarian with bone-handled steak knife in hand. While he is treated at the post hospital for a stab wound, he learns that he will be court-martialed for refusing more bomb runs and for violating leave, a minor infraction he incurs in his dash to the streets for what may be his last breath of freedom. Ironically, Aarfy, a deranged murderer, goes unpunished.

The intense fictional rhythms churn into a patterned fugue: the déjà vu of Snowden pleading for warmth forces "Yo-Yo" Yossarian to relive the futile treatment and the motherly cuddle of Snowden's chilled body. Murmuring "There, there," Yossarian suddenly brightens after recognizing Snowden's secret that man is matter:

> Drop him out a window and he'll fall. Set fire to him and he'll burn. Bury him and he'll rot like other kinds of garbage. The spirit gone, man is garbage. That was Snowden's secret. Ripeness was all. (Heller 1961, p. 450)

The news that Orr has washed up on the Swedish coast offers Yossarian an alternative to madness; for the first moment in the worsening scenario of bombing and fleeing the enemy, his eyes brim with tears of hope. Mentally boarding a rubber life raft and rowing toward Sweden, he leaps away from Nately's whore and sets out.

The novel is a veritable mine of comedy, including caricatures, surreal sight gags, illogic, death jokes, black humor, puns, incongruity, parody, and sarcasm. It served as the vehicle for a star-heavy Paramount film in 1970, featuring Alan Arkin as the antihero and Art Garfunkel as Nately. Other cast members—Martin Balsam, Richard Benjamin, Bob Newhart, Anthony Perkins, Paula Prentiss, Jon Voigt, Martin Sheen, and Orson Welles—lend an air of professionalism to an otherwise poorly received effort. The best scenes produce a surreal reflection of the disjointed novel and the fliers' rush to destruction. Most memorable is the aged Italian in the brothel who claims that the best way to survive war is to collaborate with whatever group is in power, thus outlasting temporary governments by refusing to protest. (Bermel 1982; *Contemporary Authors* 1994; *Discovering Authors* 1993; Heller 1961; Merrill 1987; Nagel 1984; Potts 1982)

See also caricature; Heller, Joseph; Irving, Washington; pun; satire; Yossarian.

 # CAT'S CRADLE

A blend of techno-fantasy, apocalyptic novel, and morality tale, Kurt Vonnegut's satiric cult classic, *Cat's Cradle* (1963), applies to his jeremiad a madcap, nonstop reader's feast—didactic chapter headings, verse, pun, parody, Christmas carols, symbolism, biblical allusion, motto, dialogue, parallelism, legend, calypso rhyme, and aphorism. The story transfers John—renamed Jonah, a lapsed Christian and mildly picaresque writer composing a book on the bombing of Hiroshima—to the fictional Republic of San Lorenzo, a microcosm in the Caribbean. John devotes himself to the Bokonon faith and to intense study of Dr. Felix Hoenikker, a progenitor of the atomic bomb who sat in his study in Ilium,

New York, and toyed with a cat's cradle. The simplistic string game relieved his stress from work on the Manhattan Project, his "last batch of brownies"— the atomic study that produced the weapon that destroyed Hiroshima and Nagasaki and precipitated the Cold War. Vonnegut's use of the cat's cradle as a symbol produces a wealth of images—infantilism, false security, animalistic pleasures, and the web of lies and deception that entrap scientists who traduce their humanism in favor of discoveries of questionable value.

As one might expect, the Hoenikkers are a sad lot. Their mother Emily died in childbirth. The oldest child, Angela, mothered her dwarf brother Newt, his twelve-year-old brother Frank, and Hoenikker himself, who had so distanced himself from his former job at the research lab of the General Forge and Foundry Company that he took refuge in studying turtles. On a venture to the Hoenikker house, John locates Dr. Asa Breed, Hoenikker's former boss, who details Hoenikker's discovery of an interlocking crystal, ethylene diamine tartrate, nicknamed ice-nine, a nugget of which can solidify a lake. Breed believes that Hoenikker died before he synthesized his compound, which has the power to dry the seas and destroy the earth. Vonnegut makes a darkly evocative jest about the Hoenikker children's discoveries of their father's corpse and ice-nine on Christmas Eve.

Vonnegut's zany string of coincidences takes John to the phallic marker on Emily Hoenikker's grave and to a freelance assignment to write about a philanthropist living in San Lorenzo, "barracuda capital of the world." There Frank, an outlaw, serves as science minister and instigator of the island "master plan" for dictator Miguel "Papa" Monzano, a parody of the eminently corrupt Papa Doc Duvalier, former president of Haiti. On the plane to San Lorenzo, John encounters Newt and Angela, who, like a human cat's cradle, reconnect a glob of loose ends in a meandering plot and fill in the evolution of Bokononism. Landing at the port city of Bolivar, named for Hispanic liberator and anticolonialist Simon Bolivar, John discovers the mockery of liberty in Papa Monzano, who arrives by limo, collapses, and receives treatment from Dr. Schlichter von Koenigswald, a former SS physician and caricature of Dr. Josef Mengele, the Nazi doctor who condemned the sick, weak, and unproductive to gas ovens. John's arrival at the "Pissant Hilton" adds another satiric touch— a meeting with American hotelier and mosaicist Philip Castle, whose piecework art suggests the driblets of data that are forming in John's mind about Hoenikker and his significance to the world.

The satire grows less humorous and more chaotic as John encounters a streak of luck in a job offer for a lucrative post as San Lorenzo's next president and an arranged marriage to Mona, a fetching model. In a formal bedside ceremony of succession, John greets Papa, who lies in a gilded lifeboat, Vonnegut's pointed symbol of hopelessness and imminent death for Papa and his heirs. On the Day of the Hundred Martyrs to Democracy ceremony, John is felled by food poisoning from tainted albatross and seeks Papa's physician, who has just discovered the old man lying dead from touching ice-nine to his lips. The doctor also reaches for the instant solidifying agent and dies instantly in a contorted state.

Vonnegut's apocalyptic finale brings one of the island's six airplanes down during an air show, upends the castle, and causes Papa and the crystal to slide into the Caribbean Sea. Vonnegut words the coda with whimsical grace:

> There was a sound like that of the gentle closing of a portal as big as the sky, the great door of heaven being closed softly. It was a grand AH-WHOOM. I opened my eyes—and all the sea was ice-nine.

The resounding cataclysm strikes worldwide; John and Mona take refuge in a bomb shelter, which John describes as a "rock womb." Seven days after their retreat, John surveys the hardened world. After Mona's death from contact with ice-nine, he joins the handful of survivors at Frank's cave for six months. The last scene shows John's encounter with Bokonon, who hands him the final sentence of the Bokonon bible, which describes how the belligerent prophet would lie supine with a history of human stupidity for a pillow and touch ice-nine while gesturing contempt heavenward at "You Know Who."

Vonnegut's Swiftian range of rhetorical devices recalls the deft eighteenth-century writer of dark humor and intricate, ingenious satire. Vonnegut toys with names: Angela, the Hoenikker family angel; Franklin, an inventor like Benjamin Franklin; Felix, named the Latin word for lucky; Newt, a grotesque homunculus; Jonah, the disobedient biblical character who is swallowed by a whale; Faust, secretary at the lab; and Castle, the philanthropist who builds dream worlds devoted to hope and mercy. The vocabulary of Bokononism lampoons religious jargon and ritual, as with boko-maru, rubbing the soles of the feet together; calypso, a verse psalm; foma, small lies; grandfalloonery, major lies; and wrang-wrang, a person who violates a godly act. Vonnegut also indulges in frequent chapter headings, concluding his book with Chapter 127, a magic number that adds up to ten, a combination of one and zero, which returns the combination to the wholeness and finality of one.

Through John, Vonnegut's Lemuel Gulliver, the reader experiences the world's demise as a result of the misapplication of technology, a major theme in science fiction. The singular viewer, his faith shaken by Bokonon's defiance of God, surveys the ruined earth, a solidified cosmos gone cold to the core. The flip side of the bomb that flattened Hiroshima, ice-nine congeals the sea and obliterates John's brief Eden and Papa's totalitarian state. Vonnegut's satire insists that despotism and scientific power are illusions—chained dragons too monstrous for human mastery. (Broer 1988; Goldsmith 1972; Klinkowitz 1982; Merrill 1989; Morse 1991; Vonnegut 1990)

See also black humor; caricature; Gulliver, Lemuel; parody; picaresque; pun; satire; slapstick; *Slaughterhouse-Five;* Swift, Jonathan; Vonnegut, Kurt; whimsy.

CATULLUS

One of satire's most caustic voices, Gaius Valerius Catullus, Rome's late Republican darling of the social-climbing set, quickly shed his country ways and, in his early twenties, embraced the questionable morals and luxuries of patronage, including Cicero among his admirers. Born in Verona to a well-connected family around 87 B.C., he met Julius Caesar on overnight stays at the family villa as the general passed back and forth on his way to the Gallic campaigns. Like Caesar, Catullus rode the meretricious fortunes of the day to Rome's height, taking his ease among the idle rich, living for a year in Bithynia while serving in a dreary civil service job, joyously returning to Rome, writing occasional verse for weddings and funerals, and earning a reputation for naughty, stinging wit. A gifted newcomer, Catullus impressed even Ovid with his dizzyingly romantic poems—five to his unfaithful boyfriend Juventius and the rest dedicated to Clodia Metelli, the upscale mistress he immortalized as Lesbia to honor Sappho, the Greek erotic versifier from the island of Lesbos. The love affair fills a quarter of Catullus's canon and alternates vilifying invective with the evidence of better days when passion fired his lust and drove him to seek the self-centered Clodia.

Poetry chronicles Catullus's love life. On good days, he cannot say enough about the rush of passion through his limbs, the sweet pangs of lust that torment him as Clodia sits opposite him at a dinner party, laughing into the eyes of her husband and drowning Catullus's senses with her allure. To the gossips, he hurls his impatient defiance and urges Clodia to realize that life is fleeting. He commands that she "live and love and count as worthless the whispers of cranky old men." Lusty and demanding, he urges:

Give me a thousand kisses, then another thousand,
Then a hundred, then a hundred thousand so that
We lose count.

When the affair dwindles to recriminations and fury, Catullus reaches deeper into invective, claiming that Clodia's brother Pulcher was "her favorite of all the family," a suggestion that she would pursue him among her ignoble amours. The poet names and vilifies six of her other lovers and lashes out: "What a woman says to her amorous lover should be written on the wind and tumbling waters." In an episode of self-evaluation, he mutters his famous "odi et amo [I hate and I love]," a bit of honesty that forces him to admit that he has lost control and, for no good reason, suffers a self-inflicted torment.

Catullus's life was filled with stress, notably because of Clodia's inconstancy and because of his own manic-depressive moments of self-doubt, jealousy, personal animosities, and loss. At times, he withdrew to his home in the Sabine hills 25 miles east of Rome in Tibur or to his manor house at Sirmio on Lake Benacus. A significant journey detailed in his verse describes a cumbersome land and sea trek to the Asian shore of Troy to reach his mortally ill brother, who died before Catullus's arrival. Attending to the traditional Roman rituals after the funeral, the poet, his eyes streaming tears, finds little comfort in bidding "ave atque vale" [hale and farewell] to mute ashes.

Three years before his death in 54 B.C., Catullus unleashed the exhibitionist side of himself by openly courting scandal. In his verse, he warns his victim, "You won't escape my iambics." He appeared at the trial of Marcus Caelius

Rufus, a false friend—one of many who bedded Clodia and bragged about the conquest. In the suit claiming that Rufus poisoned her, Cicero pled Rufus's case by sullying Clodia with imputations of indecency. Catullus, apparently cured of his lust for her, championed Cicero. A riskier turn of events pitted Catullus against Caesar and his engineer Mamurra, whom Catullus insulted by calling a prick. Of Caesar, he pens an insulting couplet:

> Nil nimium studeo, Caesar, tibi velle placere,
> Nec scire utrum sis albus an ater homo.
> [I don't paricularly care to placate you, Caesar,
> Nor do I wish to know whether you are white or black.]

Quintilian, horrified at the crudity and foolhardiness of Catullus's vitriolic attack, considered him crazy with arrogance. Perhaps because Caesar valued his friendship with Catullus's family or because he didn't seek open warfare with the youth-crazed, witty wordsmith, he made public gestures of conciliation and shared dinner at his own home and at Catullus's home in Verona.

Known as an Alexandrian for his imitation of Hellenic style, Catullus gained stature despite the trivial subjects he chose to immortalize. One of his greatest achievements was his funeral poem to a bird. Upon seeing Clodia's eyes "red and swollen with weeping," he captured the scene along with memories of her finger crooked for the pet sparrow to grasp. Courting bathos with the tiny verb *"it,"* which is Latin for "goes," to describe the bird's departure, Catullus achieves a remarkably sincere elegy to the dead bird that "takes its solitary way into the shadowy underworld, from which no one ever returns." The facile creation of these and other lines in Catullus's limited canon endeared him to Horace and Virgil in his own time and to British writers George Babington Macauley, Edmund Spenser, Ben Jonson, Robert Herrick, John Keats, Alfred Tennyson, Algernon Swinburne, and C. Day Lewis. (Bowder 1980; Catullus 1951; Feder 1986; Godolphin 1949; Hadas 1954; Howatson 1989; Knight 1981; Mantinband 1956; Radice 1973)

See also bathos; invective; satire.

CERVANTES SAAVEDRA, MIGUEL DE

Spain's classic romanticist, the author of *El Ingenioso Hidalgo Don Quixote de la Mancha* (1615) is sometimes credited with writing the first modern novel and one of satire's most influential mock epics. As star of the episodic satire, Don Quixote, the Knight of the Sad Countenance, the universal dreamer and dotard, remains unique in world literature as a good-natured but misguided idealist whose utopia exists only in his visions. So gentle is the humor of Cervantes's ridicule of romanticism that the novel's aphorisms remain constant in collections of Aesopic wisdom:

- To give the devil his due.

- No limit but the sky.

- What I have earned by the sweat of my brow.

- Time out of mind.

- There's not the least thing can be said or done, but people will talk and find fault.

- To put you in this pickle.

- Without a wink of sleep.

- A finger in every pie.

- Raise a hue and cry.

- 'Tis the part of a wise man to keep himself today for tomorrow, and not venture all his eggs in one basket.

- To turn over a new leaf.

- Honesty's the best policy.

- More knave than fool.

- I began to smell a rat.

- Don't put too fine a point to your wit for fear it should get blunted.

- Every man was not born with a silver spoon in his mouth.

In addition to lending their voices to the construction of aphorisms, the bumbling old knight astride his bony nag Rocinante and his rube sidekick, Sancho Panza, on his beloved mule have resurfaced in paintings, statuary, film, cartoon, song, legend, and musical comedy.

The creation of so lasting a figure was the work of an unusually colorful writer and civil servant, a contemporary of William Shakespeare. Cervantes was born in Alcalá de Henares outside Madrid on September 29, 1547, the fourth of seven children sired by a failed hidalgo, Rodrigo Cervantes, a surgeon and pharmacist at the University of Alcalá, and his wife, Leonor de Cortinas. Cervantes grew up in want on the ragged edge of gentility: the fine trappings of nobility were within his reach, but he never possessed them. Although his father served time in debtor's prison, Cervantes received a sound education. He read widely and grew enamored of *Amadis de Gaula [Amadis of Gaul]* (1509), a chivalric romance. After preliminary work with Jesuit tutors at the School of General Studies, Cervantes enrolled at the University of Salamanca. Under Juan López de Hoyes, he received humanistic training in all forms of literature, on which he modeled his early writings.

As Cardinal Giulio Acquaviva's chamberlain and attaché to the Vatican, Cervantes departed from Spain at age 22. During military service under Diego de Urbina, Cervantes acquired a war record heaped with commendations for heroism at Tunis, Sardinia, Sicily, Naples, Genoa, and, in October 1571, aboard the galley *La Marquesa* in the Gulf of Corinth at the Battle of Lepanto, a Christian defeat of the Ottoman Turks. He was so severely wounded by pistol fire that he suffered lung impairment and lost articulation and grip in his mangled left hand from the whack of a scimitar. On a voyage aboard the galley *Sol*, he fell into the hands of Turkish pirates and arrived at Algiers in chains. For five years he distinguished himself by trying to free 60 prisoners from an Arab slave compound. At a hearing before an Algerian tribunal, Cervantes amazed the pasha by taking full blame for the slave insurrection. The pasha was so impressed with his candor that he spared Cervantes's life.

In 1580, after Juan Gil, a Trinitarian friar, paid Cervantes's ransom of 500 gold pieces, the poet returned to his Portuguese mistress in Madrid to eke out a living cranking out predictable stage dramas. He published a pastoral idyll, *La Galatea* (1585), which earned fewer royalties than he needed to support his mistress and only daughter, Isabel Rojas de Saavedra. To end the constant need for money, in 1584 he arranged a marriage of convenience with the wealthy Catalina Salaza y Vozmediano, an unsuitable girl twenty years his junior. The dowry brought him farmland, silver, and furnishings, but the relationship was hopelessly flawed. After his father's death, Cervantes returned to his mistress and shouldered the upkeep of his daughter, sisters, and niece.

After he settled in Seville and scribbled 30 unsuccessful plays and numerous mediocre poems for other people's novels, Cervantes accepted the lucrative post of accountant for the ill-fated Spanish Armada, which fell to Queen Elizabeth I's navy in 1588. Cervantes was convicted of graft in deals involving oil and grain and was excommunicated by the church, swindled by his banker, and imprisoned in the king's lock-up in Seville. At the nadir of his writing career, he agreed, with his critic Lope de Vega, that he was "more experienced in reverses than in verses." During confinement, he created his alter ego—the master idealist, Don Quixote. Like Dante and Chaucer, Cervantes chose the language of the day—the vigorous Castilian vernacular—which he preferred to scholarly Latin or polished court Spanish. The episodic adventures of his hero, translated into French and English, attained international fame and were reprinted six times during Cervantes's life but earned him only a small cash settlement. A parody appeared in 1614; the event inspired Cervantes to complete his work and market it as one manuscript.

Upon gaining his release in 1603, Cervantes moved to Valladolid to live under the sponsorship of the Count of Lemos. He was humiliated and returned to jail following a street brawl. From 1606 until his death from diabetes on April 23, 1616, Cervantes lived in Madrid in the straitened circumstances that had defined his life and limited his career. He wrote a second segment of *Don Quixote* as well as *Novelas Exemplares* (1613), *Viaje del Parnaso* (1613), and *Ocho Comedias y Ocho Entremeses* (1615). Depressed and sick, he died without finishing *Los Trabajos de Persiles y Sigismunda* (1617), left no will, and was interred in an unmarked grave. Of himself, he concluded that he had been "blessed with the good fortune to live in folly and to die in wisdom" (Thomas and Thomas 1943, p. 47). (Bloom 1986; Boorstin 1992; Byron 1988; Cervantes 1957; Duran 1974; Gilman 1989; Nabokov 1984; Predmore 1990; Riley 1986; Russell 1985; Thomas and Thomas 1943)

See also Don Quixote; epigram; mock-heroic; parody.

CHAUCER, GEOFFREY

As the father of the English language, Geoffrey Chaucer carries a heavy load of firsts: first literate author to compose in Middle English, first English poet to use heroic verse, first English humorist, and first poet buried in Poet's Corner of Westminster Abbey. Born to a wealthy merchant household on Thames Street in London around 1340, reared at Aldgate on the city's northeastern edge, and placed in service as page to the Countess of Ulster in 1357, Chaucer—step-grandson of Richard, grandson of Robert of Ipswich, and son of John, all of whom served the wine commission as customs agents—joined a long line of civil servants and worked as a court officer under King Edward III. His service to England included the military. In 1359, during the Hundred Years War, Chaucer was captured by French forces during a botched invasion and was eventually ransomed.

A knowledgeable insider and keen observer of human motivation, Chaucer cautiously maneuvered his way along a career path—from page to valet to clerk to comptroller and port authority to Kent's justice of the peace to member of parliament and knight—in part by his talents and otherwise by the patronage of John of Gaunt, the Duke of Lancaster, the king's third son. Buffeted by subtly shifting court attitudes, the poet's rise required knowledge of finance, people, and governmental and military intrigue. During this period, he appears to have translated the satiric poem *Roman de la Rose (Romance of the Rose)* (1280) and to have composed the first portion of *Legend of Good Women* (1386) and *The Book of the Duchess* (1369), written in honor of the wife of John of Gaunt. In a public office, Chaucer was exposed to all levels and foibles of medieval England. Posted on seven trips to France, Italy, and Spain, he observed the joyous stir of humanism that had introduced the Italian Renaissance. In Florence and Genoa, he read in the original Italian the classics of Francesco Petrarch, Dante Alighieri, and Giovanni Boccaccio, the greatest poets of the Italian flowering.

On return to England, Chaucer strengthened his court position by marrying Philippa de Roet, the queen's lady-in-waiting; he fathered Thomas, Elizabeth, and Lewis, and, between lengthy ambassadorial journeys, took pleasure in domestic life. In 1374, he became comptroller of leather, wool, and wine for Richard II, Edward's successor, and occupied an office on the Thames northeast of London Bridge near the Tower. During the next decade, he made enemies who halted his political advance; as a stress-reliever after office hours, he wrote *The House of Fame* (ca. 1370), *Troilus and Criseyde* (ca. 1385), *Parliament of Fowls* (1382), and the beginning of some of the *Canterbury Tales*, a sophisticated framework narrative composed in the chivalric tradition. Around 1385, he composed the "Prologue" to the *Canterbury Tales*, considered England's first major poem in Middle English, and planned most of the extant text of an incomplete cycle of four stories each told by a cortege of pilgrims on a religious trek to Canterbury. The setting was the site of the martyrdom of Archbishop Thomas à Becket, whom King Henry II had had murdered in the cathedral. The departure of John of Gaunt for Spain in 1386 ended Chaucer's civil service

English author Geoffrey Chaucer, circa 1340–1400

employment as a customs official. That same year his wife, Philippa, died. Critics believe that the period of idleness channeled his considerable energies into writing.

Four years later, Chaucer again found favor at court and served as a treasury clerk at Windsor until 1399. He enjoyed financial security during the reign of Henry IV and advancement to the sinecure of Somerset's deputy forester. During this period, he may have composed *Treatise on the Astrolabe, Envoy to Scogan, Envoy to Bukton,* and *To His Empty Purse.* The shift in work responsibilities probably halted the composition of the *Canterbury Tales,* of which he finished only 24 of the proposed 120 stories. With royal permission to leave the king's residence, Chaucer spent his retirement in a rented home in the Garden of St. Mary's Chapel, Westminster, and rapidly declined in physique and energies. Shortly before his death on October 25, 1400, he scrawled in longhand a brief epilogue, "Farewel my bok and my devocioun!" Never acknowledging his role in literary history, Chaucer considered himself a hobby writer, but his contemporaries—John Gower, Thomas Hoccleve, Eustache Deschamps, and Thomas Usk—honored him as versifier and raconteur.

Unmentioned in early literary records, Chaucer's name receives no special tributes for his preference of vernacular "Angle-ish" over French, the cultivated language, or Latin, the scholar's and prelate's choice. For his trust in the instincts of ordinary folk and their ebullient language, Chaucer earned the title of father of the language that he applied so vividly to his high-spirited compositions, each told in a classic style appropriate to the fictional persona. Chaucer's skillful delineation of character offers a droll, often satiric jab at the wealthy, educated, or privileged as well as the low-level conniver, mountebank, malcontent, and trickster. According to his contemporary, Thomas Gascoigne, the poet rued his choice of earthly passions over piety as the central theme of his work. In the twentieth century, biographer Marchette Chute considers his earthy good humor and knowledge of real people the monument that honors him most. She concludes: "He did not do it for approval or for money or for fame. He did it for love."

Because Chaucer wrote for an elite social stratum who enjoyed royal privilege and the education and leisure to read for pleasure, he composed entertaining tales that would appeal to people for whom a reading knowledge of Anglo-Saxon, French, and Latin would be no problem. His ability to adapt the fabliau, romance, beast fable, short story, drama, and verse prologue suggests that his own reading background was considerable. Locked in his personal chest were sixty prime volumes, a valuable library greater than some medieval universities could boast. An unusual man endowed with an understated nobility and worldly knowledge, he was the perfect choice of sire for English literature. (Chaucer 1957, 1966, 1969, 1992, 1993; Chute 1946; Gardner 1977; Goring 1994; Robinson 1957; Scott 1974)

See also Canterbury Tales; Chaunticleer; fabliau; "The Miller's Tale"; satire; trickster; the Wife of Bath.

CHAUNTICLEER

One of literature's most enduring beasts, Chaunticleer or Chanticleer, literally "Sing clear," presents the staid caricature of the self-deluding he-man, the star of Geoffrey Chaucer's "The Nun's Priest's Tale." As the keeper of the widow's henyard, he glories in his magnificent crow, red comb, lofty tail, and inky black bill. Decked with gold feathers, sporting azure legs, and boasting toes with lily white claws, the rooster maintains a fine opinion of himself. For all his strut, he gave in to Lady Partlet, his mate, when she was only a week old. The pair of fowls compare with Chaucer's fictional guildsmen and their wives, and with Madam Eglantine, the Wife of Bath, and the bantyish squire, all of whom reflect the vanity and idiosyncrasy of the self-congratulatory peacock.

To milk the story for all its mock-heroic worth, Chaucer applies the lofty, elegant phraseology and diction of Homer's *Iliad*, Virgil's *Aeneid*, and Arthurian lore. Chaunticleer, like Aeneas, experiences prophetic dreams; Partlet scorns him for whimpering his misgivings, a sure sign of cowardice. To corroborate her belief that dreams are worthless, she cites Cato, the Roman censor, and urges that her rooster mate take an herbal laxative to rid his digestive tract of an offending vapor:

> Worms for a day or two I'll have to give
> As a digestive, then your laxative.
> Centaury, fumitory, caper-spurge
> And hellebore will make a splendid purge;
> And then there's laurel or the blackthorn berry,
> Ground-ivy too that makes our yard so merry;
> Peck them right up, my dear, and swallow whole.

Unconvinced, Chaunticleer counters with an illustrative story proving that dreams may presage great calamity. Turning from thoughts of murder to the beauty of Partlet's face, he concludes: "Mulier est hominis confusio [Woman is humankind's confusion]," which Chaunticleer mistranslates as "woman is man's delight and all his bliss."

Chaucer perpetuates the droll parody of the macho man in the strutting grace of the rooster, who temporarily reasserts his confidence. He copulates twenty times with his mate, then with a face as serious as a lion's frown, he strolls the yard and digs up kernels with his toes. At his call, the other six wives run to him, fueling his vanity with their admiration. Blindsided by his joy in the bright sun of March, Chaunticleer falls victim to fate, which Chaucer sharpens with a pseudo-chivalric comparison:

> My story is as true, I undertake,
> As that of good Sir Lancelot du Lake
> Who held all women in such high esteem.
> Let me return full circle to my theme.

The mention of Queen Guinevere's seducer would not have escaped the notice of the literati of Chaucer's day, nor does the modern reader fail to catch the humor of "high esteem."

By comparing the situation to the plight of Adam, Chaucer deliberately belabors Chaunticleer's failure to heed his wife's warnings and the role of women in bringing woe on men. While the head wife lies in a hazy dust bath and her sister hens bask in the sun, Chaunticleer meets his enemy, the fox, and at first jerks away in terror. The fox's soothing, ego-pleasing admiration of the rooster's voice soon convinces Chaunticleer to lower his guard, however. In the springing of the trap, Chaucer compares the violent snatching of the rooster to the murder of Richard II. Epic shrieks rend the skies louder than when Troy fell and Rome burned. Chaucer drops his noble diction with the entrance of the widow and her daughters, who cry in peasant vernacular: "Look, look! . . . O mercy, look at that! Ha! Ha! the fox!" The barnyard fills with dog, servant, Maggie the spinner, cow, calf, hogs, ducks, geese, a swarm of bees, and Jack Straw and his followers, all raising a clatter.

The falling action of the beast fable returns to the high moral tone and elegant phrasing that Chaucer introduced earlier. Tricking the fox by turning vanity against his enemy, the rooster flaps his wings and perches in a treetop. He admits that he was wrong to fall for flattery the first time, but he seems to have profited from his error. The fox, too late smart, can only remark: "Plagues be flung on all who chatter that should hold their tongue." (Chaucer 1966, 1969, 1992; Chute 1946; Gardner 1977; Keates and Hornak 1994; Robinson 1957; Scott 1974)

See also allegory; beast lore; *Canterbury Tales*; caricature; Chaucer, Geoffrey; diatribe; doggerel; satire; trickster; the Wife of Bath.

COLETTE

The pseudonym of one of the early twentieth century's most forthright individualists, Colette, who published first under the name Colette Willy, thrived on opportunities to be herself, both in action and as a writer of realistic stories, memoirs, and novels. A liberated woman before the term was invented, she pursued her work for a half-century and published 50 titles that include studies of morality, social customs, and aesthetics. All bear her unmistakable command of tone and diction, which reached their height in *The Vagabond* (1911) and *Recaptured* (1913).

Born January 28, 1873, in St.-Sauveur-en-Puisaye, Burgundy, Sidonie Gabrielle Claudine Colette was the daughter of Sido Landoy and Captain Jules-Joseph Colette, a retired military officer who lost a leg at the Battle of Magenta in 1859 and who took a desk job as the village tax agent. Colette had an older half-sister, Juliette, from Sido's first marriage, and an older brother Leopold, called Leo.

Greatly influenced by her mother, a devoted reader, Colette read adult novels in childhood. She learned by example to demand her share of the best in life and to enjoy transient pleasures while they were available. After her family's move to Châtillon-Coliquy in 1889, she met music critic and writer Henri

Gauthier-Villars, a smartly Parisian older man who encouraged her literary career by surrounding her with fascinating people. They married and settled in Paris in 1893. Villars helped her publish the Claudine novels—*Claudine à l'école [Claudine at School]* (1900), *Claudine à Paris [Claudine in Paris]* (1901), *Claudine en ménage [Claudine Married]* (1902), and *Claudine s'en va [Claudine Departs]* (1903). After 13 years, Colette wearied of Villars's social climbing and divorced him.

For four years, Colette lived the life of her protagonist in *The Vagabond* by working as a cosmetologist, immersing herself in the theatrical world, and dancing and acting in music hall productions. In 1910, she married journalist-diplomat Henry de Jouvenel, editor of *Le Matin*, and gave birth to a daughter, for whom she wrote *La Paix chez les bêtes* (*Peace among the Animals*) (1916). During World War I Colette performed humanitarian service at their country villa, which she turned into a rehabilitation center. Her selfless nursing earned her a *Legion d'Honneur*. Mirroring her tastes and maturity, Colette's writing career expanded to fashion commentary for *Le Matin, Vogue, Figaro,* and *Femina;* critical essays and reviews; and the publication of her postwar masterworks—*Chéri* (1920), *La Maison de Claudine [Claudine's House]* (1923), *Le Blé en herbe [The Ripening]* (1923), *La Fin de Chéri [The Last of Chéri]* (1926), and *Sido* (1929).

After her marriage to Maurice Goudeket in 1935, Colette's domestic contentment was disrupted by his imprisonment by the Nazis. She continued writing fiction and battled rheumatoid arthritis. Her success into her late seventies with *La Chatte [The Cat]* (1933), *Duo* (1934), *Chambre d'Hôtel* (1949), and *The Blue Light* (1949) fulfilled her ambitions. Much of her reportage contains a soupçon of wit, particularly her re-creation of a visit to a couturier in *Journey for Myself* (1949), where the clerk groused that ladies no longer wear polite underwear, only trunks, like athletes:

> No chemise, no linen drawers, no petticoat, no combinations . . . And their dress, worn next to the skin, what does it smell of, their dress that cost two thousand smackers? Of a boxing-match, Madame, a fencing championship! *Twelfth round,* unpleasant smell . . . Oh Lord! (Colette 1949, p. 68)

Revered by readers for her candor—admired especially by the fashion-mad Parisians—she received honors from the Royal Belgian Academy and the Goncourt Academy. At her death in Paris on August 3, 1954, the French government honored her with a military funeral.

Colette's fame has maintained a place among the realists of the first half of the twentieth century who filled their literary canvases with rich tones, urbane nuance, and re-creations of experience. Respected for her sensual prose, which probed the multiple styles of love, gender roles, and intimate relationships, she epitomized the coming-of-age of uninhibited female novelists. Her skill with humor, irony, and incidental satire indicates that, among her other talents, observation furnished the core of her many-sided studies of human nature, particularly in the demimonde of *la belle époque.*

Gigi (1945) is the witty story of a girl trained as a courtesan but who marries and reforms Gaston, a notorious libertine. The novel profits from delight-

French author Colette, 1873–1954

ful caricatures, particularly the imperious Tante Alicia, who studies her niece Gigi through critical eyes and questions her chaperonage, reading material, and level of boredom. Aunt Alice, the caricature of the authoritarian of an older generation making decisions for the young, has "le brillant visage de vieille femme autoritaire [the radiant face of an elderly autocrat]." A wily pragmatist in matters concerning young virgins, Alice informs Gigi that women of her station—that is, courtesans—usually marry "after" rather than "before," but, in Gigi's case, Alice lifts her glass to the rare instance of "before." In a tumble of concessions to her niece, Tante Alicia toasts a rapid advancement from ward to worldly bride:

> A nos santés, Gigi! Tu auras une khédive avec ta tasse de café. A la condition que je ne voie pas le bout de ta cigarette mouillée, et que tu fumes sans crocheter des brins de tabac en faisant *ptu-ptu*. Je te donnerai aussi un mot pour une première de chez Béchoff-David, une ancienne camarade qui n'a pas réussi. Ta garde-robe va changer. Qui ne risque rien n'a rien! [To our health, Gigi! You may have a Turkish cigarette with your coffee. On the condition that I see no moisture on the end of the cigarette, and that you smoke without spitting out shreds of tobacco with a little *ptu-ptu*. I also will give you an introduction to the house of Béchoff-David, an old friend who hasn't done well. Your wardrobe is going to change. Nothing ventured, nothing gained!]

With this cynical send-off, Gigi, a pawn of the demimonde living under prissy strictures and having no say in her future, becomes Madame Gaston Lachaille. The novel was filmed in France in 1948 and served as the nucleus of Alan Lerner's 1958 musical reprise, starring Leslie Caron, Louis Jourdain, Maurice Chevalier, and Hermione Gingold. The movie swept the Oscars: best picture, writer, director, photography, musical direction, production and costume design, editing, art direction, title song, and a special honor for Chevalier. (Blain 1990; Buck 1992; Colette 1945, 1949, 1962; Davidson and Wagner-Martin 1995; *Dictionary of Literary Biography* 1985; Lagarde and Michard 1973; Magill 1958)

See also incidental satire; irony; wit.

 # COMEDY

The comprehensive tent sheltering the far reaches of human entertainment, comedy contains elements paralleling tragedy in that characters overwhelmed by absurdity or idiocy undergo reversals of fortune (often of their own making), attain sympathy, recognize their faults, and achieve stasis, discipline, forgiveness, or even reward and elevation resulting from a necessary change of heart or behavior. In its myriad forms, comedy is identified by such various interlinking divisions and subdivisions as:

black comedy	*comédie Française*
comédie Italienne	comedy of humours
comedy of character	comedy of ideas
comedy of intrigue	comedy of manners
comedy of wit	comic relief
domestic comedy	drawing-room comedy
farce	high comedy
low comedy	middle comedy
musical comedy	new comedy
old comedy	restoration comedy
rogue comedy	romantic comedy
sentimental comedy	seriocomedy or tragicomedy

The universal element is the audience's ability to look down on the victim as inept or inferior and to profit from the experience, growth, or coming to knowledge, an intellectual restorative and spiritual cleanser that enlightens and redeems the comic protagonist. By reestablishing sanity and ousting anarchy, comedy legitimizes the curative powers of wit and fun; in good spirits, the playwright supplants with fairness the fraud or threat that has caused the impasse, antagonized the good heart, or stalled the seeker. Unwillingly shoved from hypocrisy to truth, the pilloried villain or manipulator suffers the comeuppance that restores order by trouncing chaos.

The term "comedy" derives from the Greek *komoidia* or singing and from *komos* for rustic song or processional revelry, an appropriate parentage for literature's repository of humor and delight. In a frequently quoted definition taken from the fourth and fifth chapters of the *Poetics* (mid- to late fourth century B.C.), Aristotle—writing two centuries after the loose ends of ribald Greek folk comedy gelled into an identifiable format—links comedy with tragedy for a single reason: they both imitate life. Comedy, he notes, tends toward ludicrous, imperfect beings whose interactions provide the purgative chuckle that rids the audience of pent-up tensions just as tragedy purges the viewer or reader of pity and fear.

In Greek style, the flute player led actors with padded bellies, waddling animal-headed figures, stilt-walkers, mock satyrs, and phallus-wearing punsters who formed the traditional parades. The participants imitated the wine god's adventure and celebrated changes of the agricultural seasons. These jubilant folk demonstrated a human love of dress-up and of assuming another identity, however exaggerated or preposterous. Both compelling and offensive in their absurdity, forerunners of formal comedy achieved levels of ridicule and satire that range from the apollonian control of repartee to the dionysian guffaws at uproarious, obscene comic patter.

Old comedy—the evolution of a rather strict stage convention supplanted the amateurish festival atmosphere with a strict protocol governed by the state, which underwrote performances. The archon, or city magistrate, presided over annual competitions held during the City Dionysia, or grand festival, in early April and during the Lenaean festival of the winepress in early February. As master of ceremonies, he awarded an ivy crown, basket of figs, or skin of wine to the winner, chosen by ten judges, themselves selected at random to prevent favoritism or collusion. At each gathering, troupes performed five comedies, except during wartime, when frivolity seemed inappropriate or the situation grew so testy that authorities trimmed the number to three. Interpreters of Aristotle's wording picture a set pattern:

- A formal prologue that introduces the plot, which takes place on a two-dimensional continuum—an Athenian street outside the doors of the major characters who just happen to live in adjacent buildings and encounter each other in frequent, predictable chance meetings. Note that the informational prologue takes the place of modern conventions of distributing printed programs, raising the curtain, and dimming the lights.

- The *parados,* or formal entry of the 24-member chorus, the focal performers, who sing in metered rhyme and dance in parallel segments of mirror-image choreography, a group of 12 to the right and a similar group to the left.

- The *agon,* or conflict, a debate in tetrameter lines forming the heart of the play's action, which usually derives from an irreverent or fantasy-based spoof of religion or mythology, such as talking animals, deities, or demons.

- The *parabasis*, the chorus, having removed their costume, interrupts the action to advance and address the audience directly with a summary of the author's view of the conflict.

- The *anapest*, a choric discussion of both sides of the political, religious, or social question.

- The *pnigos*, a lengthy summary sentence, usually delivered good-naturedly with gesture and mock seriousness.

- The ode, a polite song to the god or gods whose worship is central to the drama—for example, Aphrodite, goddess of passion, or Hera, goddess of marriage.

- The *epirrhema*, a digression in trochaic meter linking the conflict to current affairs.

- The antode, an antiphonal reply to the ode.

- The *antepirrhema*, a rapid shift of tone from serious to humorous or satiric mode.

- Interlinked episodes returning the actors to the stage to corroborate the author's views.

- Choric odes, a form of commentary on the action and its resolution.

- The *exodos* or conclusion of the comedy, which usually leads the three or four players to a wedding, dance, triumphal procession, or community festival.

Depending on caricature, the old comedies relied on exaggerated expressions on their masks, protruding phalluses, and the delivery of satiric, obscene, pornographic, or scatalogical lines to create the mood. The genius of the era lies in its ability to lace together the comic and grotesque behaviors of fantasy figures while lampooning real events and attitudes toward war, government, religion, and social interaction. Sexual innuendo, perversity, and improprieties of all sorts brought howls from an enthusiastic audience. Language appears to have been uncensored, although legislation attempted to control excesses.

A broad celebration of the frolics, gags, mundane entanglements, and peccadilloes of humble folk, comedy aims less at the elite and seeks a common ground in many respects closer to universal truths than tragedy. In the Western tradition, formalized merrymaking sprang from the seasonal worship of Dionysus, source of the grape and the god of fertility, both agricultural and human. In honoring the deity at the four major seasons—planting, tending, harvesting, and wine making—funsters spoofed local happenings, elections, and scandals in crude satire. In 414 B.C., the comic draw, whose scurrilous excesses stopped short of treason and libel, met its match in a law that demanded greater separation of fiction and fact. The comic muse is permanently fused with its chief marksman, Aristophanes (ca. 448–380 B.C.), Greece's father of satire. Allied with drama from the fifth century B.C., old comedy—typified by *The*

Frogs (405 B.C.), the anti-Sophoclean *Clouds* (423 B.C.), and the ribald, licentious *Lysistrata* (411 B.C.)—blends the best of the art: costuming, masks, dance, posturing and miming, sight gags, poetry, song, fantasy, and social commentary.

Middle comedy—following Athens's defeat by Sparta in the disastrous and protracted Peloponnesian War (434–404 B.C.), a repressive era in Athenian history dimmed the rowdy glow of old comedy by stretching its bounds beyond Athens to focus on safer, less fearful targets. Costumes grew more circumspect as the individualized role of the chorus diminished. Without political issues to satirize, fourth-century B.C. comedy preserved its place in Greek society by mellowing into a less prickly, more politically correct study of human foibles rather than a direct hit on the current regime, who might at any time lash back at an overzealous comic.

The playwrights were many—the Syracusan Philemon (ca. 363–264 B.C.), winner of three prizes; Diphilus (born ca. 355 B.C.), an immigrant Turk; Eubulus (fl. 380 B.C.), a parodist of Euripides; Anaxandrides of Rhodes (fl. 380–349 B.C.), winner of ten first prizes and a probable bridge with old comedy; Heniochus (fl. 350 B.C.); the prolific writer and teacher Alexis of Thurii (ca. 350–280 B.C.), whose burlesques the Roman Plautus admired; and Antiphanes (fl. 385 B.C.). However, so little remains of this era that criticism skimps on concrete examples. Manuscripts list only stage direction for the chorus's dance; the lack of lyrics suggests that the chorus lost its place as singers of satiric verse as the role of actors moved to center stage. Enough evidence remains to prove that new comedy evolved in a straight line from old comedy, passing through this troubled era without losing the humorous savor indigenous to the northwestern Mediterranean.

New comedy—Menander (ca. 343–291 B.C.), born a century after Aristophanes, inaugurated the second stage of comic evolution with new comedy. He provided a similar rich trove of wit and social satire that lambastes types—foolish or waggish slaves from a wide selection of countries and accents, the angry father, the scorned maiden, the pining young swain—rather than identifiable Athenians. A forerunner of *commedia dell'arte*, these stereotypical domestic scenes (five to a title) provided a feast of humorous home-based plays on typical plot lines (love triangle, fragmented family seeking to reunite, man-hungry female pursuing recalcitrant bachelor, local anarchy against tyrant, or greedy old man fending off hanger-on or matching wits with disreputable slaves) that wound down to a happy resolution. However, the meager fragments of Menander's genius (mainly *Dyskolos*, 316 B.C., which was discovered in recent times recorded on papyrus) leave current critics with little more than a shadow of his talent. Evidence from Roman theater proves that his comedies were the prime sources of Latin comedy, which reflect Menander's comedic skill from a distant nation speaking Latin rather than Greek.

New comedy developed a handful of quantifiable alterations:

- Removal of the chorus from its role as commentator

- Addition of comic relief in the form of two interludes breaking up the rising action, climax, and falling action of the plot

- Replacement of body padding and flopping phalluses with normal attire
- A broadening of settings from the stereotypical convention of "a street in Athens" to places colonized by Greeks or marched over or conquered during war
- A sophisticated shift from predictable intertwinings of lives to more suspense and surprise arising from expanded innovations of plot

More significant than alterations in style was Lycurgus's completion of the first of Greece's great stages, the Theater of Dionysus on the Acropolis, in 360 B.C., the prototype stage for Athens and its imitators around the Mediterranean.

Greek theatrical design proved ingenious. The semicircular theatron seated 17,000 viewers in a scooped-out incline, which provided quality acoustics to all theatergoers, from the front row to standing room at the rear. From the front two rows, preserved for priests, the choral leader, city fathers, and *ephebi* or military trainees, stone bleachers extended upward and outward to reserved seating for token holders and to the sections reserved for females and slaves. The orchestra, a circle of paving stones, served as focus; at its center stood the *thymele*, Dionysus's altar and the single most useful stage prop, depending on the play's demands on the imagination. To the right and left of the half circle extended *parados*, or entranceways, for chorus and players, flutist, and harpist.

The rectangular *skene*, or backdrop, that faced the audience provided the temple, ship's deck, forest, or street of the setting. Three doors gave the actors their entrance points. Additional *periaktoi*, or three-sided scenery, could be attached to holes in the floor in front of the central door and spun to show a change of setting; additional machinery included *pinakes* (painted scenes), metal machinery to emulate thunder and lightning, overhead *mechane* (lifts) to lower a god to stage level, and *eccyclema*, flats on wheels that stagehands slid into view to provide a separate setting or to display corpses. Across the *proscenium* or stage, the choral dances and acting spread in full view of the audience. When the chorus moved out of the way, it split into two groups and exited via ramps at each end of the stage.

Costume evolved from a simple daub of wine residue rubbed on the cheeks and lips to diaphanous robes, wigs, and thigh-high boots. The height of Greek technical achievement was the mask, a linen or hide head covering stretched over a cork or wood frame and equipped with a megaphone to project sound. So intricate and valued were these masks that they were stowed in a place of honor when not in use and viewed with an awe akin to worship. The caricatured expressions identified fear, humor, dread, wonder—a panorama of human emotion. Alongside human faces were the tails, ears, and fur, and phalluses stuffed with feathers; bird heads; insect faces; and bestial coverings that completed the mimicry of Greek comedy.

Following its tendency to imitate the best of Greek culture, Roman theater—included under the broad definition of new comedy—had its own rude beginnings in harvest mummery and wedding processions, which formalized with rehearsed Etruscan performances beginning in 364 B.C. and with the evolution of masking and mime, a wordless form of satire. When Greek colonists performed their traditional comedy for the unlettered Roman traveler during the third century B.C., a receptive audience welcomed its first comic playwright, Livius Andronicus (ca. 284–204 B.C.), to Rome to transpose Greek comedy into palatable Latin ludi, or ritual games, performed in December as part of the topsy-turvy shift of master and slave during Saturnalia, in September and October during Jovian festivals, in July to honor Apollo, and in April as worship of the earth mother. A period of Romanizing under playwrights Naevius (ca. 270–220 B.C.), Ennius (239–169 B.C.), and Caecilius Statius (ca. 235–165 B.C.) prefigured the comic masters Plautus and Terence, Rome's most revered gagmen. Of the prolific canon of Plautus, 20 titles—less than one-fifth of his output—remain; of Terence, 6 complete titles comprise his extant work.

Until Pompey built the first permanent stone stage in 55 B.C., the most sophisticated staged comedies were performed on makeshift platforms before a temporary seating arrangement. The *skene* consisted of a linear stage featuring three unopened doors; comings and goings took place from each end of the stage. Roman audiences came to expect action to the right to erupt from town; action to the left depicted movement to a harbor, woods, or a distant town. To provide conversations or action taking place beyond these confinements, the comic playwright had to add messengers and eavesdroppers, whose arrival brought news that advanced the plot, contributed to suspense, or added complications to the characters' lives.

These robust drolleries, staged by masked singers or chanters, employed stock figures (courtesans, aged misers, double-dealing slavers and financiers, swaggering warlords, wide-eyed virgins, misty-romantic lovers, blundering ne'er-do-wells, and hangers-on in search of free dinners) and predictable plots filled with meddling, lengthy soliloquies, and comic asides. In the anything-for-a-laugh style of Aristophanes, Plautus freely coined comic names and hilarious phrases and salted the action with burlesque, tap dancing, and songs suggesting vaudeville. More punctilious than Plautus, Terence preferred the formal prologue, witty repartee, and parallel plots that produced the frequent chiming of story lines on similar themes. Pantomimes set to the music of drum, cymbals, harp, lyre, flute, panpipes, and trumpet featured dancers and lavish costuming. The addition of *scabilla* or taps to shoes emphasized the importance of a lead dancer or troupe.

Continuing virtually unchanged into the Middle Ages, satiric comedy and noisy, uninhibited farce thrived—in Niccoli Machiavelli's *Mandragola* (1518) and at street level in noisy, violent Punch and Judy puppet shows—until the resurrection of comedy in the Italian *commedia dell'arte*, a peak in the history of satire. Significant alteration occurred as churchmen produced amateur Bible stories onstage, delighting in a disgruntled Noah or a suave Satan outfoxing Eve. When the purpose of Christian education gave place to a good excuse for a stage romp, the church thrust the production of morality plays into the care of guilds, who broadened sacred theater to include saint's lives and secular morality plays. In the latter, the clueless Everyman, like John Bunyan's Christian, wanders among earthly temptations on his interrupted allegorical journey to righteousness and, ultimately, heaven. In contrast to these soul-searching run-ins with the devil and his staff of evildoers, medieval theater offered varied fare during the carnival season with the Feast of Fools, featuring the Lord of Misrule, who could challenge any reveler to recite or perform a stunt as part of the entertainment.

The Renaissance revamped earlier emphasis on harum-scarum plots that jeopardize the central figures, then bring all to rights in the end. In the late sixteenth century, Sir Philip Sidney, anticipating with his *Apologie for Poetrie* (1595) the didactic dreariness of the Puritan era, sorted out the virtues and vices of comic lore and concluded that the redeeming quality must be illustrative, educative, and, above all, redemptive. Likewise, George Puttenham's *The Arte of English Poesie* (1589) underscores "amendment of man by discipline and example" and carries the definition of comedy beyond amelioration to "solace and recreation of the common people."

The chief satirist of the English Renaissance, Ben Jonson, applied to characters the medieval belief in Hippocrates's description of the four dominant body fluids—blood (joviality), phlegm (indolence), yellow bile (envy), and black bile (anger)—and the quirks, moods, and passions that overproduction, improper blend, or depletion caused in human behavior. In his masterworks—*Every Man in His Humour* (1598), *Every Man out of His Humour* (1599), and *Volpone* (1606)—Jonson showcases the best and worst of characters, all of whom function according to their inherent personalities, from grump and grouch to sunny optimist. The burgeoning of satiric comedy ceased with the Commonwealth, brought on by the 1649 Puritan upheaval that beheaded Charles I and put Oliver Cromwell in charge. For 11 years, England's playgoers survived on bootleg drama, which players hid from pursed-lipped, humorless churchmen.

During England's darker days, the life of comedy and the celebration of life passed to the Continent, where dramatists and versifiers eluded the dismal Puritan stranglehold and immersed themselves in the *joie de vivre* of France and other positive climates. During this era, Nicolas Boileau wrote his "L'Art Poetique" (1674), a broad treatise advising the comic writer to follow nature:

> Que la nature donc soit votre étude unique,
> Auteurs qui prétendez aux honneurs du comique.
> Quiconque voit bien l'homme et, d'un esprit profond,
> De tant de coeurs cachés a pénétré le fond;
> Qui sait bien ce que c'est qu'un prodigue, un avare,
> Un honnête homme, un fat, un jaloux, un bizarre,
> Sur une scène heureuse, il peut les étaler,
> Et les faire à nos yeux vivre, agir et parler.
> [Let nature be your central study,
> Authors claiming the comic honors.
> Let them envision humankind and, with a profound spirit,
> Probe to the depths of the concealed core:
> Let him know well that the prodigal, the miser,
> The honest man, the fop, the jealous, the peculiar,
> In a joyous scene, he can spread them out
> And make them live, move, and speak before our eyes.]

A decorative Grecian krater, or cup, from the third century B.C. depicts robbers attacking a miser atop his treasure chest in a scene from middle comedy.

Apparently, the exiled author absorbed Boileau's specific instructions and remained alert for the first cracks in the Puritan cabal so that humor could once more reign on British stages.

England's jubilant return to monarchy in 1660 revealed that satire had survived on the continent. Sweeping aside the overpious Puritans, the Restoration era burst into popularity with vigor and daring in Britain and France. Molière's magnificent brand of domestic satire flavored with sparkle and verbal virtuosity his best comic efforts: *Les Précieuses ridicules* (1659), *Le Misanthrope* (1666), *Tartuffe* (1669), and *Le Bourgeois gentilhomme* (1670). The British experiments in domestic and sentimental comedy (related to the French *drame bourgeois)* typify the works of William Wycherley, Sir George Etherege, and William Congreve. In the eighteenth century, the strain mutated into a puny shadow of realism with Oliver Goldsmith's *She Stoops To Conquer* (1773) and Richard Sheridan's *The School for Scandal* (1777) and *The Rivals* (1775). In contrast to the raucous good fun of novels by Henry Fielding, Laurence Sterne, and Tobias Smollett, sentimental drama deserved its demise for reducing human relationships into piddling three-hanky weepers. French comedy, in the capable hands of Denis Diderot, François Voltaire, and Pierre Beaumarchais, moved into new satiric territory. Italian comedy tinkered with the classic *commedia dell'arte* in the works of Carlo Goldoni and, to a lesser degree, with the more predictable humor of playwrights Pietro Chiari and Carlo Gozzi. Further evolution put farce ahead of sentiment in the nineteenth century with Ivan Turgenev's *A Month in the Country* (1850) and Nikolai Gogol's *The Inspector General* (1836).

Anticipating the darker tones of pre–world war satire, comedy attained a new peak as Victorian manners and morals lapsed—or imploded—and society moved resolutely toward realism. In this vein, Anton Chekhov produced *The Seagull* (1896), *Uncle Vanya* (1899), and *The Cherry Orchard* (1904). His contemporary, Oscar Wilde, returned to a melange of drawing room wit and comedy of manners with *The Importance of Being Earnest* (1895), while George Bernard Shaw, the energetic, critical force of Edwardian British comedy, produced *Arms and the Man* (1894), *Androcles and the Lion* (1912), and *Pygmalion* (1912). The latter serves as the prefeminist core of the successful play and movie *My Fair Lady* (1964); the movie version pits the insouciant Rex Harrison as Professor Higgins against a grimy but ambitious Eliza Doolittle played by Audrey Hepburn. At the same time that Shaw stimulated intellectuals, the low-brow antics of *opéra bouffe* survived ups and downs as it translated operetta into the formulaic patter of vaudeville, the bargain basement of farce.

While Noel Coward enlivened drawing room comedy with the controlled energy evidenced in *Blithe Spirit* (1941), and the more cerebral T. S. Eliot entertained thinkers with *The Cocktail Party* (1950), run-of-the-neighborhood audiences in the United States and Europe were deserting stage fare for the "flickers," starring the best of the early movie greats, Charlie Chaplin, Mae West, W. C. Fields, Buster Keaton, the Marx Brothers, and Laurel and Hardy. Chaplin earned a faithful following, as well as surveillance by the FBI, for lampooning Adolf Hitler, whom he depicted tossing the globe like a beach ball and bumping it with his posterior. The decades following silent film saw the transformation of comedy from light to heavy, from mindless to insightful.

Although no comedy of stage, radio, television, or film could fully render the devastation of war, fascism, dictatorship, or genocide, Gore Vidal's *A Visit to a Small Planet* (1955), vehicle for a Jerry Lewis comedy, prophesied the terrors of the out-of-control military complex that President Eisenhower warned of at the end of World War II. Other war-theme comedies—including Richard Hooker's *MASH* (1970) and Joseph Heller's *Catch-22* (1961)—and sentimental retrovisions such as Winston Groom's *Forrest Gump* (1995) gained steam as an endless mélange of militaristic strutters and victimizers from Franco, Lenin, and Tito to Juan Perón, Fidel Castro, Idi Amin, Saddam Hussein, and Milosovic—puffed out their chests, stocked their arms chests, and trod on the unwary. A strong runner in the category of comedy of terror, Francis Ford Coppola's *Apocalypse Now*, the 1979 film version of Joseph Conrad's *Heart of Darkness*, carried beyond the limits of psychological drama and black humor the hellish reality of a war built on lies and paranoia. In Coppola's cynical parody, set against a backdrop of Asian nations floundering against genocide, the United States reigns as superpower, gunrunner, and rogue.

Within the elastic confines of comedy live a variety of style, focus, and characterization. These subgroups, thriving in their own times, comprise significant mutations:

Comedy of humours—initiated at the height of the English Renaissance in the works of Ben Jonson, Thomas Middleton, George Chapman, Thomas Shadwell, and John Fletcher, the comedy of humours concentrated on the out-of-balance personality, which lacked or brimmed over with blood, phlegm, choler (yellow bile), or melancholy (black bile). These governing liquids produced characteristic states:

- A sanguine or roseate personality tending toward an overly romantic notion of reality

- A lethargic or phlegmatic malaise evidenced by a disinclination to take action

- Dyspepsia or choler, the characteristic grumpiness resulting from an overproduction of yellow bile

- dDepression or gloom, the cheerless state of the perpetual malcontent or potential suicide

In Jonson's words, from the induction of *Every Man out of His Humour* (1599):

. . . in every human body
The choler, melancholy, phlegm, and blood
By reason that they flow continually
In some one part, and are not continent,
Receive the name of humours. Now thus far
It may, by metaphor, apply itself
Unto the general disposition:

As when some one peculiar quality
Doth so possess a man, that it doth draw
All his affects, his spirits, and his powers,
In their confluxions, all to run one way.
This may be truly said to be a humour.

The "one peculiar quality" or eccentricity possesses the character so fully that behavior, attitude, and motivation derive from a single internal well and obscure the full display of human capabilities by eclipsing all other drives and motivations.

A classic example of the danger of imbalance is Shylock, Shakespeare's pathetically obsessed Jew whose experience with ridicule and exclusion sours his nature, throwing him into grotesque maladjustment. A less fearful character, the round-faced Sir John Falstaff, disarms all with his mirth, lust, cowardliness, and fear of death on the battlefield. Maintaining the spotlight on character, comedy of humours highlights an idiosyncratic behavior or trait prefigured or depicted in a name—Sordido, Kitely, Downright, Knowell, Havisham—a nomenclature common to centuries-old morality plays, with Everyman trapped between the admonitions of Mr. Good-Deeds and the bad example of Mr. Avaricious. Ensuing generations recognized similar black-white characterizations in *Pilgrim's Progress* that raised to puritanical heights John Bunyan's Christian allegory.

Comedy of ideas—a dramatic method of putting legs to opposing philosophies or moot arguments, the comedy of ideas presents a witty repartee between differing parties. The method became a workable model for George Bernard Shaw, who often appears to debate with himself the extremes of dialectic in *Man and Superman* (1905) and *Androcles and the Lion* (1912). The latter, setting up the Christians versus lions scenario with a makeover of Androclus, the shy Greek tailor of fable, and his lion, suitably named Tommy, comments on the nature of martyrdom and its justification, as in Androcles's ditzy lines: "Meggy: theres one chance for you. Itll take him pretty nigh twenty minutes to eat me (Im rather stringy and tough) and you can escape in less time than that." The comic *deus ex machina* in the form of a domesticated lion concludes a series of scenes that color history with the broad crayon strokes of comedy. Shaw, too much the showman to let slide a dramatic opportunity, waltzes tailor and lion past fearful Roman Circus Maximus–goers and out of the arena with the parting line, "Come, Tommy. Whilst we stand together, no cage for you: no slavery for me."

Comedy of intrigue—a convoluted interaction of mischievous but predictable characters, the comedy of intrigue—also called comedy of situation—draws strength from plot manipulation, look-alikes and confused identities, and unexpected events, a focus of William Shakespeare's *The Comedy of Errors* (ca. 1580s), the epitome of confusion with its double Dromios and the twin Antipholuses separated from their parents in a shipwreck. The closer the double sets of twins come to each other, the more confusion for other characters and audience alike. A typical ploy in the plot depicts one twin as single and confounded by the other twin's wife, who accuses him of straying. The abbess who clears up the grand misunderstanding arrives in time to stay an execution and oversee the reunion of a family that turns out to be her own. In similar vein, Ben Jonson's *Epicene, or The Silent Woman* (1609), Lope de Vega's *The Madrid Steel* (ca. 1613), Pierre Beaumarchais's *Le Barbier de Séville* (1775), and Aphra Behn's *The Rover* (1677) and *The City Heiress* (1682) create tension by stressing complications that require extensive explanation and requital.

No stranger to the twentieth-century stage, comedy of intrigue proved successful in the collaborative efforts of satirist George S. Kaufman and Moss Hart, authors of the brilliant *Once in a Lifetime* (1930), *You Can't Take It with You* (1936), and *The Man Who Came to Dinner* (1939). The third of this trio depicts the manipulative intrusion of Sheridan Whiteside, an unwelcome house guest who slips on the ice and disrupts the family's peace by demanding to be coddled. A throwback to the foppish bon vivants of eighteenth-century British drama, Sheridan represents the smooth operator who is out of his element in a normal home and who must rely on the telephone and visitors to maintain his usual court atmosphere. At the conclusion of mix-ups, conniving, and general mayhem, Kaufman and Hart set up the innocuous departure scene with a pleasant "Merry Christmas, everybody!" from Sheridan when he slips a second time, predicting another round of pampered, self-absorbed invalidism and threats of lawsuits. In these zany comedies, bizarre domestic situations, plotting, foiled love matches, and unforeseen obstacles keep the audience tittering in good spirits and mild suspense until the resolution.

Comedy of manners—a departure from the study of plot, comedy of manners, also called comedy of wit, pinpoints the interaction of characters, respectable and cynical alike, attempting to obey (or circumvent) set codes of conduct. The depth of personae depends on the satiric target: the dandy, self-absorbed man-about-town, pseudo-wit, frenzied old maid, and jealous spouse. A form of satire that relies on realistic speech rather than the vernacular of less polished entertainments, comedy of manners demands a repartee both nimble and acute, often in the form of a verbal matching of wits mimicking a duel, typified by William Congreve's *The Way of the World* (1700). Intellectual exchanges achieve the cutting sting of a duel with words yet may lapse into slapstick when servants enter the intrigues of their superiors.

Ranging over the Elizabethan and Jacobean eras, notable models of love entanglements dominate the genre, reaching a height with William Shakespeare's *Much Ado about Nothing* (1598), which Kenneth Branagh brilliantly reprised in a 1993 film version. Branagh starred as the antimarriage Benedick opposite his wife and colleague, Emma Thompson, the sharp-tongued Beatrice.

When the political turmoil of England's civil war and failed Commonwealth gave place to a restored monarchy, the Restoration comedies of Congreve and Wycherley produced rampant fooleries that gave bogus sophistication its comeuppance. Oliver Goldsmith, Richard Sheridan, and Oscar Wilde followed the pattern with suitable adaptations to time, style, and rhythms but basic adherence to old-style plots and themes. Still winning audiences in the twentieth century, comedy of manners was the appropriate choice for droll, urbane writers such as Somerset Maugham, James M. Barrie, Noel Coward, and Neil Simon.

Comedy of morals—a leaden, didactic satire, comedy of morals deliberates the hypocrisies and egregious faults of noteworthy slackers, villains, and sinners. Chief among models of suspect characters are Molière's hypochondriacs, peacocks, and shysters, the best being Tartuffe, the con artist and seducer posing as pietist. Molière's clever use of comedy as a means of improving society created a better stage vehicle for public improvement than the earlier classic tragedies of Jean Racine and Pierre Corneille, both of whom had pushed their medium beyond its years. The invigorated comedy of morals had a leveling effect on social extremes, particularly the female poseurs whom Molière humiliated with his bold satire *Les Précieuses ridicules* (1659).

Comic relief—a concentrated attempt to lighten and simultaneously heighten the seriousness of tragedy, comic relief grew out of Greek drama, forming an unpredictable fourth leg to the three titles that constituted a single performance of tragedy. Ranging from soliloquy, blackout, skit, send-up, or interlude to full episode, comic relief interposes humor that eases tensions, yet never strays far from the sober or tragic themes of its surroundings. In the hands of the best dramatists, comic relief serves as a counterpoint, a current of humor paralleling the flow of serious thought. Such a persistent light note permeates the Jacobean masques of Ben Jonson, who developed ornate allegorical scenarios into commentary on human folly.

The English touchstones of comic relief—the grave-diggers' scene preceding Ophelia's interment in William Shakespeare's *Hamlet* (ca. 1599), the bawdy rejoinders of the nurse in *Romeo and Juliet* (ca. 1593), and the dyspeptic grumblings of the porter who imagines himself attending the gates of hell in *Macbeth* (ca. 1603)—are comic departures from the tight conventions of classic tragedy. As reflections of the scrambled absurdities of real life, these vignettes insist on a world vision where tears and titters coexist. Likewise, the inept policing of Dogberry's squad in *Much Ado about Nothing* (ca. 1598) interrupts scenes of disillusion, revenge, and the fake death and interment of Hero, whose shaming produces strong audience sympathy that lessens under the diverting slapstick scenes similar in format to "Keystone Cops."

In twentieth-century comedy of the United States, the antics of Ensign Frank Pulver in the play *Mr. Roberts* (1948) lighten what could be a serious wartime power struggle between Lt. Doug Roberts and the captain of the U.S. Navy Cargo Ship *AK 601* in the spring of 1945. To relieve the tensions brought on by war, boredom, and 28 months without liberty, the authors, Thomas Heggen and Joshua Logan, insert the shenanigans of Ensign Frank Pulver, the love-starved prankster who sets off a charge of fulminate of mercury in the laundry. The play peaks when merrymakers turn the first liberty into a rout; a second dramatic peak balances the foolery with the sobering news of Doug Roberts's transfer to a destroyer bound for Okinawa and his subsequent death by Japanese kamikazes. In this example, comic relief becomes a true soldier's war on dehumanizing conditions. Expressed in a three-week-old letter from Roberts to Pulver, the moral rings true of the need for gaiety and frivolity:

> The most terrible enemy of this war is the boredom that eventually becomes a faith and, therefore, a sort of suicide—and I know now that the ones who refuse to surrender to it are the strongest of all.

In a blend of comic relief and resolution, Ensign Pulver determines to honor his mentor by jerking open the captain's door and bellowing a demand for the nightly movie, thus taking Lt. Roberts's place as the captain's chief harasser.

Commedia erudita—an Italian creation of the sixteenth century, erudite comedy makes its pilgrimage to the classic plots of Menander, Aristophanes, Terence, and Plautus, keeping faith with the satire, themes, and humor of the golden ages of Greece and Rome. Chief among playwrights of this narrow genre were Lodovico Ariosto, writer of *La Cassaria (The Strongbox)* (1508) and *I Suppositi (The Dissemblers)* (ca. 1510) and Niccoli Machiavelli, author of the cynical *Mandragola* (1518). The focus of erudite comedy was an elegant, rule-centered style emulating the classic dactylic hexameter, Homer's characteristic six-foot line.

Romantic comedy—a gentle, harmless form of humor, romantic comedy strays furthest from satire in its move toward the ideal, made-in-heaven love match, temporarily derailed by a suspicious father, cranky landlord, or shallow mix-up that requires deft reworking to a satisfying end. The ingenue, often obscured in man's garb and fake beard, represents the dream girl who is worth all the hero's efforts to win her. The height of romantic comedy falls on the denouement, a coming together of loose ends and a reconciliation between quarreling parties. Notable examples include Robert Greene's *James the Fourth* (1590) and William Shakespeare's *Two Gentlemen of Verona* (ca. 1613) and *The Merchant of Venice* (ca. 1596). A master example of romantic comedy, Shakespeare's *As You Like It* (1599), a master example of romantic comedy, hinges on the deterrents to lovers Orlando and Rosalind. Their adventures remove them from reality and place them in Eden, a forest of obvious significance, where Rosalind further rejects reality by donning men's clothing.

A modern triumph that approaches romantic overkill is Frances Goodrich and Albert Hackett's *Sobbin' Women*, which won a place among best-loved musical films as *Seven Brides for Seven Brothers* (1954). An adaptation of the legendary rape of the Sabine women, the story substitutes failed kidnap for rape. The fate-centered plot turns on a single linchpin—the collapse of a snow bank over a pass that prohibits authorities from returning seven snatched maidens to a posse of irate fathers. During a long winter in the chaste farmhouse-dormitory, the girls admire their captors from safe quarters and decide that life as farm wives appeals to them. With a deft bit of artifice the next spring, they convince their fathers that a seven-branched shotgun wedding is the only solution to a blight on family honor. Like the snow-filled pass, the theme of honor lies buried under comic scenes of sparking, dancing, teasing, and romancing.

Satiric comedy—an unwavering spotlight, satiric comedy focuses on a vice or frailty that the playwright singles out for detailed scrutiny, such as overweening pride, gluttony, disloyalty, or ambition. Epitomized by Ben Jonson's *Volpone* (1606) and *The Alchemist* (1610), satiric comedy, like *Molière's* comedy of morals, warns its audience of unscrupulous behaviors common to the manipulator, deceiver, or villain. The balance of personalities requires that the trickster fleece an equally abysmal set of marks, whose limited understanding of logic leaves them open to gulling—and to the audience's contempt.

A similar set of circumstances precedes the lengthy unbosoming of Winnie, protagonist of Amy Tan's *The Kitchen God's Wife* (1992), who chooses the joint occasion of a friend's funeral and Chinese New Year, with its strictures of setting right all quarrels and misunderstandings. Before expressing the deep grief of a disastrous feudal marriage, spousal abuse, child neglect, jail, and a farewell rape committed by her estranged husband, Winnie attends Auntie Du's pseudo-Buddhist funeral. Set in late twentieth-century San Francisco, the exotic trappings—spirit money, incense, hired mourners, and a banquet to feed the departed in the world of the dead—alternately amuse, bore, and dismay Winnie's granddaughters, who leave with their father for "ice cream over on Columbus," a droll reminder of Christopher Columbus and the U.S. reputation for trampling on outsiders' customs and traditions. Winnie, of necessity a realist when it comes to money, comments that the mourners are not mercenary because they perform a ceremonial respect for the deceased. She adds, "Maybe these ladies can do two or three funerals every day . . . earn a few dollars. Good living that way. Better than cleaning house."

Tan weaves her satiric comedy from uproar and intergenerational miscommunication. Before Winnie can begin her own mother-to-daughter housecleaning, the paper banner wishing Auntie Du a prosperous afterlife slides free from the wall and plunks on the corpse's chest "like a beauty pageant banner." The ironically failed banner contrasts the youngish funeral photo of the old lady, who has long since lost whatever womanly charms she boasted in her youth. The variance of the mourners' response to the undignified intrusion on the service underscores Tan's satire: While the older women yell "Ai-ya!," a younger Chinese-American relative, too far removed from China to share the funereal mood, shouts "Perfect landing!"

Tan returns to this satiric mode in her third adult novel, *The Hundred Secret Senses* (1995), in the characterization of Kwan, the clairvoyant whose ease in both the natural world and the world of the dead leads her to some comic conclusions about the afterlife. To her half-sister Olivia she explains that the next world is not segregated: "You love Jesus, go Jesus House. You love Allah, go Allah Land. You love sleep, go sleep." For people who have no vision of a future life, the afterlife becomes a smorgasbord: "Then you go big place, like Disneyland, many places can go try—you like, you decide. No charge, of course" (Tan 1995, p. 99).

Sentimental comedy or drama of sensibility—a frail, superficial middle-class drama devoid of the racy humor of the preceding generation, sentimental comedy (called *la comédie larmoyante* or "tear-jerkers" in France) replaced the villainy and cynicism of Restoration comedy with insipid, predictable goods and bads, veritable masks of the theater. Because English playwrights of the late 1600s moved too joyously and licentiously away from pinch-mouthed Puritans, who decamped in 1660 with the return of Charles II, Jeremy Collier foretold the collapse of amorality in his *Short View of the Immorality and Profaneness of the English Stage* (1698). Just as he predicted, the emotional pendulum corrected itself with a strong swing toward sentimental comedy, which attained the opposite excess, the sanctuary of probity, magnanimity, and mawkish tenderness. The focus of Richard Steele's *The Funeral* (1701), *The Lying Lover* (1703), and *The Tender Husband* (1704); Oliver Goldsmith's *She Stoops to Conquer*; Richard Sheridan's *The Rivals* (1775) and *The School for Scandal* (1777); and Colley Cibber's *Love's Last Shift* (1696), sentimental comedy reached a pinnacle in Steele's *The Conscious Lovers* (1722) and, for all its good intentions, vitiated itself in too pat a resolution, overstated benevolence, and too blatant a pluck on the heartstrings.

Like the sentimental comedies, the sentimental novels of eighteenth-century England play on the sympathies of readers with a revelation of cruelty that threatens to overwhelm virtue but collapses from its obvious breach of social or religious morality and, like a crumbling melon rind, falls victim to inner decay. Preceding Oliver Goldsmith's *The Vicar of Wakefield* (1766), Maria Edgeworth's *Castle Rackrent* (1800), and Jane Austen's *Sense and Sensibility* (1811) and *Northanger Abbey* (1818), Samuel Richardson's *Pamela: or Virtue Rewarded* (1740), the height of sentimental fiction, violates reality by pitting persistent womanizer against virtuous maid, whose repeated and varied protestations weary the reader. Consequently, sentimental comedy served its short-lived purpose of cleansing the stage of debauchery and an obnoxious strain of satire. As a type, the comedies remained in vogue among mediocre audiences who delighted in melodrama.

One of the treasured sentimental comedies frequently revived on U.S. stages is Mary Chase's whimsical *Harvey* (1944), filmed in 1950 and featuring one of James Stewart's most beloved comedic roles, Elwood P. Dowd, a hazy but harmless alcoholic. The title character of the plot, an invisible rabbit, causes a perpetual ruckus that jangles the nerves of Veta Louise, Elwood's nitbrained sister, and of Myrtle Mae, a waning spinster who blames her uncle's antics for reducing her chances to marry. Elwood, lost in daily rambles and bar hopping, summarizes his friendship in rose-hued splendor, recalling the bars he and Harvey frequent, the people who smile, and the memorable evenings they share with strangers who become friends.

> They talk to us. They tell us about the great big terrible things they've done and the great big wonderful things they're going to do. Their hopes, their regrets. Their loves, their hates. All very large, because nobody ever brings anything small into a bar.

Elwood's grand moment is his introduction to his friends of Harvey, who outshines what the others have to offer. Elwood believes that the others are impressed. Perpetually befogged by idealism or alcohol or both, he does not take into account the fact that his short-term friends seldom return for another conversation.

Avoiding the obvious emptiness of a life based on fantasy and self-delusion, Chase's comedy ennobles the six-foot rabbit and briefly passes along the comfort of his friendship to the psychiatrist who nearly ruins Elwood's affability with an experimental drug. In the end, Veta relents, her daughter finds a man, and Elwood is sprung from potential admission to Chumley's Rest. A benign sentimentality clings to the furry, lop-eared hallucination who follows Elwood down the road from the asylum toward home.

Theater of the absurd—a return to early forms of farce or slapstick as a mode of expressing the directionlessness of modern nihilism, theatre of the absurd, predicted in Albert Camus's *Le Mythe de Sisyphe* (1942), came of age in the 1950s in the drama of Europe and the United States. A reflection of postwar arrhythmia and rootlessness, the philosophy expressed a vacuousness of soul and a burden of meaninglessness that engulfed society, partly as a result of wartime savagery and of the encroachment of technology, with its threats to privacy and free speech. The resulting paranoia permeated literature with an aimless, drifting action made meaningful by the exhaustion and terror of its characters. Chief among writers of nihilism or theater of the absurd is Samuel Beckett, author of *Waiting for Godot* (1953). Also steeped in twentieth-century ennui is Eugène Ionesco's *La Cantatrice chauve [The Bald Soprano]* (1948), Jean Genet's *Journal du voleur [Diary of a Thief]* (1949), Edward Albee's *Who's Afraid of Virginia Woolf?* (1962) and *Tiny Alice* (1965), and Harold Pinter's *The Birthday Party* (1958) and *The Homecoming* (1965).

Tragicomedy—directed toward catastrophe, the tragicomedy emulates tragedy until it reaches a fortuitous denouement and concludes happily or at least tentatively positive. Turning on a fulcrum of jealous rage, sedition, plotting, disguise, and idealized goodness, tragicomedy pits the extremes of character against each other, as in John Fletcher's *The Faithful Shepherdess* (1610) and Shakespeare's *The Winter's Tale* (ca. 1610), which averts disaster by a bit of last-minute *deus ex machina* sleight of hand. Similarly, the potential loss of flesh in Shakespeare's *The Merchant of Venice* (ca. 1596) approaches doom, then veers away in time to settle a legal question, mitigate old enmities, and unite lovers.

A modern success in the tragicomic vein is Calder Willingham's *Rambling Rose* (1991), a play that gains strength in the movie version, which casts Laura Dern as the nubile town wench and Robert Duvall as Daddy Hillyer, a straight-arrow family man who employs Rose as governess to his three children. The parallel coming-of-age of Rose and her oldest male charge hovers at the brink of child abuse and concludes with a just-in-time wedding of Rose and David, a police officer whom she bites on the finger and later dubs "Mr. Right." The tragic implications of a conniving doctor who schemes to remove Rose's uterus and ovaries to circumvent what he calls "near nymphomania" invest the comedy with satiric derision of doctors playing God and ignorant patients who fail to demand rights to their own bodies. The rescuer—Mrs. Hillyer, champion of the oppressed, played by Diane Ladd—uses her money, humanism, and intellectual clout to intimidate the doctor and save Rose from a surgical procedure that the doctor characterizes as a benevolent female castration. (Abrams 1971; Baldick 1990; Barnet, Berman, and Burto 1960; Bermel 1982; Boileau 1965; Cuddon 1976; Drabble 1985; Feder 1986; Feinberg 1967; Flaceliere 1962; Gassner and Quinn 1969; Gray 1992; Halliwell 1995; Hammond and Scullard 1992; Hart and Kaufman 1961; Heggen and Logan 1951; Holman 1980; Howatson 1989; Mantinband 1956; McCarthur 1992; Plautus 1900; Snodgrass 1988a, 1988b; Tan 1992, 1995)

See also Aristophanes; Beckett, Samuel; Behn, Aphra; *The Birds;* black humor; burlesque; caricature; *commedia dell'arte;* Congreve, William; farce; Heller, Joseph; masque; Molière; Plautus; Restoration drama; Richardson, Samuel; satyr play; Steele, Sir Richard; Terence; theater of the absurd; Wycherley, William; *You Can't Take It with You.*

COMMEDIA DELL'ARTE

A raucous, creative, joyful phenomenon of medieval Italian drama, the *commedia dell'arte* was an extemporaneous product of highly skilled, experienced traveling troupes. This era in stage history added a note of professionalism to lighthearted market-day appearances in plazas, halls, or colonnades where peasants and vendors conducted weekly business, ate *al fresco,* and took their pleasure. Arising from the writings and acting of Angelo Beolco (1502–1542), who turned the vernacular Italian street scene into comic art in the mid-sixteenth century, the *commedia dell'arte* turned away from religious or moral drama and developed stock plots, caricatures, and scenes from the evolution of its first stereotype—*ruzzante,* the bumpkin or rube, a satiric figure whom Beolco himself enjoyed playing.

Led by a troupe director and functioning with no scenery and few props, the handful of trained actors included both male and female at a time when other countries had only men on stage playing both parts. Actors studied each comic scenario, or *lazzo*—looking for a lost hat, shying water balloons at a pompous burgher, wooing a maid with mimed gestures, questioning witnesses, or battling the hypocrisies of a powerful aristocrat—until they knew instinctively which of the set routines to apply to any given situation from zaniness to menace, melodic camp to conversational tête-à-tête. With an ear to the other actors' contributions, each participant developed a spontaneous set of lines per scene like building blocks forming a wall, punctuated with occasional bits of satire aimed at local scandal or hypocrisy. The stock prologues, soliloquys, repartee, and *canovacci* ("scripts") became repertory as precious as family heirlooms; younger generations followed their parents on the stage and spoke passages that had endured for decades. Flaminio Scala published a written version of 50 of the 700 known *lazzi* in 1611. Other playbooks provide 30 of the written commedia plays.

Similar to the Mary Hart variety of soap opera, the worldly, time-worn plots turned on the predictable ups and downs of romance: hero finds girl, soured father disapproves, hero (often in complicity with servants or girl or both) wins girl to wife and attains sizeable dowry from tight-fisted father. Adapted from loose snatches of dialogue applied ad lib, the scenes often took unexpected turns based on the players' knowledge of gossip or local happenings. Feeling their way amid laughter, catcalls, intakes of breath, and concentrated silence, skillful masked players varied their responses while holding to the basic personalities of a melange of stock figures:

- *Capitano*—the challenging suitor, excuse-finding coward, swaggering bully, or braggart warrior, a variation of Plautus's *miles gloriosus*, who carries an oversized sword to match his oversized ego

- *Pantalone*—the elderly, hook-nosed male merchant, always a gullible meddler, pinch-penny, cicerone, or bore, usually dressed in red Turkish vest and fez or cap

- *Dottore*—the learned but naive doctor of laws or grammar teacher, jealous husband, friend of pantalone, and spouter of spurious Latin phrases who dressed in the scholar's cap and gown

- *Columbina*—the sage, but humble servant or wife of *pantalone* or *dottore*, a sentimental figure often paired with Arlecchino, the simpleton serving man

- *Comico innamorato* or *amoroso*/*comica innamorata* or *amorosa*—the leading man/leading lady, unmasked and fashionably dressed for the leading lover/ingenue's part

- *Confidante* or *fantesca*—a coarse-mouthed maid, intriguer, and best friend of the *innamorata*, who acts the part of the awed country girl-come-to-town

- *Arlecchino* or *zanni*—the prototypical trickster, an amoral adolescent clown or harlequin, madcap valet, tumbler, and dancer who dressed in diamond-covered fool's cloth, wore a leather half-mask, carried a slapstick, and furthered intrigue with clever but self-defeating ruses

- *Pulcinello*—a foolish, foul-mouthed functionary, pot-bellied servant, or shrewd host or innkeeper who wore a stylized hooked nose and hump on his back, the forerunner of the British comic dupe called Punch or Jack Pudding

- *Scaramouche*—the popular central figure who dressed in black and was least bound by stereotypical behaviors and attitudes

- *Brighella* or *scapino*—the lubricious womanizer, tippler, and rascal, a hanger-on of *arlecchino* who dressed in green-trimmed costume and belt from which hung a wooden dagger and moneybag

- *Fritellino*—the penniless poser, dressed in wide white slacks and tabard with a jaunty hat and wooden sword

- *Tabarrino*—the bumbling old fool or jester dressed in green jacket and white slacks

- *Burattino*—the cringing wimp, forever cowering behind others
- *Tartaglia*—the balding, stuttering civil servant or apothecary dressed in white ruff and oversized glasses

One of the purposes of stock characters was to create rapport with the audience, which received no program but needed no help in identifying the sweet young girl, her fawning lover, and the nosy, interfering father.

The mobile troupes, who devised various methods of dividing their pay or sharing trade items paid by the audience, followed a pattern of village-by-village appearances. Troupes chose distinctive names: *Desiosi* [*The Desired*], *Uniti* [*The Unified*], *Fedeli* [*The Faithful*], and *Accesi* [*The Exuberant*]. The first noted company, led by Alberto Ganassa, covered a wide span from Paris to Mantua to Madrid from 1568 to 1583. More famous were *I Comici Gelosi* (*The Jealous Comics*), formed by Francesco Andreini (1548–1624) and his wife Isabella (1562–1604), both of whom earned lasting reputations for the stereotypical roles of *capitano* and *innamorata;* their son Giovanbattista (1578–1654) succeeded them and pushed their troupe's route east to Prague. The most renowned *arlecchino,* Tristano Martinelli (1557–1630), played on stages as far north as Austria and Germany, where companies augmented staged mime with puppetry. Pier Maria Cecchini, leader of the *Fedeli,* so impressed the emperor of Vienna that he received a title.

Troupes popularized satire across Europe. Journeying north to Paris, they taught Molière the illustrative value of comedy. Companies that performed in London entranced audiences and influenced the dramatic works of the English Renaissance, especially those by William Shakespeare and Ben Jonson. A balanced improvisational force in the broad realm of comedy that survived virtually unchanged for two centuries, the Italian *commedia dell'arte* was eclipsed by complex written drama and elaborate indoor stages. It came to an end in the 1750s when it merged with the *comédie Française* and translated Italian stage-craft into the French language. The influence of the *commedia dell'arte* survives in the witty comedies of Pierre de Marivaux and Lope de Vega; in Carlo Gozzi and Carlo Goldoni's comedies of character; and in puppetry, farce, mime, minstrel shows, vaudeville, ballet, opera, silent film, movies, and television sitcoms. (Abrams 1971; Baldick 1990; Barnet, Berman, and Burto 1960; Bermel 1982; Brockett 1968; Cuddon 1984; Drabble 1985; Gassner and Quinn 1969; Gray 1992; Holman 1980; Hornstein 1973; Roberts 1962)

See also caricature; comedy; farce; Molière; Shakespeare, William; trickster; wit.

CONGREVE, WILLIAM

The handsome, scintillating, and polished star of late Restoration drama, William Congreve produced a canon of comedy of manners that remains in production over three centuries after its introduction. A living record of the easy sexual liaisons and antipuritanical standards of the post-Commonwealth era, his epigrammatic style captures the undertones, social graces, and breezy amorality of a generation of courtiers too long repressed by priggish, domineering Puritans. Assured of his value to English literature, critics of his day compared him somewhat hastily with Molière. Although Congreve failed to live up to their judgment, he defined for the age a reasonable assessment of love on the gambler's block with social prestige as a major bargaining chip.

Born January 24, 1670, the son of a military commander in Bardsey near Leeds, Yorkshire, Congreve lived the life of the army brat in Carruckfergus outside Cork, Ireland. He attended Irish schools—Kilkenny, an upper-crust finishing school, and Trinity College in Dublin, where he became a close schoolmate of Jonathan Swift. In 1691, after settling in with his grandfather at Stretton Hall, Staffordshire, Congreve made a show of studying law at the Middle Temple. He gave up the pretense of legal scholarship when his romance parody *Incognita* was published the following year under the pseudonym Cleophil (literally "Lover of the Muse Cleo"). He followed up that publication with his translations of the satiric verse of Persius and Juvenal, completed in 1693. Befriended by John Dryden and other coffeehouse wits at the Fountain Tavern, one of London's in-crowd watering spots, he made daily contact with influential men of literature. Their encouragement led to his seven-year career as a playwright, during which he wrote admirable speaking roles for Anne Bracegirdle, a Restoration-era star for whom he maintained a lasting admiration and whose career he bolstered.

Public reception of Congreve's writings parallels the rise and fall of his fortunes, both personal and professional. His earlier titles—*The Old Bachelor* (1693) and *The Double Dealer* (1693)—fall short of his later works, which are the favored choices in anthologies of the period as well as in overviews of British comedy as a whole. The first title, presented at Drury Lane, received a stronger reception than the second, which carried Dryden's personal approval. From *The Old Bachelor*, the world has retained one sage bit of advice: "Married in haste, we may repent at leisure." A craftsman at characterization and uninhibited repartee, Congreve created pairs Prue and Ben and Valentine and Angelica for his next success, *Love for Love* (1695), a cunning suspense plot that includes a masked wedding. A scathingly satiric bit of badinage occurs in Act V between Jeremy and Tattle:

Jeremy:	Sir, I have the seeds of rhetoric and oratory in my head; I have been at Cambridge.
Tattle:	Ay! 'tis well enough for a servant to be bred at a university: but the education is a little too pedantic for a gentleman. I hope you are secret in your nature, private, close, ha?
Jeremy:	O sir, for that, sir, 'tis my chief talent: I'm as secret as the head of Nilus.
Tattle:	Ay! who is he, though? a privy counsellor?
Jeremy:	[aside] O ignorance!— [aloud] A cunning Egyptian, sir, that with his arms would overrun the country: yet nobody could ever find out his headquarters.
Tattle:	Close dog! a good whoremaster, I warrant.

English playwright William Congreve, 1670–1729

Appropriate to its promise, it was the first play staged at the new theater at Lincoln's Inn Fields.

Congreve's masterpiece characters are the admirably mated Mirabell and Millamant of *The Way of the World* (1700), his last great satiric comedy, a dizzying tangle of amours that challenged the audience's ability to follow the chase. Written in reply to Jeremy Collier's stringent attack on Restoration amorality, *The Way of the World* utilizes two familiar gathering places for London's privileged, St. James Park and a chocolate house. The play showcases an amicable array of lechers, worldly epigrams, potential fornication, and pleasingly intricate plot twists. In brilliant repartee, the principals, Mirabell and Millamant, stake out their marital territory:

> *Millamant:* I won't be called names after I'm married; positively I won't be called names.
> *Mirabell:* Names!
> *Millamant:* Aye, as wife, spouse, my dear, joy, jewel, love, sweetheart, and the rest of that nauseous cant, in which men and their wives are so fulsomely familiar—I shall never bear that . . . Let us be very strange and well-bred; let us be as strange as if we had been married a great while, and as well-bred as if we were not married at all.

From this guarded exchange of conditions, the characters strike a deal; the play concludes with a potentially happy union satirized as a boardroom contract that anticipates the twentieth-century prenuptial agreement. Because of its measured grace and fast-paced humor, it plays well as reading stage or closet comedy.

Late in Congreve's career, when public taste turned from wit to sentimental comedy, he achieved a mark of distinction—a do-nothing government job of taxi commissioner at the rate of £100 a year, followed by a similar sinecure as wine commissioner and secretary in Jamaica. For these annual incomes, he owed his old friend, Jonathan Swift. During ample leisure, Congreve worked as novelist, tragedian, and translator; he owned stock in and managed an acting company at Lincoln's Inn Fields for which he intended to write an original play each season, though he failed to fulfill his promise. After the waning of Restoration comedy, he attempted writing a masque, operatic libretto, criticism, and occasional verse, but he never attained the fame attached to his comedies. Only his tragedy *The Mourning Bride* (1697) rated public applause and popularized the classic claim that "music has charms to soothe a savage breast."

The decline of Congreve's life brought worsening health from gout and inactivity because of failing vision. At his death on January 19, 1729, from a traffic accident, he understandably bequeathed his property to Henrietta, Duchess of Marlborough, the mother of his illegitimate daughter Mary Godolphin, Duchess of Leeds. Henrietta kept an effigy of the playwright at her table and erected a plaque over his tomb in Poet's Corner of Westminster Abbey. The true measure of Congreve's felicity were the tributes from longtime friends and colleagues Alexander Pope, John Gay, Voltaire, Joseph Addison, Sir Richard Steele, and Anne Bracegirdle. (Baugh 1948; Brockett 1968; Burdick 1974;

Congreve 1953; Etherege 1953; Gassner and Quinn 1969; McMillin 1973; Roberts 1962; Wilson 1965)

See also Behn, Aphra; caricature; comedy; Dryden, John; epigram; Etherege, George; Juvenal; Persius; repartee; Restoration drama; Swift, Jonathan; Wycherley, William.

A CONNECTICUT YANKEE IN KING ARTHUR'S COURT

Mark Twain's 1886 surrealistic romance *A Connecticut Yankee in King Arthur's Court* uses well-known Arthurian lore as a framework for the author's satire on elements of his own time, namely, Victorian optimism, progress, government bureaucracy, and the control of the Catholic hierarchy. The dystopian novel opens on the narrator, a voluble stranger who reveals an anomaly to a visitor to Warwick Castle: a bullet hole in a suit of chain mail dating to the time of King Arthur. The narrator identifies himself as Hank Morgan of Hartford, Connecticut, and claims to have worked at the Colt Arms factory. After Hercules, a neighborhood bully, clouted him over the head in a fight, Hank collapses in 1879 and regains consciousness in Camelot on June 19, 528 A.D.

Twain's description of Camelot and its residents and visitors strays deliberately from the mystic lore of medieval poets. His satiric revelations about superstition and ignorance depict a world in which learning and creativity are severely restricted to an elite minority. The elaborate dress, confusing idiom, and illogic of local English citizens convince Hank that he is talking with circus performers or lunatics escaped from an asylum. Clarence, a colorful, cocky young attendant, warns Hank that Merlin has cast a spell on the dungeon. Speaking through Hank, Twain sneers at Merlin and his ilk:

> I've known Merlin seven hundred years . . . He has died and come alive again thirteen times, and traveled under a new name every time: Smith, Jones, Robinson, Jackson, Peters, Haskins, Merlin—a new alias every time he turns up. I knew him in Egypt three hundred years ago; I knew him in India five hundred years ago—he is always blethering around in my way, everywhere I go; he makes me tired. He don't amount to shucks, as a magician; knows some of the old common tricks, but has never got beyond the rudiments, and never will.

The satire, Twain style, openly challenges the bunkum of scam artists from the beginning of time, a parallel of Twain's inglorious Duke and King, the duo in *The Adventures of Huckleberry Finn* who attempt to flim-flam three trusting orphans. Hank's method of countering Merlin is frontier style at its funniest: to see his bet and double it.

The satire moves to Camelot's hierarchy after Hank appears at court. Clarence guides him to a banquet hall to appear before King Arthur, Queen

Guenever, Sir Launcelot, Sir Kay, Sir Galahad, and Merlin, Arthur's mage. The feasting halts as participants question the newcomer, stripped "naked as a pair of tongs"; they offhandedly condemn him to burn at the stake. Hank makes his own challenge, bruiting his powers with the showmanship of P. T. Barnum. Calling on his title as "supreme Grand High-yu-Muckamuck and head of the tribe," Hank insists that he can stop the sun in the sky, a feat he performs during an eclipse. The deception saves him from execution, frees him from Merlin's malice, and awards him dominance, the author's proof that medieval cruelty, sovereignty, and gullibility were linked.

Twain's syncretic utopian fantasy is a zany merger of medieval squalor and subservience, the worship of technological progress that marked the nineteenth century, and a two-edged satire, a masterly stroke, that works both for and against Hank. Unaware of his coming downfall, he boasts:

> My power was colossal; and it was not a mere name, as such things have generally been, it was the genuine article. I stood here, at the very spring and source of the second great period of the world's history . . . I was a Unique; and glad to know that that fact could not be dislodged or challenged for thirteen centuries and a half, for sure.

Hank imports U.S. amenities—soap, matches, ink, paper, batteries, and the sewing machine—and attempts to smarten up the Middle Ages. A blast of explosives establishes him as top magician but falls short of disarming his slyest enemy, the church. He sets out to systemize patenting and the military, open a democratic school system and a telegraph and telephone service, remap the kingdom, and launch an insurance bureau and a newspaper. His rise at court to his position of "the Boss" alienates both Merlin and Sir Sagramor, a vindictive knight. Ironically, Hank is so enamored of his trifling material success that he discounts growing hatred, the force that brings him down, as well as Camelot.

To broaden the range of satire, Twain moves his protagonist around the kingdom via the convention of knight-errantry. The king dispatches Hank to rescue a maiden from a trio of ogres. In the company of her loquacious sister Sandy, he sets out on horseback in cold, unyielding armor and endures his guide's run-on narrative, a chauvinistic tweak at talkative women. Hank's venture into the countryside reveals a repressive monarchy that allows feudal lords, the church, and Arthur's silky-sly sister, Morgan le Fay, to squelch civil rights. Of the dependence of the nobility on papal support, Hank grouses:

> In two or three little centuries [the Roman Catholic Church] had converted a nation of men to a nation of worms. Before the day of the Church's supremacy in the world, men were men, and held their heads up, and had a man's pride and spirit and independence; and what of greatness and position a person got, he got mainly by achievement, not by birth.

A meager mask for the author, Hank contends that the church created the concept of divine right by distorting the Beatitudes into a forced humility and meekness expected of commoners. He adds that the United States, too, suffers a remnant of *noblesse oblige* in its "dudes and dudesses," but he contends that classism has lost its force and will soon die out.

To provide two points of view, Twain manipulates the tour by having Arthur dress as a commoner and join Hank. Along the way, they witness the joviality of a band of pilgrims and the miseries of slaves under the overseer's whip. At the home of smallpox victims, Arthur takes pity on those who openly despise the king's neglect of cottage-class people. He earns Hank's regard for tenderly uniting a dying mother with her moribund daughter and for enduring an unwitting jab from a commoner:

> Ah, I know that sign: thou'st a wife at home, poor soul, and you and she have gone hungry to bed, many's the time, that the little ones might have your crust; you know what poverty is, and the daily insults of your betters, and the heavy hand of the Church and the king.

In short order, Arthur himself suffers the caprices of power after disgruntled locals unseat both king and boss and sell them to slave dealers. Hank extricates his arms from manacles and sends word to Clarence that he and the king are condemned to hang. At the crucial moment, Launcelot leads a rescue party of 500 knights mounted on bicycles like cavalry on mounts, another example of Twain's ingenuity with stock frontier comedy.

Obviously, Twain cannot allow Hank unlimited range as court innovator and reshaper of Camelot. His roving complete, Hank returns to the castle, where Sir Sagramor, his armor endowed with Merlin's magic, faces off against the Boss in the lists. Twain satirizes the set-up as Hank's bold attempt to rescue knight errantry. By ridiculing Mississippi style the tests, flags, sentinels, and combatants, Hank compounds the humor and belittles the finery of his champion, dressed in "flesh-colored tights from neck to heel, with blue silk puffings about [the] loins, and bareheaded." Against Hank rides "the iron tower and the gorgeous bed quilt [who] came gracefully pirouetting down the lists" (Twain 1963, pp. 276–277). From the stands rings out Clarence's slangy salute, "Go it, slim Jim!" Hank outmaneuvers Sir Sag's lance with a lariat until Merlin steals it. To contend against nine knights, Hank pulls two six-shooters and begins the one-man shoot-out:

> Bang! One saddle empty. Bang! another one. Bang-bang! and I bagged two. Well it was nip and tuck with us, and I knew it. If I spent the eleventh shot without convincing these people, the twelfth man would kill me, sure.

Twain, as light in his style as Hank on a cow pony, departs from medieval satire to dime western ploy, then returns to southern dialect to gloat, "And Brer Merlin? His stock was flat again."

Twain's love of children surfaces in the novel's denouement, replacing satire with a melodrama that the Clemens family had lived during the illness of Langdon, who died in babyhood, and of Olivia, Susy, Clara, and Jean, who predeceased their father. At home again, Hank, who has deserted his Connecticut fiancée, Puss Flanagan, and married the affable Sandy, learns that croup endangers the life of his daughter, Hello-Central. Launcelot endears himself to the family by sitting up at night and keeping the steam kettle stoked with sulphur to ease the child's labored breathing. Twain pauses in his sentimental

Political cartoonist Dan Beard illustrated Mark Twain's *A Connecticut Yankee in King Arthur's Court*. Twain described King Arthur's era as a society in which the church ruled the king, the king ruled noblemen, and noblemen ruled freemen.

home-fires story with a keen glance at Sir Launcelot, suited in armor and striding toward the stock board, which he chairs. The farewell to Hello-Central reflects Twain's soft side:

> Well, he stood watch and watch with me, right straight through, for three days and nights, till the child was out of danger; then he took her up in his great arms and kissed her, with his plumes falling about her golden head, then laid her softly in Sandy's lap again and took his stately way down the vast hall, between the ranks of admiring men-at-arms and menials, and so disappeared. (Twain 1963, p. 288)

A doctor sends Hank, Sandy, and Hello-Central on an extended sea voyage. Underneath his professional diagnosis and cure lurks a scheme to keep Hank out of the way while authorities override his progressive schools, private ownership of property, demotion of the aristocracy, and other futuristic ideas.

The plot resolution pits Hank against the toughest obstacle—the church. Defying an interdiction, he and Clarence set up a stronghold to ward off the insidious Mordred, who undercuts Arthur's authority and dignity by pressing for action on Sir Launcelot's infatuation with Queen Guenever. In Chapter 43, Hank's self-deprecating vernacular mourns:

> Ah, what a donkey I was! . . . The Church, the nobles, and the gentry then turned one grand, all-disapproving frown upon them and shriveled them into sheep! From that moment the sheep had begun to gather to the fold—that is to say, the camps—and offer their valueless lives and their valuable wool to the "righteous cause."

The erupting war channels the might of the kingdom in a wasteful battle for control. Mordred fells Arthur. Ecclesiastical minions maneuver the Boss, Clarence, and fifty-two assistants into a cave.

In the ensuing slaughter, Hank halts an attack by 30,000 knights with dynamite, electric fence, and Gatling gun. The rebels' loss turns into victory as a ring of decaying bodies immures Hank and his staff and spreads contagion to their cave. After Hank is wounded and falls victim to Merlin's black magic, Clarence continues the handwritten account of the siege. Merlin's spell puts Hank into a deep sleep, which ends at Warwick Castle, where the visitor encounters him. Nearing death, Hank picks at the coverlet, shouts commands to his workers, and calls to his wife. Thirteen centuries away from Hartford, his hello-girl, and the arms factory, he dies.

Twain's story functions both as adventure tale and as satire. On the light side, he harnesses wit and comedy to a familiar story and garnishes with touches of frontier humor. For example, Launcelot speaks his obvious love for Guenever with a single glance "that would have got him shot in Arkansas." The implication that illicit amours flourish in all levels of society and periods of history adds to Hank's obvious understanding of court life and his ability to manipulate it to his benefit. At a formal banquet, Hank notes that modesty and moderation are not necessary adjuncts to good manners. Women and clerics put away gallons of wine and laugh at racy jokes. The evening ends with drunkenness, hilarity, quarrels, and a few wastrels under the table. The didacticism of these passages portrays the prude in Twain, who may have submitted his manuscripts to his prim wife Olivia for censorship.

Along with titters and raw jest, Twain structures enough handicaps and medieval challenges to maintain a modicum of tension in the Boss's life. Hank's unfamiliarity with armor becomes a monumental impediment as he rides out for the first time:

> The first ten or fifteen times I wanted my handkerchief I didn't seem to care; I got along, and said never mind, it isn't any matter, and dropped it out of my mind. But now it was different; I wanted it all the time; it was nag, nag, nag, right along, and no rest; I couldn't get it out of my mind; and so at last I lost my temper and said hang a man that would make a suit of armor without any pockets in it. (Twain 1963, pp. 75–76)

Twain's humor, whether set in nineteenth-century Hartford or medieval Camelot, returns to the flaws and yearnings of humankind. Stretching from the minor flaws that make people comical and interesting to the cruelty and corruption that make them monsters, the satiric panorama hits high and low, lampooning Arthur for his ignorance, Clarence for his poor spelling, Merlin for his old-world stock of magic tricks, and Hank for his arrogance. (Budd 1983; Hoffman 1988; Kesterson 1979; Rasmussen 1995; Twain 1963)

See also comedy; didacticism; Morgan, Hank; satire; Twain, Mark.

"THE COQUETTE'S HEART"

One of the most frequently cited excerpts from the *Spectator*, a journal published by Joseph Addison and Richard Steele from 1709 to 1712, "The Coquette's

Heart," a companion essay to "The Bean's Head," demonstrates Addison's light touch with satire and his ability to maneuver words and images into an inventive essay. The feature was published as No. 218, Tuesday, January 22, 1712, near the end of the paper's tenure. It begins in classical style with a Latin epigraph from Virgil noting, "Pectoribus inhians spirantia consulit exta" ("Holding his breath, he studied the steamy entrails"). Like a Roman augur examining an excised organ, Addison, caught in a dream, adopts an objective tone, suggesting the scientific curiosity of a physician or physiologist. He notes that the operator slices into the flirt's heart and finds circuitous passageways of a number and type unknown in any other animal. Outside, he adds, the pericardium displays "millions of little scars" where Cupid's arrows have attempted to penetrate but made no entry through the tough exterior and into the inner chambers.

Patiently, Addison works layer by layer to the core. Beyond the pericardium, the heart's structure offers satiric evidence of the shallow nature of the coquette. The organ's inconstant liquid reminds Addison of mercury in that it rises and falls like a thermometer "to show the change of weather." Upon fuller study, the liquid makes no differentiation in atmosphere, but it does indicate "the qualities of those persons who entered the room," whether clod or coxcomb. The intertwined fibers are twisted "like a Gordian knot," the nerves grow directly from the eyes rather than from the brain, and the organ as a whole seems light and hollow. The essayist comments that the owner of the heart, while she was alive and attracting suitors, gave little encouragement. At the core, Addison identifies a miniature of a beau whom the *Spectator* had previously featured. The essayist concludes archly with a lab experiment:

> Accordingly, we laid [the heart] into a pan of burning coals, when we observed in it a certain salamandrine quality that made it capable of living in the midst of fire and flame, without being consumed or so much as singed.

The observers stand around the flame-engulfed heart and observe a singular phenomenon—it sighs, cracks, and dissolves into "smoke and vapor." This final image, a nimble bit of humor, demonstrates Addison's skill with satire: he labels coquetry a lightweight artifice endured by the men who worship shallow, self-absorbed women. (Addison 1973; Baugh 1948; Inglis and Spear 1952; Steele 1973)

See also Addison, Joseph; epigram; satire; *The Spectator*.

 # THE COUNTRY WIFE

William Wycherley's third and most critically debated comedy of manners, produced in London in 1675, demonstrates the quandary that leads admirers to laud the playwright's honest depiction of Restoration-era debauchery. Simultaneously, the sly grace and seeming triumph of low morals produced a vocal condemnation of stage productions rife with cynicism, casual fornication, and unseemly flouting of respectability. The play, which depicts the rural maiden introduced to the London smart set, is a high-spirited, frolicsome piece. It abstains from overt moralizing and didactic speeches and lets the playgoer deduce from the action the author's intent. Mistress Margery Pinchwife, the female protagonist, and Horner, the libidinous cuckolder and despoiler of women, are based on popular caricatures from Molière's urbane comedies, the fount from which Restoration comedy draws its energy and comic leer. Wycherley carries the sophisticated French model to extremes by proclaiming his protagonist a "horner" or giver of horns, a double-fingered gesture used from ancient times to indicate that a husband has been debased by a trickster who has enjoyed sexual intimacy with his wife.

The plot reveals an open field for Horner's debauchery after Dr. Quack spreads the word that Horner has contracted venereal disease, which a French doctor is unable to cure. According to false rumor, Horner is supposedly impotent, victim of an "English-French disaster," and no longer a threat to wives. Free to pursue Mrs. Squeamish, Lady Fidget, and Mrs. Dainty Fidget, Horner succeeds in bedding them all. None of the three means anything to him beyond a conquest to add to his list. To Mrs. Squeamish's outrage, he counters, "[Men] must let you win at cards, or we lose your hearts; and if you make an assignation, 'tis at a goldsmith's, jeweller's, or china-house," Horner's proof that women sell their favors like strumpets. Lady Fidget and Horner carry the heated exchange to a moot point:

Lady Fidget: Well, Harry Common, I hope you can be true to three. Swear; but 'tis to no purpose to require your oath, for you are as often forsworn as you swear to new women.

Horner: Come, faith, Madam, let us e'en pardon one another; for all the difference I find betwixt we men and you women, we forswear ourselves at the beginning of an amour, you as long as it lasts.

With a clearing away of pretense, the two settle the battle of the sexes by disclosing the obvious: both men and women behave like vendors selling their wares and, consequently, deserve the disillusion that accompanies love that originates in the social marketplace.

Wycherley relishes the climax when each woman realizes that she is not alone in sharing Horner's sexual favors. He presses Lady Fidget into the role of spokesperson to conceal the trio's shame in being gulled:

Well, then, there's no remedy, sister sharers; let us not fall out but have a care of our honor, the jewel of most value and use, which shines yet to the world unsuspected, though it be counterfeit.

Cloaked in false respectability, the three compromised women feel safe from public scorn but not from their own misgivings and free-floating distrust of male-female relationships.

Unknown to them, Margery Pinchwife, the barnyard housewife, outstrips them in treachery and sexual drive. Margery schemes to win Horner by posing as her sister-in-law, Alithea. Proclaiming herself sick of Pinchwife and sick for

Horner, she bears symptoms of "the London disease called love" and grows nauseated at the sight of her husband. Flaunting her power over her quarry, she envisions the next step in the plot:

> As in other fevers, my own chamber is tedious to me, and I would fain be removed to his, and then methinks I should be well. Ah, poor Mr. Horner! Well, I cannot, will not stay here; therefore I'll make an end of my letter to him, which shall be a finer letter than my last, because I have studied it like anything. Oh sick sick! (Harris 1953, p. 129)

The concluding line verbalizes the ambiguity of Wycherley's play. Ironically, Margery has made herself sick with longing for a better man than her grumpy, jealous husband. Yet, the sickness applies to society at large, the arena of England's amoral sideshow that Wycherley so keenly lampoons.

The playwright appeases the sophisticated audience's love of complicated subplots by producing a second restless woman, who becomes Margery's foil. The counterrhythms of Alithea's betrothal to a lame-brain poser produce considerable satire. Sparkish, lacking the alert sense of public chicanery that forms the backdrop of Restoration comedy, remains sure of himself. After Pinchwife locks Margery indoors to keep her safe from seducers, Sparkish gloats:

> Lord, how shy you are of your wife! But let me tell you, Brother, we men of wit have amongst us a saying that cuckolding, like the small-pox, comes with a fear; and you may keep your wife as much as you will out of danger of infection, but if her constitution incline her to't, she'll have it sooner or later, by the world, say they. (Harris 1953, p. 131)

The pun on "pox," a common name for syphilis, names the consequence of promiscuity, a real threat in Wycherley's day, but among the posturing social climbers of Restoration drama, fear of public ridicule outdistances concern about infection. On the sly, Alithea considers dumping Sparkish for a more considerable man, Harcourt, who is Horner's friend. The tie with Sparkish holds until he accuses her of adultery with Horner. At last revealing himself both petty and foolish, Sparkish loses Alithea, who was far beyond his worth from the beginning. To her detriment, she also proves foolish for remaining true to him.

The conclusion of the farce maintains more than a nominal tie with conventional morality. Alithea appears safely captivated by Harcourt. Margery, although mismated to a humorless scold, gives up hopes of landing Horner. The trio of false wives remain fair game for Horner, whose behavior is the least affected by the preceding scenes. Wycherley further clouds the moral intent of his work by closing with a dance of cuckolds and Horner's advice:

> Vain fops but court and dress, and keep a pother,
> To pass for women's men with one another;
> But he who aims by women to be priz'd.
> First by the men, you see, must be despis'd.

Lady Fidget counters Horner's quatrain with an epilogue. Summoning relentless philanderers who hide behind vizard masks, she tears down their macho posturings and show of gallantry. Her conclusion defies the Horners of society with a warning:

> But, gallants, have a care, faith, what you do.
> The world, which to no man his due will give,
> You by experience know you can deceive,
> And men may still believe you vigorous,
> But then we women—there's no cozening us.

Wycherley's running competition between the women who flirt and the men who chase them ends in a tie. Neither side can claim the stronger position because the moral bankruptcy of the perennial coquette and the tireless skirt-chaser relies on a willing supply of each type. Thus Wycherley satirizes his age for producing people of low character and chides the audience for laughing at stage models of themselves. (Baugh 1948; Brockett 1968; Burdick 1974; Gassner 1969; Kunitz and Haycraft 1952; McMillin 1973; Person 1988; Roberts 1962; Wilson 1965; Wycherley 1953)

See also Behn, Aphra; caricature; comedy; Congreve, William; double entendre; Etherege, George; farce; Molière; repartee; Restoration drama; Wycherley, William.

COWARD, NOEL

A model of unconventional, anti-Victorian sophistication, Sir Noel Pierce Coward, like his English forebears in Restoration comedy, delighted audiences with numerous satiric farces. A canny observer of manners and customs, he focused on the staccato repartee of the vacuous smart set and their aimlessness, amorality, and disillusion. Drawing on these raw materials, he managed, produced, wrote, and acted for the stage; produced and directed original screenplays; composed and performed operetta and stylish tunes and lyrics for cabaret revues; and wrote extensive and often mordant insider's views of the theatrical world. The eminently singable "Mad Dogs and Englishmen" proved such a hit that he sang it on request of Winston Churchill and Franklin Roosevelt aboard the HMS *Prince of Wales*. Coward was a workaholic who made himself wealthy by the age of 40 and is often described as a member of the suave, agnostic smart set that he so skillfully spoofed.

The son of Violet Veitch Coward, a stereotypical stage mother, and out-at-elbows piano salesman Arthur Coward, Noel Coward was born December 16, 1899, in Teddington-on-Thames, Middlesex. While performing in stage shows in childhood, he attended day school in Surrey and boarded at Chapel Royal School in Clapham. By 14, Coward was the veteran of several performances as the star of *Peter Pan*. In his early teens, he was drawn to the postwar Dixieland boom and left school permanently to write songs for BBC radio. He never failed with lyrics and tunes, but he did lose his singing job. To employer André Charlot he quipped, "I don't mind criticism, so long as it's restricted to unqualified praise" (Bickerdyke 1995, p. 52).

More to Coward's taste was preparation for a career in drama, for which impresario Italia Conti tutored him. He debuted as playwright in 1917 with *The Last Trick,* a melodrama, only months before he was drafted for service. Dismissed for a tubercular infection, he served with the Artists' Rifles at Gidea Park, a home guard for medical rejects, until he injured his head in a fall and was honorably discharged. He labored seven years composing stage exposés of London's seamier side before scoring with a domestic drama, *The Vortex* (1924), and two comedies, *Fallen Angels* (1925) and *Hay Fever* (1925), his favorite farce. From astute observer of the privileged, Coward slid into a sardonic mode brought on by the postwar disenchantment and regret that permeate *Post Mortem* (1930), an overview of an era by a soldier returned to earth as a ghost, and *Cavalcade* (1931), an ironic consideration of English life that the critics misread as nostalgia.

Coward wrote one of his most revealing domestic satires, *Private Lives* (1930), while recovering from flu in Shanghai. The show starred Coward, Gertrude Lawrence, and Laurence Olivier in its debut at the Phoenix Theatre in London. It garnered instant success in Britain and the United States and was frequently acted in local theater productions. The story is a durable plot that brings together two ex-spouses who have married other mates and find themselves booked at the same honeymoon retreat. Brisk, uncompromising give-and-take dramatizes such evenly matched set-tos as this exchange between Amanda and Victor, her new husband:

Victor:	It's no use being cross.
Amanda:	You're a pompous ass.
Victor:	Mandy!
Amanda:	Pompous ass, that's what I said, and that's what I meant. Blown out with your own importance.
Victor:	Mandy, control yourself.
Amanda:	Get away from me. I can't bear to think I'm married to such rugged grandeur.
Victor:	I'll be in the bar.

On the opposite side of the stage, Elyot and Sibyl part in an equal state of indignation to dine separately and fume over their marital discontent. After Amanda and Elyot settle differences, they leave their former mates to reprise the squabbles that caused their original divorce. Ironically, each thinks the other shallow and pigheaded, terms that could describe all four.

An arty film, *The Scoundrel,* in which Coward starred in 1935, and a lighter, less cynical comedy, *Blithe Spirit* (1941), the spoof of a ghost-haunted husband, preceded wartime patriotic productions—*This Happy Breed* (1942) and *Brief Encounter* (1944)—which Coward adapted for film and for which otherwise disappointing venture he earned an Oscar nomination. Obviously productive, the war years were also a turning point for most of Britain and particularly for Coward. He supported the war effort by entertaining camps of soldiers and

Usually urbane, English actor and playwright Noel Coward, left, sang and danced in the musical comedy skit *Red Peppers* with musical comedy star Gertrude Lawrence in 1936.

collecting funds. In the aftermath, the demand for gritty postwar realism and theater of the absurd passed by Coward, who continued to write polished pieces for stage and film, but to a diminished audience. Following numerous revivals of *Private Lives* and a brief stint as nightclub performer, Coward was knighted in 1970. He retired to Switzerland and the Caribbean; he died in his sleep of heart failure on March 26, 1973, at Firefly, his island home in St. Mary, Jamaica. His posthumous *Noel Coward Diaries* (1982) provides glimpses of the theatrical milieu and snipes at his critics and competition. Two years after its publication, a plaque was unveiled in Westminster Abbey with the simple notation, "A Talent to Amuse." (Baugh 1948; Bickerdyke 1995; Brockett 1968; Coward 1965; Gassner and Quinn 1969; Kunitz 1942; Lesley 1976; Roberts 1962)

See also comedy; farce; repartee; Restoration drama; theater of the absurd; wit.

DIATRIBE

Diatribe is verbal abuse, bluster, vilification, or tirade that ranges beyond rationality. The word is derived from the Greek for *expend* or *lecture*, and it is the rhetorical device most commonly employed in camp, invective, or splenetic monologue. Originally created as ethical discourse equivalent to a moral sermon, diatribe degenerated into polemics, bombast, hectoring, and embittered carping. In numerous instances—Iago's evil spoutings in William Shakespeare's *Othello* (ca. 1603), lengthy rationalization in Sinclair Lewis's *Babbitt* (1922), Merlin's complaints against the Boss in Mark Twain's *A Connecticut Yankee in King Arthur's Court* (1889), and the angry retort of the Baron's son to Candide's intention to marry his sister Cunégonde in Voltaire's *Candide* (1759)—diatribe serves as a vehicle for the emotionally immature or maladjusted personality, whose uninterrupted monologue or aside discloses meaty chunks of discontent, disillusion, or confusion. A frequently quoted diatribe from American literature is from Chapter 5 of Mark Twain's *The Adventures of Huckleberry Finn* (1876). "Huck's Father—The Fond Parent" reveals Pap Finn's irrational fear of government and opposition to rights for blacks, especially those with a superior education. Toward the conclusion of the seriocomic diatribe, Twain returns to humor by having Pap admit his greatest weakness: "Thinks I, what is the country a-coming to? It was 'lection day, and I was just about to go and vote myself if I warn't too drunk to get there."

The diatribe derives from Greek stoic masters Hesiod, Bion, Crates, and Teles. It was a favorite of classical Rome, and survives in the satiric works of Horace, Seneca, Lucan, Persius, Juvenal, and Epictetus, stoic mentor to Marcus Aurelius. In a characteristic rumble against connivers like his wastrel brother, Hesiod cautions:

> Here is the law, as Zeus established it for human beings;
> as for fish, and wild animals, and the flying birds, they
> feed on each other, since there is no idea of justice among
> them; but to men he gave justice, and she in the end is proved
> the best thing they have.

Such black-and-white logic permeates Hesiod's *Works and Days* (sixth century B.C.), a humorless work devoted to probity and worthy examples. Detailing the

161

farmer's hard work on stony soil, Hesiod's equally stony prose, like Ecclesiasticus and Jeremiah in the Old Testament or the sermons of Cotton Mather, shuns wit and humor in favor of accusation.

In controlled masterpieces, particularly Horace's comments on critics, diatribe rises above the level of harangue to studied, sometimes elegant didacticism. In the opening book of his *Sermones* (30 B.C.), Horace, a soul-satisfied homebody, rails against the work-driven laborer:

> The man who turns the heavy earth
> With his unyielding plow or the rascally sharp innkeeper
> Or the soldier or undaunted sailors who set out across
> Any old sea, all say they put up with such work
> To retire safe and sure in old age when they've scraped up enough
> To subsist on. . . .

However, Horace muses, while the ant lives off its stores, the workaholic continues grabbing for more, letting "not blistering summer, not winter, not fire, flood, or sword" halt the continual money lust that overruns body and soul.

Lucius Annaeus Seneca, the humorless master of Roman diatribe, replaces the ease and grace of Horace's light-paced sermonettes with a thundering puritanism worthy of Jonathan Edwards. Although Seneca clearly triumphs intellectually over illogic and shilly-shallying, he too often allows himself an excess of ultimata that defeats satire. His plays swamp the few examples of Menippean satire, such as *Apocolocyntosis [The Pumpkinification]* (ca. A.D. 55), in which his polemics share the stage with light patter, a witty scenario on Claudius's appointment to godhood, and some personal scores settled with lampoon, jest, anecdote, and more lethal skewers. Philosophical to a fault, Seneca grew so enamored of his own voice that he marred the poesy of his nine surviving tragedies. His name survives not in the honor roll of comics but in the adjective "senecan," a synonym for overblown bombast, a segment of language that Peter Roget's *Thesaurus* correctly assigns to the category "inelegance of language" along with *grandiloquence, rant, hot air,* and *balderdashy.*

The Renaissance, a time of free-spirited, inventive literature, produced diatribe as a balance to vignette, spoof, dialogue, and other lighter genres. A deliciously funny harangue occurs in Book II, Chapter 8 of Miguel de Cervantes's *Don Quixote* (1615) when the Don, stripped of his armor and standing in his underwear, requests a moment of privacy with his companion Sancho Panza in order to take him down several pegs for insolence:

> Tell me now, you clown of today and noodle of yesterday—do you think it was right of you to offend and insult a duenna so worthy of reverence and respect as that one? . . . Remember, you sinner, that well-bred and honourable servants cause their master to be respected, and that one of the greatest advantages which princes possess over other men is that they have servants as good as themselves to wait on them.

The plentiful irony of this passage is the inappropriate timing of the comeuppance, which Sancho may have deserved on numerous earlier occasions but not on this one. Incapable of seeing that the duenna is mocking him, Don Quixote persists to a wise Sancho, who would "bite off his tongue rather than utter a word that was not fitting and well-considered."

A harangue like Don Quixote's that vents personal irritation or a grudge may launch a well-aimed venomous dart that pains, denounces, or destroys; such a relaxing of restraint, however, extends no quarter to the repentant sinner, no mercy to the villain, and no gleanings of wisdom to the audience. Also referred to as phillipic, vituperation, or jeremiad, the literary diatribe wastes momentum when it abandons humor, compassion, and forgiveness as necessary adjuncts to restoring order or justice. Thus, the fulminator, overwhelmed by corrosive, self-limiting anger, loses control; at full throttle, the outburst gives off heat, but no light, as exemplified in "Gareth and Lynette," a segment of Alfred Tennyson's *Idylls of the King* (1885). In this exchange, Sir Lancelot and Sir Kay the Seneschal discuss the future of Gareth, an untried youth:

> Then Lancelot standing near: "Sir Seneschal,
> Sleuthhound thou knowest, and gray, and all the hounds;
> A horse thou knowest, a man thou dost not know.
> Broad brows and fair, a fluent hair and fine,
> High nose, a nostril large and fine, and hands
> Large, fair, and fine!—Some young lad's mystery—
> But, or from sheepcote or king's hall, the boy
> Is noble-natured. Treat him with all grace,
> Lest he should come to shame thy judging of him."
> Then Kay: "What murmurest thou of mystery?
> Think ye this fellow will poison the King's dish?
> Nay, for he spake too fool-like; mystery!
> Tut, an the lad were noble, he had asked
> For horse and armor; fair and fine, forsooth!
> Sir Fine-face, Sir Fair-hands? but see thou to it
> That thine own fineness, Lancelot, some fine day
> Undo thee not—and leave my man to me."

Typically, the berater, like Kay, the kitchen manager, riddles the message with illogic and personal vendetta, in this case, his envy of Lancelot's fame and glamor, confusing subject and substance with personal distaste or festering jealousy. In addition, the speech serves the poet as a portent of the death of Camelot, which is brought on by Lancelot's "undoing." More often the rhetorical weapon of the political candidate, court judge, or critic than of the writer, diatribe loses its way in such a rush of self-righteous pontification, piety, self-important posturing, judgment, or prejudice.

Not all diatribe falls short of satire's aims. A satiric use of diatribe in Jerome Lawrence and Robert E. Lee's *Inherit the Wind* (1955), a frequently revived historical drama, works like the pursuing race-car driver drafting off the lead car. While populist orator and prosecuting attorney Matthew Harrison Brady grandstands at the trial of a Tennessee biology teacher accused of violating biblical principles by teaching evolution, defense lawyer Henry Drummond lets the hot air gust him into pointed one-liners, saving him the effort of deflating a pompous windbag who eventually outsmarts himself. Rising during testimony of a schoolchild, Brady prates his fundamentalist cause and booms at the judge:

> Your Honor, the defense makes the same old error of all Godless men! They confuse material things with the great spiritual realities of the Revealed Word! Why do you bewilder this child? Does Right have no meaning to you, sir?

Drummond mumbles: "'Right' has no meaning to me whatsoever! *Truth* has meaning—as a direction." Thus the badinage proceeds, with Drummond reeling in his catch with the skill of an experienced angler and playing him out on the line until, weary with self-wasting exertion, Brady struggles no more.

In an unexpected twist, Drummond, inhibited by a biased venue and judge, calls Brady to the stand to serve as a Bible expert. Drummond undercuts his adversary's rickety logic and trounces him by making the audience laugh. Brady, still cloaked in bombastic fervor, gives away his weak position by growing defensive:

> All of you know what I stand for! What I believe! I believe, I believe in the truth of the Book of Genesis! Exodus, Leviticus, Numbers, Deuteronomy, Joshua, Judges, Ruth, First Samuel, Second Samuel, First Kings, Second Kings.

No longer facing a formidable opponent, Drummond excuses Brady without letting him complete the list. These dramatic courtroom scenes, adapted from the verbal sparring of orator William Jennings Bryan and attorney Clarence Darrow, depict the fomentation of a pious would-be contender for the White House who dies on the campaign trail, ostensibly from the verbal exertions expended in behalf of narrow-mindedness and intolerance. (Cervantes Saavedra, Miguel de 1957; Feinberg 1967; Hammond and Scullard 1992; Hesiod 1973; Holman 1980; Horace 1891; Howatson 1989; Lawrence and Lee 1960; Loban, Holmstrom, and Cook 1958; McArthur 1992; Twain 1962a)

See also The Adventures of Huckleberry Finn; camp; *Candide*; Cervantes Saavedra, Miguel de; didacticism; *Don Quixote*; Horace; invective; Juvenal; Lewis, Sinclair; satire; Twain, Mark; Voltaire, François.

DIDACTICISM

A step beyond satire, didacticism derives from the Greek term for *instructive;* it loses the force of satire by muffling its humor in a hollow, cliché-ridden, or pious show of persuasion, intellectual skill, experience, or expertise. "The Influence of the Aristocracy on Snobs," by William Makepeace Thackeray, offers a particularly overt example of the genre. In a virulent attack on toadying, Mammon worship, and other social evidences of prestige and privilege, Thackeray's essay ends with an anticlimactic rhetorical—and didactic—question: "But how should it be otherwise in a country where Lordolatry is part of our creed, and where our children are brought up to respect the 'Peerage' as the Englishman's second Bible?"

As much a part of sermons, diatribes, and homilies as of satire, didacticism permeates classic literature by Hesiod, Virgil, Cicero, Horace, Seneca, and Lucretius, and its aphorisms peek through the humor of Aristophanes. A common example occurs in the conclusion to *The Frogs* (405 B.C.), when the chorus exults:

> Happy the man who possesses
> An intellect sharpened and fine—
> (And the fortune of many expresses
> The truth oft his lesson of mine!) . . .
> Graceless the man who professes
> To nestle in Socrates' heart,
> Abandoning music, and stresses
> His scorn for the tragic art!
> To talk with pompous phrase and word
> Of high philosophy,
> To spend a life of idleness
> And hair-dissecting foolishness,
> Oh! Surely this is quite absurd
> And proves insanity!

Didacticism suits the chorus, whose purpose is to enlighten the audience on the meaning and value of reliving the characters' experiences.

Didactic lines from less lofty speakers temper advice with wit and compassion, as demonstrated by this encounter in William Shakespeare's *The Tempest* (ca. 1610) between Prospero and his future son-in-law in which the elder warns the younger of the dangers of premarital sex:

> Then, as my gift, and thine own acquisition
> Worthily purchased, take my daughter. But
> If thou dost break her virgin-knot before
> All sanctimonious ceremonies may
> With full and holy rite be minist'red,
> No sweet aspersion shall the heavens let fall
> To make this contract grow; but barren hate,
> Sour-eyed disdain, and discord shall bestrew
> The union of your bed with weeds so loathly
> That you shall hate it both. Therefore take heed,
> As Hymen's lamp shall light you.

By enshrouding his hospitable, forgiving nature in the carping expected of the father of the bride, Prospero abandons the endearing tone that sets the mood of the play. Still, the playgoer may forgive the father for seeking to spare his sheltered daughter from rancor, which was the cause of their marooning on the island of Bermuda.

Unlike Prospero, who curbs instructive monologue, literary characters abound who never miss an opportunity to mount the pulpit. A frequent rhetorical digression in Miguel de Cervantes's *Don Quixote* (1615), the maundering old knight's didacticism grows ponderous and tiresome when he reaches into the most obscure origins of his romanticism for the lesson Sancho should learn. In protecting himself from ridicule by association in Book II, Chapter 8, Don Quixote speaks in aphorism to remind Sancho that the noble who pairs himself with a foolish servant looks even more the fool:

> Do you not see, you unlucky bane of mine, that if they find out you are a coarse clod-hopper or a clownish loony, they will think that I am some roaming quack or a knight of straw? No, no, Sancho, my friend, shun such pitfalls, for he who trips into being a droll chatterbox, at the first stumble drops into a despised clown. Bridle your tongue, reflect and chew the cud before you let your words escape from your mouth, and remember that we have arrived at a point whence, by the help of God and the strength of my arm, we shall come forth greatly advanced both in fame and fortune.

The humor of the Don's miniature lesson in self-restraint lies in his own ludicrous situation—not Sancho's—and in the picture of serving girls lingering outside the door, holding hands over mouths to keep from laughing out loud at an elderly gentleman too daft to see that no one believes him a knight. Ironically, the Don's delusions defame Sancho, who is too loyal to the old man to divert him from his search for worthy duties by which to honor his idealized lady, Dulcinea del Toboso.

A lighter version of didacticism appears in the satire that fuels the tongue-in-cheek humor of R. J. Heathorn's "Learn with BOOK," published in a 1962 edition of *Punch*. The essay consists of a witty take-off on the reader's desire for an electronic gizmo to make learning convenient and fun. As Heathorn patiently explains, BOOK, an acronym for Built-in Orderly Organized Knowledge, is composed of covers and pages, fits easily into the hand, and can be stored on an ordinary shelf with little fuss or upkeep. BOOK "requires no further cost; no batteries or wires are needed, since the motive power, thanks to the ingenious device patented by the makers, is supplied by the brain of the user." The author promises that, with the self-explanatory BOOK, the reader will succeed. (Abrams 1971; Baldick 1990; Barnet, Berman, and Burto 1960; Cervantes Saavedra 1957; Cuddon 1976; Feinberg 1967; Gray 1992; Hammond and Scullard 1992; Heathorn 1958; Henry 1995; Holman 1980; Howatson 1989; MacKendrick and Howe 1952; Mantinband 1956; Shakespeare 1966; Thackeray 1967)

See also Cervantes Saavedra, Miguel de; diatribe; *Don Quixote*; epigram; Horace; political satire; Shakespeare, William.

DOGGEREL

A crude, trivial, or occasionally topical snatch of throwaway rhyme, doggerel is either poorly executed verse, an awkward advertising slogan, or a roughshod, arrhythmic burlesque or mockery of more dignified efforts. Derived from a diminutive or derogation of dog or dog Latin, doggerel has survived at the outer edge of literary propriety as a hint of antiliterature, a glimpse of shallow wordsmithy and illogic that fails or refuses to observe literary convention. A strong characteristic of doggerel is rocking-horse rhythm, cascading verses, and forced or slant rhyme, as demonstrated by John Skelton's "The Tunning of Elinour Rumming" (ca. 1550):

> Maud Ruggy thither skipped;
> She was ugly hipped,
> And ugly thick lipped,
> Like an onion sided,
> Like tan ledder hided.
> She had her so guided
> Between the cup and the wall
> That she was therewithal
> Into a palsy fall;
> With that her head shaked,
> And her hands quaked;
> One's head would have ached
> To see her naked!

This tumbling effusion of bawdy couplets, rhyming aabbbcccddd, has fixed the term "skeltonics" on later models of doggerel influenced by Skelton's bouncy, asymmetric scribblings.

A more artful use of doggerel is evident in Geoffrey Chaucer's *Canterbury Tales* (1387). After the host of the Tabard Inn insists, Chaucer begins his turn and recites a tedious, lengthy rhyme in the heroic tradition. His Sir Thopas, a type of warrior who would have much in common with Don Quixote, clatters on in jangly trios of tetrameter/trimeter rhyming aabccb, going nowhere:

> His goode steede al he bistrood,
> And forth upon his wey he glood
> As sparcle out of the bronde;
> Upon his creest he bar a tour,
> And therinne stiked a lilie flour,—
> God shilde his cors fro shondel!
> [His good horse he straddled,
> And away he rode
> Like a sparkle out of a torch;
> Upon his crest he wore a tower,
> And on it stuck a lily flower,—
> God shield his body from harm!]

A good-natured gibe at himself, the 200-line verse canters along until the host, wearied by the nothingness of nonsense romanticism, cries,

> Namoore of this, for Goddes dignitee
> . . . for thou makest me
> So wery of thy verray lewednesse.

Pleading tired ears, the host begs Chaucer to leave off his "rym dogerel," which is "nat worth a toord!"

Doggerel can be used for other humorous or mock-serious purposes, such as the vehicle for an under-the-table reply to a public attack. In the controversy concerning the authenticity of Aphra Behn's plays, critics have named her friends John Hoyle and Edward Ravenscroft the ghostwriters. Alexander Radcliffe refers to the scandal in his satiric *The Ramble: News from Hell* (1682):

> Amongst this Heptarchy of Wit
> The censuring Age have thought it fit,
> To damn a Woman, 'cause 'tis said
> The Plays she vends she never made.
> But that a grays inn lawyer does 'em
> Who unto her was Friend in Bosom,
> So not presenting Scarf and Hood
> New Plays and Songs are full as good.

The allegations fit a pattern of misogynist lies and innuendo against a woman who had the courage to earn her living as a secret agent and writer. No proof of literary piracy emerged to substantiate the accusation of these jingly couplets.

A less damning satire on unprofessional professionals occurs in the frolicsome doggerel of Molière, the French funnyman who wrote *The Imaginary Invalid* (1673), his best work. The play closes with 22 doctors, a medical student, 8 surgeons, and 6 pharmacists all dancing to the vocalized cracked-brain finale, composed in macaronic, or mingled language, verse:

> May all his anni
> Be to him boni
> And favorable ever
> Et n'habere never
> Quam plaguas, poxas,
> Fievras, pluresias
> Bloody effusions and dissenterias.

The shrill, macaronic refrain flees further from any known system of grammar with a jolly chant calling for the hypochondriac to:

> Vivat, vivat, vivat, vivat, forever vivat
> Novus doctor, qui tam bene speakat,
> Mille, mille annis, manget and bibat,
> Et bleedat and killat.

The vibrance of the rhythm and shreds of meaning hammer out the general idea that the well-reputed "novus doctor" (Latin for new or strange doctor) should live a thousand years, eat and drink, and continue to bleed and kill his patients.

In a more recent example of doggerel, a modern short story, "The First Sally (A) OR Trurl's Electronic Bard," by Stanislaw Lem, posits the invention of a machine that can make up songs. In a rush of alliteration, it gushes:

> Seduced, shaggy Samson snored.
> She scissored short. Sorely shorn,
> Soon shackled slave, Samson sighed,
> Silently scheming,
> Sightlessly seeking
> Some savage, spectacular suicide.

The parody of the biblical story of Samson and Delilah demonstrates the brilliance of Trurl's doggerel machine, which can even perform in pantomime for deaf technicians.

Another example of monotonous cadence and brainless rhymes is the macaronic blend of ecclesiastical Latin, English, French, and Italian that Salvatore, the doomed hunchback, sings to visitors in Umberto Eco's *The Name of the Rose* (1980). The pathetic shambles of a monk suffers from a severe mental defect; he mutters:

> Penitenziagite! Watch out for the draco who cometh in
> futurum to gnaw your anima! Death is super now! Pray the
> Santo Pater come to liberar nos a malo and all our sin! Ha
> ha, you like this negromanzia de Domini Nostri Jesu Christi!
> Et anco jois m'es dols e plazer m'es dolors. . . . Cave el diabolo!
> [Repent ye! Watch out for the dragon who will come to gnaw
> your soul. Death now hovers over you! Pray that the Holy
> Father will come to free us from sin! You like this black
> magic in the name of our Lord Jesus Christ! And again gladness
> is sweet to me and pleasure is my grief. . . . Beware the devil!]

He concludes that Satan lies in wait to snap at his heels. But Salvatore claims he is not stupid and asks for prayers to Christ to rescue the monastery and refectory. And the rest, he adds, is "not worth excrement. Amen. No?" Salvatore's gibberish forms an ominous contrapuntal undertone to the pious mouthings of a priestly body bent on concealing murder from a visiting priest, Father William. William's servant boy surmises that the convergent bits, like bricolage, form a jagged, shackly Babelish tongue reflecting the unholy state of humanity after the fall of Adam.

Another form of doggerel, juvenilia, can indicate the future themes and tendencies of a writer. From a Freudian standpoint, these immature works resurrected from a writer's childhood hint at raw, inexact modes of thought that evolve into mature themes, style, and tone. A memorable example is Jane Austen's epitaph for Charlotte:

> Here lies our friend who having promis-ed
> That unto two she would be marrie-ed
> Threw her sweet Body & her lovely face
> Into the Stream that runs thro' Portland Place.

From the late twentieth century, rap and its accompanying jerky music, a similar example of bobbling, lack-logic rhyme, has been criticized as the legacy of children who learned versification from Dr. Seuss books, cereal ads, and Saturday morning cartoons. An offshoot of the fast-forward disc jockey patter of radio, rap is an evolving form of ghetto juvenilia first identified in 1979 with the recording "Rapper's Delight," by the Sugarhill Gang.

Other works of nonsense or choplogic reflect the oral traditions of black culture. In their memoir, *Having Our Say: The Delany Sisters' First 100 Years* (1995), centenarians Sadie and Bessie Delany interweave aphorism, folk wisdom, and anecdotes with two rhymes that reflect the doggerel that white vaudevillians perpetrated upon black society during the painful Jim Crow era. According to Bessie, Sadie is wrong in assuming that a black candidate can win the American presidency. In proof, Bessie recites a scurrilous, racist line from minstrel shows of the 1890s:

> Oh my, what fun
> In Washington
> I bettya every coon
> From coontown will be there
> Oh my, what fun
> In Washington
> When the coon sits in that presidential chair.

Children of the Delany sisters' era also sang about the preacher who violates his Sunday by hunting a grizzly bear. The upshot of the hapless hunter's encounter with the bear is a prayer that the God who rescued Daniel, Jonah, and Shadrach, Mesach, and Abednego spare the minister also. If the Almighty has other intentions, the minister prays, "But Lord, if you can't help me, *Please don't help that bear!*" (Baldick 1990; Chaucer 1957; Cuddon 1976; Delany and Delany 1994; Drabble 1985; Eco 1983; Gassner and Quinn 1969; Gray 1992; Hardy and Laing 1987; Henry 1995; Highet 1962; Hitchcock and Sadie 1980; Holman 1980; Lem 1991; McArthur 1992; Padgett 1987; Radcliffe 1915; Skelton 1954)

See also Austen, Jane; Behn, Aphra; *Canterbury Tales;* Carroll, Lewis; Chaucer, Geoffrey; jingle; Molière; rap.

DON QUIXOTE

The Knight of the Rueful Figure, Miguel de Cervantes's imaginative dreamer and the central character of Spain's epic episodic novel, *El Ingenioso Hidalgo Don Quixote de la Mancha* (1615), is the classic figure of the self-deluding romantic seeking a quest. In Part 1, Chapter 1, Señor Alonso Quixano, at age 50 a devoted reader and idealist, is so entranced by chivalric lore that he sells arable land to buy books, most written by his favorite romance writer, Amadis of Gaul. He alters his name to Don Quixote, garbs himself in outdated oddments culled from his great-grandfather's armory, and sets out one hot July morning on his rawboned nag, Rocinante, to champion right over wrong. The author fills the would-be hero's head with a swirl of aims:

> He would not delay putting his designs into operation any longer, for he was spurred on by the conviction that the world needed his immediate presence: so many were the grievances he intended to rectify, the wrongs he resolved to set right, the harms he meant to redress, the abuses he would reform and the debts he would discharge.

Knighted by an indulgent innkeeper, he frees a young man from bondage and is battered by a vicious muleteer. The ignoble return from the abortive first sally contrasts with a grand departure: his devoted neighbor, Pedro Alonso, rescues the deluded old cavalier from a ditch and escorts him home, where Don Quixote's niece Antonia and the Don's housekeeper put him to bed and patch up his wounds.

Cervantes lampoons the monomaniacal don, who is completely taken in by the high ideals of chivalric lore. Against a plethora of obstacles, Don Quixote persists in his calling as knight errant by joining with Sancho Panza, his appointed squire, to search for challenges to right and truth. Don Quixote jousts with windmills, fights an innkeeper over a winsome barmaid, and launches a siege against a torchlight funeral procession. In a benevolent act, he frees a truculent ruffian and famed trickster, Ginés de Pasamonte, from a coffle of galley slaves. The felon repays him by beating him, stripping him down to his underwear, and stealing Dapple, Sancho's mule. The description is typical of Cervantes's use of *reductio ad absurdum*:

> The ass, Rocinante, Sancho and Don Quixote remained alone. The ass, with drooping head, stood shaking his ears every now and then as if he thought the storm of stones was not yet over. . . . Don Quixote was most downcast to see himself so ill-treated by those to whom he had done such service.

Sancho, the don's foil, comments:

> Though I'm only a rough clod-hopper of a fellow, I've a smattering of what is called good government: so don't repent of having taken my advice, but mount Rocinante (if you're able; if not, I'll give you a hand) and follow me. I've a shrewd notion that for the present we'll need our heels more than our hands.

The irony of the pair is their grounding in opposing philosophies: Don Quixote remounts to continue his glorious, impossible task; Sancho, vigilant against the pursuers, plans to move deeper into the Sierra Morena to lay low until the way is safe for a retreat.

Cervantes spreads the satire of his knight from laughable champion to ridiculous ladies' man. Deluded by his concept of the perfect unattainable maiden, Don Quixote casts Dulcinea in the role. Wandering toward the mountains, he mourns for her and dispatches Sancho with a message. The don's friends, Nicholas the barber and the local curate, halt Sancho on his mission and plot to lure the old man back home once more. Don Quixote continues to thrust himself into dangerous escapades, intercedes in failed love affairs, and falls into the clutches of scamps, rascals, and losers. Against a background of deceit and potential harm, he maintains faith in Dulcinea and the abstract concept of chivalry. As he rededicates himself to the quest, he insists that the true knight, before engaging in a great feat of arms, should seek the protection of his idealized lady and recite his mantra of faith and devotion. With her shimmering image before him, Don Quixote—like Dante illuminated by the saintly Beatrice—presses on, not in the least daunted by recurrent disasters.

Cervantes presses the parody of chivalric romance by giving Don Quixote repeated opportunities to turn back; at the same time, the author intensifies the reader's admiration for the beat-up old antihero who, like Joseph Heller's Yossarian and Charles Portis's Rooster Cogburn, refuses to quit. Don Quixote and Sancho arrive finally at the island of Barataria on July 21, 1614. The duke and duchess, who intend to mock the wayfarers, undergo a metamorphosis common to readers of Cervantes: they experience a change of heart and sympathize with the old man's refusal to give in to disillusion. They award Sancho a governorship, which he attempts to rule but then abandons partly in disgust and partly because of homesickness for his family. Unlike his master, Sancho is rooted in reality and recognizes that romance lies in the eye of the beholder.

Cervantes ends the episodic journey with the aged knight's denunciation of the false philosophy that inspired him. Again at La Mancha, Don Quixote recuperates. He contracts a dangerous fever, then returns to normalcy and renounces the false persona of the knight-errant and the folly and deception of romance literature. In Part 2, Chapter 16, he declares to his niece with the vehemence of a reformed fanatic:

> I am now the sworn enemy of Amadis of Gaul, and his innumerable brood: I now abhor all profane stories of knight-errantry, for I know only too well through Heaven's mercy and through my own personal experience the great danger of reading them.

After orally composing his will, the old man dies. Samson, seeking to immortalize the nobility, altruism, and charity of his friend, writes that Don Quixote "reck'd the world of little prize, and was a bugbear in men's eyes; but had the fortune in his age to live a fool and die a sage."

Because he preserves Don Quixote's adherence to the ideals of chivalry, particularly justice and innocence, Cervantes deflects satire from the final scenes to allow the reader to admire a latter-day paladin—a courageous, wise, relentless pursuer of truth. As both benefactor and victim of a profane world, Don Quixote maintains his exuberance and challenges all comers, whatever the size, number, or strength. He proclaims in Part 2, Chapter 1:

> But our depraved times do not deserve to enjoy so great a blessing as did those in which knights errant undertook and carried on their shoulders the defence of kingdoms, the protection of damsels, the succour of orphans and wards, the chastisement of the proud, and the rewarding of the humble.

At the end of his failed quest, the self-sacrificing don looks beyond drubbings and pratfalls, a lost ear and ruined armor, unseatings, ridicule, and robberies to his most painful shortcoming—the failure to help others. The humor and parody of Don Quixote's missions lie not in his failures but in his delusion, the unfailing belief in a book definition of valor, "a virtue that lies between the two extremes of cowardice on the one hand and temerity on the other."

Flawed, but at heart right-thinking, Don Quixote satisfies the human need to believe in a code of behavior and a purity of purpose that transcend the ugliness, squalor, greed, sacrilege, rapacity, and treachery of the real world. He expresses to Sancho this need to sacrifice:

> When the head aches all the other members suffer; and so, being your lord and master, I am your head, and you are a part of me since you are my servant; and thus the evil that touches or shall touch me should hurt you, and what touches you should give pain to me.

In clinging to an impossible standard of gentility derived from a lifelong study of romance, the old man epitomizes the seeker. Like Sir Galahad, the don dedicates his mythic quest to a transcendent ideal that lives in his mind and heart and on the pages of his favorite books. Forever removed from the vicious observers who derided his going forth, he refuses to lie in the gutter. As Sancho reminds his dying master:

> You must remember, too, sir, from your books on knight-errantry how common it was for knights to jostle one another out of the saddle, and he who's lying low today may be crowning his victory tomorrow.

The reality of the deathbed scene lifts the satire from mockery to a noble tribute to "Alonso Quixano the Good, commonly known as Don Quixote of La Mancha." (Bloom 1986; Byron 1988; Castiglione 1976; Cervantes Saavedra 1957; Duran 1974; Gilman 1989; Mack 1962; Nabokov 1984; Predmore 1990; Riley 1986; Russell 1985)

See also Cervantes Saavedra, Miguel de; epigram; lampoon; mock epic; trickster.

DOUBLE ENTENDRE

A relative of punning, *double entendre*—literally, "to hear twice"—is a term meaning deliberate ambiguity. The phrase refers to an implied double meaning, the second of which is often sexual, scurrilous, smutty, or, at the least, risqué. In much European satiric verse and drama, for example, word-play on a swordsman's skill with his weapon generally carries an implied parallel to his sexual prowess, the size of his penis, or his macho reputation. Another common double meaning attends "horns," the invisible but public joke at the expense of a cuckolded husband who often is unaware of his wife's infidelity. The lavish punning on simple terms such as "top" and "fall" arouses laughter from a reader or playgoer who recognizes the author's intent to call up visions of a seducer atop a maiden, whose fall is moral rather than physical. A more elaborate allusion to sexual intercourse occurs in the opening scenes of William Shakespeare's *Othello* (ca. 1603) when the villain Iago crudely informs Brabante that his newlywed daughter Desdemona and Othello the Moor "are now making the beast with two backs," a vivid jest on the face-to-face or "missionary" coital position.

At his bawdy best in a spirited passage from Act II, Scene i of *The Taming of the Shrew* (ca. 1589), Shakespeare strikes sparks between Petruchio and his intended on the would-be suitor's first meeting with the notorious "Kate the curst." Their punning bristles with sexual innuendo and animal images:

Petruchio:	Come, come, you wasp; i' faith you are too angry.
Katharina:	If I be waspish, best beware my sting.
Petruchio:	My remedy is then to pluck it out.
Katharina:	Ay, if the fool could find it where it lies.

Petruchio:	Who knows not where a wasp does wear his sting?
	In his tail.
Katharina:	In his tongue.
Petruchio:	Whose tongue?
Katharina:	Yours, if you talk of tales; and so farewell.
Petruchio:	What! with my tongue in your tail?

The implication of cunnilingus derived from a deliberate blurring of the homophones tail/tale is not lost on the modern audience any more than it was on Shakespeare's contemporaries. The macho tone of rough wordplay precedes sleep deprivation, starvation, and the physical and emotional pummeling that Petruchio employs to remake the cursed Kate into an amenable, loving bride.

Segueing into a new set of images equally sexual in implication, the scene demonstrates the playwright's facility with *double entendre*. Shakespeare parallels the bald sexual jest of tongue in tail with the ensuing repartee, which introduces the double meaning of "cock," a face-saving word thrust that proceeds from Kate's slapping her suitor:

Petruchio:	I swear I'll cuff you, if you strike again.
Katharina:	So may you lose your arms:
	If you strike me, you are no gentleman,
	And if no gentleman, why then no arms.
Petruchio:	A herald, Kate? O, put me in thy books!
Katharina:	What is your crest? a coxcomb?
Petruchio:	A combless cock, so Kate will be my hen.
Katharina:	No cock of mine; you crow too like a craven.

Because Kate declines to lower her standards of womanly conduct, the phallic wordplay remains innocently anchored in the barnyard. An even match of saucy ill-humor, the exchange suggests that a perverse kind of respect hovers at the outer edges of both minds—an appreciation for lightly cloaked libido that could produce an admirable mating. However, both characters must play out their respective hostility toward marriage before the resolution and finale, a courtly gesture from Kate, who relents with grace: "My hand is ready; may it do him ease." No less popular today than in Elizabethan time, *double entendre* remains the refuge of the scamp who cloaks shocking or pungent badinage in innocent pretense. (Baldick 1990; Cuddon 1976; Drabble 1985; Gassner 1969; Gray 1992; Holman 1980; McArthur 1992; Shakespeare 1957, 1963)

See also pun; repartee; Restoration drama; Shakespeare, William.

DRYDEN, JOHN

One of England's most versatile writers and its first literary critic, John Dryden belongs in the forefront of verse satirists and comic dramatists. After studying the Roman classics and taking Geoffrey Chaucer, William Shakespeare, Ben Jonson, and, to a lesser degree, John Milton as his masters, Dryden developed a reputation for balance, clarity, and metrical precision. He rewrote Renaissance drama to the taste of the seventeenth century, which demanded reason, restraint, and respect for the unities of time, place, and action. To his works he appended meticulous prefaces explaining his views on wit and humor and listing the criteria by which they should be judged. The impetus to his critical evaluation was, in part, his Puritan upbringing, but also a riposte to Jeremy Collier's infamous attack on Restoration comedy, which Dryden soundly trounced with reason and elegance. Because of his monumental influence on contemporaries, his era was known as the Age of Dryden, yet, the monetary return on his notoriety was pitifully slim.

A native of Aldwinkle All Saints, Northamptonshire, Dryden was born of rural stock on August 9, 1631. He entered Westminster School at age 15 and completed a bachelor's degree at Trinity College, Cambridge. For two years, he served as clerk to Secretary of State John Thurloe. A royalist, Dryden came to manhood during the Commonwealth and composed an obligatory ode on Oliver Cromwell's death, *Heroique Stanzas* (1658). At age 29, Dryden welcomed Charles II and the restoration of both monarchy and theater with the publication of *Astraea Redux* and *To His Sacred Majesty*. Dryden married Lady Elizabeth Howard, sister of his collaborator, Sir Robert Howard, in 1663 and sired three sons. That same year, Dryden was elected to the Royal Society, an attainment attesting to his sobriety and scholarship. Like Samuel Pepys's diary, Dryden's verse *Annus Mirabilis* (1667) comments on the zeitgeist, especially the furor created by an outbreak of bubonic plague, the Dutch War, and the London Fire of 1666, which put him out of work until theaters could be rebuilt.

Unlike writers who could count on patronage or inheritance to support them while they dabbled at art, Dryden wrote professionally as his only means of earning a living. Having received a minor inheritance, he welcomed what freelance work his publisher, Henry Herringman, could provide. During the 1660s and into the 1670s, Dryden steadily poured out witty stanzas and comic songs to flesh out his farces and comedies, including *The Wild Gallant* (1663), *The Rival Ladies* (1664), and *Secret Love, or the Maiden Queen* (1666). His accomplished comic skills continued with *Sir Martin Mar-All* (1667) and *An Evening's Love, or, The Mock Astrologer* (1671). He was surprisingly reticent in public, giving little clue to the mirth he was capable of generating for the stage. His place among Will's Coffeehouse wits hinged on literary achievement and his considerable influence on lesser writers.

A high point of Restoration comedy is Dryden's comic masterwork, *Marriage à la Mode* (1673), which abounds in lighthearted characters, clever repartee, and *double entendre*, some of which derives from models translated from Molière. A glimpse of Dryden's craftsmanship appears in his song proposing a facetious rhetorical question about the purpose of marriage:

> Why should a foolish marriage vow,
>   Which long ago was made,
> Oblige us to each other now,
>   When passion is decay'd?
> We lov'd, and we lov'd out in us both;
> But our marriage is dead, when the pleasure is fled:
>   'Twas pleasure first made it an oath.

Essayist Samuel Pepys reports on the stage production of *Marriage à la Mode*, noting the marvel of Nell Gwyn, a former theater orange seller and the mistress of Charles II, in the starring role as Doralice. Her husband, Rhodophil, bewails his marriage in the strongest possible terms: "The greatest misfortune imaginable is fallen upon me. In one word, I am married, wretchedly married, and have been above these two years." Dryden escapes the cynicism of a potential double adultery by having Rhodophil reevaluate his love for Doralice after his friend Palamede attempts to seduce her. A parallel plot reveals that Rhodophil ogles Palamede's fiancée, whom Palamede begins to love in earnest. The upshot of the double dalliance is that both couples adhere to monogamy by abandoning their silly fantasies. This moral conclusion is central to Dryden's defense of comedy as "divertisement and delight" and his denial that amorality is essential to the farcical representations of matrimony.

While living on Fleet Street and thriving from the company of local wits, Dryden succeeded with tragicomedies and uplifting heroic drama, a short-lived genre: *The Indian Emperor* (1665), *Secret Love* (1667), *Tyrannic Love* (1669), *Almanzor and Almahide* (1672), and *Aurengzebe* (1675), the last of the great rhymed stage epics. These heavy offerings, however well intentioned, met with George Villiers's parody, *The Rehearsal* (1671), a burlesque of Dryden, who is called the Poet Bayes, played by an actor wearing Dryden's typical dress. Undaunted, Dryden survived the ridicule and met audience expectations with his greatest stageplay, *All for Love, or the World Well Lost* (1678), a retelling of William Shakespeare's tragedy of Antony and Cleopatra reset in Restoration high tragedy. In 1668, Dryden published both *An Essay of Dramatic Poesy* and *A Defence of an Essay of Dramatic Poesy*, his learned discourse on the use of the rhymed couplet in stage drama and the establishment of standards of diction for serious writing. His audience appeal earned him sole rights to produce plays for Killigrew's company, to whom he promised three titles annually in exchange for a tenth of the gate, which averaged nearly £400 a year.

Dryden dedicated the last two decades of his career to satire, in part because his arrangement with Killigrew ended in a financial muddle. The first and perhaps most popular satire, *Absalom and Achitophel* (1681), a biblical parody composed at the expense of the Earl of Shaftesbury, grew out of failed Whig attempts to squelch an incipient Catholic branch on the royal genealogy of Charles II. In a subtle gesture to John Milton's gravity, Dryden's brimming couplets chortle:

> Of these the false Achitophel was first,
> A name to all succeeding ages curst:
> For close designs and crooked counsels fit,
> Sagacious, bold, and turbulent of wit,
> Restless, unfixed in principles and place,
> In power unpleased, impatient of disgrace.

He followed with two more episodes mocking the failed Whig leader: *The Medall: A Satyre against Sedition* (1682), a biting ridicule of Shaftesbury's acquittal for treason and his release from the Tower of London, and *Mac Flecknoe, or a*

English critic and dramatist John Dryden, 1631–1700

Satyr upon the True-Blew-Protestant Poet, T. S. (1682), a more personal attack on Dryden's enemy, Thomas Shadwell. The final satire, *The Hind and the Panther* (1687), an allegorical beast fable and apologia, defends Dryden's conversion from Anglicanism to Catholicism in response to the crowning of James II. The work painted a brave front on a decision that cost the poet much gibing for an about-face to please the new Papist king. During this sincere self-study, he withdrew to the home of his friend, Lord Clifford of Devon, for solace and solitude.

The success of Dryden's first two eras of creative output earned him the title poet laureate and the honorary title of Historiographer-Royal in 1670. The pay of £200 was largely an honorarium, which was delayed by treasury incompetence or royal lapse. With the accession of William and Mary in 1688, Dryden lost his court appointment altogether—ironically, to his enemy Thomas Shadwell—and, like Alexander Pope, was forced to move farther from town and to pay the double taxes levied against Catholics.

Because of his political realignment, Dryden became the hireling of the Count of Abingdon, who commissioned "Eleonora," a poem to honor the dead countess. Dryden grasped at translation as a means of adding to his declining income. He wrote sporadically for the theater but could no longer count on the waning popularity of the stage as a prime employer. At age 66, he published his translations of Ovid, Juvenal, Theocritus, Horace, Persius, and Virgil; the success of the complete works of Virgil brought in a windfall of £1,400. Shortly before Dryden's death on May 1, 1700, he withdrew to Cotterstock and completed *Fables Ancient and Modern,* a jolly collection adapted from Chaucer, Boccaccio, Ovid, and Homer concluding with "The Secular Masque." His last days were marred by such ill health and poverty that he wrote up to his final hour. His friends took up a free-will donation to pay for his burial. He is interred in an honorable spot—Poets' Corner of Westminster Abbey. (Bermel 1982; Brockett 1968; Burdick 1974; Drabble 1985; Dryden 1953, 1959, 1973; Eagle and Stephens 1992; Gassner and Quinn 1969; Highet 1962; Hornstein 1973; Kunitz 1952; Magill 1958; Magnusson 1990; Person 1988; Pollard 1970; Roberts 1962; Van Doren 1936; Wilson 1965)

See also allegory; beast lore; burlesque; *double entendre;* farce; masque; Molière; parody; Pope, Alexander; repartee; Restoration drama; satire.

THE DUNCIAD

A Restoration-era model of private griefs aired Juvenalian style, Alexander Pope's *The Dunciad* (1728) has undergone a series of reevaluations from its publication date to the present. Originally labeled by a host of anti-Pope critics as a self-aggrandizing diatribe, the satire has gained appreciable acclaim for its articulate style, emulation of the epic, and droll comedic images. Pope was overcharged with disgust after the publication of Lewis Theobald's studies in Shakespeare. Pope selected the critic to serve as king of dunces in his tribute to dullness. The storm of protest and laughter that resulted inspired Pope's *Dunciad Variorum* (1729), an updated version of his first two volumes. Completed in 1743 with two more volumes, *The Dunciad* altered its course from satirizing Lewis Theobald to ridiculing Colley Cibber, a second-rate writer whom Pope selected as the epitome of mediocrity. The preface that publishers appended suggests an unnamed writer's touch and perspective. Critics speculate that Pope's friend, Jonathan Swift, was the only author skillful enough to compose an introduction for *The Dunciad*.

In Pope's four-book microcosm, humankind struggles to defeat its bestial side and promote nobler instincts. Writers in particular are wont to favor the ambitious, self-indulgent aspects of their personalities to the detriment of reason and logic. The title, a derivative of Homer's *Iliad* and Virgil's *Aeneid*, means "sons of dunces," a prediction that the era of fools and dullards is prologue to a genealogical deluge of dullness. William Cleland's tongue-in-cheek letter to Pope's publisher introduces the personal bias for which Pope's work is lambasted:

> If Obscurity or poverty were to exempt a man from satire, much more should Folly or Dulness, which are still more involuntary; nay, as much so as personal Deformity. But even this will not help them: Deformity becomes an object of Ridicule when a man sets up for being handsome; and so must Dulness when he sets up for a Wit.

Because Pope suffered from a severe skeletal malformation, he appears to speak through Cleland, who maligns Pope's mockers. The alternative explanation for the letter is that Pope concocted the lengthy introduction as a mask for his venom, which concludes, gracefully and tastefully, with a note to the *cognoscenti*:

> As to his Poem, those alone are capable of doing it justice, who, to use the words of a great writer, know how hard it is (with regard both to his subject and his manner) *vetustis dare novitatem, obsoletis nitorem, obscuris lucem, fastiditis gratiam* [to give novelty to the out-of-fashion, allure to the obsolete, light to the dim, and grace to the fussbudgets].

The intense, concentrated effort, resulting in four books opposing the publication of dense, uninspired works, contains dated references to paltry hack writers and critics of the early eighteenth century. Ironically, it is Pope's challenge to them that preserves their names and works from well-deserved oblivion.

Book I launches his poem with a call to the muse, the epic poet recounts the era of Queen Anne and asks that no reader mourn the dull past, for she has spread her wings over developing possibilities "to hatch a new Saturnian age of Lead." Sequestered in the "Cave of Poverty and Poetry," Bays attempts to prosper amid a chaos of literary devices and traditions by burning the classic masters and tossing on the pyre the also-rans of the day. The Queen douses the fire, rescues the soggy dreck from extinction, then elevates Bays to the post of Poet Laureate.

In Book II, as king of dunces, Bays looks over a court clogged with patrons, booksellers, critics, and phantom poets. With mock piety, the ritual turns to high ceremony:

> In office here fair Cloacina stands,
> And ministers to Jove with purest hands.
> Forth from the heap she picked her votary's prayer,
> And placed it next him, a distinction rare!

The fecal goddess, whose name derives from the Latin for sewer, has collected filthy jests by eavesdropping on "linkboys vile, and watermen obscene." The scatalogical references attest to Pope's fervor in lampooning the worst of England's poetasters, who compete in classic games of tickling, vociferation, and diving in hellish, fetid waters.

Pope ends Book II with an exciting conclusion to the final event of literature's Olympic games: Arnall is drawn into a lair of brown-stained nymphs swimming in muck, who compete for his affections:

> . . . sinking to the chin,
> Smit with his mien, the Mud Nymphs sucked him in:
> How young Lutetia, softer than the down,
> Nigrina black, and Merdamante brown,
> Vied for his love in jetty bowers below,
> As Hylas fair was ravished long ago.
> Then sung, how shown him by the Nut-brown maids
> A branch of Styx here rises from the Shades,
> That tinctured as it runs with Lethe's streams,
> And wafting Vapours from the Land of Dreams.

The audience, composed of "Three college Sophs, and three pert Templars," possess similar tastes and talents. To the panoply of literary competition, they send up a unified hum as "they stretch, they yawn, they doze." The triumphant day ends appropriately with "soft gifts of Sleep."

In Book III, the goddess is pleased that the king of dunces has made a grand showing and removes him to her throne to sleep with his head on her lap. Like Aeneas following the Cumaean sibyl into the underworld, the king dreams of a visit to the River Lethe, where the shoddiest of publishing firms readies souls of future dullards and ignoble critics for their passage on earth:

> Millions and millions on these banks he views,
> Thick as the stars of night, or morning dews,
> As thick as bees o'er vernal blossoms fly,
> As thick as eggs at Ward in Pillory.

A parody of Aeneas's journey to the underworld in the *Aeneid*, this segment gives Pope another opportunity to catalogue the hundred worst: Popple, Durfey, Ward, Horneck, Goode, Roome, "Each Songster, Riddler, every nameless name," all forgettable except for Pope's temporary spotlight on their inadequacy.

Book IV prefaces the establishment of a "kingdom of Dulness." A single ray of light searches the anarchy on earth:

> Now flamed the Dog star's unpropitious ray,
> Smote every Brain, and withered every Bay;
> Sick was the Sun, the Owl forsook his bower,

The moon-struck Prophet felt the madding hour:
Then rose the Seed of Chaos, and of Night,
To blot out Order, and extinguish Light,
Of dull and venal a new World to mold,
And bring Saturnian days of Lead and Gold.

Pope emphasizes that science, wit, logic, and rhetoric are helpless to halt the progress of philistinism over London; universities do nothing to abate the publication of ill-favored literature. Parading like mummers, the philosophers, freethinkers, and other anomalies await a taste of the cup of oblivion and anticipate the meaningless honoraria and privileges that deck the unworthy. Pope concludes with an anthem honoring the coming spate of poetasters. In a fitting fade-out for his hilarious allegory, truth slinks back to her cave, leaving philosophy, religion, and morality to die unchampioned. Like stage tragedy, the mock epic ends with a falling curtain, which cloaks the audience in darkness.

Often accused of compensating for withered limbs, diminished height, and humped back by sharpening his pen and dipping it in vitriol, Pope had a nobler impetus to write satire: he gagged on the materialism, pseudo-intellectualism, and shallowness of his age. Never far removed from quarrels with venal popinjays and would-be literati, he published four versions of *The Dunciad* as a frontal assault on the worst of the lot: Edmund Curll, the least principled of book pirates; bluestocking Lady Mary Wortley Montagu, Pope's false friend; John Dennis, a crotchety critic; John Oldmixion, a minor historian; poet laureate Colley Cibber; and Lewis Theobald, a critic who denounced Pope for publishing an updated edition of Shakespeare's works. (Bermel 1982; Drabble 1985; Eagle 1992; Highet 1962; Hornstein 1973; Kunitz and Haycraft 1952; Magill 1958; Magnusson 1990; Person 1988; Pollard 1970; Pope 1965)

See also Addison, Joseph; allegory; bathos; caricature; diatribe; Horace; Juvenal; mock-heroic; Pope, Alexander; *The Rape of the Lock;* satire; scatology; *The Spectator;* Steele, Sir Richard; Swift, Jonathan.

DÜRRENMATT, FRIEDRICH

One of the post–World War II nihilists, Friedrich Dürrenmatt epitomizes the writers of the chaotic era in which survivors questioned both values and religion in a world devastated by bombs and genocide. The senseless destruction that decimated the Jewish population, flattened Hiroshima and Nagasaki, burned Dresden, and bombed much of London and Berlin affected creative minds with depleted spirits and restlessness. These artists came to terms with militarism through abstract art, cinema verité, and an experimental theater that searched for meaning amid chaos. Inherently humorous in their juxtapositions, the plays of Dürrenmatt and his contemporaries posed a challenging puzzle for critics and playgoers, who confronted a new, scathing type of satire.

Born in Konolfingen, Berne province, on January 5, 1921, Friedrich Dürrenmatt, Swiss novelist and dramatist, was the grandson of a disgruntled satirist and the son of a Protestant parson in a rural parish. Interested in art in his youth, Dürrenmatt attended the University of Bern and Zurich. He turned to literature in his mid-twenties, learned the trade of fiction writer and critic, and acquired enough patrons to support him. His first play, *Es steht geschrieben* [*Thus It Is Written*] (1947), demonstrates the importance of Bertolt Brecht, whose experimental drama nudged a generation of dramatists from complacency into expressionism. Black humor and the looming fate of humanity fills Dürrenmatt's canon, including *Die Ehe des Herrn Mississippi* [*The Marriage of Mr. Mississippi*] (1952), *Der Besuch der alten Dame* [*The Visit*] (1956), *Romulus der Grosse* [*Romulus the Great*] (1957), and *Die Physiker* (*The Physicists*) (1962). In these major works, the pitiful stratagems to avoid destiny impel individuals to perform good and worthwhile acts, which, in the overall accounting, change the human situation very little and abandon the viewer to a maze of fantasy, irony, and frustration.

As a proponent of the absurdist movement, Dürrenmatt explored the themes of futility and corruption, the interlinking forces that pull his characters into a vortex of negation. By writing grim, pessimistic dramas, he achieves a form of grace through compassion for the small-minded beings reaching up and out of their despair. In *The Visit,* set in Güllen, a provincial, German-speaking burg similar to Dürrenmatt's home, the village thrums with anticipation of the visit of 63-year-old Madame Claire Wascher Zachanassian, the world's wealthiest woman, who has a reputation for generosity to German towns. A clutch of town boosters awaits her arrival. One euphemistically lists her holdings: "Armenian Oil, Western Railways, North Broadcasting Company and the Hong Kong-uh-Amusement District." The welcoming committee pressures Alfred, the local storekeeper and her former lover, to persuade her to invest in the tumble-down village, which lives on dreams of past glories. The men seem diffident. The priest insists that God is their hope; the schoolmaster reminds him dolefully, "But God won't pay."

At the railroad depot, the visitor arrives with an entourage of two blind eunuchs, Husband VII (named "Moby"), Butler Boby, and an empty coffin. Her appearance startles the dreamers, who discover that Claire, a crippled, self-indulgent old matriarch carried in a sedan chair, has halted the express train rather than bother with the local. To quiet the complaining railway inspector, she hands him a $4,000 bribe. In anticipation of shared memories, Alfred reaches for her hand and seizes ivory, one of several prostheses that have marred her former loveliness since a plane crash in Afghanistan. He conceals his revulsion and extracts a promise that she will invest in her old hometown.

Dürrenmatt builds audience expectations in parallel with the hopes of the town. At a formal dinner, Claire jolts both audience and burghers with an unforeseen stipulation: her offer of a billion dollars requires one sacrifice—Alfred's life. The vengeful Claire reveals that in 1910, Alfred spurned her and bribed two witnesses to deny that he sired Claire's unborn child; Claire had to leave Güllen and work as a prostitute in Hamburg. She searched until she located the witnesses, her two bearers, whom she ordered blinded and castrated. In her anguish at reliving the past, she snarls, "The world turned me into a whore, I shall turn the world into a brothel."

The mayor refuses Claire's deal; Alfred insists on justice and promises that he will not complain. The townspeople, misguidedly believing that they will profit from Claire's visit, ignore the moral crisis and spend extravagantly. They turn against Alfred and circle like vultures as the media covers his murder. At the conclusion of the grotesque execution, his corpse is covered with a checkered tablecloth. All disclaim any part in his death: the doctor deduces that he died of a heart attack; the mayor claims that joy killed him. Before a refurbished depot and prosperous villagers, Claire's staff gathers Alfred's remains and places them in the coffin. Impersonal in her charity, Claire passes her check to the mayor on her way to Capri, where a tomb awaits the victim of her vengeance.

Dürrenmatt's lethal satire, heightened by a chorus of villagers in evening wear and formal suits, parodies the high moral tone of a Greek tragedy. The first chorus laments volcanoes, earthquakes, tidal waves, and the atomic bomb; the antiphony decries human treacheries that deprive the poor and nurture greed. The symbolic train, bearing in and out of the world its human freight, carries Madame Claire, her entourage, and the coffin out of town to huzzahs from the mayor, who hails the arrival of boom times. Like a phoenix, Güllen considers itself reborn and prays that no calamity will return it to squalor. (Brockett 1968; Dürrenmatt 1981; Gassner and Quinn 1969; Magnusson 1990)

See also black humor; Brecht, Bertolt; parody; satire; theater of the absurd.

EPIGRAM

A brisk comment, observation, or didactic proverb—sometimes ponderous, waggish, or roguish—the epigram must meet a single criterion: it must illuminate wit in brief. In the clever rendition of Samuel Taylor Coleridge, the epigram is "A dwarfish whole,/Its body brevity, and wit its soul." Whether laced with paradox, replete with religious homiletics, chiseled into elegant epitaph or votive tablet, or honed into a spare antithesis, epigram is the core of the satirist's diet. Built on sagacity, intelligence, reflection, and a wordsmith's love of pithy rhetoric, epigram, derived from the Greek for "inscription," models a truism well stated, as in Lao-Tzu's "Nature is not human-hearted" from the *Tao Te Ching* or the Slovenian saw, "Never whisper to the deaf or wink at the blind." Undergirding its power to impress or instruct is restraint, the writer's inner ear for "enough said."

Often so far removed from the source that it stands apart from the original sentiment, the epigram attains a life of its own, as is the case with "Sweets to the sweet," the parting phrase Queen Gertrude utters over the open grave of Ophelia, her intended daughter-in-law, following the demented girl's accidental drowning in a willow-shaded brook in William Shakespeare's *Hamlet* (ca. 1599). In context, the introductory words suit a somber occasion:

> Sweets to the sweet: farewell!
> I hop'd thou shouldst have been my Hamlet's wife;
> I thought thy bride-bed to have deck'd, sweet maid,
> And not have strew'd thy grave.

A wistfully sad farewell, the phrase, which precedes virulent fighting and the deaths of the remaining major characters, has slid from tragedy to sappy cliché and now accompanies vases of sweetheart roses, flowery valentines, and Godiva chocolates.

The joy of the intelligentsia and punsters, the ammunition of politicians and satirists, the epigram was also the mainstay of Confucius, Lao Tzu, Mohammed, David the Psalmist, and Jesus. It sparks works by classic Greek and Roman playwrights and orators, from Aristophanes, Plato, and Demosthenes to Cicero, Martial, and Juvenal. Letter writers such as Pliny the

Younger and literati of the stature of Horace and Virgil left a wealth of one-liners as familiar as Virgil's "Love conquers all." Meleager (ca. 100 B.C.) compiled a collection of favorites that he entitled *Stephanos* or *The Garland*; an anonymous collector gathered the favorite ancient Mediterranean aphorisms into *The Greek Anthology* (A.D. 925). Whether modeled on the timeline form of *Bartlett's Familiar Quotations* or classed by gender (*The Beacon Book of Quotations by Women*), theme (*The Great Quotations*), place (*The International Dictionary of Quotations*), or type (*The Oxford Book of Literary Anecdotes*), subsequent compendia are standard reference books or computer CDs frequently consulted by the writer, reader, scholar, politician, layout editor, and after-dinner speaker.

A true literary form, the epigram may combine numerous rhetorical devices to impart its grain of wisdom. These examples embody wit, chagrin, spirit, and grace:

Adage:	I hate a pot-companion with a memory. (Erasmus, *The Praise of Folly*, 1509)
Allegory:	He that riseth late must trot all day, and shall scarce overtake his business at night; while Laziness travels so slowly, that Poverty soon overtakes him. (Benjamin Franklin, *Poor Richard's Almanack,* 1784)
Anticlimax:	They told me how Mr. Gladstone read Homer for fun, which I thought served him right; and that it would be a great pleasure to me after life. (Winston Churchill, 1930)
Antithesis:	I have changed my ministers, but I have not changed my measures. . . . (Queen Anne, speech, 1711)
Apostrophe:	O kind missionary, O compassionate missionary, leave China! come home and convert these Christians! (Mark Twain, *Europe and Elsewhere*, 1923)
Dialect:	Watch out w'en youer gittin' all you want. Fatten' hogs ain't in luck. (Joel Chandler Harris, *Nights with Uncle Remus*, 1883)
Direct address:	Brothers! I have listened to a great many talks from our Great Father. But they always began and ended in this—"Get a little farther; you are too near me." (Speckled Snake, speech to the Creeks, 1829)
Epitaph:	Here lies my wife: here let her lie! Now she's at rest, and so am I. (John Dryden)
Humor:	Until you've lost your reputation, you never realize what burden it was or what freedom really is. (Margaret Mitchell, *Gone with the Wind*, 1936)
Hyperbole:	I wasn't used to children and they were getting on my nerves. Worse, it appeared that I was a child, too. I hadn't known that before; I thought I was just short. (Florence King, *Confessions of a Failed Southern Lady*, 1985)
Paradox:	When I give food to the poor, they call me a saint. When I

ask why the poor have no food, they call me a Communist. (Don Helder Camara)

Parallelism: Humor to me, Heaven help me, takes in many things. There must be courage; there must be no awe. There must be criticism, for humor, to my mind, is encapsulated in criticism. There must be a disciplined eye and a wild mind. There must be a magnificent disregard for your reader, for if he cannot follow you, there is nothing you can do about it. (Dorothy Parker, *The Most of S. J. Perelman*, 1953)

Periodic sentence: It's one of the tragic ironies of the theater that only one man in it can count on steady work—the night watchman. (Tallulah Bankhead, *Tallulah*, 1952)

Repetition: Our lives are frittered away by detail. . . . Simplify, simplify. (Henry David Thoreau, *Walden*, 1854)

Repetitive cognates: Man proposes but God disposes. (Thomas à Kempis, *Imitation of Christ*, ca. 1420)

Rhetorical question: How could a better ending be arranged?
Could one change people? Can the world be changed?
Would new gods do the trick? Will atheism?
Moral rearmament? Materialism? (Bertolt Brecht, *The Good Woman of Setzuan*, 1940)

Rhymed couplet: "Lord!" cried my Lady Wormwood (who loves tattle, And puts much salt and pepper in her prattle). (Richard Sheridan, *The School for Scandal*, 1777)

Understatement: The three great stumbling blocks in a girl's education . . . *homard a l'Américaine* [American lobster], a boiled egg, and asparagus. (Colette, *Gigi*, 1942)

Whimsy: Strange, when you come to think of it, that of all the countless folk who have lived before our time on this planet not one is known in history or in legend as having died of laughter. (Max Beerbohm, *Laughter*, 1911)

Wit: For what I have published I can only hope to be pardoned; for what I have burned I deserve to be praised. (Alexander Pope)

Whether salty, instructive, or wickedly lascivious, the epigram addresses, reproves, and summarizes much of history and literature in monuments and chapter headings, tombstones, needlepoint samplers, and wedding rings. By nature concise, aphoristic sayings may follow either verse or prose style. At its best, the epigram gains thrust and meaning from a clever coupling of metered lines ending in masculine or feminine rhyme. For example:

Feminine: Men seldom make passes
At girls who wear glasses.
(Dorothy Parker, "News Item")

MAXIMS AND MORALS

FROM

DR. FRANKLIN:

BEING

INCITEMENTS TO INDUSTRY, FRUGALITY AND PRUDENCE.

He who by the plough would thrive,
Himself should either hold or drive.

LONDON:

PRINTED FOR DARTON AND HARVEY,
GRACECHURCH-STREET.

1807.

American inventor, statesman, and wit Benjamin Franklin wrote epigrams, short poems, some of which were published in *Maxims and Morals* in 1807.

Masculine: License my roving hands, and let them go,
Before, behind, between, above, below.
(John Donne, "To His Mistress Going to Bed")

However, the difficulty of encompassing so compressed a twist of humor and logic in a translation—especially from classic Hebrew, Greek, or Latin or from outdated Native American, Asian, or African tongues to modern European languages—usually yields only a hint of the original cadence and underlying meaning. The most succinct, for example, Virgil's "anguis in herba" or "a snake in the grass," is fair game for even beginning translators. A more demanding turn of phrase, Pliny the Elder's "sal Atticum" or "Attic wit," presents a minor challenge, especially the second English word, which substitutes the abstraction "wit" for the concrete Latin "salt." A greater challenge is North Carolina's motto "Esse Quam Videri" or "to be rather than to seem," which offers a false semblance of one-for-one translation despite the fact that the English phrase doubles the number of words necessary to capture the brief Latin maxim and murders the rhythmic trimeter. One of the most compact of Terence's lines, "suo quoque mos [literally, to each his own custom]," has undergone an unusual translation in that the English version is more abstract: "to each his own."

In context, epigrams often express a satiric or didactic message that lifts the passage from the mundane to a higher or more meaningful plane. In Thornton Wilder's *The Matchmaker* (1954), a comedy that has resurfaced numerous times, including the Broadway play and film *Hello, Dolly* (1969), the central character, Dolly Levi, pauses for a heart-stirring moment in the final scene to address the spirit of Ephraim, her deceased husband. To justify her decision to remarry, she tells him: "There comes a moment in everybody's life when he must decide whether he'll live among human beings or not—a fool among fools or a fool alone." The wistful tone presides over a lengthy soliloquy in which Dolly expresses the hardships of widowhood and earning a living. She rounds out her tender speech with the pragmaticism that energizes her character: "Money, I've always felt, money—pardon my expression—is like manure; it's not worth a thing unless it's spread about encouraging young things to grow." The comic aphorism mirrors the conclusion, in which a young couple decide to marry during the weighty discussion of Horace Vandergelder, who doesn't yet recognize that Dolly is the future Mrs. Vandergelder. (Abrams 1971; Auden and Kronenberger 1966; Abrams 1971; Baldick 1990; Barnet, Berman, and Burto 1960; Brecht 1967; Churchill 1967; Cuddon 1984; Drabble 1985; Ehrlich 1985; *Encarta* 1994; Erasmus 1941; Feinberg 1967; Franklin 1987; Gassner and Quinn 1969; Gray 1992; Hammond and Scullard 1992; Holman 1980; Hornstein 1973; Howatson 1989; Kaplan 1992; Levin and Hyman 1958; Maggio 1992; Man-tinband 1956; Rawson and Miner 1986; Seldes 1967; Shakespeare 1967; Sheridan 1967; Sutherland 1975; Turner 1974; Wilder 1958)

See also allegory; Aristophanes; Beerbohm, Max; Brecht, Bertolt; Colette; didacticism; Dryden, John; Franklin, Benjamin; Harris, Joel Chandler; Horace; hyperbole; Juvenal; King, Florence; Martial; Parker, Dorothy; Pope, Alexander; pun; *Sermones*; Shakespeare, William; Terence; Twain, Mark; whimsy; wit.

EPISTOLARY NOVEL

A stylized form of long fiction, the epistolary novel records its action and commentary in letter form, as in Aphra Behn's *Love Letters between a Nobleman and His Sister* (1682). The most famous epistolary fiction dates to the eighteenth century: Samuel Richardson's *Pamela* (1741) and *Clarissa Harlowe* (1748), Tobias Smollett's *Humphrey Clinker* (1771), Henri Rousseau's *La Nouvelle Héloise* (1761), Fanny Burney's *Evelina* (1778), and Choderlos de Laclos's *Les Liaisons dangereuses* (1782), which Christopher Hampton adapted into a play and Oscar-winning screenplay, *Dangerous Liaisons* (1988), starring Glenn Close, John Malkovich, and Michelle Pfeiffer. More recent epistolary novels include J. P. Marquand's *The Late George Apley* (1937), Saul Bellow's *Herzog* (1964), and John Barth's *Letters* (1979).

A limited form of expression, the epistolary novel, which is usually reflective, lacks spontaneity and surprise. Just as retold jokes lose their sparkle and spur-of-the-moment anecdotes stale in the retelling, epistolary form, by its constraints on point of view, covers a narrow sphere of interest. Described by Martin Buber as an "I-Thou" relationship, the tête-à-tête exchange between two parties encourages intimacy, while simultaneously drawing invisible walls around both parties. In like fashion, verse apostrophe follows the conventions of speaker to receiver, as in this stanza from Robert Burns's "Epistle to J. Lapraik" (1786):

> Your critic-folk may cock their nose,
> And say, "How can you e'er propose,
> You wha ken hardly verse frae prose,
>   To mak a sang?"
> But, by your leaves, my learnèd foes,
>   Ye're maybe wrang.

In its own way, the verse demonstrates epistolary style; however, the one-sided nature of writer to receiver contrasts with the greater opportunity of the novelist to develop a two-sided give and take. A novelist can thus explore more deeply satire's malleability by enhancing caricature or advancing opposing sides of a squabble or controversy, which Burns indicates he combats in his letter to a critic.

The epistolary novel often requires the narrator to recount a complex conversation in order to maintain ongoing relationships between characters. Because of its intimate, first-person approach to events and their interpretation, a fictional letter story, like the journal or diary, often produces humor or dramatic irony beyond the ken of the speaker or speakers, as in the case with Celie, protagonist of Alice Walker's *The Color Purple* (1982). Immediately after discovering that her abusive husband, called "Mr.," has stashed 30 years' worth of correspondence from her beloved sister Nettie, who has been living in Africa, Celie writes to God. Still in shock, she reports a philosophical discussion of murder she holds with Shug Avery, who urges her not to kill:

> But it so hard, I say, while Shug empty her suitcase and put the letters inside.
> Hard to be Christ too, say Shug. But he manage. Remember that. Thou Shalt

> Not Kill, He said. And probably wanted to add on to that, Starting with me.
> He knowed the fools he was dealing with.

As Alice Walker demonstrates, even the subjects of deities and murder enrich satire aimed at a cruel patriarchy that pushes women to desperate acts. (Abrams 1971; Baldick 1990; Burns 1948; Cuddon 1984; Drabble 1985; Ehrlich 1985; *Encarta* 1994; Gassner 1969; Gray 1992; Hampton 1985; Holman 1980; Hornstein 1973; Walker 1982)

See also African-American satire; Behn, Aphra; caricature; Richardson, Samuel.

ERASMUS, DESIDERIUS

The learned Dutch humanist, correspondent, and benefactor of learning who was painted by Hans Holbein and admired by Renaissance humanists, Desiderius Erasmus achieved recognition early in his career for his satiric *Encomium Moriae [The Praise of Folly]* (1509). Born in Gouda or Rotterdam on October 26 or 27, 1466, he was the second child of the illicit union of Margaret and Father Roger Gerard. His foster father, Peter Winckel, tutored him in elementary subjects. From 1475 to 1483, Erasmus and his older brother Peter attended the ultraliberal St. Lebwin's School of the Brothers of the Common Life in Deventer and served as choirboys at Utrecht. In 1484, his parents died of plague. Unpleasant experiences in the closed campus of Hertogenbosch repelled Erasmus from the stringently guarded side of the cloister, which he later embraced after Catholicism flowered from the influence of early Renaissance humanism. Never completely won over to religion but left with little choice after his guardians spent his inheritance, he maintained a love of the pagan satirists—Juvenal, Martial, Lucian, and Terence—whose wit colored his thinking and prose.

Peter took leave of his brother to enter a cloister at Sion outside Delft; Erasmus—having settled on a patronym other than that of his father—entered the priesthood in Steyn as an Augustinian, then came under the patronage of Henry of Bergen, the bishop of Cambrai. Freed from the monastery, Erasmus traveled Europe and studied theology at the University of Paris, where physical illness presaged his heart-weariness with irksome dogma. In one of his despairing moods, he complained that pious nitpickers preached more sermons on giving up butter and cheese for Lent than on love for humanity. He taught rhetoric in Lubeck from his original satiric text, *The Colloquies of Erasmus* (ca. 1510). After securing William Blount, Lord Mountjoy, as a dependable patron, Erasmus tutored in Italy, obtained his doctorate at Turin, lectured on Greek and the writings of St. Jerome from 1511 to 1514 at Queen's College, Cambridge, and debated aspects of humanism with Thomas More, John Colet, William Latimer, and other scholars of his day.

The canon of Erasmus's works before the *Encomium* includes his *Adagia*

[*Adages*] (1500), a respectable assortment of 3,000 classical epigrams. One of his oft-quoted comments in the *Adagia*—"In the country of the blind the one-eyed man is king"—epitomizes his exasperation with church pedants who fail to recognize parishioners' needs. A more risqué lampoon against the pope appeared in 1514, the anonymous *Julius exclusus* [*Julius Shut Out (of Heaven)*]. Erasmus went through the motions of denying authorship, but he appears to have written out of spite toward church hierarchy and papal malfeasance.

Upon losing his freedom and being recalled to monastic life in 1514, Erasmus implored the pope to allow him to continue the scholarly life. Pope Leo X agreed to his request and allowed him to dispense with his Augustinian habit as well. In 1516, as the culmination to Erasmus's studies in Greek, he edited the *Novum instrumentum*, a translation of the New Testament, and dedicated the volume to Leo. The work, which corrected six hundred textual errors, may have served William Tyndale in his translation of an English Bible and provided church reformers with a more substantial working text.

At the beginning of the Reformation, Erasmus kept in contact with leading sources of religious unrest but maintained a neutral stand. He studied sacred languages from 1517 to 1521 at Louvain; after settling in Basel, he produced significant tomes of scholarly discourse on early church doctrine and is considered the first New Testament scholar. Although Erasmus supported freedoms of devotion and worship, his tract "Free Will" (1524) appears to contradict the teachings of Martin Luther, which he spurned for the chaos they caused and the mean-spirited aggression that arose against Catholicism and holy relics. Near the end of his life, Erasmus grew weak from lifelong illness, gave up writing, and withdrew to a protective cell at Basel at a time when the Vatican council was considering him for a cardinal's post. Having settled his affairs and sold his books, he died July 12, 1536, without a mitre; he was vilified by the next two popes, who banned his writings.

An influence on François Rabelais, Erasmus nurtured pre-Renaissance individuality. He dedicated to Thomas More *The Praise of Folly*, a study in irony written in a week while Erasmus recovered from illness in England. The satire follows the Lucian style and remained in vogue throughout the Renaissance. A fulsome lay sermon attacking rhetoricians, attorneys, sophists, logicians, preachers, scientists, tipplers, ignoramuses, fops, egotists, ascetics, and prelates, *The Praise of Folly* exhibits some of the frustrations and paradoxes of the author's life, which he dedicated to morality and truth. The work is a four-part parody of corruption that covers folly's introduction, her functions in human delight, her disciples, and Christian fools. A monologue spoken by the symbolic figure Folly, a talkative female who comments on all branches of society, the comic essay ultimately allows folly to triumph over wisdom. *The Praise of Folly* so delighted Erasmus's humanist colleagues that he journeyed to Paris in 1511 to have the work printed in secret. Before the end of the year, it had gone through seven printings.

Translated by Sir Thomas Chaloner in 1549, *The Praise of Folly* opens with Chaloner's epistle, then launches its fervid philosophy from a female perspective. Folly notes that she is reviled by many as foolish or profane, but she retaliates with strong sense:

> Whereas men come forth disguised, one in one array, another in another, each playing his part till at last the maker of the play or book-bearer causeth theim to avoid the scaffold, and yet sometime maketh one man come in two or three times with sundry parts and apparail, as who before represented a king, being clothed all in purple, having no more but shifted himself a little should shew himself again like an wobegone miser.

Folly extends the metaphor of the stage with a note that good Christians, who claim to look forward to heaven, have little reason to complain when their lives end and the new role begins.

The energetic prose that Erasmus puts into the mouth of his speaker lampoons those who take ecclesiastical excess as a right and privilege. Among the ramblings of Mistress Folly are these quotable comments:

- Nothing is more fond than prudence out of season.

- It is folly alone that stays the fugue of Youth and beats off louring Old Age.

- They may attack me with an army of six hundred syllogisms; and if I do not recant, they will proclaim me a heretic.

A strong vein of irony points to holy men who spend much time in learning and books, then behave as though they have learned little. Folly claims that they roar like asses in their monasteries, feeding "sainets' ears with a mervailous melody." Outwardly dressed in sackcloth, they take care to hide fine linens nearer the skin. Having given up women and wine, they delight in debating the finer points of ritual and ceremony, but give no thought to modeling themselves after Christ. In their haste to embrace the name of Grey Friars, Benedictines, Jacobites, and Augustinians, they reject so fitting a name as Christian.

In the final chapter, the speaker grows serious about her subject in a reminder that Christ's sacrifice was a recompense for foolish humankind and that his teachings tended toward the silly and trivial—"children, lilies, mustard-seed, and sparrows—witless things and deficient in sense, living their lives by the guidance of nature with no art or anxious care." Out of patience with martyrdom, the self-righteous speaker plunges into didactic mode as she upbraids the clergy for overlooking sin, treating enemies as friends, and giving up pleasure, food, sleep, rest, and content in the pursuit of the Christian principle of *summum bonum* (the greatest good). At the end of her peroration, Folly admits that she has "long since forgotten myself and run out of bounds." With a hasty apology for her *satura*, she concludes with a command to "Applaud . . . live . . . drink . . . O most distinguished initiates of Folly!" (Drabble 1985; Eagle and Stephens 1992; Erasmus 1941, 1954; Gentz 1973; Magill 1958)

See also didacticism; epigram; folly literature; irony; Juvenal; Martial; parody; Rabelais, François; satire; Terence.

ETHEREGE, GEORGE

A dashing blade in post-Puritan England, George Etherege fits many descriptions: diplomat, skeptic, courtier, hedonist, deist, libertine, wit, and gentleman. Born in Maidenhead, Berkshire, in 1634, Etherege traveled Europe with his father and was apprenticed to a Buckinghamshire law office. He was only 15 when his father died, the same year that the Puritans drove the monarchists from England. Reared by his grandfather, Etherege withdrew to Paris during the Commonwealth, studied law, and honed his considerable talent at writing frivolous, entertaining comedy of manners, the prevailing style of the post-Puritan period. At an impressionable age, he thrived in the refined milieu of continental graces, dance, and entertaining repartee. When he returned to England in 1663, he found himself the center of interest for his charm and natural skill in conversation.

Etherege's first play, *The Comical Revenge, or Love in a Tub* (1664), a cynical farce, brought him to the attention of the court wits, King Charles's inner circle and the most powerful influences on court entertainment. Etherege's next work, *She Would If She Could* (1668), which, due to poor casting, failed to profit, became a solid audience-pleaser in notable revivals and influenced William Congreve, who learned from Etherege's mistakes. Following its production, Etherege joined the Privy Chamber as secretary to Sir Daniel Harvey and from 1668 to 1771 served as ambassador to Turkey. Upon his return to England, he rejoined the vibrant theater life of the late eighteenth century by composing a prologue for the opening of the Dorset Garden Theater.

Etherege's final work, *The Man of Mode, or Sir Fopling Flutter* (1676), is a blatant satire on Harriet and Dorimant, mirror images of the aristocratic, fashion-obsessed playgoers who patronized the Restoration stage. Beginning with an open censure of England's excesses following the demise of the Puritan commonwealth, the prologue sneers frankly:

> But I'm afraid that while to France we go,
> To bring you home fine dresses, dance, and show,
> The stage, like you, will but more foppish grow.
> Of foreign wares why should we fetch the sum,
> When we can be so richly served at home?

Etherege charges that actors thrive on human folly as doctors live by disease. So rife is England with fools that a new character crops up each day begging to be satirized.

The Man of Mode, composed of a series of facile seductions, pits the rake Dorimant against a tough-minded Harriet. The two spar with words that unmask their vacuous, contrived mannerisms:

> *Dorimant:* As I followed you, I observed how you were pleased when the fops cried, "She's handsome—very handsome! By God she is!" and whispered aloud your name. The thousand several forms you put your face into, then to make yourself more agreeable! How wantonly you played with your head, flung back your locks, and looked smiling over your shoulder at 'em!

> *Harriet:*   I do not go begging the men's, as you do the ladies', good liking, with a sly softness in your looks and a gentle slowness in your bows as you pass 'em-as thus, sir. Is not this like you?

The play prompts an ambiguous pairing of Harriet and Dorimant, settling neither the question of faithfulness nor the matter of who captured whom. The final fillip of the epilogue furthers Etherege's blunt disdain of London's fops who study refined graces, practice cravat-tying, and twirl the tails of perukes in self-satisfied gestures. But no individual need worry about being ridiculed, for, Etherege assures them, "No one fool is hunted from the herd."

Etherege's plots—the arranged betrothals and trysts that sparked the English aristocracy's social intrigues—furnished likely settings for droll satire of fashions, behaviors, and unforeseen menages. Although Alexander Radcliffe fulminated against Etherege for stealing private conversations from the Dog and Partridge, a Fleet street pub, John Dryden, England's first literary critic, lauded the fine style of Etherege's characterization in a quatrain from *MacFlecknoe*:

> Let Gentle George in triumph tread the stage,
> Make Dorimant betray, and Loveit rage;
> Let Cully, Cockwood, Fopling charm the pit,
> And in their folly show the writer's wit.

Knighted by Charles II in 1680 and financially settled for life by his marriage to a wealthy widow, Etherege was himself an example of the pragmatic lifestyle. He moved in and out of public service, serving from 1685 to 1689 as James II's representative to the council of Ratisbon, Germany, about which he kept up a telling correspondence until his death in Paris in 1691. (Baugh 1948; Brockett 1968; Burdick 1974; Etherege 1953; Gassner and Quinn 1969; McMillin 1973; Roberts 1962; Wilson 1965)

See also Behn, Aphra; caricature; comedy; Congreve, William; *The Country Wife;* Dryden, John; repartee; Restoration drama; satire; Wycherley, William.

FABLIAU

A brief ribald tale, the fabliau, a staple verse satire of the Middle Ages, draws on folk anecdote for racy stories often employing scurrilous talk, indecent behavior, revenge motifs, personal indignities, and irreverence, especially borne by the lower classes toward authority, the church, and the elite or pseudo-elite. For good reason, all but 20 of the extant 150 fabliaux are anonymous. Derived from the diminutive of the Latin *fabula* or "discourse," the fabliau, a favorite recitation of wandering scops and gleemen, is basically earthy good fun, often demanding poetic justice for the tormentor, patriarch, or manipulative spouse. The masters of the fabliau were the French, who employed a series of 300 to 400 couplets in octameter to express their cynical, low-life fare over three and a half centuries (1150–1400), when more polished fiction paralleled the growth of the middle class. Like the Italian *commedia dell'arte*, French fabliau concocts myriad plots from the stock figures of rural or village life: the deceptive wife, impetuous lover, coarse neighbor, sly rascal, greedy pinch-purse, nitwit servant, self-important doctor, and irreverent reverend. Significant to the ending is a measure of comeuppance for the trickster, who is not allowed a clean getaway. An obvious antithesis of the formulaic courtly love romance, the fabliau dethrones women from idealized perches and depicts them as willing co-conspirators in duping their husbands out of money or stealing away from the hearth for a romp with a passing tinker or lusty monk.

Raw, comedic folk tales like fabliaux are a staple worldwide in the larder of brief satiric lore. Their occurrence in Asian compendia, oral African lore, Native American song, and the more structured versions in the *Decameron* (1353) by the Italian master Giovanni Boccaccio feeds the universal stock with pungent stories that, but for the costume and dialect, are virtually interchangeable. Written from a whimsical, carnivalesque viewpoint, these plot-heavy stories lack intricacy and character development. Boccaccio's intent is to tease and amuse with droll disclosures or blatantly bawdy jest. His themes encompass human frailties—hypocrisy, ignorance, greed, carnality, religious prejudice, and everyday rascality. The saving grace of his bumptious, frivolous mirth lies in the enjoyment of life, a quality common to the *Carmina Burana* and other collected ribaldry of the Middle Ages.

In the style of Boccaccio's scurrilous tales, the most famous English fabliau, Geoffrey Chaucer's "The Miller's Tale" (1387), spoofs the courtly romance with a risqué plot about a stolen kiss on a posterior "cheek" thrust out a window. Chaucer's fabliaux include:

- "The Reeve's Tale," a domestic entanglement in which clerks get even with a miller for stealing grain by seducing his wife

- "The Merchant's Tale," a comic gulling of the aged, blind January by his libidinous wife May, who copulates with a lover in a pear tree at the strategic moment when January regains his sight

- "The Shipman's Tale," a complex intrigue involving a bawdy wife, stingy husband, and lustful churchman, each of whom repays the other with quid pro quo venality.

The fabliau's joking tone persists through the mock-serious moral, which, in deference to its coarse, rowdy jest, does not embrace the sober control and didacticism of a fable.

Literary imitations of the fabliau are common to masters of short, tightly constructed fiction, notably Anton Chekhov. In his "A Slander," an upper-class wedding brings together the host, Sergei Kapitonich Ahineev, and his wait staff. Because Vankin, a passing usher, hears Ahineev smacking his lips over the jellied sturgeon, he implies that Marfa, the cook, was kissing someone. The more Ahineev tries to squelch the idea that he has bussed the cook, the more the rumor spreads. Within a week, Ahineev's home life founders, his reputation is in tatters, and the upright Vankin claims innocence of the slander. Still in the dark about his guilty coverup of a nonincident, Ahineev ends the story looking for a culprit: "But who, then, who?" (Abrams 1971; Baldick 1990; Barnet, Berman, and Burto 1960; Chekhov 1958; Cuddon 1984; Drabble 1985; Gassner and Quinn 1969; Gray 1992; Holman 1980; Hornstein 1973; Thomas and Thomas 1943)

See also Carmina Burana; Chaucer, Geoffrey; *commedia dell'arte*; didacticism; "The Miller's Tale"; parody; trickster.

FALSTAFF, SIR JOHN

An outrageous, many-sided roisterer who functions as comic relief, despoiler of the innocent, soldier, boaster, brigand, spendthrift, companion, cutpurse, and lay-about, William Shakespeare's Sir John Falstaff is his most satiric characterization. Falstaff retains so lifelike an after-image in the playgoer's mind that he becomes almost palpable. A model figure for satire and frisky comedy, he embodies the Elizabethan distaste for sedate Puritans and the increasingly cumbrous bureaucracy that circumscribed English citizens, often forcing them out of the city to seek entertainment in theaters, which the pious condemned as pleasures of the devil. An amiable scofflaw, Falstaff carries the rank of

Sir John Falstaff woos Mrs. Ford in William Shakespeare's *The Merry Wives of Windsor*. Falstaff, a comic character, first appeared in *Henry IV*.

captain but guards more closely than honor his own precious hide. A realist above all, he knows that wars terrorize, maim, and kill and prides himself in an amoral philosophy that allows much leverage in matters of honesty, courage, and virtue. A comic iconoclast as eager to laugh at himself as to ridicule another, Falstaff stands out among the stock theatrical figure of the self-important *miles gloriosus,* the boastful soldier that dates to ancient classical drama and the *commedia dell'arte* and strides the kabuki stage as the *aragoto,* the menacing military man.

One of the challenges of the critic is to separate Falstaff the ingenuous liar and rogue from Falstaff the scrupulously honest scapegrace. Introduced in

Henvy IV, Parts 1 and 2 (ca. 1596–1597), Falstaff, who is in his late fifties, wenches, drinks to excess, and gorges himself into obesity. In self-jest in Act I of *Henry IV, Part 1*, to Prince Hal, his royal companion who delights in slumming with a handful of highwaymen and mocking scripture, Falstaff accuses:

> Thou has done much harm upon me, Hal; God forgive thee for it! Before I knew thee, Hal, I knew nothing; and now am I, if a man should speak truly, little better than one of the wicked. I must give over this life, and I will give it over: by the Lord, an I do not, I am a villain; I'll be damned for never a king's son in Christendom.

The plan to rob Canterbury pilgrims at the Gadshill junction at four in the morning causes Hal to ponder whether he truly wants to join the band. Falstaff razzes him with the truth about how much honesty attaches to a royal name: "There's neither honesty, manhood, nor good fellowship in thee, nor thou camest not of the blood royal, if thou darest not stand for ten shillings."

Shakespeare uses Hal as devil's advocate and leader into temptation. At the Boar's Head Tavern, Falstaff falls for a delightful parody as Hal imitates the bold warrior Hotspur and draws Falstaff into a pack of lies. In a delightful dramatic irony, the unsuspecting captain expands his bravery with grand hyperbole, then learns that Prince Hal pulled off the prank that spoiled his thievery. Quickly turning the tables on Hal, Falstaff plays the role of the King and chastises Hal for consorting with common outlaws:

> Shall the son of England prove a thief and take purses? a question to be asked. There is a thing, Harry, which thou hast often heard of and it is known to many in our land by the name of pitch: this pitch, as ancient writers do report, doth defile; so doth the company thou keepest: for, Harry, now I do not speak to thee in drink but in tears, not in pleasure but in passion, not in words only, but in woes also: and yet there is a virtuous man whom I have often noted in thy company, but I know not his name. . . . A goodly portly man, i' faith, and a corpulent; of a cheerful look, a pleasing eye and a most noble carriage; and, as I think, his age some fifty, or, by'r lady inclining to three score; and now I remember me, his name is Falstaff.

Later, grown pensive and diffident, Falstaff presents his doubt-ridden credo of honor in a brief summary:

> I was as virtuously given as a gentleman need to be; virtuous enough; swore little; diced not above seven times a week; paid money that I borrowed, three or four times; lived well and in good compass; and now I live out of all order, out of all compass.

The melancholy musings, out of kilter with Falstaff's usual swagger and repartee, foretells a side of the old soldier that becomes clear as battle nears and Falstaff must display his conscripts, the worst of a lot of ancients whom he has taken into his unit in place of men who have bought their deferment at £300 each. No fast talk will get the grand mischief-maker out of this scrape.

The theme of honor, which holds together the disparate parts of the plot, forces from Falstaff some of his most self-revelatory commentary. After Hal allows Falstaff to parade the pathetic band of has-been soldiers, Falstaff notes that the worst of military might is good enough to stop bullets. The thought of dying on the field unsettles the old captain, who discourses to himself one of Shakespeare's memorable treatises on heroism:

> . . . honour pricks me on. Yea, but how if honour prick me off when I come on? how then? Can honour set to a leg? no: or an arm? no: or take away the grief of a wound? no. Honour hath no skill in surgery, then? no. What is honour? a word. What is in that word honour? air. A trim reckoning! Who hath it? he that died o'Wednesday. Doth he feel it? no. Doth he hear it? no. 'Tis insensible then. Yea, to the dead. But will it not live with the living? no. Why? Detraction will not suffer it.

The chivalric code, skillfully stripped of its mystique, replaces Falstaff's braggadocio with sobering thoughts, skillfully debated in parallel questions and self-evident answers. In a swift dismissal of military duplicity, Falstaff settles on the side of self-preservation: "Therefore I'll none of it. Honour is a mere scutcheon; and so ends my catechism." After the battle concludes in Scene IV, Falstaff, mistaken for a corpse and marked for embalming, stabs the corpse of the enemy, just to assure himself that Hotspur is really dead. Then he hoists him in a shoulder carry and trudges off. In his concluding speech, Falstaff, expecting a reward, puns on "growing great" and promises to swear off drink and to live "cleanly as a nobleman should do."

Grown pudgier in *Henry IV, Part 2*, Falstaff requires a suit made from 22 yards of satin and deserves the barmaid's complaint that "there's a whole merchant's venture of Bordeaux stuff in him, you have not seen a hulk better stuff'd in the hold." His old friend Hal's accession to England's throne as Henry V sobers Falstaff considerably, even though the two plays, taken as a unit, serve as a single coming-of-age motif for the next Tudor monarch. Newly crowned and filled with the majesty of office, Hal yanks the humor out of their former relationship by banning Falstaff from within ten miles of the king's presence and warning in the pompous royal "we": "As we hear you do reform yourselves, we will, according to your strengths and qualities, give you advancement." The irony of Hal's reformation is lost on Falstaff, who knew him when he courted grifters and barflies and who suspects that, in private, Hal is still the bon vivant. As though ridding himself of offal, Hal departs, leaving the lord chief justice to deal with an embarrassing relic of the king's disreputable past.

When Falstaff reappears in Shakespeare's working-class morality play *The Merry Wives of Windsor* (ca. 1597), one of the playwright's best-loved so-called women's plays, the aged good-timer has resituated himself as the victim in a masquelike comedy rather than the comic relief in a pair of history plays. The butt of Mrs. Ford and Mrs. Page's manipulative humor, he tries to gull them out of their superiority over men by faking love letters to prove them false to their husbands. In a comic debacle, Falstaff pretends to woo Mrs. Ford. When he learns that her husband approaches, Falstaff hides in a basket of soiled clothes and is dumped in a mucky ditch in Datchet-lane. The second attempt to stain

Mrs. Ford's honor forces Falstaff to dress in women's clothes and flee from a merciless drubbing. Indignant, he complains,

> I was beaten myself into all the colors of the rainbow; and I was like to be apprehended for the witch of Brainford. But that my admirable dexterity of wit, my counterfeiting the action of an old woman, deliver'd me, the knave constable had set me i' th' stocks, i' th' common stocks, for a witch.

Pride, a major component in his makeup, disallows any comparison to a common thug. To Falstaff, being caught is not so grievous as being lumped together with less worthy louts.

The concluding scene destroys the remaining shreds of Falstaff's dignity after tormentors pinch and scorch him. Disguised in a stag's head, he realizes that he has been duped by two female tricksters and falls into a gray funk:

> Have I laid my brain in the sun and dried it, that it wants matter to prevent so gross o'erreaching as this? Am I ridden with a Welsh goat too? Shall I have a coxcomb of frieze? 'Tis time I were chok'd with a piece of toasted cheese.

As satiric farce, the play depicts a slice of Elizabethan pub life. To the detriment of Falstaff, he is removed from the company of military men. The unfamiliar setting deflates his brashness and he is soundly trounced. Because the recurrent figure of Falstaff disappears from Shakespeare's stage plays, critics have surmised that Will Kempe, the professional clown for whom Shakespeare wrote the part of Falstaff, had departed in 1599, leaving no one to flesh out a fuller, subtler satiric role. (Bentley 1961; Bermel 1982; Boorstin 1992; Boyce 1990; Campbell 1943; Chute 1949, 1951; Gassner and Quinn 1969; Muir and Schoenbaum 1971; Sandler 1986; Shakespeare 1974)

See also black humor; caricature; *commedia dell'arte;* diatribe; epigram; farce; hyperbole; incidental satire; irony; pun; sarcasm; Shakespeare, William; trickster.

FARCE

At the far end from serious satire and more sedentary, cerebral comedy, farce occupies a low comedic niche of crude, knockabout, but harmless, amoral hilarity alongside burlesque, camp, situation comedy, and slapstick. Derived from the Latin for "stuffed," the word names a French improvisation tagged onto a play performed in the style of the Greek satyr play or miracle plays such as the *Wakefield Noah* or *The Second Shepherd's Play* (ca. 1450). The extemporaneous nature of farce implies the broad, ragtag rigmarole of slamming doors, sexual innuendo, and coincidental buffeting that compounds a hearty, rollicking stage show. Usually limited in scope and length, farce tends toward skit or blackout, which may end with the collapse of a structure, barroom horseplay, or the explosion of a clown car. The controlling element of farce is confusion or anarchy—the multiple mistaken identities that have the police chasing the wrong suspect, the students running the school, or the father excoriating the wrong suitor. Most significant is the physical energy that impels pursuer and prey round and about, sometimes colliding in mock surprise, scoring with a pie in the face, or assaulting the mark with a madcap, pitiless assault. These set pieces—called *lazzi* in *commedia dell'arte, sotie* in medieval French vaudeville, and shtick on Broadway—require a bit of acting, mugging, asides, and tumbling and a flare for timing, without which these fast-paced scenes would collapse into meaningless mayhem.

Like *commedia dell'arte*, farce draws on make-believe violence, such as striking the panicky adversary with an inflated pig's bladder-on-a-stick, and peoples its scenarios with a host of satiric stock figures, notably the haughty judge or lawyer or the dim-witted servant or flunky. A significant part of Aristophanes's successful *Clouds* and *Wasps* in fifth-century Greece, farce derives from earlier Megaran vaudeville and remains alive in movies, revues, circuses, and local talent shows. The simultaneous launching of Italian *phylax*, or mumming, brought farce to village stages. With a change of scenery, a few new hats and pairs of baggy pants, Aristophanes's comedies became Plautus's *Menaechmi* (second century B.C.), which evolved from the *fabulae Atellanae*, or Atellan farces. In Italy, the torch passed from the *zanni* of the *commedia dell'arte* to France's beloved Molière. Brief vignettes of English farce, pioneered by John Heywood's *The Foure P's* (1545), serve as comic relief in more serious works of the English Renaissance, notably William Shakespeare's most vigorous comedies: *The Comedy of Errors* (ca. 1580), *The Taming of the Shrew* (ca. 1589), *The Merry Wives of Windsor* (ca. 1597), and *Twelfth Night* (ca. 1599). The best alliance of Shakespearean comedy and farce occurs in *Much Ado about Nothing* (ca. 1598), in which Officer Dogberry botches a night patrol that witnesses the undoing of Hero, a virtuous maiden.

In the Restoration era, John Dryden, England's first literary critic, attempted to characterize farce with the reason and control expected in his era. He summarized on the side of incongruity: "A farce is that in poetry, which grotesque is in a picture. The persons and action of a farce are all unnatural, and the manners false, inconsisting with the characters of mankind." In his preface to *An Evening's Love* (1671), the author and critic contends that farce is a lesser form of comedy because it turns to the "monstrous and chimerical" to vent laughter at its whimsy. He notes the irony that farce is more likely to succeed by happenstance because audiences respond to zaniness rather than to the carefully engineered workings of fine comedy.

This left-handed compliment from John Dryden is not the final word on farce. Resurrected in the late Victorian era in Brandon Thomas's *Charley's Aunt* (1892) and Oscar Wilde's *The Importance of Being Earnest* (1895), variations of farce adorned American vaudeville and enlivened the classic cinema foolery of Charlie Chaplin's *Modern Times* (1936), the prophetic, satiric nightmare that depicts the assembly-line worker being pummeled and devoured by a mechanized maw filled with gears, conveyor belts, and cams. Likewise, the screen performances of Buster Keaton, the Marx Brothers, and Laurel and Hardy combine raucous, sometimes picaresque villainy and multiple or serial conflicts as ramshackle and lack-logic as a Rube Goldberg invention. Beginning in the mid-1950s, television showcased the great farceurs of the era: Lucille Ball, Benny

Brandon Thomas wrote *Charley's Aunt* in 1892 as a Victorian farce. In a reprise on Broadway as *Where's Charley?* in 1949, Charley (Ray Bolger) chaperones at tea and pours from a top hat.

Hill, Carol Burnett, Jackie Gleason, and the Three Stooges, all of whom owe homage to their humble farcical forebears of ancient Greece.

The Hollywood farce, with its backup of skilled stunt players and special effects, has advanced the typical improbability of farce from humbler, less eye- and ear-assaulting interaction to silent and early talking movies, with their improbable train wrecks, faked fistfights, and falls from skyscrapers. More recent farcical comedies include Joe Orton's *What the Butler Saw* (1969) and Neil Simon's bedroom farce *The Last of the Red Hot Lovers* (1972), which was made into a movie starring Alan Arkin as the restaurateur and self-styled ladies' man targeting females played by noted comics Paula Prentiss and Sally Kellerman. In these models, farce approaches satire but emphasizes capricious escapades that leave the unstated moral at best optional. A major Broadway contribution to farce, Burt Shevelove and Larry Gelbart's *A Funny Thing Happened on the Way to the Forum* (1962) manages to joke about slavery, lechery, adultery, leprosy, and death while satirizing the patriarchal system of mating, the play's focus. The 1966 film version brought together the considerable talent of the era's best comics: the goo-goo-eyed Zero Mostel, smirky Phil Silvers, and dog-faced Buster Keaton. In 1963, a similar farce—William and Tania Rose's *It's a Mad Mad Mad World*—utilized spirited, at times frantic, pursuits in planes and cars and numerous explosions and cinematic catastrophe. The *tour de force* farce titillated the audience by stockpiling cameos featuring Spencer Tracy,

Jimmy Durante, Milton Berle, Sid Caesar, Ethel Merman, Buddy Hackett, Mickey Rooney, Dick Shawn, Phil Silvers, Terry Thomas, Jonathan Winters, Edie Adams, Dorothy Provine, Eddie Anderson, Jim Backus, William Demarest, Peter Falk, Paul Ford, Ben Blue, Buster Keaton, Joe E. Brown, Carl Reiner, the Three Stooges, ZaSu Pitts, Jack Benny, and Jerry Lewis—surely the longest list of comic skill on a single cinema credit list. Evidently, farce will remain in style as long as people are willing to sit through pseudo-violent clowning to get a good laugh. (Abrams 1971; Baldick 1990; Barnet, Berman, and Burto 1960; Cuddon 1984; Dryden 1973; Gassner and Quinn 1969; Gray 1992; Highet 1962; Holman 1980; Wilson 1965)

See also Aristophanes; black humor; burlesque; camp; comedy; *commedia dell'arte*; Dryden, John; Molière; picaresque; Shakespeare, William; slapstick; whimsy; Wilde, Oscar.

FINN, HUCK

Mark Twain's contribution to world literature includes more than travelogs and frontier "stretchers"; perhaps his most endearing satiric creation is the portrait of a boy torn between the joys of the Mississippi River and the constricting expectations of a genteel society. American fiction's prototypical scamp, Huckleberry, son of Pap Finn, appears as a friend of the title character in *The Adventures of Tom Sawyer* (1876) and stars in *The Adventures of Huckleberry Finn* (1884). Huck's bad influence on good children makes him popular with Tom and his pals but raises suspicion and doubt in churchgoing, ear-washing, mannerly folk who nurture the same respectable practices in their offspring. Approximately 13 years old, Huck, the outcast, "idle and lawless and vulgar," has been around and knows that not all parents deserve obedience and reverence. Partly in awe of his own character, Twain says of his youthful pariah:

> Huckleberry came and went, at his own free will. He slept on doorsteps in fine weather and in empty hogsheads in wet; he did not have to go to school or to church, or call any being master or obey anybody; he could go fishing or swimming when and where he chose, and stay as long as it suited him; nobody forbade him to fight; he could sit up as late as he pleased; he was always the first boy that went barefoot in the spring and the last to resume leather in the fall; he never had to wash, nor put on clean clothes; he could swear wonderfully.

As the motherless son of a vituperative, trashy, sometimes violent alcoholic, Huck savors independence, partly as a means of survival, but also as a blessedly innocent hymn to life. Critics have surmised, not without cause, that the idealized Huck was Twain himself before Livy Clemens took over his life and remade him according to the demands of middle-class Buffalo, New York.

Taming Huck is a chancy affair. After locating $12,000 in *The Adventures of Tom Sawyer,* Huck and Tom share the money, which Judge Thatcher banks for them. Huck accepts the generosity of the Widow Douglas, who considers him "a poor lost lamb" and wants to "sivilize" him. While under her roof, he lives the standard routine of clean clothes, elbows off the table, and a bed with fresh linen. In Huck's words, the botheration wears him down:

> The widow rung a bell for supper, and you had to come to time. When you got to the table you couldn't go right to eating, but you had to wait for the widow to tuck down her head and grumble a little over the victuals, though there warn't really anything the matter with them—that is, nothing only everything was cooked by itself. In a barrel of odds and ends it is different; things get mixed up, and the juice kind of swaps around, and the things go better.

Having tasted the sweet joy of doing as he pleases, Huck struggles with arbitrary rules against smoking. He notes the hypocrisy of the widow's distaste for the practice, but her acceptance of snuff. He adds, "Of course that was all right, because she done it herself."

A persistent obstacle to Huck's contentment is the widow's sister, Miss Watson, who coaches him in spelling and whose list of don'ts extends to posture and deportment. Obsessed with hell and damnation, she tries to Christianize him. Huck maintains skepticism about an afterlife where his friends are not welcome: "I asked her if she reckoned Tom Sawyer would go there, and she said not by a considerable sight. I was glad about that, because I wanted him and me to be together." Still, Huck fears the supernatural and courts a host of charms and spells that remove warts with spunkwater and keep him safe from harm—but not safe from the evils of an abusive father or a nation founded on a narrow form of liberty meant only for people with white skin.

Twain's satire on the worthy example of do-gooders places Huck in one of literature's most researched, discussed, and debated dilemmas. After he runs away to protect himself from the fearful effects of Pap's alcoholic delirium, Huck encounters Jim, Miss Watson's runaway slave, and adds to his list of negatives the pejorative of "low-down abolitionist." Acting on observations of Jim's kindness, good nature, and genuine feeling for family, Huck divests himself of prejudice and embraces damnation as the price of aiding a black friend on his flight north. The powerful wrestlings with self and society occur in Chapter 31, containing the famous letter to Miss Watson. At first, Huck kneels in prayer, "But the words wouldn't come. Why wouldn't they? It warn't no use to try and hide it from Him. . . . You can't pray a lie—I found that out." Compromising his peace of mind, which he has just established by freeing himself from sin, he renounces the confession he plans to mail to Miss Watson: "'All right, then, I'll go to hell'—and tore it up." A pragmatist at heart, Huck concludes, "As long as I was in, and in for good, I might as well go the whole hog."

Throughout the development of Huck's character, the nature of truth and Huck's willingness to express it form the conflict of each episode. To escape the locked cabin, Huck saws free, then goes to elaborate pains to create a crime scene that implicates his father in murder by leaving Pap's whetstone and dragging a sack to leave a trail resembling the removal of a human corpse toward the creek. When the ferry party searches for Huck's corpse, Huck watches from

Huckleberry Finn, hero of Mark Twain's 1884 satirical novel *Adventures of Huckleberry Finn*, is the eternally "idle and lawless and vulgar" thirteen-year-old protagonist. Illustrator E. W. Kemble armed Huck with a rifle and an infectious grin for the frontispiece of the book.

shore and names the familiar faces on deck. On the river run, Huck leaves Jim safe aboard the raft and scours the neighborhood vegetable patches and henhouses for food, then rationalizes his theft of sweet corn and chicken so that his conscience can bear the load of more sins. When bounty hunters prey on the raft, Huck sizes up their fears and pretends to call to them for help, then lets slip that contagion may harm them. The satire ricochets off Huck and onto the dregs of society who would steal the boy's slave and profit from Jim's misery. Twain gets his revenge on the scavengers by having a 13-year-old outwit, outlie, and outmaneuver them.

Twain's satire on the rapacious Duke and King sets up a contrast between a pair of caricatures of frontier frauds and Huck, a harmless youth whose crimes spring from need. At the crucial moment in the conning of the Wilks girls, Huck comes upon a reward for virtue that is new to him. Mary Jane, the first female to touch Huck's heart with romance, expresses her misgivings about packing for England because she grieves for her slaves, whom the Duke and King divided and sold. Without thought to his role in serious crime, Huck spills the truth, but admits, "It's a rough gang, them two frauds, and I'm fixed so I got to travel with them awhile longer, whether I want to or not—I druther not tell you why." Concealing his intention to transport Jim to a free state, Huck presses Mary Jane into action with his backwoods gallantry: "I don't want no better book than what your face is. A body can set down and read it off like coarse print." Twain, a skilled worker of audiences, knows that Huck's pure-hearted admission of love strikes the appropriate note, particularly poignant in an unlettered dialect.

A mix of sentiment, chivalry, boy fun, and satire, Twain's final chapters run a dizzying gauntlet between resolution and Tom Sawyer's creation of more obstacles. Twain's satire feeds on the romantic mindset of boys brought up on pirate lore, twisted tales of the French Revolution, and the interference of adults who place no value on imagination. A comic exchange between Huck and Aunt Sally concerns Huck's theft of butter, which he tucks under his hat. When trickles of yellow liquid ooze down his forehead, she exclaims: "For the land's sake, what is the matter with the child? He's got the brain fever as shore as you're born, and they're oozing out!" The truth of where supplies have been disappearing brings out the mother in Aunt Sally, who, like the Widow Douglas, is ready to forgive rapscallions.

In two quick pages, Twain polishes off Huck's major adventure by accounting for Pap's disappearance (he is found dead in the floating house), ownership of Jim (Miss Watson's will frees him), and Tom's lies to Aunt Sally (she forgives his pranks; he wears a bullet on a watch guard as memento of the trip to Pikesville). In a rush of humor and self-derision, the author speaks through Huck: "If I'd 'a' knowed what a trouble it was to make a book I wouldn't 'a' tackled it, and ain't a-going to no more." The final sentences set up the premise for Twain's unfinished novel, *Huck Finn and Tom Sawyer among the Indians*, by nudging Huck further from adult tyranny and into "the territory," where he doesn't anticipate a need for civility. (Budd 1983; Hoffman 1988; Kesterson 1979; Rasmussen 1995; Twain 1962a, 1962b)

See also caricature; comedy; *A Connecticut Yankee in King Arthur's Court;* diatribe; didacticism; Morgan, Hank; satire; Twain, Mark.

LA FOLLE JOURNÉE OU LE MARIAGE DE FIGARO

Pierre-Augustin Caron de Beaumarchais, author of *Le Barbier de Séville [The Barber of Seville]* (1774), revived his comic character Figaro a decade later in *La Folle journée ou le mariage de Figaro [The Foolish Day's Work, or The Marriage of Figaro]* (1784), a second romantic comedy set in eighteenth-century Spain. Continuing the story of Count Almaviva, who stole the ward of Dr. Bartholo, married her, and has lived three years in happiness, the first act opens on the castle of Aguas Frescas, where Count Almaviva governs Andalusia. In the first scene, Figaro, the trickster, spends the morning of his wedding day measuring the room for a marriage bed, which he longs to share with Suzanne, lady-in-waiting to the Countess Rosine.

The major plot complication occurs when Figaro realizes that the count has wearied of Rosine and now dallies with Suzanne, who owes him the infamous *droit de seigneur,* or the right to her virginity, if she marries in his realm. The resourceful barber nurses a grudge against the count for having thought up an errand to France to part Figaro from Suzanne. He mutters rebelliously:

> While I'm galloping in one direction you'll be progressing nicely in another—with my little wife! I shall be fighting my way through rain and mud for the greater glory of your family while you are condescending to cooperate in the increase of mine. A pretty sort of reciprocity!

Finding Dr. Bartholo at the door, Figaro insults him as well. Marceline, the housekeeper, matches wits with Bartholo in summing up Figaro's qualities:

Bartholo:	That worthless scoundrel!
Marceline:	Never angry, always good-humored, living for the pleasure of the moment, worrying as little about the future as the past, carefree and . . . generous . . . generous as . . .
Bartholo:	As a thief!
Marceline:	As a lord! He's utterly charming!

Marceline complicates the story by holding Figaro to a promise to marry her if he defaults on a loan. A surprise discovery that Figaro is her illegitimate child, fathered by Dr. Bartholo, redirects the action from revenge to reconciliation: Marceline forgives the debt, marries Bartholo, and accepts Figaro as a son.

Meanwhile, Beaumarchais turns an attempted assignation into a romp. Before the count can steal Suzanne, Figaro plots to dress Chérubin, a page, in women's clothes to trick the count. The countess and Suzanne foil the count's plans for a secret tryst in the park, where his wife poses as his love object. Figaro interrupts the romantic idyll with a hefty list of his financial and personal setbacks, an obvious parody of Beaumarchais's topsy-turvy business dealings and troubles with lawsuits:

I dine out in style, and so-called fashionable people throw open their houses to me—keeping three-quarters of the profits for themselves. I could well have restored my fortunes: I even began to understand that in making money *savoir-faire* is more important than true knowledge. But since everybody was involved in some form of swindle and at the same time demanding honesty from me, I inevitably went under again.

The wooing scene and its comic disguises revitalize the count's waning marriage. The author triples the love interest with two more pairings: Figaro marries the feisty Suzanne and earns a fat purse in the bargain, and the hapless page marries a serving girl.

Beaumarchais admits more cynicism into his second play featuring Figaro. In the final scene, a masterpiece of interwoven remarks, slaps, and assorted epithets, there is a scramble for a garter and a concluding song. Suzanne interjects a feminist slant:

> Let a husband break his vows
> It's just a joke the world allows—
> But should a wife like freedom take
> The world will punish her mistake.

Figaro joins in with a wry reminder that wives can always find a way to elude their husband's watch. The judge concludes that the playwright has created a story "true to life/All the fuss, the hubbub-strife." The play closes on a questioning note, as though the author admits to a loving, trusting resolution for the stage only while acknowledging that real life cannot count on perpetual marital bliss and fidelity. (*Amadeus* 1984; Beaumarchais 1964; Cross 1947; Magill 1958; Magnusson 1990)

See also Le Barbier de Séville; Beaumarchais, Pierre-Augustin Caron de; comedy; *commedia dell'arte*; farce; Plautus; repartee; satire; trickster.

FOLLY LITERATURE

An overdone, quasi-legitimate study of foolishness, folly literature, a satire of human idiosyncrasies, has maintained an irregular hold on popularity. It succeeds best when cleverly illustrated by a skilled cartoonist or caricaturist. Perhaps best known as the branch of comedy that champions nonsense or the absurd, folly collections gain strength through multiple examples of ridicule, whimsy, or Rabelaisian fantasy as methods of pillorying the ignorant. Notable collectors of two-dimensional silliness include these:

- Poggio Bracciolini, a papal scribe and compiler of *Facetiae,* which William Caxton published three decades later under the title *Fables of Poge the Florentine* (1484).

- Sebastian Brant, author of *Das Narrenschiff* or *Ship of Fools* (1494), a tedious listing of 112 shipmates displaying idiosyncratic brands of asininity, venality, affectation, and foppery. The upshot of this literary lark is that the ship goes nowhere, but the satire was widely translated and appreciated, particularly by the French and by Desiderius Erasmus, Europe's noted humanist.

- The anonymous collections of reprised medieval fabliaux, picaresque scrapes, and exempla under the titles *A Hundred Merry Tales* (1526), an amusing bagatelle that Shakespeare drew on, and *Merry Tales and Quick Answers* (1535), a set of droll stories capped with a moral.

- John Skelton's *Merie Tales Newly Imprinted & Made by Maister Skelton Poet Laureate* (1567), a loose chronicle of episodic misadventures featuring Skelton and written "very pleasant for the recreation of the mind."

- Thomas Nashe's motley scrapbag, *The Unfortunate Traveller, or the Life of Jacke Wilton* (1594), an ungainly array of parody, satire, and whimsy featuring Jack the soldier, a self-serving rascal as long-lived as the first-person accounts of Archilochus. Jack's misdeeds prefigure the questionable morals of William Shakespeare's Falstaff, Daniel Defoe's Moll Flanders, François Rabelais's Gargantua, Henry Fielding's Tom Jones, John Gay's Macheath, and assorted raggle-taggle adventurers.

A bit more elevated in tone and complex of style than Bracciolini's waggish *Facetiae*, Nashe's picaresque soldiery, and Brant's travel lore is Erasmus's best-selling *Encomium Moriae or In Praise of Folly* (1511), an anticlerical romp jotted down in Latin, dedicated to Thomas More, and translated into English by Sir Thomas Chaloner. In the voice of the comely, evil-tongued wench known only by the allegorical name of Folly who "[doth] glad both the gods and men," the work provides Erasmus an outlet for humorous social commentary on the state of holy orders in his day:

> Nor they look not how to resemble Christ, but sooner how amongs theimselves to be dissemblable, esteeming further a great part of their felicity to consist in the names of their orders. For some of them rejoice to be called Grey Friars, some White, these Colletes, they Minors, other observants, other Crossed, some Benedictines, some Bernardines, these Carmelites, those Augustines, these Guilhermites, those Jacobites, etc. As who saith it were too sclender a name for theim to be called bare Christians.

The seventeenth, eighteenth, and nineteenth centuries frequently reprised this anecdotal mode of comedy with numerous fool books or jest books. Thomas Dekker's *Gull's Hornbook* (1609) cast literary poignards at dandies, strutters, gadabouts, and pompous aristocrats. Alexander Pope's various editions of *The Dunciad* (1728, 1743), which lampoons Pope's critics, Colley Cibber and Lewis Theobald, who panned Pope's edition of Shakespeare, preceded Voltaire's master foolbook, *Candide* (1759), a travelog replete with poseurs, shysters, and ignoramuses. A perennial favorite since the Victorian era is Edward Lear's *A Book of Nonsense* (1846), an illustrated book of limericks written to entertain Lear's grandchildren; less successful is Katherine Anne Porter's *Ship of Fools*

(1962), which follows a group of shipmates sailing from Mexico to pre–World War II Germany. A failed offshoot of fool lore, Porter's novel groups an unremarkable mix of travelers—obstreperous children, a bickering couple, and a heterogeneous band of meddlers, users, drunks, and exhibitionists. (Cuddon 1984; Drabble 1985; Erasmus 1954; Gray 1992; Henry 1995; Hornstein 1973; Rollins and Baker 1954)

See also Archilochus; burlesque; *Candide; Carmina Burana;* comedy; Falstaff, Sir John; Gay, John; limerick; Pope, Alexander; Rabelais, François; Shakespeare, William; Voltaire, François; whimsy.

FRANKLIN, BENJAMIN

One of colonial America's Renaissance men, Benjamin Franklin excelled as journalist and literary hoaxer, philosopher, adviser, statesman, and publisher. A civic gadfly, clerk of the Pennsylvania Assembly, and inventor of the parlor stove, glass harmonica, lightning rod, electrostatic generator, desk chair, and bifocal glasses, he gave full range to his many talents and interests and profited from most of his endeavors. To give back to the city that nurtured him, he improved life for his neighbors by initiating a home guard, lending library, fire and police departments, Freemasonry, street and school improvements, an improved postal system, city hospital, public inoculation against smallpox, philanthropic aids to the destitute, and the University of Pennsylvania. When he retired at age 44, he devoted himself to scientific experimentation. For discoveries concerning electricity, the Gulf Stream, and the tracking of weather fronts, he was elected to the French Academy of Sciences and the Royal Society, Britain's most prestigious scientific enclave and disseminator of learned articles.

A laboring-class Bostonian, Franklin was born January 17, 1706, the tenth of Josiah and Abiah Folger Franklin's 17 children, and remained rooted in the ordinary citizen's point of view. Requiring an errand boy and wick cutter, his father, who manufactured soap and candles, ended the boy's formal education in 1716 after brief tutoring and a year at the Boston Grammar School. Benjamin wanted to go to sea, but his father apprenticed him at age 12 for five years to printer James Franklin, Benjamin's half-brother. While working for James's anti-Tory newspaper, the *New England Courant*, Franklin composed the "Dogood Papers" under the pseudonym Silence Dogood, the chatty wife of a minister. The papers lampoon self-important Bostonians in the manner of Joseph Addison's gently satiric essays in *The Spectator*, which Franklin used as a textbook and vocabulary strengthener. One installment purports to advise the writers of funeral elegies:

> Having chose the person, take all his virtues, excellencies, etc., and if he have not enough, you may borrow some to make up a sufficient quantity: To these add his last words, dying expressions, etc., if they are to be had; mix all these together, and be sure you strain them well. Then season all with a handful or two of melancholy expressions, such as dreadful, deadly, cruel cold death,

unhappy fate, weeping eyes, etc. Having mixed all these ingredients well, put them into the empty scull of some young Harvard (but in case you have ne'er a one at hand, you may use your own); there let them ferment for the space of a fortnight, and by that time they will be incorporated into a body.

The advice concludes with a witty postcript to "Hypercarpus [hypercritical]," who had previously assailed Franklin's essay on pride.

Franklin ended his apprenticeship abruptly after a disagreement over James's high-handed tyranny and the suppression of the press. Because James encouraged local employers not to hire his nettlesome younger brother, the 17-year-old Franklin gave up plans to move to New York and fled to Philadelphia, where he found similar work with Samuel Keimer. While journeying to England to purchase equipment for his press, Franklin discovered that he had been cheated by a patron, Governor Keith, and had to take temporary employment as a printer's devil to earn his fare home. During an 18 months' sojourn in England, he composed a deistic tract, *A Dissertation on Liberty and Necessity, Pleasure and Pain* (1725), evidence that Franklin's promise had blossomed from jocular wit to a mature and sober adult talent.

Intellectual pursuits drove Franklin to read and better himself and to form the first American adult education class, the Junto Club. By age 24, Franklin, posing under the pseudonym of Critico, had published at least 6 of the 32 "Busy-Body Papers" for the *American Weekly Mercury* as a satiric means of driving his old employer Keimer out of business. Franklin succeeded, bought out his competitor, and began publishing his own paper, the *Pennsylvania Gazette*, which flourished for 37 years and introduced such journalistic staples as weather reports and political cartoons. One of his barbed, tongue-in-cheek articles describes a witch-dunking in Mount Holly, New Jersey, on October 22, 1730:

> The more thinking part of the spectators were of opinion that any Person so bound and placed in the water (unless they were mere skin and bones), would swim, till their breath was gone, and their lungs filled with water. But it being the general Belief of the Populace that the Women's shifts and the garters with which they were bound helped to support them, it is said they are to be tried again the next warm weather, naked.

Frequently, readers misread his satire and missed the subtle humor that became his trademark, thus contributing to his reputation as an unprincipled scamp.

A pragmatist and worthy colonist, Franklin grew wealthy and content but did not always please others with his live-and-let-live views. In September 1730, he married Deborah Read Rogers, a grass widow who was mother of Franklin's children, Sarah and Francis Folger Franklin ("Young Franky," who died in 1736 of smallpox), and stepmother to Franklin's illegitimate son William. A frequenter of prostitutes, Franklin made no apologies for obeying his "hard-to-be-govern'd Passion of Youth" and composed a satiric essay, "The Speech of Polly Baker" (1747) as a defense of a woman trapped by society's double standard after her seducer, a magistrate, deserts her. To her accusers at a Connecticut hearing, she parries the court's censure with a blunt question:

What must poor young women do, whom customs and nature forbid to solicit the men, and who cannot force themselves upon husbands, when the laws take no care to provide them any, and yet severely punish them if they do their duty without them; the duty of the first and great command of nature and nature's God, increase and multiply.

Polly concludes that society castigates her with disgrace and a public whipping, when they ought to "have a statue erected to my memory."

Franklin's most beloved publication, *Poor Richard's Almanack* (1733–1758), packed a handy array of information under the subtitle:

containing the Lunations, Eclipses, Planets Motions and Aspects, Weather, Sun and Moon's rising and setting, Highwater & besides many pleasant and witty Verses, Jests and Sayings, Author's Motive of Writing, Prediction of the Death of his Friend Mr. Titan Leeds, Moon no Cuckold, Batchelor's Folly, Parson's Wine and Baker's Pudding, Short Visits, Kings and Bears, New Fashions, Game for Kisses, Katherine's Love, Different Sentiments, Signs of a Tempest, Death of a Fisherman, Conjugal Debate, Men and Melons, H. the Prodigal, Breakfast in Bed, Oyster Lawsuit, & by Richard Saunders, Philomat [lover of learning].

The popular annual sold 10,000 copies per issue and quickly built his fortune. The first issue began with one of Franklin's literary jokes: a witty falsified death notice of Titan Leeds, his competitor. The almanac derives its name from Franklin's fictional persona, Richard "Dick" Saunders, whom Leeds claims to have found sleeping and

entered your left nostril, ascended into your brain, found out where the ends of those nerves were fastened that move your right hand and fingers, by the help of which I am now writing unknown to you.

A compendium of homespun epigrams, humor, and advice, the almanac earned readers' respect for its wisdom and appreciation of common sense and frugality, two of Franklin's notable traits. A less sanguine form of satire drives his Swiftian objection to the English penal system's deportation of criminals to the colonies:

Our mother knows what is best for us. What is a little housebreaking, shoplifting, or highway robbing; what is a son now and then corrupted and hanged, a daughter debauched and poxed, a wife stabbed, a husband's throat cut, or a child's brains beat out with an axe, compared with this "improvement and well being of the people of the Colonies"!

Because he earned the trust of his contemporaries as the Colonies' defender and foremost publisher and printer, he helped the Albany Congress of 1754 determine how the Colonies could be better governed. He impressed Tory leaders with reasonable protest against the Stamp Act, an unfair tax on colonists.

After Franklin advanced to the diplomatic level, he joined libertarians who agitated for freedom from the British crown. Two of his satires—"Rules by Which a Great Empire May Be Reduced to a Small One" (1773) and "Edict by the King of Prussia" (1773)—pressed for the rescinding of the Townshend Acts and warned the English that the empire would be nibbled away like a cookie, from the distant edges inward. To his sister, Jane Mecom, Franklin wrote that he hoped the satires "held up a Looking-Glass in which some Ministers may see their ugly faces, & the Nation its Injustice." A firm separation between patriots and Tories pressed Franklin onto the committee composing the Declaration of Independence. In 1778, he helped negotiate the Treaty of Paris, guaranteeing France's military alliance with the colonists. In the after-hours of these tedious ambassadorial meetings, he surveyed the eccentricities of French salon society and continued to write satire as a pastime. A plainly dressed man of the people, he won the hearts of the French and became a cult figure.

On Franklin's return to the Market Street Wharf in 1785, he received a hero's welcome. His body was weakened from chronic bladder stones, but his mind was quick-witted. He served the Constitutional Convention as a delegate and proposed successfully that the body accept the Constitution without further wrangling. Attended by Mary Hewson, who followed him from Passy, France, he struggled with ill health and injuries from a fall and was borne to public functions in a sedan chair because he could not tolerate a jouncing carriage. He spent his final years pressing for humane treatment of Indians and an end to the slave trade, penning a forceful editorial letter "On the Slave Trade," which appeared in the *Federal Gazette.* After drawing up a will, he attempted to finish his autobiography for the edification of his son William. Edited by his grandson and secretary, William Temple Franklin, the autobiography remained unfinished at Franklin's death on April 17, 1790. His funeral in Philadelphia was sumptuous; from a prison in France, Louis XVI lauded the crafty American for his wisdom and love of liberty. (Clark 1983; Franklin 1982, 1987; Hart 1983)

See also Addison, Joseph; epigram; lampoon; parody; satire; *The Spectator;* Swift, Jonathan.

A FUNNY THING HAPPENED ON THE WAY TO THE FORUM

A labor of joy for the lover of puns, immodest jest, and outright belly laughs, Burt Shevelove and Larry Gelbart's *A Funny Thing Happened on the Way to the Forum* (1962) took four years to write, refine, and rewrite. It draws on Gelbart's experience writing for Jack Paar, Danny Kaye, Art Carney, and Bob Hope. To Gelbart's multiple awards and collaborations, Shevelove added directing and writing talent, which he applied to *No, No, Nanette* (1971) and television comedies featuring Jack Benny, Barbra Streisand, Art Carney, Judy Garland, and Frank Sinatra.

A Funny Thing. . . replicates on the musical stage the quick-witted humor of classic authors, mainly Aristophanes and his heir, Plautus, the third-century Roman funnyman and caricaturist who influenced the gamut of European comedy from the *commedia dell'arte* to Molière's *L'Avare* and William Shakespeare's *The Comedy of Errors.* With music by Stephen Sondheim, composer for *West Side Story* and *Gypsy,* the Broadway staple burgeoned into a twisted noodle of plots and counterplots pitting uppity slaves against aging lechers, coaxing courtesans, and a calculating, supercilious social matron. The Broadway opener won Tony awards for best musical, producer, book, director, supporting actor, and lead actor (David Burns and Zero Mostel played Senex and Pseudolus, respectively). The 1966 movie version, starring Mostel, Phil Silvers, and Buster Keaton, won an Oscar for music director Ken Thorne.

Setting the work, appropriately, in Rome during the Empire, in front of the doors of the elderly Senex, the flesh peddler Marcus Lycus, and the wandering Erronius, the authors supply their low-comic farce with a wealth of disguise motifs, unrequited love, mistaken identities, pratfalls, and fools waiting to be gulled. Pagan, vulgar, and uproarious to the last, the plot depends on frenetic pacing as a procession of caricatures strolls past, involving themselves in the grand scheme. Central to the humor is the underlying meaning of the names: Senex, old man; Erronius, from the verb to wander; Pseudolus, false; Domina, lady of the house; Miles Gloriosus, boastful soldier; Tintinnabula, jingle bells; and Philia, love. Other names—Hysterium, Panacea, Geminae, Vibrata, Gymnasia, Prologus, and Hero—require no translation.

The play opens like a revue: the players sing the delights of "comedy tonight." With appropriate piety, Prologus invokes Thespis, the legendary first actor. On her way out of her front door, Domina, an all-controlling mother, indicates that Pseudolus is to keep an eye on Hero, whom she wishes to remain virginal. To match her fervor, Hero enters and sings a song that is ripe with new love. Pseudolus does not object to love but cringes at the news that Hero is sparking a courtesan employed in the despicable house of Marcus Lycus. Throwaway lines swell the growing farce, as in Lycus's observation that the eunuch will "never learn. You'll be a eunuch all your life!"

The plot thickens early when Pseudolus learns that the girl Philia, a virgin from Crete, is the property of Miles Gloriosus. To delay delivery of the girl to her new owner, Pseudolus, the perennial slick underling, casts a sigh for Crete, which he claims is overrun with plague. By rigging a fake funeral, calling in a soothsayer, and reuniting a brother and sister separated in childhood, Pseudolus earns his freedom. The cast summarizes:

> Free! Free! Free! Free! Free!
> Nothing for kings,
> Nothing for crowns,
> Something for lovers, liars and clowns!

The satire—broad-based, universal, and unfailingly lively—ribs humdrum marriages, witless masters, and dreary prudery that saps young love of vitality. Because the playwrights set out to honor a satirist rather than ridicule a victim, they succeed in re-creating some of the pyrotechnics of ancient Roman comedy. (Bermel 1982; Shevelove and Gelbart 1991)

See also Aristophanes; caricature; comedy; *commedia dell'arte;* farce; Plautus; pun; satire; trickster.

GARDNER, JOHN

Unlike most academics, John Champlin Gardner, Jr., flourished on multiple planes: as critic and adviser to aspiring writers and teachers; as founder of a literary journal and contributor to scholarly quarterlies; and as poet, editor, translator, radio scriptwriter, and producer of bestsellers, libretti, verse, and young adult fables. At the heart of his genius lay a love for medieval literature, Arthurian lore, and the traditions of Chaucer, Dante, and the Gawain-poet, the raw materials of his own creations. Gardner was born July 21, 1933, in Batavia, New York, to dairyman John Gardner, Sr., and Priscilla Jones Gardner, a high school English teacher. He studied at DePauw, Washington University, and the State University of Iowa, from which he received an M.A. and a Ph.D. in medieval studies and an enduring respect for Anglo-Saxon literature and the works of Geoffrey Chaucer. The promise of Gardner's interests and skills brought multiple fellowships from the Woodrow Wilson, Danforth, and Guggenheim foundations. He made pilgrimages to a string of college English departments, teaching a year or two, serving as writer in residence, and encouraging gifted students. He died in a motorcycle accident in Susquehanna, Pennsylvania, on September 14, 1982.

An iconoclast, Gardner explored the outer fringes of creativity, publishing brilliant works and earning an NEA award, National Book Critics Circle award, Armstrong Prize, and kudos from *Time* and *Newsweek*. His best work is the anomalous modern quasi-medieval classic, *Grendel* (1971), a philosophical novel that is the obverse of the Anglo-Saxon epic *Beowulf*. Gardner gives a monster's-eye view of the chaotic milieu that spawned Grendel, a vengeful stalker who roams the periphery of the human realm and, like a fretful peafowl, debates with himself a nettlesome exile and a looming knowledge of earthly impermanence.

Opening *in medias res* outside Heorot hall, the novel examines Grendel in the twelfth year of his war with King Hrothgar and his murderous Danes. The incessant chant of Grendel's self-doubt and insecurity forms a counterpoint to the brutish Danes, boasting and guzzling, too intent on bestial concerns to listen to the tempered rhythms of the Shaper, their song-philosopher, who built the hall "by the power of his songs: created with casual words its grave mor(t)ality" and thrums out their saga to inattentive ears. Ironically, the stalker absorbs the lore that the Danes discount as so much noise:

"Why can't these creatures discover a little dignity?" I ask the sky. The sky says nothing, predictably. I make a face, uplift a defiant middle finger, and give an obscene little kick. The sky ignores me, forever unimpressed. Him too I hate.

The humor of the apostate Grendel defying God precedes a satiric quandary—Grendel's self-entrapment in a forked oak and the wails that bring his mother. Like cavalry arriving at a trot, she rescues him from the Danes, whom Grendel classifies as "thinking creatures, pattern makers, the most dangerous thing I'd ever met." In her lair, she snuggles her fitful offspring in a perverse rendition of madonna and child.

As humankind stretches intrusive tentacles far into the forest, Grendel grows wild with bloodlust, moody with alienation. Drawn by the soothing sound of the blind harper, a parallel of Homer, the monster eavesdrops on Hrothgar, whose comic vulgarity defies explanation:

I laugh, crumple over; I can't help myself. In the darkness, I alone see clear as day. While they squeal and screech and bump into each other, I silently sack up my dead and withdraw to the woods. I eat and laugh and eat until I can barely walk . . . and all at once I am filled with gloom again.

An unseen mourner at the Shaper's cremation, Grendel observes the symbolic end of the wise old man, whose head explodes and whose mouth and ears ooze blood. Grendel cannot escape the truth that death comes to all creatures, wise and foolish. To still the maddening dismay that clings and cankers and gives him no rest, he consults the Dragon, a stealthy, xenophobic survivor devoid of illusions. The news is not good: there will be no end to the nightly voyeurism until order replaces Hrothgar's anarchy.

The suspenseful narrative moves toward denouement with the arrival of 15 Geat heroes who surpass Unferth, Heorot's antihero, whom Grendel once buried in a deluge of apples. Their beardless leader looms, a Gibraltar of a man who commands the fractious Danes' respect. At last able to face a worthy challenger, Grendel ceases tramping the frosty heath and enters the mead hall to grapple with the upstart. Simultaneously with the death grip on his arm comes the death knowledge that he has avoided, rationalized, and defied. In parody of the twenty-third psalm, he intones, "The world is my bone-cave, I shall not want." The hole in the shoulder where an arm once fit pours blood; Grendel first bawls for his mother, then bows his head to doom. Hurtling himself into a black abyss, he exerts a power that derives from his will to end the agony, to end life. His pain-glazed eyes stare up at the animals that gather around to gloat. Flaunting his newfound experience with approaching death, he whispers up to them, "Poor Grendel's had an accident. . . . *So may you all.*"

A perplexing, doom-ridden novel based on a gut-yearning for humankind and gnawing cosmic fears, *Grendel* has found a unique niche in high school and college reading lists for its bravura study of point of view and existentialism. Although Gardner never convinced all the critics of his sincerity, never shook off the mantle of boy wonder in overdrive, his clever mix of prose devices moves readers to accept a worldview fraught with themes of respect for

American critic, writer, and musician John Gardner in 1977

tradition versus despair, rootlessness, and self-annihilation. Central to his dramatic gift is his command of literary style, ranging from pun, metaphor, and sense impression to incongruity, parody, and satire, the sharpest and most enlightening spear points in the writer's arsenal. (*Contemporary Authors* 1994; *Contemporary Literary Criticism* 1974; Cowart 1983; *Dictionary of Literary Biography* 1978; Gardner 1971, 1984; Morace and Van Spanckeren 1982)

    See also Chaucer, Geoffrey; parody; pun; satire.

GARGANTUA AND PANTAGRUEL

A roistering, dizzyingly inventive five-part satiric epic novel about a family of giants, *Gargantua and Pantagruel* introduces a lusty protagonist who, with mate Badebec, produces the untameable Pantagruel, the "Ever-Thirsty," grandson of Grandgousier, the king of Utopia. Rabelais's 259 chapters follow a meandering path through a comic milieu teeming with life at its crudest, funniest, and most irreverent. He inaugurated this invigorating tale in 1532 and dedicated it to sots and syphilitics. Fittingly, it was cranked out on the underground press and banned by the Sorbonne for lewdness. Nine years after his death in 1553, the final version appeared with a questionable addendum that carries the main character on a long Odyssean voyage. The novel offers a convoluted blend of outrageous humor, insatiable curiosity, and worldly wisdom; indeed, the author envisioned the finished work as a rich feast and urged his readers to peel away the exterior layers like outer skins from an onion and suck meaning from its pages like marrow from bones. Categorized by its enemies as earthy pornography and a bacchic debauch and championed by its fans as a refreshingly unbowdlerized slam on dry dogma and rigorous pedantry, *Gargantua and Pantagruel*—subtitled "The Grand and Inestimable Chronicles of the Great and Enormous Giant Gargantua"—opens with a friendly verse urging friends to drop affectation and welcome mirth as a cure for grief.

Rabelais spares no prudish sensibilities in his description of the lusty priapic protagonist. Gargantua is born with an oversized phallus and with prophetic words in his mouth: "I want drink! Bring me drink!" After extensive home tutoring, he studies Gothic calligraphy at the University of Paris, joins forces with his pal Panurge, and keeps up a steady enmity against the Dipsodes or "Thirsty Ones." The book contains a loose stream-of-consciousness retelling of the quixotic adventures of two giants—father and son—and their retinue through a surrealistic maelstrom of brawls, travels, and encounters. In mock-epic form, the episodic novel leads the pair to the underworld and parodies ecclesiastical excesses, war and politics, and the medieval education system. In a farcical visit to a sibyl, Panurge observes her preparing to prophesy:

> I saw her take off one of her clogs—we call them *sabots*—put her apron over her head, as priests do their amice when about to sing the Mass, and tie it under her throat with an ancient piece of striped and spotted cloth. Then all muffled up, she took a long swig from the bottle, extracted three crowns from the ramscod purse, put them in three walnut shells, and placed them on the bottom of a pot of feathers. Next she swept her broom three times across the hearth and threw half a faggot of briar and a branch of dry laurel on the fire, watching them burn in silence, and noticing that in burning they made no crackling or noise of any kind.

Rabelais's obvious dig at clerical ritual recalls a similar scene in Virgil's *Aeneid* when the Cumalan sybil prepares to guide Aeneas to the underworld. The mystical mumbo-jumbo sends Panurge into a panic, which the satirist turns to salacious fun. During his pell-mell dash from the sibyl, Panurge glances back and sees that the Sybil has "hitched up her gown, petticoat, and smock to her armpits, and showed them her arse." Panurge cries, "there's the sibyl's cavern."

In his most famous segment, Chapters 52–57 of Book I, *The Abbey of Thélème*, Rabelais employs visionary style in an epicurean vignette that the author intends as a gesture to the endearing fictional humanist Frère Jean. The abbey (the French *thélème* comes from the Greek word for desire or will) is a closed sybaritic commune that ignores the usual rules of chastity, poverty, self-denial, and obedience and in their place lauds marriage, luxury, enjoyment, and personal freedom epitomized by the precept "Do as you will." The inmates, who come from a privileged background of education and gentility, embrace virtue, courtesy, and honor. Like the perfect Renaissance knight in Castiglione's *The Courtier* (1528), they are educated to "read, write, sing, play upon several musical instruments, speak five or six languages, and readily compose in them all, both in verse and prose." Encompassing the Renaissance spirit of sampling at will both experience and learning, *The Abbey of Thélème* asserts the individual's right to throw off the yoke of scholasticism and civil authoritarianism in favor of the unbridled pursuit of personal preference. At the idealized court of Thélème, a local intelligentsia relishes a deformalized internal order free of clerical restraints, servitude, punishment, cumbrous laws, politics, taxation, and popery.

The abbey is a splendid château of the Loire Valley, where Gargantua promotes to the post of abbot Frère Jean des Entomeures, a monk who aided Gargantua in battle. The goal of the commune of Thélème reflects the height of Renaissance interests: a pleasurable absorption in learning, enjoyment, luxury, and beauty. Inhabitants—"jollie Friars and Nuns"—Rabelais describes as

> lively, jovial, handsome, brisk, gay, witty, frolicsome, cheerful, merry, frisky, spruce, jocund, courteous furtherers of trade, and in a word, all worthy gentle blades . . . ladies of high birth, delicious, stately, charming, full of mirth, ingenious, lovely, miniard, proper, fair. Magnetic, graceful, splendid, pleasant, rare, obliging, sprightly, virtuous, young, salacious, kind, neat, quick, feat, bright, compt, ripe, choice, dear, precious, alluring, courtly, comely, fine, compleat, wise, personable, ravishing, and sweet.

Thélèmites reside under the benign rule of a wealthy patron who provides servants to do menial chores and artisans to supply gold, jewels, embroidery, clothing, and tapestries. Each resident enjoys the freedom to expand mind and body to perfection, whether or not utility is served.

Essential to liberty is the absence of a cloistered compound and all timepieces. Rabelais insists that too stout a confinement produces "a store of murmur, envy, and mutual conspiracy." Liberated in spirit as well as practice from the Church custom of canonical hours marked by tolling bells, inmates expend no energy in following the precise schedules of an overregulated convent. Gargantua declares, "the greatest loss of time that I know is to count the hours, what good comes of it?" Activity, he insists, should be guided by "judgment and discretion" rather than a pull on the bell rope. Therefore, "None did awake them, none did offer to constrain them to eat, drink, nor to do any other thing."

Daily life at the abbey consists of such purposeful and pleasurable activity as hawking, riding, swimming, dramatic performances, tilting, and hunting. Unlike the drab garments worn by prelates, sumptuous garb brightens the residents, who disport themselves in Europe's latest styles cut from lavish fabrics and sewn with embellishments. Pairing of lords and ladies produces life mates who later marry and transport their "good devotion and amity" into the world beyond Thélème. Their marriages—an uplifting alternative to the burden of priestly celibacy—exemplify the ideal of lifetime devotion, "in no less vigor and fervency than at the very day of their wedding." Renaissance readers had no difficulty in interpreting the author's message: suitably wedded church wardens set better examples for parishioners than the crabbed, mateless priests who made lame efforts to advise others on conjugal relationships.

Rabelais formulates his religious commune on a belief that people, if given the opportunity, live honorably and decently without the constant intervention of moralistic clergy. Boldly refuting Catholic notions that humans are born to sin, he trusts natural tendencies toward goodness. Going one step further, Rabelais turns didactic and lays the blame for human debauchery and evil on church doctrine, which, he claims, furthers suspicions that people cannot escape innate depravity. By disproving the self-fulfilling prophecy that the human race always pursues evil, Gargantua shatters the core Christian doctrine of original sin at the same time that he produces a lively, jovial atmosphere in which to thrive and be happy. (Bishop 1965; Boorstin 1992; Lewis 1969; Mack 1962; Manguel 1987; Pollard 1970; Putnam 1993; Rabelais 1955; Screech 1980; Thomas and Thomas 1943)

See also didacticism; mock epic; parody; Rabelais, François; satire.

GAY, JOHN

Best known for his long-lived *The Beggar's Opera* (1728), ironist and satirist John Gay was born to a prosperous middle-class family in Barnstaple, Devonshire, in September 1685. After an unremarkable grammar school education, he was apprenticed to a London draper and silk mercer. At the age of 27, he served as scribe to the Duchess of Monmouth, prepared for a career in journalism with the *British Apollo,* and, with the encouragement of the Scriblerus Club—regular literary sessions held by Thomas Parnell, Alexander Pope, Dr. John Arbuthnot, and Jonathan Swift—began composing verse burlesque. His pamphlet *The Present State of Wit* (1711) drew on the success of the coffeehouse wits, particularly Joseph Addison and Richard Steele, producers of *The Tatler* and *The Spectator.* Influenced by Pope, Gay wrote the didactic Horatian poem *Rural Sports* (1713) and a mock epic, *The Fan* (1714). Further experiments with comic and satiric modes resulted in *The What-D'Ye-Call-It* (1715) and *Trivia; or, The Art of Walking the Streets of London* (1716). The latter, a satiric eclogue, uses mock-epic devices to heighten the humor of wearing appropriate shoes, avoiding street filth, dodging sedan chairs, and keeping a dry overcoat.

Because of poor financial management, Gay lost his investment in the South Sea company and incurred disfavor at court. He survived with the patronage of a string of notables and stayed at Amesbury Abbey with the Duke and Duchess of Queensberry, where he wrote *The Beggar's Opera*, and at Queensberry House in Edinburgh, where he formed a close friendship with painter Allan Ramsay. With a Tory faction headed by Pope and Arbuthnot, Gay collaborated on a play, *Three Hours after Marriage* (1717), a flop. He fared no better with *The Captives* (1724), a tragedy performed at Drury Lane. However, the success of his satiric *Fables* (1727) and *The Beggar's Opera* (1728), an antiromantic ballad opera suggested by Jonathan Swift and produced by John Rich at Lincoln's Inn Fields Theatre, preserved his name among satirists and earned him a fortune. The play remains a frequently revived musical. Gay gleaned further earnings on a sequel, *Polly* (1729), which satirized Sir Robert Walpole. Because the Lord Chamberlain banned Gay's political satire as too dangerous for public performance, he gleefully sold the work as a *roman à clef*. The first production opened in 1732 to a packed house at the Private Theatre in Kilkenny, Ireland.

Shortly before Gay died of intestinal abscess in London on December 4, 1732, he completed the libretto for Georg Friedrich Handel's *Acis and Galatea* (1732) and the opera *Achilles* (1733). Gay was buried in Westminster Abbey beneath a doggerel couplet fitting for a satirist: "Life is a jest, and all things show it;/I thought so once, and now I know it." The resilience of his good humor survives in Bertolt Brecht and Kurt Weill's *The Threepenny Opera* (1928), an adaptation of *The Beggar's Opera*. Despite numerous setbacks, Gay left a legacy of £6,000, a considerable sum for a writer in his day. (Baugh 1948; Brockett 1968; Burdick 1974; Drabble 1985; Feinberg 1967; Fowler 1989; Gay 1932, 1952; Magill 1958; Pollard 1970; Roberts 1962; Thomas and Thomas 1943; Woods 1947)

See also Addison, Joseph; *The Beggar's Opera*; Brecht, Bertolt; burlesque; didacticism; doggerel; farce; Horace; mock epic; Pope, Alexander; *The Spectator*; Steele, Sir Richard; Swift, Jonathan; *The Tatler*; wit.

GILBERT, SIR WILLIAM SCHWENCK

England's light-hearted satirist and librettist William Gilbert survives in literary memory as one-half of the combination of Gilbert and Sullivan. Their gentle farce, laced with slapstick, clichés, sight gags, whimsy, doggerel, witty patter lampooning the establishment, euphemism, puns, and musical comedy, supplied the English-speaking world with decades of stage entertainment that needled the pomposity, complacency, smugness, hypocrisy, sentimentality, and prudery of Victorians. Born in London on November 18, 1836, to Ann Morris and William Gilbert, retired naval surgeon, Gilbert was educated at Boulogne, Great Ealing School, and King's College, London. In 1838, he was kidnapped by Italian bandits, ransomed for £25, and returned without harm, an incident that may have inspired the harum-scarum plots and harmless scrapes of his

A caricature of English librettist William Schwenck Gilbert, left, with composer Arthur Seymour Sullivan, right.

comic operas. He began writing plays in childhood and had advanced to burlesque by his late teens.

Gilbert entered the army during the Crimean War and was annoyed that he received no commission for his service in the 5th West Yorkshire Militia and Royal Aberdeen Highlanders. On return to civilian life, he graduated from the University of London in 1857. He clerked at the education department office of the Privy Council, another likely source of fodder for satire. When he inherited £300 from his aunt, he resigned civil service with its myriad drudgeries and pettifogging bureaucrats and returned to serious study of law at Clement's Inn. His practice caused a free-floating discontent that only writing could diminish.

In 1861, Gilbert, his mind fertile with the snafus of army life and civil service, began submitting to *Fun, Punch,* and the *Piccadilly Annual* the humorous, self-illustrated verse that he later published as *Bab Ballads* (1869) and *More Bab Ballads* (1873). His success inspired his moniker of "doggerel bard," a title in which he took pride. A colleague, Thomas William Robertson, encouraged him to compose a Christmas piece for the stage; *Dulcamara, or the Little Duck and the Great Quack* (1866) took Gilbert only ten days to finish. After his first taste of stage success and a check for £30, he attempted fantasy, fiction, serious drama, and a parody of Alfred Tennyson's *The Princess.*

In 1869, at the request of John Hollingshead, Gaiety Theatre manager, to compose a stage spectacle, Gilbert joined Sullivan, a serious composer of oratorios and incidental music for Shakespeare's plays. The two wrote satiric musicals known as the Savoy Operas, beginning with *Thespis, or the Gods Grown Old* (1871) and the one-act sellout, *Trial by Jury* (1875), their first success. Both sticklers for stage propriety, Gilbert and Sullivan insisted that costumes cover the body, that male roles be played by men, and that female roles be played by women. The duo rose in popularity with *The Sorcerer* (1877), *H.M.S. Pinafore* (1878), *The Pirates of Penzance* (1879), *Patience, or Bunthorne's Bride* (1881), *Iolanthe, or the Peer and the Peri* (1882), *Princess Ida, or Castle Adamant* (1884), and *The Mikado, or the Town of Titipu* (1885), one of their best-received stage farces. Their success spread to the United States, where critics raved in the review pages and newly formed repertory companies headed west with makeshift versions of *Pinafore.*

Originally basing Gilbert and Sullivan at the Opéra Comique, impresario Richard D'Oyly Carte built the Savoy Theatre, the first theater in England to use electric lights. The Savoyards produced the duo's later work, including *Ruddigore, or the Witch's Curse* (1887), *The Yeomen of the Guard* (1888), *The Gondoliers* (1889), and *The Grand Duke* (1896), a cynical piece that failed with Victorian playgoers. Of the latter works, *Yeomen* was Gilbert's favorite; Queen Victoria preferred *Gondoliers.* A quarrel—variously blamed on the price of a carpet, box office receipts, and Sullivan's intention to write serious opera—ended two decades of successful collaboration. When Sullivan retired, Gilbert continued with *Rosencrantz and Guildenstern* (1891), *Fallen Fairies* (1909), and *The Hooligans* (1911) but groused that his serious works were rewarded with indifference while his "twaddle" proved most entertaining.

Gilbert's private life with Lucy Agnes Blois Turner Gilbert centered on Grim's Dyke, their estate in Middlesex. Except for gout and arthritis, his health was good enough for motoring and photography. He enjoyed gardening, fruit propagation, and a quiet gentrification after his public performance of 70-plus stage works, of which 14 are officially known as "Gilbert and Sullivan operas." In 1907, Edward VII conferred knighthood on him at Buckingham Palace; because of the number of people receiving the same honor, Gilbert referred to it as a "tin-pot, two-penny-half-penny sort of distinction." Gilbert died at Harrow Weald on May 29, 1911, in an appropriately dashing misadventure—he suffered heart failure or drowned while he tried to save a young girl from a tumble into his swimming pool. His ashes are interred near his home at Great Stanmore Church cemetery.

A whole generation of audiences grew up on Gilbert's satire, which was regularly reprised in chanteys, skits, and whole shows for community theater, vaudeville, and stage revues. Favorite lines achieved recognition level with much of England, for example, the patter about swearing from *H.M.S. Pinafore:*

Captain:	Bad language or abuse,
	I never, never use,
	Whatever the emergency;
	Though "Bother it" I may
	Occasionally say,
	I never use a big, big D—
All:	What, never?
Captain:	No, never!
All:	What never?
Captain:	Hardly ever!
All:	Hardly ever swears a big, big D—
	Then give three cheers, and one cheer more,
	For the well-bred Captain of the Pinafore!

Another favorite, a twit at the excesses of colonialism and the self-importance of the bureaucracy, comes from the Pirate King in Act I of *The Pirates of Penzance:*

When I sally forth to seek my prey
I help myself in a royal way:
I sink a few more ships, it's true,
Than a well-bred monarch ought to do;
But many a king on a first-class throne,
If he wants to call his crown his own,
Must manage somehow to get through
More dirty work than ever I do,
Though I am a Pirate King.

The grace and good humor of Gilbert's most famous caricatures passed muster with all levels of society—even Queen Victoria and Edward VII—and survived the censorious Victorian era unscathed, whereas his later works ventured further from whimsical cartoonesque figures into a reality that audiences shunned. (Bermel 1982; Brockett 1968; Burdick 1974; Gassner and Quinn 1969;

Gilbert 1967, 1992; Gilbert and Sullivan 1962; Roberts 1962; *Something about the Author* 1984)

See also burlesque; caricature; doggerel; farce; lampoon; *The Mikado;* parody; satire; whimsy; wit.

GULLIVER, LEMUEL

A fictional native of Redriff, Nottinghamshire, England, Lemuel Gulliver serves as antihero of Jonathan Swift's satiric, dystopian *Gulliver's Travels* (1727). A learned but misguided idealist, Gulliver is a caricature of the educated ne'er-do-well and gadabout. The third of five sons, he stood to inherit nothing. To prepare himself for a profession, he attended Emmanuel College, Cambridge, but did not complete a degree.

Swift spools out the continued misapplication of experience in Gulliver's adulthood. True to form, he maintains high standards without learning how to apply them to real situations. To set himself up in a profession, he studies under James Bates, a London surgeon, attends lectures in Leyden, studies navigation and mathematics, and attempts to earn a living practicing medicine. He marries Mary Burton Gulliver, opens a medical practice in Old Jury, but never prospers. To aid his family, he works briefly as ship's surgeon on the *Swallow*. In this early stage of character exposition, Swift's keen satire remains partially sheathed under hints that the focus of *Gulliver's Travels* is a naive young seeker who, like the swallow, remains on the alert for a place to nest, but, at the same time, "swallows" a series of false impressions.

Swift's satiric chronicle is precise. On May 4, 1699, Gulliver makes a metaphoric leap at destiny by putting to sea aboard the *Antelope* as ship's surgeon and sailing from Bristol to the East Indies. He ventures into remarkable societies where ideologies contrast sharply with the worlds he has known and emulated. An ingenuous, sheltered observer, Lemuel peers down on tiny Lilliputians performing trivial rope stunts and leaping over sticks before their emperor; involving themselves in petty squabbles, such as which end of an egg should be cracked first; and confining their children in public nurseries apart from their parents. In recompense for his disturbance of their nation, his minute jailers determine that:

> In three Days your Friend the Secretary will be directed to come to your House, and read before you the Articles of Impeachment; and then to signify the great *Lenity* and Favour of his Majesty and Council; whereby you are only condemned to the Loss of your Eyes, which his Majesty doth not question you will gratefully and humbly submit to.

As serious as the blinding of Oedipus and Lear, the harsh symbolism of Gulliver's punishment for seeing too much seems out of balance among the otherwise foolish, at times entertaining foibles of a tiny, mean-spirited race. Gulliver has the gumption to shove off from shore and seek less desperate penalty for being different.

His second voyage reverses his adventures by allying him with gross giants, the Brobdingnags, whose magnified human qualities disgust and alienate the observer from his hosts. He reflects from his glimpse of the wetnurse's breast:

> Upon the fair skins of our *English* Ladies, who appear so beautiful to us, only because they are of our own size, and their Defects not to be seen but through a magnifying Glass, where we find by Experiment that the smoothest and whitest Skins look rough and coarse, and ill coloured.

Upon escaping the giants, Gulliver uses nail parings and hair clippings to prove to his rescuers that the Brobdingnagians were as he described them. Displaying a bit of maturity, Gulliver remarks, "I winked at my own Littleness, as People do at their own Faults."

This small proof of logic and reason is a false start, for Gulliver loses ground in his last two voyages. As a result of his regression, the third and fourth encounters stand closer to the heart of Swift's criticisms of human behavior. Reported as incisively as the first half of his sea adventures, the encounters with Laputa and the land of the Houyhnhnms intensify the guileless sailor's inability to maintain perspective. He is so taken with the lifestyle of the horses that he conceives a plan "to send a sufficient Number of their Inhabitants for civilizing *Europe;* by teaching us the first Principles of Honour, Justice, Truth, Temperance, publick Spirit, Fortitude, Chastity, Friendship, Benevolence, and Fidelity." By withdrawing to a stable on his return to Redriff, Gulliver is blinded by what he recognizes in himself as a full range of bestial qualities. He is immobilized from taking action against illogic or from appreciating his better nature. Swift depicts his antihero as a disconcertingly simple-witted booby who distances himself from his wife and children. His adventures so demoralized him that he is unable to cope with even the smell of his human family.

As though *Gulliver's Travels* had appeared only recently, critics continue to debate the paradoxical, immensely puzzling novel with fresh insights and applications. At first castigating and reviling Gulliver as a misanthropic narrator, critics later appreciated the parody after deducing the source of his name—a portmanteau word that merges "gullible" and "traveler." When they ceased to jeer, they began to value Swift's refined gift for irony, caricature, and parody. At length, the reading public delighted in Gulliver, an irrational, fusty old hermit. He has since become a standard figure in young adult literature, often recreated on a simpler level in satiric cartoons and children's stories. (Drabble 1985; Harrison 1967; Hornstein 1973; Johnson 1968; Magill 1958; Manguel and Guadalupi 1987; Pollard 1970; Swift 1958; Woods 1947)

See also caricature; *Gulliver's Travels;* parody; pun; satire; Swift, Jonathan; whimsy.

 # GULLIVER'S TRAVELS

Labeled the greatest of English satires and the favorite work to survive the eighteenth century, Jonathan Swift's masterly, perplexing adventure tale,

Gulliver's Travels, applies utopian and anti-utopian precepts to the correction of society's ills. Published in 1726, the work was an immediate success and has maintained an uncontested position in English literature. Achieving what the "gullible traveler" assumes to be utopia in the horseland of the Houyhnhnms, Gulliver loses his objectivity, deserts his family, and moves into the stable to live with horses, whom his distorted value system classes above humanity.

Book I begins on May 4, 1699, with the *Swallow*'s voyage from Bristol, England, around Africa's horn to the East Indies. Shipwrecked by collision with a boulder northwest of Van Diemen's Land on November 5, Lemuel Gulliver sets out in a punt that overturns. He swims ashore and sleeps for nine hours. On awakening, he realizes that he is bound hand and foot—a captive in Lilliput, a land ruled by people only six inches high. Drugged into stupor, Gulliver is transported by flatcar at great physical hardship to his conquerors, who install him nearer the royal palace. There he gains the citizens' respect and is allowed to rove and to question Reldresal, an imperial private secretary who serves as Gulliver's official liaison.

The petty Lilliputians display myriad peculiarities. Swift delights in ridiculing their writing that slants from corner to corner "like Ladies in England," their belief that the world is flat, and their burial of the dead feet upward so that they will stand upright on the day of resurrection. In court trials of state crime, if the defendant is proved innocent, the state executes the accuser. The legal system also dispenses rewards for good behavior by naming worthy citizens Snilpalls or Legals. To acquire honors, Lilliputians dance on ropes or leap over sticks, thus earning wisps of thread from Emperor Golbasto. The convoluted nature of Lilliputian society replicates the idiocies of court life in Swift's time and the beliefs and behaviors of people who hesitate to think for themselves.

Swift—who outraged England with *A Modest Proposal* (1729), an ingenuous proposal that the Irish sell their children as livestock—puts much thought into Lilliput's children, who are highly valued. Parents produce only the number of offspring they intend to support. To bring up a family in Lilliputian fashion, parents expect no gratitude from their offspring. With a smirk, Swift notes that "Parents are the last of all others to be trusted with the Education of their own Children." Young Lilliputians attend public nurseries and are indoctrinated into a rigid social station. Upper-class males attend rigorous schools that teach moral values. Lower-class males and females, who never converse with the top stratum, receive education commensurate with their needs. The agricultural caste, which keeps children at home, is left illiterate. The rigidity of Lilliputian child care ridicules the English system, which creates caste-conscious adults who have more loyalty to social class than to home and nuclear family.

In Chapter 6, Swift explores the utopian qualities of Lilliput. The courts maintain order by enacting strong laws against treason, fraud, and false testimony. To assure the best in government, the nation demands a high standard of ethics and religiosity from its bureaucracy. He notes that each person who reaches the age of 73 and can prove a lawful character earns "the Title of Snilpall, or Legal, which is added to his Name." Yet, for all the idealism of the Platonic concept, the Lilliputian spirit never rises above its petty infighting, cruelties, jockeying for court position, and envy. The comic symbol of justice is ridiculous:

> with six Eyes, two before, as many behind, and on each Side one, to signify Circumspection; with a Bag of Gold open in her right Hand, and a Sword sheathed in her left, to shew she is more disposed to reward than to punish.

Gulliver's interpretation of Lilliputians' love of justice alters after he learns that they will spare him the death penalty and tender a benevolent punishment of blinding.

Swift toys with his nation of homunculi by playing with the disparity in dimensions. The emperor grants his guest freedom but requires certain compromises, notably that the giant man will enter town by the road and take care not to squash Lilliputians. To achieve military objectives, Gulliver vows to aid in fights with the enemy, to carry urgent messages, and to survey the kingdom in exchange for enough food to sustain 1,728 locals. Gulliver accepts these strictures and ventures into Mildendo, Lilliput's capital. He reaches the breaking point, however, during the Lilliputian war with Blefuscu. Towing warships like model boats in a pond, he ends the miniature sea battle and is rewarded with the title of Nardac. Like the British titles of duke, earl, and viscount, the reward is meaningless.

The stint as war hero ends with strained relations between Gulliver and the emperor and the narrow escape from blinding. After Gulliver refuses to loot Blefuscu on behalf of the emperor of Lilliput, he earns the spite of Flimnap, the imperial treasurer, and Skyresh Bolgolam, head of the navy, and faces a charge of treason. A more embarrassing gaffe is Gulliver's decision to save the palace from fire by urinating on the flames. The empress expresses her contempt and anger for this pubic display of Gulliver's privates. The emperor ends the contretemps by extending a pardon. Swift also exploits the difference in physical size by placing Gulliver in a scandal; the absurdity of a sexual liaison with a female thumbkin epitomizes Swift's coarser jests and signals a deviation from the more serious goals of satire.

The tribulations of Swift's puppet man grow ever more absurd. The burden of feeding so large a guest leads Flimnap to suggest ousting the giant. The emperor rejects the possibility of capital punishment and proposes putting out Gulliver's eyes as a more humane punishment for insubordination. On learning of the danger he faces, Gulliver wades across to Blefuscu, where he takes refuge. The first adventure ends in Chapter 8 against the backdrop of ongoing militaristic nitter-natter between Lilliput and Blefuscu. Gulliver maintains his autonomy by locating a beached boat. He repairs it, collects 300 miniature sheep and 100 oxen to slaughter, and departs on September 24, 1701. On September 26, he locates a passing English merchant vessel and returns to England. The only reward he gains from his four months at sea is a lucrative sideshow of Lilliputian animals. Swift tweaks the English merchant with a deadpan comment ending in a pun on fleece: "I find the Breed is considerably increased, especially the Sheep; which I hope will prove much to the Advantage of the Woollen Manufacture, by the Fineness of the Fleeces."

Restless for adventure at the beginning of Book II, Gulliver boards the *Adventure* on June 20, 1702, and sets sail from Liverpool toward Surat. Throughout the winter, the ship is grounded at the Cape of Good Hope for repairs. Captain John Nicholas comes down with ague, holding up the voyage until March. The crew sets out again, but, in June 1703, a storm at sea ends Gulliver's second voyage, also bound for the East Indies. During a search for water, Gulliver separates from the crew, who hurry away from oversized pursuers. On a 6,000-mile-long volcanic peninsula in the northwestern Pacific, he is marooned among the Brobdingnagians, a nation of 60-foot giants. In vain he hides among stalks of grain, where a farmer apprehends him from the ungentle hands of children. Gulliver reflects that the Lilliputians would have rejoiced over a people as proportionately small as he was to the Brobdingnagians. Swift spoofs female squeamishness in describing Gulliver's encounter with the farmer's wife, who screams at sight of a little man much as English women scream "at the Sight of a Toad or a Spider."

To supply a caretaker for Gulliver, Swift creates Glumdalclitch, a nine-year-old farm girl and one of the author's most endearing characters. Much as a child plays with a doll, Glumdalclitch watches over her charge, dresses and undresses him, and tends to his hygiene until the farmer can put him on display. By market day, Gulliver has learned enough of the native tongue to understand what his captors and viewers think of him. The farmer earns a sizable income from the ten-week journey to 18 towns to display his homunculus, who suffers from the rigors of trying to keep up with giants and from the undignified capers he must perform to earn his keeper's living. The farmer resolves to get all out of the declining little captive he can before Gulliver dies.

Swift differentiates between male and female treatment of the freakish miniature man after the queen purchases him and retains Glumdalclitch as Gulliver's attendant. Probing hands turn him this way and that as though manipulating a piece of clockwork; examiners determine that he is a *Lusus Naturae* (a freak). The Brobdingnagian philosopher-king, who attempts to rule by wise and compassionate laws, dismays Gulliver by permitting the grossness and cruelty of his oversized subjects. Resolved to survive this misfortune as he did his previous journey, Gulliver entertains at court by telling sea adventures and survives the frequent plots of the queen's dwarf, who tries to drown his competition in a cream pitcher.

In Chapter 6, Swift moves closer to his puppet's mask while summarizing English history. Over a period of five audiences, the king listens to Gulliver's description of England, takes notes, and deprecates its past. To Gulliver, English exploits are noble, but to the king's discerning eye, there are too many uprisings and too much violence:

> He was perfectly astonished with the historical Account I gave him of our Affairs during the last Century; protesting it was only an Heap of Conspiracies, rebellions, Murders, Massacres, Revolutions, Banishments: the very worst Effects that Avarice, Faction, Hypocrisy, Perfidiousness, Cruelty, Rage, Madness, Hatred, envy, Lust, Malice, and Ambition could produce.

Hearing of a nation so embroiled in treachery, mean-spiritedness, court intrigue, and insanity leads the king to conclude what Swift has already implied: that the English are "the most pernicious race of little odious Vermin that Nature ever suffered to crawl upon the Surface of the Earth." Swift ends this philosophical standoff with irony. Disdaining a nation that employs gunpowder, the king—who previously had allowed the dwarf to torment Gulliver—lauds the Brobdingnagian values, morality, and penchant for verse and mathematics.

As in Book I, Gulliver's patience wears thin. He tolerates a court role for two years, but secretly pines for home and family. As a reward for his congeniality, the queen devises a traveling coach and transports him to the seashore. An eagle snatches up the conveyance and carries it far out to sea before dropping it. English sailors aboard the *New-Holland* save Gulliver from drowning. They ferry him safely home to England and his wife and daughter by June 3, 1706. Gulliver's wife complains that these adventures should come to an end, but he doubts that he can override his evil destiny.

In Book III, Swift's protagonist is curiously uninterested in settling in with his family. For ten days, Gulliver insists that he has had enough of roving; then he accepts a generous offer of twice the salary and a staff of three. After convincing his wife that the voyage may benefit the children, Gulliver joins the *Hopewell*, a symbolic name that indicates his wide-eyed view of the world; on August 5, 1706, the ship sails from Fort St. George toward Tonquin (China). The crew weathers a severe gale, which is followed by boarding by Japanese pirates, who debate Gulliver's fate. Gulliver is surprised to obtain mercy from the non-Christian Japanese captain, but none from their Dutch translator, whom he considers "a Brother Christian." The crew sets Gulliver adrift in a canoe bearing four days' provisions. He nears some islands and camps under an overhanging crag. Establishing a home base, he explores other islands in the group and subsists on bird eggs.

Swift's penchant for whimsy turns this adventure into a fantasy: Just as Gulliver loses heart, the flying island of Laputa appears above him. At his gesture of need, the Laputans lower a seat and, by means of pulleys, raise him to their island, which functions and maneuvers through the manipulation of a lodestone, or magnet. The Laputans exhibit curious peculiarities: they hold their heads tilted so one eye can gaze up and the other down; as students of science and math, they apply their skills to control the Balnibarbi, an earthbound people on whom they drop rocks. If the surface of Balnibarbi were not so irregular, Laputans would land the entire island on the citizens below and crush them.

Gulliver requests a visit to Balnibarbi and is befriended by the ruler, Munodi. In Lagado, capital of the country, Gulliver comes upon ruined farmsteads and cities. The people explain that project leaders at the academy create unworkable plans, such as grinding ice into gunpowder, breeding fleeceless sheep, and building houses from the roof down to the foundation. These extremes of illogic destroy people and habitations. Gulliver moves on to Maldonada, capital of Glubbdubdrib, an island governed by a sorcerer capable of recalling the dead to life. To satisfy his curiosity about historical figures, Gulliver has the magician restore Alexander, Hannibal, Caesar, Pompey, Aristotle, and Homer so he can interview them. The theme of evil forms a single strand as the historical parade passes by.

Arriving at the island of Luggnagg, Gulliver engages an interpreter. Through him, Gulliver learns that 1,500 residents called Struldbrugs are immortal. He at first welcomes the thought of living forever, but then he realizes that the sufferings of old age create insurmountable problems for the deathless Luggnaggians, who grow weak, fretful, and sad. Through intervention of the king of Luggnagg, Gulliver ends a three-month stay by boarding the *Glanguenstald* on May 7 and pressing on to Japan to take passage on the *Amboyna* for Amsterdam. By April 10, 1710, Gulliver arrives safely home after an absence of five and a half years.

In Book IV, Gulliver lives for five months in harmony with his family. In September 1710, he takes control of a merchant vessel that calls into the port of Barbados in the Leeward Islands to hire replacements for crewmen who have died of fever. Along the way to Madagascar, Gulliver learns that the new mariners are brigands. They incarcerate Gulliver and set him adrift in a longboat. He arrives at a land populated by foul-smelling, tailless beasts. Amid a polarized society where a race of horse-creatures revile and segregate the Yahoos, a repulsive species of humanoids, the horse-people, known as Houyhnhnms, rescue Gulliver from Yahoo attack. In a land of health and happiness, the Houyhnhnms live in a self-styled utopia by demonstrating the extreme of Plato's concept of reason. The Yahoos, who epitomize passion, mimic the side of human nature that bestializes and perverts behavior. Because Gulliver is wearing clothing, the Houyhnhnms seem unaware at first that he bears strong resemblance to a Yahoo.

Employing a kind of teeter-totter character study, Swift depicts ebullient Gulliver in the role of Houyhnhnm student and the dour Houyhnhnms as suspicious mentors. Happy at last to find a people he can admire and emulate, Gulliver embraces the philosophy of the Houyhnhnms because they approach life with wisdom and logic and behave judiciously. By learning the local language and locating food to supplement the horse diet of oats, he thrives while contemplating the beauties of the ideal land, particularly the uselessness of a word for "falsehood." As he grows more enamored of the Houyhnhnms' noble nature, however, they begin to suspect that his gloves, vest, pants, and shoes conceal a loathed Yahoo. Thus, in this idyllic setting, Swift refuses Gulliver the haven he has sought in four voyages from his homeland.

Unable to suppress the bestial side of his nature, Gulliver offends the Houyhnhnms by relating that Englishmen ride on horses' backs and often war on neighboring nations. Gulliver's mild-mannered host compliments his guest, but is horrified at such historical motifs as hunger, violence, wine-bibbing, greed, and graft. In contrast to the illogic of England, the Houyhnhnms display virtue and reason in their choice of mates, who are selected on the basis of color, strength, beauty, and a sincere effort to upgrade the race. By cultivating temperance, hard work, exercise, and cleanliness, the Houyhnhnms have arrived at a state of sturdy resilience, which Gulliver admires. With well-controlled irony, Swift notes that, for all their virtues, the Houyhnhnms are a sterile race, ingrown and uncreative because of their insular lifestyle.

At the climax of Book IV, the Houyhnhnm assembly debates the long-standing question of genocide—whether Yahoos should be tolerated or exterminated. During this period, Gulliver grows more at home among the philosophical horse-people, but the Houyhnhnms fear that he may betray them to the ravening Yahoos, with whom he has much in common. Like the biblical Adam, Gulliver is forced out of his Eden by decree. He swoons at the news that he must depart; however, he concurs with their logic. Just as Swift himself came to acknowledge his humanity among disgusting human beings, Gulliver accepts the sentence of living with his own undeniable breed.

Swift seems to enjoy the conclusion of the idyll and the distortion of the protagonist's rationality and sense of proportion. On February 15, 1715, distraught over losing his utopian ideal and after a tearful leave-taking of his host, Gulliver departs in a crude canoe covered with Yahoo skins and fitted with sails from the same source. His friend, the Sorrel Nag, weeps, "Take Care of thy self, gentle Yahoo." Borne by Portuguese ship to Lisbon on November 5, 1715, and, two weeks later, from there to England, he is greeted by his wife, who feared that her husband had died. He berates himself for copulating with his wife, a woman who resembles a female Yahoo and has given birth during his absence to another child.

Swift's four-part quest comes to fruition at this stage of Gulliver's introspection. As lacking in imagination as his Houyhnhnm hosts, Gulliver fails to put together the four-part dissection he has viewed: first the Lilliputians; second, their opposites, the Brobdingnags; finally, after a digression among the absurd choplogic of the Laputan adventure, the clash of the Yahoos and the Houyhnhnms. He is so traumatized by the tremendous difference between the latter pair that he disdains food touched by human hands and abandons his family. He purchases two stallions with the intention of teaching them the Houyhnhnm language and spends his evenings in conversation with them. Unable to bear human contact, he stops his nose with herbs to ward off the repulsive Yahoo smell of his wife and shuns all humankind.

Throughout literature, the *modus operandi* of satire is the classification of individuals who exhibit an excess of one of the four humors. Whether the cad of Restoration stage, Roman comedy's trickster, or the louts and brigands in the novels of T. Coraghessan Boyle and John Gardner, the driving force of satiric characterization is the hyperbole that twists a human personality into a caricature. Swift's redirection of caricature generalizes from individuals to whole nations: the picayune Lilliputians, coarse Brobdingnags, witless Struldbrugs, carnal Yahoos, and dry, academic Houyhnhnms. The crowning irony of Gulliver's interaction with these boobies and boors is his failure to recognize himself as a worthy, good-intentioned traveler who possesses a fair blend of the best in humanity. (Drabble 1985; Harrison 1967; Hornstein 1973; Johnson

1968; Magill 1958; Manguel and Guadalupi 1987; Miller 1967; Pollard 1970; Rexroth 1969; Swift 1958; Thomas 1943; Woods 1947)

See also Boyle, T. Coraghessan; caricature; Gardner, John; Gulliver, Lemuel; hyperbole; satire; Swift, Jonathan; trickster.

THE HANDMAID'S TALE

Margaret Atwood's chilling, satiric stream-of-consciousness fantasy, published in Canada in 1985 and filmed by Cinecom in 1990, speculates on where and how contemporary society is likely to derail and destroy itself. Set in the late twentieth century in the fictional Republic of Gilead, the novel uses black humor, puns, and Swiftian satire in its depiction of a futuristic, barbed-wire enclosure outside Boston. Against a backdrop of indistinct sectarian religious wars, Gilead is ruled by authoritarian fundamentalist Christians—enemies of homosexuals, dissidents, adulterers, divorcees, and nonfundamentalist religious sects such as Baptists, Presbyterians, Catholics, Jews, Jehovah's Witnesses, and Quakers. Following the "President's Day Massacre," which kills the U.S. president and members of Congress, the country suspends constitutional rights and experiences nuclear war. The novel reviews a chaotic history, described in taped narratives by an unidentified female bondswoman known only as Offred. On June 25, 2195, the Twelfth Symposium studying Gileadean history convenes at the University of Denay, Nunavit—a pun on "Deny none of it"—where Professor Pieixoto surmises that Offred was the concubine of Commander Frederick Waterford, a highly placed official who was killed during a purge of liberals for harboring a subversive.

As the central intelligence, Offred wars against dehumanization while trying to learn the fate of her family. Modestly clad in a wide-sleeved, ankle-length scarlet mother hubbard, gloves, and overdress topped by a winged wimple and undergirded by petticoat, red stockings, and white cotton bloomers, 33-year-old Offred lives immured on the second story of the commander's house and serves Gilead as a breeder. An ominous presence in her pristine room is the missing light fixture from which the former Offred hanged herself rather than wait to be annihilated for inability to conceive. Named "Of Fred," a pun that also yields "off-red," the Handmaid replaces her predecessor as the handmaid of the aging Commander of the Faithful—later identified as Frederick Waterford—chief of the Eyes, Gilead's security force—who services her in monthly ritual matings.

A matter-of-fact narrator, Offred recounts the rapid transformation of Gilead from freewheeling mart of Feels on Wheels, Bun-Dle Buggies, and Pornomarts to a puritanical concentration camp. She describes the swift loss of job, financial control, and identity that precedes the usurpation of her body by the state. Offred is a literary foil to both her militant mother, a dedicated women's libber, and Moira, a hoydenish, irrepressible lesbian college friend who organizes an "underwhore party" to peddle slinky lingerie to college classmates. Moira resurfaces at the Rachel and Leah Re-education Center, slangily dubbed the Red Center, where women are interned by a female-controlled brainwashing regimen. Set up in an abandoned high school gymnasium and run by the schoolmarmish Aunt Lydia and her amazon phalanx, the Red Center forces fertile white breeders like Offred and Moira into compliance with matings mandated by the misogynist hierarchy. Moira rebels and makes an abortive flight to Salem before being captured and forced into whoredom.

A particularly twisted form of satire, the caricature of Aunt Lydia, a khaki-clad, teacherly termagant, reveals a sadistic matron posing as counselor of Gilead's young females. Alert and attentive, Aunt Lydia, armed with electric cattle prod and whistle, surveys the girls to stamp out the rebellious, disobedient, conniving, or immodest among the faithful. Mouthing a philosophy of either/or's, Aunt Lydia influences Offred, one of her pupils, through martinetlike repetition of such platitudes as "They also serve who only stand and wait," a wryly humorous citation from John Milton's sonnet on blindness. Skilled as an indoctrinator, Lydia urges, "Think of it as being in the army." Like her peers, Aunt Sara and Aunt Elizabeth, Aunt Lydia is named for a product, Lydia Pinkham, a vegetable and alcohol elixir that women of the early twentieth century took as a health restorative and tonic for "women's complaints." In similar vein, Sara and Elizabeth lampoon the sweetly feminine founders of Sara Lee desserts and Elizabeth Arden cosmetics.

Atwood tightens the tension in her fable as Lydia and her cohorts fail to program Offred, a bright pseudo-collaborator who skillfully works the system against itself. Aswirl in her brain are doubts about the future, fear for her loved ones, a controlled urge for suicide, suspicions that her lover may spy for the Eyes, a spy unit, and concern that she has no lotion to maintain her smooth complexion. She relives scenes in which Luke is shot during a dash for the Canadian border or fantasizes that he is imprisoned and tortured. Her dreams and thoughts turn frequently to the old days: "Why did they buy so many different clothes, in the old days? To trick the men into thinking they were several different women." Her words echo with longing, "I want to go to bed, make love, right now. I think the word *relish*. I could eat a horse." In a parody of the Lord's Prayer, she speaks her frustration at the absence of love in her life.

The end of the novel carries the reader two centuries into the future to 2195, out of range of proof that Offred, a diarist of 30 cassette tapes, was able to escape Gilead and reunite with her past. Professor Pieixoto, who studies the evidence and presents his views at a symposium of experts, assumes that she migrated to Bangor, Maine, and found shelter with Quakers by trusting the "Underground Frailroad," a pun on similar routes taken by fleeing slaves before the American Civil War. Pieixoto deduces that Offred emigrated to either

Canada or England and, to protect her family, may have lived out her life in seclusion.

Reflecting real episodes of violence, censorship, arch-conservatism, and anti-female measures throughout Canada, the United States, Iran, Romania, and Russia, *The Handmaid's Tale* focuses its dark humor on ultra-right-wing sexist coercion. The few women who retain fertility in second marriages and illegal liaisons are torn from husbands and lovers and rationed out as Handmaids to breed children for the elite echelon, the Commanders of the Faithful. The remaining female population scuttles about under the eye of a repressive patriarchal regime, reciting bromides about the family, performing public prayers and executions, and rejoicing at the birth of healthy babies.

Atwood's study of women persecuting women offers thoughtful satiric commentary on femininity. Under the discipline of a Martha or household guard and the tight-lipped care of Rita and Cora, the Commander's suspicious, short-tempered servants, Offred lives in a pleasant, demure late-Victorian home in a chaste upstairs cell. Without reading material, television, cosmetics, cigarettes, tea, or coffee, she readies her body for motherhood. In Chapter 11, she goes to the doctor and repulses his offer to impregnate her to spare her an ignoble death for failure to conceive. Her mind returns to the cry of Rachel in the book of Genesis, "Give me children, or else I die." In Serena's parlor, Offred prepares for required copulation as a gospel hymn—"Come to the Church in the Wildwood"—rings spiritedly with *double entendre*.

Atwood highlights enmity between different levels of women by pitting Offred against Serena Joy, the commander's wife. A former evangelist and singer, Serena limps arthritically about her garden, lops off symbolic spent tulip heads, and glowers at Offred. Each month, Serena supervises the passionless ritual intercourse intended to provide the family with a child. In the sitting room, with the house staff present, the Commander reads from Scripture, a privilege forbidden to women of any status. Upstairs in a canopied bed, he mounts Offred, who lies supine between the spread thighs of the Commander's wife. Offred appears to comply with the perverse procedures while secretly courting the commander during illicit night visits and simultaneously conducting an affair with Nick, the commander's macho chauffeur. She bargains with the commander to learn the fate of her husband Luke and militant feminist mother and schemes to escape and reunite with her young daughter.

Ostensibly a decent, compliant soldier, the commander follows the prescribed mating ritual to provide Gilead with children during a period of declining birth rate. Offred's doctor suggests that the commander may be sterile, a condition that afflicts many survivors of nuclear contamination. Atwood imbues the commander with contrast: the needful lover and aging bon vivant. On the first unauthorized "date" with the gray-haired commander, Offred creeps downstairs to an off-limits hideaway for a game of Scrabble, at which she excels by spelling prolix, quartz, quandary, sylph, and rhythm. Expecting perversion, possibly torture, she is surprised that he craves affection, a commodity long since banned in pious, repressive Gilead. In exchange, she asks for hand lotion and information about the outside world. A fatherly man at home, the commander, his spirit as dry of passion as Offred's skin is of moisture, savors the sight of her hands stroking on lotion.

One of Atwood's most pointed satires occurs on a festive occasion when Commander Fred dresses his Handmaid in high heels, makeup, and sequined and feathered costume, cloaks her from observation, and escorts her by private car to Jezebel's, a garish night spot staffed by whores and designed to improve trade relations with Arab and Japanese businessmen. As though squiring a paid escort, he offers her a drink and describes the purpose of prostitution in Gilead, where, theoretically, immoral practices no longer exist. Atwood drains the nightclub fantasy of its allure by closing in on the expected conclusion—seduction in a motel. The commander leads Offred to a room for the type of copulation that people once took for granted—the sexual union of consenting adults. Without his uniform, he appears shrunken and old. Offred, appalled at a situation that requires her to act the part of call girl, lingers in the bathroom before performing her part without passion or meaning.

After a difficult evening with Commander Fred, Offred retires to her room to cower in the closet as she represses hysteria. The dreary, repetitive cycle of grocery shopping with Handmaid Ofglen, anticipating pregnancy, Prayvaganzas, Salvagings, and birthings locks Offred in a circumscribed lifestyle that revolves around her menstrual cycle, the proof that her monthly matings have yet to bring sperm and egg together. Her survival hinges on being able to conceive within three years. At the novel's climax, events press Offred to desperation. After Ofglen's arrest, Offred panics that Ofglen will implicate her in the conspiracies of Mayday, an underground rebel network. When Offred returns to the commander's door, she encounters Serena Joy dangling a sequined costume in hand to indicate that she knows of Offred's clandestine rendezvous with the commander.

Atwood presses Offred toward an unappealing set of alternatives. Repulsed by contemplation of fire, suicide, escape to her lover Nick, pleading for the commander's mercy, flight, or murder of Serena Joy, Offred opts for Nick "the private eye," a satiric allusion to Nick and Nora Charles of "The Thin Man," a popular pair of movie detectives. Before Offred takes action, Nick bursts into her room and insists that she accompany two unidentified men in a police van. As Offred complies with an arrest for revealing state secrets, the commander objects to the lack of a search warrant. Her captors ignore him and thrust Offred into the van. Atwood concludes the novel with an insider's twist—a rapid flight to the future to gain a brief glimpse at the past.

Critics have responded with a mix of praise and censure for Atwood's dire fable and its too witty, too detached conclusion. Some readers declare her premise—that the United States could be easily commandeered by right-wing, misogynist fascists—a workable satire, but an unlikely eventuality. Others admire her ingenious use of the feminist apologia as a basis to ridicule aspects of society already in evidence—the resurgence of fascism, fundamentalism, antiabortion sentiment, and blatant misogyny. Most critics find the work historically possible, exacting, and so charged with warning that they proclaim it a feminist *1984* and satiric dystopian classic on a par with those of Aldous Huxley and George Orwell. (Atwood 1972; *Contemporary Authors* 1994; *Contemporary Authors New Revision Series* 1989; *Contemporary Literary Criticism* 1987; Davidson 1986; *Discovering Authors* 1993; Dreifus 1992; Hammer 1990; Ingersoll 1991; *Major Twentieth-Century Writers* 1990; McCombs 1988; Van Spanckeren and Castro 1988; Wilson 1993)

See also Atwood, Margaret; black humor; double entendre; parody; pun; Swift, Jonathan.

HARRIS, JOEL CHANDLER

The reality behind the pseudonymous Uncle Remus, teller of West African beast fables, Joel Chandler Harris was a Southern journalist, editor, and peacemaker during the troubled Reconstruction era. A native of Eatonton, Georgia, he was born December 9, 1848, from an unlikely mating between Mary Harris and an unnamed Irish laborer, who wooed and bedded her, then left her to cope with an infant. The outlook for Harris was limited until he met Joseph Addison Turner, editor of the *Countryman*, a weekly journal. At Turnwold plantation, Harris, a shy, curious child, served as printer's devil and educated himself by reading from the manor's considerable library and through contact with Uncle George Terrell and Old Harbert, the American equivalent of African griots.

When the Civil War ended Turner's fortune and his paper, Harris moved on in 1866 to typeset the *Macon Telegraph*. Greater opportunities came in the form of an assistant's post on the *New Orleans Crescent Monthly*, where he became friends with humorist Mark Twain and local colorist Lafcadio Hearn. Later career moves include editor of the Forsythe, Georgia, *Monroe Advertiser* from 1867 to 1870 and writer for the *Savannah Morning News*. An outbreak of yellow fever in 1876 forced Harris and wife Esther LaRose inland to Atlanta, the city most intimately connected with his development as editor and teller of the Uncle Remus stories. As editor and adviser to Henry Grady, proponent of the New South, Harris helped to shape the future of the conciliatory *Atlanta Constitution*, where he edited and wrote over the next quarter century. To house a large family, he built Wren's Nest, his country home, now a museum and garden on Atlanta's outer edge.

A chance reading of an inaccurate article—William Owens's "Folklore of Southern Negroes" in *Lippincott's Magazine* (December 1877)—impelled Harris to pen a rebuttal, "Negro Folklore: The Story of Mr. Rabbit and Mr. Fox, as Told by Uncle Remus," published July 20, 1879. Perhaps realizing the trove of slave narrative that he had absorbed in his youth, he began collecting, ordering, and compiling stories as a sideline to his job as journalist. Some of his search took him to Daufuskie Islanders living near Hilton Head, North Carolina. In his mid-fifties, Harris turned his writing from editorials and economic news to the lore he remembered from Turnwold. He presented the Uncle Remus stories first in the *Constitution;* on his own, he published *Uncle Remus: His Songs*

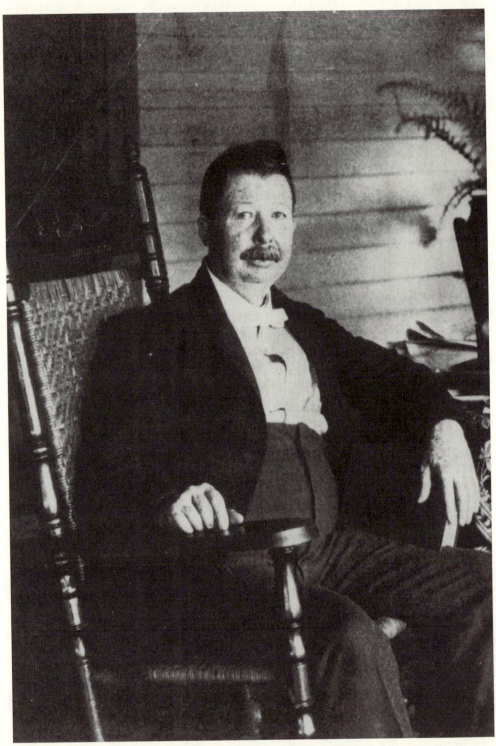

American teller of Uncle Remus tales Joel Chandler Harris in 1900

and *His Sayings* (1880) and *Nights with Uncle Remus* (1883)—the latter introduces Daddy Jack, a Gullah narrator whose complex dialect inhibited the popularity of the work. Harris's knowledge of a variety of character types and dialects became the basis for *Mingo and Other Sketches in Black and White* (1884), *Free Joe and Other Georgian Sketches* (1887), and *Daddy Jack the Runaway, and Other Stories Told After Dark* (1889). In addition, Harris published 20 more volumes, including *Gabriel Tolliver* (1902), a reflective study of Reconstruction; novels and novellas; a fictional autobiography, *On the Plantation* (1892); short story collections; and children's stories. His final work, *Uncle Remus and the Little Boy* (1910), was published posthumously.

In 1907, Harris, with the help of his son Julian, collected the tales in *Uncle Remus's Magazine,* which Don Marquis helped edit. The journal merged with *Home* magazine after Harris's death from nephritis on July 3, 1908. Critical studies of his stories and of their African beginnings indicate that Harris did more than transmit folklore: his inventive style and command of dialect broadened the trickster tales into recognizable short stories and a valuable insight into Negro folklore. Popularized by Walt Disney's double Oscar-winning *Song of the South* (1946), which was the first film to blend human and animated characters, the mischievous Br'er Rabbit and his critter pals accompany Uncle Remus down a country road, sing "Zip-a-Dee-Do-Dah," and act out the famous Tarbaby story, initiated by the voice of James Baskett playing the lovable Negro narrator. The story follows a blend of Harris originals, "Br'er Rabbit, Br'er Fox, and the Tar Baby," published November 16, 1879. After Uncle Remus initiates his young listener into the self-sufficiency of the trickster rabbit, he spins out the humorous Tarbaby incident in which the rabbit's curiosity and stubbornness nearly cost him his life. Stalked by Br'er Fox, the rabbit is unaware of the snare and comes "pacin' down de road-lippity-clippity, clippity-lippity-dez ez sassy ez a jay-bird."

Harris's study of West African lore in a Georgia plantation setting amalgamated universal beast lore and the influence of the American South. A victim of plantation manners, Br'er Rabbit insists that the silent Tarbaby reply to his greeting. Further refusal ignites the rabbit's temper. Blows to the Tarbaby's body stick the rabbit, paw and foot, to the phony figure. To the boy's questions about how Br'er Rabbit eludes the fox, Uncle Remus replies, "He mout, en den agin he moutent. Some say Jedge B'ar come 'long en loosed 'im—some say he didn't." The suspense is the hallmark of the plot, which turns on a constant tension between large menacing animals and their smaller, wiser victims. (Dorson 1959; Ehrlich and Carruth 1982; Harris 1952; Perkins 1991; Wilson and Ferris 1989)

See also beast lore; satire; trickster; Twain, Mark.

 # HART, MOSS

Sharing with George S. Kaufman the success of *You Can't Take It with You* (1936), Moss Hart won a place on Broadway, in community theater revivals, and in anthologies that sets the whimsical comedy among America's finest stage satires. Hart attained his first win with *Once in a Lifetime* (1930) and followed with *Face the Music* (1932), a satire on New York City graft; a serious study of art, *Merrily We Roll Along* (1934); and *I'd Rather Be Right* (1937), a satire on the presidency of Franklin Roosevelt; later winners include *The Man Who Came to Dinner* (1939) and *George Washington Slept Here* (1940). His bestselling autobiography, *Act One* (1959), credits New York, his hometown, with allowing him to be creative. He comments on dreaming, "For those who did, it unlocked its gates and its treasures, not caring who they were or where they came from." Born in the Bronx on October 24, 1904, to Barnett and Lillian Solomon Hart, Moss Hart—who grew rich on his first Broadway hit and bought a country home and a house on New York's Sutton Place—grew up in a colorless tenement and wrote plays as an escape. At age ten, he quit school to go to work. His training with the Thalian Players and the hands-on job experience as floorwalker at Macy's and summer camp social director in the Catskills preceded an acting role in Eugene O'Neill's *The Emperor Jones* and less lucrative spots in summer stock.

Hart enjoyed close friendships with the outstanding figures of American criticism and literary productivity—Alexander Woollcott, Ben Hecht, Cornelia Otis Skinner, Cole Porter, and Thornton Wilder. He shared a writers' escape at a stone summer cottage at Neshobe Island on Lake Bomoseen, Vermont. Hart's New Hope, Pennsylvania, farm on Aquetong Road was convenient to Kaufman's Bucks County estate and writer's haven, Barley Sheaf Farm. The duo's first collaboration was *Once in a Lifetime* (1930), a satire that lampooned Hollywood, where it was filmed in 1933. Kaufman and Hart later focused on Woollcott's demanding traits by writing *The Man Who Came to Dinner* (1939), a successful comedy about an unexpected houseguest who exasperates his hosts. The main character, Whiteside, proves so daunting to his nurse that she exclaims:

> After one month with you, Mr. Whiteside, I am going to work in a munitions factory. From now on, anything I can do to help exterminate the human race will fill me with the greatest of pleasure. If Florence Nightingale had ever nursed YOU, Mr. Whiteside, she would have married Jack the Ripper.

Hart's later writing shifted from satire and comedy to collaboration with Kurt Weill on a musical, *Lady in the Dark* (1941); *Winged Victory* (1944), a late–World War II play filmed by George Cukor for Daryl F. Zanuck; a study of anti-Semitism, *Gentleman's Agreement* (1947), which won Academy Awards for best picture, director, and supporting actress; *Hans Christian Andersen* (1954), a troubled movie starring Danny Kaye; and the 1954 version of *A Star Is Born*. His stage direction of *My Fair Lady* (1956) and *Camelot* (1961) solidified his name as a show business achiever. Two years after his death in Palm Springs, California, on December 20, 1961, his autobiography was filmed, starring George Hamilton as Hart and Jason Robards as Kaufman. (Burdick 1974; Ehrlich and Carruth 1982; Halliwell 1995; Hart 1961; Katz 1982; Kunitz 1942; Magnusson 1990)

See also Algonquin Club; Kaufman, George S.; Parker, Dorothy; repartee; whimsy; *You Can't Take It with You*.

HARVEY

A Pulitzer Prize-winning classic comedy of manners, *Harvey* (1944) derives from author Mary Chase's attempt to take people's minds off World War II. A whimsical spoof of social class and its close call with a tony insane asylum, the play is irrevocably connected with actor James Stewart, who played protagonist Elwood P. Dowd in the 1950 movie and in the Hallmark Hall of Fame reprise aired March 20, 1972. Although Chase enjoyed a smashing career with four Broadway plays, children's works, and name recognition in her own day, she failed to outlive the fame of her star invisible character, Harvey, a six-foot-plus pooka, a Celtic supernatural being that takes the form of a rabbit. Seen only by Elwood, a sweet-natured midwestern lush, the rabbit escorts him daily for martinis and chats with a variety of workers, cab drivers, tipplers, and chance acquaintances. To assure himself and Harvey of drinking partners, Elwood hands out calling cards.

Chase, who reworked her farce 50 times to straighten out a devilish kink, was a Denver native with a natural flair for off-the-wall comedy. She shared with Elwood's sister Veta an affinity for the pathfinder's spirit. As Veta Louise Simmons explains to the society editor of the *Evening News Bee:* "My mother, you know . . . the late Marcella Pinkney Dowd, pioneer cultural leader—she came here by ox-team as a child and she founded the Wednesday forum." Born February 25, 1907, Chase was the daughter of Irish immigrant Mary McDonough, who kept house for four brothers prospecting in the Rockies, and Frank Dernard Coyle, a failed prospector turned flour salesman. A rowdy bibliophile with a love of her Uncle Timothy's recitations of Irish lore and a yen to teach herself classical Greek, Mary attended local schools and the University of Denver and graduated from the University of Colorado at Boulder. After a seven-year stint as reporter for the *Rocky Mountain News,* she gave up the city beat, picketed for liberal causes, and, when not otherwise engaged, reared Michael, Colin, and Jerry, the three sons born to her and reporter Robert Lamont Chase. Her postmotherhood career revived with a job as a stringer, lobbyist, radio scriptwriter, and publicist for UPI. She also served as publicity director for the Teamsters' Union in the 1940s. Already a successful author of plays for screen and stage after completing her first play, *Now I've Done It,* as part of a WPA project, Chase published "He's Our Baby" (1945) in *Ladies' Home Journal.* She reached her height—and the William McLeod Raine award—with *Harvey,* which preceded two more Broadway plays: *Mrs. McThing* (1952), starring Helen Hayes, and *Bernardine* (1952), a study of teenagers.

From the outset, *Harvey* presented unique problems. Director Antoinette Perry's staging difficulties with a rubbery rabbit ended when producer Brocker Pemberton transformed Elwood's companion into a hallucination. Elwood, first played by vaudevillian Frank Fay, then by Jimmy Stewart, overwhelms the drama with a warmth suited to an unruffleable alcoholic—described by his niece as the "biggest screwball in town." He allows his sister to maneuver him into Chumley's Rest to receive serum number 977, a formulation guaranteed to make him as normal as everybody else. The film version won Josephine

Hull an Oscar for playing Veta and Stewart an Academy Award nomination.

The satire of Chase's *Harvey* focuses on the social aspirations of Veta's daughter Myrtle Mae, an old maid whom her mother describes as "charming in a modish Rancho Rose toned crepe, picked up at the girdle with a touch of magenta on emerald." A hurried discussion of family problems precedes an afternoon musicale:

Myrtle:	Why did [Grandmother] have to leave all her property to Uncle Elwood?
Veta:	Well, I suppose it was because she died in his arms. People are sentimental about things like that.
Myrtle:	You always say that and it doesn't make sense. She couldn't make out her will after she died, could she?
Veta:	Don't be didactic, Myrtle Mae. It's not becoming in a young girl, and men loathe it.

Veta's attempt to introduce Myrtle to local society ends in disaster in what appears to be a Dowd family pattern: Elwood arrives unexpectedly, introduces the prize guest, Aunt Ethel Chauvenet, to his hallucination, and scares everybody away. Ironically, Veta, who depends on Elwood for a home since her departure from Des Moines, decides that living with him is unbearable in the extreme. She resolves to have him committed.

Scene 2 intensifies the satire on social climbers after Veta takes her compliant brother to an upscale clinic run by Dr. William R. Chumley, a caricature of a reclusive socialite psychiatrist who is more interested in a cocktail party than in the admittance of patients. In her agitation over commitment proceedings, Veta demands to see Chumley and, temporarily placated by Dr. Sanderson, his staff psychiatrist, admits, "Every once in a while I see that big white rabbit myself. Now isn't that terrible? . . . And what's more—he's every bit as big as Elwood says he is." Dr. Sanderson concludes that Veta, a charmingly jittery ditz with a tendency toward melodrama, is a "cunning psychopath" and that the clinic has admitted the wrong patient. Sanderson patronizes Dowd to cover up the clinic's mistake, then confides to Nurse Kelly:

All he does is hang around bars. He doesn't work. All that corny bowing and getting up out of his chair every time a woman makes a move. Why he's as outdated as a cast-iron deer. But you'd sit with him in a bar and let him flatter you—You're a wonderful girl, Kelly.

Sanderson's cynicism prepares for the next crisis—the realization that Dowd is the patient and that Sanderson has let him escape. Dr. Chumley heightens the social satire by defining a psychiatrist's function—"to tell the difference between those who are reasonable, and those who merely talk and act reasonably."

Chase emphasizes the central theme of *Harvey* in frequent references to people's dreams and hopes. A little wistful in his reminiscence, Elwood sums up a need for attention and acceptance in his description of evenings with Harvey and the friends they make at the bar:

Elwood P. Dowd (James Stewart) gazes fondly at his portrait with a Celtic pooka manifested as a rabbit (Harvey) in the 1950 movie, which was based on Mary Chase's comedy of manners play *Harvey*.

> They come over. They sit with us. They drink with us. They talk to us. They tell about the big terrible things they have done. The big wonderful things they will do. Their hopes, their regrets, their loves, their hates.

Elwood concludes that "nobody ever brings anything small into a bar." The line appropriately describes Harvey, who outdistances anything the other patrons boast of. In the falling action, Dr. Chumley sequesters himself with Elwood to discuss his own fantasy: he longs to meet a pretty, sympathetic woman in Akron at a cottage camp under a grove of maples. His dream scenario extends to two weeks of tender head pats, cold beer, and her voice crooning, "Poor thing! Oh, you poor, poor thing!"

The appeal of *Harvey* reaches beyond ridicule to the larger issue of social acceptance, which some critics were unwilling to accord a play about a polite but hazy inebriate. At the resolution, the satire—on pompous psychiatrists, a social-climbing sister who freeloads on her brother, an unmarried niece who wants to sell the house immediately after Elwood's commitment, and the off-center thinking of Elwood, who compensates for his dinginess with a thorough interest in other people, especially strangers—gives the stage back to comedy and the sentimental reunion of Elwood and his inept, scheming sister. After she halts the treatment to end his hallucinations, she throws herself into his arms. Elwood, who understands how a hard day of decision making has exceeded her limitations, accepts her and departs with a query for Dr. Chumley: "Doctor, for years I've known what my family thinks of Harvey. But I've often wondered what Harvey's family thinks of me." (Chase 1958; *Contemporary Authors* 1994; Roberts 1962; Rothe 1949)

See also caricature; farce; irony; whimsy.

HELLER, JOSEPH

One of the outstanding satirists of the twentieth century, Joseph Heller produced a stir with his masterly first novel, *Catch-22* (1961), one of the most varied, entertaining, and edifying examples of the sustained satiric novel. The center of a spirited debate, Heller has been alternately praised for denouncing the antihumanism of technowar and censured for praising a falsifier and wartime gold brick. Yossarian, the character at the heart of the debate, seems unbearably aware not only of the waste of soldiers in an insatiable war machine, but the waste of human cries against a stony-hearted bureaucracy. The screen version of *Catch-22*, filmed by Paramount Pictures in 1970, became a cult classic for antiwar protesters and boosted Heller's recognition as one of the era's most compelling humanists and complex novelists of his time.

The third child of Lena and Isaac Heller, a bakery truck driver, Joseph "Joe" Heller, the second son of first-generation Russian-Jewish immigrants, was born May 1, 1923, in the Coney Island section of Brooklyn, where he worked in childhood as a Western Union delivery boy. The unanticipated death of his father in surgery in 1928 left Heller with a wry appreciation for black humor, the cosmic joke that claims humanity for its victim. As readers may guess from a close reading of *Catch-22*, Heller came of age in time to serve in World War II as wing bombardier on 60 missions aboard a B-25, a key setting of the novel and the constant terror of Yossarian, Heller's fictional mask. A decorated war hero, Phi Beta Kappan, and Fulbright scholar at Oxford with a B.A. from New York University and an M.A. from Columbia, Heller was a professor of English, drama, and creative writing at Yale, Pennsylvania State, and City College of New York. He opted to write ad copy for *Time, Look*, and *McCalls* during the 1950s; under the pseudonym Max Orange he scripted episodes of *McHale's Navy*; then, with his first novel well under way, he took up fiction full time. Heller turned out quality short fiction for *Cosmopolitan, Atlantic Monthly*, and *Esquire*; contributed to *New Republic, Smart, Nation*, and other periodicals; and collaborated on screenplays (*Sex and the Single Girl, Casino Royale, Dirty Dingus Magee*, and *Of Men and Women*); but he didn't feel that he had met the challenge until his antiwar novel brought him recognition.

Heller's later works—*We Bombed in New Haven* (1968), the one-act stage version of *Catch-22* (1971), another portion of the novel published as *Clevinger's Trial* (1974), *Something Happened* (1974), *Good as Gold* (1979), and *God Knows* (1985), a humorously anachronistic study of King David's declining years—lack the gutsy, existential humor of *Catch-22*. A rough bout with Guillain-Barré syndrome beginning December 12, 1981, temporarily sidelined Heller. Sum-

American satirist Joseph Heller in 1963

marizing his three weeks of intensive care for gradual paralysis, he reflects: "I could hear, I could answer, I could joke, I could laugh; and compulsive and insatiable was my appetite for distraction." He spent six months at the Rusk Institute of Rehabilitation Medicine and left in a wheelchair. During this stressful period, he turned to the friendship of his regular gang, the Gourmet Club, composed of Mario Puzo, Mel Brooks, and Speed Vogel, who served as live-in companion, nurse, and co-author of Heller's autobiographical *No Laughing Matter* (1986). Heller, who feared that his career was compromised by nerve damage, survived to receive two French prizes, the Prix Interallie and the Prix Medicis Étranger. He continues to develop the character John Yossarian in a sequel to *Catch-22*. (Bermel 1982; *Contemporary Authors* 1994; *Discovering Authors* 1993; Heller 1961; Heller and Vogel 1986; Merrill 1987; Nagel 1984; Potts 1982)

See also caricature; *Catch-22*; satire; Yossarian.

HENLEY, BETH

Named along with Marsha Norman as one of the strong emerging dramatic voices from the late twentieth-century South, Beth Henley produced a multiple winner with *Crimes of the Heart*, a satiric glimpse into the lives of a quirky, off-center, small-town "family with a past." Winner of the New York Drama Critic's Award, a Tony, and a Pulitzer Prize, the play opened at the Actors Theatre of Louisville in February 1979 before its New York debut at the Manhattan Theatre Club in 1980, followed by presentation at the John Golden Theatre in New York City on November 4, 1981. *Crimes of the Heart* worked well on film in the 1986 version, which starred Jessica Lange, Diane Keaton, and Sissy Spacek, who was nominated for an Oscar.

Henley has good reason to choose the South as the setting for her plays. The daughter of actor Elizabeth Josephine Becker and attorney Charles Boyce was born May 8, 1952, in Jackson, Mississippi. After earning a B.F.A. from Southern Methodist University in 1974 and completing a year's graduate study in drama at the University of Illinois, Henley acted at Dallas's Theatre Three, taught at SMU, and directed the Dallas Minority Repertory Theatre. In 1975, she taught acting and voice at the University of Illinois. Discouraged with the paucity of roles available for southern females, she turned to drama and screenwriting. Her canon, beginning with a class assignment, *Am I Blue?* (1973), contains an energetic burst of comic and satiric artistry for stage, television, and cinema, including *Morgan's Daughters* (1979), *Miss Firecracker Contest* (1980), *The Wake of Jamey Foster* (1982), *The Debutante Ball* (1985), *The Lucky Spot* (1986), and *True Stories* (1986). Critics squeezed out so-so ratings for her screenplay *Nobody's Fool* (1986), which lacks the candor, compassion, and quixotic jest of *Crimes of the Heart*. A similar fate assailed *Miss Firecracker* (1989), a seriocomic study of a wayward spirit who seeks acceptance in a paltry Fourth of July beauty contest. Ably acted by Holly Hunter and Mary Steenburgen, the movie overshot audience expectations with its emphasis on near-miss bathos that bemuses rather than entertains.

At home with the southern gothic modes of Eudora Welty, William Faulkner, and Flannery O'Connor, Henley succeeds with *Crimes of the Heart* because she gives full play to the offbeat eccentricities of the three orphaned McGrath sisters of Hazlehurst, Mississippi, whose father—who they recall had nice teeth—deserted the family when the girls were young. The mother's depression and suicide give a clue to the family's extremes of behavior: she hanged her cat and herself so that she wouldn't have to die alone. In the opening scene, set "five years after Hurricane Camille," the daughters—Babe, Meg, and Lenny—muddle through multiple failures with marriage, career, and male-female relationships. A revealing moment depicts spinster Lenny alone in the kitchen of the family homeplace, where she attempts to set candles on cookies while she sings "Happy Birthday" to herself.

The height of the play is Babe's misguided attempt to murder her husband Zackery, a state senator from Copiah County and patriarchal tyrant who discovers her fling with Willie Jay, a local black youth. The satiric caricature of the meddling family malcontent, Cousin Chick, bears the community's disdain for Babe's crazy attempted murder. Chick refers to Babe's shooting of Zackery as "this heinous crime" and "manslaughter with intent to commit murder" and high-handedly orders Babe to cooperate with the attorney, "that nice-looking young Lloyd boy." Babe defies Chick's melodramatic demand for a confession with her stubborn explanation of the shooting, "I just didn't like his stinking looks! And I don't like yours much, either, Chick the Stick!" In Act II, Babe carries on a one-sided phone call with Zackery that dawdles along with "Uh huh . . . uh huh . . . Oh, I'm sorry. . . . Please don't scream." Defiant in the face of jail time for attempted murder, she looks forward to a respite from her over-bearing mate and his spying sister Lucille and an opportunity to learn to play her new sax.

Unresolved family failures overhang the play like dusty valances. The girls relive their mother's sorrow and inertia—the days that she sat on the back porch steps, smoked, and flung ashes at bugs and ants. In defiance of claims that she should be "put away" for acting crazy like her mother, Babe retorts that their mother wasn't crazy, only the victim of "a very bad day." The sisters' sibling rivalries sound picayunish, particularly Lenny's contention that Grandmama sewed "twelve golden jingle bells" in Meg's skirt when the other girls got only three each, but their unity in hard times holds steady, proving that their mother's death brought them together against a callous community and troubled family life.

As the play winds down to a satisfying denouement, Henley turns from satire to comedy. Babe and Lenny discuss Zackery's condition and the death of Billy Boy, an aged horse struck by lightning. Babe consoles, "Life sure can be miserable" (Henley 1981, p. 97). The attorney discovers that Zackery's attempt to blackmail Babe has crumbled in the welter of scandal that attaches to the senator. Chick's diatribe against "you trashy McGraths and your trashy ways: hanging yourselves in cellars; carrying on with married men; shooting your own husbands" ignites Lenny's dormant anger; Lenny grabs a broom and runs Chick up a mimosa tree. The play concludes with birthday cake for breakfast and the girls at last developing emotionally into women. (Buck 1992; *Contemporary Authors* 1994; *Contemporary Literary Criticism* 1983; Davidson and Wagner-Martin 1995; *Dictionary of Literary Biography* 1987; Hargrove 1984; Henley 1981; Laughlin 1986)

See also bathos; black humor; caricature; comedy; diatribe; Norman, Marsha.

HORACE

A polished poet and satirist, Horace produced his *Sermones* (Satires or Chats, 35–30 B.C.) at a crucial point in Roman history, beginning less than a decade after Julius Caesar's assassination. Horace continued writing during the set-tling-in years of Caesar Augustus, Rome's first emperor and the founder of the

Roman poet and satirist Horace, 65–8 B.C.

Pax Romana, a treasured respite from a decade of civil anarchy. Horace was eminently qualified for the job of Rome's chief satirist, for, whether joshing a bore at the dinner table or questioning the values of grumblers, he gained a reputation for tolerance, open-mindedness, self-control, and versatility. Untainted by privilege or soft city life, Quintus Horatius Flaccus was a country boy born December 8, 65 B.C., in Venusia, a mountain town in Apulia on the Appian Way near Mount Vultur. The motherless son of a freedman (no doubt manumitted by the illustratious Horatii, from whom he adopted a patronym) and probably an only child, Horace profited from his father's upright behavior and wise husbandry of income from his job as provincial tax collector and part-time clerk to an auctioneer. A first-generation college man, Horace—dark-haired, stocky, but handsome at age 12—attended classes under the notorious rhetorician Orbilius, the Mr. Chips of Rome's prep-school elite whose texts derived primarily from Homer and Livy. Because the boy had no servants to attend him, his father accompanied him to Rome and, acting as *paedagogus* (body servant), supplied daily valet service and chaperonage to and from class. In later years, Horace notes in his *Sermones* that the example of his ambitious, sober parent was the basis for his later contentment.

After a tough beginning curriculum of Greek and Roman classics, Horace emulated the most serious students by journeying to Athens' best philosophy school in 44 B.C. He was classmate to two aristocrats, Marcus Valerius Messalla and Cicero's unruly son Marcus, who introduced him to dinner parties and the city's youthful intelligentsia. The college idyll ceased with Rome's revolution. A victim of the zeitgeist, Horace, as conservative as his father, was outraged by Caesar's assassination and, as a tribune and legion commander on Brutus's staff, allied with the doomed republican faction. His legion met defeat in 42 B.C. at Philippi in northern Greece, where co-conspirators Brutus and Cassius fell to the combined armies of Marc Antony and Octavian, Caesar's nephew and heir. Not entirely successful as a soldier, Horace, imitating the Greek Archilochus, recalls in his satire of army days that sitting by the firelight with comrades outweighed dropping his shield and fleeing to save his hide.

After Octavian—later known as Augustus Caesar—began pulling together the shreds of Rome and stitching the seams that would form an empire, he granted well-intentioned men like Horace an amnesty. The poet did some growing up in his early twenties and, following his father's loss of fortune and subsequent death, grudgingly concluded that the self-proclaimed Emperor Augustus was good for the battered nation. Augustus, keen on hiring the most promising men, offered Horace a position as his private secretary; according to Suetonius's biographical sketch, Horace opted for a mundane job as a treasury clerk in the quaestor's office. The choice proved auspicious for his growth as a writer, for he filled the daily ennui of desk work with brief scribblings that grew into his satires and epodes. As he reflects in a letter to Julius Flores on the shift in his life, Horace exults that the twists of fortune yanked him from his idealistic search for truths *inter silvas Academi* (among the groves of Academe) to a lost political cause and into poverty, from which he emerged a writer.

Critical commentary on Horace's development notes the scattered loyalties and emotional chaos common to thoughtful citizens who survived the bloodbath brought on by ten years of civil war. When the paranoia subsided, he discovered that the writer's life agreed with him. At the age of 25, Horace had ingratiated himself with the best of Rome's literate world—Varius Rufus and Virgil, who was Augustus's propagandist and the better of the two budding epic poets. With these powerful friends, in the spring of 38 B.C., Horace met Gaius Cilnius Maecenas, a refined nobleman and able imperial adviser who at first snubbed the struggling poet because Horace claimed no aristocratic ties. At length, Horace proved his genius and acquired patronage in

Maecenas's stable of writers, including Propertius, Varius, and Virgil. In 33 B.C., Maecenas provided him a tidy manor in the Sabine foothills outside Tivoli, which employed a steward and eight slaves and produced wine, olives, and small grains. This pleasing getaway only a day's ride out of the city afforded Horace the leisure to pursue philosophy, entertain friends, and craft his verse. The warmth between Maecenas and Horace persisted to the end of their lives.

The success of Horace's *Sermones* preceded a string of balanced, polished literary successes: a sequel to the satires and, five years later, his *Epodes* (Refrains). Not content within these confines, Horace expanded his métier to a series of *Carmina* (Songs), published in 23 B.C. in the style of Homer, Sappho, Pindar, Alcaeus, Bacchylides, and other Greek classic poets. At the age of 45, Horace completed 20 *Epistulae,* a series of formal verse letters to his friends and, at the emperor's request, one addressed to Augustus. At this stage in his mastery of precise, lyric Latin, Horace was ready for the crowning reward— the post of poet laureate after Virgil's death in 17 B.C. For the occasion of the Secular Games, Horace presented Augustus the *Carmen Saeculare* (Secular Hymns); hand-picked youth choirs intoned the blend of patriotic and liturgical verses to Diana and Apollo. The positive reception of his staid, balanced lines earned him a second task—the composition of poems honoring the military triumphs of Drusus Nero, Claudius, and Tiberius in the Alpine campaigns. Without pause—except for therapeutic trips to Baiae in southern Italy each winter on the advice of his doctor, Antonius Musa, who treated him for an undisclosed ailment—Horace labored on with a fourth volume of odes, 20 verse letters, and, in 20 B.C., his *Ars Poetica,* or *Epistula ad Pisones,* a literary credo that secured his position among classic masters.

Still the letter-perfect student who recalled the sharp whacks of Orbilius's stylus, Horace had maintained his boyhood habits of attention to detail and pride in work. Without warning, in early fall of 8 B.C., after nine years as Rome's revered poet, Horace suffered a stunning loss in the death of Maecenas, whose final words bade the emperor "Horati Flacci ut mei esto memor. [As a favor to me, be mindful of Horace.]" Still in mourning, the poet, prematurely gray, stout, and lacking the robust health of his youth, died suddenly on November 27 that same year, an event he predicted when he contemplated life without his patron. Lacking heirs and too weak to complete the seal on his will, he gave verbal instructions leaving all to Augustus. Cremated and interred on the Esquiline Hill beside Maecenas, the poet earned the genuine grief of a generation of writers and readers who valued him among Rome's most literate, respected citizens. To his credit, his odes became a standard text of Roman schoolboys in his day and after.

A human example of the Latin *satura,* or medley, Horace perplexes critics who try to classify him as Epicurean, stoic, or Aristotelian. No simple task, the study of Horatian satire continues as classical scholars debate the tasteful, articulate amalgam of mordant satire, gay urbanity, everyday grace, country charm, and old-fashioned republican ethics, the latter an heirloom of a devoted, self-sacrificing father. A crafter of memorable epigram, Horace is best known for these, in both Latin and English translation:

- Carpe diem [Seize the day]

- in medias res [in the middle of things]

- aurea mediocritas [the golden mean]

- Non omnis morior [I shall not altogether die]

- nil admirari [nothing to be proud of]

- Odi profanum vulgus [I hate the common mob]

- Ars est celare artem [It is an art to conceal art]

- Dulce et decorum est pro patria mori [It is sweet and fitting to die for one's country]

The most prominent theme in his prolific eclectic verses proceeds from observation and experience: the value of the balanced life and the wisdom to appreciate simple pleasures.

In a carefully worded rumination on human contentment, Horace states his creed in Book 1 of the *Sermones:* "Why is it, Maecenas, that no living person remains satisfied with the confines of a life, whether chosen or allotted by fate? Why do people grow envious of others?" As though replying to his own question, Horace concludes that moderation requires each person to take stock of self and value the degree of happiness that life offers. An influence on his contemporaries as well as on St. Jerome, Dante Alighieri, Francesco Petrarch, Michel Montaigne, Ben Jonson, Alexander Pope, Joseph Addison, Richard Steele, Samuel Johnson, Robert Herrick, Henry Fielding, George Byron, Pierre de Ronsard, Louis MacNeice, and A. E. Housman, Horace holds a place among the classic masters of Latin literature and world satire. (Bowder 1980; Feder 1986; Godolphin 1949; Hadas 1954; Horace 1888, 1891, 1892, 1899, 1902, 1909, 1959; Howatson 1989; Knight 1981; Mantinband 1956; Monagan 1985; Moskovit 1983; Radice 1973; Rudd 1982; Shackleton 1982)

See also Addison, Joseph; Archilochus; epigram; Juvenal; Martial; Pope, Alexander; satire; *Sermones;* Steele, Sir Richard.

HYPERBOLE

Necessary to satire's instructive aim, hyperbole or exaggeration heightens humor or satiric exposition by carrying to unusual or extravagant lengths the obvious confines of definition or action. Essential to the drollery of Alexander Pope's *The Rape of the Lock* (1714), hyperbole, which derives from the Greek for overshot or thrown beyond, lifts a mundane card game from its petty social milieu and places it in the mock-heroic realm of the battlefield alongside calculated military conquests where participants, aided by winged sylphs, risk lives rather than mere reputations. In a genuine historical milieu, William

Shakespeare boldly overstates for effect the perceived position of the title character in his tragedy *Julius Caesar* (1599). The precipitating scene shows the cynical, manipulative Cassius nudging Brutus into a murderous cabal with this epic hyperbole comparing the Roman dictator to the famed lighthouse in the harbor at Rhodes:

> Why, man, he doth bestride the narrow world
> Like a Colossus, and we petty men
> Walk under his huge legs and peep about
> To find ourselves dishonourable graves.

Carried beyond a literal meaning, such overcasting emphasizes the quality that Cassius insists is Caesar's most fearful flaw—the straddling legs of power that overawe Roman citizens and reduce the populace to cowering hinds. An added fillip is the irony of the denouement, in which Caesar rises to the level of martyr while Brutus and Cassius are indeed interred in "dishonourable graves."

Hyperbole serves the purpose and style of Charles Dickens, Victorian England's needling conscience who refused to overlook the horrors of the workhouse, shame-riddled homes to unwed mothers, orphaned children, and the elderly, unemployable, and handicapped. In Chapter 2 of *Oliver Twist*, the author depicts the governing board in exaggerated satire:

> The members of this board were very sage, deep, philosophical men; and when they came to turn their attention to the workhouse, they found out at once, what ordinary folks would never have discovered—the poor people liked it! It was a regular place of public entertainment for the poorer classes; a tavern where there was nothing to pay; a public breakfast, dinner, tea, and supper all the year round; a brick and mortar elysium, where it was all play and no work.

Rising to a classic overreckoning—the "brick and mortar elysium"—Dickens faults the cynicism and insensitivity of powerful men who, like Caesar, overpower and undervalue the helpless folk whose lives they direct.

Because of its adaptability to almost any literary effort, overstatement supplies the writer with a flexible, all-purpose figure of speech. In Isak Dinesen's metaphysical tale "Babette's Feast" (1953), the title character arrives in Norway from Paris under bizarre conditions and vows that, if the minister's daughters do not give her a job, she will die. Immediately upon assuming the role of cook for their mission to the elderly poor, Babette learns the skills of Scandinavian cookery and bargains efficiently in her new language. As the story reaches its height, Babette cooks a multicourse version of the Last Supper, which alters the moral behavior and outlook of a failing religious cell. The house fills with a heavenly light, as if a number of small halos had blended

> into one glorious radiance. Taciturn old people received the gift of tongues; ears that for years had been almost deaf were opened to it. Time itself had merged into eternity.

The ironic conclusion counters the spare, abstemious Lutheran sect with the generosity and self-assurance of a strong ego who believes that the artist demands one concession from the world: "Give me leave to do my utmost."

Similarly, hyperbole, an integral part of Laura Esquivel's feminist fable *Like Water for Chocolate* (1992), overreaches fact to lighten the conflict that constrains and subverts the heroine's life—a feudal marriage that condemns Tita to a life of sublimated libido. By channeling her emotions into a love of cooking, she makes bearable the yearning for the man her parents choose for her sister. At Tita's birth, Esquivel prefigures grief by creating a seriosymbolic kitchen birthing scene:

> And before my great-grandmother could let out a word or even a whimper, Tita made her entrance into this world, prematurely, right there on the kitchen table amid the smells of simmering noodle soup, thyme, bay leaves, and cilantro, steamed milk, garlic, and of course, onion. . . . Nacha swept up the residue the tears had left on the red stone floor. There was enough salt to fill a ten-pound sack—it was used for cooking and lasted a long time.

In the 1991 film version, scripted by Esquivel, the tenuous hold on her sex drive keeps Tita's temper at a slow simmer, "like water for chocolate," which must be controlled to keep the tricky, unpredictable goo from burning. So, too, does her control of tears stanch a greater display of tears capable of supplying the kitchen with salt. (Abrams 1971; Baldick 1990; Barnet, Berman, and Burto 1960; Cuddon 1976; Dickens 1986; Dinesen 1958; Drabble 1985; Esquivel 1992; Feinberg 1967; Gassner and Quinn 1969; Gray 1992; Halliwell 1995; Holman 1980; McArthur 1992; Pollard 1970; Shakespeare 1967)

See also Pope, Alexander; *The Rape of the Lock;* satire; Shakespeare, William.

THE IMPORTANCE OF BEING EARNEST

The long-lived and best-loved English satiric comedy of the Victorian period, Oscar Wilde's *The Importance of Being Earnest: A Trivial Comedy for Serious People* (1895) earned him worldwide fame and buoyed his spirits and his purse during a two-year confinement to prison for homosexuality. Studded with wry witticisms, puns, caricatures, and sparkling epigrams, the play evolved from a pun on Ernest/earnest. It details the frivolity, chicanery, and premarital behaviors of John "Jack" Worthing (the real name of the wicked flirt Ernest) and Algernon "Algy" Moncrieff (the true identity of the hypochondriac Bunbury, who uses ill health as a cover for illicit activities). The story is set in Algernon's flat in London and a country manor in Hertfordshire; it gains momentum after Lady Augusta Bracknell searches for personal information about Ernest. While the fictitious Ernest pursues Gwendolen Fairfax, Algernon's cousin, Algernon courts Cecily Cardew, Jack's ward.

Wilde's satire stands out as a rare example of a successful revival of the Restoration comedy of manners. His contrived plot turns on the duplicity of both men: Algernon must conceal his peccadilloes from his Aunt Augusta and decides to rename himself Ernest to deflect scandal from his real identity; likewise, Jack asks the Reverend Canon Chasuble, D.D., to rechristen him with the name of Ernest, his alter ego. A ridiculous denouement reveals two unlikely coincidences: that Jack is really Algernon's elder brother and that Jack was christened Ernest in honor of his father, General Ernest John Moncrieff. The two girls arrive at the Bracknell manor house on the day that Jack adopts deep mourning for the death of Ernest. At the same time, Algernon poses as Ernest, leading the girls to presume that they have fallen in love with the same man.

The quibbles over permission for the girls' betrothals turn up a hilariously patriarchal obstacle—a stipulation in Cecily's grandfather's will that she not marry until she comes of age at 35. At the height of the confusion, Cecily's absent-minded governess, Miss Letitia Prism, reveals that, to conceal the birth of a child named Ernest to Lady Bracknell's sister, she placed him in a "capacious hand-bag" and her novel in a pram. She inadvertently carried the infant from Lord Bracknell's residence to the cloakroom of Victoria Station. Lady Bracknell, who is far more concerned with class proprieties than with Jack's ego, remarks:

> To be born, or at any rate bred, in a hand-bag, whether it had handles or not, seems to me to display a contempt for the ordinary decencies of family life that reminds one of the worst excesses of the French Revolution.

To Jack's request for advice, Lady Bracknell urges him to "acquire some relations as soon as possible, and to make a definite effort to produce at any rate one parent, of either sex, before the season is quite over."

First presented at London's St. James's Theater, the farce earned critical kudos for its intricate dialogue, mock seriousness, and brilliant caricature. An example of light comedy shows Jack reaching for a sandwich:

Algernon:	Please don't touch the cucumber sandwiches. They are ordered specially for Aunt Augusta.
Jack:	Well, you have been eating them all the time.
Algernon:	That is quite a different matter. She is my aunt.

Wilde's self-assured touch quickly redirects humorous dialogue to satire with a minute shift of diction, as in these lines:

Lady Bracknell:	I had some crumpets with Lady Harbury, who seems to me to be living entirely for pleasure now.
Algernon:	I hear her hair has turned quite gold from grief.
Lady Bracknell:	It certainly has changed its colour. From what cause I, of course, cannot say.

Compared to the harmless drolleries of William S. Gilbert, *The Importance of Being Earnest* boldly attacks the self-deception and hypocrisies of Wilde's age, notably religion, politics, matrimony, and the high moral tone for which Victorianism is known. On a literary plane, the comedy parodies the mid-nineteenth century's taste for sentimental comedies in which all obstacles work out in favor of true love. (Bermel 1982; Brockett 1968; Gassner and Quinn 1969; Grigson 1963; Hornstein 1973; Magill 1958; McArthur 1992; Miller 1989; Wilde 1954, 1995)

See also caricature; comedy; epigram; farce; Gilbert, William S.; parody; pun; repartee; satire; Wilde, Oscar.

INCIDENTAL SATIRE

Satire, a major genre in verse, drama, novel, essay, and short story, may provide a glimmer of recognition or coming to knowledge in any literary work. Itself a rhetorical device that can enhance meaning when included alongside metaphor, sense impression, alliteration, personification, or cadence, incidental satire often carries the tipped barb that makes the initial prod of the reader's consciousness. An amusing segment of John van Druten's *I Remember Mama* (1944) uses incidental satire to characterize the loosening of old world bonds on immigrant women. Mama, the wonder worker and family savant, settles her unwed sister Trina's quandary over permission to marry Mr. Thorkelson.

Countering the iron-willed Sigurd, who ridicules the groom's size, and Jenny, who considers the engagement an old maid's fantasy, Mama proves equal to their cruelty and spite. If Trina laughs, Mama will reveal "the time before your wedding when your husband try to run away." Similarly prepared for Sigurd's defection, Mama has a second secret ace in the hole: the disastrous wedding night when Sigurd cried and Ole, the groom, sent her back to her mother. Obviously not a scheming woman, Mama typifies the resourceful housewifely power broker who recognizes the appropriate time to strike a deal.

Attuned toward political power-mongering, William J. Lederer and Eugene Burdick, authors of *The Ugly American* (1958), select incidental satire as the vehicle for the climax of their novel—the speech of Burmese journalist U Maung Swe. To explain why Americans fail in Asian diplomacy, Swe relies on history and his experience in the United States to jolt ambassadors at a dinner party in Rangoon: "Poor America. It took the British a hundred years to lose their prestige in Asia. America has managed to lose hers in ten years." Step by step, he turns the insulting evaluation of American ineptitude into a lengthy list of faults: isolation, pretense, ostentation, defensiveness, and ignorance. From satire to lecture, Swe shifts the mood from comedy toward fiasco—Russian tactics undercut American bumbling amateurism. Skillfully, Lederer and Burdick dazzle the reader with a swift backpedaling that begins in jest and coasts at deadly speed toward the crash of recognition.

In *A Raisin in the Sun* (1959), one of the major plays by a black female author, Lorraine Hansberry breaks the intensity of social drama with several satiric scenes depicting Beneatha Younger, a postadolescent college student whose neo-Black hauteur casts her in ridiculous confrontations over faddish intentions to "find herself." When Beneatha introduces the Nigerian Asagai to Mrs. Younger, Mama embarrasses her daughter with frank American ignorance and dialect:

> I think it's so sad the way our American Negroes don't know nothing about Africa 'cept Tarzan and all that. All that money they pour into these churches when they ought to be helping you people over there drive out them French and Englishmen done taken away your land.

In Act II, Beneatha demonstrates her superior knowledge by promenading in authentic Yoruba headdress and cooling herself with an oriental fan. Her American suitor, George Murchison, interrupts with a sarcastic put-down, "Let's face it, baby, your heritage is nothing but a bunch of raggedy-assed spirituals and some grass huts."

A seriocomic historical drama intended as a reexamination of the thinking and influence of Henry David Thoreau, Jerome Lawrence and Robert E. Lee's *The Night Thoreau Spent in Jail* (1971) parades phantoms of the philosopher's early years before his eyes in Act I as though resurrecting the dead. A sore spot between Henry and his brother John is the flirtation of Ellen Sewell, who enjoys tormenting both brothers, even though she accedes to her father's rejection of male members of the Thoreau family. John is perplexed that she wants a proposal from Henry so that she can reject it:

Henry:	It's an outrage! She wants to wear *both* of our scalps on her petticoat strings!
John:	She won't marry you, and she won't marry me. But I think she'd marry *us* in a minute.
Henry:	That's carrying Unitarianism too far!

This and other risible arguments with the past overlie tormenting memories of John's death from tetanus and the tension that lay between two brothers similar enough to share celibacy, yet disconnected in the core of their personal philosophies. Serving more as reflections of Henry's ability to mock his own fatuousness rather than as comic relief, Lawrence and Lee's incidental satire becomes a tool by which the collaborators mine the bright flecks of humor and compassion that lie hidden in the protagonist's ideal-burdened spirit.

In some instances, incidental satire momentarily singles out a pervasive human fault. A humorous episode in the harrowing flight of rabbits in Richard Adams's *Watership Down* (1972) depicts Hazel reminding Bigwig that a warren without does is doomed. Adams, stepping into the narrative, remarks tongue-in-cheek:

> It may seem incredible that the rabbits had given no thought to so vital a matter. But men have made the same mistake more than once—left the whole business out of account, or been content to trust to luck and the fortune of war.

The satire intensifies with Bigwig's discovery of Hyzenthlay, the clairvoyant insider female, who surprises him with a talent that had eluded him: "He had stumbled, quite unexpectedly, upon what he needed most of all, a strong, sensible friend who would think on her own account and help to bear his burden." The inclusion of a bit of feminism, however restrained, adds to the theme of widening horizons, a physical landscape suddenly stretched to welcome sexual freedom to the overall loosening of bonds on a venturesome band of rabbits.

Incidental satire can serve tone and characterization as well as plot and theme. In Leonore Fleischer's novel *Agnes of God* (1985), based on John Pielmeier's screenplay, the inevitable clash between Mother Miriam Ruth, head of Les Petites Soeurs de Marie Magdalen, and the psychiatrist Dr. Martha Livingston lightens in a shared moment at a symbolically edenic garden gazebo where Martha feeds her nicotine habit. Mother Miriam Ruth, stolid and unapproachable, confesses that she was once addicted to cigarette smoking. The two, like school girls, sneak a smoke. Martha begins a teasing discussion of the saints and their attitudes toward tobacco, if it had been available to them. Miriam snickers, "Saint Ignatius, I think, would smoke cigars and then stub them out on the soles of his feet." Peter, she decides, would have opted for a pipe. Martha selects "You've come a long way, baby" as the slogan suiting Mary Magdalene's up-front style. Miriam rounds out the role-playing with Saint Joan chewing tobacco. At the same time that the witty repartee unmasks the fallible woman behind Mother Miriam Ruth's mask, the shared mimickry returns Martha to her assignment—determining whether Agnes, a strangely innocent novice, could have murdered the infant she secretly conceived and

Incidental satire provides a moment of humor in the 1985 movie *Agnes of God* when Mother Miriam Ruth (Anne Bancroft) and psychiatrist Dr. Martha Livingston (Jane Fonda) sneak a smoke and reveal a moment of humanity.

gave birth to. By opening a fissure in Mother Miriam's reserve, Martha discloses a satiric view of sainthood and a glimpse of her own failure to reconcile her personal distaste for piety.

The use of exaggeration to create incidental satire completes a poignant mating after long denial in Laura Esquivel's *Like Water for Chocolate* (1992). Tita, who has held her emotions in check over a bumpy trail of family woes, maintains her sanity by staying in the kitchen and tending her temper at a near-boil, which is the correct temperature of water for chocolate. Death removes her mother and sister, and her niece Esperanza is married; in mid-life, Tita responds generously to Pedro's love, which he had offered since they were teens. Ironically, the exertion kills him. Before he can flee down the tunnel to a nebulous afterlife, Tita stuffs her mouth with homemade matches and sets off a charge that ignites the lovers, their final trysting place, and the whole ranch. An intriguing ending to folk romance, the bursts of sparks appear to enhance Esperanza's wedding, but really celebrate the liberation of all women in love.

Incidental satire requires verbal agility and thematic perception and precision. A mishandling of gripping spots of ridicule, Michael Crichton's *Jurassic Park* (1990) demonstrates the author's inept manipulation of character. From the beginning, Crichton sketches the typical computer nerd, Dennis Nedry, as fat, slovenly, complacent, ill-tempered, impatient, shallow, and venal. When a staff member searches for Nedry to locate the cause of a temporary system shutdown, he imagines the computer whiz hiding in the toilet to read comic books. Crichton's unnecessary tip-off is the obvious scrambling of "nerdy" to produce Nedry's last name. A parallel to Nedry, Ian Malcolm, computer-addicted mathematician from the University of Texas, displays the quirky "deplorable excess of personality" that Crichton snatches for him from the bottomless sack of scientific misfits dating back to the Faust legend and Francis Bacon. Dressing in either gray or black and ogling the only adult female on the mission, Malcolm thrusts his acerbic wit and exhibitionistic prodigality on the audience at large, making a fool of himself and casting suspicion on chaos theory, his career focus, and, ironically, the cause of the failure of Jurassic Park.

A prodigy at concocting twentieth-century techno-thrillers, Crichton relentlessly showcases his strength—scientific acumen. By vaulting through suspenseful action and pressing the reader to a multifaceted resolution, the author drains characters of realism. Regressing to the oddball and mad-scientist stereotypes, denigrating Nedry's competence, and trivializing Malcolm's study as "the latest scientific fad," Crichton overshoots the incidental satire he strives to achieve. Because of these colossal structural errors, he reduces his personae to shadow figures cast on a screen by an obvious master manipulator. Had he taken more time in crafting Ian Malcolm's coming to knowledge that "life on earth can take care of itself," the shift in focus from power over matter to power over self might have given the novel a stronger character base to support the clangor of technological disorder that overwhelms it. (Adams 1972; Crichton 1990; Esquivel 1992; Feinberg 1967; Fleischer 1985; Hansberry 1988; Lawrence and Lee 1972; Lederer and Burdick 1958; Snodgrass 1995; van Druten 1961)

See also African-American satire; pun; repartee; sarcasm; satire.

INCONGRUITY

The base upon which humor and satire is built, incongruity spotlights the incompatibility of elements that produces a snicker of recognition from the reader or audience. Ranging from a surface unsuitability of manners or dress to anachronisms, cross-dressing, androgyny, and the deeper mismating of philosophies, incongruity covers a plethora of imbalances in character, style, theme, setting, tone, and mood:

- Liza Doolittle's attempt at polite small talk in George Bernard Shaw's *Pygmalion* (1912)

- The main character's frequent reincarnations in *Orlando* (1928), Virginia Woolf's biography of an androgyne

- The hayseed's straw hat and overalls in the grand emerald court in L. Frank Baum's *The Wizard of Oz* (1939)

- A simplistic, tongue-in-cheek solution to segregation in Harry Golden's "The Vertical Negro" (1956)

- The semi-barbaric king attempting to prove himself an enlightened despot in Richard Rodgers and Oscar Hammerstein's *The King and I* (1951)

- The tart's garish get-ups and flouncing mannerisms in Neil Simon's *Sweet Charity* (1969) and Billy Wilder and I. A. L. Diamond's *Irma la Douce* (1963)

- Cynic vs. romantic in Jean Giraudoux's screenplay *The Madwoman of Chaillot* (1969)

- Manipulator or dictator vs. lover of freedom in Kurt Vonnegut's *Cat's Cradle* (1973)

- Female impersonation in Anne Fine's *Alias Madam Doubtfire* (1988)

A facile tool of the parodist, incongruous events and ideas lampoon the structure and purpose of the original. Notable among parodies is Henry Fielding's pseudonymous *An Apology for the Life of Mrs. Shamela Andrews* (1741), the obverse of Samuel Richardson's *Pamela, or Virtue Rewarded* (1740–1741). Fielding's duplicitous heroine appears as chaste as Richardson's pious goody-goody until certain correspondence reveals a brazen strumpet and manipulator, thus exposing the overdrawn goodness of Pam the sham. This obvious disharmony is the lever that lifts the reader's awareness to a more subtle—and often more humorous or significant—layer of meaning.

Marriage between unlike mates is often the basis for incongruity. In Jessamyn West's historical novel *Except for Me and Thee* (1949), the yoking of a female Quaker minister with a less-than-zealous Quaker orchardist produces the kind of marital compromise on which comedy feeds. The gentle domestic humor of male pragmatism at war with female piety, which begins with West's *The Friendly Persuasion* (1945), turns to a glimpse of street-level discussions of slavery, the Civil War, and the Quaker role in the underground railroad in West's sequel. When conscience ousts Jess Birdwell from his bed and into the sporting clothes of Enoch, his non-Quaker hired man, Eliza registers more shock at the change in dress than in her husband's decision to aid runaway slaves. The unlikely pose of male clotheshorse surprises and amuses Eliza, who considers him a "sheep in wolf's clothing." Partly in riposte, but more in fondness for his wife, Jess replies, "This is the first, and I hope the last, time, Eliza, thee's ever going to be kissed by a man of fashion. Best make the most of it." The quippy Pennsylvania-style repartee pulls the Birdwells to and fro over a bumpy washboard of religious hairsplitting and domestic entanglement. West, revealing poignant family and community decisions made against a backdrop of sweeping political change, chooses incongruity as a form of safety valve—the comic relief intended to ease the ethical dyspepsia that unsettles a nation.

Incongruity fuels a cottage industry in contemporary putdowns as new as the latest gossip rag and as indigenous to the English language as broadside ballads and *The Tatler* and *The Spectator*. A witty phenomenon of the mid-1990s, James Finn Garner's *Politically Correct Bedtime Stories* (1994) and *Once upon a*

More Enlightened Time (1995) and Cathy Crimmins and Tom Maeder's arch, anti-conservative *Newt Gingrich's Bedtime Stories for Orphans* (1995) demonstrate continued audience demand for entertaining incongruity. The first two utilize mismatches in a facetious spoof of political correctness by retelling familiar fairy tales from the point of view of a society gone overboard on fairness and equity. In Garner's second book, he lampoons feminism by placing in "Hansel and Gretel" the following unlikely turn of events in the confrontation between the lost children and the witch:

> The wommon laughed. "No, no, my dear. I'm not a witch, I'm a Wiccan. I'm no more evil than anyone else, and I certainly don't eat little pre-adults, like all the rumors would have you believe. I worship nature and the Goddess, and mix herbs and natural potions to help people. Really."

The absurdity of prejudice-cleansed terms such as "wommon" rather than "woman" and "pre-adults" rather than "children" carries to extremes the liberal tendency to overdo their search for the fabled "level playing field" and smirks at the 1990s evenhanded acceptance of herbalists, naturopaths, latter-day Wiccans, goddess worship, and other forms of alternative culture without weighing the likelihood of deception, sacrilege, or fraud.

In like fashion, Crimmins and Maeder's satire, *Newt Gingrich's Bedtime Stories for Orphans,* spins a wry web out of the suggestion of the speaker of the U.S. House of Representatives that social agencies place in state orphanages all children who live on welfare. By skillful juxtaposition, the authors ridicule conservative politicos' victimization of the poor, right-wing insistence on prayer at public gatherings, and Republican disregard for the needy. As an introduction, the authors note that "Uncle Newt's" orphanage visits are always festive:

> The work day in the orphanage industries is cut short so that the boys and girls can display their drill team exercises on the parade ground. Then it's prayer session and dinner with an extra helping of gruel, followed by a half-hour discussion of the principles of self-government.

The deft use of terms that call to mind Dickensian workhouses (extra helping of gruel), fundamentalist piety (prayer session), and Mao's regimented Chinese followers (team exercises on the parade ground) reminds the reader that satire may entertain while attuning the alert reader to potential dictatorship by ultraconservatives. In subsequent chapters, the slim booklet associates the homes of the three little pigs with subsidized housing and parodies a sing-along or "Newt-enanny" by altering familiar titles to "I've Been Tearing Down the Amtrak" ("I've Been Working on the Railroad"), "Where Has Genny Flowers Gone?" ("Where Have All the Flowers Gone?"), "School Lunch Hot, School Lunch Cold" ("Pease Porridge Hot, Pease Porridge Cold"), and "House, House for a Change" ("Home, Home on the Range"). The supplanting of childhood lore with political in-fighting tweaks the natural dissonance of politics, one of the more vicious focuses of comedy. (Crimmins and Maeder 1995; Feinberg 1967; Garner 1994, 1995; Henry 1995; Highet 1962; West 1969)

See also Cat's Cradle; comedy; *The King and I;* parody; political satire; satire; Shaw, George Bernard; Simon, Neil; *The Spectator; The Tatler;* Vonnegut, Kurt.

INVECTIVE

A distortion of satire, invective steps beyond the two-pronged intent to entertain and instruct by forgetting the first tine. Basically hurtful, vituperative, humiliating, and, above all, humorless, the invective of speech, poem, article, or editorial inveighs heavily against its object, victimizing with cutting insults, denunciation, slander, or ridicule. A common literary phenomenon in which personal vendetta motivates the author or speaker, invective outstrips the diatribe in scorn and hatred to become a vehicle for distaste, contempt, and loathing. As a genre, invective dates to the earliest writings and derives from the Latin for "borne against," a visual image of a killer force broadsiding its target. In clandestine form, the device may fuel the vituperative *roman à clef*, for example, John Gay's *Polly* (1729), a "key novel" that reveals the names of characters to those close to the subject. The most anthologized of Western invective includes these classical models:

- Archilochus's extant verse (seventh century B.C.)

- Demosthenes's denunciations of Philip of Macedon (349–344 B.C.)

- Lucillus's *Sermones* (second century B.C.)

- Martial's *Epigrammata* (75 B.C.)

- Catullus's verse (ca. 60 B.C.)

- Persius's *First Satire* (first century A.D.)

- Juvenal's epigrams (first century A.D.)

Renaissance literature contains extremes of temper and carefully honed denunciations, for example, the nose-to-nose confrontation between Kent and Oswald in Act II, Scene ii of William Shakespeare's *King Lear* (1605):

Kent: Fellow, I know thee.
Oswald: What does thou know me for?
Kent: A knave, a rascal, an eater of broken meats; a base, proud, shallow, beggarly, three-suited, hundred-pound, filthy, worsted-stocking knave; a lily-livered, action-taking, whoreson, glass-gazing, superserviceable, finical rogue; one-trunk-inheriting slave; one that wouldst be a bawd in way of good service, and art nothing but the composition of a knave, beggar, coward, pander, and the son and heir of a mongrel bitch; one whom I will beat into clamorous whining if thou deny'st the least syllable of thy addition.

Although spirited and colorful, the charge against Kent's victim is lost in the welter of abuse, which gives off heat but no light. Flanked by other examples from *Coriolanus*, *Troilus and Cressida*, *Cymbeline*, and *Timon of Athens*, the passage reflects a similar trend in works by Ben Jonson, Thomas Lodge, and John Marston. Later English experts at character assassination and unbridled fulmination include Alexander Pope, Samuel Butler, John Dryden, Tobias Smollett, George Byron, Charles Dickens, Algernon Swinburne, and George Bernard Shaw.

The example that permeates most discussions of invective is Jonathan Swift's *Gulliver's Travels* (1726), a fantasy dystopia so choked with the author's antipathy toward English elitism that the reader is at times overpowered by the venomous outpouring and wonders at the sanity of its composer. In Chapter 6 of Book 4, "A Voyage to the Houyhnhnms," Gulliver repudiates England for encouraging poverty by exporting its produce:

> But, in order to feed the luxury and Intemperance of the Males, and the Vanity of the Females, we sent away the greatest Part of our necessary Things to other Countries, from whence in Return we brought the materials of Diseases, Folly, and Vice, to spend among ourselves. Hence it follows of Necessity, that vast Numbers of our People are compelled to seek their Livelihood by Begging, Robbing, Stealing, Cheating, Pimping, Forswearing, Flattering, Suborning, Forging, Gaming, Lying, Fawning, Hectoring, Voting, Scribling, Stargazing, Poysoning, Whoring, Canting, Libelling, Free-thinking, and the like Occupations.

The derogatory tone of the author destroys his mask—Lemuel Gulliver—and reveals the hand of the puppeteer pulling the strings to open the jaws of his central character. Gulliver speaks Swift's personal revilement, which is out of place and, to the detriment of the piece, out of control. (Abrams 1971; Barnet, Berman, and Burto 1960; Cuddon 1976; Drabble 1985; Feinberg 1967; Gray 1992; Holman 1980; Shakespeare 1957; Swift 1958)

See also Archilochus; diatribe; Dryden, John; *Gulliver's Travels*; irony; Juvenal; Martial; satire; Shakespeare, William; Swift, Jonathan.

IRONY

A sophisticated, multifaceted tool in the writer's kit, irony derives from the Greek for "dissembling." In stage use, the Greek *eiron*, or trickster, played the simpleton, yet, to the audience's delight, repeatedly outfoxed the *alazon*, the conceited know-it-all. Also known as tongue-in-cheek humor, irony is a broad term for words or actions that say or indicate less than or the opposite of their meaning. James D. Houston captures a glib truism in the change in attitude toward the gas purchaser in "Gasoline" (1973):

> My pumps runneth over, they would say. Now the pumps are drying up. And no one can explain it. Some say the world supply of fuel is running out. They wag their heads and say your next tankful could be your last.

The implied contrast between buyer's market and seller's market demonstrates a change in treatment of the journeyer in need of a fill-up.

The epitome of English irony is Jonathan Swift's "A Modest Proposal" (1729), a first-person essay in which a naive altruist suggests that the struggling Irish raise children as livestock and sell them to the English for food and a source of fine leather for gloves. The bitter irony, aimed at the mercenary British who rob the Irish of their autonomy while ridiculing their large families, effectively publicizes the plight of a people in bondage to unfeeling over-lords. The innocent speaker distances himself from any profit motive, claiming: "I have no Children, by which I can propose to get a single Penny; the youngest being nine Years old, and my Wife past Child-bearing." Swift's success in sustaining the irony thus hinges on restraint and the ability to play-act the bumbling do-gooder.

In lighter versions of irony, characters' actions innocently collide, derailing expectations—for example, the arrival on the wrong evening of supercilious dinner guests—the daughter's potential in-laws—in Moss Hart and George S. Kaufman's *You Can't Take It with You* (1936). These inconsistencies of behavior produce funny scenes or revelations of character, as in the case of the uncomfortable in-laws, who learn something from the laid-back Sycamore family about relaxing, indulging idiosyncratic hobbies, and dropping pretensions.

Irony need not be didactic. Perhaps the best loved of O. Henry's stories, "The Gift of the Magi," merely underscores the appropriate union of two people who deserve each other. The biblical title hints at the endearing selflessness of Jim and Della, a husband and wife who are too poor to offer fine Christmas gifts to each other. To surprise Jim, Della sells her hair to a wigmaker and applies the money to an elegant fob for his pocket watch. Meanwhile, Jim pawns his watch to buy Della combs for her hair. The irony results in a facile statement of the Christmas theme that has become a classic holiday reading.

Gradations and styles of irony assist the analyst in defining the subtleties of this rhetorical device:

Verbal irony. In its most lethal form, verbal irony is capable of stirring characters to catastrophic action. In print, verbal irony lacks the opportunity for the sneer, smirk, moue, or insouciant shrug. A demanding rhetorical device, written irony requires a masterly pen stroke or italics, underlining, or all caps to indicate a discrepancy between what is expected and what actually occurs.

One of literature's most effective examples of verbal irony appears in Act III, Scene ii, the electric moment at the climax of William Shakespeare's *Julius Caesar* when Marc Antony makes good on his promise to thrust Rome into a state of enraged anarchy. From the fickle funeral attendees who applauded Brutus's call for patriotism, Antony skillfully elicits the overturn of the republic. To achieve this end and to avenge Caesar's brutal murder, Antony ingratiates himself to the assassins:

> Here under leave of Brutus and the rest
> (For Brutus is an honourable man:
> So are they all, all honourable men),
> Come I to speak in Caesar's funeral.

Playing the innocent, he pretends gratitude for an opportunity that he will in fact turn against Caesar's killers. The scene spools out deliciously, making it one of the choicest moments on the Renaissance stage. Seven more times Antony tosses the word "honourable" at his audience, skillfully twisting the word into a taunt, an accusation, and, finally, an implicit accusation of disloyalty and murder.

To prevent his irony from overshooting the grasp of an unlettered mob, Antony introduces his speech as a traditional act of funeral oratory, a gesture expected of colleagues: "He was my friend, faithful and just to me." Antony then asks the rabble whether they have forgotten their own gratitude and love. With skillful mock innocence, he inquires, "What cause withholds you then to mourn for him?" Tension, a valuable adjunct to irony, builds while Antony manipulates public response. In a decorous end to this toying with emotions, Antony, as though overcome with grief, pauses to gain his composure.

Gradually, nuance gives way to clear evidence of murder. Snatching the cloak from the corpse, Antony points to the encrusted stab wounds inflicted by men claiming to be supporters and colleagues. The ruse is plain—Antony, having been pulled aside on arrival at the Senate, was not present at the assassination and has no idea who struck where on Caesar's body. Feigning surprise at the behavior of such "honourable" men, Antony reaches further into his stock of verbal irony to strengthen his well-meaning pose:

> I come not, friends, to steal away your hearts.
> I am no orator, as Brutus is,
> But (as you know me all) a plain blunt man
> That love my friend; and that they know full well
> That gave me public leave to speak of him.
> For I have neither writ, nor words, nor worth,
> Action, nor utterance, nor the power of speech
> To stir men's blood. I only speak right on.

Like Mephistopheles chortling at his hellish powers, Antony, admiring the eruption of chaos, mutters, "Now let it work." His trickery is as old as politics, as fresh as the twentieth-century chicanery of Louisiana governor Huey "King Fish" Long, Alabama governor George Corley Wallace, or North Carolina senator Jesse Helms. It is no wonder that students of irony have returned to this double-bladed speech again and again, fascinated by the metamorphosis that prefaces ten years of civil war, multiple executions, and the downfall of the Roman republic.

Robert Tallman's television adaptation of Evelyn Waugh's *The Man Who Liked Dickens* (1954) provides another example of verbal irony. Henty, a man held captive in the Amazon to read sentimental scenes from Dickens's novels to the tyrannical McMaster, leaves an obvious message in the back of his watch. After Mrs. Henty arrives in search of her husband and learns that Henty died in the encampment, she hears her companion reading phrases from a page concealed in her husband's pocket watch:

> After having been long in danger . . . at the hands of the villagers . . . seized with great violence . . . held here against my will . . . for the love of heaven, of justice, of generosity, I supplicate you to succor and release me from this prison of horror.

In Waugh's original version, McMaster torments Henty by admitting that a rescue party came to the village and left with the watch as a souvenir and a visit to Henty's supposed grave. The virulent McMaster, living up to his name, forces Henty to continue reading from Dickens and comments on *Little Dorrit:* "There are passages in that book I can never hear without the temptation to weep."

Similarly, Ira Levin and Mac Hyman's *No Time for Sergeants* (1956) interweaves verbal irony in a crucial scene involving tyranny and subjection. Without realizing the implications of his actions, Private Will Stockdale, the backwoods protagonist, destroys his devious superior officer, Sergeant King, by praising his kindness in making Will P.L.O. (Permanent Latrine Orderly). Will's insistent voice interrupts King's excuses to the captain with a good-old-boy joviality about the sergeant's many "kindnesses":

> He solves our problems for us, and he helps us out on our difficult days of military service, and I reckon he's just about the best danged sergeant there is in the whole danged Air Force!

The savvy captain realizes that King has singled out an innocent for humiliating toilet cleaning, and he turns the irony on King by promising that, if Will does not complete basic training with his group, King, a 12-year veteran, will "in all probability be a permanent latrine orderly. P.L.O.!"

Tragic irony. Characters bring about their own downfall in the playing out of tragic irony. The prototype in Western literature, Sophocles' *Oedipus Rex* (ca. 429 B.C.), depicts the king's search for the cause of a plague in Thebes. The task leads him to an answer that demands his destruction, for Oedipus himself is unknowingly the cause of the gods' punishment. A form of cosmic irony, the pitiless god-driven joke turns on the king and faults him for his failure to connect the killing of an arrogant traveler with the roadside death of the former king of Thebes. At last free from ignorance concerning the weighty guilt that has burdened his realm, Oedipus knows that he alone can pay the penalty. He cries out with the voice of a human king driven to the extremes of self-understanding:

> Lost! Ah lost! At last it's blazing clear.
> Light of my eyes, good-bye—my final gaze!
> My birth all sprung revealed from those it never should;
> myself entwined with those I never could;
> and I the killer of those I never would.

Rushing offstage, he blinds himself at the moment of full vision. The bitter visual proof of his coming to knowledge is the streaming gore from his eyes, which he gouges out with the brooch from his dead wife's dress. Returned to stage, he makes a final confession:

> Yes, I should be free,
> Free from parricide;
> Not pointed out as wedded
> To the one who weaned me.
> Now I'm god-abandoned
> A son of sin and sorrows,
> All incest-stained with the womb that bore me.
> O Oedipus, your portion!

Blinded by the truth foretold to his parents in his childhood, he offers his hands to his daughters and pursues a solitary way from Thebes in a vain search for respite and forgiveness.

As replete with funerals, suicides, and sufferings as Greek tragedy, the eighteenth-century classic Chinese novel, *The Dream of the Red Chamber*, was begun by Tsao Hsueh-chin in the first decade of the century and completed around 1791 by Kao Ngo. The book details the decline of Chinese feudalism and the men and women who schemed and plotted to increase their social status while sacrificing the happiness of those around them. The central figure, Chia Pao-yu, a spoiled prodigy born with a dazzling piece of jade in his mouth, exerts the rights of male over female by breaking hearts in perpetual flirtations common to the Grand View Garden. Yet the social system defeats him by denying him Lin Tai-yu, who never gains favor with the powerful Dowager's family and thus loses Pao-yu. The tragic irony that ends Lin Tai-yu's life consigns Pao-yu to spartan Buddhist otherworldliness in complete contrast to the courtly favors, whims, and concessions that marked his growing-up years.

Dramatic irony. A significant situational or structural incongruity, dramatic irony places characters or speakers in circumstances beyond their understanding. The audience or reader, wise to inside information, may laugh at humorous misunderstandings or a mix-up of identities or may shudder at impending doom that the innocent character either fails to see or misperceives as harmless. In George Eliot's *Silas Marner* (1861), the rising action thrusts Silas into the night in search of redress for the theft of his money. The path of the limited village of Raveloe takes him to the center of life and justice—the Rainbow Inn, where local experts discuss cows and ghosts in local dialect, which is well oiled with ale. The landlord, setting himself up as an expert, declares: "These's folks, i' my opinion, they can't see ghos'es, not if they stood as plain as a pikestaff before 'em." At the height of the controversy, Silas, his buggy eyes protruding and his limbs atwitch "like the antennae of startled insects," walks into the common room. For an instant, the party studies Silas while he catches his breath. His timing proves so convincing that Jem Rodney refuses the landlord's command to grab Silas out of fear that "he's been robbed, and murdered too, for what I know." Eliot's witty situational irony underscores gentle humor at the expense of Raveloe's self-appointed aficionados of the occult.

At the conclusion of Chinua Achebe's disastrous *Things Fall Apart* (1959), the author deliberately plays out the tragic resolution with a counter-harmony of irony. After Okonkwo does the unthinkable—hangs himself—for a series of crimes he has committed out of obedience to cultural demands, the commissioner summarizes the destruction of a tribal leader in "a reasonable paragraph." He assigns his work the title *The Pacification of the Primitive Tribes of the Lower Niger,* a broad overview that swallows Okonkwo's tragedy like the ocean sweeping over a pebble. Less lethal a form of dramatic irony is Roald Dahl's "Lamb to the Slaughter" (1954), a frequently anthologized short story in which a wife murders her husband by bludgeoning him with a frozen leg of lamb. While police officers search the premises for a murder weapon, the widow/murderer cooks and serves the haunch of meat to the unsuspecting authorities, urging,

"It'd be a favour to me if you'd eat it up. Then you can go on with your work again afterwards." True to the definition of dramatic irony, the audience shares complicity with the wife and laughs at the ignorant diners, who continue to ponder the murderer's method.

Thomas Berger's *Little Big Man* (1965) presents the pathetic situation of Amelia, a teen prostitute in a raw sin den in Kansas City. Oblivious to the implied comparison between prostitution and polygamy, the girl snuffles and narrates her early life in Salt Lake City in a respectable family. She describes her mother married in her teens to a notable Mormon and adds:

> You would know the name right off if I was to tell it. Now, outside folks have a funny idea about Mormons on account of the number of wives they take, but I tell you that is the reason why you won't find a den of iniquity like this in Salt Lake. . . . All we did was work and pray from early in the morning until night.

Unaware of the humor she generates with the depiction of Mormon peculiarities, Amelia explains that Woodbine, a neighbor with "only six wives," wanted to add her to the household. Dismayed, she ran away, spurning the opportunity to join model Mormon women in harem-style family life. As Amelia describes her self-perceived shame: "whereas instead of a device of pleasure to any man who comes down the road I would have been an honored Mormon wife." Narrator Jack Crabb, a frontier sage despite his lack of experience with women, comments that such hard-luck stories are common to women of easy virtue, all of whom claim to have come from "good families."

The use of irony to account for reprehensible behavior also prefaces small crimes and, with a deft mix of hyperbole, blows out of proportion a blip of a misdeed in Alfred Uhry's Pulitzer Prize-winning *Driving Miss Daisy* (1987). A gently remonstrative exchange depicts the early morning arrival of Hoke the chauffeur after his employer, Boolie Werthen, has heard his mother's complaint that Hoke has stolen a can of salmon. Bristly and ramrod straight at the scene of the "crime" in the 1988 movie version, Miss Daisy, played by Jessica Tandy, says nothing as Hoke, played by Morgan Freeman, presents a can of salmon wrapped in a humble brown grocery sack. She winces slightly when he explains that he rejected the desiccated pork chop she had left for his lunch the previous day and had opted for salmon without first asking her permission. Unaware that his actions raise him in the family's estimation while passing blame to his stingy passenger, Hoke hangs up his coat and cheerfully awaits the confrontation. Thus the ironist establishes a rapport with the audience by sharing knowledge of the chauffeur's fate that Hoke himself is denied. (Abrams 1971; Achebe 1959; Baldick 1990; Barnet, Berman, and Burto 1960; Berger 1965; *Contemporary Authors* 1994; Cuddon 1976; Dahl 1995; Eliot 1960; Feinberg 1967; Gassner and Quinn 1969; Gray 1992; Halliwell 1995; Henry 1995; Holman 1980; Houston 1973; Levin and Hyman 1958; McArthur 1992; Shakespeare 1967; Sophocles 1958; Swift 1958; Tsao Hsueh-Chin 1958; Uhry 1990; Waugh 1958; Wu 1961)

See also hyperbole; incongruity; sarcasm; Shakespeare, William; Swift, Jonathan.

IRVING, WASHINGTON

A noted man of letters and observer of picturesque landscapes and human idiosyncrasies, Washington Irving was one of America's first originals. The last of a family of 11, he endured frequent medical treatment for tuberculosis and paused for intermittent rest cures, which gave him the leisure for introspection and evaluation of human nature. In defiance of a persistent cough and lung weakness that presaged a short, limited life, he flourished as the father of the American short story and as a notable diplomat. Irving produced a cornucopia of romantic tales, sketches, plays, a novel, biographies, essays, vignettes, miscellanies, and satires flavored with a conservative tone in a variety of styles ranging from imitations of Joseph Addison's neoclassic essays to Goldsmith's sentimentality to Byronesque exotica. His fame on both sides of the Atlantic places him in a category with Mark Twain and James Fenimore Cooper, who also entertained European readers with keen observations of life in the United States.

Irving was a first-generation New Yorker. He was born to Sarah Sanders and William Irving, a prosperous hardware dealer and no-nonsense Scotch Calvinist, in lower Manhattan on April 3, 1783, in the final week of the American Revolution. Irving bore the name of George Washington, the country's savior. A known scamp, Irving preferred prowling the wharf, watching amateur theatricals, and investigating legends and ghost sightings to attending classes in Benjamin Romaine's private school, which his father had hoped would tame him. When players set up at a local theater, Irving, like Huck Finn, climbed out his bedroom window to catch the final act. Irving's unimpressive academic record, particularly in math, prohibited entrance to Columbia University. After studying law and clerking for attorney Brockholst Livingston, he worked as a stringer for his brother Peter's newspapers, the *Corrector* and the *Morning Chronicle,* for which Irving published the droll letters of Jonathan Oldstyle, Gent., a satiric examination of manners and attitudes of New Yorkers. From 1804 to 1806, Irving lived in France and recovered from consumption. He made rigorous side trips through Europe that took him to public hangings, the ballet, troop departures for the Napoleonic wars, and the pirate-infested shores of Sicily. He returned with extensive journal entries animated with the people and events he encountered, especially dance, opera, theater, and social interaction.

On his return to New York, Irving opened a Wall Street law firm with his brother John but took little interest in the profession. Attracted to writers, Irving, along with brothers Peter and William and brother-in-law James Kirke Paulding, dubbed themselves the "Nine Worthies" and founded *Salmagundi; or, the Whim-Whams and Opinions of Launcelot Longstaff, Esq. and Others,* a short-lived satiric journal named for a spicy meat sauce. The periodical produced 20 issues from 1807 to 1808 under the pseudonyms of Anthony Evergreen, Jeremy Cockloft the Younger, Will Wizard, and Pindar Cockloft, Esq. Similar to the English *Spectator,* it concentrated on informative, whimsical, and witty caricatures; parodies of America's earliest presidents; and essays on New Yorkers.

In the editor's words, the staff took to heart the mission of satire: "to instruct the young, reform the old, correct the city, and castigate the age."

Irving preferred broad-based satire. To the delight of New York insiders, he challenged his compatriots to spoof "the fairest, the finest, the most accomplished, the most bewitching, and the most ineffable beings that walk, creep, crawl, swim, fly, float, or vegitate [sic] in any or all of the four elements." A favorite series of his humorous writings were the concocted letters of the fictional Mustapha-Rub-a-Dub Keli Khan, who purported to inform friend Asem Haachem of political opinions of the era. Assorted other works skewered the elite Ding Dongs and Sophie Sparkles, self-indulgent rakes, windy backbenchers, busybodies, and bombastic actors. His touch was sharp but light and rarely didactic.

Irving's literary career took an inauspicious turn shortly before he published America's first comic burlesque, a spoof of the historical guidebook entitled *A History of New York, from the Beginning of the World to the End of the Dutch Dynasty* (1809), a melange of fact and buffoonery spoken through the fictional persona of Diedrich Knickerbocker, a Dutch pedant whose name came to symbolize New Yorkers. Irving extended the humor of his comic fictional observer by taking out newspaper ads requesting information about Knickerbocker's disappearance. Although his work brought raves from critics and titters from readers, Dutch residents were not amused at a lampoon of the governor of New Amsterdam, whom Irving characterized as five feet six in height, five feet six in girth, and bearing "the appearance of a beer barrel on skids." During the stressful time when Irving came under fire of irate readers of Dutch ancestry, he also suffered the double loss of his father and of his fiancée, Matilda Hoffman.

Grief undermined the author's energies. He retired briefly to tutor the children of Judge William Van Ness at Lindenwald in Kinderhook, New York, the setting of the notorious ride of the headless horseman. As a partner in P & E Irving, the family cutlery trade, he traveled to Washington, D.C., where he petitioned Congress to assist the flagging New York market. During the War of 1812, he divided his time between serving as attaché to Governor Tompkins and editing the *Analectic Magazine,* a Philadelphia-based journal rife with the author's patriotism and bemusement at varied citizen responses to the war years. Although he disliked editing, he earned $1,500 annually and kept up a column and critical articles as part of his duties.

At the age of 33, after the death of his mother and eldest brother William, Irving unintentionally chose the life of the expatriate. He settled in Liverpool, England, as representative for the foundering family trade at the Goree Arcade. When the company went bankrupt, he visited his brother-in-law in Birmingham, West Midlands, to relieve chronic melancholia. Forced to write for a living, Irving became America's first professional author, completing *The Sketch Book of Geoffrey Crayon, Gent.* (1818), an entertaining seven-part serial, and followed with *Bracebridge Hall, or the Humourists: A Medley* (1822), a financially successful collection of comic vignettes, ghost stories, travelogs, essays, supernatural tales, and reflections. These vivid beginnings contained his three most famous stories, "The Spectre Bridegroom"; "Rip Van Winkle," set in the mountains around Kaatskill [Catskill], New York; and "The Legend of Sleepy Hollow," a ghost legend still featured in numerous cartoons. This triad preserves Irving's most famous caricatures: Ichabod Crane, the scrawny man of learning and butt of local pranksters who enjoy taunting the diffident schoolmaster; Dame Van Winkle of the scalding tongue; and Rip Van Winkle, a tattered ne'er-do-well. The author's spirited fun at the expense of henpecked husbands extends to Rip's henpecked dog Wolf, who "was as courageous an animal as ever scoured the woods; but what courage can withstand the ever-during and all-besetting terrors of a woman's tongue?" In her presence, the cowering beast wilted and "sneaked about with a gallows air," casting many a sidelong glance at Dame Van Winkle, and at the least flourish of a broomstick or ladle he would fly to the door with yelping precipitation.

The public's enjoyment of such droll, irreverent lampoons brought Irving instant fame and the friendship and respect of Sir Walter Scott, Thomas Moore, and George Byron. In Paris, Irving wrote stage plays in collaboration with John Howard Payne. Irving settled in London and worked in the Reading Room of the British Museum while composing *Tales of a Traveler* (1824), a critically disastrous blend of 32 short pieces published under his real name and including more of Knickerbocker's anecdotes, a perusal of the legends of the pirate Captain Kidd, and the acclaimed "Devil and Tom Walker." In the latter, the author halts a gripping story of a man's deal with an ominous, dark Satan to interject a quip about the protagonist's wife. A parallel of Rip Van Winkle's shrewish mate, Irving surmises that Tom's wife

> had probably attempted to deal with the black man as she had been accustomed to deal with her husband; but though a female scold is generally considered a match for the devil, yet in this instance she appears to have had the worse of it. She must have died game, however; for it is said Tom noticed many prints of cloven feet deeply stamped about the tree and found handfuls of hair, that looked as if they had been plucked from the coarse shock of the woodman.

Following Irving's failed courtship of Mary Shelley, a lengthy sojourn in Spain sparked his interest in biography and history, as reflected in *The Life and Voyages of Christopher Columbus* (1828) and *The Conquest of Granada* (1829). The adoring Spanish awarded him membership in the Real Academia de la Historia. In England he received a history medal from the Royal Society of Literature and an honorary degree from Oxford.

On Irving's return to New York in 1832, he discovered his work in vogue, his name as well known among readers as those of Ichabod Crane and Rip Van Winkle, and his presence requested at the president's mansion for a dinner in his honor. He capitalized on his popularity with *The Alhambra* (1832), an architectural guide collected with miscellaneous Spanish sketches and a satire on King Boabdil, the tearful, ineffectual Spanish monarch. Irving's month-long trek for a fact-finding commission took him west to study locations for the resettlement of the Cherokee nation and gave him material for *A Tour of the*

Prairies (1835), a study of Indians and buffaloes on the plains; *Astoria* (1836), an overview of the fur trade; and *The Adventures of Captain Bonneville, U.S.A.* (1837), a study of mountaineers of the Rockies. The triad was published over a century later as his *Western Journals.* Subsequent ambassadorial appointments returned him to Spain and England as cultural liaison until, in his mid-sixties, he refused further political offices. He retired to Sunnyside, his country estate on the Hudson River near Tarrytown, New York, and lived with his niece Sarah Paris. Still productive until his death from heart failure at Irvington, New York, on November 28, 1859, he conducted research, managed the library of John Jacob Astor, contributed to *Knickerbocker Magazine,* and wrote *The Lives of Mahomet and His Successors* (1850), *Wolfert's Roost and Miscellanies* (1855), and his critically acclaimed five-volume *Life of George Washington* (1859). Irving is buried in Sleepy Hollow Cemetery. (Bowden 1981; Carlson 1979; Cowie 1951; Eagle and Stephens 1992; Ehrlich and Carruth 1982; Hart 1983; Irving 1855, 1978, 1983, 1987; Malia 1983; Miller 1989)

See also Addison, Joseph; burlesque; caricature; *The Spectator;* whimsy.

 JINGLE

The onamotopoetic jingle imitates a sound, melody, or cadence, often sacrificing sense for sound. The frequent accompaniment to radio or television advertisement, this simplistic chanting of illogical or pseudo-logical patter, lighthearted tra-la-las, alliterated feminine rhymes, and punched-up masculine rhyme forms part of the charm of nonsense literature. Jingle figures in the gibes and wit of music hall verse, popular in the 1800s. One piece, "Do It No More," leaves unspecified the "it" not to be done, but the conversation overheard between V and A leaves little doubt that the author refers to English royalty and their growing family:

> We kindly do treat 'em
> And seldom do beat 'em,
> So Albert, dear Albert,
> We'll do it no more.

In Renaissance drama, jingles often repeated sounds and lines, as in Benedick's song from William Shakespeare's *Much Ado about Nothing* (ca. 1589):

> Sigh no more, ladies, sigh no more,
> Men were deceivers ever;
> One foot in sea and one on shore,
> To one thing constant never:
> Then sigh not so, but let them go,
> And be you blithe and bonny;
> Converting all your sounds of woe
> Into Hey nonny, nonny.

The repeated syllable that closes this and the second octet verbalizes the gist of the jingle in its suggestion of "nonsense," the focus of doggerel. A unifying factor in Kenneth Branagh's production of *Much Ado about Nothing* (1993), the jingle's thumping rhythm begins the play and concludes it in a joyous dance and chorus.

An example of homespun verse from anonymous cowboy lore suggests the scurrilous nature of less decorous forms of jingle:

Carnation milk, the best in the land
Comes to the table in a little red can.
No tits to pull; no hay to pitch.
Just punch a hole in the son-of-a-bitch.

For all its rustic idiocy, the jingle carries a kernel of truth—farm life is neither enjoyable nor ennobling. The person who best speaks for the ignoble labors of the farmhand is the one who enjoys a respite from dairy labor by creaming coffee with a squirt from a punctured tin. Another aspect of this gem of satire is the convenience of tinned milk for the herder, who may be too far from dairy animals and stores to have access to milk and thus drinks coffee with neither fresh nor canned cream.

One of the most recited jingles of nineteenth-century English literature is Lewis Carroll's "Jabberwocky," the *tour de force* creation of portmanteau words that tell the tale of the stalker's victory over the jabber-beast. Written to entertain Carroll's siblings, the poem first appeared in pseudo-Anglo-Saxon script in *Misch-Masch*, then recurs—written backwards—in Chapter 1 of *Through the Looking-Glass* (1872). Carroll emphasizes the most abstract of his mock-heroic quatrains by repeating the first one as the poem's closure:

'Twas brillig and the slithy toves
    Did gyre and gimble in the wabe:
All mimsy were the borogoves,
    And the mome raths outgrabe.

The jingle lampoons the heroics of hunter against prey with glimpses of jaws, claws, the Jubjub bird, and the "frumious Bandersnatch." To survive this mock-serious quarry, the hunter uses his "vorpal sword" as he seeks "the manxome foe." Teasingly staging the contemplative man in contest against a wily beast, Carroll paints him "in uffish thought" until the Jabberwock interrupts his thinking and, "whiffling through the tulgey wood," burbles as it approaches. The set-to ends with deft snicker-snacks of the blade. The hero's reward is a parent's cry of "O frabjous day! Callooh! Callay! / He chortled in his joy." Carroll's combination of snorting and chuckling produced "chortle," a useful blend that survives the jingle in current dictionaries.

In twentieth-century dystopia, incidental satire ridicules the clangor of advertisement, which exemplifies much of the discordance that wearies and dismays. Aldous Huxley parodies the blend of hype and public carnality in *Brave New World* (1939). At Westminster Abbey, on the night of Henry's date with Lenina Crowne, "Calvin Stopes and His Sixteen Sexophonists" boop out "All the Latest Synthetic Music":

Bottle of mine, it's you I've always wanted!
Bottle of mind, why was I ever decanted?
    Skies are blue inside of you,
    The weather's always fine;
For
There ain't no Bottle in all the world
Like that dear little Bottle of mine.

Five-steppers dancing to the scent- and color-dispensing organ dip and sway their troubles away to "slow Malthusian Blues," which emulate the pre-decantation atmosphere that cloaked budding fetuses. The cheer of the pop jingle contrasts with "the depressing stars [which] had travelled quite some way across the heavens," Huxley's poignant satire on a society that prefers canned happiness to nature.

American novelist and dystopist Ray Bradbury creates a brilliant counter-point between Guy Montag's disordered thoughts set against the jolt of a train and the gibberish of an alliterated toothpaste ad in *Fahrenheit 451* (1953):

> "Denham's. Spelled: D-E-N-"
> They toil not, neither do they . . .
> A fierce whisper of hot sand through empty sieve.
> *"Denham's does it!"*
> Consider the lilies, the lilies, the lilies . . .
> "Denham's dental detergent."
> "Shut up, shut up, shut up!"

The alliterated nonsense repeats d-d-d as Guy rushes toward his salvation, a meeting with a fellow defier of a repressive state. Along the route, more Ds clutter Guy's thoughts: Denham, Dentifrice, Dandy, Dental, Detergent. To Guy, the sound is "radio vomit . . . a great tonload of music made of tin, copper, silver, chromium, and brass." Like a jackhammer, the strung-out Ds pound the people into submission, a fate Guy eludes at peril to his family and home. (Bradbury 1953; Branagh 1993; Carroll 1960; Cuddon 1984; Davison 1971; Drabble 1985; Gray 1992; Holman 1992; Huxley 194)

See also Carroll, Lewis; doggerel; limerick; mock-heroic; Shakespeare, William.

JUVENAL

A misanthropic, suspicious, bitter, unforgiving aphorist, Decimus Junius Juvenalis earned an unenviable niche among Rome's most ill-tempered, out-spoken satirists and remains an example of the hardliner who takes no prison-ers. Born in Aquinum, southeast of Rome, in about A.D. 60, Juvenal was the son of a well-to-do freedman and was reared in country ease along the Via Latina, the route that set him on his way to an unavoidable collision with the Roman Empire. From a strong background in stoic philosophy, oratory, verse, and gram-mar, probably gained in a Roman school, he earned a civil-service post. An incomplete votive tablet containing part of his name suggests he served the empire as a military legate in Britain or as an Aquinian magistrate and priest, although his sneers at mythological gods indicate his disinclination for ancient Roman religious rites. The fragments bear out this reconstruction:

> C[ere]ri sacrum [D. Iu]nius Iuvenalis trib. coh[ortis I] Dalmatarum, II vir quinq[uennalis] flamen divi Vespasiani vovit dedicav[it q]ue sua pec[unia].

[Sacred to the goddess Ceres, D. Junius Juvenal, tribune of the Dalmation co-hort, priest of the deified Vespasian pledged and dedicated this with his own money.]

To suit his solitary bent, Juvenal established a reclusive, no doubt money-starved existence on his farm at Tibur, rumored to be a gift from the emperor Hadrian, who may have sponsored the poet. When finances allowed, Juvenal enjoyed entertaining in his Roman apartments; he kept himself in pocket money by associating with the rich. Except for his friend Martial, he apparently took few people into his confidence. As tight as a miser's money chest, he concealed whatever personal hurts or financial setbacks might have launched his cas-cade of gibes, although he shared with a clutch of disgruntled republicans his idealization of the Roman past and his distaste for emperors and their toadies.

Inflamed by the tyranny of Domitian's disastrous fifteen-year rule from A.D. 81 to 96, Juvenal began his writing career at age 50, a safe enough period of time after the emperor's death to avoid political reprisals, and continued spit-ting out indignant barbs until his death in A.D. 140. Assuming the role of critic, adviser, nostalgic patriot, and, to the bemusement of critics, cheated bisexual, he puts himself into his *Satirae* (ca. A.D. 110–127) so artfully and humorlessly that critics hesitate to accept any scenario as autobiographical. In the opening sally, Juvenal stakes out the territory he intends to reconnoiter:

> Quidquid agunt homines, votum timor ira voluptas gaudia discursus, nostri farrago libelli est. [Whatever people do—oath, fear, anger, pleasure, joys, amuse-ments—is the motley subject of our little book.]

So broad a salvo testifies to the author's seriousness of purpose and hints at his underlying motivation; that is, to explore the behaviors of one of Rome's least attractive historical periods.

Juvenal's finely honed hexametric epigrams waste no words and, for the scholarly, remain catchphrases needing no translation:

- Mens sana in corpore sano [a sound mind in a sound body]
- Panem et circenses [bread and circuses, the handouts that Roman politicians distributed to maintain popularity and a semblance of public contentment]
- Probitas laudatur et alget [Honesty is praised and shivers]
- Nemo repente fuit turpissimus [No one suddenly becomes wicked]
- Rara avis [a rare bird]
- Saevior armis luxuria [luxury, deadlier than war]
- Quis custodiet ipsos custodes? [Who will watch the watchers?]
- Difficile est saturam non scribere [It's hard not to write satire]

From snitty to grievously ironic to darkly brooding, his style puts him on the defensive front line, itching for a one-two punch at Rome's decadent set. He

Roman satirist Decimus Junius Juvenalis, circa 55–140

seems to labor under a child's sense of justice and fair play and must thrash in frustration when his world vision proves false. In a frivolous mood, he once trod perilously close to public apostasy by proposing that Romans add money to their list of Pax, Victoria, Virtus, Concordia [peace, victory, strength, harmony] and other allegorical deities. More to his detriment, Juvenal is said to have infuriated the emperor by lampooning Paris, a stage performer in imperial favor until his death in A.D. 83. Because the barbed criticism reflected poorly on Domitian's fondness for flatterers, the emperor confiscated the versifier's land and posted him to Syene, Egypt, where Juvenal endured for four years (until the death of the emperor) the boredom and rigors of a spartan military outpost.

The list of Juvenal's targets reads like a synopsis of a daily gossip rag full of "morning after" details. Only 16 of his satires remain, but even from that relatively small corpus shrieks the shrill oratory of a soapbox spoiler. With what appears to be personal scores to settle, he rails at Rome's most egregious no-goods: prostitutes, posturing social climbers, seedy foreign investors, pushy women, tyrants and egotists, sodomites, flesh peddlers, skirt-chasers, assassins, mountebanks, and fraudulent religious fanatics. For Rome, in short, he has little good to say:

> What of the fact that the nation excels in flattery, praising the talk of an ignorant patron, the looks of one who is ugly, comparing the stalk-like neck of a weakling to Hercules' muscles as he holds the giant Antaeus aloft well clear of the ground, admiring a squeaky voice which sounds as wretched as that of the cock, which seizes his partner's crest in the act of mating?

Juvenal claims to be so well supplied with such material that he can't resist writing nasty, gloom-laden couplets that picture his homeland sliding down the sewer. Females, in particular, fall victim to his venom, for he accuses women of demanding gifts, whining for attention, and poisoning men who fail to slake their lust. Of the adultress's faithlessness and duplicity, he claims:

> She meets the adulterer bathed, perfumed, and dressed,
> But rots in filth at home, a very pest!
> For him she breathes of nard; for him alone
> She makes the sweets of Araby her own;
> For him, at length, she ventures to uncase,
> Scales the first layer of roughcast from her face . . .
> But tell me yet; this thing, thus daubed and oiled,
> Thus poulticed, plastered, baked by turns and boiled,
> Thus with pomatums, ointments, lackered o'er,
> Is it a face, Ursidius, or a sore?

To escape these foul, vice-ridden snares, Juvenal dedicates his last satire, an unfinished paean, to the soldier, who at least can get out of town and survive on order and merit rather than patronage and guile.

Though neglected in his own time, Juvenal's work was frequently contrasted with that of Horace, a genial satirist whose style lacks the raw lashes of Juvenal's rancorous whip. Less frequently is he compared with Martial, who achieved fame in Juvenal's day yet never equaled the clever wit of his contemporary. In the fourth century, a new edition with commentary, perhaps the work of Servius the grammarian, brought the *Satirae* into public favor. A favorite of John Skelton and John Donne, Juvenal rose to importance during the eighteenth century and became a *cause célèbre* of Samuel Johnson, John Dryden, and Jonathan Swift; later appreciative writers include George Byron, T. S. Eliot, and Victor Hugo. (Ehrlich 1985; Feder 1986; Godolphin 1949; Hadas 1954; Hammond and Scullard 1992; Howatson 1989; Juvenal 1890, 1892, 1992; Mantinband 1956; Pollard 1970; Radice 1973; Snodgrass 1988)

See also Dryden, John; Horace; invective; Martial; satire; Swift, Jonathan.

KABUKI

The most recent form of drama to develop in Japan, kabuki originated about 1600, the beginning of the Genroku period, when the collapse of a rigid feudal social structure enabled the rise of a middle class and spread more evenly the nation's wealth among crafters and merchants. The era parallels the popularity of Elizabethan drama during the English Renaissance. During its first century of growth, kabuki theater blended singing, dancing, spectacle, and orchestral accompaniment of drums, flutes, samisen or shamisen, and wooden batabata (clappers). Kabuki actors emulated *bunruku* (puppet shows), adopting the flexed joints and stylized eyelids, mouth, and eyebrows of the puppets. Similar to Michael Jackson's moon-walking, the technique of *ningyo buri* (jerky hand manipulation) guided the actor's limbs to give the impression of wooden, socially motivated behaviors, as in *Hidakagawa Iriai Zakura* (1759), the story of a prince who meets his mistress on the sly.

Kabuki evolved from innovations to the vigorous Buddhist *odori* (literally "shocking dances") performed by Izuma no Okuni or O Kuni, a priestess and comic or folk dancer. In 1603, kabuki made its first appearance on a platform erected in the dry Kamo River bed at the Shinto shrine of Izumo. Izuma's husband and dance partner, the former samurai lancer Nagoya Sansaburo, redirected her art from religious dance to secular entertainment, which they named *kabuki*. Sanjuro, a colleague and probably second husband to Okuni, brought to Izuma's second collaboration a knowledge of farcical *kyogen* (literally "mad words" or interludes), exemplified three centuries later in *The Zen Substitute* (1910), a confused-identity play in which a drunken husband brags to his servant about carousing with a courtesan, then learns that the servant is really his wife in disguise.

Kabuki productions became so popular that Izuma moved her stage show to Edo, Japan's former capital, in 1607 and performed in the shogun's castle. Her repertoire, the obverse of formal Japanese traditional theater, included innovative low-comic slapstick that had enormous appeal. Other data about her life suggest several possibilities: that she died in 1613, that she returned to her village to enter a convent, and that she was succeeded by a daughter and a granddaughter bearing the names Okuni II and Okuni III.

An actor-centered performance set to jolly plucks on the samisen, kabuki was the impetus of Kyoto's courtesan kabuki or all-female troupes, often geishas or women of suspect reputation because of their erotic performances and because they belonged to the *kawaramono*, Japan's untouchables, riverbed beggars who performed such lowly work as grave digging, tanning, and collection of night soil. As *kawaramono*, actors received no welcome from the four stations of society—warrior, farmer, crafter, and merchant (and, therefore, like Europe's gypsy troupes, remained at the edge of respectability)—until their acceptance by the imperial family in 1879. Among the moneyed Edo merchant class, Okuni broke the barriers of social class and earned fame for dressing in men's clothing. She played boisterous or comic drunks, which were set roles, or *kata*, that resemble the *lazzi* of the *commedia dell'arte*.

Under the fiat of the Tokugawa shoguns, kabuki made a radical shift to young male troupes in 1629 after puritanical laws barred women from the stage, even as puppeteers. Within a quarter-century, young men were involved in the same network of scandals that had ended female troupes. In 1652, the kabuki stage passed into the hands of *otokogata* (mature men) whom authorities, mindful of strict Confucian principles, watched for signs of frivolity or sacrilege. An example of such stage impropriety occurs in *Narukami* (1742), a one-act play in which a trickster priestess seduces a priest and causes him to release the rain god, whom he holds in captivity. Owing to the high quality of their acting and public behavior, these performers mixed with society's best and passed their stock roles and innovative techniques to their offspring to create *ie no gei* (family tradition), a longstanding source of pride in stagecraft and in plays that writers composed just to showcase their talents. The families devised crests—for instance, a fan and oak leaves, group of boxes, and two scrolls—to decorate dressing-room doors, towels, or curtains and to indicate their membership in a prestigious theatrical lineage.

In the seventeenth century, kabuki exploded in popularity, continuing to adapt its two-dimensional style from the emulation of puppetry. It produced two star performers: Ichikawa Danjuro of Tokyo (1660–1704), a favorite in history plays who was stabbed to death at his peak by a rival, and Sakata Tojuro (1644–1709), a leading heartthrob in domestic comedy. A visual feast, kabuki coordinated colorful costumes; *kumadori* (masklike makeup), which emphasizes facial muscles; and the strum of the three-string *samisen*. Vivid scenery required sets that were slid from the wings into grooves, rotating stages, hinged flap sets, and simulated weather changes. Entertainers energized the stage with flagrant melodrama, violence, and overacting. Written plots were of little significance until the influence of Chikamatsu Monzaemon (1653–1724), the master dramatist who altered kabuki from freelance acting to a literary skill. A connecting link between puppet theater and kabuki, Chikamatsu wrote more than 150 plays for the two genres, often heavily tinged with fantasy. For the first time, plays contained an action that was broken into two acts and that followed the identifiable dramatic structure of rising action, climax, and falling action. Unfortunately for theater history, commentary is limited to early critics, for none of Chikamatsu's works survives.

Chikamatsu and his follower, Takedo Izumo (1691–1756), master tragedian, wrote solely for Osaka's doll theater. Izumo produced a major addition to kabuki canon, *Kanadehon Chushingura (The Treasury of Loyal Retainers)* (1748), an eleven-act play that runs an entire day and expresses the theme of vengeance because of dishonor done to a lady. For the first time, the writer's name deserved audience attention. Unlike the stiffly traditional *no* plays, kabuki, like the *no* tradition's farcical *kyogen*, allowed broad leeway with comedy, satire, and spectacle, which often introduced anachronism and improvisation to loosely connected acts. Simultaneously, dance schools developing talent for the stage taught choreography especially for the needs of kabuki. The dancers learned to express the intense feelings of each character by overacting sobs, alarm, admiration, dismay, or other emotions. Their interpretation took precedence over the play, for which there was no director.

Kabuki's literary style, which is largely episodic and blended from a variety of moods, is comprised of three categories:

- *Jidaimono*, historical drama

- *Sewamono*, plays about domestic situations or the lives of commoners

- *Shosagoto*, dance or spectacle

In addition, playwrights added *chariba* (scenes of comic relief) that might exaggerate a sad scene, for example, to the point that it would elicit laughter. Two generations of playwrights—Tsuruya Namboku (1755–1829) and the author of 360 of kabuki's most respected works, Mokuami Kawatake (1816–1893)—linked drama to realism by adding servants and thieves as focal characters rather

A Japanese audience of the 1740s attends a kabuki performance where actors, center, take their places by moving through the audience on a raised stage, or "flower walk."

than centering on aristocrats, as in the old style. Taking his cue from changes in social structure, Kawatake concentrated his plots on the decadence of the aristocracy, who no longer deserved the reverence of ordinary Japanese. A strongly satiric play, *Ningen Ganji Kane Yo No Naka* (1879), adapted from Edward Bulwer-Lytton's comedy *Money* (1840), ridicules a grasping foster parent who mistreats his ward until the boy comes into money. The boy exposes the old man's avarice, then marries a servant girl who has suffered similar misfortune at the hands of the foster father.

Kabuki has remained popular with the Japanese through regular revivals of classic titles and the inventive creations of modern playwrights. Some critics maintain that the burgeoning tourist trade has forced up the price of tickets beyond the reach of average Japanese playgoers. When plays fill an entire day, producers create *midori*, a varied genre and acting style that often blends parts of dramas and scenes from a mix of sources and highlights contrast by skillful juxtaposition. Cosmopolitan audiences used to television and movies expect technical artistry:

- Scene changes, elevators, flying apparatus, and walkways

- Trap doors to serve as entrances for ghosts and spirits and as underground passageways

- Stage lighting to replace the old-fashioned *sashidashi*, or lights thrust on poles from the wings to highlight facial expressions

- Pools of water and mud for dunking players

- Wavy boards simulating the ocean

- Fake blood and costumes that slip to the floor to reveal blood-stained bandages

- Sound effects and animal noises.

A camp element of casting is the continued use of the *onnagata* (stylized female impersonators), who intensify femininity and womanly emotions by expressive mime, eye movements, coy manipulation of the traditional fan, rapid costume change, and artful or suggestive posturing and muscular facial distortion to overplay the role of the butch female, who is often broad-shouldered and decked with tattoos. Against the overdone stereotype of womanhood, the samurai warrior stands grim-faced, stoic, unmoved by the coy female; the counterbalance produces the tension of the story. Other stereotypical characters include bandit, pirate, pilgrim, loyal client, and child. To heighten the appearance of a stock figure, procession, or band of travelers, the actor may leap into view along the *hanamichi* (literally "flower path"), an extended runway that fans out between rows of viewers to the back of the auditorium. Actors, some of whom enjoy the fame of Hollywood movie stars, such as Bando Tamasaburo, a noted female impersonator, attract fans.

Twentieth-century realists took an interest in plays by George Bernard Shaw, Henrik Ibsen, John Millington Synge, Leo Tolstoy, August Strindberg, and Anton

Chekhov and forced a radical alteration of tradition with the upsurge of pro-Communist, proletarian *shingeki* theater. An underground Little Theater movement, *shingeki* replaced the pretentious mannerisms of kabuki with modern dance, music, and irony as a social statement. For example, *Musuko* (1923), a one-act play, offers a snowy stage to which a young criminal returns in time to overhear his father bragging to a police officer about the son's blameless career. Another successful work is *Nemuru Ga Rakuda Monogatari* (1929), a three-act comic play depicting the death of a blustering villager from eating blowfish. The ironic genre was short-lived: the political scene of the 1930s found working-class theater philosophically unacceptable. Other attempts to update theater have had meager success; kabuki, an exotic seventeenth-century relic, holds its position as Japan's revered stage tradition. (Bermel 1982; Brockett 1968; Burdick 1974; Cavendish 1970; Gassner and Quinn 1969; Hartnell 1983; Hughes 1938; Izumo 1971; Leiter 1979; Perkins 1991)

See also camp; comedy; comic relief; *commedia dell'arte;* Shaw, George Bernard; slapstick; trickster.

KAUFMAN, GEORGE S.

One of America's noted wits of the 1930s and a member of the Algonquin Club, George Simon Kaufman worked as journalist and theater reviewer before launching a 30-year career in comedy. His skill kept his name in Broadway lights for decades and guaranteed him a spot at the famous Algonquin Hotel's Round Table, a daily lunch meeting of witty friends, including Dorothy Parker, Alexander Woollcott, and Heywood Broun. Kaufman's musical, *Of Thee I Sing* (1931) was the first in the genre to receive a Pulitzer Prize; the second, *Dinner at Eight* (1932), and *The Man Who Came to Dinner* (1939) received high critical acclaim for their comic ingenuity and repartee.

Born in Pittsburgh on November 16, 1889, to Nettie Schamberg Myers and Joseph S. Kaufman, Kaufman gave the study of law barely a semester before leaving school and working as a surveyor. Before finding his niche in writing, he worked as an Allegheny County tax clerk, a secretary, and a ribbon seller. In heady years as columnist for the *Washington Times, New York Evening Mail,* and *New York Times,* Kaufman lived a double life of city exhibitionism and country seclusion on his Bucks County, Pennsylvania, estate, Barley Sheaf Farm. He produced *The Butter and Egg Man* (1925) alone before settling on collaboration as a method of producing fiction. He wrote with Ring Lardner, Alexander Woollcott, Marc Connelly, Edna Ferber, George Gershwin, and Moss Hart, with whom he produced *Merrily We Roll Along* (1934), *You Can't Take It with You* (1936), *The Man Who Came to Dinner,* and *George Washington Slept Here* (1940). On his own, Kaufman wrote the tremendously lucrative *A Night at the Opera* (1935), a Marx Brothers hit; in 1946, he assisted J. P. Marquand in dramatizing *The Late George Apley,* a Pulitzer Prize-winning novel, and directed *The Senator Was Indiscreet* (1947), a political satire starring William Powell as a dim-witted

American playwright George S. Kaufman, 1889–1961

politician. After a distinguished career in musicals and Hollywood screenplays, Kaufman returned to New York. He died at his Park Avenue home on June 2, 1961. (Bermel 1982; Ehrlich and Carruth 1982; Hart 1961; Katz 1982; Kunitz 1942; Magnusson 1990)

See also comedy; Hart, Moss; *Harvey*; Parker, Dorothy; political satire; repartee; satire; whimsy; *You Can't Take It with You.*

KING, FLORENCE

One of the treasures of southern satire, Florence King fits the "unique" category enough times to retire the loving cup. An only child, she is the daughter of freelance jazz trombonist Herbert Frederick King, a mild-mannered Britisher, and Louise Ruding King, an outspoken baseball fan who was living in Washington, D.C., when Florence was born January 5, 1936. If the biographer can accept the testimony of King's rollicking *Confessions of a Failed Southern Lady* (1985), life at the King home bore little resemblance to "Father Knows Best." The news of Louise's pregnancy "brought Granny to Park Road on winged Enna Jettick feet." Her maternal grandmother, whom Florence identifies as a member of "the Daughters," that is, United Daughters of the Confederacy, attempted with limited success to instill southern gentility in her granddaughter by example and force. A closing quatrain in *Reflections in a Jaundiced Eye* (1989) offers the counterpoint to Granny's monomania:

> Regarding our Democrazy
> And all of those who love it,
> I'll quote my angel mother now
> And end by saying "Shove it."

The result was an uncompromising amalgam of southern cussedness and smart-mouth retorts spoken in the crisp British enunciation that Florence gained from the gentle, perennially underemployed Herb. Randy and daring in her teens, she admits, "I failed to 'draw the line,' i.e., I let [a date] touch me 'up top.' Covered tit was for the fifth date and bare tit was for the sixth date, so when I let him unhook my bra, I was two tits too early."

King earned a bachelor's degree from American University in 1957 and, after a year of graduate work at the University of Mississippi, she tried teaching history in Suitland, Maryland, and filing for a realty firm before finding a passion worth her labor—writing for the *Raleigh News and Observer*, for which she earned a North Carolina Press award; reviewing books for *Newsday* and the *New York Times*; writing a column for *National Review* and articles for *Cosmo, Ms., Playgirl, Southern Magazine*, and *Penthouse*; and penning soft porn "eroticas" for *Uncensored Confessions*. Not altogether proud of her bodice-rippers, which she published under an assortment of pseudonyms, King claims that the discipline of steady composition in the limited genre taught her the rudiments of fiction.

Since 1975, King has taken top place among America's best satiric essayists with a steady flow of hilariously readable commentary. In her words, the appeal of her take-no-prisoners style is partly gender based: she's a "woman who rips the teats off sacred cows." Fiercely conservative, antidemocratic, and proindividual, she has been described as an "unreconstructed Southerner, gun-toting right-wing feminist, high-church Episcopal atheist, postmenopausal misanthropic monarchist." Her "legitimate" satire began with *Southern Ladies and Gentlemen* (1975), a spin-off of her years writing up debutante soirees and tea parties for the press. In the Afterword of the 1993 edition, she adds to her list of good ol' boys, prom trotters, hoydens, daddy's girls, gracious do-gooders, invalids with pelvic disorders, and dowagers with hot flashes the latest regional outrage—the homogenized South, vitiated by waves of insipid northern climbers:

> If Oakland has no there, Damnyuppies have no from. Whatever ethnic background they once possessed has faded with the geographical and psychological distance they have put between themselves and their origins. Most of them seem to have no distinctive traits, habits, or accents—just master's degrees.

Her later titles—*WASP, Where Is Thy Sting* (1976); *He: An Irreverent Look at the American Male* (1978); and *When Sisterhood Was in Flower* (1982)—spotlight inconsistencies in American behaviors, particularly those springing from religious fervor or political prejudice. In *WASP,* she leaps to conclusions about uppity women whose shopping list reads like a post-Victorian shaped verse apologia:

Alpo
9-Lives
Harper's
tomato juice
Worcestershire
Tabasco
vodka
food.

The third, *Sisterhood,* opens with a parody of *Moby Dick* ("Call me Isabel") and lampoons half-baked philosophies of radical feminists.

On a personal note, King assesses home and family traditions with *Confessions of a Failed Southern Lady,* a pseudo-autobiographical memoir of the King family. Her jests about mismated parents, precocity, and a tyrannical grandmother vibrate with enough audacious truth to suggest actual memories rather than blatant exaggeration. The mélange of a mother reading the sports page and chainsmoking Lucky Strikes, Granny counseling women who suffer from tilted womb, and Herb quietly suffering the out-of-sync household supplies a verisimilitude that screams, "This poor waif grew up in a madhouse." The turn to gay college confessional in the last quarter of the book provides insight into the solitude and diffidence that plagued King's childhood and teen years.

Returning to the seriocomic essay in her next three works, she attacks the U.S. penchant for crisis hotlines and ACLU causes in *Reflections in a Jaundiced*

Eye. With a pathologist's glee, she launches wickedly raw, Swiftian attacks on American values and pursues a personal vendetta against feminist polemicist Andrea Dworkin in *Lump It or Leave It* (1991). Similarly uncompromising studies of human character grace *With Charity for None* (1992). In *Lump It*, King opines: "An America without -ists is like an egg without salt, so defenders of the environment and animal-rights advocates are doing their bit to smoke out and hunt down new villains." In 1995, she reprised earlier essays in a collection, *The Florence King Reader*, of some of her funniest and most irreverent caricatures, including a seventies flower child and a hare-brained medievalist.

In one of the inevitable confrontations between contemporaries of comparable wit and verve, Florence King clashed with Molly Ivins, political satirist for the *Fort Worth Star-Telegram*. In August 1995, King published "Molly Ivins, Plagiarist" in *American Entertainment;* Ivins had little choice but to apologize for withholding credit for significant citations. Ivins, who considers herself a populist, shares little of the harsher tones of King, self-described as "slightly to the right of Vlad the Impaler." The dust-up arose from King's critique of Ivins's 1991 collection *Molly Ivins Can't Say Those Things, Can She?* Four years after the successful volume appeared in print, King saw segments in Ivins's chapter "Magnolias and Moonshine" that derived from King's *Southern Ladies and Gentlemen*, published twenty years earlier. (*Authors in the News* 1976; *Contemporary Authors* 1994; *Dictionary of Literary Biography* 1986; Groer 1995; Ivins 1991; King 1975, 1989, 1990, 1995)

See also burlesque; caricature; lampoon; political satire; satire; Swift, Jonathan.

THE KING AND I

A success in autobiography, lecture, print and film biography, stage musical, and film musical comedy, the story of Anna Leonowens, a Welsh schoolteacher who tutored the royal children of Siam, has engaged the imagination of readers and viewers for decades. The story intermingles international concerns—Wales with Siam, England with its colonies, and the United States with followers of Harriet Beecher Stowe's *Uncle Tom's Cabin* (1852) and Abraham Lincoln's *Emancipation Proclamation*. Margaret Landon's version of Leonowens's life, a biography titled *Anna and the King of Siam* (1943), takes a realistic approach to the convoluted story of Anna Harriette Crawford, born in Carnarvon, Wales, on November 5, 1834, reared in India after her father's death in 1849, and married at age seventeen to her choice of suitors—Major Thomas Louis Leonowens, an officer of the commissariat. While living in Singapore with son Louis and daughter Avis in 1857, Anna suffered the loss of her husband, who died within hours of contracting a fever.

A doomed attempt to support herself by forming a private school preceded Anna's acceptance of an invitation in 1862 from Phra Maha Mongut, King of Siam, to teach the royal children. Her years in the classroom with wives, concubines, children, and the crown prince, Chulalongkorn, cemented a life-long friendship with the future king, who applied his lessons from Anna's classroom to Siam's third-world problems. His reign is credited with liberal laws, notably amnesty for political prisoners, religious freedom, and gradual termination of serfdom and slavery, which ended in 1905. Anna composed memoirs for the *Atlantic Monthly*, wrote an autobiography, *The English Governess at the Siamese Court*, and lectured to the cream of New England literary society, including James Russell Lowell, Sarah Orne Jewett, Oliver Wendell Holmes, Julia Ward Howe, William Cullen Bryant, Henry Wadsworth Longfellow, and Anna's philosophical idols, abolitionist Stowe and transcendentalist Ralph Waldo Emerson.

On March 29, 1951, Richard Rodgers and Oscar Hammerstein, America's most talented musical comedy duo, raised the curtain on *The King and I*, their satiric, highly romanticized version of Anna Leonowens's life at the Siamese court. Devoid of the vicious court intrigue and cruel vendettas that the historical Phra Maha Mongut gloried in, the play concentrates on one of satire's most common motifs: a patriarchal male coping with a woman liberated from Victorianism, male bondage, and self-doubt. The comic, often fiery exchanges between the king and his royal tutor produce a satisfying, sometimes roseate study of world order in the early 1860s. The inevitable clashes in dialogue and lyrics—more a battle of the sexes than the struggle of a self-important king to outwit a visiting teacher—instruct both adults' sons in the necessity of an open mind and elicit a carefully balanced compromise when cultures collide.

At the opening of the story, Anna, garbed in the voluminous skirts, hoops, and high-necked bodices of the Victorian era, must accustom herself to men stripped to the waist and prostrating themselves toadlike before her. At length, Anna acclimates herself to the style of dress and pace of a royal court, which holds her at bay as a gesture of control from a king over a lowly woman. To prove herself a verbal equal, Anna steels herself against cultural surprises and maintains a sense of humor:

> *Anna:* The fireworks—
> *King:* Best fireworks I ever see at funeral. How you like my acrobats?
> *Anna:* Splendid, Your Majesty. Best acrobats I have ever seen at funeral.

To turn the king into a laughable caricature, the authors give him a verbal tic—the repetition of significant words. During the argument over promises to Anna of a private residence, the king exclaims, "House? House? What is this about House?" The significance of Anna's demands, an outgrowth of her insecurity so close to the royal harem, becomes apparent as she describes the pain of widowhood and her need to rely on herself rather than male authority in a land where women count for little.

The satire takes a political stance as the king, also unsure of himself, tackles international difficulties. An obvious target of Britain's growing colonial empire, Siam lumbers into the Industrial Age still burdened with backward tools, superstition, and outdated information. The king intends for Siam to remain a sovereign state. The concept of chauvinistic regard for one's country becomes the subject of Anna's lessons to the royal students. The king, who eavesdrops on Anna's classes and gleans from the prince the focus of their studies, probes the Western world's concept of individual worth and democratic rule and even studies the biblical story of creation in an effort to gauge his European adversaries. Out of anger at his autocratic rule, Anna characterizes Siam:

> A land where there is talk of honor, and a wish for Siam to take her place among the modern nations of the world! Where there is talk of great changes, but where everything still remains according to the wishes of the King!

Anna's son and the crown prince puzzle over their parents' intractability. The king, without expressing verbally his need for a compromise, indicates that he will speak his mind if Anna will be certain that her head never rises above the level of his. In hoopskirts, Anna does her best to crouch to floor level and concentrates on resolving his fears for Siam.

The authors' satiric intent becomes clear when Anna, won over by the endearingly stubborn patriarch, tries to serve him as secretary and composes a formal letter from Mongut to "President Abra-Hom Lingkong in America" offering elephants as wartime beasts of burden. The king, in traditional style, begins his letter:

> From Phra Maha Mongut, by the blessing of the highest super agency in the world of the whole Universe, the King of Siam, the Sovereign of all tributary countries adjacent and around in every direction, etcetera, etcetera, etcetera.

The arrival of emissary Sir Edward Ramsay from Singapore pushes Mongut to extract advice from a woman. To supply him answers while he thinks out loud, she playacts an echo, as though Mongut solves his own image problem and fends off a possible takeover. She ventures:

> . . . my guess is that you will not fight with Sir Edward. . . . You will entertain him and his party in an especially grand manner. In this way you will make them all witnesses in your favor.

Anna concludes that Ramsay will return to Queen Victoria with a favorable report that Mongut is not a barbarian. To impress Ramsay with Siam's awareness of world events, Anna arranges a dinner, dresses the women in European hoopskirts, and choreographs a highly stylized pantomime of *Uncle Tom's Cabin*. The after-dinner dissection of conversation and impressions produces a reversal of Anna's discomfiture on arrival: Mongut puts on his jacket to indicate that he disapproves of Anna's fashionable evening décolletage. He implies that, by Siamese standards, dancing in the arms of Sir Edward Ramsay is immoral. The irony, both subtle and humorous, presents a view of manners and social customs from both sides of the globe and questions European standards regarding the parts of the anatomy that one may display without shame and the way in which men and women behave on the dance floor.

The drama's falling action ties the failed escapes of a palace slave and an emissary to Anna's intention to assist Mongut in abolishing slavery, the focus of her meddling in Siamese affairs. In a romance-charged scene, the king holds the whip over the slave girl. Anna attacks his pride:

She's only a child. She was running away because she was unhappy. Can't you understand that? Your majesty, I beg of you—don't throw away everything you've done. This girl hurt your vanity. She didn't hurt your heart. You haven't got a heart. You've never loved anyone. You never will.

The king retaliates by equating strength with kingship. He humiliates himself by raising the whip, then hurling it aside. The sudden denouement carries the focus from heartlessness to heart disease. The next time Anna appears before Mongut, he lies dying before his harem, minister, and children. Chulalongkorn, who has learned much from Anna and from Mongut's self-centered autocracy, makes his first proclamations as king: "First, I would proclaim for coming New Year—fireworks. . . . Also boat races," his personal choice of entertainment. Then he moves into the role of king by supplanting the custom of kowtowing with the European bow and curtsy.

The gently romantic nip and tuck between teacher and king contains strong irony and situational satire:

- The king, who tries to prove that he is not a barbarian, sets women to sew and prepare for the dinner and threatens a hundred strokes with the whip if they fail.

- The Siamese women who attend the formal dinner see their first monocle and hide themselves from "evil eye" by hoisting their European hoop-skirts over their heads.

- During an evening intended to prove Mongut an enlightened monarch, he sets a team of palace spies on Ramsay's party to learn how well he has achieved his mission.

- When Sir Edward inquires about the size of Mongut's family, the king replies, "Seventy-seven now, but I am not married very long."

The strongest irony—the parallel plot that compares a runaway slave girl and her pursuers to Eliza fleeing Simon Legree—departs from the real Mongut, who did not flinch from a cruel, capricious torture set up outside Anna's window to prove to her that the King intended to control his slaves, even if he had to maim and execute them to subdue them. In the Rodgers and Hammerstein version, Mongut dies before the matter of slave discipline is settled. Despite its departure from realism, the musical comedy remains a favorite of audiences in frequent revivals and in the values-rich songs "Hello Young Lovers," "Whistle a Happy Tune," and "Getting to Know You." The 1956 film won four Academy Award nominations and three Oscars, one for Yul Brynner's unforgettable role as the king. (Landon 1944; Rodgers and Hammerstein 1958)

See also Hart, Moss; Kaufman, George S.; satire.

LAMPOON

A pungent, personal satiric diatribe, lampoon, derived from the French *lampons* or "let us swig," draws a bead on a victim and attacks with spirit and excess. Rougher, coarser, and more apt to exaggerate than wit, parody, burlesque, or more graceful forms of satire, lampoon remembers, holds a grudge, and forgives nothing. Destructive rather than instructive, the lampoon anticipates the downfall of its object, whether from public humiliation or exposure of deceit or crime. A keen-edged slice at Thomas Shadwell appears in John Dryden's *Absalom and Achitophel* (1681), which pictures Og, the poet's Cro-Magnon designation for his enemy, rolling home from the Treason Tavern, monstrously bloated with "foul corrupted matter," obese and god-cursed. Thus reducing Og to the worst of God's sinners, Dryden ridicules his enemy's substantial girth, which he pictures as concocted from satanic batter and deserving of damnation.

In the eighteenth century, Alexander Pope produced an equally scurrilous attack in "An Epistle from Mr. Pope, to Dr. Arbuthnot" (1735). The frolicsome fervor with which Pope sallies forth suggests a particular delight in lacerating Lord Hervey, a noxious contemporary:

> Eternal smiles his emptiness betray,
> As shallow streams run dimpling all the way,
> Whether in florid importance he speaks,
> And, as the prompter breathes, the puppet squeaks,
> Or at the ear of *Eve*, familiar Toad,
> Half froth, half venom, spits himself abroad,
> In puns, or politicks, or tales, or lyes,
> Or spite, or smut, or rymes, or blasphemies,
> His wit all see-saw, between *that* and *this*,
> Now high, now low, now master up, now miss,
> And he himself one vile Antithesis.

This vicious, wickedly humorous caricature, which equates Lord Hervey with a poisonous toad, the puppet of Satan in his assault on Eve in the Garden of Eden, serves as the raw, unbridled vehicle of Pope's riposte. Were it not so wittily contrived, the guided missile of Pope's hatred could easily turn against him by baring his injurious purpose without supplying the reader with frequent chuckles at his inventiveness. (Barnet, Berman, and Burto 1960; Cuddon 1984; Gray 1992; Henry 1995; Holman and Harmon 1992; Pope 1932)

See also diatribe; Dryden, John; invective; Pope, Alexander; wit.

LEONARD, HUGH

A resourceful, productive stage and screenwriter and adapter, Irishman Hugh Leonard transcends the stereotype of idiomatic Irish satirist to address a universal audience. Born John Keyes Byrne in Dublin on November 6, 1926, to gardener Nicholas Keyes and Margaret Doyle Byrne, Leonard grew up during the unsteady years of World War II. He was brought up Catholic and educated at Dum Laoghaire. Leonard worked at the Department of Lands until his early thirties, when he dropped his real name and assumed a new identity as writer for television and theater. From scriptwriter for Granada TV in Manchester, England, he graduated to the self-discipline of freelance writing, taking time out in 1976 for a stint as literary editor for Ireland's prestigious Abbey Theatre.

A prodigious craftsman and adapter of a lengthy list of titles by Conan Doyle, Charles Dickens, Fyodor Dostoevsky, Gustave Flaubert, Somerset Maugham, Guy de Maupassant, Saki, and Emily Brontë, Leonard took particular delight in *Stephen D.* (1962), a stage version of James Joyce's *Portrait of the Artist as a Young Man*. Leonard achieved name recognition with his autobiographical *Da* (1973), which earned him a Tony, New York Drama Critics Circle award, and Outer Critics Circle award. His notable plays include *Barracks* (1969), *Patrick Pearse Hotel* (1971), *Summer* (1974), *Some of My Best Friends Are Husbands* (1976), *Liam Liar* (1976), *Time Was* (1981), and *A Life* (1981). One of his best comedies, *The Au Pair Man* (1968), parodies Queen Elizabeth in the initials of the protagonist, Mrs. Elizabeth Rogers (E. R. for Elizabeth Regina).

Comfortable in all comedy's arenas, Leonard created his most sensitive backward glance in *Da*, the parting of foster son and foster father after the old man's death. The work debuted August 9, 1973, in the Olney Theatre in Olney, Maryland, before its big-city presentations in Chicago and New York. A witty ghost play, *Da*—the kernel of the 1988 film that Leonard adapted for the comic skills of Barnard Hughes and Martin Sheen—calls home a wayward son to make peace with his departed father, who refuses to leave until the two have had a man-to-man thrashing out of old grudges and misunderstandings. Alternately bald and graceful in its vigorous pursuit of settlement, the play triggers laughter in the Irish sense of "wake," the traditional, ale-soaked, home-centered celebration of a departed soul.

Leonard achieves wry satire by lacing his play with incongruity. Set in the kitchen of the family home, the action carries expatriate Charlie Tynan to Dublin for his father's funeral. In clearing out debris from his family's personal effects, Charlie encounters the ghost of Da, whose good humor leads him to an irreligious note that rain is expected: "Yis, the angels'll be having a pee." The observation leads casually to Da's work as a gardener specializing in roses and to Charlie's hurry to be rid of the onus of memories—doggerel from his courtship days, his first job, shared comic songs, and coming-to-manhood with his adoptive parents. He adds:

> Your nephew Paddy got the TV set, I gave the radio to Maureen and Tom, and Mrs. Dunne next door got my sincere thanks for her many kindness and in consequence thereof has said she'll never talk to me again.

Charlie uplifts the depression with the thought that "An hour from now that fire will go out and there'll be no one here to light it. I'll be rid of you." The understated humor hangs on the "riddance," the parting with past that Leonard insists is an illusion.

The conversation takes a surreal turn as Young Charlie butts in, inflicting his callow point of view on the adult conversation. Charlie growls, "Ignore him." While the adult Charlie tries to speak with Drumm, his former employer and a caricature of the meddler, Da interrupts with scurrilous working-class jest, "There was a young fella went to confession. 'Father,' says he, 'I rode a girl from Cork.' 'Yerra, boy,' says the priest, 'sure 'twas better than walking.'" The falling action derides the manipulating scoundrel Drumm, who lords over Charlie a private bit of news that Da left his foster son £135. Charlie concludes that the money accrued from checks that he sent his father to ease his life by padding his inadequate pension.

The crucial dust-up in *Da* amounts to a critical issue among adopted children and their parents: who will love whom and in what form. The final argument depicts Charlie as longing for the one thing that a foster son lacks—the opportunity to give back a portion of the life his voluntary parents so willingly gave. To Charlie, Da is an ignoramus, a hanger-on, yet, with love and dogged intensity, the ghost of old man Tynan follows his son out the door into the rain, still mouthing barroom ditties and clinging to his only child as firmly as any father, biological or adoptive. (Anderson 1971; *Contemporary Authors* 1994; Leonard 1973)

See also caricature; doggerel; Hart, Moss; Kaufman, George S.; Saki; satire.

 # LEWIS, SINCLAIR

A controversial, dominant figure in American literature of the 1920s and 1930s, Sinclair Lewis—satirist, dynamic realist, and the first American Nobel Prize–winner for literature—reproduced national self-consciousness with keen caricature tinged with sarcasm. A midwesterner, he studied the heartland for tell-tale impulses, behaviors, tics, and speech patterns. He concluded that Americans were developing a demoralizing national character by such slow increments that they were unaware of idiosyncrasies and faults that would develop into crises. His sure-footed analysis presaged the post–Eisenhower Era dryrot and the 1970s drop-out society that rejected America's spiritual bankruptcy.

A native of Sauk Center, Minnesota, Harry Sinclair "Red" Lewis, the son of a Canadian mother, Emma Kermott, and Dr. Emmett J. Lewis, a rural general practitioner, was born February 7, 1885. He grew up at loose ends, never content among classmates or with his two brothers. Before college, he wrote for local newspapers and studied briefly at Oberlin Academy in Ohio, his first departure from home. At Yale University, Lewis drifted to the outer rim of social life, a restless genius and loner who dwelt apart from the activities and tastes of the eastern in-crowd. In his senior year, he interrupted his studies to join a group of socialists at Upton Sinclair's Helicon Home Colony, New Jersey, an idyllic experimental commune where he willingly served as furnace attendant until poverty forced him back to college. His first writings stemmed from this period, during which he edited the Yale literary magazine.

In 1908, Lewis began his real education. From coast to coast and south to Panama, he freelanced, ghostwrote for Jack London, and worked at journalism and editing, a truer study of human nature than he had acquired at Yale. The author's incipient alcoholism and the pace of writing hack novels, penning short fiction for the *Saturday Evening Post* and *Harper's*, and moving from job to job destroyed his first marriage to Grace Livingston Hegger, a writer for *Vogue* and mother of their son Wells, who was killed in World War II. At 35, after intense research and incubation, Lewis produced his first telling blow to the national self-concept with *Main Street* (1920), an antisentimental, iconoclastic satire that initiated a streak of five classic American novels and added the term "main street" to the national lingo. The critical uproar had barely subsided when he finished *Babbitt* (1922), a novel so palpably antiprovincial that it broadened English vocabulary a second time with "babbitt," a jeering synonym for the middle-brow hustler, a proponent of mindless cronyism. In Lewis's Dickensian description of the Zenith cityscape:

> All about him the city was hustling for hustling's sake. Men in motors were hustling to pass one another in the hustling traffic. . . . Men were hustling . . . to gallop across the sidewalk, to hurl themselves into buildings, into hustling express elevators. . . . Men who had made five thousand, year before last, and ten thousand last year, were urging on nerve-yelping bodies and parched brains so they might make twenty thousand this year; and the men who had broken down after making their twenty thousand were hustling, to catch trains to hustle through the vacations which the hustling doctors had ordered.

Lewis's brilliant debunking of babbittry disclosed the smug, simple-minded cultural wasteland that enveloped the Zenith cosmos in stifling, provincial sameness.

In conceiving the character of Zenith realtor George Folansbee Babbitt, Lewis strikes precipitously near the milieu from which he came—the complacent conformity and intolerance to change that produced shallow, uninitiated businessmen and "America first" boosterism. The novel mocks the Republican Party as the fount of conservative snobbery and the Rotary Club as an empty ritual— a directionless wheel doomed to churn in the mire of a single rut. A word cartoon, *Babbitt* derides the stable, social-climbing materialist, who thrives in

America's boom years by adhering to flexible principles and perpetually joining and championing the establishment's commercial enterprises with membership in the Clan of Good Fellows, Good Citizens League, Elks, and Boosters'
Club. A small-statured entrepreneur far below the John Jacob Astors and the
J. P. Morgans, Babbitt lives for the safety net that will sustain his limited gains
in an economic market he scarcely understands and can never master. His stressful perch on the edge pushes and tugs at his precarious balance, leaving him
no peace of mind or pride in achievement.

For Babbitt, the criterion of action is the outcome for business. Whatever
hoists his self-image of virile male and one of the guys becomes his life aim
and the excuse for self-indulgent evenings at his clubs. For the sake of commercial success, he willingly puts himself into the castrating clutches of "mechanical business, mechanical religion, mechanical golf and dinner parties, and
mechanical conversation with mechanical friends." Even worship takes on a
monetary value as a bogus act "respectable to do, and beneficial to one's business, to be seen going to services." In one of his most humorous tweaks of
parochial middle-class superficiality, Lewis pictures the men of Babbitt's Presbyterian Sunday School in a morally slipshod commercial venture to oust the
Central Methodist Church from prominence by applying PR to the problem of
recruiting new members.

Lewis bolsters the satire of stale repetition with frequent jabs at advertising, which determines what symbols of ownership people will buy to prove
their worthiness to a social class as banal as Babbitt. In Chapter 4, Lewis ribs
the packaging of burial plans with grotesque ad copy:

DO YOU RESPECT YOUR LOVED ONES?

When the last sad rites of bereavement are over, do you know for certain
that you have done your best for the Departed? You haven't unless they lie
in the Cemetery Beautiful

LINDEN LANE

the only strictly up-to-date burial place in or near Zenith, where exquisitely
gardened plots look from daisy-dotted hill-slopes across the smiling fields of
Dorchester.

A quintessential mediocrity, Babbitt exults in his ability to sell consumer strategies to Babbitt clones. Ironically, he loses himself in his acquiescence to the
group his flack targets. Unaware of his abdication of individuality, he deliberately abandons American freedoms by limiting his choices to those of the
frontrunners, "Chan Mott and his weedy old Wildwood Cemetery."

The climactic moment in his coming-to-knowledge is the realization that
his ailing wife Myra is mortal and could die, leaving him bereft of the security
that he intends to build for middle age. In the dawn light after a harried night
brought on by an inflamed appendix, she becomes "not merely A Woman, to
be contrasted with other women, but his own self." They reestablish former
intimacy, a ramshackle marriage shored up with illusion. Because he prefers
the shadow to reality, Babbitt himself is sapped of life—a sleepless, enervated

image of middle-class yes-men all negating individuality in their rush toward the cultural ideal of success. At the collapse of his ideal, his inability to relax on vacation in Maine, and the foundering of his doomed relationship with an enticing widow, Mrs. Tanis Judique, he is forced to admit to son Ted, "I've never done a single thing I've wanted to in my whole life!"

Babbitt succeeds as social satire for its convincing picture of family dysfunction, snobbery, hypocrisy, and insincerity. In a column for the *Baltimore Evening Sun* dated December 21, 1925, H. L. Mencken, an admirer of Lewis, defended the caricature as suitably "petty and piddling . . . so full of highfaluting fraud and bombast—that he talks like a millionaire and a chautauqua orator rolled into one." As standardized as a hot-water heater built on an assembly line, Babbitt mouths the perpetual brag that his country, his ideals, his house, his family life are the best to be had, yet, in private, he realizes that he has no home, only the requisite gadgetry and trappings of status. A sham on all fronts, he takes his opinions from conservative editorials and lives a humorless, empty respectability. The pitiable day-planner in which he jots the minutes and hours of a drab life testifies to the minutiae that comprise his vapid existence. Lewis captures the terrorizing moment when the antihero realizes his predicament:

> In his journey there was no appearance of flight, but he was fleeing, and four days afterward he was on the Zenith train. He knew that he was slinking back not because it was what he longed to do but because it was all he could do. He scanned again his discovery that he could never run away from Zenith and family and office, because in his own brain he bore the office and the family and every street and disquiet and illusion of Zenith.

In the end, Babbitt lapses into tragicomedy as he loses self in a maze of perfunctory gestures.

With the publication of *Arrowsmith* (1925), which depicted some of his misgivings about his father's profession, Lewis again touched a brash and revealing truth about medicine as science and as business, a topic that, by the 1990s, had become national scandal. Twice more he achieved literary greatness: with *Elmer Gantry* (1927), an antimythic satire of the religious huckster, and with *Dodsworth* (1929), a dismal picture of the upper-class miasma from which the main character flees to wander Europe in search of his misplaced values. Because Lewis believed other writers more deserving, he rejected the 1926 Pulitzer Prize. Four years later, he did accept the Nobel, then made a speech in Stockholm naming Theodore Dreiser, John Dos Passos, Ernest Hemingway, Thomas Wolfe, James Branch Cabell, Willa Cather, and Upton Sinclair as better writers than himself.

The Depression years put an end to Lewis's fame, as he replaced his middle-class themes with the challenge of joblessness and the nation's mounting socialism. His subsequent novels never reached the pungency, photographic detail, or vision of his five best. In 1935, he married noted journalist and radio commentator Dorothy Thompson and sired a second son, Michael, before the breakup of the marriage. Her influence on his work sparked a minor success with *It Can't Happen Here* (1935), a speculative novel on fascism in America.

While his fiction declined in popularity, he wrote columns for *Newsweek* and *Esquire*. Still unsettled and unfulfilled, Lewis died alone of heart disease in Rome, Italy, on January 10, 1951. His ashes were returned to his beginnings, Sauk Center. (Cowie 1951; Davidson and Wagner-Martin 1995; *Discovering Authors* 1993; Grigson 1963; Hart 1983; Kunitz 1942; Lewis 1980; Mencken 1991)
    See also caricature; irony; Mencken, H. L.; sarcasm; satire.

LIMERICK

A rigid form of occasional or light verse, doggerel, or unsigned ribaldry, the limerick—inexplicably named for a town and county in Ireland that may have appeared in a recurring refrain—is a late-blooming metrical form amalgamated from children's and soldiers' rhymes and sketchy, off-color Irish folk verse honoring such questionable practices as bribing, wenching, tippling, gambling, and rebelling against authority. An early example is the self-pitying "The Wearin' O' the Green," circulated anonymously around 1795. Diction in limerick tends to be blatantly raffish, bawdy, or outright pornographic or scatalogical. In the extreme, the limerick writer's choice of gutter terms for body functions or for anatomical parts reduces its impact to the babbling jingles of naughty adolescents. The saving grace of the best examples is a clever restraint in the final line that satisfies the intent reader without lowering the verse to scurrilous vulgarity.
    The verse adheres to a five-line pattern that announces itself on the page with a pair of indented lines that precede the conclusion:

A wickedly smart-mouthed apostate
Chose nuns, clerks, and popes to berate.
    But when he fell dead,
    His soul sank like lead,
And decamped to stoke coal in a low state.

Verses one, two, and five carry three beats blending anapaestic and iambic rhythm; lines three and four drop one of the beats, thus producing a pair of rollicking dimeters among trimeters at a significant, often climactic moment in the action. At their most frivolous, limericks use fantasy and sublimation to express anger, contempt, or prurience. The tone frequently flouts authority, explores fear, or vents hostility. For example, the preceding example implies a dread of retribution for sins committed on earth and displays an anticlerical bent. Victims other than church hierarchy include women, the aged or handicapped, homosexuals, royalty, police, and various minority races, nationalities, and religions.
    The rhyme scheme of the limerick mirrors the beat with its variance of aabba; the longer lines conclude in feminine rhymes (Arden/garden/pardon) and the shorter ones in masculine rhyme (Flo/go, hips/lips). End words may mimic a higher level of poetic skill with a number of mock-humorous shortcuts:

- Slant or forced rhyme (Vassar/surpass her/Alas, sir)

- Sight rhyme (bough/though/through/rough)

- Garbled or humorously applied foreign terms (Reno/Bambino/ Mara-schino; got o'er/*emptor*/*por favor*)

- Dialect or slang (concern 'em/confirm 'em/gosh dern 'em)

- Made-up place names that echo an important element in the second line: "A cheery young thing from South Mickle/Had a terrible yen for sweet pickle."

Composed *ad libitum* in challenge matches or as party or barroom liveners, the limerick is deceptively simple on the surface, yet it requires a knowledge of metrics, facility with varied styles of rhyme, and a sense of balance, timing, and wit. In most limericks, the complication appears in the two short lines, which may be written as two dimeter lines: "Of beet, lime, salt, dill/She had gotten her fill," or as a single tetrameter with internal rhyme: "Of beet, lime, salt, dill she had gotten her fill," a four-beat line that falls easily into two loose dimeters if broken after "dill." Whatever method of versification the poet chooses, the obligatory last line must round out the verse with a witty solution to a problem or a stinging, suggestive, or titillating closure at the expense of the subject, as in "Only sweet pickle could assuage her deep tickle."

Frequently found scribbled on the walls in military camps or fraternity houses or as filler at the ends of columns in tabloid papers, the limerick remains popular for its anonymous hit-and-run zest, a quality not always shared by the object of the jest, for example, old maids, pompous ministers, timorous lovers, scandal-ridden governors, or unattractive persons of either sex. Employed by Alfred Tennyson, Algernon Swinburne, Rudyard Kipling, Robert Louis Stevenson, Dante Gabriel Rossetti, W. H. Auden, Robert Frost, W. S. Gilbert, Hilaire Belloc, Sir John Betjeman, Ogden Nash, and the limerick master Edward Lear, author of *The Book of Nonsense* (1846), the limerick reached fad proportions in England after *Punch* magazine invited participants to send in verses for a contest. The craze spread to the United States during the Civil War, when Charles Godfrey Leland popularized the cult form in *Ye Book of Copperheads* (1863), a jab at midwestern Democrats who opposed war against the Confederacy for the purpose of ending slavery. Despite its residence beyond the pale of respectability, the book served the Red Cross as an effective method of raising relief funds for victims of the war. (Abrams 1971; Barnet, Berman, and Burto 1960; Cuddon 1984; Drabble 1985; Gray 1992; Holman and Harmon 1992; Legman 1991; McArthur 1992; Muir 1954; Padgett 1987)

See also doggerel; jingle; scatology; wit.

 # LUCAN

A minor figure in Rome's Silver Age (A.D. 14–117) who died without fulfilling his considerable promise, Marcus Annaeus Lucanus (not to be confused with the Greek satirist Lucian [A.D. 120–180]) deserves a place among the satirists of his day, albeit a small billing alongside Martial and Juvenal. Coming so soon after the end of the Golden Age (83 B.C.–A.D. 14) and the limpid beauties of Horace's verse, Lucan suffered by comparison with the giants of his time. Born in A.D. 39, the son of a knight, grandson of the elder Seneca, and nephew of the later Seneca, Lucan had lived less than a year in his native Corduba (Cordova, Spain) when his father, Marcus Annaeus Mela, hurried him away to Rome to be reared in the stoic philosophy. The regimen suited the boy, who from early childhood displayed brilliance and a flair for rhetoric. According to Suetonius, the emperor Nero recalled Lucan from his studies in Athens to adorn the court. Under the tutelage of an ambitious household and encouraged by royal support, Lucan pursued an imperial commission and in A.D. 64 received a judgeship. The sinecure of augur (priest in charge of interpreting omens) increased his status. On his own merit, he charmed his way to the imperial inner circle and performed so wittily at table that the envious Nero stomped out of the room. Lucan pressed the battle of egos with daring words and discourtesies. The emperor, a deluded poetaster, resented Lucan's glib anecdotes and barred him from composing or reading subsequent verses aloud.

Wary of the edict and smarting with repressed anger, Lucan hid his spite and composed in private a set of satires along with an array of other works—essays, libretti, epistles, speeches, court verse, a drama on Medea, epigrams, harangue, and his most famous work, the ten-volume *Pharsalia*. All that remains of Lucan's verse, this balky, overly heroic poem opens with obligatory flattery of the monarch, then defiantly praises a high point in Rome's republican history—Julius Caesar's war against Pompey. The unfinished work ends at the Battle of Pharsalus. All that remains of Lucan's rapier-sharp satire is a bit of comic understatement from Book I, "If the victor had the gods on his side, the vanquished had Cato." Apparently, Lucan intended the epic to follow Caesar to his assassination in 44 B.C., but palace intrigue cut short the poet's career before his twenty-sixth birthday. Listed among Piso's collection of conspirators seeking to rid Rome of the lunatic Nero, Lucan and his teacher Cornutus were betrayed and condemned to public execution. The poet used his skills one last time to gain a reprieve: He named his mother a co-conspirator and cooperated with Nero's tribunal. Lucan earned a small concession—the opportunity of a private death, the same fate chosen by Lucan's father and his uncles, Gallio and Seneca. On April 30, after a lordly feast, Lucan wrote a farewell note to his father, bid his doctor slit his arteries, and died joyfully spouting gore and original verse in defiance of Nero's orders. One of his salient lines would have been most appropriate: in Book VIII of the *Pharsalia*, he had noted, "We all praise fidelity; but the true friend pays the penalty when he supports those whom Fortune crushes."

Lucan's stiff, didactic work brought jeers from Martial, who satirized the satirist, but time preserved the cadence and sweep of the epic, which outlasted the gibes. Resurrected during the Middle Ages and openly admired by Dante Alighieri, Michel Montaigne, Christopher Marlowe, Robert Southey, Percy Bysshe Shelley, and Thomas Macauley, Lucan achieved honor as defender of

Rome's republican former glory and detractor of its ignominy under Nero. Idealistic and daring, the poet died in vigorous youth, much like Shelley and Byron. (Drabble 1985; Feder 1986; Godolphin 1949; Hadas 1954; Hammond and Scullard 1992; Hornstein 1973; Howatson 1989; Mantinband 1956; Radice 1973)

See also didacticism; Horace; Juvenal; Martial; Petronius; satire.

MAN AND SUPERMAN

One of George Bernard Shaw's early successes and most philosophical, "talky" farces, *Man and Superman*, an imaginative comedy of manners, was presented in 1905 at London's Court Theatre. The play mirrors the situations of Restoration romantic satire with the vitality and fresh insights of post-Victorian feminism. The producer chose to remove one of Shaw's digressions, its detachable third act, a car trip to Spain and a dream scenario that sets the protagonist, handsome, rakish Jack Tanner, in hell. The purpose of the fantasy is to place Jack in the stead of his ancestor, Don Juan Tenorio, to debate Satan; Jack's childhood friend, Ann Whitefield; and her foster father, Roebuck "Granny" Ramsden.

In a resetting of the stereotypical woman-chases-perennial-bachelor, Ann, a London virago who acts the part of the liberated women, pursues Jack because he seems to be likely husband material. Lacking interest in Tanner's *Revolutionist's Handbook,* she boldly courts a love match. To rid himself of a grasping female, Jack wants her to marry Octavius "Tavy" Robinson, a romantic and poet whom Ann disdains with the taunting nickname of Ricky-Ticky-Tavy, after the mongoose in Rudyard Kipling's short story. Ann proves herself too slick for Octavius by tricking him into believing that she must marry Jack, a cynical libertine, because he is the pick of her widowed mother and recently deceased father.

After Ann concocts lie after lie in a deceptive structure meant to trap Jack, he accuses Ann (in Act IV) of flirtation, bullying, and hypocrisy, the last being the worst of her sins. To Jack, an ineffectual jabberer given to lengthy tirades, the elaborate machinery that forces him to the altar becomes unbearable. Against constraint, he bitterly charges her with stalking him from their youth and denounces her use of marriage as a form of entrapment to prove her the conqueror. Ironically struggling to flee, Jack embraces Ann as though he cannot fend off the *élan vital,* the vital spark that is her emotional power over him. In the end, the couple reach a truce: they agree to marry at the registry office three days hence; Ann bids him to keep on talking.

Shaw, the comedic master of the late Edwardian age, empowers *Man and Superman* with satire's most skillful adjuncts:

- caricature, in the portrait of Malone, a moneyed American

- whimsy, particularly the lengthy dream sequence that reveals Jack's most personal beliefs and misgivings

- wit, obvious in the numerous verbal sparring matches between lovers and between parent and child

- incongruity, for example, the choice of a roué like Jack Tanner as co-guardian for Ann Whitefield

- humor, especially Ann's adoring imaginative efforts to wear down a man who spurns her and the whole institution of marriage

- didacticism, displayed in Shaw's insistence that marriage is a battle for dominance

- dramatic irony, evident in Jack's receipt of a note that unmasks Ann's ruses

- hyperbole, a title that mocks the image Jack maintains of himself and his right to choose his destiny

- repartee, the darting, continual set-to between stalker and quarry

The strength of Shaw's play lies in the creation of Ann, a willful female. While displaying no curiosity about Jack's handbook on vigorous human behavior, she epitomizes the character he envisions. The irony, of course, lies in the fact that she is more vital than Jack. (Bermel 1982; Brockett 1968; Gassner and Quinn 1969; Grigson 1963; Hill 1978; Hornstein 1973; Johnson 1968; Kunitz 1942; Magill 1958; Negley and Patrick 1952; Shaw 1950)

See also caricature; didacticism; hyperbole; incongruity; irony; *Pygmalion;* repartee; satire; Shaw, George Bernard; whimsy; wit.

MARTIAL

A champion and master of epigram as an adaptable art form, Marcus Valerius Martialis rode the crest of the literary wave that buoyed Horace and Juvenal to lasting fame and influence and established Rome as the birthplace of literary satire. Born in March around A.D. 38 and named in honor of the month and, appropriately, the god of war, Martial was the son of Flaccilla and Valerius Fronto, residents of Bilbilis, Spain, a gritty mining burg on Rome's frontier that kept the army supplied with spear points, breastplates, and wagon wheels. Unlike the more polished Roman verse masters, Martial did not get his basic education from cosmopolitan grammarians. Suitably schooled on the frontier and well read in Ovid and Catullus, Martial studied rhetoric and law and opened a law office in Rome in A.D. 63. Against the competition of insider attorneys and writers, Martial barely survived and lived on the third floor of a boardinghouse on the Quirinal among other ambitious immigrants.

Like Juvenal, Martial tells little about his parents, childhood, and daily life. He established himself with three top-flight patrons—orator and educator

Quintilian and fellow Spaniards Seneca and Lucan; the latter pair, for their part in the anti-imperial Piso conspiracy, were forced to take the "Roman way of death" and quietly slit their wrists after a failed plot to kill Nero. Lucan was only 25 at the time. Befriended by four colleagues—technical writer and surveyor Frontinus, epicist Silius Italicus, essayist Pliny the Younger, and satirist Juvenal—Martial entered a more bearable phase of city life among the literati and bought or received as a gift a scrap of rural acreage near Nomentum, a half-day's ride north of Rome. To maintain a steady income, the poet wrote what his patrons wanted to hear, whether buttery praise or justification for the times, which, under Domitian, were unsettlingly stern and capricious. The obverse of the conservative, hard-driving Horace, Martial lounged his way into foyers in time for dinner with a smile and a wink for anyone registering shock at his effrontery.

To the consternation of some, Martial openly compared himself with Catullus and Lucan, Rome's best aphorists. In A.D. 80, Martial published *Liber Spectaculorum* [*A Book of Spectacles*], a somewhat amateurish series of 33 brief occasional verses composed in honor of Titus, who opened the Colosseum, originally known as the Flavian Amphitheater. The architectural wonder opened to a ga-ga audience glimpsing the inauguration of Rome's romance with blood sport, the empire's failing that history can neither euphemize nor forgive. Martial contrasts the water sports, underwater ballet, and mock armada launched in the flooded arena with the laceration of a sow from whose abdomen emerge living offspring, a gruesome image of the perverted birth pangs that produced a monstrous trio, Caligula, Nero, and Domitian. Skilled with mood pieces, belly laughs, and subtle digs, Martial took it all in—the crowds, the grifters, and the klutzes—and turned his unflatteringly keen observations into history's most fascinating sociological study. Of his style, he claims, "My verse bears the whiff of our humanity"; of his objectivity, he comments, "My pages are naughty, but my life is blameless."

Four years later, Martial followed with 350 couplets in companion volumes: *Xenia* [*Guest Gifts*] and *Apophoreta* [*Party Favors*], both an outgrowth of Saturnalia, the jolly Roman yuletide held in honor of Saturn the week of December 17 and marked by the droll exchange of roles between slave and master. Within a year, Martial began his masterpiece, the twelve books jointly labeled *Epigrammata* [*Epigrams*] (A.D. 85), which focused his talents on satire during his last twelve years in Rome, which were interrupted by a sabbatical in Cisalpine Gaul, and his subsequent four years in Spain. Daring and frank, he opens his first book with a disclaimer to the prissy or weak-stomached reader. His panorama of Romans covers guller and gulled, sodomite, coquette and beau, perennial kisser of friends, and retching, hungover drunk.

Martial's trademark periodic style saves the zinger for the end, an idiosyncratic detail similar to O. Henry's surprise endings and the final twist of an Alfred Hitchcock mystery movie. In one zippy bit of holiday musing, he notes:

All the Saturnalia over!
  And no little gift—ah no!

Such as Galla sent her lover—
    Sent her Martial years ago.
So roll past, my dull December,
    And, when you your nuts will crack
On the first of March, remember,
    Galla, I shall pay you back.

Mixed in satura or medley style alongside seamy pornography are the yearning lines of an unquiet heart longing to leave Rome for good and withdraw to full tables, warm fireplaces, fresh food, quiet evenings, and genuine friendships—the rich country fare of his boyhood.

Departure from the city was a mixed blessing. After Domitian's death brought a new rule and a gentler Rome under Titus, Martial received an honorarium: an equestrian tribuneship complete with the *ius trium liberorum* (the right of three children), a tax break meant to encourage families, but which the emperor redirected to a solitary bachelor. However, the political honeymoon ended rancorously, leaving Martial out of step and out of favor. Despite his fame in street and banquet hall, he withdrew from a clamoring public, perhaps because of tenuous health or disenchantment with patronage. Dispatched home to Bilbilis in his early to mid-fifties through the agency of Pliny, Martial settled for a marriage to Marcella, a local art patron with whom he shared "a bed not puritanical yet decent" during his remaining years.

As his insightful pen sharpened with memories of Rome's cynicism, Martial lampooned the sleaziest characters his mind dredged up. A surprising number of verses revert to tenderness, particularly the epitaph of Erotion, whom he memorializes with a sober farewell:

Let not her shuddering spirit fear to meet
The ghosts, but soothe her lest she be afraid.
How should a baby heart be undismayed
To pass the lair where Cerberus is laid?
The little six-year maiden gently greet . . .
Lie softly on her, kindly earth; her feet,
Such tiny feet, on thee were lightly laid.

Lionized for his quick-witted one-liners, Martial retains a secure place in satire's canon for his ability to prick the overblown ego and spotlight Rome's obscenely bulging underbelly. His energetic verse strikes left and right, wounding or maiming where it will; it earned him the everlasting loathing of Statius, a contemporary writer whom Martial ridiculed in print. Of his own fame, Martial quips, "Yet soft, my books, no haste, nor hurry fate;/If fame must wait on death, then let it wait." The discriminating audience, among them Juvenal and Pliny, had reason to mourn Martial's passing in A.D. 102. His felicity of phrasing influenced Robert Burns, Johann Goethe, Oscar Wilde, Ogden Nash, Ezra Pound, and Dorothy Parker. (*Encarta* 1994; Feder 1986; Godolphin 1949; Hadas 1954; Hammond and Scullard 1992; Howatson 1989; Mantinband 1956; Martial 1981; Radice 1973; Snodgrass 1988)

See also Horace; Juvenal; Parker, Dorothy; satire; Wilde, Oscar.

MASH

In his frank, brief foreword to the twentieth century's most successful antiwar novel/movie/television series/dress-up cult, Richard Hooker dedicates his fiction to the staff of the Mobile Army Surgical Hospitals. His comic satire asserts that Americans survived the Korean War by applying skill and compassion to patients and zany good humor to relieve frustration, tension, ennui, and stress brought on by exertion, army regulations, and the cruelty of unending barrage. In one of the rare instances when a work expands far beyond its creator's expectations, *MASH* (1968) formed the basis for the 1970 film version (spelled M*A*S*H, Hollywood style) and earned an Oscar for adaptor Ring Lardner, as well as nominations for best picture, best director (Robert Altman), and best female lead (Sally Kellerman). A phenomenon on television from 1971 to 1981 and in frequent reruns, the series won awards for the acting of Alan Alda as star surgeon Hawkeye Pierce and earned praise for a cohesive cast, including Mike Farrell, McLean Stevenson, Harry Morgan, Larry Linville, Loretta Swit, Gary Burghof, Jamie Farr, Charles Ogden Stiers, and William Christopher.

The original novel is attributed to Richard Hooker, pseudonym of Dr. H. Richard "Horny" Hornberger, surgeon on staff at Thayer Hospital in Waterville, Maine, following service in the 8055th MASH unit after he was drafted for the Korean War. *MASH* suffered five years of pink slips before ghostwriter W. C. Heinz edited it and split $100,000 with Hornberger for the film rights and $1,000 for each television episode. Hornberger's sequel, *Mash Goes to Maine* (1971), spawned eleven spin-offs—*Mash Goes to Paris, London, New Orleans, Hollywood, Las Vegas, Miami, Morocco, Vienna, Montreal,* and *Moscow*—written over a four-year period in collaboration with war-novel specialist William Edmund Butterworth III, a native of Newark, New Jersey. The final sequel, *MASH Mania* (1977), Hornberger wrote in its entirety.

The film version, which coincided with the 1970s antiwar fervor associated with American involvement in Vietnam, won international fame at the Cannes Film Festival and critical acclaim for stars Elliott Gould, Donald Sutherland, and Tom Skerritt. Perhaps because Donald Sutherland fit the novel's conception of Hawkeye, Hornberger approved the movie wholeheartedly but did not cotton to the television series. Because the antiwar flavor violates his conservative bent, the surgeon/novelist distanced himself from the liberal views espoused by the writers of the postnovel bonanza, especially the wise-cracking pacifist Hawkeye. Still at home on Crabapple Cove, Hornberger remains aloof from MASH mania and covets his privacy.

The novel's appeal compares with that of Joseph Heller's dark classic *Catch-22* (1961) in its irreverent study of the regularities of army expectations and the irregularities of war and warriors. The characters, a microcosm of the United States, bring to the 4077th MASH experiences from a variety of backgrounds, including endearing farmboy Corporal Radar O'Reilly, the undersized signal corpsman whose ability to hear and identify incoming weapons and vehicles gives the crack trauma team its edge on approaching victims. In addition to exhaustion, crippling injury, and death, the team shares a penchant for alcohol, pranks, and razzing each other's idiosyncrasies. The setting, a satiric glimpse at war's exigencies, juxtaposes the lab with "the Painless Polish Poker and Dental Clinic, then the mess hall, the PX, the shower tent, the barber shop, and the enlisted men's tents."

The urge to rob war of reality forms the major motif of Hooker's humor, which ranges from slapstick ball games and drunk scenes to ribald penis jokes about Captain Walter Koskousko Waldowski to the zany imposture of two surgeons claiming to be chaplains. The officers' tent goes by the name of the Swamp, and the priest, who tries to be an okay-Joe, good-naturedly accepts the moniker of Dago Red. During one of an endless string of impromptu parties, the group celebrates the advancement of Trapper John McIntyre to chief surgeon. The group indulges in doggerel verse followed by coarse references to chief nurse Major Margaret Houlihan, a regular-army type who takes offense at deviation from army regulations. Promoted from the original reference to the "goose girl," Houlihan earns her permanent nickname, Hot Lips, for her obvious attraction to Captain Burns, whose loss of control at the unmilitary shenanigans nets him a transfer stateside.

Pranks flow at a rapid pace as the doctors become more adept at sabotaging regular channels. While collecting six thousand dollars to send houseboy Ho-Jon to medical school, the men distribute photographs of a phony Jesus who tours units in a makeshift passion play. An emergency in Kokura puts Hawkeye and Trapper in line for a quick surgery, then some golf. They elect instead to help a Eurasian infant who needs immediate thoracic surgery. The repartee surrounding brief skits ties together the loose plot into a satiric whole— a comic view of the human methods of staying sane in the blood, muck, shattered organs, and insanity of Korea. Emergency cases either pour into the 4077th or dry to a trickle. At the height of Hawkeye's desperation, he comments, "When you live in this sort of situation long enough, you either get to love a few people or to hate them, and we've been pretty lucky." (*Contemporary Authors* 1969; Hooker 1961; Walker 1994; Waters 1983)

See also black humor; *Catch-22;* doggerel; Heller, Joseph; satire.

MASQUE

An imaginative form of holiday mummery or guest entertainment, similar to that employed in William Shakespeare's *As You Like It* (ca. 1599), *The Tempest* (ca. 1610), and *Much Ado about Nothing* (ca. 1598), the masque derives its name and style from processions of masked figures in torchlit community frolics such as May Queen courts, harvest balls, Twelfth Night frivolity, Mardi Gras parades, and the Caribbean Carnaval. Introduced in its early Renaissance form in 1512 by Henry VIII, who adapted style and tone from Lorenzo de Medici's symbolic displays, the English court masque at first shocked staid aristocrats unaccustomed to Italian entertainments calling for ladies to dance with masked men. Shortly, masque evolved into a high-toned verse drama that adorned court performances and resembled an elaborate tableau or skit in which costume, pose, choreography, floats, and staging superseded action or character development. Peopled with mythological monsters, deities, king and queen of fairies and their gamesome court, witches and their familiars, pastoral figures, and leering satyrs and fauns, the masque required complicated stage machinery, lighting, and movement coordinated with music. The mask is often preceded or interrupted by an antimasque or burlesque similar to the Greek satyr play; its serious or lyric nature contrasts with competing figures bent on clowning and mugging, grotesque behaviors, or raucous arguments.

Shakespeare's pageantry in *Much Ado about Nothing* provides a backdrop for a bit of badinage between Beatrice and Benedick, a bickering pair who are drawn to each other but are unwilling to give up their independence. Masked, Benedick refuses to reveal his identity. Beatrice uses the opportunity to needle him about the real Benedick:

Beatrice:	I am sure you know him well enough.
Benedick:	Not I, believe me.
Beatrice:	Did he never make you laugh?
Benedick:	I pray you, what is he?
Beatrice:	Why, he is the Prince's jester, a very dull fool. Only his gift is in devising impossible slanders. None but libertines delight in him, and the commendation is not in his wit but in his villainy, for he both pleases men and angers them, and then they laugh at him and beat him.

Beatrice's unflattering cameo impels Benedick to move on and later swear vengeance against her sharp-tongued criticism and gibes at his expense. Come full circle by the end of the play, Benedick calls for a prenuptial dance "that we may lighten our own hearts and our wives' heels."

Despite its lowly beginnings in folk festival, the Jacobean masque reached its height as an elaborate form of entertainment for ladies and gentlemen of quality following the swift rise in stage sophistication during the Elizabethan era. Sparked by a triad—the technical wizardry of Inigo Jones, who studied with Italian architect Andrea Palladio; the musical scores of Alfonso Ferrabosco; and the delightful scripts of Ben Jonson—1605 saw the beginning of a series of sophisticated masques, particularly the *Masque of Blackness* (1605) and the *Masque of Beauty* (1608). Thomas Campion, gifted in both verse and melody, composed the *Masque in Honor of the Marriage of Lord Hayes* (1607). These costly extravaganzas, similar to bowl-game half-time shows or Winter Olympics finales, pursued a single theme that later influenced stage plays, pantomime, opera, the French Folies Bergère, and ballet. The decline of masque began with the clash of Jones and Jonson, two egos fighting for the upper hand in an argument over spectacle (Jones) and poetry (Jonson). As a comic or satiric balance to serious or allegorical themes, Jonson supported antimasque (derived from antic masque, also spelled antemasque, meaning "before the masque"). He lost his job as court masque manager during the reign of Charles I, whose licentious reign preceded the Puritan backlash and eleven years of the English Commonwealth. (Abrams 1971; Barnet, Berman, and Burto 1960; Cuddon 1984; Drabble 1985; *Encarta* 1994; Gray 1992; Holman and Harmon 1992; Hornstein 1973)

See also comedy; repartee; satire; satyr play; Shakespeare, William.

McMILLAN, TERRY

One of America's most vigorous upstarts, Terry L. McMillan, master caricaturist, burst onto the fiction scene in the late 1980s with *Mama* (1987) and parlayed her first iridescent bubble on the bestseller list into a long-running series of successes. Her second comedy smash, *Waiting to Exhale* (1992), the intertwined story of Savannah, Bernie, Gloria, and Robin, four professional women finding love as best they can and bonding against rebuffs, broke records for autograph sessions and public readings and found immediate reception with movie companies, which bid the price of McMillan's original up to $700,000.

A native of Port Huron, Michigan, McMillan was born on October 18, 1951, to Edward Lewis McMillan and Madeline Washington Tillman. McMillan's mother, a tough version of the protagonist in *Mama*, survived divorce in 1964 and reared five children on domestic work and factory pay. A spokeswoman for black society, McMillan faced the dearth of knowledge of black history that others of her generation have known. Like James Baldwin and Toni Morrison, she absorbed her race's culture from reading and experienced an apotheosis with Alex Haley's *The Autobiography of Malcolm X* (1965), the genesis of McMillan's black pride.

After graduation from the University of California at Berkeley and completion of an M.F.A. from Columbia University, McMillan taught at the Universities of Wyoming and Arizona while turning out her first three novels. A boost from the National Endowment for the Arts in 1988 assisted her emerging talent. She published her first novel while working as a typist and living the familiar struggle of the single parent, a standard feature of her autobiographical fiction. An energetic self-promoter, McMillan made the rounds of book stores, petitioned chain stores to sell her fiction, and gave interviews to television talk show hosts.

The astounding rise of McMillan to the upper echelons of American fiction did not come without cost. Her one-time lover Leonard Welch sued her for casting him as a villain and dopehead in *Disappearing Acts* (1989), McMillan's second novel, which she dedicated to her son Solomon Welch. A ruling in her favor established a truth that fiction writers instinctively trust: that the best of writing transforms real experiences into art, however close to or distant from reality it may lie in its finished state. Like Alice Walker, McMillan has borne a disproportionate amount of scorn for purported male-bashing and an undeserved reputation for trash-mouth characters. Her honest depiction of

American novelist Terry McMillan in June 1992

contemporary male-female relations answers both complaints with the one-word explanation—verisimilitude.

Rich in caricature and working-class seriocomedy, *Mama* tells the story of Mildred Peacock, a can-do parent of five who rejects rejection and outfoxes a drunkard mate by surviving on wisecracks and determination. In a peaceful moment by a pool, Mama relaxes by taking stock of her children, bad or good:

> She hadn't taken a nerve pill since she didn't know when, and even though she hadn't met that perfect somebody yet, right now this water was giving her all she needed—a little cooling off.

Realistically evaluating the battles she could win against sure losses, she remains candid about the detriments that hold her back:

> Mildred did not appreciate Acquilla dying a month before Angel's wedding, especially since she hadn't come up with her part of the money yet. Her daddy had asked if Mildred could come back. . . . He was her daddy, but this time around, somebody else was going to have to carry the weight.

As the strength ebbs into empty VO bottles, Mildred applies her honesty to self-evaluation:

> What happened to all my strength? She closed her eyes as if she'd been hyp-notized. . . . When she woke up, Mildred was forty-eight years old and soaking wet from the waist down.

Still well endowed with spunk and strength equal to her burdens, Mildred wrecks her car in the snow on the way to Mercy Hospital to visit son Curly and lies back on the seat to contemplate God and fate. Certain that her sins deserve worse than she's getting, she sighs, "I betcha this is some kind of game, ain't it. But I'm gon' tell you something, bud. I'm gon' make it past the finish line." (Chambers 1995; *Contemporary Authors* 1994; Fein 1992; McMillan 1987, 1989a, 1989b; Norment 1995; Smith 1992; Steinberg 1992)

See also African-American satire; caricature; satire.

 # MENAECHMI

Plautus established some of comedy's conventions, notably the mix-ups and confusion of separated families, people with the same name, plots to bring lovers together, and the grand resolution of all tangles in the final dramatic moments. His masterpiece, the *Menaechmi* [*The Twin Menaechmi*] (ca. 186 B.C.) turns on the repeated mistaken identity of twins who were separated in childhood. The prologue explains how a merchant from Syracuse, a prosperous Greek colony in Sicily, lost his seven-year-old son Menaechmus at the Tarentum market. Kidnapped by a trader from Epidamnum, the boy grew up apart from his family. After the father grieved himself to death, the boy's grandfather named the remaining twin Menaechmus.

Plautus introduces the lost son in comic subterfuge: a wealthy man after the death of his foster father, the Epidamnium Menaechmus appears in Act I in the ridiculous role of deceiving husband. Stuffing a woman's garb under his mantle, he sneaks away from his shrewish wife and slips next door to his mistress Erotium to offer the dress as a gift. She plans a meal for him while he and Peniculus, the local freeloader, stroll to the bar for a drink. Meanwhile, the complication enters in the form of the Syracusan Menaechmus, who has been traveling with his slave Messenio from port to port in a six-year search for his lost brother. The typical complainer, Messenio generalizes that

> Epidamnus is filled with roués, booze-hounds, con artists and ne'er-do-wells. The city's women are immodest. For good reason, the town earns its name, for its atmosphere leads all comers to damnation.

The lines illustrate Plautus's skill with puns, plot complication, and stock figures, notably the scurrilous, brash body servant.

Plautus sets up a situation that keeps the audience tense with laughter in anticipation of confused identity. Immediately, Erotium and the cook mistake the Syracusan for his twin. Erotium coos:

> What are you doing in the street, my sweet? You should come in and make yourself at home. Dinner is cooked, the doors swing wide, and your place is set. Enter and take your spot whenever you're ready.

The foreign twin, startled, but poised enough to accept a free meal after spending most of his cash on the search, complies with Erotium's invitation. On afternoon errands for his hostess, the Syracusan Menaechmus departs just as his double appears.

Plautus segues entrances and exits with the skill required of a juggling of look-alikes. The ensuing mix-ups over embroidered goods and baubles and harangues over lawsuits grow rowdy and comic when the wronged wife sets up a howl that Menaechmus is stealing her personal belongings to give to his mistress. Even the freeloader scratches his head in confusion at a meeting with the second Menaechmus. Caught in the squeeze between scolding wife and miffed lover, the Epidamnian Menaechmus reaches the low point of his fortunes when he tries to placate both women. Heaping self-pity on his guilty head for being booted into the street by both wife and mistress, he wails, "I am the most excluded of men."

Like a comic opera, the caterwauling and accusations move from duet to trio to motet as the Syracusan Menaechmus and the father-in-law of the Epidamnian Menaechmus add their complaints to the grand chorus. The Syracusan escapes to the harbor by faking a collapse. In his absence, the Epidamnian Menaechmus runs afoul of the busybody father-in-law with doctor in tow. The apotheosis occurs when the entourage prepares to haul Menaechmus to the lunatic asylum. Harried to the limit, the Epidamnian Menaechmus wonders in an aside why his day has been filled with odd goings-on. He pleads, "Heaven help me."

In a comedic fugue, Plautus orchestrates the expanding and contracting tensions, which subside with a swift, insight-filled resolution. The brothers reunite and engage in a happy explanation of the day's misidentifications. The hasty setting to rights includes a journey to Syracuse and the manumission of Messenio. A clever manipulator, the rapscallion gets the last word. He plans to earn a hefty commission by auctioning the Epidamnian Menaechmus's property. To the audience he chortles, "In a week's time, I'm hosting a dandy yard sale here . . . and if I get any takers, I'm putting the wife on the block."

Plautus's *Menaechmi* rings true to a long heritage of farcical story lines. Into the twentieth century, the seedy mooch, complaining wife, interfering in-law, and deceiving husband remain staple comic figures. The freedom of Messenio, which contrasts the compromised position of the wife, concludes with a misogynistic putdown that might have come from a Maggie and Jiggs cartoon, a snide remark from W. C. Fields, or an installment of Jackie Gleason and Audrey Meadows's series *The Honeymooners*. The satiric anti-marriage jest appears timeless. (Feder 1986; Godolphin 1949; Hadas 1954; Hammond and Scullard 1992; Hornstein 1973; Howatson 1989; Mantinband 1956; Plautus 1900; Radice 1973)

See also The Beggar's Opera; caricature; comedy; *commedia dell'arte*; farce; *A Funny Thing Happened on the Way to the Forum*; Gay, John; Menander; Molière; Plautus; Shakespeare, William; slapstick; Terence.

MENANDER

More legend than flesh, Menander dominates the comedy of the ancient world. Because so little remains of his plays, he teases theater historians with shining shards of wit, which exist in fragments of original manuscripts, in critical commentary, and among the compendia of epigrams compiled during the ancient period. One of his oft-repeated statements demonstrates his ready comebacks: "My comedy is complete. I've got the whole thing in my head. All that's left is to write the words." A native of Cephisia, an Attic borough, Menander (originally Menandros) appears to have been born in 342 B.C. to a wealthy family. Eyewitness accounts describe him as suave and good-looking with a touch of complacency and devil-may-care. Mad for theater and oblivious to the political headlines made by his contemporary, Alexander the Great, Menander perfected his craft under Theophrastus, who studied with Aristotle. Among Menander's cronies were Epicurus, the arbiter of refined pleasures; Demetrius, a naval commander; and Alexis of Thurii, the impetus for new comedy and writer of 245 plays.

At home in his country manor at Piraeus, the harbor town southeast of Athens, Menander appears to have enjoyed both city excursions and rural quiet and to have made friends easily. He nested comfortably first with the fiercely loyal Glycera—who described him in a letter as a terrific lover—and later with Thaïs, but he avoided marriage and never established a family. His surroundings suited him so completely that he rejected an opportunity to visit Ptolemy I's palace in Alexandria. Legend describes his drowning at the shore off Piraeus in 291 B.C. Both Quintilian and Martial mourned the fact that Menander received inadequate acclaim until after his death, largely because of his use of dialect, which excluded his works from use as school texts.

Like Aristophanes, Menander began his life's work in his late teens. *Orge* [*Anger*] (321 B.C.), his first staged play and the first of eight titles to win top prize, prefaced a library of 108 formulaic plays composed in koine Greek and cranked out over a thirty-year career. Striking out in a less raucous direction than Aristophanes's energetic comedies, Menander's drawing-room comedies avoided song and dance, baggy-pants horseplay, phallic humor, and prickly satire. In place of earthy jests he developed graceful, upscale romantic comedies designed for men like Epicurus, who preferred a moral or a reconciliation to a festival. By appealing to a limited audience, Menander lacked the standing-room-only popularity of Aristophanes and Philemon, a popular rival. However, Menander's work had a classic touch—an energy and staying power that influenced Rome's evolving stagecraft, particularly that of Terence, who may have drowned on a voyage home from Greece carrying fresh Latin translations of Menander's plays.

For centuries, so little was left of Menander's canon that it would fit on a modest sheaf of pages. Over a six-decade span, researchers in Egypt recovered papyrus strips used to wrap law scrolls. Beginning in 1898 and concluding in 1959, various contributors patched together *Dyskolos* [*The Grump*], the humanistic story of a changed man, for which Menander won first place in 316 B.C. at the January Lenaea. Added to segments of *Heros* [*The Family God*], *Samia* [*The Girl from Samos*], *Epitrepontes* [*Arbitration*], *Georgas* [*The Farmer*], *Colax* [*The Flatterer*], *Periceiromene* [*The Shearing of Glycera*], *Aspis* [*The Shield*], and *Sicyonius* [*The Sicyonian*] and of Roman adaptations of original plays, the extant lines give critics enough material to form a sketchy summation of style and content. Clearly, Menander followed the convention of stock characters—the skinflint uncle, tricky slaves, conceited man about town, winsome courtesan, simpleton heir, military strutter, and charming ingenue. Combined in plots calling for unrequited love, family reunions, chance encounters, and comic misunderstandings, Menander's personae form the basis on which Roman farce and *commedia dell'arte* grew; adaptations of his style influenced Molière, Richard Sheridan, and the writers of Restoration drama.

Menander exceeded the audience's expectations by individualizing his characters and by harmonizing details such as accent, class behaviors, and local customs. In *The Shearing of Glycera*, for example, the focal character is the stereotypical twin separated at birth from her brother Moschion. While chatting with him, Glycera incurs the hot temper of her lover Polemon, a bullying warrior. Without allowing her to explain her relationship to Moschion, Polemon lops off Glycera's hair and leaves her the object of public ridicule. The potential for an unforeseen incestuous relationship stalks the action until Glycera produces baby clothes. An aged meddler recognizes the needlework and claims Glycera as one of his twins. The subtle satire mocks Polemon, the graceless military man who must conquer himself before he can win back the girl he humiliated.

Best known for *The Arbitration*, a richly ironic, woman-centered play featuring the trials of Pamphila, a wife raped by her own husband and forced to abandon her child, Menander enjoyed numerous revivals and was even quoted in one of St. Paul's epistles: "Evil communications corrupt good manners" (I Corinthians 33). Menander's *Deus ex machina* (God in a machine) survives in standard literary terms denoting rescue from an unforeseen source. Other memorable one-liners include these:

- We survive the best way we can.
- I call a spade a spade.
- Marriage is a necessary evil.
- The one who runs may survive to fight again.
- Whom God loves dies young.
- Riches cover a multitude of woes.
- Nothing human lies outside my field of interests.

To preserve Menander's place among Athens' best writers, the sons of the sculptor Praxiteles made a bronze bust of him for the Theater of Dionysus. (Feder 1986; Gassner and Quinn 1969; Godolphin 1949; Hadas 1954; Hammond and Scullard 1992; Hornstein 1973; Howatson 1989; Mantinband 1956; Plautus 1973)

See also Aristophanes; comedy; *commedia dell'arte*; epigram; irony; Molière; Plautus; satire; Terence.

MENCKEN, H. L.

Dubbed the "Sage of Baltimore," the curmudgeonly aphorist, humorist, satirist, and critic of ideas H. L. Mencken established an unenviable place as the prickliest pear in America's literary cactus bed. His puckish delight in invective and diatribe that skewered the egos of the proud and deflated overblown sentimentality brought him devoted fans and a sizable number of enemies. Literary historians compare him to Sinclair Lewis, whose satiric novels cover the same territory as Mencken's snitty one-liners. Both Lewis and Mencken despised the smug parochialism and self-deception of the ebullient post–World War I era. In the introduction to *The Vintage Mencken*, Alastair Cooke notes that Mencken emulated Friedrich Nietzsche and George Bernard Shaw and aimed

> to be the native American Voltaire, the enemy of all puritans, the heretic in the Sunday School, the one-man demolition crew of the genteel tradition, the unregenerate neighborhood brat who stretches a string in the alley to trip the bourgeoisie on its pious homeward journey. (Mencken 1983, p. ix)

Mencken's one-of-a-kind wit has endeared his name and style to would-be Menckens who lack the color, control, and chutzpah to reprise the master satirist.

The first of four children of Anna Abhou and August Mencken, Henry Louis Mencken was born September 12, 1880, in Baltimore, Maryland, and claimed kin with complacent German burghers. His paternal grandfather settled in Baltimore and opened a cigar factory. Likewise inspired by the Puritan work ethic, Mencken's father and uncle flourished in the tobacco business. August forced on his son the tasks of office boy, cigar seller, and assistant bookkeeper. Mencken preferred newsgathering and, in his teens, operated his own printing press and studied journalism through correspondence courses. He attended private school at Friedrich Knapp's Institute and earned a superb record at Baltimore Polytechnic, from which he graduated in 1896. The day after his father's death in January 1899, Mencken began a daily job hunt at the Baltimore *Herald* and refused to accept the editor's rejection. Mencken worked free, then wrote obituaries and was eventually assigned a police beat. His first printed contribution to journalism was a five-line blip about a horse thief. The power of the press sparked a glint of mischief that remained his beacon for a half century.

A staff writer, editor, and columnist under the heading "The Free Lance," Mencken worked for the *Baltimore Sun* most of his career and earned a reputation as libertarian, free-thinker, iconoclast, skeptic, and subjective critic of artsy writing, particularly professorial rantings and poetry, both of which he abominated. He advanced to editor of the *Evening Herald* in 1904, covered political conventions, submitted essays to most of the journals of his day, and produced serious critical works on his idols, Shaw and Nietzsche. When news reporting began to pall on him in 1906, Mencken departed permanently from the newsroom and stuck to criticism and commentary, even when his fingers itched to return to his first love.

With drama critic George Jean Nathan, Mencken shared the editorial role for *The Smart Set: A Magazine of Cleverness* in 1914 and collaborated on two plays, *The Artist* (1912) and *Heliogabalus* (1920). He also produced *A Book of Burlesques* (1916) and *A Book of Prefaces* (1917), which Richard Wright adopted as a writing text. The partnership of Nathan and Mencken survived to serve an intellectual audience with *The American Mercury* from 1924 to 1933, which covered the boom years of realists Willa Cather and Eugene O'Neill; poet Ezra Pound; naturalists Theodore Dreiser, Sinclair Lewis, James Branch Cabell, and Sherwood Anderson; utopist Aldous Huxley; and novelists James Joyce, F. Scott Fitzgerald, Joseph Conrad, D. H. Lawrence, and Somerset Maugham. Because prejudice against Germans deprived Mencken of a forum in the popular press during World War I, he produced and revised six volumes of *The American Language* (1919–1948), a bestseller and impetus to scholarly research into American linguistic contributions from baseball and railroad slang to immigrant phrases, radio patter, and energetic vulgarisms. To rib the man-in-the-street slang, he freely translated the Declaration of Independence into vernacular English. During these supercharged years, frequent trips to Chicago and New York found him grousing over the latter city as "a third-rate Babylon" and rejoicing to return to Baltimore.

American humorist and satirist H. L. Mencken in 1935

Mencken lost his following during the Roosevelt years, when national danger turned readers away from cheap shots at a president they revered as a savior. Readers who had hated Mencken's egalitarianism took umbrage at his frequent crowing, for example, "I am thus opposed to all the paternalisms now prevailing, whether communism, Nazism, Fascism, or the New Deal" and "I belong to no party. I am my own party" (Mencken 1991, p. lviii). At age 50, for the only time in his life, Mencken moved from his Hollins Street home after he married writer Sarah Powell Haardt. When she died five years later, he was too sad to remain in their flat, and he returned to the Mencken family rowhouse. Six years before he was felled by a stroke, he published *A New Dictionary of Quotations, on Historical Principles* (1942) and followed with a three-volume comic memoir, *Heathen Days, 1890–1936* (1943). Aphasic and paralyzed, he was a virtual prisoner in his sickbed and depended on the care of his brother and a few friends. He died of heart failure on January 29, 1956, and was cremated and interred next to his wife in the Loudon Park Cemetery. The Enoch Pratt Library displays Mencken memorabilia, including his desk and typewriter; his collected letters on literary criticism were published in 1961.

Laden with jubilant hyperbole and impudent, often aggressive wit, Mencken's quotable lines resound with honesty and disgust, which he leveled at varied targets, ranging from Christian Scientists and chiropractors to prudes, the FBI, Holy Rollers, censorship, and the self-promoting British, whom he suspected of operating American politics like a long-distance puppeteer. His parodies emulate traditions dating from Roman satire to Samuel Johnson's dictionary. From the era of the Scopes Monkey Trial came some of his brightest literary pyrotechnics. Banking on a firsthand view of "the ninth-rate country town" of Dayton, Tennessee, during the trial of July 1925, Mencken referred to the average Tennessean as "Homo Neanderthalensis" and ridiculed Freemasons, Ku Kluxers, glossalalia, and fundamentalism. Of the latter, he roars:

> So far the exegetes who roar and snuffle in the town have found . . . only blazing ratifications and reinforcements of Genesis. Darwin is the devil with seven tails and nine horns. Scopes, though he is disguised by flannel pantaloons and a Beta Theta Pi haircut, is the harlot of Babylon. Darrow is Beelzebub in person.

With financing wheedled from the *Sun,* Mencken hired Clarence Darrow to face one of his long-time favorite objects of verbal abuse, William Jennings Bryan, and finagled an additional $100 to pay John Scopes's fine. Mencken concluded his day-by-day series with a tribute to Darrow: "On the one side was bigotry, ignorance, hatred, superstition, every sort of blackness that the human mind is capable of. On the other side was sense."

For his years of travel and thumping out splenetic commentary two-fingered style on a portable typewriter, Mencken earned his star as an individualist and defender of the underdog, whether the badgered agnostic, friendly German Jew, or beleaguered bootlegger. He won an award from the *Nation* in 1932 for honest reportage. His obdurate, at times self-glorifying satiric style often swamped the victim in a single stroke. He targeted especially the idols of mass culture, including Valentino; President Woodrow Wilson, who led America into World War I; and FDR, who repeated the action in December 1941. A clever wordsmith who invented wherever he found a dearth of appropriate terminology, Mencken coined the terms "Homo boobiensis," "booboisie," "bozart," and the "Bible Belt," after experimenting with "the Hookworm Belt, the Hog-and-Hominy Belt, the Total Immersion Belt, and so on." His wildcatter's style influenced radio newscasters and columnists, particularly Menckenesque humorist Florence King. (*Contemporary Authors* 1994; Grigson 1963; Hart 1983; Kunitz 1942; McArthur 1992; Mencken 1983, 1991)

See also burlesque; diatribe; epigram; invective; King, Florence; Lewis, Sinclair; parody; satire.

THE MIKADO

One of William S. Gilbert and Arthur Sullivan's most quoted and revived comic operas, *The Mikado, or the Town of Titipu* (1885), presents a veneer of Japan spread thinly over a farcical jab at Victorian England, the author's favorite satiric milieu. The play received so much attention that the British Embassy requested a brief hiatus during a diplomatic call by Japanese dignitaries lest the visitors should feel slighted. Gilbert's comment reveals a droll wit:

> A delicate and polite action on the part of a guest towards a host. The rights in the piece do not revert to me for three years; by that time we shall probably be at war with Japan about India, and they will offer me a high price to permit it to be played.

The loss of three days' box office apparently made little difference to Gilbert's sizeable income from his string of light musicals, which he later deprecated as "twaddle."

The well-mined scenario of young love thwarted by old conceits emerges in Act I with the hasty arrival of Nanki-Poo, a rich boy disguised as a wandering troubadour who has run away from home to escape the Mikado's imperial decree that he marry Katisha. Among Nanki-Poo's romantic plaints lurks cutting satire of the English penchant for forging an empire:

> But if patriotic sentiment is wanted,
> I've patriotic ballads cut and dried;
> For where'er our country's banner may be planted,
> All other local banners are defied!
> Our warriors, in serried ranks assembled,
> Never quail—or they conceal it if they do—
> And I shouldn't be surprised if nations trembled
> Before the mighty troops of Titipu!

The turn of plot pits Nanki-Poo against Ko-Ko, a disreputable tailor and the region's Lord High executioner, who has been cited for flirting, a capital offense in Titipu. Ko-Ko's chances for the hand of Yum-Yum brighten when Ko-

Ko tries to force the despondent Nanki-Poo into taking Ko-Ko's place at the execution.

Gilbert is at his best in depicting Pooh-Bah, the foil of Ko-Ko, a posturing bureaucrat who claims "pre-Adamite ancestral descent" and deigns to take a salary, although accepting money for service to the state demeans him. It is Pooh-Bah's duty to explain to the Mikado, the emperor of Japan, the legal technicalities of the recent execution. The Mikado believes that, precisely according to law, his errant son and crown prince has been beheaded. Nanki-Poo, who has married Yum-Yum, fears that the elderly, spiteful Katisha will demand his death and the living burial of his bride, which Yum-Yum classifies as a "stuffy death." To stave off disaster, Nanki-Poo convinces Ko-Ko to court Katisha. The play ends with multiple reassessments: Nanki-Poo has his love, Katisha is safely wedded to Ko-Ko, and the Mikado still has an heir. With razzle-dazzle illogic, Ko-Ko sums up:

> When your Majesty says, "Let a thing be done," it's as good as done—practically, it is done—because your Majesty's will is law. Your Majesty says, "Kill a gentleman," and a gentleman is towed off to be killed. Consequently, that gentleman is as good as dead—practically, he is dead—and if he is dead, why not say so?

The irreverent costume melodrama is so filled with song, inanities, and comic reversals that no one takes offense at Gilbert's witticisms, for example:

> *Yum-Yum:* . . . in Japan girls do not arrive at years of discretion until they are fifty.
>
> *Nanki-Poo:* True; from seventeen to forty-nine are considered years of indiscretion.

Other ridicule of snobbery, pomposity, sexism, and unprincipled selfishness wedges itself tidily among interlinking limericks, comic trios, death jokes, sentimental dialogue, and Ko-Ko's "Titwillow" song, one of the most resilient of Sullivan's melodies. (Bermel 1982; Brockett 1968; Burdick 1974; Gassner and Quinn 1969; Gilbert and Sullivan 1962; Gilbert 1967, 1992; Roberts 1962; *Something about the Author* 1984)

See also black humor; burlesque; caricature; doggerel; farce; Gilbert, William S.; limerick; parody; satire; whimsy.

 # "THE MILLER'S TALE"

One of the coarsest stories from medieval times, "The Miller's Tale" earns its foul savor from a single act—a kiss on the behind. As a natural part of rowdy fun and practical jokes, the fabliau belongs to the folk satire tradition, which often champions a tit-for-tat sense of justice. Told by Chaucer's scummiest pilgrim, the story depicts a pair of foils: Nicholas the astrology student and his landlord, John the jealous carpenter of Oxford. A common thread in such scurrilous narratives is the young wife, Alison, who married unwisely a man much too old to serve her needs. Chaucer comments:

> A man should marry someone like himself;
> A man should pick an equal for his mate.
> Youth and old age are often in debate.
> However, he had fallen in the snare,
> And had to bear his cross as others bear.

Nicholas's intimacy with the family brings him into close contact with Alison. Her weak objections give way to a natural order of love that the hearer finds appropriate. Thus, Alison agrees to help Nicholas cuckold John.

The addition of Absalon, a second young clerk who finds Alison attractive, complicates Chaucer's plot. After eyeing her in church, Absalon, a flouncing fop, steals beneath her window at night and sings of passion. The carpenter awakens and rejoices that Alison takes no interest in the serenade. The incident weakens John's jealousy and leaves him open to trickery. Nicholas pretends to be dead, then rises from a vision to warn John that a flood is about to engulf the region. Ironically, John thinks not of himself but exclaims: "Alas, my wife! My little Alison! Is she to drown?" To prepare for disaster, Nicholas urges John to nail three tubs to the ceiling of the house and provision each with food and water. That night, the couple and John take their places in the tubs, ostensibly to pray for mercy; after John falls fast asleep from his toil, Nicholas and Alison tiptoe off to bed.

During the evening, Chaucer's notorious kissing scene occurs when Absalon returns to beg Alison's favors. She thrusts her bare buttocks out the window frame for Absalon to kiss. The fastidious parish clerk feels scratchy pubic hair, realizes he has been duped, and departs in shame. To Nicholas's chuckles, Absalon vows revenge. He retaliates by acquiring a hot poker and summoning Alison to the window for a second kiss. Chaucer saucily notes:

> The fiery heat of love by now had cooled,
> For from that time he kissed her hinder parts
> He didn't give a tinker's curse for tarts;
> His malady was cured by this endeavor
> And he defied all paramours whatever.

Nicholas, who had arisen to relieve his bladder, hears Absalon at the window. Nicholas joins in the fun and "stuck out his arse, a handsome piece of work,/ Buttocks and all, as far as to the haunch." He commits the worst of insults to Absalon's delicate sensibilities by expelling gas. The outraged youth stabs Nicholas's backside with the poker. Because Nicholas cries for water to ease the burn, John awakens with a start and jostles the tub from the ceiling. The fall breaks his arm and provokes his neighbors to ridicule his foolishness.

Chaucer's conclusion to this uncouth narrative attempts to restore it to a moral level: Alison gets her man, John's peculiar behavior earns him his neighbor's contempt, Absalon is grievously insulted, and Nicholas, the wife-despoiler, loses a patch of skin from his posterior. The return to the subject of marriage appears to link "The Miller's Tale" with others in Chaucer's study of matrimony. If read as parody, the story allows the author to use levity and wit to prick the overnoble stories like "The Knight's Tale," a boring rehash of unattainable ladies, courtly knights who love from a distance, and purified love that sees no action below the waist. For Chaucer's wholesomely diverse group of gadabouts, the burst of foul gas comes as a relief from the pent-up sameness of chivalric lore. (Chaucer 1959, 1969, 1992; Chute 1946; Gardner 1977; Scott 1974)

See also Canterbury Tales; Chaunticleer; fabliau; parody; trickster; the Wife of Bath.

 # MOCK EPIC

A humorous, satiric, or heroicomical poem composed in elevated style, the mock epic is a sophisticated literary work that follows classic epic conventions:

- a hero—almost always male—who is capable of superhuman deeds and whose actions determine the fate of a tribe, nation, or race, as with Moses' leadership of the Hebrews from Egypt in *Exodus*

- a setting on a grand scale, such as John Milton's placement of *Paradise Lost* in heaven, earth, and hell

- *in medias res*, or the act of opening the narrative in the middle of the action, for example, the framework narrative in Homer's *Odyssey*

- the epic question of how the situation escalated to a desperate state

- a prefatory invocation to a muse or deity—for instance, the title character's dependence on Manitou in Henry Wadsworth Longfellow's epic poem *Hiawatha*

- lofty arguments and grand discourse that avoid lowly or slangy dialogue, vulgarity, or dialect—for example, Aeneas's exhortation of his surviving followers after a storm in Virgil's *Aeneid*

- vaunting ego, strutting, or bragging as a ceremonial or ritual show of manhood, especially the performance of warriors at Patroclus's funeral in Homer's *Iliad*

- epic simile or Homeric simile comparing at length something on the battlefield with objects or situations not available to soldiers during war

- intervention of supernatural beings, whether gods, fates, sprites, sylphs, or fairies

- stock epithets or set patterns of description—for example, imitations of Homer's "rosy-fingered dawn" or Virgil's "swift-footed Rumor"

The History of Tom Thumbe, the Little, for his small stature surnamed, King ARTHVRS Dwarfe:

Whose Life and aduentures containe many strange and wonderfull accidents, published for *the delight of merry Time-spenders.*

Imprinted at London for *Tho: Langley.* 1621.

A traditional figure in English literature, Tom Thumb's adventures included his being carried off by a bird. These mock-heroic tales were published in *The History of Tom Thumbe, the Little* in 1621.

- catalogs of ships, equipment, or warriors—for instance, Virgil's list of troops who defend Alba Longa against the incursion of Aeneas and his men in the *Aeneid*

- prophetic dreams or visions that reveal the fate of characters or an unforeseen turn of events

As a vehicle of comedy, mock epic creates humor or satire by applying the lofty elements of epic to unworthy characters or events, for example, the fox stalking Chaunticleer, Geoffrey Chaucer's vaunting, self-congratulatory rooster.

A natural outgrowth of the revival of classical literary elements in the late seventeenth and early eighteenth centuries, mock epic pokes fun at self-conscious loftiness and high-flown language or unmasks quacks, humbugs, or bogus philosophies. Usually divided into cantos, the mock epic may follow Homeric style and begin *in medias res*, then review the events that precipitated the conflict. Resolution usually precedes a crucial or supernatural event; a charming application of a mystic conclusion is the transformation of Belinda's hair into a constellation in Alexander Pope's *The Rape of the Lock* (1714). Other examples of mock epic include these:

- The anonymous Greek *Batrachomyomachia* [*The Battle of the Frogs and Mice*] (sixth century B.C.)

- Geoffrey Chaucer's *The Nun's Priest's Tale* (1387)

- Edmund Spenser's *Muiopotmos* (1591)

- Alessandro Tassoni's *La Secchia Rapita* [*The Rape of the Bucket*] (1622)

- Nicolas Boileau's *Le Lutrin* (1683)

- Samuel Garth's *The Dispensary* (1699)

- Jonathan Swift's *The Battle of the Books* (1704)

- Alexander Pope's *The Dunciad* (1728–1743)

- John Hookham Frere's *Whistlecraft* (1817)

(Bermel 1982; Cuddon 1984; Gray 1992; Holman and Harmon 1992; Padgett 1987)
    See also burlesque; Chaucer, Geoffrey; Chaunticleer; *The Dunciad*; incongruity; parody; Pope, Alexander; *The Rape of the Lock*; Swift, Jonathan.

 # MOCK-HEROIC

Not as constrained by elaborate conventions as the longer mock epic, mock-heroic or heroicomical verse nevertheless emulates the aura of the mock epic by reproducing several of its aspects. The opposite of classic or dignified, *mock-heroic* is an adjective that describes ironic literature of varying length composed according to grand or elegant standards about a humble or ludicrous topic—

for example, John Dryden's *MacFlecknoe* (1682), John Phillips's *The Splendid Shilling: An Imitation of Milton* (1705), Henry Fielding's *Tom Thumb* (1730), Thomas Gray's "Ode on the Death of a Favourite Cat, Drowned in a Tub of Gold Fishes" (1748), and George Byron's *Don Juan* (1824). Phillips, a splendid joker, contrasts the epic spiritual struggle of the pinchpenny who huddles by a cheerless, friendless hearth and rewards his penury with fantasy:

> . . . I Labour with eternal Drought,
> And restless Wish, and Rave; my parched Throat
> Finds no Relief, nor heavy Eyes Repose:
> But if a Slumber haply does Invade
> My weary Limbs, my Fancy's still awake,
> Thoughtful of Drink, and Eager in a Dream,
> Tipples Imaginary Pots of Ale . . .

Purposely depriving himself of "John-Apple" and other forms of alcoholic refreshment, he foresees greater trials in his future, which is "By time subdu'd, (what will not Time subdue!)." He imagines a ship loaded with mariners who are engulfed with the monsters Scylla and Charybdis of Homeric fame: "They stare, they lave, they pump, they swear, they prey:/(Vain Efforts!)." Soaked in a superfluity of liquid and foam, they vanish into the deep.

Similarly freighted with water imagery and the threat of a watery death, Gray's mock-heroic cat epic draws out the allure of angelic fish shapes swimming by in gleaming gold, "their scaly armour's Tyrian hue" catching the demure tabby's eye and holding her in thrall. The comedic version of hand-to-hand combat pits animal against animal, paw against fin, while deities spurn the cat's cries:

> The slipp'ry verge her feet beguil'd,
>   She tumbled headlong in.
> Eight times emerging from the flood
> She mew'd to ev'ry watry God,
>   Some speedy aid to send.
> No Dolphin came, no Nereid stirr'd:
> Nor cruel Tom, nor Susan heard.
>   A Fav'rite has no friend!

Tongue-in-cheek, Gray winds down the dramatic drowning to a pseudo-Homeric warning: "Know, one false step is ne'er retriev'd." With the epic writer's didactic close, Gray concludes the 42-line verse with the heavy lesson that the greedy heart was not meant to possess every shiny bauble. He sighs, in conclusion, "Nor all, that glisters, gold."

In 1824, George Gordon, Lord Byron, wrote to his publisher that his mock heroic, *Don Juan,* had no plan. He exclaimed, "the Soul of such writing is its licence." At his death, Byron had completed 16 cantos of his facetious ottava rima, which he had begun writing when he composed *Beppo: A Venetian Story* (1818) and developed to greater economy and skill with subsequent practice. Lightheartedly punning and alluding to poets and figures of his time, Byron comments freely on how and where he will follow epic style or deviate from it. In Canto 4 he introduces Lord Nelson, the British naval hero:

Nelson was once Britannia's god of war,
    And still should be so, but the tide is turned;
There's no more to be said of Trafalgar,
    'Tis with our hero quietly inurned;
Because the army's grown more popular,
    At which the naval people are concerned,
Besides, the prince is all for the land-service,
Forgetting Duncan, Nelson, Howe, and Jervis.

The irreverent rhyming of "is turned" with "inurned" and "land-service" with "and Jervis" indicates that Byron is cleverly concealing poetic mastery and commentary under a bantering, slapdash style. Left incomplete in Greece after Byron's untimely death, the work was intended to follow the antihero through conversion to Methodism and on to hell.

Not all mock-heroic ends with such ludicrous misfortune. A favorite from children's literature, Lewis Carroll's "Jabberwocky" steeps its nonsense words in the lore of pursuit, the survivalist's glee in facing an unknown challenger, defeating it on its own turf, and nabbing the trophy, the lopped-off head. A peal of rejoicing that follows the homeward procession begins with a portmanteau verb (gallop + triumph) to produce "galumphing," a pseudo-epic action suited to the victor. To return to the menace of the opening lines, Carroll repeats his enigmatic quatrain, a reminder that the season for Jabberwocks affords the hunter no rest. (Byron 1959; Carroll 1960; Cuddon 1984; Drabble 1985; Gray 1992; Gray, T. 1932; Henry 1995; Holman and Harmon 1992; Padgett 1987; Philips 1932)

See also burlesque; Carroll, Lewis; didacticism; Dryden, John; irony; mock epic; parody; satire.

MOLIÈRE

A notable farceur in an era of tragedians, a creator of ornate diversions, and the strongest single influence on seventeenth- and eighteenth-century drama, Frenchman Molière managed and directed a theatrical company that performed satiric treasures. He developed a style known as *pièce à thèse*, or thesis drama, a play that presents a problem and provides a solution. At a time when England became a fundamentalist-dominated commonwealth, closed its theaters, and made its communities inhospitable to playwrights, English writers and dramatists fled to the Continent to absorb the wonder of the mid–seventeenth-century French stage and the plays and spectacles of Molière.

Born January 15, 1622, in Paris, Jean Baptiste Poquelin was the son and eldest of the six children of Marie Cressé and prosperous furniture dealer and upholsterer Jean Poquelin, the king's *valet de chambre*, a hereditary post that required three months' work each year for a stipend of 300 livres. Little data remain of Molière's early life except that he was short, spoke with a noticeable impediment, and developed a hiccup that became his stage trademark. His mother died when he was ten; his father married Catherine Fleurette, a widow with two daughters. At a Jesuit school, the Collège de Clermont, he mastered Latin and Greek and studied law at Orléans. At the age of twenty, Molière got to see more of the world by accompanying King Louis XIII to Narbonne and Lyons in his father's place as royal upholsterer. Visits to the royal performances at the Hôtel de Bourgogne struck the respondent chord that turned Molière from law to an iffy and despised profession—acting in comedy. Making his choice official in 1643, he voluntarily vacated rights to his father's title and royal pension.

While master of the L'Illustre Théâtre, a company he formed with the Béjart family—Madeleine, Geneviève, Louis, Joseph, and Marie Hervé—he developed a love for Madeleine, who served as business adviser and lead actor in roles he wrote to suit their mutual talents. Bankrolled by Gaston, Duc d'Orléans, the brother of Louis XIII, the company met stiff competition from the royal company. Molière, who at first concentrated on tragedy, the métier of serious stage art, distanced his company from the tennis court at the Port de Nesle and emigrated from Rouen to Paris before foundering from lack of funds. He was cast into debtor's prison until his father could sign a note covering the company's losses.

A new start took the fledgling troupe to Lyons, where they performed with Charles Dufresne's company in rural settings in Nantes, Montpellier, Béziers, and Toulouse and sought new patronage from the Duc d'Épernon. Molière introduced *L'Étourdi ou les contretemps* [*The Scatterbrain, or The Blunders*] (1655), which he based on an Italian farce written by Barbieri, and *Le Dépit amoureux* [*The Amourous Quarrel*] (1656). Comedy brought prosperity and an expanded company. Three years later, the playwright returned to the Louvre in Paris to present Corneille's *Nicomède* (ca. 1650), followed by a brief original farce with ballet, *Le Docteur amoureux* [*The Lovelorn Doctor*]. The approval of the young Louis XIV and the patronage of Phillipe, Duc d'Orléans, assured anchorage for the company at Le Petit-Bourbon near the Louvre, where farces brought more profits than did tragedies. Molière studied the Italian company of Scaramouche, his mentor, who shared the theater on alternate nights, and learned from the Italian *commedia dell'arte* that laughter is better than sermons.

Intensely competitive with the established theatrical community, Molière opened at the Louvre on November 18, 1659, with his first one-act comedy of manners, *Les Précieuses ridicules* [*The Ridiculous Bluestockings*], an outrageous, but successful satire that ridiculed pretentious speech, poufy wigs, overtrimmed costumes, euphuisms, and absurd mannerisms through inventive caricature of social-climbing young women. The elite were not amused and retaliated by having Molière's theater demolished. Nonetheless, by currying favor with Louis XIV, Molière managed to continue lampooning the less adroit curriers of favor and reforming them through ridicule. To the king's delight, Molière performed *Les Fâcheux* [*The Impertinents*] (1662) twice for the court's pleasure. During his courtship of Armande Béjart, whom he married in 1662, Molière, more than twice her age, acted the lead in *L'École des maris* [*The School for Husbands*] (1661) and *L'École des femmes* [*The School for Wives*] (1662), a mocking binocular view of older men married to younger women and the constricted expectations society held for young women. In 1663, to critical commentary from his detractors, he issued *La Critique de l'Ecole des femmes* and *L'Impromptu de Versailles*.

Bold experiment based on the *commedia dell'arte* in the mid-1660s brought Molière to a crisis. He incurred the displeasure of both church and laity with his character comedy, *Tartuffe, ou l'hypocrite* [*Tartuffe, or The Hypocrite*] (1664), which the archbishop banned from public performance on grounds of impiety, and with *Don Juan, ou Le Festin de pierre* [*Don Juan, or The Feast of the Stone*] (1665). This audacious change in style and purpose ended his friendship with colleague and supporter Jean Racine. The break cost him Racine's *Alexandre*, which passed to another troupe, but Molière's troupe earned the title of *Troupe du roi* (The King's Troupe), a headliner's achievement that carried a hefty purse of 1,000 livres annually. In 1666, after a nonstop schedule of writing, acting, and directing, Molière was felled by pleurisy in both lungs. His financial picture brightened with a barrage of entertaining, enlightening comedies, ballets, and spectacles:

- *Don Juan, L'Amour médecin* [*Love's the Best Doctor*] (1665)

- *Le Médecin malgré lui* [*The Doctor in Spite of Himself*] (1666)

- *Ballet of Muses* (1666), performed to music by Jean-Baptiste Lully

- *La Pastorale comique* [*The Comic Pastoral*] (1666)

- A masterwork, *Le Misanthrope* (1666)

Notwithstanding the rise of his company's fortunes, he still gambled and lost money on Corneille's *Attila*, a leaden tragedy. Some of Molière's works were pirated, some never published. His personal woes kept him off balance: his son Louis died in infancy and Armande was unfaithful with Michel Baron, one of Molière's protégés; she took two-year-old daughter Esprit-Madeleine and deserted her husband. To strengthen his weakening body, Molière withdrew to Auteuil and adopted a stringent milk diet. He continued producing at his best:

- *L'Avare* [*The Miser*] (1668)

- *Amphitryon; Georges Dandin, ou le Marie confondu* [*George Dandin, or The Confused Husband*] (1668)

- *Monsieur de Pourceaugnac* (1669), a court farce

- The comedy-ballet *Le Bourgeois gentilhomme* [*The Bourgeois Gentleman*] (1670)

- *Les Amants magnifiques* [*The Magnificent Lovers*] (1670), a comic ballet suggested by the king

- *Psyché* (1670), a tragicomic ballet written in collaboration with Pierre Corneille and Philippe Quinault

- *Les Femmes savantes* [*The Learned Ladies*] (1672)

- *Les Fourberies de Scapin* [*The Cheats of Scapin*] (1672)

In 1671, shortly after the death of Madeleine Béjart, Armande returned to Molière and bore him a third child, Pierre-Jean-Baptiste, who survived only three weeks. The king exhibited his sympathy and support by standing as godfather. Neurasthenic from fever and stress, Molière had to write and produce at a killing pace to keep up with the whims of court, counter the connivance of the church, and pay for his wife's expensive taste in decor. The night before his death, the playwright was performing *Le Malade imaginaire* [*The Hypochondriac*], a vigorous part that compromised his weakened lungs. At his death from exhaustion, convulsion, and lung hemorrhage the next night—February 17, 1673—Molière completed his part, then was carried to the rue de Richelieu barely conscious. The church refused burial for his remains in holy ground, a common response of prelates to actors. Armande had to grovel before the hypocritical Archbishop de Champvallon and the king to acquire a plot at St. Joseph's Cemetery, where Molière was buried February 21 at night by torchlight without a priest's blessing or absolution.

Ironically, Molière, the toast of the age of Louis XIV, died wealthy in money, friends, and influence but scorned by tragedians, prelates, and the social elite. One of France's most adept, unconventional stage mimes, he became the giant of his métier, the pioneer of serious satiric comedy. His commentary on humor left a model for his followers:

> Incongruity is the heart of the comic . . . it follows that all lying, disguise, cheating, dissimulation, all outward show different from the reality, all contradiction in fact between actions that proceed from a single source, all this is in essence comic.

His lines ring with wit and truth:

- We die only once, but for such a long time!

- There is no rampart that will hold out against malice.

- Those whose conduct gives room for talk are always the first to attack their neighbors.

- Cover that bosom that I must not see: souls are wounded by such things.

- The more we love our friends, the less we flatter them; it is by excusing nothing that pure love shows itself.

- If everyone were clothed with integrity, if every heart were just, frank, kindly, the other virtues would be well-nigh useless, since their chief purpose is to make us bear with patience the injustice of our fellows.

- I prefer an accommodating vice to an obstinate virtue.

- A learned fool is more foolish than an ignorant one.

Often compared to the rubbery movie characters mimed by Charlie Chaplin, Molière was one of the Western world's masters of satire, which he grounded on urbane, vital incongruities and realistic portraits of the miser, hypocrite, snooty lord, clubwoman, parvenu, seducer, pedant, sycophant, and flirt. Success set him above his contemporaries, Racine and Corneille, whose works exist only in textbooks. In honor of an immense cult following, the Comédie Française was renamed the House of Molière. (Baugh 1948; Bermel 1982; Brockett 1968; Burdick 1974; Gassner and Quinn 1969; Guicharnaud 1967; Molière 1965; Roberts 1962)

See also caricature; *commedia dell'arte;* doggerel; epigram; farce; incongruity; satire; *Tartuffe.*

MORGAN, HANK

The self-important protagonist of Mark Twain's satiric historical novel, *A Connecticut Yankee in King Arthur's Court* (1886), Hank Morgan exemplifies Twain's vision of the puffed-up, self-satisfied New Englander. A metal worker at the Colt Arms factory, Hank typifies the bustling enterprise and faith in progress common to the New World at the time of his inexplicable transfer from Hartford, Connecticut, to sixth-century Camelot. On a self-directed mission to upgrade the era, Hank looks at medieval life as a romantic challenge:

> I was just another Robinson Crusoe cast away on an uninhabited island, with no society but some more or less tame animals, and if I wanted to make life bearable I must do as he did—invent, contrive, create, reorganize things; set brain and hand to work, and keep them busy. Well that was in my line.

As his words indicate, Hank, a deluded idealist and sometime swaggerer, becomes an antihero, a bumbler who brings about his downfall by attempting too much change in a medieval environment. Beset by callous monarchy, Church treachery, and centuries of ignorance and superstition, he unseats himself by discounting the political clout of the envious courtiers and clergy.

Twain achieves comedy in the creation of his protagonist, a whiz-bang optimist and man-of-all-trades. By wearing the guise of the mage, Hank, dubbed The Boss, sets up a progressive alliance of capitalistic workers, baseball teams, democratic schools, insurance agencies, improved transportation, newspapers, and industrial expansion. Faithful to the nineteenth-century ideal of universal betterment, Hank falls for his era's self-deception, a chicanery based on gadgetry. Confident that he can overcome repression with invention, he neglects the political structure that democratization replaces. The enmity of knights, Church prelates, and Merlin the Magician erupts into medieval warfare, which defeats Hank's plans to raise the working class to the standards of the nineteenth-century United States. The satire of both the Middle Ages and Hank's New World ingenuity creates a useful tension that Twain exploits to characterize human frailty at both ends of the spectrum—the unlearned past and his own vainglorious era, both ripe for downfall.

As history and myth dictate, Arthur's utopia must collapse, despite the organizational legerdemain that places Hank and Clarence at the forefront of a progressive Camelot. Part of the pathos of Hank's demise is a betrayal of honor and trust, virtues he expects from gentlefolk. A husband and father not unlike Twain himself, Hank gladly sets aside national concerns and ferries wife and child to more healthful surroundings until his sickly daughter Hello-Central can recover from life-threatening bronchitis. On his return, he realizes how cold malice has gathered strength and outmaneuvered his modern contrivances. Too late, Hank challenges the Church's duplicity in getting him out of the way; too late, he proclaims his republic and dispatches his 52 assistants as though they were Confederate soldiers. He ignores the one unnamed soldier who speaks the horror of civil war:

> But think—the matter is altered—all England is marching against us! Oh, sir, consider! Reflect! These people are our people, they are bone of our bone, flesh of our flesh, we love them—do not ask us to destroy our nation!

The Boss hastily proclaims the Battle of the Sand Belt a victory, but a slight wound and attendance by Merlin end Hank's power with a sleep that lasts thirteen centuries, a magic number rife with supernatural implications.

Twain's creation of Hank Morgan is one of America's finest satiric moments. The author intends for the reader to see that serious flaws stand in the way of Hank's modernized Camelot, not the least of which is egotism. More insidious is Hank's dependence on weaponry and gunpowder. In the end, he faces off against hosts of mailed and mounted knights and kills them with electrified fences. Camelot's end is swift and surprisingly detrimental to Hank. The victor, ringed about by three tiers of decaying corpses, lives out his final hours a virtual prisoner of his own craft. Ironically overcome by the redoubtable Merlin, an officious humbug who refuses to bow to competition, Hank hibernates into Twain's time and dies in Warwick Castle after passing a detailed journal to the narrator. Still clinging to his medieval mirage, Hank, while breathing his last, calls: "It is the king! The drawbridge, there! Man the battlements—turn out the—" and dies while "getting up his last 'effect.'"

Twain's Hank, ever the brash, pushy optimist, never doubts that his brand of technological know-how will rescue him. The combined efforts of his workers produce a pyrrhic victory. Clarence, the Boss's hand-picked assistant and budding genius, takes up the narrative in a handwritten manuscript. Thirteen centuries later in the final moments at Warwick, the awakening Hank, too frail to last long, gasps out his disillusion:

> I thought that Clarence and I and a handful of my cadets fought and exterminated the whole chivalry of England! . . . Yes, I seemed to have flown back out of that age into this of ours, and then forward to it again, and was set down, a stranger and forlorn in that strange England, with an abyss of thirteen centuries yawning between me and you! between me and my home and my friends! between me and all that is dear to me, all that could make life worth the living! It was awful—awfuler than you can ever imagine.

Still calling his minions to arms, Hank, in the voice of a top sergeant, lies on his deathbed in a state of hallucination. His mind clings to his wife and trusts his young corps of engineers to overcome the foe and renew his plans for a sixth-century utopia. His body, sunken under the spell of Merlin and revived briefly in the nineteenth century, gradually slips away. (Budd 1983; Hoffman 1988; Kesterson 1979; Rasmussen 1995; Twain 1963)

See also caricature; comedy; *A Connecticut Yankee in King Arthur's Court;* didacticism; satire; Twain, Mark.

NORMAN, MARSHA

A Pulitzer Prize–winning playwright with a gift for cold, lacerating honesty, Marsha Norman has applied skill and innovation to her best works: *Getting Out* (1977) and *'night Mother* (1982), first presented December 1982 at the American Repertory Theatre in Cambridge, Massachusetts. A native of Louisville, Kentucky, Norman, the daughter of realtor Billie Lee and Bertha Mae Conley Williams, grew up in the stifling confines of Christian fundamentalism, an isolating force that colored her childhood. She graduated from Agnes Scott with a B.A. in philosophy in 1969, received an M.A.T. from the University of Louisiana in 1971, and taught for the Kentucky Department of Health and in Jefferson County Schools before working for the Kentucky Arts Commission in 1974. After editing and reviewing for the *Louisville Times* from 1974 to 1979, Norman worked with emotionally disturbed children at the Kentucky Central State Hospital, her source of empathy for tormented people.

After succeeding with *Getting Out,* the transformation of Arlie the crazy into Arlene the recovering schizophrenic prostitute, Norman received a National Endowment for the Arts grant in 1978 as well as the John Gassner New Playwright's Medallion, a George Oppenheimer–Newsday award, and the Outer Critics Circle award. Norman has written a remarkable number of dramas: *Third and Oak* (1978), *It's the Willingness* (1978), *Circus* (1979), *The Holdup* (1980), *In Trouble at Fifteen* (1980), and her most successful play, *'night Mother*, which earned both the Pulitzer Prize and a Tony. Continuing to turn out high-quality plays for stage and screen, Norman published *Traveler in the Dark* (1984), *Sarah and Abraham* (1988), and *D. Boone* (1992). Her apt blend of music and dialogue won her a second Tony for *Secret Garden* (1991), a reworking of the Frances Hodgson Burnett children's classic.

Frequently compared to Beth Henley, the author of *Crimes of the Heart*, who also focuses on failed interpersonal relationships, Norman chooses a universality of language and setting to place her characters at large among humankind and gives them free rein over an enveloping black humor. The engaging one-liners of *'night Mother* pit mother Thelma Cates against daughter Jessie in a farewell wrangle over Jessie's impending suicide, which seems like the sensible conclusion to the daughter's dead-end life of giving without getting, trying and not succeeding, and planning for no attainable aims. The 1986 film version, starring Sissy Spacek and Anne Bancroft, preserves the two-character drift of dialogue that rehashes old griefs without providing enough hope to stop Jessie from carrying out her intended suicide.

Norman's explicit instructions for characters and setting depict Jessie as in control to the point of making peace with death more easily than making peace with her mother. Thelma, an aging manipulator who lives on a rural lane and expects daily attendance by her daughter, realizes that the cluttered emotional baggage of her daughter's life parallels the clutter of their living quarters, which give the outward appearance of feminine niceties but shed no warmth on the emotionally arid pair. The portentous humor in Thelma's retorts to Jessie's dead-serious admission opens the way to an evening of prickly give and take:

Jessie: I'm through talking, Mama . . .
Thelma: You'll miss. You'll just wind up a vegetable. How would you like that? Shoot your ear off?

The mundane quality of kitchen-based dialogue satirizes the failed lives of two women centered in such temporal concerns as cupcakes, dish detergent, Christmas lists, and Jessie's son's escapades with drugs.

The grim satiric humor that plays through the dialogue like arced lightning occasionally illuminates a memorable image. To Jessie, ending a fruitless existence is an opportunity to get off the bus when she wishes. Thelma inanely suggests buying a dog, then retorts sarcastically, "You're not having a good time!" To express her views on eccentricities, she cites Agnes Fletcher, a pyromaniac who wears whistles around her neck and buys expensive birds. Thelma claims, "It's that okra she eats. You can't just willy-nilly eat okra two meals a day and expect to get away with it. Made her crazy." With the stark conclusion of the play, satire gives way to realism as a shot ends Jessie's arguments with son, mother, and self. (Buck 1992; *Contemporary Authors* 1994; *Contemporary Literary Criticism* 1983; Davidson and Wagner-Martin 1995; *Dictionary of Literary Biography* 1985; Norman 1983; Schroeder 1989; Spencer 1987)

See also black humor; caricature; diatribe; Henley, Beth; sarcasm.

ORWELL, GEORGE

In Part 3, Chapter 3 of *1984*, Orwell warned, "If you want a picture of the future, imagine a boot stamping on a human face—forever." Obviously, if these words encapsulated the thrust of his prose, he would belong among apocalyptic writers rather than satirists. As England's mid-twentieth-century foremost political satirist, iconoclast, and libertarian, George Orwell carries the field as the primary cassandra for a world he feared was rushing toward technocratic nightmare. Famed for his nonconformist patriotism and for two dystopian novels, *Animal Farm* (1945) and *1984* (1949), he emulates the acerbity of Juvenal and Jonathan Swift, the intellectualism of his contemporary George Bernard Shaw, and the literary skills of Joseph Addison and Voltaire. His dystopian satire provided the English language with the terms "Orwellian," "doublethink," "newspeak," and "Big Brother." A polite anarchist and uncompromising champion of freedom, he wrote the definitive antitotalitarian novels to follow World War II.

A child of the British Empire, Eric Arthur Blair, the son of Ida Mabel Limouzin, Anglo-French daughter of a teak merchant, and Eric Blair, Sr., a narcotics agent, was born on July 23, 1903, in Motihari, Bengal. At age four, he and his two sisters, Margaret and Avril, sailed for England, where he entered Eastbourne's St. Cyprian's Boys' School. As a young sahib repatriated to an unfamiliar milieu, he grew uncomfortably aware of British snobbery and sarcastically labeled his family one of the "landless gentry." Homesickness and shame of his chubby frame robbed him of energy and friends. Lonely and asocial, he longed to return to bright colors, warmth, and the welcome of India. While living among the sons of upper-crust families, he came to despise petty elitism and favor-currying as well as minuscule rules that he was frequently accused of breaking. As he describes in the autobiographical *Such, Such Were the Joys* (1953), he escaped the drabness of his new life by retreating into his preferred studies, language and literature, especially his favorite authors, Swift and Kipling. Orwell distinguished himself at age 11 by publishing a poem about the death of Field Marshal Kitchener, a British hero. A promising student, Orwell won scholarships to Eton and Winchester and chose Eton, where Aldous Huxley was a member of the staff.

During World War I, Orwell, a diligent reader and debater, preferred pacifist and socialist issues. Although labeled a leftist and rebel, he kept his distance from overtly anticonservative politics. He chose a career in social service and rose to the rank of sergeant in the Burmese police. In *Burmese Days* (1934), he summarizes the depravity of the job that quickly exhausted youthful enthusiasm, leaving each officer nursing "a wrecked liver and a pine-apple backside from sitting in cane chairs":

> And what debauchery! They swilled whisky which they privately hated, they stood round the piano bawling songs of insane filthiness and silliness, they squandered rupees by the hundred on aged Jewish whores with the faces of crocodiles. That too had been a formative period.

In the latter chapters, he observes that a combination of the effects of despotism often forced officers to commit suicide, an event that provoked little remark or internal investigation.

An unwilling "pukka sahib," Orwell obviously despised the assignment, as demonstrated by his much anthologized essay, "Shooting an Elephant" (1950), in which he penned a caustic slam at Queen Victoria, symbol of the empire, in the collapsing bulk of a "grandmotherly" elephant:

> He looked suddenly stricken, shrunken, immensely old, as though the frightful impact of the bullet had paralyzed him . . . he sagged flabbily to his knees. His mouth slobbered. An enormous senility seemed to have settled upon him.

The awful truth of a white man policing an alien district of southern Burma settled in with the awareness that the elephant was worth more than the coolie it had mangled. By January 1927, Orwell so disliked the racism implicit in service to arrogant British imperialists that, while on leave in England, he telegraphed his resignation from the imperial police force and took up writing. While wandering France and Great Britain, he adopted the pen name George Orwell from an English river.

Influenced by Jack London's *The People of the Abyss* (1903), Orwell expiated his guilt at his role in subjugating Asians. To study the low end of the working class, he drifted through menial jobs in pub kitchens and slept in sheepcots and cheap slum hostels. By 1933, these humbling experiences provided him material for *Down and Out in Paris and London* (1933). Over the next three years, he published three unprofitable titles—*Burmese Days, A Clergyman's Daughter* (1935), and *Keep the Aspidistra Flying* (1936)—while teaching at Hawthorne High School for Boys in Hayes, Middlesex, and clerking part time in a Hampstead book store. In 1936, Orwell wed Eileen O'Shaughnessy, a journalist and teacher. During the late 1930s, the couple operated a pub and grocery in Wallington, Hertfordshire.

On a trip to a depressed industrial area in Manchester, financed by Jewish scholar Israel Gollancz, founder of the Left Book Club, an anti-Fascist, anti-Nazi publishing house, Orwell kept a diary in the early months of 1937. These writings evolved into *The Road to Wigan Pier* (1937), a humorless overview of his political views on joblessness and other discouraging realities faced by unskilled laborers. In his political commentary, he wrote that all avenues of society—work, finance, religion, education, marriage, and family—are political and that no one can avoid political issues. To Orwell, politics, with its basis in untruth, evasion, foolishness, animosity, and schizophrenia, was untrustworthy and more than a shade dishonorable.

As Europe entered a troubled age, Orwell joined Spain's POUM, a Marxist Republican militia fighting Generalissimo Francisco Franco and fascism, and served as war correspondent. In June 1937, after five months at the Aragon front, Orwell caught a sniper's bullet in the throat. He recovered from paralysis and aphasia and continued writing anti-fascist propaganda but discovered that his libertarian beliefs were out of favor as communism gained power. Fearful of a purge led by Communist hardliners, he and his wife fled across the Pyrenees mountains to France and thence to England and settled on a Hertfordshire farm, where he raised hens and grew vegetables until Nazi bombings drove him out. As a result of their escape from imminent execution, Orwell channeled his intense anticommunism into *Homage to Catalonia* (1938) and a nostalgic yearning for the English ideal in *Coming Up for Air* (1939), his first successful novel.

Orwell's socialistic beliefs gained strength and bolstered his literary career. He composed "As I Please," a literary column for the *London Tribune*, and published *Inside the Whale and Other Essays* (1940), *The Lion and the Unicorn: Socialism and the English Genius* (1940), and freelance critiques and articles in other journals and newspapers. Abandoning his characteristic humanism after Axis powers overran eastern Europe, he sought a commission in the army but was declared ineligible because of consumptive lungs. He enlisted in the national militia, served the BBC as their Indian editor, edited the left-wing *Tribune*, and made antitotalitarian broadcasts overseas.

The most lucrative portion of Orwell's career began at the end of the war, when he wrote his classic Swiftian satire, *Animal Farm*, an internationally bestselling fantasy novel incorporating his experiences at Wallington. So uncompromising was his dystopian beast fable that it went unpublished for a year until Orwell could locate a company willing to tackle anti-authoritarianism. While polishing *Dickens, Dali, and Others: Studies in Popular Culture* in 1946, he suffered a worsening of his tuberculosis and the unexpected death of Eileen during a routine hysterectomy.

Although grief-stricken, terminally ill, and frequently bedridden, Orwell elected to keep his adopted infant, Richard Horatio. With the help of a sister, the family settled off Scotland's west coast at Barnhill on Jura, Argylls, a windswept, isolated island of the Inner Hebrides. He recognized the brevity of his time, and in January 1949, before hospitalization at a sanitarium in Gloucestershire, England, he completed *1984*, a dispirited dystopian classic that he originally intended to call *The Last Man in Europe*. During a brief rally in strength, he detailed the indignities of the English boarding school system. In a final attempt to reestablish life and health, he wed Sonia Mary Brownell in 1949. Within months, as he made plans to retire to a Swiss sanitarium, he collapsed, sick and exhausted from recurrent lung hemorrhage.

On his deathbed Orwell asked that no biography be written about him. He composed both his will and an understated epitaph:

Here Lies
Eric Arthur Blair
Born June 25th 1903
Died January 21st 1950

In a rural churchyard in the village of Sutton Courtenay, his remains lie buried near the end of an avenue of yews.

A master of nonfiction, he was ironically hailed as the era's famed novelist. His needle-sharp epigrams continue to express his journalistic power:

- One could not even dignify him with the name of stuffed shirt. He was simply a hole in the air.

- The great enemy of clear language is insincerity.

- The object of persecution is persecution. The object of torture is torture. The object of power is power.

- God save us from self-pity!

- Everyone is free in England; we sell our souls in public and buy them back in private, among our friends. But even friendship can hardly exist when every white man is a cog in the wheels of despotism.

His essays, polemics, and correspondence were gathered into four volumes, which were published in 1968. Both *Animal Farm* and *1984* were filmed in 1955: the former as an unsuccessful cartoon diatribe, the latter as a drama starring Michael Redgrave and Edmond O'Brien. A reprise in 1984, starring John Hurt and Richard Burton, deviated from Orwell's antitotalitarian intent. (Buitehuis and Nadel 1988; Crick 1980; *Discovering Authors* 1993; Ferrell 1988; Gardner 1987; Miller 1989; Orwell 1946, 1958, 1962, 1983, 1984; Reilly 1989)

See also Animal Farm; diatribe; epigram; satire; Shaw, George Bernard; Swift, Jonathan; Voltaire, François.

PARKER, DOROTHY

Viking Press's *Portable Dorothy Parker* (1944) holds a singular distinction: along with Shakespeare and the Bible, it is the only Viking edition that has remained in continuous print. One of U.S. literature's most misunderstood satirists, Dorothy Parker, author of ironic light verse and short fiction, lived a public life of cynical gaiety and bohemianism conducted at regular Round Table lunches in the dining room of New York's Algonquin Hotel. Of herself, her sexuality, and her taste for Haig and Haig, she noted, "They say of me, and so they should,/ It's doubtful if I come to good."

Parker's deceptively flippant writing presaged the feminism of the 1960s with examinations of the emptiness of women's lives, hypocrisy between the sexes, and women's self-destruction from dependence on men for money and self-esteem. In a 1928 essay for the *New Yorker*, Parker expressed her sympathy with society's victims, saying of Isadora Duncan's bravura self-expression, "There was never a place for her in the ranks of the terrible, slow army of the cautious. She ran ahead, where there were no paths." Much at home with cynicism, according to a memoir by Somerset Maugham, she wrote off-the-cuff at a dinner party:

> Higgledy Piggledy, my white hen;
> She lays eggs for gentlemen.
> You cannot persuade her with gun or lariat
> To come across for the proletariat.

In private, her exhibitionism gave place to intense unhappiness, alcoholism, and suicidal thoughts generated by low self-image and debilitating bouts of depression and loneliness.

Born Dorothy Rothschild on August 22, 1893, in West End near Long Branch, New Jersey, she was the last of four children of teacher Elizabeth A. "Eliza" Marston and J. Henry Rothschild, a Talmudic scholar, clothing merchant, and factory manager. Along with brothers Harry and Bert and sister Helen, Dorothy grew up at 57 West 68th Street in New York City. After her mother's death in 1898 and her father's remarriage, Parker was forced to attend the exclusive Blessed Sacrament Academy and eluded an unhappy relationship with her starchy Scotch Presbyterian stepmother by cultivating impertinent rejoinders and asides, which became her trademark. Having been expelled for ridiculing the concept of immaculate conception as "spontaneous combustion," she attended Miss Dana's Seminary, a prestigious bastion for polite young ladies in Morristown, New Jersey.

Following her father's death in 1913, Parker, left penniless, played the piano at a dancing school, penned verses for the *Saturday Evening Post*, and wrote captions for *Vogue* before establishing her prominence as drama and book critic. Beginning as critic for *Vanity Fair* and *Ainslee's* in the late 1910s, she was fired from her early jobs because of her caustic reviews. She then launched the "Constant Reader" column of the *New Yorker*, a new effort and the least restrictive role for a flamboyant wit. Also enticing to an exacting writer, the magazine became an open venue for her short stories, which depict the hypocrisy that slaughters hope and love.

In June 1917, Parker gained a gentile surname by marrying Connecticut financier Edwin "Eddie" Pond Parker II. Because of his emotional trauma, morphine addiction, and alcoholism exacerbated by experiences in France during World War I, Eddie was an unsuitable mate for a restless, profane, amoral woman like Dorothy, whose love affairs were casual, brief, and predictable and whose consumption of alcohol was legendary. One peccadillo—a torrid fling with playboy Charlie MacArthur—left her pregnant and hopeless. The resultant abortion filled her with guilt that she had waited until the fetus had fully formed; she attempted suicide by slashing her wrists. Unrepentant, however, she alternately cuckolded, abandoned, and, in 1928, discarded husband Eddie. Free to swing with the expatriates, she traveled France with Ernest Hemingway, her literary idol, and joined the entourage of F. Scott and Zelda Fitzgerald at their seaside villa in Cap d'Antibes on the French Riviera, the watering spot of an urbane, inconstant flock. She returned to New York with worldly experience but an easily wounded ego that regularly leaned on superficial support.

During her 32-year career at the *New Yorker*, Parker refined her satiric gift and produced a first poetry collection, *Enough Rope* (1926). She began writing freelance, sometimes living on the dole of friends. Her next three verse collections, *Sunset Gun* (1928), *Death and Taxes* (1931), and *Not So Deep as a Well* (1936), contributed to her reputation for spare, lacerating humor and achieved a rare distinction for poetry by becoming bestsellers. A wickedly brash but tidy aphorist, she achieved name recognition for sprinkling *bons mots* in her own epitaph ("Excuse my dust") and in these lines:

- Men seldom make passes
  At girls who wear glasses.

- The humorist has never been happy anyhow. Today he's whistling past worse graveyards to worse tunes.

- She whose body's young and cool
  Has no need of dancing school.

American satirist Dorothy Parker in 1932

- Brevity is the soul of lingerie.

- Every love's the love before in a duller dress.

- The two most beautiful words in the English language are "check enclosed."

- It's not the tragedies that kill us, it's the messes.

- [She] ran the gamut of emotion from A to B.

- Scratch a king and find a fool.

- One more drink and I'll be under the host.

- This is not a novel to be tossed aside lightly. It should be thrown with great force.

- You can't teach an old dogma new tricks.

- The affair between Margot Asquith and Margot Asquith will live as one of the prettiest love stories in all literature.

Housed in a hotel room in lieu of a permanent home, she composed the 1929 O. Henry Award–winning "Big Blonde," "A Telephone Call," and other stories that appear in *Laments for the Living* (1930), *After Such Pleasures* (1933), and *Here Lies* (1939).

In 1933, Parker sought a revived career in Hollywood scriptwriting and collaborated with her second—and third—husband, actor Alan Campbell, on the 1937 version of *A Star Is Born*, which won an Oscar nomination for script. Her seventeen forgettable scripts crowd the only other notable one, *The Little Foxes* (1941), for which lead writer Lillian Hellman got an Oscar nomination and all the credit. The heady days of high wages afforded Alan and Dorothy a Beverly Hills mansion and a getaway in Bucks County, Pennsylvania, which in 1935 served her during recovery from a miscarriage.

In 1937, Parker, a devout left-winger, ventured into war coverage, sailed with Alan to Spain, and covered the Spanish Civil War for the Communist journal the *Masses*. During the McCarthy era, her support of communism in the 1930s and an arrest in Boston for singing the "Internationale" to protest the execution of Sacco and Vanzetti cost her future assignments after her name appeared on the dread Hollywood blacklist of 1949. Three failed plays—*Close Harmony* (1924), *The Coast of Illyria* (1949), and *Ladies of the Corridor* (1963)— convinced her that dramatist and drama critic are distinctly different skills, the latter being more to her taste. A widow sunk in pessimism and bitterness after her husband's apparent suicide, she mourned the loss of her best friend, Robert Benchley, and consoled herself with a reliance on S. J. Perelman, who adored and attended "Dorrie" at her physical and emotional worst. After drying out at a rehabilitation hospital, she attempted a new entry into fiction in 1958 with a short stint as reviewer for *Esquire,* then ceased to write, battled increasing debt, and died alone—except for poodle C'est Tout—in her Upper East Side suite in the Volney Hotel on June 7, 1967.

Few cronies survived from her coterie; Dorothy Parker had designated friend Lillian Hellman as executor. Hellman and Zero Mostel spoke briefly at a funeral service that Parker insisted not be held; 150 mourners attended and listened to Bach's "Air on a G-String," a title she had found amusing. The *New York Times* printed a lengthy obituary, citing her wide readership and fame as a wit and Hollywood scriptwriter. She willed her private papers and $20,000 to Dr. Martin Luther King, Jr., and the NAACP. Her lawyers mailed her ashes to NAACP headquarters in Baltimore for interment in the memorial gardens. (Broun 1991; Buck 1992; Davidson and Wagner-Martin 1995; Ehrlich and Carruth 1982; Frewin 1986; Hart 1983; Katz 1982; Keats 1970; Maggio 1992; Meade 1987; Parker 1976, 1994; Perkins 1991; Time-Life Books, 1969)

See also Algonquin Club; epigram; satire.

 # PARODY

A keen, creative form of mimicry or indirect commentary, parody, which is similar to political cartoons and caricature, derives from the Greek for "false song" and parallels the tone, diction, style, or themes of a serious work to create incongruity, disparagement, or dissonance. A clever, often spitefully cutting method of ridiculing or lampooning pompous or erudite authors, actors, or notables, parody derides words, situations, sentimentality, posturing, and overblown rhetoric through exaggeration or misapplication—by casting as animals, for example, in the place of the self-important, which is the essence of Walt Disney's animated film *The Lion King* (1995). Pastiche, a lesser wing of the genre, ignores the substance and imitates only the style of a work, whether writing, dance, fashion, decor, or architecture, as with the numerous send-ups of the *pas de deux* and *corps de ballet* scenes in Peter Ilyich Tchaikovsky's *Swan Lake*.

One of the earliest parodies, the anonymous and undated *Batrachomyomachia* [*The Battle of the Frogs and Mice*] (sixth century B.C.), carries to epic extremes Athena's war on vermin in a comic spoof of Homer's *Iliad*. Both Plato and Aristophanes succeeded with parody, as did the Roman poet Catullus and satirists Lucian and Petronius Arbiter, author of *The Satyricon* (A.D. 60), a matchless Roman parody of manners and epic lore whittled down by time to only 1 of 16 books. Less interested in secular life, medieval parodists found pompous prelates, with their over-refined mannerisms, licentiousness, and pseudo-scholasticism, to be a natural target and filled miracle plays with witty put-downs. Geoffrey Chaucer's tedious, meandering "Tale of Sir Thopas" (1387), a brief, self-denigrating interpolated scene in the *Canterbury Tales*, prefigures the mock romantic so nimbly lampooned in the Renaissance by François Rabelais's *Gargantua and Pantagruel* (1532) and Miguel de Cervantes's *Don Quixote* (1615).

Perhaps a true test of an author's significance, the parody aims at the great to bring them low. The English Renaissance produced its idiosyncratic mockery—William Shakespeare ridiculing John Lyly, Christopher Marlowe skewering Shakespeare, and Sir John Suckling reprising the ponderous John Donne. The venerable John Milton met his detractor in John Philips's *The Splendid Shilling* (1701); John Dryden's *The Conquest of Granada* fell to the buffoonery of George Villiers's *The Rehearsal* (1671). The eighteenth and nineteenth centuries continued the one-upmanship of writer-parodist with Henry Fielding's *Shamela* (1741) deriding Samuel Richardson's *Pamela* (1740). More recent times have inspired a curious lot of funsters: Lewis Carroll's mockery of Henry Wadsworth Longfellow's tortuous meter and drawn-out images in *Hiawatha* (1855), John Squire's parody of Thomas Gray's *Elegy Written in a Country Churchyard* (1751), John Gardner's ribbing of *Beowulf* with *Grendel* (1971), and Monty Python's screenplay on the Holy Grail ridiculing Arthurian lore.

Children's literature, also a source of classics restated in comic exaggeration or burlesque, appeals to readers who respond to old beast fables or fairy tales retold from an updated point of view. *The True Story of the Three Little Pigs!* (1989), Jon Scieszka's witty reworking of "The Three Little Pigs," allows Alexander T. "Al" Wolf to give his version of life as a carnivore and to explain why meat-eaters devour sheep, rabbits, and pigs. While baking a cake for his granny, Al runs out of sugar and goes a-borrowing to the homes of neighboring pigs. By chance, Al has a sneezy cold and unintentionally blows away the first two neighbors. Being a meat-eater, he can't waste the pork he finds in the rubble, so he devours the first two pigs.

Scieszka produces the appropriate motivation for destruction by creating a "Your old lady wears army boots" face-off. The third house, made of bricks, is the residence of a rude pig who refuses to give the wolf the needed sugar and yells, "And your old granny can sit on a pin!" Al decides that such rudeness deserves the brunt of his anger. In retrospect, Al declares that the media "jazzed up the story" to create a big and bad image. In breezy style, Al, now serving time in the "pig penn," concludes, "That's it. The real story. I was framed." The retelling has its purpose: it exposes children to one of the facts of modern life— the power of the press.

In 1992, Jon Scieszka and Lane Smith teamed up in a clever parody of fairy tales and bookmaking called *The Stinky Cheese Man and Other Fairly Stupid Tales*. In addition to parodied tales, the book contains a title page marked "Title Page," an upside-down dedication page with space left blank for the reader to designate the dedicatee, and a copy of the surgeon general's warning on cigarette packs, which the authors tailor to the humor of their whimsical book. The tale of Chicken Licken, which parodies Chicken Little's misadventures, describes the familiar panic of the bird who surmises that the sky is falling. On the way to warn the president, Chicken Licken gathers the usual entourage—Ducky Lucky, Goosey Loosey, and Cocky Locky. The narrator interrupts to warn that he forgot to print the table of contents, but the trail of fowl hurry to catch a plane to Washington. The characters make a poor judgment call when they encounter Foxy Loxy, who escorts them to his cave to eat them. The birds elude the fox but die anyway because the table of contents collapses and crushes all of them. The silliness of the parody engages and entertains young readers while completing a didactic purpose—explaining the parts of a book, displaying a variety of fonts and point sizes, and rehashing a funky version of the Little Red Hen. (Abrams 1971; Barnet, Berman, and Burto 1960; Cuddon 1984; Drabble 1985; Feinberg 1967; Gray 1992; Hadas 1954; Hammond and Scullard 1992; Henry 1995; Holman and Harmon 1992; McArthur 1992; Mantinband 1956; Scieszka 1989; Scieszka and Smith 1992)

See also Aristophanes; *Canterbury Tales;* Catullus; Cervantes Saavedra, Miguel de; Chaucer, Geoffrey; *Don Quixote; Gargantua and Pantagruel;* Petronius; Rabelais, François; Richardson, Samuel; satire; *Satyricon;* whimsy.

PERSIUS

A painstaking satirist who lacked the sparkle of Horace and the prolixity of Lucan, Persius remains on the second tier of satirists behind front-benchers Martial and Juvenal. For much of Persius's biography, historians turn to Suetonius. Born Aulus Persius Flaccus in Volterra, Etruria, in A.D. 34, he enjoyed the privilege of Etruscan equestrian status and studied under the best, Remmius Palaemon, Verginius, and Lucius Annaeus Cornutus, Lucan's instructor. Along with the poet Lucan and his friend Thrasea Paetus, a firm-minded consul of the old school, Persius studied stoicism and imitated the rhetoric of Horace and Lucilius. He adopted the unassuming, mild-mannered air of the dedicated scholar with a touch of the bold, nostalgic mourners of Rome's heyday, the Republic, which had ended in a massive, decade-long civil purge beginning in 44 B.C. with the assassination of Julius Caesar.

Persius's major works, published in *libelli* (pamphlets), tended toward diatribe and ironic hexameters interrupted by digression; a minor travelogue is lost in antiquity. Smug in his boyish thrill at achieving fame early in his career, he smirks:

> But, sure, 'tis pleasant, as we walk, to see
> The pointed finger, hear the loud "That's he,"
> On every side:—and seems it, in your sight,
> So poor a trifle, that whate'er we write
> Is introduced to every school of note,
> And taught the youth of quality by rote?

Hampered by tendencies toward personal reflections on the era ("Let them look upon virtue and pine because they have lost her"), motherly advice ("Challenge disease at the first sign"), and pious sermonizing ("Explain, priests, the purpose of gold in a holy place"), Persius often mystified his readers with indecipherable sentiments. An iconoclast at heart, he challenged the public to abandon polished niceties written by purple-clad imperial poetasters and to respond wholeheartedly to lusty verse.

Persius died young in A.D. 62, afflicted with an unspecified stomach ailment, leaving two million sesterces to his sister and mother, unpublishable works for Cornutus to destroy, and a farewell letter to his mother. His friend

Caesius Bassus gathered up his six satires—which Perseus characterizes as "tasting of chewed nails"—and edited and published them. *The Satirae* (ca. A.D. 63), rich with portraiture, achieved a modicum of demand and the support of Martial, his admirer; however, the contrived versification, awkward caesura, common street Latin, and ponderous allusions lessened his impact. Because Persius distanced theme and subject from later generations, readers and translators wrestled with the burden of his personal remarks:

> O yet suppress this carping mood.
> Impossible! I could not if I would;
> For nature framed me of satiric mold,
> And spleen, too petulant to be controlled.

Much valued in the Middle Ages, Persius also influenced the works of John Donne and John Dryden. (Drabble 1985; Feder 1986; Godolphin 1949; Hadas 1954; Hammond and Scullard 1992; Hornstein 1973; Howatson 1989; Mantinband 1956; Radice 1973)

See also diatribe; Dryden, John; epigram; Horace; Juvenal; Martial; Petronius; satire.

 # PETRONIUS

Possibly Rome's most admired Epicurean and slyest peep-and-tell novelist, Gaius (or Titus) Petronius Arbiter Niger appears to have led a double existence: in public, he was Petronius Arbiter, Nero's *arbiter elegantiae* (protocol officer or judge of good taste); in the privacy of his office, Petronius Arbiter was the word-charged, punning scribbler of the ancient world's dirty little classic, the *Satyricon* (A.D. 60). Judging by the scarcity of other people named Arbiter and the time in which the book was published, critics tend to believe that Nero's courtly Petronius and the author were the same person. Born in Massilia (Marseilles on the French Riviera) around A.D. 20, Petronius carried little personal baggage into the public forum. Of Petronius's public career, Tacitus assures the reader that Petronius stood out from the ordinary in polish and sophistication, although he was inclined to yawn at the ordinary entertainments that no longer satisfied his jaded palate. The remains of some lyrics and elegies bear little evidence of the masterwork for which Petronius earned his place among satirists.

Deliberately patronizing the bizarre whims of a Nero, a demented emperor, Petronius rose rapidly in the imperial inner circle and served as consul and as governor to Bithynia, west of modern Turkey on the south shore of the Black Sea. As one might expect in a political situation so unstable as the degenerate Roman Empire, the poet trod tenuous ground and, as the emperor's cat's paw, performed deeds fated to cost him his life at the height of his writing career. With the completion of the *Satyricon*, his book of satyrs, he fell in with or was implicated with Piso, a failed conspirator who plotted to kill the emperor.

Petronius, who was betrayed by the oily, fawning Ofonius Tigellinus, a shifty Praetorian honor guardsman who bettered his chances of political appointment by citing the Pisonian cabal for treason, decoded the fearful message from Nero to wait at the official coastal spa at Cumae until the emperor could return from Campania.

Adept at Roman scheming, Petronius, waggishly dubbed the "author of the purest impurities," may have suffered from knowing too much: for a certainty, he knew that stalling would not offset the emperor's displeasure and fabled vengeance. Discreetly as he lived, he opened his veins and bled to death, but not before smashing a valuable murrhine vase to keep it out of Nero's greedy mitts. Tacitus's *Annals* (A.D. 66) summarize, "Within a few days, indeed, there perished in one and the same batch, Annaeus Mela, Cerialis Anicius, Rufius Crispinus and Petronius." At the public disclosure in 65 A.D., poets Lucan and Quintilian were likewise obliged to take the Roman way out of scandal by killing themselves. The public, wise in the underhanded ways of Nero's court, raised no outcry.

Appearing in print about the time of Petronius's demise, the *Satyricon* (at first called *Patronii Arbitri Saturicon)* and its bold Chapter 15 entitled "Cena Trimalchionis" ("Trimalchio's Feast") bear the seeds of disenchantment with a bawdy entourage, nonstop fun-seeking, and dreary, aimless drift. As satire, the work epitomizes the aim of instruction through ridicule. Petronius, whom Tacitus accuses of sleeping by day and serving as master of revels each night, may have burned out on the stress of party-hearty fraternity hijinx. Surmise leaves a thousand questions about Petronius's career as Nero's voluptuary and about Tigellinus's jealousy, which may have spawned an egregious lie costing the lives of some of Rome's most talented men. By bribing Petronius's valet, Tigellinus appears to have compounded earlier charges about friendship with the conspirator Scaevinus. The death scene is legendary: opening and closing the slit wrist while carrying on his usual badinage with friends, Petronius appears to have conducted his own Cena Trimalchio with himself as the main course.

Calm to the end, Petronius gave parting gifts and floggings to his staff as merit or fault demanded, recited verse on the question of life after death, mailed to the emperor a personal satire (possibly a copy of the *Satyricon)* ridiculing Nero and his vice-ridden court, and destroyed his signet ring. The substance of epigrams from the *Satyricon* leaves doubt concerning Nero's understanding of Petronius's aims. What did he have to fear from the man who coined such phrases as "Not worth his salt," "My heart was in my mouth," "the great majority," "natural curls," and "One good turn deserves another"? Whatever the reason, when Nero received the satire and news of Petronius's death, he immediately cast out Silia, a senator's wife whose only crime was befriending Petronius. (Drabble 1985; Feder 1986; Godolphin 1949; Hadas 1954; Hammond and Scullard 1992; Hornstein 1973; Howatson 1989; Mantinband 1956; Petronius 1925, 1934; Radice 1973)

See also Lucan; picaresque; pun; satire; *Satyricon.*

PHAEDRUS

One of ancient literature's shadow figures, Phaedrus reveals himself almost entirely through his collection of terse fables, a Greek genre he adapted for a Roman audience. The title of his fragmented collection, *Phaedri, Augusti liberti, fabularum aesopiarum libri* [*The Books of Aesop's fables by Phaedrus, Augustus's Freedman*] (ca. A.D. 48), sums up the world's picture of the compiler. Living in the imperial palace during the establishment of the Roman Empire, the candid narrator appends a note of joy that Aesop, a slave, received a high honor—a statue in Athens. That Phaedrus's own life in bondage was tenuous is obvious in one of the poet's tidbits of personal data: Phaedrus admits having angered Sejanus, Tiberius's untrustworthy Praetorian Guard and personal handler, who was executed in A.D. 31 for plotting against the emperor.

Born in the mountain town of Pieria, Thessaly, around 15 B.C., Phaedrus may have been the son of a teacher, but was transported to Italy at an early age and educated. At some point—either in Thessaly or Rome—he came in contact with an anthology of Aesop's fables, most likely that of Demetrius of Phalerum (fourth century B.C.). Greatly praised by La Fontaine, his own imitator, Phaedrus survived to old age and died around A.D. 50. He readily describes his career as a refiner of Aesop's original verse morality tales, then adds in the prologue to Book 4 that he enlarged Aesop's canon with some stories and anecdotes of his own. Of Phaedrus's published books of *fabella*, five remain; half of the 94 tales are beast fables.

The brief, tightly knit style of Phaedrus's fables demonstrates the skill of the poet both as writer and as translator of Aesop's fables. An example in five lines demonstrates incisive writing at its briefest—one sentence:

> Two bags full of faults have been fitted onto us
> By Jupiter, one weighed down by our own,
> Hanging behind us, the other heavy
> With other people's, plainly pendant
> In front of us, easy for our eyes to observe.

Tales of greed, impetuosity, and self-delusion follow the same pattern, paring satiric lessons into simple, easily digested fables. Their graceful, genteel prologues reveal a refined sensibility and a light touch that professes to amuse by concocting a bit of fun. A humorous thrust at the puffed-up poseur is number 24, "The Frog Who Burst Himself and the Bull," in which a foolhardy frog ignores his limitations and his friends' discouragement and tries to inflate himself to the size of a bull:

> He filled his frame even fuller
> And asked them again, and again the answer
> Was "No." So, baffled and belligerent, he blew
> And blew and blew and blew until he burst.

Begun with a moral, the tale proposes to illustrate presumption, a fatal flaw that leads to ruin.

A bit of pure Phaedrian satire appears in the protracted prologue to Book 3, which the poet directs to his patron Eutychus, a charioteer for the Green team and a workaholic too busy to read. Phaedrus lampoons him with irony that, while attending to studies that will increase his income, Eutychus distances himself from "the mansion of the Muses," a jest on Phaedrus's homeland, Pieria. Phaedrus claims that, from childhood, he has ignored the "lure of money, and . . . lived for art, with Athene's aid." He concludes with a rhetorical question about the fate of people who never satisfy their lust for money. Further on, Phaedrus declares, "My purpose is not to pillory any person, but to illustrate life and the ways of the world," then returns to a bantering tone when he challenges Eutychus to read the poems and offer Phaedrus some "candid criticism."

The publication of Phaedrus's volumes must have received critical attention, which Phaedrus reports as of no concern to him. Unwittingly, while commenting in the prologue to Book 3 on the difficulties of slavery, he defines the nature of satire:

> Slaves are exposed to incessant hazards.
> Unable openly to express what he wanted,
> One of them projected his personal opinions
> Into fictional fables and found shelter
> From carping critics in comic inventions. (Phaedrus 1992, p. xv)

This masked merriment is the fail-safe for the satirist, who conceals a demand for justice and liberty for the oppressed under layers of buffoonery and wit. Concluded with a moral, the stories redeem themselves through didacticism, the cloak that mimics the sugar-coated pill. (Feder 1986; Hadas 1954; Hammond and Scullard 1992; Howatson 1989; Mantinband 1956; Phaedrus 1992; Radice 1973)

See also Aesop; beast lore; didacticism; epigram; pun; satire; trickster; wit.

 # PICARESQUE

Derived from the Latin for "to prick" and the Spanish for "rascal," the picaresque tale or novel focuses on the picaro or picaroon, an unfettered, amoral rogue or endearingly clever trickster often widely versed in thievery, deception, and varying degrees of related crime. Claimed by the Spanish, yet found worldwide in song, lore, and beast fables from the ancient Romans—Petronius's *Satyricon* (A.D. 60) and Apuleius's *The Golden Ass* (ca. A.D. 160)—to modern detective fare and countless soldiers of fortune, the fully developed picaresque novel dates to the sixteenth century and the works of Mateo Alemán, Francisco Quevedo, and Miguel de Cervantes as well as anonymous scribblers, one of whom penned a bestseller, *La Vida de Lazarillo de tormes y de sus fortunas y adversidades* (1554). The French produced a cluster of tales featuring Reynard the fox as well as these works:

- François Rabelais's *Gargantua and Pantagruel* (1564), the latter pair loosely strung together from outlandish misadventures of a giant baby

- Alain-René LeSage's four-volume adventure series *Gil Blas* (1735)

- Voltaire's *Candide* (1759)

English picaroons dominate the works of a number of authors:

- Thomas Nashe's *The Unfortunate Traveller, or The Life of Jack Wilton* (1594)

- Daniel Defoe's *The Fortunes and Misfortunes of the Famous Moll Flanders* (1722)

- Henry Fielding's *Jonathan Wild* (1743) and *Tom Jones* (1749)

- Tobias Smollett's *The Adventures of Roderick Random* (1748), *The Adventures of Peregrine Pickle* (1751), and *Ferdinand, Count Fathom* (1753)

The British romantic and Victorian eras evolved their own brand of picaroon:

- George Byron's *Don Juan* (1824)

- Sir Walter Scott's *Memoirs of Vidoq* (1829)

- William Makepeace Thackeray's *Vanity Fair* (1848) and *Memoirs of Barry Lyndon* (1852)

The modern age has produced an updated slate of picaros, from Ian Fleming's 007 to George Lucas's Indiana Jones and Luke Skywalker.

Picaresque literature obeys an idiosyncratic set of conventions: low-level buffoonery, cliff-hangers, close shaves, near disasters, and outlandish pranks, disguises, or ruses, which may exaggerate scatology, cross-dressing, or sexual detail to vivid and unnecessary lengths. The style tends toward first-person episodic adventure lore or chronicles narrated by a low-class, self-sufficient, but shiftless male, who may speak the prejudices of an underclass, untouchable, or outcast toward the hypocritical overlord or against the peacockery of high society. The novel is often sparsely tied together by a change of scenery, resurrected adversary, or new set of obstacles: a cuckolded husband, robbery victim, indignant mate, or mistaken identity. Thematic or character development is uncharacteristic of the picaresque novel, but realism may present a worldview from the level of the born loser, a prevalent device of T. Coraghessan Boyle's *Water Music* (1982), *East Is East* (1990), and *The Road to Wellville* (1993). (Abrams 1971; Barnet, Berman, and Burto 1960; Cuddon 1984; Drabble 1985; Gray 1992; Henry 1995; Holman and Harmon 1992)

See also *The Adventures of Huckleberry Finn*; Boyle, T. Coraghessan; *Candide*; Cervantes Saavedra, Miguel de; *Gargantua and Pantagruel*; Petronius; Rabelais, François; scatology; trickster.

 # PLATO

A central figure in Greece's Golden Age, Plato was a writer of intriguing dialogues and chronicler of Socrates's humanistic thought on goodness and the best form of education for Athenian aristocrats. The offspring of Perictione and Ariston, the conjunction of two illustrious family lines, Aristocles, nick-named Plato or "broad shoulders," was born in 428 B.C. He received a quality education in music, literature, and mathematics and began writing in his youth. In childhood, he suffered the addition of Pyrilampes, his stepfather, to the family soon after Ariston's death. The close examination of his relatives' and stepfather's political plottings and the tyrannic manipulations of his country's lackluster tyrants following the Peloponnesian War turned Plato away from his initial choice of a career in civil service.

The most grievous lesson of Plato's coming-to-knowledge was the trial of his mentor, Socrates, a selfless teacher accused of sacrilege. The court called 501 jury members to hear the testimony and vote their opinion on charges that Socrates corrupted young minds. Although Plato claims to have been absent because of illness, internal evidence in his writing suggests otherwise. Before impanelment, Socrates declared "either acquit me or not; but whatever you do, know that I shall never alter my ways, not even if I have to die many times." The court found him guilty in a vote of 281 to 220; the charge carried a death penalty. Socrates expressed surprise that the vote was not more one-sided against him. In 399 B.C., after a brief confinement in jail, he was forced to drink a cup of hemlock, after which he calmly lay down and dictated a few minor errands before the poison stopped his heart.

In flight from grief, self, and the hypocrisy of his homeland, Plato visited Megara outside Corinth to soak up wisdom and comfort from Euclid, a phi-losopher and mathematician proclaimed the father of geometry. In the quiet of his friend's library, Plato studied and recomposed his rattled spirit. In his mid-thirties, he served honorably in the military, then settled in Egypt to study astronomy and later in Cyrene to learn mathematics from Theodorus. Disillu-sioned by the disorder and waste of the political arena, Plato pursued the ideal community, a human gathering spot devoted to goodness. Drawing on mysti-cism as his *modus operandi*, the philosopher mused over human interaction with nature. A contrast to the polemical essays of his maturer years, he wrote the *Symposium* (ca. early fourth century B.C.), his venture into satire, which details a night of drinking during which Socrates tries to make sense while other guests pontificate and carouse.

While sojourning with Dionysius I in Syracusa, Sicily, in 388 B.C., Plato so piqued his host's ire with his empirical axioms that he was booted out, lodged on a Spartan freighter, and placed on the auction block in Aegina's slave mar-ket, where the dealer dickered with his friend Anniceris, a Cyrenian, over a suitable price for a useless philosopher. The incident did not deter Plato from his study of lands and peoples. In Tarentum, he met Archytas, the town mayor, who was a student of Pythagorean logic. Plato left southern Italy and returned home. Equipped with a holistic philosophy, he taught at the Academea. At age 41, he opened his own finishing school near Colonus and remained content for 38 years. Students from all parts of the Mediterranean arrived to study logic, astronomy, and Plato's specialty, mathematics. To the illustrious student body, he stressed his one requirement: "No one shall enter who knows no geometry."

During this period of scholarship and self-development, Plato worked on his private crusade, the *Apologia* and *Euthyphro,* a formal vindication of his mentor Socrates written in dialogue form.

After the first two decades at his academy, Plato left on an extended sabbatical to conduct an experiment. Hired in 367 B.C. to tutor Dionysius II, Plato accepted the task and made an agreement with the boy's uncle Dion to produce the world's first philosopher-king, Plato's ideal of the enlightened ruler. The boy proved an unsuitable candidate. Turning on both his tutor and uncle, he accused them of treason and ended his lessons in philosophy. After returning to his school, Plato had but a few years' reprieve from the Sicilian debacle when Dionysius requested his advice on local political discontent. Once more, Plato failed to satisfy the squabbling parties and returned to Greece. Dionysius, in flight from his greedy uncle, settled in Corinth; the next year, he was executed. Plato came under suspicion for meddling in Syracusan politics and wrote two formal letters expressing his innocence. In Plato's absence, Eudoxus, his former pupil, ran the school and pursued the master's passion for mathematics, particularly solid geometry and calculus. Less skilled in astronomy, Eudoxus drew up a complex study of the earth as the center of a universe that swirled planets in orbit around it. His studies in rational hedonism and metaphysics forced Plato to repudiate Eudoxus's teachings by publishing his own theories, *Philebus* and *Parmenides.*

On a return trip to Sicily in his late seventies, Plato complied with the local government by providing them a system of government suited to the Greek colony. Still tinkering with its finer points, Plato died on the island. His canon— 13 epistles and 42 dialogues, some serious, some farcical—remains unharmed; the academy did not fare as well. Against the advice of Xenocrates and Aristotle, directors passed the school to an unworthy successor, Plato's nephew Speusippus, Potone's son. Twelve years later, Xenocrates seized control and remained principal until 314 B.C. Plato's academy survived until A.D. 529, when the emperor Justinian closed it. Still, the light of Plato's search for truth continued into future generations; his utopian masterpiece, the *Politeia (Republic* or *State)* influenced Aristotle, Alexander the Great, Plotinus, St. Augustine, Immanuel Kant, Friedrich Nietzsche, and Husserl. (Feder 1986; Flaceliere 1962; Hadas 1954; Hammond and Scullard 1992; Hornstein 1973; Howatson 1989; Plato 1956; Radice 1973; Snodgrass 1988; Warner 1958)

See also Aristophanes; farce; parody; satire.

PLAUTUS

The strongest voice in Rome's early period (514–240 B.C.), the playwright Plautus performed a major literary service in introducing the fledgling Roman audience to Greek comedy. Influenced by new comedy (320–250 B.C.) and the works of Philemon, Diphilus, Apollodorus, Alexis, and Menander, Plautus created his own zany theatrical farces, initiating Rome's considerable contribution to the world of satire and simultaneously preserving what little remains of Menander's comic style, now lost except for fragments. A difficult figure to trace, Titus Maccius Plautus was probably born poor in Sarsina, Umbria, around 254 B.C. and may have taken a pseudonym from "Mac the Clown," the classic Roman jester. According to Aulus Gellius, the playwright arrived in Rome in boyhood and sought a career in entertainment, probably as a stagehand or carpenter. After losing his bankroll in an all-or-nothing investment in trade, he took a job hauling sacks in a flour mill and wrote when he found time.

Already a gifted mime, Plautus drew on trusted stagecraft and wrote three hit shows. Spread over his 25-year career were notable successes, including *Stichus* (200 B.C.), a preface to the plebeian games, and *Pseudolus* (191 B.C.), the evening's entertainment preceding dedication of the Magna Mater, a temple on the Palatine. All guesses at his output are academic; only 20 complete plays survive. Classed as Romanized Greek drama, his *fabulae palliatae* ("stories dressed in Greek cloaks") center on the working-class spirit and vernacular. Fleshed out with country dance, *cantica* (complex recitative), myth, caricature, ribald jokes and pranks, slapstick and pratfalls, farce, parallel plots, and traditional festival fare, Plautus's canon maintains the guise of Greek place- names, but reflects the earthy, often risqué good times of Rome's formative years. One of his characteristic devices is the creation of outlandish caricature names, such as Vaniloquidorus Verginesvendonides Nugiepiloquides Argentumextenebronides Tedigniloquides Nugides Palponides Quodsemelarripides Numquameripides ("Blabberodorus Maidvendorovich Lightchatterson Cashcreweroutstein Ibn Saidwhatyoudeserve MacTrifle McBlarney Whatonceyougetyourhandson Neverpartwithitski"). Occasionally true to Greek decorum, he swelled his chorus in verbal mayhem and may have resorted to masks to exaggerate emotions, but he carefully shielded the viewer by removing all physical violence offstage. Hints of greater literary capabilities and a bent for improvisation appear in frequent malapropisms, witty repartee, alliteration, parody of Roman customs, blended accents, original flute accompaniment, tragicomic themes in *Amphytrion*, didacticism in *Rudens*, and the acrostic verse that initiates *Captivi [The Captives]*.

Playing to the balcony by lacing scenes with vaudevillian patter and amusements, Plautus knew how to draw the crowds, as evidenced by revivals of *Menaechmi [The Twin Menaechmi]*, *Captivi*, and *Amphytrion*, the playwright's big three. His inclusion of a curtain call and concluding verse in straightforward appeal to the audience appears at the end of *Captivi*:

> Spectatores, ad pudicos mores facta haec fabulast,
> Neque in hac subigitationes sunt neque ulla amatio
> Nec pueri suppositio nec argenti circumductio,
> Neque ubi amans adulescens scortum liberet clam suum patrem.
> Huius modi paucas poetae reperiunt comedias,
> Ubi boni meliores fiant. Nunc vos, si vobis placet,
> Et si placuimus neque odio fuimus, signum hoc mittite,
> Qui pudicitae esse voltis praemium: plausum date.
> [Viewers, this tale was composed according to pure standards,

There were no strong-arm tactics nor love affair
Nor coercion of youths nor payoffs,
Nor did any young swain solicit a strumpet in secret from his father.
Poets write few comedy in this style,
Such that the good become better. Now you, if you choose,
And if we have pleased and not bored you, give us a sign,
As a reward for virtue: clap hands!]

Plautus need not have asked for the obvious. The country's gratitude is evident in the playwright's achievement of Roman citizenship, a significant status in his day, and in the great gap he left unfilled by writers of equal felicity and stature.

At his death in 184 B.C., Plautus had earned an honorable spot for the comic playwright among Rome's statesmen, moralists, and orators. As boastful as Roman culture permitted, he inscribed his own epitaph as though composing stage directions:

Postquam est mortem aptus Plautus, comedia luget
Scaena est deserta ac dein risus, ludus, iocusque
Et numeri innumeri simul omnes collacrumarunt.
[After the clever Plautus dies, comedy mourns,
the stage is deserted, and then laughter, fun, and joking
and countless stanzas in a single chorus break into tears.]

His works maintained their appeal for over five hundred years, prompted Julius Caesar to praise their comic energy, and influenced the comedy writers who followed. Owing thanks to Plautus are Italy's *commedia dell'arte*, Molière, Nicholas Udall, William Shakespeare, John Gay, Ben Jonson, John Dryden, and the rollicking stagecraft of Thomas Heywood and Jean Giraudoux. Likewise a fan, Henry VIII called for two revivals in 1526. (Bermel 1982; Feder 1986; Gassner and Quinn 1969; Godolphin 1949; Hadas 1954; Hammond and Scullard 1992; Hornstein 1973; Howatson 1989; Mantinband 1956; Plautus 1900; Radice 1973)

See also The Beggar's Opera; caricature; comedy; *commedia dell'arte*; didacticism; Dryden, John; farce; *A Funny Thing Happened on the Way to the Forum*; Gay, John; Menander; Molière; parody; satire; Shakespeare, William; slapstick; Terence; wit.

POLITICAL SATIRE

A daily reminder that satire lives outside books, the stage, and electronic media, political satire keeps alive the greatest hope of the satirist: that the object of ridicule—whether Lucrezia Borgia, Adolf Hitler, Idi Amin, Evita Peron, or Everyman—will acknowledge the pointed ridicule in an essay, song, editorial, comic strip, or cartoon and will alter inappropriate behavior. During extended periods of public scandal, political satire informs and entertains newspaper readers and electronic news purveyors with witty putdowns, saucy revelations, and sobering reminders that unchecked villainy, ranging from public exhibitionism to mass crime, by nature of its harm or contagion, becomes everyone's business. Writers and artists Andy Rooney, Molly Ivins, Thomas Nast, Ellen Goodman, Gary Larson, Doug Marlette, Florence King, and Erma Bombeck each have had their say over a period of public unrest at the extramarital affairs of the Prince of Wales, the misdirection of the O. J. Simpson trial, the venality of the Iran-Contra cover-up, and the folly of such lotharios and self-promoters as Senator Bob Packwood, entrepreneur Donald Trump, and televangelists Jim and Tammy Bakker. The media wits achieve an impact by speaking to the confusion or dismay of society at unfolding stages in the situation, from the height of crisis to resolution and afterthought. Long after the danger is past, it is the political satirist's responsibility to keep alive the outrage that prevents future bounders and brigands from invading government, entertainment, education, religion, and private life.

The eighteenth century, one of Europe's liveliest periods of public commentary, provoked the print caricatures of Arthur Pond, George Townshend's comic portraits for the *London Magazine* and *Town and Country,* Hogarth's delightful prints, Voltaire's classic *Candide* (1759), and spirited public debate of manners, morals, and political practices that permeated a century of unrest. As a means of sounding out thought on a variety of issues, the chief authority on language and a regular fulminator at the Literary Club, Doctor Samuel Johnson allied himself with thoughtful men—statesman Edmund Burke, painter Joshua Reynolds, actor David Garrick, playwrights Oliver Goldsmith and Richard Sheridan, and friend and biographer James Boswell. After nine years' work, Johnson published a satiric *Dictionary of the English Language* (1755), one of the high points of the era. His compilation of 40,000 entries sold so well that he issued five editions during his life.

Unlike current dictionaries, Johnson's whimsical, sardonic commentary was meant to standardize spelling and usage and to stimulate thought on difficult issues for which no consensus existed:

- Oats: a grain which in England is generally given to horses, but in Scotland supports the people.

- Pension: In England it is generally understood to mean pay given to a state hireling for treason to his country.

- Tory: one who adheres to the ancient constitution of the State and the apostolical hierarchy of the Church of England; opposed to a Whig.

- Whig: the name of a faction.

The satiric twist of Johnson's political commentary indicates his sympathy with Scottish poverty and disapproval of paying pensions to civil servants suspected of disloyalty, along with a humorous swipe at one-sidedness in categorizing political parties.

More open-handed a slur on political matters is Max Beerbohm's "Ballade Tragique à Double Refrain" (1910), a blatant—and unsigned—comic dialogue between two unidentified staff members in the household of King George and Queen Mary. The Lord-in-Waiting declares:

> Slow pass the hours—ah, passing slow!
>   My doom is worse than anything
> Conceived by Edgar Allan Poe:
>   The Queen is duller than the King.

In a brisk riposte, the Lord-in-Waiting insists:

> Lady, your mind is wandering:
>   You babble what you do not mean.
> Remember, to your heartening,
>   The King is duller than the Queen.

The badinage continues for six stanzas, ending with a blending of voices in an uproarious murder-suicide. To prove his point, the lord stabs the lady, drinks strychnine, and claims his martyrdom to a single belief that "the King-is-duller than—the Queen." The upshot of Beerbohm's wry mockery was the delay of his knighthood for two decades.

The Victorian era yielded one of England's greatest contributions to caricature—*Punch*, an anti-Albert vehicle that lampooned the amateurish dabbling of a German prince in English architecture and design. Begun in 1841, *Punch* employed Henry Mayhew, Richard Doyle, John Tenniel, Harry Furniss, and novelist William Makepeace Thackeray as prickers of the self-important, whom weekly woodcuts lampooned without mercy. On the other side of the Atlantic, Thomas Nast, the U.S. giant of cartooning, established his niche at *Harper's* and rose to fame as the victimizer of a succession of scoundrels, grifters, wardheelers, and boobs who figured in President Grant's venal administration. It was Nast who solidified the American image of Santa Claus and established the elephant and donkey as symbols of the Republican and Democratic parties, respectively.

U.S. writers, though lacking a royal family to ridicule, have suffered no absence of subjects for satire. In 1846, James Russell Lowell began a series of verse satires in a somewhat tedious unlettered dialect for the *Boston Courier*. His subject, the unpopular Mexican War, received the scorn of his comic persona, Hosea Biglow, a Massachusetts farmer, and Hosea's friend, Birdofredom Sawin. The nine-letter series featured an antiphonal satiric voice in the editorial commentary of Homer Wilbur, pastor of the First Church in Jaalam. The second political satire series, which contains Latinate doggerel and was published in the *Atlantic Monthly* during the Civil War, takes a Union slant in the burlesque of Confederate politics and the unmanageable muddle caused by Reconstruction.

In recent times, satire has teamed with cartooning to produce some of the United States' most distinctive political lampooning. In October 1952, Harvey Kurtzman lobbed the first issue of *Mad*, a comic book produced by Bill Elder, Wally Wood, and Jack Davis that departed from animal caricatures, outlandish fantasy, and teen humor to smack serious subjects with pie-in-the-face parody,

Political satirists use elements of comedy, parody, ridicule, and irony. Alfred E. Newman, the gap-toothed persona of *MAD Magazine*, prepares to blacken one of President Jimmy Carter's teeth. The art is in the style of *Mad*'s traditional gloves-off satire.

incongruity, and lethal satire. Among visual humor and exaggerated human features were silly actions that spoofed Superman with Superduperman, whose penetrating gaze allowed him to spy on women's toilets; Picasso's art blended with an antic collage of cut-outs; and a pun-laced antitelevision backlash, including mindless cowboy plots parodied in the Lone Stranger, who is deserted at the stake by his faithful companion Pronto. For the next two decades, the concept of a satiric comic magazine triggered a list of imitators, most short-lived: *Panic, Wacko, Humbug, Help!, Trash, Blast, Tales Calculated to Drive You Bats, Not Brand Echh, Nuts, Cracked, Sick, Plop,* and *Arrgh!* Espousing underground antiestablishment sentiment, these magazines cloaked teen readers in an aura of counterculture cachet.

One political satire with staying power is Harry Golden's "Vertical Negro Plan" (1956), a product of preintegration unrest in the United States. Opening with a tongue-in-cheek examination of the chafing spots exacerbated by public integration, Golden, a Jewish journalist from Charlotte, North Carolina, proposes that hostile races avoid problems of school desks and restaurant seats by remaining on foot. "Since no one in the South pays the slightest attention to a vertical negro," blacks pose no risk of offense and, at the same time, "save millions of dollars, to say nothing of eliminating forever any danger to our public education system upon which rests the destiny, hopes, and happiness of this society." Mimicking the tone and style of Jonathan Swift's "A Modest Proposal," the essayist pretends to view his suggestion as a bonanza to public goodwill.

An adjunct to Golden's suggestion is his "White Baby Plan." By posing as nannies of white children, black caretakers can enter movie theaters and, simultaneously, end problems of day-care for working mothers. Golden can't resist adding:

> Eventually the Negro community can set up a factory and manufacture white babies made of plastic, and when they want to go to the opera or to a concert, all they need do is carry that plastic doll in their arms.

By cranking out fake babies with blond hair and blue eyes, the black manufacturers assure themselves "the very best seats in the house." A second poke at segregation is the "Golden 'Out-of-Order' Plan," which will force whites to use water fountains set aside for blacks by putting out of commission the "white-only" facilities. He concludes wickedly that the sign must remain in effect for two years and cautions, "We must do this thing gradually."

Late twentieth-century political satire invents new twists on earlier period pieces through blatant caricature and parody, such as Kurt Vonnegut's pointedly satiric cocktail party on the Caribbean island of San Lorenzo in *Cat's Cradle* (1963). While observing an air show celebrating the Day of a Hundred Martyrs to Democracy, guests at the dictator's castle eat albatross canapés and drink acetone cocktails while observing the six-plane air force firing on paper cutouts of Stalin, Russia's post–World War II dictator; Fidel Castro, puppet dictator of Cuba; Adolf Hitler and Mussolini, Axis leaders during World War II; "some old jap," a humorous poke at American lack of interest in their old enemy Tojo; Karl Marx, founder of communism; Kaiser Bill, the fomenter of World War I; and old Mao, the leader who ousted the Japanese invaders from China and replaced their regime with Chinese communism. Vonnegut's use of paper for his targets indicates that human enemies are far less deadly than the real destroyer of dictator Papa Monzano, ice-nine, Vonnegut's fictional end-of-the-world compound that solidifies the oceans.

A similar but shorter work of black humor is Tom Wolfe's satiric essay *Mau-Mauing the Flak Catchers* (1970), a study of the establishment's dealings with Black Panthers. Wolfe credits one "genius in the art of confrontation" who sliced a shortcut to what the white negotiator refers to as "meaningful dialogue":

> He would just show up with a crocus sack full of revolvers, ice picks, fish knives, switchblades, hatchets, blackjacks, gravity knives, straight razors, hand grenades, blow guns, bazookas, Molotov cocktails, tank rippers, unbelievable stuff, and he'd dump it all out on somebody's shiny walnut conference table.

The juxtaposition works its magic: bureaucrats are quick to protect themselves by hiring the Mafia-style "Ethnic Catering Service," which they rationalize gives jobs to the hard-core unemployed.

A perennial favorite among U.S. political editorialists is Molly Ivins, columnist for the *Fort Worth Star-Telegram* and pundit on CBS's *Sixty Minutes*. Her witty populist putdowns center on the idiocies of national politics and Texas's anointed knuckleheads who inhabit the legislature, which she dubs "the lege." An Ivin's election-year quip appearing in the Lincoln, Nebraska, *Star* on September 27, 1995, pricks the hopeful bubbles that floated General Colin Powell's name among the growing list of potential candidates. To the wishful flock who named Powell, of Jamaican parentage, as proof that the United States is no longer racist, Ivins trounces their hopes: "I hate to point out the obvious again, but Powell is not a very black man. I speak only of hue: he is what is known in some circles as light 'n bright." Ivins's ready wit draws blood as surely as a rawhide whip and flicks torment to right and left and particularly to the fringe. Of the unpredictable sloganeering of candidate wannabe Ross Perot, she deflates his overblown oratory with quips about his "chihuahua voice."

Print cartoons contain their own brand of barb through the wizardry of computerized images, touch-tone colorizing, and multilith print. The gentler comics of manners—*Peanuts, Sally Forth, For Better or Worse, Kathy*, and *Dennis the Menace*—pursue age-old glimpses of marriages at their most perplexing, unruly children, urban morality, and the post–World War II materialism that perpetuates "keeping up with the Jones." A broadside condemnation of political insensitivity comes from *The Wizard of Id*, whose diminutive king flinches at the Lone Haranguer's nightly call, "The King is a fink!" More pointed is Garry Trudeau's *Doonesbury*, the long-running strip that zeroes in on contemporary leaders as well as on stock figures and objects of public scorn. His depiction of Ronald Reagan as addle-pated and George Bush as intellectually bankrupt helped bring down a twelve-year Republican occupancy of the White House. A depiction of O. J. Simpson going door to door looking for a fit for a leather glove pokes fun at a potentially volatile racial backlash following the popular football player's acquittal in a savage double-murder trial. (Beerbohm 1967; Benton 1989; Drabble 1985; Golden 1958, 1972; Ivins 1991, 1995; Johnson 1952; Lowell 1992; McArthur 1992; Wolfe 1970)

See also Beerbohm, Max; *The Beggar's Opera; Candide; Cat's Cradle;* doggerel; incongruity; King, Florence; parody; repartee; satire; Swift, Jonathan; Voltaire, François; Vonnegut, Kurt; wit.

POPE, ALEXANDER

Both revered and feared in the Augustan Age for his keen wit and exacting literary skill, Alexander Pope mastered the essay and the epigram and lifted satire to one of Britain's higher arts. Because of his Catholicism and his combative disposition, he received little patronage yet accumulated more wealth from publication than any other writer of his time. Pope was born in London to Editha Turner and Alexander Pope, a wealthy linen merchant, on May 21, 1688, and grew up at Binfield Lodge, Windsor Forest. Pope was the grandson of an Anglican minister, but he carried the stigma of Catholicism during a time when religion determined his public reception. Laws prevented his family from sending him to a university, from buying land, and from residing within ten miles of London's outer limits. Public aversion and double taxes made clear the scorn that Anglicans felt for "Romans." Pope made do with private instruction from priests. He taught himself through readings in English, Latin, Greek, Italian, and French authors and cultivated a taste for Horace's satires.

For much of his life, Pope was limited to home activities because of recurrent migraine headaches and Pott's disease, a type of tuberculosis that deformed his spine, shriveled his muscles, and dwarfed him to subnormal height. To compensate, he developed a keen mind that gained him admittance to London's vanguard of wit that met at Will's coffeehouse. Despite being a generation younger than his colleagues, Pope later joined the Whig enclave at Buttons's coffeehouse. When challenged by a detractor, Pope once hurled a witty quatrain:

> Sir I admit your general rule,
> That every poet is a fool:
> But you yourself may serve to show it,
> That every fool is not a poet.

To the chagrin of his enemy, the success of Pope's ready retort had rhymers all over London citing his putdown.

At age 21, Pope published *Pastorals* (1709), which Joseph Addison praised in No. 253 of *The Spectator*. Pope followed with his most famous verse work, *Essay on Criticism* (1711), a compendium of advice from which readers extracted popular epigrams:

- A little learning is a dangerous thing;
  Drink deep, or taste not the Pierian spring:
  There shallow draughts intoxicate the brain,
  and drinking largely sobers us again.

- True wit is nature to advantage dress'd,
  What oft was thought, but ne'er so well express'd.
  True ease in writing comes from art, not chance,
  As those move easiest who have learn'd to dance.

- To err is human, to forgive divine.
  For fools rush in where angels fear to tread.

English essayist Alexander Pope, 1688–1744

The work details the method by which the writer can tame disordered thoughts, follow nature, and learn polish and grace from the classics. Its control and vision suggest that Pope had been writing early in his childhood and had himself mastered the literary precepts he recommends.

In his mid-twenties, Pope completed his first mock epic, *The Rape of the Lock* (1712), a masterpiece of understatement and an incisive view of the trivialities of his day. His published bestselling versions of Homer, which he translated with the aid of assistants Elijah Fenton and William Broome in an austere tower in Stanton Harcourt, earned considerable royalties; a six-volume edition of Shakespeare received widespread acceptance. On May 14, 1712, Pope abandoned himself to lighter works by contributing "Messiah, A Sacred Eclogue" to No. 378 of *The Spectator;* the next year, he wrote for the April 27 issue of Richard Steele's *Guardian.* In 1718, Pope and his widowed mother left their house in Chiswick and established a spectacular riverside home, Crossdeep, at Twickenham, Middlesex, on the Thames, where he developed his love of landscaping, which is adorned with private grottoes lined with crystals. He pursued Lady Mary Wortley Montagu, to whom he sent a copy of his *Eloisa to Abelard* (1717), and devoted much of his spare time to Martha Blount's companionship, but he remained unmarried. When Edmund Curll ridiculed Lady Mary, Pope slipped an emetic into his wine and published a description of Curll's discomfort. Of his affection for Martha, he teasingly wrote of her departure from city life:

> She went, to plain-work, and to purling brooks,
> Old-fashion'd halls, dull aunts, and croaking rooks.
> She went from Op'ra, park, assembly, play,
> To morning-walks, and pray'rs three hours a day;
> Or o'er cold coffee, trifle with the spoon,
> Count the slow clock, and dine exact at noon;
> Divert her eyes with pictures in the fire,
> Hum half a tune, tell stories to the squire;
> Up to her godly garret after sev'n
> There starve and pray, for that's the way to heav'n.

Like Mary, who remained constant in her friendship, Pope's other friends were devoted to his keen insights and helped defend him from a respectable list of enemies, including Addison, whom he alienated. Other detractors he deliberately antagonized by publishing *The Dunciad* (1728), a second mock-heroic and caustic satire deliberately skewering adversaries, both personal and professional, which he upgraded the rest of his days with new victims of his spite and their laughable foibles. So virulent was his distaste for dolts and dullards such as Lewis Theobald and Colley Cibber that he immortalized their dullness in verse and earned for himself the nickname "the wicked wasp of Twickenham." Pope's last major works—*Peri Bathous: or of the Art of Sinking in Poetry* (1727), *Essay on Man* (1734), "An Epistle from Mr. Pope, to Dr. Arbuthnot" (1735), and *Imitations of Horace* (1737)—round out a considerable neoclassic canon that influenced his contemporaries and succeeding generations.

Friendship with Jonathan Swift, John Gay, and others of the Scriblerus Club, as well as the thrill of sailing off the Isle of Wight with Lord Peterborough, ornamented Pope's home-centered life. He varied the daily rhythm with informal gatherings in his ornate gardens and at friends' homes. Health care dominated much of his time. He attended his mother until her death at age 91. When arthritis gripped his spine, he wore a laced linen body brace and took the healing waters at Bath. His attendants kept him wrapped in layers of warm clothing, washed him, and, night or day, helped him into and out of chairs and bed, where he wrote at a portable desk. At his death from asthma and congestive heart failure on May 30, 1744, he was considered one of England's finest writers. A pedant on the subject of the rhymed couplet, he championed clear modules of thought that the romantic age ridiculed as rigid, uninspiring, and laughable. Later study of his work restored his position so strongly that his era was named the Age of Pope. (Bermel 1982; Drabble 1985; Eagle and Stephens 1992; Highet 1962; Hornstein 1973; Kunitz and Haycrraft 1952; Magill 1958; Magnusson 1990; Padgett 1987; Person 1988; Pollard 1970; Pope 1965)

See also Addison, Joseph; bathos; *The Dunciad;* Gay, John; Horace; *The Rape of the Lock; The Spectator;* Steele, Sir Richard; Swift, Jonathan.

LES PRÉCIEUSES RIDICULES

Molière's one-act farce ridiculing the pretentious, oh-so-dainty social climbers of the French salons, *Les Précieuses ridicules* debuted for King Louis XIV in 1659. An experiment in satire, the production was one of the genre's strongest ventures into the realm of public chastisement. It opened November 18 at the Hôtel de Petit Bourbon, starring Molière in the droll part of Mascarille, and set Paris in titters at the self-absorbed social set of bluestockings who fancied themselves discerning and tasteful. The humor so devastated the self-appointed trendsetters that they sank into decline rather than subject themselves to more ridicule. Molière's enemies retaliated by having his theater torn down, ostensibly to accommodate an expansion of the Louvre.

The humor derives from a plot device as old as theater: two coddled, conceited drawing-room chits spurn their suitors, La Grange and Du Croisy, and demand better. Gorgibus, who is father to Magdelon and uncle to Cathos, chides the girls' vanities:

> Those hussies are trying to ruin me, with their lip salve. All I see around is whites of eggs, virgin-milk, and a hundred other groceries I don't recognize. Since we have been here they have used up the fat of a dozen pigs at least; and four menservants could live on the sheep's trotters they get rid of.

The "precious ones," who consider themselves too chic, too delicate for an open proposal of marriage, advise Gorgibus on the current fashion in courtship, which calls for gallantry and concealed passion. The girls expect sighing, weeping, high drama, fashion, reproaches, despair, abduction, and consequences as a part of their overly romanticized notion of citified love. To Gorgibus, their talk is rubbish.

The suitors, stung, but game for revenge against rank snobbery, disguise their servants as courtiers and send them in service to charm the ladies with blandishments and ornate gestures. Mascarille, La Grange's valet, arrives in a sedan chair and presents Magdelon an epic verse:

> "You stole my heart," that is you robbed me, you carried it away. "Stop thief! Stop thief! Stop thief! Stop thief! Stop thief!" Wouldn't you say it was a man shouting and running after a robber to try to catch him? "Stop thief! Stop thief! Stop thief! Stop thief! Stop thief!"

Magdelon agrees that the poem is witty, the style she prefers from suitors. Tuning his voice to offset the difficulty of the weather, Mascarille again launches into a chorus of "Stop Thief!" The girls admire his ribbons and effusive gallantry.

The Vicomte de Jodelet, the pose of Du Croisy's manservant, joins Mascarille. The two compete to impress the girls with name-dropping, polished manners, curled wigs, and skill on the dance floor. In the midst of a successful courtship, the masters burst in on the servants and yank them back into line. After a verbal drubbing from Gorgibus for the scorn this incident will bring from his enemies, the "precious ones" are horrified and sick with shame. Trapped by their gullibility and "fantasticalities," they are mortified. Gorgibus blames their silliness on immersion in "novels, verses, songs and sonnets" and curses them roundly. (Baugh 1948; Bermel 1982; Brockett 1968; Burdick 1974; Gassner and Quinn 1969; Guicharnaud 1967; Molière 1965; Roberts 1962)

See also Le Bourgeois gentilhomme; caricature; *commedia dell'arte;* farce; incongruity; Molière; satire; *Tartuffe.*

PRIDE AND PREJUDICE

Jane Austen wrote her first novel, originally entitled *First Impressions*, in 1797. Because she found no publisher, she destroyed the prototype. The second writing, completed in 1812 and published the next year, appeared as *Pride and Prejudice*, which may have drawn heavily on the original work but utilizes later events as material. Restricted to a bourgeois milieu, Austen's dispassionate novel—unlike William Thackeray's broad-based *Vanity Fair* (1848) with its multinational sweep—views a narrow stratum of society in which a limited number of characters interact. Her droll observations show a keen awareness of manners and decorum, which Georgian England judged as a sign of character, and of the eligible male's value to a man-hungry clutch of eligible daughters. With a facetious wit that strikes close to black humor and reveals her inner musing on old-maidhood, Austen observes, "It is a truth universally acknowledged, that a single man in possession of a good fortune, must be in want of a wife." A paean to matrimony replete with irony, caricature, and restrained humor, the novel—sometimes classified as social farce—delineates the importance of pairings to the stability of the middle-class family and to the economic and emotional well-being of the gentry.

At Longbourn, Hertfordshire, Mr. and Mrs. Bennet and their five daughters anticipate that cousin William Collins will inherit the Bennet property, which is entailed to pass on only to a male heir. Austen excels at revealing contrasts in the Bennet family by presenting the ironic, lackadaisical Bennet against his wife, a mercenary social engineer driven to make promising matches for her daughters. Of Mrs. Bennet, Austen comments:

> She was a woman of mean understanding, little information, and uncertain temper. . . . The business of her life was to get her daughters married; its solace was visiting and news.

The meat-market aspect of competing for eligible mates reduces the Bennet girls' mother to an ignoble stature, but bearably so when she contemplates the alternative of sharing her life with three spinsters. Mrs. Bennet's recitation of how and with whom her daughters dance at the ball produces the bearish grunt that typifies Mr. Bennet's attitude to contrived matchmaking with the pick of beaux: "For God's sake, say no more of his partners. Oh! that he had sprained his ankle on the first dance!"

Facing limited choices, the characters begin the traditional mating ritual. In due course, Jane, the eldest and most beautiful daughter, falls in love with Charles Bingley. Fitzwilliam Darcy, Bingley's aristocratic friend, is a wealthy and eligible bachelor who offends Mrs. Bennet with his conceited, condescending air. On being upbraided for refusing to join in the dance, Darcy rejects the suggestion of asking Elizabeth, the second Bennet daughter and the protagonist of the novel. He sniffs:

> She is tolerable; but not handsome enough to tempt me; and I am in no humour at present to give consequence to young ladies who are slighted by other men. You had better return to your partner and enjoy her smiles, for you are wasting your time with me.

Jane's triumph at the expense of Elizabeth leads to clashes in the post-ball evaluation. To Jane's joy at being asked by Mr. Bingley, Elizabeth quips, "I give you leave to like him. You have liked many a stupider person."

In a private moment at a subsequent ball at Longbourn, Darcy dances with Elizabeth without holding up his end of the obligatory conversation. Elizabeth, who speaks her mind without giving a thought to humiliating her partner or breaching the bounds of good manners, reminds him that he must enter into the small talk with some pittance about the room size or number of guests. Darcy smiles and agrees to be more engaging, to which Elizabeth—in a voice that rings with the author's sardonic wit—replies:

> We are each of an unsocial, taciturn disposition, unwilling to speak, unless we expect to say something that will amaze the whole room, and be handed down to posterity with all the *éclat* of a proverb.

The verbal dueling of this small but intense coterie of marriageable young people spools out like a string of major skirmishes preceding a decisive battle.

With her outspoken manner, Elizabeth appears to hold the best of the field with Darcy clinging to a bare second.

Bad blood between the meddlesome Bingley sisters and the younger Bennets and their mother disrupts Jane's romance. In vain, William Collins unsuccessfully courts his cousin Elizabeth, summing the positive points of the union as awkwardly as if he were rendering a financial report. He admits that he chooses her as a form of atonement for inheriting the Bennet estate. Overeager to the point of absurdity, Mrs. Bennet bursts into the parlor in a flurry of congratulations and assurances that Lizzy can be brought around to Mr. Collins's proposal. When Mrs. Bennet draws her husband in as unwilling mediator, she declares that Lizzy must marry Collins or cut all ties with her mother. Knowing his wife to be a fool on the subject of matrimony, Bennet drolly observes, "Your mother will never see you again if you do *not* marry Mr. Collins, and I will never see you again if you do."

On the rebound, the silly, foppish Collins successfully woos Charlotte Lucas, Elizabeth's friend, and quickly weds her. While visiting the newlyweds, Elizabeth continues making caustic observations. When Charlotte's young sister Maria calls her to the window, Elizabeth observes Collins's obsequious fuss over Lady De Bourgh (who just happens to be Darcy's aunt) and remarks, "And is this all? . . . I expected at least that the pigs were got into the garden, and here is nothing but Lady Catherine and her daughter." Elizabeth's insouciance, dry wit, and freedom from social hypocrisy charm Darcy, but his insensitive behavior causes Elizabeth to dwell on his faults.

The major event that brings the novel to its peak reveals Austen's sense of propriety. On vacation near Pemberley, Darcy's estate, Elizabeth accidentally meets him again and, just as the two begin to forge a warm relationship, learns that her heedless youngest sister Lydia has eloped to Gretna Green with her suitor, George Wickham, a man whom Elizabeth considers imprudent. Elizabeth's bear-all façade crumbles. Distressed that Lydia resides unwed with a bounder, she exclaims to Darcy: "*You* know him too well to doubt the rest. She has no money, no connections, nothing that can tempt him to—she is lost forever." The melodrama bears out the hypocritical principles of mother Bennet, who examines potential matings with the calculation of a horse trader. Collins picks this tense period to pen a prissy letter lamenting Lydia's licentiousness and crisply and dispassionately advises Bennet to "throw off your unworthy child from our affection forever, and leave her to reap the fruits of her own heinous offence."

From a decidedly female point of view, the denouement brings all to rights. Uncle Edward Gardiner reports that Lydia and Wickham will marry. After a fortnight sequestered upstairs in mortification, Mrs. Bennet reappears at the dinner table; Lydia marries Mr. Wickham at St. Clements and, after three months of living like an amoral bohemian, flashes her ring and boasts of her good fortune. Bingley again woos Jane; Darcy proposes to Elizabeth. Lady Catherine tries to intervene, but Elizabeth refuses the intimidation of wealth and privilege. The girls accept their beaux; very much in character, Mrs. Bennet exults, "Ten thousand a year! Oh, Lord! What will become of me. I shall go distracted."

A remarkably vigorous, honest, and sensible character, Elizabeth speaks the author's own gentle view of satire: "Follies and nonsense, whims and inconsistencies do divert me, I own, and I laugh at them whenever I can." The ease with which Austen navigates the intricacies of familial and social intercourse derives from experience with letters, whisperings, gossip, dance-floor exchanges, furtive courtships, and tearful partings. Her ironic tone coats all the maneuverings and countermoves, surprise turns of plot, and smooth resolution with the savoir-faire of a keen observer who has heard similar cynical matchmakers meddling in young people's affairs and who finds the whole admixture a necessary but laughable social mechanism. (Austen 1961; Baugh 1948; Buck 1992; Chapman 1948; Drabble 1985; Hainer 1995; Halperin 1984; Hornstein 1973; Lovett and Hughesl 1932; O'Neill 1970)

See also Austen, Jane; caricature; comedy; farce; irony; satire; Thackeray, William Makepeace; *Vanity Fair;* wit.

 # PUN

The word "pun" derived in the mid-seventeenth century from the Italian fencing term "fine point" for its quick-witted stab during a significant moment, reemergence of a theme, or impasse in repartee. The pun is a literary device linking incongruous or ambiguous meanings with words that sound alike or words that suggest humorous, ridiculous, sexual, or undignified or debased connotations. The plays on homophones all/awl and sole/soul in the opening lines of William Shakespeare's tragedy *Julius Caesar* (ca. 1599) furnish one example of the genre:

Marullus:	But what trade art thou? Answer me directly.
Cobbler:	A trade, sir, that I hope I may use with a safe conscience, which is indeed, sir, a mender of bad soles.
Flavius:	What trade, thou knave? Thou naughty knave, what trade?
Cobbler:	Nay, I beseech you sir, be not out with me, yet if thou be out, sir. I can mend you.
Marullus:	What mean'st thou by that? Mend me, thou saucy fellow?
Cobbler:	Why, sir, cobble you.
Flavius:	Thou art a cobbler, art thou?
Cobbler:	Truly sir, all that I live by is with the awl. I meddle with no tradesman's matters nor women's matters, but withal—I am indeed, sir, a surgeon to old shoes.

Developing from the Greek paronomasia or "false naming," everyday conversational puns like those of Shakespeare provoke groans of dismay and grimaces or disparagement, yet they remain a favorite of comics and satirists at all levels, from newspaper headlines to sophisticated drawing room comedy.

Dating from Roman times in the play on names in Cicero's orations, puns find a surprisingly large following among religious writers, including Bede and Isidore. The book of Genesis opens with a pun on the Hebrew *adamah* or *earth* and the first man, Adam, who is punished for breaking God's commandment by being forced to live a hard life, plow the earth, then die and return to the dust from which he was shaped. The sturdiest—and perhaps most problematic—pun in Christendom occurs in Matthew 16:18 when Christ commissions Peter to establish the Holy Church, an act Peter initiates with the reassembly of the twelve apostles. The line, known as the Petrine Supremacy, plays on the dual meaning of the Greek name Peter (Petros), which repeats the root word of rock (petra): "And I say also unto thee, That thou art Peter, and upon this rock I will build my church; and the gates of hell shall not prevail against it." (Note that in Aramaic, Christ's native tongue, the line would carry a direct, one-for-one Semitic pun: "You are *Kepha,* and on this *kepha* I will build my church.") A subsequent reference in Paul's letter to the Ephesians (2:19–22) calls up the expanded construction metaphor:

> Now therefore ye are no more strangers and foreigners, but fellow citizens with the saints, and of the household of God; And are built upon the foundation of the apostles and prophets, Jesus Christ himself being the chief corner stone; In whom all the building fitly framed together groweth unto an holy temple in the Lord: In whom ye also are builded together for an habitation of God through the Spirit.

The Petrine Supremacy holds such centrality and power in Catholic dogma that the Vulgate version of Christ's pun is inscribed in gold letters around the dome, which Michelangelo designed as the crown of St. Peter's Basilica. Written in the Latin of St. Jerome, the line reads: "Tu es Petrus, et super hanc petram aedificabo Ecclesiam meam." The First Vatican Council of 1870 established this sentence as the validation of papal authority.

A specific form of punning, the spoonerism, named for W. A. Spooner (1844–1930), a dean and churchman of New College, Oxford, involves the reversal of initial or consonant sounds or syllables: lead spoon/sped loon. In the opening line of a British music hall ballad, "One of the Deathless Army," the speaker, a member of the territorial army that guarded and kept peace in the British Empire, begins his chorus with a deliberate spoonerism:

> I am a bolger sold—
> > I mean I'm a soldier bold,
> I'm not so young as I used to be
> > Before I got so old.

The implication that the soldier has been sold a bill of goods and has spent his youth in service to the crown permeates the song, raising it from the humdrum soldier's complaint to a thrust at soldiering as an unfulfilling, wasteful life's work. In a similar spirit of revelation from U.S. popular culture, the spoonerism was a favorite of Archie Bunker on the popular satiric TV series *All in the Family* and carried some of Archie's funniest nitwittish observations, especially his objection to "noodle frontity" during a nude antiwar march.

A keen punster in verse is novelist Marge Piercy, best known for her *tour de force* dystopic fantasy *Woman on the Edge of Time* (1976). In sharp-edged feminist black humor, she lambastes society in the poem "The Grey Flannel Sexual

Harassment Suit" for acknowledging charges of sexual harassment only when they apply to paragons, that is, the immaculate housekeeper, churchgoer, clean-living goody-goody who has "known" her father alone, a sly reference to the biblical definition of "known" in the carnal sense. The best candidate for redress, Piercy insists, is ideally a virgin who is a regular churchgoer. So pure must this victim be that the only acceptable race is white, a natural blonde; the minister may pat her on the head if he wears gloves and the angels who visit her are, of necessity, all female. (Abbott 1969; Abrams 1971; Barnet, Berman, and Burto 1960; Cuddon 1984; Davison 1971; Drabble 1985; Ekstrom 1995; Gentz 1973; Gray 1992; Henry 1995; Holman and Harmon 1992; Johnson 1994; Mantinband 1956; Mays 1988; McCarthur 1992; Piercy 1995)

See also black humor; comedy; double entendre; limerick; scatology; wit.

PYGMALION

George Bernard Shaw's play (1912) derives its title from a Greek myth in Ovid's *Metamorphoses* about a disdainful sculptor who neglects the love of women and suffers for his rejection by falling in love with a marble statue. The work has achieved phenomenal success in frequent stage revivals and in the musical adaptation, *My Fair Lady*, which won seven Oscars and four Academy Award nominations for Alan Jay Lerner's 1964 film version, starring Rex Harrison as Henry Higgins and Audrey Hepburn as Eliza Doolittle. A social satire rather than a romantic comedy, the play depicts Professor Higgins's skill in applying speech refinements and upper-class manners to turn a "squashed cabbage leaf" of a street vendor into a polished lady, then hands him the dilemma of accommodating her spirit, outlook, and future to the grandness of her manners and diction.

Act I opens on a rainy night in Covent Garden outside the opera house, where Higgins, always on the lookout for interesting speech characteristics to reproduce in his notebook, takes down snatches of talk in an arcane phonetic alphabet. From the jostling, ill-tempered crowd, Shaw tosses in bits of satiric observation: Eliza, the violet-seller, bawls repeatedly that she's "a respectable girl," that is, not a prostitute; a bystander takes in the outward appearance of her supposed accuser and concludes, "It's all right; he's a gentleman. Look at his boots." By coincidence, Higgins meets a second bystander and recognizes him as "Colonel Pickering, the author of Spoken Sanscrit." Higgins claims that he has extended his hobby into a comfy living by refining upstarts who "begin in Kentish Town with £80 a year, and end in Park Lane with a hundred thousand." To protect them from the label of parvenu, Higgins offers lessons that pare away unrefined argot and replace it with the accepted diction of the elite.

Shaw shifts the focus from the salvation of a street girl to the impossible man of science. The second act shifts to Higgins's lab, where he reveals the worst of his character: he sees his clients as experiments rather than human

Professor Henry Higgins (Rex Harrison) notes the Cockney dialect of flower seller Eliza Doolittle (Julie Andrews) in *My Fair Lady*, a musical based on George Bernard Shaw's 1912 play *Pygmalion*. Pygmalion, a character in Greek mythology, was a sculptor who fell in love with a statue he created.

beings. When Eliza arrives to inquire about lessons, Higgins and Pickering join for a teasing bit of doggerel juggling variations of the name "Elizabeth":

Eliza, Elizabeth, Betsy and Bess,
They went to the woods to get a bird's nes':
They found a nest with four eggs in it:
They took one apiece, and left three in it.

In a jocular mood at the challenge Eliza presents to his theory, Higgins makes a bet with Pickering that Eliza can pass the social test of the ambassador's garden party. Eliza's lower-class prudery amuses Higgins, who orders Mrs. Pearce, the housekeeper, to scrub her with "Monkey Brand" and burn her clothes. Leaping light-years beyond Eliza's comprehension, Higgins startles the girl into a defense of her reputation. To settle the matter of propriety, he hands her into the care of Mrs. Pearce.

The satiric element continues to skewer Higgins, who selects his mother's weekly "at-home" as a social testing ground for a new, improved Eliza. Behaving abominably while coaching Eliza, Higgins, like a nettlesome infant, annoys his refined mother by accepting the visiting Eynsford Hill family as guinea pigs rather than guests. Higgins—offering a glimpse of the fractious, irrepressible Shaw himself—observes Eliza at her lower-class worst. To questions about the weather, Eliza develops a run of conversation that ends in her aunt's questionable death. Archly suspicious, Eliza inquires:

What call would a woman with that strength in her have to die of influenza?
What become of her new straw hat that should have come to me? Somebody
pinched it; and what I say is, them as pinched it done her in.

The social insecurity of the out-at-elbows Eynsford Hills glares as openly as Eliza's inability to conduct normal drawing-room chitchat. After the guests depart, Mrs. Higgins, wise in the full requirements of respectability, admits to her son, "She's a triumph of your art and of her dressmaker's; but if you support for a moment that she doesn't give herself away in every sentence she utters, you must be perfectly cracked about her."

The anticlimax proves Higgins as naive as Eliza is out of place. After Eliza wins Higgins's bet by charming guests at the party, she explodes with Shaw's focal theme: "There can't be any feelings between the like of you and the like of me." Higgins's riposte to the question of manners states Shaw's personal credo:

The great secret, Eliza, is not having bad manners or good manners or any
other particular sort of manners, but having the same manners for all human
souls. In short, behaving as if you were in Heaven, where there are no third
class carriages, and one soul is as good as another.

Shaky on her new social legs, Eliza demands independence from her mentor. Ironically, Higgins is in a position to claim victory whether she stays or goes. The closing lines leave untold Eliza's future, whether wife of Freddie Eynsford Hill or a duke, or again a flower-seller. Whatever Eliza chooses, she remains a tribute to the speech coach's art and to the false evaluations of the social elite who look at surface details in defining quality. (Bermel 1982; Brockett 1968; Gassner and Quinn 1969; Grigson 1963; Hill 1978; Hornstein 1973; Johnson 1968; Kunitz 1942; Magill 1958; Negley and Patrick 1952; Shaw 1952)

See also *Androcles and the Lion; Back to Methuselah;* beast lore; doggerel; irony; repartee; satire; Shaw, George Bernard; wit.

RABELAIS, FRANÇOIS

The famed rebel and idealist of the French Renaissance, François Rabelais, a raconteur, savant, propagandist, naturalist, linguist, and satirist, is best known for *Gargantua and Pantagruel* (1562), a jolly, full-bodied satire that he alternately edited and added to for years. Laced with almost every style of humor, his episodic fantasy explodes with energy and bold ideas—a starburst of sensual delights as an antidote to the dour, uncompromising religiosity of the Middle Ages. Son of Antoine Rabelais, an attorney, and native of La Devinière near Chinon in Touraine, Rabelais was born around 1494. In 1520, he entered Abbaye de Seuillé in Fontenay, a heavily regulated Franciscan monastery that forbade the study of classical literature. In contrast to his contemporary, John Calvin, the strict Protestant who governed Geneva by theocratic fiat, Rabelais rejoiced in human goodness and jocularity and met regularly with a literary gathering influenced by the Dutch humanist Desiderius Erasmus to discuss the roles of men and women in society. So cogent were Rabelais's writings on freedom that they influenced the drafters of America's Declaration of Independence, especially Thomas Jefferson, who was a knowledgeable francophile.

Censured by closed-minded prelates who disdained pagan, radical notions and confiscated his private library, Rabelais transferred to the Benedictines at Abbaye de Maillezais in Angiers, a less repressive religious house, where, with the blessing of Pope Clement VII, he could more freely study classical languages, astronomy, and medicine and enter the priesthood. In 1526, Rabelais revoked his vows, monasticism, and clerical robes and lived openly in Paris and Montpellier with his mistress, a widow who bore him two children. At the Faculty of Medicine of Montpellier, he pursued a broad-based humanism consisting of philosophy, anatomy, and law. He graduated in 1537 and practiced law at the bar of Lyons, although he doubted the justice of the profession. In his words, "Our laws are like cobwebs; the silly little flies are stopped, caught and destroyed therein, but the stronger ones break them, and force and carry them whichsoever they please."

In his thirties, Rabelais took a greater interest in medicine than in his former profession as lawyer. He turned his genius to the new science of anatomy by conducting formal dissections, for which he invented a precise surgical scalpel, the gluttotomon. On his own, he translated Galen and Hippocrates for less adept medical students to read, edited contemporary medical texts, and attended as personal physician his patron, Cardinal Jean du Bellay, who suffered from acute sciatica. On semi-official business with the cardinal and later with the cardinal's brother, Guillaume Seigneur de Langey, Rabelais made several extended tours of Italy and lived in Turin, where he added a reading knowledge of Arabic to his polyglot list.

In 1532, under the pseudonym Alcofribas, Rabelais published the first segment of his five-part *Gargantua et Pantagruel*. Drawing on his overactive imagination, he evolved a country squabble into a meandering, picaresque ramble, which he filled with puns, comic dialogues, parody, coinages, aphorism, riddles, misogyny, professional lore, political mockery, barroom jest, educational theory, rhyme, and open ridicule. Turns of plot depict Gargantua flimflamming the gullible and pulling pranks as impossible as stealing the bells of Notre Dame Cathedral and placing them on his horse's harness. Essentially, the work conceals erudition under silliness and coarse, scatological humor and centers on *joie de vivre*, appreciation of nature, and an all-embracing trust in curiosity, knowledge, experimentation, and deformalized worship. This example of his untranslatable nonsense verse comes from "A Tetrastich in the Lanternish Language":

> Brismarg dalgotbrick nubstzne zos,
> Isquebsz prusq: albok crinqs Zacbac.
> Mizbe dilbarskz morp nipp stancz bos,
> Strombtz, Panurge, walmap quost gruszbac.

The poem epitomizes Rabelais's scorn of a society governed by petty rules, even the rules of the Lanternish language. A witty, bold satirist, he risked ridicule and apostasy in order to quell medieval superstitions and ossification and to invigorate readers with Renaissance freedom. Because of his liberal musings and ribaldry, he offended conservative elements and was forced to flee France.

With the intervention of Clement's successor, Pope Paul III, Rabelais, still under du Bellay's protection, returned to the Benedictine order in 1535 and took up serious hospital work and anatomy lectures. The censorious, fuddy-duddy staff repudiated the famed joker and punster, who saw his printer Dolet burned at the stake for heresy in Paris in 1546. Rabelais advanced to a curacy and continued writing madcap, festive satire. Late in his life, still influenced by his motto "Rire est le propre de l'homme [Laughter suits humankind]," he returned to Paris and was named Meudon's curé. His death on April 9, 1553, preceded the publication of a fifth segment of his satiric novel and, in subsequent centuries, a public outpouring of admiration for his buffoonery from Michel de Montaigne, Jean de La Fontaine, Honoré de Balzac, Jonathan Swift, and Laurence Sterne.

The success of *Gargantua and Pantagruel* supplied linguistics with a useful eponym. The adjective "rabelaisian" means robust, vigorous, extravagant, and naturalistic. Connotatively, "rabelaisian" carries a hint of coarse, crude exhibitionism, the down side of the author's unbounded curiosity and energy. The word appeared early in the nineteenth century and identifies forms of caricature or parody that pillory dogma, bigotry, cant, fundamentalism, pedantry, conformity, and other forms of narrow-mindedness. "Rabelaisian" eventually typified the Renaissance itself, with its exuberant embrace of change, earthly pastimes, humor, creativity, and liberal arts. (Bishop 1965; Boorstin 1992; Lewis 1969; Mack 1962; Manguel and Guadalupi 1987; Padgett 1987; Pollard 1970; Putnam 1993; Rabelais 1955; Screech 1980; Thomas and Thomas 1943)

See also doggerel; epigram; Erasmus, Desiderius; *Gargantua and Pantagruel*; picaresque; pun; satire; scatology; Swift, Jonathan; wit.

RAP

A loose, shallow form of overlapping rhyme derived from the fast-talking spiel of radio disc jockeys, disco spinners, scat singers, political demagogues, prison inmates, and street ministers, rap as a form of mock-heroic insult exchange and hype has been alternately known as "playing the dozens," "toasting," "sounding," "dissing or dishing," "signifying," and "capping." The verbal meter, percussive rhythm, and Afro-centric themes combine with the hallmarks of adolescence: exhibitionism and rebellion against authority. The style, which permeates novels, poetry, drama, and screenplays, reflects an earlier oral ancestry that taps a mesmerizing power in the griot's storytelling, antiphonal minister-and-congregation litany, oral genealogies, the fighter Muhammad Ali's bluff puffery, and the shaman's heady command of curses, incantations, and gris-gris or voodoo magic. Like drama, jest, and burlesque, rap occupies its own corner of performance that supplies a cathartic relief of racial, social, religious, and personal tensions by responding with taunts or retorts to an enemy, unfair law, or social stigma. The general perception of rap's unsettling alienation, childish methods and argot, gangster aura, and questionable taste, however, imprisons its splenetic rhyme on the outer edge of asocial, antisocial, racist, or militant behaviors including vulgar or juvenile graffiti, sidewalk strutting and breakdancing, martial face-offs, and incendiary audio techno-wizardry.

The popular rhythmic sound indigenous to New York's poorest neighborhoods evolved in 1979 as a separate division of the music industry. The premier album, "Rapper's Delight," features the Sugarhill Gang in a mélange of blunt street lingo chanted or spoken to minimal musical accompaniment, often only nonmelodic drum riffs or percussion blends. Set in an urban scene rife with hatred, racial discontent, misogyny, fragmented family, and gun lore, the monochromatic versification, usually composed in couplets or quatrains, gives the impression of precocious improvisation. For example:

> I got no worries, all set to be cool;
> Don't need no mama, no time in school.
> Settin' my pace to suit myself,
> Shootin' up stuff from off the shelf.

Strongly judgmental of marginalization and insistent on the rights of black Americans to their own lifestyle, rap mixes nonsensical, sing-song lines about drugs, explicit details of sexual liaisons, police corruption and brutality, Euro-centric education, discrimination, and joblessness into a string of politically inflammatory diatribe. The dynamic, pervasive patter, accompanied by an exaggerated strut and macho posturing, is so common to the daily routine of young black males that, since the 1970s, it has accompanied their everyday activities through cassette and CD earphones, portable oversized players lightheartedly named "ghetto blasters" or "boom boxes," and oversized car speakers.

After rap melded with Jamaican reggae to form a calypso hybrid, sometimes known as funk, the style caught on rapidly with young teens from urban ghettos and spawned a blended black/Caribbean/Latino culture of jerky, expressionless imitators, tangentially identified by droopy pants, untied sneakers, and ball caps worn backwards and by carnivalesque lounges and street scenes where performers break-dance and scrawl prorap grafitti. African-American rappers speak in monotone of their antiwhite, anti-Semitic, anti-authority agitation, shock talk (sodomy, fellatio, torture, bondage, sadomasochism, gang rape, scatology), and bluff blarney set to an offbeat iambic rhythm grouped in fours. Graphic lyrics, often looped together by slant rhyme, have become the specialty of numerous short-lived imitators with teasingly caricatured names—Afrika Bombaataa, Funkadelic, Grandmaster Flash, Dr. Dre, 2 Live Crew, Run-DMC, Soul Sonic Force, Snoop Doggy Dogg, Fearless Four, Ice Cube, LL Cool J, M. C. Hammer, Beastie Boys, Queen Latifah, Sister Souljah, Salt N Peppa, Treacherous Three, Niggas with Attitude, Kurtis Blow, and Fat Boys—plus a lesser number of white hip-hoppers, Jewish rappers, gospel and Christian groups, and New Wave performers.

The phenomenon, which gives the illusion of power via verbal subjugation of enemies, rivals, or fears, alarms adults because of the insistence on self-delusion, violence, materialism, sadism, pornography, and hopelessness. Humor and satire are limited, sometimes pointedly vindictive, and peculiarly self-derogatory in instances where the speaker boasts of criminal activity, gay-bashing, cop-killing, or female abuse. Initially, few authorities on adolescent behavior predicted a long life for the hypnotic recitatives, yet, in 1986, the style went gold with its first million-selling recording, "Raisin' Hell," and appeared on a Bart Simpson cartoon, on Japanese television, and as "Yo! MTV Raps" on cable. The impertinent subcultural phenomenon maintains a hold on the junior high radio and recorded music market, especially in the inner city and the Caribbean. As a political, guerillaesque force, rap has created its enemies among the far-right religious factions who would curtail First Amendment rights for minors by imposing arbitrary censorship, a coding system, and parental and school control of the sale and broadcast of scurrilous, uninhibited rap lyrics to young teens enamored of bad-ass rappers. Less strident voices predict that soft rap will acquire a sizeable share of the market. In the mid-1990s, advertisers and other exploiters were weakening rap by extracting its verbal gibes and replacing them with commercial or didactic messages. (Blair 1993; Farley 1996; Hardy and Laing 1987; Henry 1995; Highet 1962; Hitchcock and Sadie 1980; Krohn and Suazo 1995; McArthur 1992; Padgett 1987; Panati 1991; Rickelman 1992; Spencer 1992; Stern and Stern 1992)

See also caricature; diatribe; didacticism; doggerel; jingle; mock-heroic; scatology.

THE RAPE OF THE LOCK

Alexander Pope's bravura creation of his mock-heroic *The Rape of the Lock: An Heroical-Comical Poem* (1714) functions as an ingenious critique of the early eighteenth-century milieu. Filled with epic diction, zeugma, paradox, bathos, and understatement, the poet first captured in two cantos—then expanded to five cantos—a verbal duel that mimics a physical assault. Delightfully playful, the poem represents one of Pope's few exercises in writing for entertainment, yet it maintains his high standards for classical style, strict cadence and rhyme, and unity of tone and action. The poem opens with a tribute to Belinda (Arabella Fermor), who may have commissioned the work. In his envoi, Pope tells Arabella that he originally meant to entertain a few young ladies with gentle satire of their foibles. He introduces the sylphs, his demi-deities, who perform the divine interventions that further the action, derived from a real attack by Lord Petre on Arabella's hair.

Canto I: The poet, a facile reader of the classics, opens with the standard epic question—"What dire offence from amorous causes springs/What mighty contests rise from trivial things,/I sing"—and proceeds to a dedication to his muse, poet John Caryll, and a review of the cause ("what strange motive, Goddess! could compel/A well-bred Lord t'assault a gentle belle?"). At sunrise, Belinda lies asleep under the watch of her guardian sylph, Ariel, who tries to warn her of the enemy—man. Belinda hears nothing until her lapdog Shock awakens her with a lick. Like Achilles arming for battle, Belinda sits before her dressing table and "begins the sacred rites of pride," requiring a potpourri of combs, pins, "Puffs, Powders, Patches, Bibles, Billet-doux." The triviality of elements of the toilet table indicate Pope's intent to parody epic and, simultaneously, tease coquettes for their childish wiles.

Canto II: Leaning heavily on the ponderous style and subject of John Milton's *Paradise Lost,* Pope carries the events of the morning back to their cosmic beginnings and heralds dire omens for the future. The felicitous verse that accompanies Belinda's fateful day moves in and out of trivialities, juxtaposing the shallow with the important:

> But what, or where, the fates have wrapped in night.
> Whether the nymph shall break Diana's law,
> Or some frail China jar receive a flaw;
> Or stain her honour, or her new brocade;
> Forget her prayers, or miss a masquerade;
> Or lose her heart, or necklace, at a ball;
> Or whether Heaven has doomed that Shock must fall.

The implication that loss of virginity (the breaking of Diana's law of chastity) and a spot on brocade belong in the same series of disasters undercuts the actual dread of the ensuing events, which compromise the real Arabella Fermor and nearly lead to a court battle. To protect the fictional Belinda from danger, the poet dispatches Zephyretta to the fan, Brillante to Belinda's earrings, Momentilla to her watch, and Crispissa to her hairdo. Fifty more sylphs guard the hooped petticoat. Ariel, the chief sylph, remains in charge of Shock. The punishment for failure is steep: any sylph neglecting Belinda may be stopped in a bottle, pierced with pins, plunged into face cream, wedged in a needle's eye, stuck with gum, or dried up in alum.

Canto III: Pope introduces the setting as a field of battle—Hampton Court, ruled by Queen Anne, "whom three realms obey/Dost sometimes counsel take—and sometimes Tea." As the day ends, justices at court determine the doom of criminals while Belinda prepares for a game of Ombre, in which the cards themselves become warriors. After calling spades trumps, Belinda leads off against the baron and defeats him in one canny play of the king. With lyrical grace, Pope reverberates to the sky the winner's shouts of joy. The serving of coffee sends disruptive vapors into the baron's head and causes him to plot how he can steal a lock of Belinda's hair. In classic Greek style, the act itself must stretch out to epic proportions:

> The Peer now spreads the glittering Forfex wide,
> T' enclose the Lock; now joins it, to divide.
> Even then, before the fatal engine closed,
> A wretched Sylph too fondly interposed;
> Fate urged the shears, and cut the Sylph in twain,
> (But airy substance soon unites again)
> The meeting points the sacred hair dissever
> From the fair head, for ever, and for ever!

Obviously enjoying the *reductio ad absurdum* of the theft of hair, Pope immortalizes the sylph who is temporarily hacked apart. Belinda's scream prompts an epic comparison: "Not louder shrieks to pitying heaven are cast,/When husbands, or when lap dogs breathe their last." This segment is often quoted as a model of bathos, for the deaths of husbands and lap dogs are equally distressing to muddle-headed women like Belinda.

Canto IV: In mock anguish, Pope depicts Belinda's distress as bordering on hysteria. He elaborates the grievous snatching of a curl with six parallel lines:

> Not youthful kings in battle seized alive,
> Not scornful virgins who their charms survive,
> Not ardent lovers robbed of all their bliss,
> Not ancient ladies when refused a kiss,
> Not tyrants fierce that unrepenting die,
> Not Cynthia when her manteau's pinned awry,
> E'er felt such rage, resentment, and despair,
> As thou, sad Virgin! for thy ravished Hair.

Decking Belinda's emotions in ornate images, Pope dispatches the gnome Umbriel to the queen for a bag of sobs and sighs, a humorous parody of Odysseus's receipt of the bag of winds from King Aeolus. The dumping of pure emotion on Belinda's head shoves her over the brink of anguish; she recounts the torments of combing, conditioning, curling, and dressing her locks.

Belinda's petition to Sir Plume produces one of Pope's wittiest caricatures—the ineffectual fop with "round unthinking face." At Belinda's request, he fulminates:

> "My Lord, why, what the devil?
> Zounds! damn the lock! 'fore Gad, you must be civil!
> Plague on't! 'tis past a jest—nay prithee, pox!
> Give her the hair"—he spoke, and rapped his box.

The compounded epithets and unmasculine challenge to a cad satirizes a real defender in the fray, Sir George Brown, who took offense that Pope put sputtering nonsense in his mouth and demoted him from a serious character to witless fluff. Belinda, bereft of a champion, rues her failure to heed the omens. Pope carries his ridicule beyond the brink of decorum by having Belinda wish that the baron had "been content to seize / Hairs less in sight or any hairs but these!"

Canto V: Unstoppable in her rage, Belinda, the "fierce Virago," moves against her attacker; around her group the sprites to watch and assist. Pope, like Homer and Virgil, depicts fate as a balance beam, which favors the lock over the beaux' wits. Belinda's use of snuff and a bodkin as weapons deflates the mounting clash. At the peak of her ire, she commands that the baron give back the lock. Pope steps in with a metaphysical transformation: the treasured prize, which is no longer in the villain's hand, has transcended mortal worship and risen to heaven among the snuffboxes, tweezer cases, broken vows, hearts bound with ribbons, and other inconsequential objects. The satiric intent tempers to a mild joy in Belinda's fame as her lock of hair becomes a comet that inscribes her name amid the stars.

The Rape of the Lock, a poet's triumph of wit and classic art, displays more than Pope's involvement in a minor spat. By developing the theme of beauty as a social entity on a par with virginity and honor, he tweaks the self-absorbed eighteenth-century female who has little more to occupy her time than flirtations, card games, lap dogs, and a fit of the sulks over a suitor's unmannerly behavior. The battle between the belles and beaux exemplifies the wasted energies of a generation that expends its potential on the whims of peacockery and games of ombre and loo. In backhanded fashion, the poem does what Pope claims—it immortalizes Arabella Fermor's lost lock as a symbol of a shallow period in English history. (Bermel 1982; Drabble 1985; Eagle and Stephens 1992; Highet 1962; Hornstein 1973; Kunitz and Haycraft 1952; Magill 1958; Magnusson 1990; Person 1988; Pollard 1970; Pope 1965)

See also Addison, Joseph; bathos; caricature; Horace; mock-heroic; Pope, Alexander; satire; *The Spectator;* Steele, Sir Richard.

REPARTEE

A witty exchange of words during a verbal duel, repartee, a form of rejoinder or insulting or belittling "comeback," derives from the French for return trip.

The key to the volley established by witty or bitter badinage is that participants keep an even exchange, giving as good as they get. Repartee refers to both protracted and short exchanges. In Ring Lardner's *The Young Immigrants* (1920), for example, the elements of repartee are reduced to riposte:

> "Are you lost, daddy?" I asked tenderly.
> "Shut up," he explained.

In Book 2, Chapter 8 of Miguel de Cervantes's *Don Quixote*, a lengthy, scintillating tit for tat occurs after the tenderhearted Sancho Panza requests Doña Rodriguez de Grijalba, a duenna, to care for his mount Dapple. Her retorts set in context the scrambled values of both speakers:

> "Go mind your own ass: we duennas are not used to jobs of that kind."
> "Faith, and I've heard my master tell," quoth Sancho, "and, mind you, he's a wizard for stories—of how Launcelot when he came from Britain, said that ladies waited on him, and duennas on his nag; and, when it comes to my ass, I wouldn't swap him for Sir Launcelot's horse."
> "If you are a jester, brother," said the duenna, "keep your jokes for the right occasion where they'll be paid for, from me you'll get naught but a 'fig.'" [i.e., double entendre for an obscene gesture]
> "In that case," quoth Sancho, "'tis sure to be a ripe one, and if years count, you certainly won't lose the trick by too few points."
> "Whoreson knave," said the duenna, blazing with anger, "if I'm old or no, that is God's business, not yours, you garlic-stuffed rascal!"

Sancho bests his opponent, who drops the weapons of repartee and takes up diatribe and insults as the next best—but obviously second-rate—methods of verbal assault.

Drama, a natural setting for repartee, has provided writers with an arena for verbal fisticuffs, whether serious, comic, or satiric. Masters of the vivid, energetic give and take of evenly matched adversaries, George Etherege, William Wycherley, Aphra Behn, and William Congreve established repartee as one of the crowning literary achievements of the Restoration stage by animating characters who are skilled in turning against a detractor the bite of a nasty or caustic remark. Later practitioners of clever word sparring include Oscar Wilde, George Bernard Shaw, Dorothy Parker, Noel Coward, Mary Chase, Ring Lardner, Anita Loos, Neil Simon, and T. Coraghessan Boyle.

An example of repartee as spark to a rather tame domestic comedy is Howard Lindsay and Russell Crouse's *Life with Father* (1939), a play that ran for 3,224 Broadway performances and has been revived in school and community theaters for most of the twentieth century. The cliché of cagey wife besting boastful, overbearing husband is as old as the Greeks; in classic form, the exchanges between Vinnie and Clare Day uplift the comedy to a nip-and-tuck game of marital manipulation versus tyranny. In a husband-knows-best voice, Clare begins with complaints that he can't run the house on a sound business basis because Vinnie keeps no record of her expenditures. The discussion soon exceeds Clare's ability to cope with Vinnie's illogic concerning the purchase of a replacement coffeepot:

Vinnie:	I couldn't get another imported one. That little shop has stopped selling them. They said the tariff wouldn't let them. And that's your fault, Clare, because you're always voting to raise the tariff.
Clare:	The tariff protects America against cheap foreign labor. Now I find among my bills—
Vinnie:	The tariff does nothing but raise the prices and that's hard on everybody, especially the farmer.
Clare:	I wish to God you wouldn't talk about things you don't know a damn thing about!

The household accounts take second place to a wrangle about Vinnie's attendance at Miss Gulick's lectures on politics. Clare considers it an outrage that "a pack of idle-minded females" pay a dollar admission to hear another woman gabble about current events.

Back on track, Lindsay and Crouse's domestic satire proves the self-important banker no match for his wife. Vinnie begins adding up her purchases since Clare gave her six dollars to buy a new coffeepot: four and a half for an umbrella, two dollars for the wash. In Vinnie's summation, Clare owes her a dollar and fifty cents beyond the cost of the new coffeepot, which she charged. Playing the stock wounded wife, Vinnie blubbers:

> I don't know what you expect of me, I tire myself out chasing up and down those stairs all day long—trying to look after your comfort—to bring up our children—I do the mending and the marketing—as if that isn't enough, you expect me to be an expert bookkeeper, too.

Clare, the knowledgeable New York businessman, caves in, the victim once more of a spouse who turns on emotion and womanly ineptitude to end an unsavory evening of going over the household accounts.

Other forms of fiction, short and long, flesh out significant scenes with repartee that builds suspense and draws the reader into the spirit of time, place, and action. One of the first evidences of Mark Twain's promise was "The Celebrated Jumping Frog of Calaveras County" (1867), a sprightly western yarn long on wit and local color. At the beginning of the bet, Smiley, the protagonist, lures his sucker with a frog:

> "Well," Smiley says, easy and careless, "He's good enough for one thing, I should judge—he can outjump any frog in Calaveras County."
>
> The feller took the box again, and took another long, particular look, and give it back to Smiley, and says, very deliberate, "Well," he says, "I don't see no p'ints about that frog that's any better 'n any other frog."
>
> "Maybe you don't," Smiley says. "Maybe you understand frogs and maybe you don't understand 'em; maybe you've had experience, and maybe you ain't only a amature, as it were. Anyways, I've got my opinion, and I'll resk forty dollars that he can outjump any frog in Calaveras County."
>
> And the feller studied a minute, and then says, kinder sadlike, "Well, I'm ony a stranger here, and I ain't got no frog, but if I had a frog, I'd bet you."

And so the carnivalesque quality of sucker and bait play out, turning tables on Smiley, who is fool enough to leave his frog in the hands of an opponent. Twain's cool handling of the closed-mouth con artist prefigures a full range of hucksters and glib talkers, all of whom he caricatures as a type commonly preying on the foolish in a variety of settings: Mississippi riverboats, New England city halls, southern dry goods stores, the goldfields of the West, and around the world.

Not all repartee is built on hilarity. A repository of the menace and meaningless exchanges of absurdist literature, Heinrich Böll's "My Melancholy Face" dissolves into a succession of blips that passes for interrogation:

> "Occupation?"
> "Simple Comrade."
> "Born?"
> "1.1 one," I said.
> "Last employment?"
> "Prisoner. . . ."
> "Former offense?"
> "Happy face."

In a brief explanation, the interviewee recounts a seemingly harmless smile on a day of state mourning honoring the death of "the chief." The chillingly humorless repartee concludes with the examiner knocking out three front teeth preparatory to a horrendous going-over by torture experts. The speaker concludes disconsolately that he must "try to have no face at all anymore."

In the second half of the twentieth century, repartee surfaces in realistic, whimsical, and dramatic fiction, for example, the old-against-young meeting of the minds between a stubborn girl and the horse dealer who cheated her father in Charles Portis's *True Grit* (1968). Dickering over gelded ponies that Colonel G. Stonehill sold the late Frank Ross as breeder stock, Mattie insists that the seedy huckster reimburse her for the loss of her father's mount and also return the money he received for the ponies. Stonehill, an able, unprincipled negotiator, agrees that Mattie should consult an attorney if she deems the matter worth a lawsuit. Mattie implies that a widow with three small children may obtain the court's sympathies. Stonehill threatens to consult his lawyer. Mattie retorts:

> And I will take it up with mine. I will send him a message by telegraph and he will be here on the evening train. He will make money and I will make money and your lawyer will make money and you, Mr. Licensed Auctioneer, will foot the bill.

Stonehill relents and accepts her offer, which she presents in writing ready for his signature. Mattie, anticipating a ride into Indian territory after her father's killer, returns to Stonehill to buy a pony. Their meeting has an inauspicious beginning. Stonehill comments:

> "I just received word that a young girl fell head first into a fifty-foot well on the Towson Road. I thought perhaps it was you."
> "No, it was not I."
> "She was drowned, they say."
> "I am not surprised."

Mattie dismisses Stonehill's roistering with her spare, dry wit and argues him down to a reasonable price. Before she completes her business in Fort Smith, the exchange turns to lively sallies on both sides. Mattie notes:

> "You think I am wrong."
> "I think you are wrongheaded."
> "We will see."
> "Yes, I am afraid so."

Her preparations complete, Mattie disengages from her battle of wits with Stonehill and turns her strong Calvinistic values on a Texas ranger named LaBoeuf and U.S. Marshal Rooster Cogburn, filling the remainder of the book with frequent examples of the comic repartee that enlivens the 1969 cinema version, starring Kim Darby as Mattie, John Wayne as Rooster, and Glen Campbell as Ranger LaBoeuf.

Other examples demonstrate the flexibility of repartee as a comic or satiric device suited to an array of conversants and quibblers. In Harvey Fierstein's *Torch Song Trilogy* (1979), a camp classic on stage and in a film starring the author, Anne Bancroft, and Matthew Broderick, the central exchange is between mother and son. The stereotypical Jewish mother needles her unmarried and obviously gay son to seek a "nice girl" and raise children:

Ma:	What's the matter; you don't want children?
Arnold:	Not the kind you mean.
Ma:	The kind I mean have two arms, two legs, a mother, father, and Chicken Pox. How many kinds are there?
Arnold:	You'd be surprised.

A guardedly hostile dust-up between mother and child when the child is well into adulthood, the repartee demonstrates the frustration of each participant with unrealistic expectations—Arnold pursues an adult relationship with a mother who denies his sexual preference and devalues his love relationships. The only warfare permitted between the two is a symbolic loosing of verbal darts.

The darts between Henry II and Eleanor of Aquitaine in James Goldman's *The Lion in Winter* (1968) carry repartee to a different level of enmity. Because their three surviving male offspring leave them with a killer, a schemer, and a dullard, the king and queen have good reason to conduct a verbal yuletide shoving match as Henry contemplates the need to name an heir to the throne:

John:	You're a failure as a father, you know that?
Henry:	I'm sorry, John.
John:	Not yet you're not. But I'll do something terrible and you'll be sorry then.
Eleanor:	Did you rehearse all this or are you improvising?
Henry:	Good God, woman, face the facts.
Eleanor:	Which ones? We've got so many.

Character assassination, deception, and counterplots precipitate Henry's desperate act of confining his sons to the dungeon and plotting to marry Alais and sire more sons. The caustic verbal joust deepens old wounds with harsher re-criminations:

Eleanor: What kind of spindly, ricket-ridden, milky, semiwitted, wizened,
            dim-eyed, gammy-handed, limpy line of things will you beget?
Henry: It's sweet of you to care.

The even balance between brainy queen and grandstanding king ends the Christmas visit of Eleanor in a hilarious truce, suggesting that their relationship will continue in one-upmanship until one of them dies. (Abrams 1971; Baldick 1990; Barnet, Berman, and Burto 1960; Böll 1991; Cervantes Saavedra 1957; Fierstein 1979; Goldman 1968; Gray 1992; Holman and Harmon 1992; Lindsay and Crouse 1961; Portis 1968; Twain 1995)

See also Behn, Aphra; camp; Cervantes Saavedra, Miguel de; Congreve, William; diatribe; *Don Quixote*; double entendre; Etherege, George; Parker, Dorothy; satire; Shaw, George Bernard; theater of the absurd; wit; Wycherley, William.

RESTORATION DRAMA

The outpouring of comedies of manners that marked Charles II's accession to England's throne concluded one of the nation's most ignoble and jarring periods. Preceded by the rise of the Puritan Roundheads to political power, the collapse of monarchy prefaced the unthinkable—the public execution of Charles I on January 20, 1649; expulsion of the ousted Charles II to Scilly and his court retainers to exile in France and other European refuges; and the establishment of a commonwealth under the hand of Oliver Cromwell. Even in the early eighteenth century, dissension between Cavaliers (Royalists) and Roundheads (Puritans) caused daily unrest, as revealed in No. 125 of *The Spectator*, published Tuesday, July 24, 1711:

> There cannot a greater judgment befall a country than such a dreadful spirit of division as rends a government into two distinct people and makes them greater strangers and more averse to one another than if they were actually two different nations.

Along with killing the king and banning dance, dicing, cock fighting, and card playing, Cromwell, intending to halt the scandalous relationships between male actors and the boys of the company who played women's roles, also slew the heart of English drama by closing the theater in 1649. The absence of drama deprived the populace of stage entertainment for a dismal eleven years, when Cromwell's death and the inadequacy of his witless son Richard brought down the fanatic cabal and, on May 25, 1660, restored England's royal family.

Because this contretemps followed the energetic Elizabethan and Jacobean eras of theatrical wizardry and humanism, the loss bred a virulent hatred for religious fanatics and caused regular violations of city ordinances against satiric stage presentations known as "drolls." Like the raids on liquor stills of the

Prohibition era, the Puritan destroyers of sets, confiscators of costumes and props, and jailers of actors provoked public merriment of set-tos as outrageous as the antics of Keystone Cops. Vindictive government minions subjected companies to flogging, pillorying, and branding, but audiences continued to welcome a diversion from the long-faced Puritans. Despite all the police vigilance against mirth, one theater, the Red Bull, survived the wrecking crew the entire eleven years and was still in operation in the Restoration, but the notable stages—the Globe, Whitehall, Blackfriars, and Salisbury Court—were reduced to rubble or recycled as arenas for bear baiting or variety acts such as juggling, rope walking, and sword swallowing. When a formal setting guaranteed a raid, acting companies rescheduled their contraband productions to tennis courts and inn yards.

The joy and gaiety of a country set free of censorious fundamentalists enlivened satire and farce, which became the most available outlets for revolt against oppression, disillusion, and despair. Derived from the rich vein of French satiric jest acted by Molière and his theatrical compatriots, the notably rich English satire disparaged religion and power-mad members of the clergy. After an interim of reprises of the works of William Shakespeare, Ben Jonson, and Francis Beaumont and John Fletcher, the Restoration era produced its own stars: poet and critic John Dryden, diarist Samuel Pepys, philosopher John Locke, playwright and novelist Aphra Behn, and satirist John Rochester, one of the king's court wits. A full, invigorating era of witty, lusty Restoration comedy of manners showcased the works of William Congreve, George Etherege, and William Wycherley. A blend of music, dance, prose, and occasional verse, the plays centered on love and its tenuous alliance with matrimony but reached the local level with blatant character assassination, *romans à clef*, and references to real scandals that later generations are unlikely to decode. The cast ranged over a profusion of stock figures: the lace-cuffed dandy, the scolding brothel keeper, man-hungry widows, and the schemers, gourmands, rogues, libertines, and sweet young things who rounded out a community of libidinous folk intent on pleasure.

Over a significant period of stage history, the theater was performing the task set forth in the definition of satire—deliberately reforming public misbehaviors by publicly mocking them. The controlling element of Restoration comedy was the intellectual side of wit, a fancy-free blend of repartee, puns, double entendre, and subtle sparks of illumination, which Dryden proclaimed the high points of stage fare. Critics of Restoration humor have determined that wit is an innate substance, like one of the humors. It is either born a part of the personality or is forever lacking, an absence epitomized by the humorless Puritans. The narrowing of the field to possessors of wit also limited the subject matter of comedy of manners, which depicts sophisticates and their illusions about le beau monde.

When Nell Gwynn, Elizabeth Knepp, Anne Bracegirdle, and Elizabeth Barry took roles in plays steeped in sexual intrigue and scurrilous double entendre, the theater reached its height of bawdiness; proper theatergoers stayed home and left the stage to a narrowed audience—a prominent king's box for Charles

II and his guests and seating for a small circle of court adventurers and would-be aristocrats who had little reputation to lose by openly promoting scandalous plays. Women who ventured into the theater covered their eyes with vizard masks in a half-hearted show of guarding their reputations. Pulpits thundered in religious backlash. Playwrights responded with a strong case for their reflection of life as it was in 1660 and for some decades afterward until the English had spit out the remaining ill savor of Puritan censorship. The theater became the social setting in which reputations were made, alliances established, publications advertised, and romances furthered. A reverse of William Shakespeare's arrangement, the ticket sellers charged just a few pence for the balcony and high prices for the pit and the edge of the stage, where the fops, writers, and exhibitionists sat, often ignoring the play to bandy words and make a show of their fashionable dress and ornate mannerisms.

Restoration comedies offered innovative entertainment featuring caricatures of such abstract personae as Sir Wilfull Witwoud, Sir Positive At-all, Dashwell, Fainall, Lady Wishfort, Sir Martin Mar-All, Captain Bluffe, Sir Novelty Fashion, Mockmode, Mrs. Loveit, and Sir Fopling Flutter. Players dressed in contemporary clothing enhanced by lengthy trains, eye patches, beauty marks, stage makeup, wigs, beards, and false noses. The general tenor of amorality—sometimes called antimorality—faltered late in the period with the crowning of William and Mary and the 1698 publication of Jeremy Collier's arbitrary attack on theatrics, *A Short View of the Immorality and Profaneness of the English Stage,* which urged playwrights to rid the stage of immodesty, swearing, smut, sacrilege, wickedness, and other shows of libertinism. Collier bade them write plays:

> to expose the singularities of pride and fancy, to make folly and falsehood contemptible, and to bring everything that is ill under infamy and neglect. . . . The end of comedy is the exposing of knavery and making lewdness ridiculous.

An anonymous riposte appeared that same year claiming that "comedy will no less shame us out of our follies." But Collier's views won out over the exuberant randiness of earlier writers. The Restoration's hedonistic fervor collapsed entirely with the accession of Queen Anne, whose disinterest in theater returned the stage to the middle classes and a newer venue, sentimental comedy. (Baugh 1948; Bermel 1982; Brockett 1968; Burdick 1974; Gassner and Quinn 1969; Harris 1953; Inglis 1952; McMillin 1973; Norman 1995; Pepys 1926; Roberts 1962; Wilson 1965)

See also Behn, Aphra; caricature; comedy; Congreve, William; *The Country Wife;* double entendre; Dryden, John; Etherege, George; repartee; satire; *The Spectator;* wit; Wycherley, William.

REYNARD THE FOX

The ubiquitous trickster of medieval European beast fables, Reynard or Renard the Fox sprang from the vigorous, amoral tales that salted the more elegiac verses of courtly romance. A spark of texture and comic relief, Reynard plays the comic middle class harassed by privileged nobles and pompous churchmen. Like Uncle Remus's Br'er Rabbit, Reynard must abandon noble thoughts and gestures and rely on quick-witted action to preserve his life and independence. One version depicts the fox up against a rape charge. Finding his wife, Hersent, in a compromising circumstance—stuck in a fox hole while hunting—the wolf yanks her free, then assaults her physically and verbally:

> Do you think I'm blind,
> You vile, stinking, shameless whore—
> You got what you were asking for!
> I saw Renard as he straddled your tail
> To cuckold me, and he did not fail!

At the trial, Hersent claims that she chased the fox into his hole, followed him in, and got stuck because of her girth. Reynard ran out a back entrance and mounted her while she flailed to pull herself out of the tunnel entrance. To the king's question, Hersent claims that Ysengrin was a witness.

The king, uncertain that this scenario proves Reynard's guilt, consults a special legate from Lombardy. In humorous contrast to the straightforward, graphic testimony, the camel quotes from book three of the law:

> De concordia officiales
> Item matrimoniales
> Quando sunt adulterante
> Abscondito or in flagrante,
> Primo: interrogazione!
> [Concerning cases of a violation
> of the harmony of authorities or
> spouses, whether the adultery be
> hidden or out in the open,
> First: interrogate!]

In a bewildering circumlocution, the camel's ponderous retort meanders along without openly declaring the bourgeoisie a deviant, aggressive class who take what they want. He advises the king to punish Reynard with penitence, and either stone or burn him. The camel concludes: "Res ipse loquitur, Rex [The thing speaks for itself, King], what is a ruler for?" (Evans 1989; Harvey and Heseltine 1959; Hollier 1989; "Renard the Fox" 1994; Strayer 1989)

See also beast lore; Harris, Joel Chandler; trickster.

RICHARDSON, SAMUEL

Hailed as father of the English novel and the first name in epistolary stylists, Samuel Richardson, a Fleet Street printer and late-in-life arrival in the fiction business, produced satire of uncommonly fine proportions but concealed it so cleverly beneath bourgeois priggishness that critics are hesitant to label it true

Samuel Richardson, left, reads to a circle of literary friends from the manuscript of *Sir Charles Grandison* in the 1751 drawing. The novel, published in 1754, was to be his last.

satire. Buyers snapped up his psychological novel *Pamela* (1740), which he based on a real person, and enjoyed the droll, detailed passages that became the author's trademark. Richardson intended his work as a letter-writing manual, but, influenced by a pious upbringing, could not miss an opportunity of applying moral principles to realistic situations. The title page defines Richardson's purpose and his major stumbling-block—the inability to find a suitable stopping place:

> Now first published in order to cultivate the Principles of Virtue and Religion in the Minds of the Youth of both Sexes. A Narrative which has its Foundation in Truth and Nature; and at the same time that it agreeably entertains, by a Variety of curious and affecting Incidents, is entirely divested of all those Images, which, in too many Pieces calculated for Amusement only, tend to inflame the Minds they should instruct.

As a monument to the class differences that often brought ruin to young female members of a household wait staff, *Pamela* details the turning of the tables on a determined roué who must marry the woman he pursues for casual sex.

That a novelist of Richardson's skill should evolve from a printshop seems unlikely yet fitting for a writer who chose a working-class heroine as his fictional voice. Born the son of a carpenter in Marckworth near Derby, England, in mid-August 1689, Samuel Richardson lived in poverty and obtained a meager education. Like others in his position, he read his way to learning and developed so legible a handwriting that he hired out as a scribe and adviser to girls attempting to compose love letters. In lieu of a divinity degree, he apprenticed in his late teens to John Wilde, a printer, and enrolled with the powerful Stationers' Company, which controlled England's publishing industry during the seventeenth century.

In midlife, Richardson opened his own print shop and married Martha, Wilde's daughter. Widowed a decade later, he lost all six of his children, who died in childhood. The trauma of these losses undermined his health. In 1733, his family life prospered with marriage to Elizabeth Leake, who bore him four thriving daughters out of his second set of six children. By thrift and hard work, he succeeded in business, producing fliers, penny broadsides, texts, biography, religious tracts, chronicles, and journals. As printer for the House of Commons and warden of the Stationers' Company in the late 1730s, he profited enough to publish his own works and to purchase a country getaway, the Grange at North End, and, in 1754, bought Parson's Green, a more commodious retreat.

At age 50, Richardson returned to his boyhood interest in correspondence and began composing the letters that form the bestselling novel *Pamela, or Virtue Rewarded*. The romantic satire of 15-year-old Pamela Andrews typifies the plight of the female servant class. After the death of her employer, Lady B., Pamela must continue to work for the heir, Lady B.'s son, Mr. B., and to elude his advances, which compromise her situation as a lone female with no one to defend her honor. With the meager support of Chaplain Williams, Pamela maintains her virginity while recording in a diary and in letters to her parents Mr. B.'s daily onslaught on decorum, decency, and modesty. At Pamela's lowest point, her would-be seducer offers to keep her as a mistress and attempts to rape her. Pamela's retreat and caution salvage her virtue until the two agree on marriage.

Richardson plays a tricky game of brinksmanship, alternately assailing the reader with salacious cat-and-mouse games, then retreating to high-minded moral lectures. In an example of an ambiguous set of messages, he depicts Pamela as protective of her diary, which she sews into her underskirts alongside her hips. In direct confrontation with her base employer, she retorts:

> "Why," said I, "should your so much obliged Pamela refuse to answer this question? Cruel as I have thought you, and dangerous as your views to my honesty have been; you, Sir, are the only person living that was ever more than indifferent to me; and before I knew this to be what I now blush to call it, I could not hate you, or wish you ill, though, from my soul, the attempts you made were shocking and most distasteful to me."

In her cries to heaven, she begs the Almighty to keep her unpolluted from the lascivious master who scorns her "humble estate" and sneers at her duty to spotless maidenhood. Chastened by this bulwark of virtue, Mr. B. replies that he intends to "learn the degree of kindness sufficient to recompense you." Thus, Richardson, balancing the tedious platitude with suspense, both annoys and titillates, playing both sides of the question to his literary advantage.

Received by knowledgeable readers as a hallmark of fiction and a clever delineation of aristocratic vice, *Pamela* suffered from checkered reviews by stuffier, narrow-minded factions that labeled the work trash. As forbidden fruit unpopular with Puritans, the work became a Continental *cause célèbre* and boosted the author to best-loved status among bluestockings, who bombarded the saucy letter-writer with love notes. By 1741, Richardson wrote a sequel, *Pamela in Her Exalted Condition*, which spawned *Shamela*, an anonymous parody attributed to Henry Fielding, but never formally acknowledged. Richardson's next effort, the more straightforward tragic novel *Clarissa, or The History of a Young Lady* (1747), succeeded, again finding adoring fans across Europe who were not put off by the author's middle-class sanctimony. His last novel, the pedestrian *Sir Charles Grandison* (1754), an epistolary novel from the male perspective, fell flat, leaving critics to conclude that Richardson was at his best when viewing life from the more constrained female point of view.

The onset of Parkinson's disease competed with Richardson's drive to write. In his declining years, he enjoyed friendship with Dr. Samuel Johnson and other literati and took the waters at Bath among the fashionable set. He remained a frontrunner in the publishing world until his death from stroke at Parson's Green outside London on July 4, 1761. A vain, boring man, he would probably be surprised and quite pleased to learn of the battle of Pamelists and anti-Pamelists since the rise of feminist criticism. (Baugh 1948; Cowler 1969; Drabble 1985; Feinberg 1967; Fowler 1989; Magill 1958; Pollard 1970; Woods 1947)

See also epistolary novel; parody; satire.

SAKI

One of England's keenest spoofers of Victorianism, Hector Hugh "Hugo" Munro, writing under the name of the cupbearer in Omar Khayyam's *Rubaiyat*, disarms his reader with the lightest sting of self-realization. A social satirist of the first order, his eccentric short fiction debunks titles, priggishness, gluttony, social status, private clubs, and other humbuggery of the Edwardian middle class. In an effort to get at the heart of snobbery, he located what he considered the strongest impediment to class relations—the human desire to feel superior to one's contemporaries. He displays his insecurity among the "beautiful people" and the socially aggressive with his most memorable aphorisms:

- Women with perfect profiles are seldom agreeable.
- No more privacy than a goldfish.
- The art of public life consists in knowing exactly where to stop and going a bit farther.

Saki demonstrates his light touch in "The Storyteller" with a description of Bertha, a young woman who earns rewards for good behavior:

> She was so good . . . that she won several medals for goodness, which she always wore pinned onto her dress. There was a medal for obedience, another medal for punctuality, and a third for good behavior. They were large metal medals, and they clicked against one another as she walked. No other child in town where she lived had as many as three medals, so everybody knew that she must be an extra good child.

Saki ends the updated beast fable with an ironic twist: after Bertha hides under myrtle from a wolf, her trembling causes her medals to clink. The wolf finds her and devours all but bits of clothing, shoes, and the three medals. The story demonstrates Saki's puckish wit and his enjoyment of turning upside down the expectations of the average reader.

Saki was of Scottish ancestry, son of an inspector-general of the Burmese police and a mother from clan McNab. He was born December 18, 1870, in Akyab in the British colony of Burma, the second son and youngest of three children. In 1872, he and his brother Charlie and sister Ethel were separated from their widowed father and dispatched to Broadgate Villa in Pilton outside

Barnstaple, North Devon. The trio lived with a loving grandmother and combated the tyranny of two shrewish maiden aunts, Charlotte and Augusta, who believed that fresh air and rambles on the green were bad for children and insisted on the reading of High Church catechism on Sunday afternoons.

Reflecting on his lackluster boyhood, Saki skewers the family's "fearsome silences" and repressive confinement in "Sredni Vashtar," the story of Conradin, a fragile child who, like Saki, was not expected to live and who took refuge in a backyard shed. In the context of Conradin's particularly painful spat with his mother, Saki comments on the powerlessness of children:

> But Conradin said nothing: there was nothing to be said. Something perhaps in his white set face gave her a momentary qualm, for at tea that afternoon there was toast on the table, a delicacy which she usually banned on the ground that it was bad for him; also because the making of it "gave trouble," a deadly offence in the middle-class feminine eye.

Of this repressive aspect of Saki's childhood, Christopher Morley quips acerbically, "Aunts and werewolves were two of his specialities."

To attain peace of mind in a frazzled domestic arrangement, Saki withdrew to quiet nooks to sketch, made friends with animals, collected bird nests, and anticipated the infrequent visits of his favorite uncle, Wellesley, and his grandfather Mercer. Every four years, he enjoyed a six-week visit from his father, who had advanced to the rank of major in the Bengal Staff Corps. Freed from the misery of matriarchy, Saki, like the pathetic retriever his aunt kept chained on the back lot, thrilled to rough and tumble as though getting in enough play to satisfy him for the next four years. After graduating from Exmouth and Bedford Grammar School, Saki traveled with his retired father to France, Germany, Austria, and Switzerland.

At age 23, Saki followed the example of his grandfather, a colonel in the Indian army, and his father and brother and accepted a civil service post with the Burmese military police. He wrote home delightfully witty letters about life on horseback:

> During the night, the frogs and owls and lizards have necessarily lots to say to each other, and whenever my pony hears another neigh she whinnies back, and being a mare always insists on having the last word. As to the dogs they go on at intervals during the twenty-four hours, like the Cherubim which rest not day or night.

Over Saki's thirteen months of duty, the Burmese climate and seven bouts of malaria weakened his health to the degree that return to England was a must.

After rehabilitation in Devonshire, Saki settled in London in 1896 and wrote a political humor series, "Alice in Westminster," for the *Westminster Gazette*. His pro-Tory cartoons soon branched out to the *Westminster Alice, Daily Express, Bystander,* and *Morning Post*. Commissioned as a war correspondent, he traveled Poland, France, and the Balkans and spent two years in St. Petersburg, Russia, the source of his *Rise of the Russian Empire* (1900). On the side, he composed short satirical stories, which he published anonymously as the *Not So Stories* (1902), and a collection (which first appeared as a serial) entitled

Reginald (1904), followed by *Reginald in Russia* (1910), *The Chronicles of Clovis* (1912), *Beasts and Super-Beasts* (1914), and two novels. On his return, he lived in Surrey, where his unmarried sister Ethel kept house and served as hostess.

By nature a nonviolent man who championed animal rights, Saki nonetheless enlisted as a private in the British 22nd Royal Fusiliers at the beginning of World War I; he demanded the military accept his enlistment despite four previous rejections for being too old and physically unfit. After promotion to lance-sergeant in September 1916, Saki, still itchy for a bayonet charge that would put him in the thick of battle against England's enemy, came down with recurring malaria. A sniper shot him dead in a foxhole on the northern end of the Western Front at Beaumont-Hamel on November 13, 1916, an unheroic end of the protracted Battle of the Sommes, which cost 1,270,000 lives. To honor his friend and colleague, Christopher Morley wrote a generous eulogy that summarizes the lighter role of the satirist:

> The smiling bitter rubaiyat from which Hector Munro took his pseudonym were effectively symbolic of his own gift. The empty glass we turn down for him is the fragile, hollow-stemmed goblet meant for dryest champagne; it is of the finest crystal. Occasionally at his table we are aware that he was also a still wine of elect vintage; but for the most part he preferred to sparkle and fume with incessant bubbles of wit; a wit for which such words as satire, cynicism, sophistry, are all too gassy.

To fill gaps in public knowledge of the man who lived a vicarious double life as journalist and mirthful satirist, Saki's sister Ethel composed his biography, a reflective character study and comprehensive collection of anecdotes and letters, which is appended to his posthumous collection *The Square Egg* (1924).

Because of his Anglo-Burmese upbringing and embattled life with his harpy aunts, Saki shares a palpable empathy for children of motherless, loveless, or fragmented families and for the eccentricities of a man unsure of his place at the table. His caricature glories in a Dickensian naming of fops, losers, and social climbers—Ada Spelvexit, Sir James Beanquest, Clovis Sangrail, and Hortensia Bavvel. One of his whimsical collections—*The Toys of Peace* (1919), which features his chief loves, children and animals—appeared posthumously. Beloved for his lightly humorous stories, he continues to please readers with three frequently anthologized titles: "The Storyteller," the tale of a bachelor's attempt to amuse some bored children; "Tobermory," the dilemma of an English house party ruined by a nosy cat who suddenly learns to talk; and "The Open Window," Saki's brief masterpiece that flaunts the cruel mendacity of Vera, a girl who specializes in "romance at short notice." (Eagle and Stephens 1992; Grigson 1963; Kunitz 1942; Saki 1958a, 1958b, 1967)

See also political satire; satire; whimsy.

SARCASM

Common to ordinary conversation, sarcasm turns a simple statement upside down and spiteful. The extreme negative end of criticism, sarcasm, which derives from the Greek for "to rip flesh," allows the speaker to wear a mask and to insult or belittle while playing the role of the victim—the scorned wife, impatient landlord, hypercritical military officer, or enraged politician. Along with words go any combination of a set of contradictory gestures—a thrust of the hip, wave of the hand, drumming fingers, toss of the head, arched eyebrow, flared nostrils, sniff of disapproval, or downturned lips, all part of the arsenal of the skilled kabuki player, intricately articulated marionette, and comic vaudevillian. In written sarcasm, the choice sign-off often lobs a final bombshell, as with François Villon's "No, I Am Not as Others Are," in which he assures all that death will rob the living of wind, gall the heart, and wring out drops of sweat and futile prayers for deliverance. Playing devil's advocate, Villon poses sardonically, "Body of woman . . . must thou be spoiled in bone and skin? Yes, or else go alive to heaven."

Sarcasm's affinity for incongruity speaks volumes, making single words, phrases, and sentences do the work of a page of straight invective. For example, in Tennessee Williams's *Cat on a Hot Tin Roof* (1955), the virulent Mae, daughter-in-law of Big Daddy and chief detractor of the favorite son, Brick, strikes while Brick is fighting alcoholism and extreme depression. As Brick hobbles about on crutches, Gooper, Mae's husband, compares his injury to being sidelined at the Sugar Bowl or Rose Bowl. At Gooper's uncertainty about which bowl game Brick starred in, Mae sneers, "The punch bowl, honey, it was the punch bowl, the cut-glass punch bowl!" Gooper plays along with her undercutting of the favored son, forcing Brick's wife to defend his name against obvious slander and his patrimony from a concerted grab.

A similarly sarcastic exchange occurs in the final tangle between the corrupt judge and Roy Hobbs, wonder athlete in Bernard Malamud's *The Natural* (1952). The judge, who is adept at turning shards of aphorism into a shallow display of wisdom, believes that Roy is won over to a cynical sell-out of the Knights baseball team. To the judge's surprise, however, his man proves cannier and better equipped to discuss dishonesty than the judge anticipates. The formerly one-sided exchange tips in Roy's favor when he recalls a line from Isaiah 5:20: "Woe unto him who calls evil good and good evil." The judge, silenced by an Old Testament prophet, has no recourse.

The unrestrained use of sarcasm betrays the satirist's strategy, displaying a faulty understanding of the vitriol that sarcasm releases. By contrast, an example of the careful deployment of bitter words occurs in the last chapters of John Steinbeck's *Travels with Charley* (1962), a reflective, counterclockwise around-the-United-States travelog begun for the purpose of research. The zeitgeist carries Steinbeck from New England west to the Pacific, south to Monterey, California, and east to New Orleans late in 1960 during the media circus that accompanies enrollment of black students in white southern schools. To demonize the people who line sidewalks to revile Negro school children, Steinbeck comments:

I had seen photographs in the papers every day and motion pictures on the television screen. What made the newsmen love the story was a group of stout middle-aged women who, by some curious definition of the word "mother," gathered every day to scream invectives at children.

Before tackling the subject of overt racism, Steinbeck steps back to poke fun at himself camouflaged in "an old blue jacket and my British navy cap on the supposition that in a seaport no one ever looks at a sailor any more than a waiter is inspected in a restaurant." True to Steinbeck's prediction, no one risks missing a moment of sidewalk histrionics to study the features of the scruffy, Nobel Prize-winning author standing anonymously among locals.

Safely masked, the author moves in for a journalist's assessment of the head cheerleader—Nellie, a blowzy vulgarian built like a bull, "not tall, but . . . ample and full-busted." Like a camera recording the bare truth of something ugly and obscene, he views the almost comic pairing of the gibes and jingo "bestial and filthy and degenerate." In the brief scene that follows, observers become an enraged citizenry turned rabble whose sole purpose is stopping a single doll-sized black child from following federal marshals into a local school. Steinbeck compares his visceral reflex against crude catcalls to the audience's flinch at the theatricality of a circus barker:

> Anyone who has been near the theater would know that these speeches were not spontaneous. They were tried and memorized and carefully rehearsed. This was theater. I watched the intent faces of the listening crowd and they were the faces of an audience. Where there was applause, it was for a performer.

The sarcasm lauds well-delivered lines; the implied distaste reveals the author's revulsion at a "witch's sabbath." Combatting nausea, he stares long at the "Big Muddy" while contemplating misguided efforts to preserve segregation. He infers that "the end is not in question. It's the means—the dreadful uncertainty of the means."

Loosening the restraints is often possible when an author sets up a character to be the assassin's mouthpiece. Unlike Steinbeck's personal evaluation of racism's hot mamas, Daniel Keyes creates a retarded adult, Charlie Gordon, protagonist of *Flowers for Algernon* (1966), who profits from psychosurgery. Flying the stratosphere far above the cumulus-bound scientists at a convention, Charlie, a genius who is still wobbly in the area of self-control and interpersonal relationships, spies his counterpart, the mouse Algernon. An obvious setback to the mouse spells trouble for Charlie, who experiences the momentary coming-to-knowledge that a life of hyperbrilliance is about to end in an unimaginably grotesque slide back to mental retardation, exaggerated mannerisms, and pranks and misunderstandings at his old job as gofer at a bakery.

The situational irony hangs heavy at the climactic moment. For the first time, Charlie views photos and film footage of himself in his early moronic stage, typified by a "dull, vacuous facial expression." The audience's careless perusal of Charlie reduces him, robs him of humanity and negates the hopes that have taken shape in a once sterile soul. The audience laughs at the hopeless T-maze races against a smart mouse as Charlie tries to convince himself that "they were not gawking curiosity seekers, but scientists here in search of knowledge." On a visit to the Warren State Home and Training School, where he will probably live after he regresses, Charlie suffers the humiliation of a tongue-lashing from Winslow, the school supervisor:

> Well, how many people do you know who are prepared to take a grown man into his arms and let him nurse with the bottle? . . . You can't understand it, can you, from way up there in your research ivory tower? What do you know about being shut out from every human experience as our patients have been?

The irony anticipates the unexpected for Winslow, who assumes that sparks will fly from Charlie's wounded ego. Comforted to know that the supervisor is unashamed to express compassion for the handicapped, Charlie leaves with the first glimmer of promise on his gray horizon.

The acme of emotional regression occurs at Mrs. Neimur's cocktail party, where Charlie behaves like a self-indulgent whiner. Neimur laughs: "What did you expect? This experiment was calculated to raise your intelligence, not to make you popular." Dripping with a sarcasm that expresses his disdain for scientific meddling in human life, Charlie responds: "The hitch is that I'm a person." Finding himself on tenuous ground, Charlie consoles himself that, when he worked in the bakery, he had friends. In the privacy of the bathroom, Charlie berates himself for arrogance and self-absorption. Then, summoning courage and a touch of nobility, he drops the sarcasm and self-pity and returns to the role of objective observer. Symbolically interring his former self, Charlie buries Algernon's remains in the backyard and weeps as he places wild flowers on the minuscule grave.

A similar unleashing of sarcasm in Paul Zindel's Pulitzer Prize-winning play *The Effect of Gamma Rays on Man-in-the-Moon Marigolds* (1970) questions the satirist's ability to control sarcasm as a means to revelation. Throughout a brutal exchange bordering on child abuse, Beatrice Hunsdorfer (ironically named from the Latin for blessed) sneers at Tillie: "No, my dear, the fortress of knowledge is not going to be blessed with your presence today. I have a good number of exciting duties for you to take care of, not the least of which is rabbit droppings." Reflecting on the injustice of marriage and family, Beatrice blames her husband for being "the wrong man" and warns Tillie and Ruth about men who will weight them down with "two stones around your neck for the rest of your life." The stark torment of being mother to two girls, one severely epileptic, and hired keeper of a senile old woman pushes the snide retorts too far into sarcasm to generate much satire or humor. A comedy only in the barest sense, *The Effect of Gamma Rays on Man-in-the-Moon Marigolds* drowns in the bitter words of a mother who offers little guidance or love to the three people obstructing her freedom. Beatrice overmilks sarcasm and finds it dry and unyielding, devoid of even a moment's uplift. (Abrams 1971; Barnet, Berman, and Burto 1960; Gassner and Quinn 1969; Gray 1992; Halliwell 1994; Henry 1995; Holman 1980; Keyes 1967; Malamud 1952; McArthur 1992; Steinbeck 1962; Villon 1967; Williams 1958; Zindel 1972)

See also incongruity; invective; irony; kabuki.

SATIRE

A vigorous, sharply pointed, and, at times, embarrassingly or cruelly effective rhetorical device or genre, satire—the art of telling truth through laughter— blazes with vitality on stage and television, in advertising, puppetry, novels, biography, or verse. Satire dates to ancient Greece and Rome, particularly the witty comedies of Aristophanes, Plautus, Terence, and Menander and the barbed verse of Archilochus, Lucan, Persius, Juvenal, Martial, and Horace. The term "satire" derives from the Latin *satur* or full, the root of *satura* or medley, a mixed fare that jigs to its own rhythms to add spice and texture to the literary diet, whether fable, dialogue, anecdote, didactic verse, irony, jest, or epigram. At one time, a forced connection with the Greek *satyr* muddled critical thinking until the intervention of Swiss classical scholar Isaac Casaubon and his *De Satyra Poesi* (1605). Rescued from this unnatural connection with the satyr, a randy, demonic wood sprite from Greek mythology, the term currently resides alongside more respectable synonyms such as censure, denunciation, exposé, and impeachment, in such variously humorous, titillating, piquant, and mordant satiric classics as these:

- Aristophanes, *The Birds* (414 B.C.)

- Horace, *Sermones* (35 B.C.)

- Juvenal, *Satirae* (A.D. 110–127)

- *Le Roman de Renard* (ca. 1100–1200)

- *Carmina Burana* (1200s)

- William Langland, *The Vision of William Concerning Piers the Plowman* (1300s)

- Geoffrey Chaucer, "The Miller's Tale" and "The Nun's Priest's Tale" (1387)

- Sebastian Brant, *Das Narrenschiff* (1494)

- Desiderius Erasmus, *Encomium Moriae* (1509)

- François Rabelais, *Gargantua and Pantagruel* (1553)

- William Shakespeare, *The Taming of the Shrew* (ca. 1589)

- Miguel de Cervantes, *Don Quixote* (1605–1615)

- William Wycherley, *The Country Wife* (1675)

- Samuel Butler, *Hudibras* (1678)

- Aphra Behn, *The Rover* (1677)

- John Dryden, *Absalom and Achitophel* (1682)

- Jonathan Swift, "A Modest Proposal" (1720) and *Gulliver's Travels* (1727)

- John Gay, *The Beggar's Opera* (1728)

- Alexander Pope, *The Dunciad* (1743)

- François Voltaire, *Candide* (1759)

- Tobias Smollet, *The Expedition of Humphry Clinker* (1771)

- Robert Browning, "Soliloquy of the Spanish Cloister" (1842)

- Lewis Carroll, *Alice in Wonderland* (1865)

The twentieth century has reached its peaks of satiric skills in drama and novel, with some rare examples of verse achieving acclaim:

- Ambrose Bierce, *Devil's Dictionary* (1906)

- Sinclair Lewis, *Babbitt* (1922)

- Aldous Huxley, *Brave New World* (1932)

- George Orwell, *Animal Farm* (1945)

- Samuel Beckett, *Waiting for Godot* (1952)

- Joseph Heller, *Catch-22* (1961)

- Florence King, *Southern Ladies and Gentlemen* (1975)

- Terry McMillan, *Mama* (1987)

- Margaret Atwood, *The Robber Bride* (1993)

- T. Coraghessan Boyle, *East Is East* (1990)

- Marge Piercy, "The Grey Flannel Sexual Harassment Suit" (1995)

At home in many settings, satire often dominates dramatic scenes, as in the coming together of a community for the annual stoning in Shirley Jackson's "The Lottery" (1948) and the concentration of the wait staff to align table settings for a strategy meeting that would align Europe with the dictatorship of Adolf Hitler in Kazuo Ishiguro's *Remains of the Day* (1990). Satire also flourishes in the whimsy of Theodore Geisel (Dr. Seuss), as he describes Grinch and his dog Max in the children's holiday classic fable *How the Grinch Stole Christmas* (1957), as well as in the naughty-nice den trysts in Margaret Atwood's *The Handmaid's Tale* (1985) where Offred plays Scrabble with Commander Fred and coats her dry skin with forbidden lotion, or in Florence King's depiction of the parlor dust bunnies left by the recalcitrant southern housekeeper caught up in a frenzy of silver polishing in *Confessions of a Failed Southern Lady* (1986).

As a rule, satire pulls to the middle ground, the common denominator. A cleanser of public acrimony or defilement, satire is intended to ridicule or belittle an individual or collective human aberration—weakness, idiosyncrasy, folly, pretense, pomposity, sloth, manipulation, wickedness, or outright crime—to reform the individual and to restore probity to the era. Psychologically, the literary mode serves the writer as a form of verbal assassination of society's evils—a safe sublimation of rage that channels bluster into witty, even-handed expressions of distaste or indignation or kiss-and-tell confessional. Thus, the pattern of great eras of satire parallels eras of public excess, hardship, impropriety, and aberration, notably post-Republican Rome, Britain's Restoration Era, and America's Prohibition Era and Great Depression.

Growing out of preliterate local contests involving rustic extempore, music, and witty dialogues, Roman satire—the first use of the medium as an identifiable genre—served two polished professionals, Ennius (239–169 B.C.) and his nephew, Marcus Pacuvius (220–130 B.C.), whose experimental works survive in tatters and in their influence on the second stage of satiric evolution, the *Lucili ritu* or Lucilian style, the autobiographical, sometimes pornographic style of Gaius Lucilius (102–1 B.C.), author of irreverent satires. Written in formal hexameters, these commentaries in turn undergirded the height of Roman satire, the verse of Horace (65–8 B.C.), Persius (A.D. 34–62), and Juvenal (A.D. second century), who composed in dactylic hexameter. Of these three, Horace, a smooth joker, produced the greatest library of wit with the least number of personal reprisals. Perseus, also a survivalist, let slip a single zinger at Nero, which a friend smudged on a posthumous manuscript before sending it to the publisher. Sparing himself the law courts or an unamused Nemesis, Juvenal, a wise student of Horace's caution, chose only deceased victims for his salient gibes and covered most of Rome's checkered history. A fourth satirist, Marcus Terentius Varro (116–27 B.C.), returned to Greek models and produced an astounding 150 volumes, which were seized by the second provisional government and survive in fragments. The successors to this quartet—Seneca (ca. 4 B.C.–A.D. 65) and Petronius Arbiter (first century A.D.)—grew bold in their disenchantment with the emperors who succeeded Augustus. Seneca lampooned Emperor Claudius in *Apocolocyntosis [The Pumpkinification]* (ca. A.D. 55). Petronius, the most daring of post-Augustan satirists, penned a picaresque feast, his *Satyricon* (A.D. 60), Rome's height of social exposé.

A long dry season during the rise of Christianity left satire virtually untapped until the Middle Ages, when wandering singing poets called troubadours or *trouvères* (from the French for "invent") earned their supper and whatever patronage they could coax from audiences who listened to their original music. Alternating a stock of secular themes from love to war to local squabbles, troubadours and hired jongleurs plucked lute and bowed fiddle while entertaining with love plaints, rounds, dirges, and evensongs interspersed with spicy *sirvente* (political satires) based on local interests. Polished craftsmen Geoffrey Chaucer, William Langland, and François Villon revived and replenished the world's stock of pungent, scathing humor. Other writers followed with less well-known works, such as Thomas Drant's *Medicinable Morall* (1566) and *Arte of Poetrie* (1567), both adaptations of Horace. The puppet play of Hans Sachs, *Kasper Conjures Up the Devil* (1551), ridiculed the deceitful wife and lascivious priest whom Kasper maneuvers into playing Satan. Yet another lull preceded satire's heyday, the cultivated, self-absorbed eighteenth century, which spawned salon wit and some of theater's most revered comedies.

Satire produces a twist of logic—a distortion of reality that enlightens readers about unadmirable character traits by applying incongruity, humor, irony, and wit to such laughable or deplorable character types as social climbers, do-gooders, governmental grafters, mischievous grifters, or vain aristocrats.

The tradition of satire as a means of uplifting mortals from vice carries over from fable and fabliau to the utopian novel, which attempts to create the perfect world, and the dystopian novel, which pinpoints the flaws in philosophies and governments that tinker in vain with earthly bureaucracies. In contrast, comedy of manners directs the humor toward graphic foibles that can be depicted through sight gags, pratfalls, and incongruity. Political cartoon, a pictorial enhancement of satire, relies on incongruity, caricature, and visual absurdities, as found in Gary Larson's *The Far Side*, a pictorial bestiary that depicts animals living in human settings and behaving like humanity at its most absurd.

The style of satire tends to overt, sophisticated, mock-serious, or formalized ridicule or protest stated by a first-person narrator who is often a scantily concealed persona masking the satirist. This method of isolating human pretense, deception, conceit, or hypocrisy can vary from the gentle jest, pun, or *mot juste* of the needler to the stinging jabs and lacerations of the most indignant panegyric or diatribe, as in the works of Jonathan Swift, Britain's most renowned satirist and shaper of irony. Concealed in the folds of humor, however genteel, good-humored, sarcastic, or blatant, satire enables the writer to afflict the pompous, unscrupulous, or infamous, then take refuge in the laughter of the audience, thus shielding the originator from reprisal. A skillful example is Robert Browning's "Soliloquy of the Spanish Cloister" (1842), a venomous bluster set in a religious house:

> Gr-r-r-then go, my heart's abhorrence!
>   Water your damned flower-pots, do!
> If hate killed men, Brother Lawrence,
>   God's blood, would not mine kill you!
> What! your myrtle-bush wants trimming?
>   Oh, that rose has prior claims—
> Needs its leaden vase filled brimming?
>   Hell dry you up with its flames!
>
> At the meal we sit stogether:
>   *Salve tibi!* I must hear
> Wise talk of the kind of weather,
>   Sort of season, time of year:
> Not a plenteous cork-crop: scarcely
>   Dare we hope oak-galls, I doubt:
> What's the Latin name for "parsley"!
>   What's the Greek name for Swine's Snout?

Balancing the thin line between diatribe and hilarity, Browning concludes the satanic snarl of the speaker with a blend of blessing and sniping, *"Plena gratia/ Ave, Virgo!* G-r-r-you swine!" Browning demonstrates that the position of the satirist is tenuous, for, without a firm handhold on tone and diction, the needler slips off a lofty pedestal reserved for the guardians of truth and tumbles into the mire of the supercilious prig, thin-skinned whiner, or fastidious aesthete.

Satire is not limited to essay or editorial; it also accommodates itself to sudden enlightening revelations of amusement, dismay, or disgust in chant,

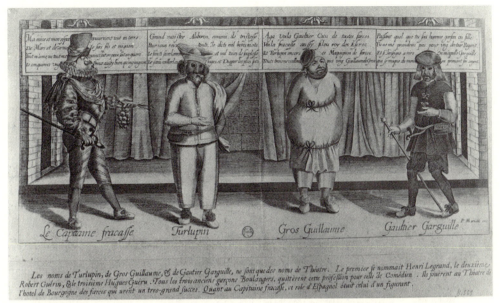

Stylized characters in seventeenth-century French satiric comedy include, left to right, a braggart Captain Fracasse, Turlupin, Gros Guillaume, and Gauthier Garguille.

song, verse, epic, drama, comic strip, cartoon, monologue, editorial, children's literature, whimsy, and short and long fiction. It may lurk in parody, understatement, mockery, burlesque, irony, caricature, or mock epic, as demonstrated by Bernard de Mandeville's mock utopian *Fable of the Bees* (1705), or, more directly, in invective, the vitriolic weapon of political cartoonists. Several variants require specific definition:

Horatian satire: The least offensive and easiest to swallow, Horace's graceful, stylistically perfect couplets spawned a branch of satire that seeks to lessen the blow, to soften the satirist's jab with a cushion of lush, punctiliously composed verse. Filled with witty wordplay, punning, energetic antithesis, droll understatement, and rhetorical turns of phrase, the satires of the Horatian school appear to aim more at art than comeuppance. Memorable as essay, verse, or aphorism for cunning putdowns, this mode of humor may cast doubts on human faults, yet offers quarter to the quarry, however vile the offense.

An example of the exacting but flexible aim of the Horatian satirist occurs in Robert Frost's quirky eulogy to Jerry McCormic, the dead insect in "Departmental: The End of My Ant Jerry." The poet's pretense at inept dactylic trimeter and comic rhymes enhances the aura of a stultifying regimentation, a bureaucratic snafu of "formic" proportions that has occluded funeral arrangements for a "selfless forager," one of the anthill's better citizens. With mock-heroic touches, Frost formalizes the lying in state and a petal shroud, suitably cleancut, understated proofs of "his people's" final gesture of fondness and remembrance. Appropriately embalmed with "ichor of nettle," Jerry in death reminds the reader of the rigidity and formality of mortuary protocol, a soulless obsequy that is irksomely sanitized. By the time the mortician, antennae "calmly atwiddle," hoists Jerry's carcass, tosses it upward, and carts it away, the onlookers have turned to their own affairs. Unable to resist a final caustic couplet, Frost concludes that the semblance of dignity, however exacting, ignores a need for warmth.

Juvenalian satire: The obverse of Horatian satire, the Juvenalian assault spares no hurts and takes no prisoners. An intense, fine-tuned attack on the world's seedier sins, the Juvenalian school sets out at a trot and quickens the pace, never pausing to let the victim catch wind and hope for escape. More self-righteous than Horatian style, Juvenalian satire stokes its furnace with the heat of dismay, shock, and outrage. The smallest phrase raises its hackles for a deeper plunge into loathing. For obvious reasons, the Juvenalian variety of needling is the weapon of choice for the political satirist or pernicious columnist, who often must hit and run in a small space.

A worthy example is the lacerating examination of U.S. morals in Florence King's *Reflections in a Jaundiced Eye* (1989). Cutting to tatters the bunting-draped niceties of American chauvinism, King is quick to swipe at the national urge to set elected officials and their families on a pedestal:

> Americans are the Uriah Heeps of democracy, wringing our hands over equal rights from the depths of a purple velvet closet. Though few will admit it, in many ways we already have a monarchy.

Her even-handed examples cover both parties, the Republican Nixons and the Democratic Roosevelts and especially the Kennedys, whom Americans revere for their refined style.

Satire Bernesque: a rollicking branch of satire derived from the grotesque-ries of Francesco Berni (ca. 1490–1536), a Tuscan poet given to whimsical characterizations, stylized paradox, conceits, picaresque heroes, and monstrous, misbegotten comparisons. Berni's facetious good fun fuels the shenanigans of François Rabelais's title heroes, *Gargantua and Pantagruel* (1553), and permeates the satires of George Byron, notably *Beppo* (1818) and *Don Juan* (1824). Rabelais's irrepressible adventurers grow so out of control that their long list of sins and misdoings has raised Rabelaisian to an equivalent of Bernesque.

Satire Ménippée: A minor genre, Menippean satire takes its name from the cynic philosopher Menippus of Gadara (third century B.C.), who inspired both Varro and Lucian to create a literary potpourri—a blend of prose and poetry into an outpouring of dialectic during Nero's troubled reign (A.D. 54–68). A fanciful, self-conscious bit of roistering, satire Ménippée requires familiarity with various styles, control, and a deft touch in pacing and texturizing humor and wit. A monograph—*États généraux* (1593)—written by Jean Leroy and a handful of gleeful cohorts (Jean Passerat, Florent, Chrétien, Pierre Pithou, Nicolas Rapin, and Jacques Gillot) pilloried the Catholic Ligue and extolled the French Protestant king, Henri IV, in an energetic concoction of burlesque, parody, caricature, and irony. The pamphlet, laced with inside jokes, ridicules the aristocracy, the Ligue's chief supporters. Other examples of the Menippean genre include:

- François Rabelais, *Gargantua and Pantagruel* (1553)
- Robert Burton's *Anatomy of Melancholy* (1621)

- Voltaire, *Candide* (1759)

- Thomas Love Peacock, *Nightmare Abbey* (1818)

- Lewis Carroll, *Alice in Wonderland* (1865)

- Aldous Huxley, *Point Counter Point* (1928)

Satiric comedy: Satiric comedy derives its farcical, slapstick energy from burlesque, sight gags, and rampant overstatement of human foolery. The drama of choice for some of theater's greatest farceurs, satiric comedy served Aristophanes, Plautus, Ben Jonson, Richard Sheridan, Molière, Nikolai Gogol, and George Bernard Shaw well. A relatively recent example of satiric comedy is Burt Shevelove and Larry Gelbart, authors of *A Funny Thing Happened on the Way to the Forum* (1963), a take-off on Plautine comedy that Stephen Sondheim developed into a successful stage romp. Full of comic repartee, puns, and naughtiness, the play focuses on the machinations of Pseudolus the trickster, played by Phil Silvers in the 1966 film version. Attempting to save the maiden from the lusty captain, he invents a plague that kills Cretans by the thousands:

Lycus:	But this girl is healthy. She goes smiling through the day.
Pseudolus:	She doesn't! I thought you knew. When they start to smile, the end is near.
Lycus:	No!
Pseudolus:	Yes. I am told it is lovely now in Crete. Everyone lying there, smiling.

A masterpiece of manipulation, Pseudolus's conniving and impromptu lies make fools of lord and slave alike, proving with his indiscriminate deception that folly, an equal-opportunity mocker, permeates all strata.

A crucial rhetorical weapon for the fiction writer, the satire of Miguel de Cervantes, Jane Austen, Mark Twain, Aldous Huxley, George Orwell, T. Coraghessan Boyle, Harvey Fierstein, Florence King, and Margaret Atwood serves as a necessary vehicle for effective criticism of society's failings, as demonstrated in *Don Quixote* (1615), *Pride and Prejudice* (1813), *A Connecticut Yankee in King Arthur's Court* (1886), *Brave New World* (1932), *Animal Farm* (1945), *Torch Song Trilogy* (1979), *Confessions of a Failed Southern Lady* (1985), and *The Robber Bride* (1993). (Abrams 1971; Barnet, Berman, and Burto 1960; Browning 1949; Cuddon 1984; Drabble 1985; *Encarta* 1994; Feder 1986; Frost 1962; Gassner and Quinn 1969; Gray 1992; Hadas 1954; Hammond and Scullard 1992; Henry 1995; Holman 1992; Hornstein 1973; Howatson 1989; Ishiguro 1990; Jackson 1982; Lovett and Hughesl 1932; Padgett 1987; Pollard 1970; Sheedy 1972; Shevelove and Gelbart 1991; Simmen 1972; Snodgrass 1987, 1988a, 1988b)

See also *Alice in Wonderland; Animal Farm;* Aristophanes; Atwood, Margaret; Austen, Jane; Babbitt; Beckett, Samuel; *The Beggar's Opera;* Behn, Aphra; *The Birds;* Boyle, T. Coraghessan; *Brave New World; Candide; The Canterbury Tales;* Carroll, Lewis; *Catch-22;* Chaucer, Geoffrey; *A Connecticut Yankee in King Arthur's Court;* diatribe; *Don Quixote;* Dryden, John; epigram; Erasmus, Desiderius; *Gargantua and Pantagruel;* Gay, John; *Gulliver's Travels; The Handmaid's Tale;* Heller, Joseph; Horace; invective; Juvenal; kabuki; King, Florence; Lewis, Sinclair;

Lucan; McMillan, Terry; Plautus; *Pride and Prejudice;* Rabelais, François; Swift, Jonathan; Voltaire, François; whimsy; Wycherley, William.

SATYR PLAY

In the classic Greek tradition, the satyr play is an outgrowth of Pisistratus's contest of triads at the City Dionysia attributed to the Athenian comic playwright Pratinas of Philus (fl. 520–515 B.C.), Aristophanes's rival. The short comic sketch allowed the viewer a reprieve from heavy tension and a return to Dionysian themes, including heady worship rituals involving wine, revelry, lechery, mock machismo, mythic lore, and uninhibited pleasure-seeking. The tragedian rounded out three tragedies with a brief satyr play, a low comedy, skit, or burlesque similar to the modern blackout. Based on clowning, costumes, mumming, and satire of local officials or aristocracy, the satyr play focused on coarse belly laughs and the lecherous antics and posturings of an animal-headed Silenus, Dionysus's mentor, leading a herd of satyrs, who were half-human, half-goat. A balance to tragedy's catharsis of pity and fear, as described in Chapter 4 of Aristotle's *Poetics*, the satyr play lightened the emotional load with a bit of fluff.

A serious impediment to the study of satyr plays is the lack of recognizable models. One satyr play, Euripides's *Cyclops* (438 B.C.), exists in its entirety among segments of Sophocles's *Ichneutae [Trackers]* (ca. 495 B.C.) and Aeschylus's *Diktyoulkoi [The Net-Drawers]* (ca. 450 B.C.). Of the 50 works of Pratinas, the master of satyr plays, nothing remains except his star Papposilenus, the too-smart-for-his-own-good instigator of devilment, and the brief statement that Pratinas's son Aristias reproduced his father's works in 467 B.C., earning for himself second prize. An ambiguous blend of wisdom and turpitude with a face resembling Socrates, Papposilenus became popular in Athenian vase art around 420 B.C., suggesting that Pratinas reached his zenith in the last two decades of the fifth century B.C. The leering satyr survives in other art—painting, mosaic, pottery—and in spirit, as evidenced by medieval and Renaissance tricksters, the best being William Shakespeare's irrepressible Sir John Falstaff. Pratinas achieved a reputation based on gag-charged plays, which influenced the Roman versions still in vogue in Augustus's day when Horace composed the rules for their composition in his *Ars Poetica* (20 B.C.). (Cuddon 1984; Drabble 1985; Feder 1986; Gassner and Quinn 1969; Gray 1992; Hammond and Scullard 1992; Henry 1995; Holman and Harmon 1992; Howatson 1989; Tripp 1970)

See also burlesque; comedy; Falstaff, Sir John; Horace; satire; trickster.

 SATYRICON

The undisputed Roman masterpiece of picaresque fiction, ludicrous burlesque, and comic romance, Gaius Petronius Arbiter's *Satyricon,* which was written around A.D. 63–65, appears to have reached the hands of readers about the time of the author's death following involvement in a foiled plot against the emperor Nero. Titled *The Book of Satyrs*, the work conjures up mental pictures of the lecherous, fur-haunched goatmen of Greek mythology along with wordplay linking satyric lechery with the aphrodisiac satyricon. A symbol of licentious debauchery and the antithesis of the Epicurean credo "Nothing in excess," Petronius's narrative loosens all the bonds, explores sexual intoxication, and commits the ultimate outrage for a variety of occasions. Badly flawed by time and by a hodgepodge of incorrect citations in other authors' works, the remaining book of the novel's sixteen chapters received a historical reprieve in 1650 when a Dalmatian antiquarian located the gem of Petronius's work, the *Cena Trimalchionis [Trimalchio's Feast]*.

Dotted with interpolations and flawed readings, the *Satyricon*, unlike Greek satire, departs from mythological characters and characterizes monstrous human follies. To depict the extremes of youthful libido, Petronius features the disjointed coming-of-age of three scamps: the Greek Encolpius and his groveling, pretty-boy lover Giton, and their troublemaking companion Ascyltos, who roam Magna Graecia—Campania, the city of Naples, Croton, and southern Italy—on their way to Tarentum in company with the coarsest and worst of local riffraff, sybarites, and scofflaws. While spending themselves further into debt at inns, brothels, public baths, bars, markets, and the shrine of Priapus, the raffish trio encounters a rogue's gallery:

- the lovely siren Tryphaena, batted back and forth from Encolpius to Giton

- Professor Agamemnon, a tiresome bore passing for a "monument of learning"

- the boastful Captain Lichas, whose macho strut limps to a halt after Encolpius seduces Tryphaena

- Quartilla, an oversexed maid given to harsh-tongued harangue and reckless sexual debauchery

- Lycurgus, kidnapper and despoiler of young men

- the grasping Philumena, too old for courtship, but still lively enough to arrange profitable marriages for her children

- Enothea, who delivers a bathetic eulogy over a dead goose

- the stereotypical mad poet, Eumolpus, the ingenuous fool fleeing a stoning after giving an obnoxious public reading

The supporting cast covers the police blotter—flashers, wife abusers, slobbering catamites and pedophiles, venal procurers, rapists, and temple robbers. The madcap pace moves from cliffhanger to escape and on to no particular end while Petronius salts in commentary on faulty education, poor upbringing, and lack of self-discipline.

The story appears to leap about, deviating from the reader's expectation of a plot, theme, or structure. The story, a frail parody of Odysseus and Aeneas's

Roman Gaius Petronius Arbiter's *Satyricon*, or *The Book of Satyrs*, written circa A.D. 63–65, was adapted as a movie by Italian director Federico Fellini. Here, Vernacchio (Fanfulla), a depraved actor, plays a lyre in a scene from the 1969 movie.

meandering journeys, reveals that Eumolpus's manhood falters because of a slight to Priapus, the god symbolized in Roman trinket stalls by a nobly erect phallus jutting forward from plump testicles. To restore his vigor, he invites Philomela to "sacrifice to the rearward Venus." Complaining of rheumatism and gout, he implores the help of Corax, who lies under his master "to hoist him up and down with his back." The ribald gymnastics result in a combined rhythm that moves Eumolpus closer to climax. With a shout, he calls for more action and "suspended between his servant and his mistress, enjoyed himself as if in a swing." Even with Encolpius's help, however, the group sex fails, but the old man takes comfort in admiring Encolpius's privates, which the youth bares with a flip of his tunic.

In contrast to less focused episodes, the chapters entitled *Cena Trimalchionis,* on a linguistic par with Plautus's bawdy vernacular plays, exploit the stereotype of the nouveau riche, a Gaius-come-lately to imperial success who flaunts money with no thought to courtesy or taste. Prefaced by the trumpet's call and the service of liveried flunkies, dinner includes smoking sausages alongside delicate plums, pomegranate seeds, and dormice in honeyed poppy sauce. The speeches of the host Trimalchio, a middle-brow freedman who picks his teeth; his companion Habinnas; and their associates illustrate the undereducated low Latin *(lingua Romana rusticana)*, a slangy, graceless patois reminiscent of the English Cockney or the southern redneck: "to piss hot and drink cold" and "the sweat poured down my crotch." Most memorable of Petronius's lines is the motto "Vivamus, dum licet esse [Let us live while we can]."

Stretching out in mock-heroic overkill, the lengthy gala reprieves Trimalchio's ostentation with each new dish, including the dropped silver salver that Trimalchio tosses into the trash heap along with broken crockery. A table mate boasts to the wide-eyed Encolpius, "[Trimalchio's] lands reach as far as the kites fly, and his money breeds money." To prove his worth, Trimalchio organizes a bingo game and displays a grabbag of prizes: a side of bacon, a neck pillow, "lamprey and a letter, a mouse and a frog tied together, and a bundle of beet-root."

At a tense moment in the lavish supper, Ascyltos loses his composure and laughs uncontrollably at his host's dimwittedness. In defense of Trimalchio, Hermeros, a loyal freedman, launches into his best oratory:

> You! with your mammy's milk scarce dry on your lips, you can't say boo! to a goose; you crock, you limp scrap of soaked leather, you may be supple, but you're no good. Are you richer than other folk? Then dine twice over, and sup twice!

Giton compounds the offense by joining in the uproar, which concludes with the watchdog smashing a chandelier. Trimalchio concludes the feast with the text of his tomb inscription, which names him "C. Pompeius Trimalchio, a Second Maecenas," after Rome's famous patron of the arts.

Petronius's satire offers multiple possibilities for interpretation. If taken as low comedy directed at the know-nothing parvenu (perhaps autobiographical in its arch irony), the *Cena Trimalchionis* serves the purpose of satire in revealing the upstart's faulty upbringing and unwise display of ignorance by, for example, ordering a servant to bring a pot in which the bumbler can relieve himself before proceeding with the next course. If read as a roman à clef and sweeping generalization on Roman moral corruption in the fifth decade of the empire, the piece moves up a notch in skillful parody, cleverly depicting an entire nation as vapid, materialistic, and deserving of the welter of public behaviors and imperial depravity that violated its former seemliness and decorum. If the work is a roman à clef, the story obviously disguises Nero as Trimalchio, a persona certain to keep underground Rome snickering as copies passed from hand to hand and readers whooped at Rome's self-assured smart set. Assuming that Petronius was targeting Nero's moral bankruptcy, editor John Dunlop remarked in 1876 that the poet creates "too fine a veil for so deformed a body."

A version of Menippean satire with its blend of verse and prose, Petronius's *Satyricon* offers enough of a glimpse of imperial Rome to convince the reader that "judge of good taste" might have been a nickname freighted with sarcasm and a tinge of contempt. The chaotic array of vivid stanzas features numerous promising starts: a fabliau about the resourceful matron of Ephesus, riddles, erotica, lycanthropy and witchcraft, charming billets doux, harangues laced with malapropisms, a takeoff on Lucan's *Pharsalia*, a brief overview of the fall of Troy *(Troiae Halosis)*, a fitting tribute to Nero's disastrous reign, and a public execution. The subject of Henryk Sienkiewicz's moralistic *Quo Vadis* (1912), the work was more fittingly treated in Federico Fellini's *Satyricon* (1969), a bold, scenic satire that applies Petronius's formula to a camera-eye view of the sexual dabblings of a young Roman whom the author displays in crayon-bright scenarios and a sensuous melange of grotesquerie, obscenity, jollity, and lust loosely linked with frail dialogue and audacious stunts. For all its flaws, the film earned Fellini an Oscar nomination for directing. (Drabble 1985; Feder 1986; Godolphin 1949; Hadas 1954; Hammond and Scullard 1992; Hornstein 1973; Howatson 1989; Mantinband 1956; Petronius 1925, 1934; Radice 1973)

See also burlesque; comedy; fabliau; parody; Petronius; picaresque; Plautus; satire.

SCATOLOGY

Scatology is a scientific or paleontological term that describes the study of excreta or, more specifically, of animal dung, scat, or coprolites as a repository of data on nutrition, disease, and digestive and excretory habits of living organisms or fossils. In a literary sense, scatology and coprolalia, both forms of pornography, name a subset of satire or comedy that takes its humor from foul or crude talk, coarse jest, pornography, coprophilia, zoophilia, pederasty, necrophilia, fetishism, or inappropriate or facetious commentary on the sound, smell, or appearance of human or animal bowel functions, expulsion of flatus, and excretion. Satire is a natural source of scatological humor. One of the most joyous of Renaissance scatologists, François Rabelais, depicts his foul-mouthed, uninhibited character Gargantua in the act of making up rhymes:

Shittard
Squittard,
Crackard,
Turdous,
Thy bung
Has flung
Some dung
On us.
Filthard,
Cackard,
Stinkard,
May you burn with St. Anthony's fire
   If all
   Your foul
   Arseholes
Are not well wiped ere you retire.

In a more recent novel, a comic example of the scientist's study appears in Michael Crichton's *Jurassic Park* (1990), in which zoologists dig up to their elbows in a monstrous glob of dinosaur feces to determine the illness that afflicts a triceratops. In a broader sense, the term also names any obsession with obscenity or immodesty. For example, in Act II, scene ii of William Shakespeare's *Antony and Cleopatra* (1607), the smirking Agrippa comments on the Egyptian queen, "Royal wench! She made great Caesar lay his sword to bed; he plowed her, and she cropp'd." Such metaphoric comparisons of penis to plow and vagina to fertile field are indigenous to symbolic language, statuary, mosaic, fresco, and particularly to hymns and paeans to fertility gods, notably the Roman Priapus.

Most often, scatology defines an egregious nastiness, an urge to repel or provoke disgust. In twentieth-century young adult literature, Holden Caulfield from J. D. Salinger's *The Catcher in the Rye* (1951) ridicules Stradlater, an insecure classmate who picks at his acne and squeezes pustules, and about a presentation by Ossenburg, a wealthy undertaker who drives a Cadillac and receives a grandstand cheer for funding a dormitory and regular donations of money to Pencey High. With one quick anecdote, Holden deflates the aggrandizement of a pep talk about Ossenburg praying to Jesus:

> He was telling us all about what a swell guy he was, what a hot-shot and all, then all of a sudden this guy sitting in the row in front of me, Edgar Marsalla, laid this terrific fart. It was a very crude thing to do, in chapel and all, but it was also quite amusing. Old Marsalla. He damn near blew the roof off.

Salinger adds that the headmaster, Mr. Thurmer, visits compulsory study hall the next night to scold "the boy that had created the disturbance in chapel," whom Thurmer deems unfit to be a Pencey student. The boys, impressed with

Marsalla's skill, encourage a repeat performance, but Marsalla "wasn't in the right mood."

The "commodic wit" that is the norm of smutty, offensive adolescent humor and grafitti becomes a symptom of arrested emotional development or serious mental disturbance in adult characters and writers. A pathological interest in body effluvia applies particularly well to T. Coraghessan Boyle's frequent and detailed descriptions of disease and his listing of wens, ulceration, intestinal gas, fistulas, vomiting, rheumy eyes, pus, and sweat. His most intense study of miserable human conditions occurs in *Water Music* (1983), a picaresque novel that describes a fictional character in England in tandem with a study of Mungo Park, the adventurer who attempts to locate the source of the Niger River by slogging through wretched jungle at the mercy of unpleasant weather, heat, insects, snakes, and disease.

In a broader sense, scatology also names bawdy talk, for example, the low comic element that permeates folk lyrics, limericks, medieval satire, and fabliaux. A part of the earthy humor in Geoffrey Chaucer's "The Tale of Sir Thopas" (1387), scatology takes the form of evaluation: the story is "not worth a toord." More repulsive to most readers is the ribald "Miller's Tale," in which Alison, during an amorous intrigue with Nicholas, rejects Absalon's plea for a kiss, then relents and presents her posterior at the window. Absalon realizes that he has been tricked into kissing "her nether eye" and complains about her scratchy pubic hair.

The most perplexing of scatologists, Jonathan Swift, a churchman and satirist who was fond of François Rabelais's *Gargantua and Pantagruel* (1593), frequently lingers longer than necessary over low comic scenes. His interest in anatomical detail in *Gulliver's Travels*, for example, manifests itself in his emphasis on the British pronunciation of Mr. Bates, a homophone for masturbates; in ludicrous accusations that the giant Gulliver carries on a secret amour with the Lilliputian wife of a court official; and in the outrageous comic scene in which Gulliver urinates on a palace fire to stop its spread. A more pointed digression—Chapter 8 of *A Tale of a Tub* (1704)—wanders on inanely about the Aeolists and summarizes:

> For, after certain Gripings, the Wind and Vapours issuing forth; having first by their Turbulence and Convulsions within, caused an Earthquake in Man's little World; distorted the Mouth, bloated the Cheeks, and gave the eyes a terrible kind of Relievo. At which Junctures, all their Belches were received for Sacred, the Sourer the better, and swallowed with infinite Consolation by their meager Devotees.

This aspect of Swift's dark, incomprehensibly vitriolic satire of the evolution of religious sects from Catholicism has incurred the greatest criticism of otherwise finely honed, focused satire.

In contrast to Swift's overkill, Laura Esquivel's *Like Water for Chocolate* (1992) releases Tita, the protagonist, from an untimely pregnancy by "loosing a violent menstrual flow" and, in the denouement, disposes of a cruel, possessive sister in an illness that causes extreme flatulence:

> At first Pedro didn't find it odd that he could hear Rosaura breaking wind
> even with the door closed. He began to notice the unpleasant noises when one
> lasted so long it seemed it would never end.

Esquivel pictures Pedro trying to concentrate on reading rather than on "his wife's digestive problems." Meanwhile, the floor shakes, the lights blink, and a smell permeates the area, even though he walks around the bedroom holding burning charcoal and a bit of sugar in a spoon. Esquivel's description, unlike Swift's scholarly dissertation, proceeds naturally from outspoken peasant fiction.

Swift's protégé, John Gay, produced similarly dung-laden passages in the satiric mock Virgilian eclogue *Trivia; or, The Art of Walking the Streets of London* (1716). Unlike Swift, Gay controls his jest with humorous word play, as in his description of Cloacina, goddess of excrement, whom he names for cloaca, the Latin for sewer:

> Then Cloacina (Goddess of the tide
> Whose sable streams beneath the city glide)
> Indulg'd the modish flame; the town she rov'd,
> A mortal scavenger she saw, she lov'd;
> The muddy spots that dry'd upon his face,
> Like female patches, heighten'd ev'ry grace:
> She gaz'd; she sigh'd. For love can beauties spy
> In what seems faults to ev'ry common eye.

The political intent of Gay's poem lies in the comparison of "brown spots" to the makeup patches that fashionable women applied to face, neck, and shoulders. In some cases, the shape and placement of the patches indicated their wearer's political affiliation.

A more recent study of the eighteenth century returns to Swift's manic concern with scatology through an evaluation of insanity in England's King George III. Yorkshireman Alan Bennett's darkly comic parable, *The Madness of George III* (1993) is the impetus for the cinema adaptation, *The Madness of King George* (1994), which earned the playwright an Oscar nomination. The play's depiction of the excesses of medical treatment, especially for the insane, extend to cupping and bloodletting, restraints, pap feeding, purges, and one physician's obsession with the king's "motions," a euphemism for bowel movements. After the most rigorous purge, George declares that his fourteen motions could have manured the neighboring fields. In repeated episodes, medical descriptions of the color of the king's "water," or urine, the shape and quantity of his stool, and frequent views of the king in diapers or his "small clothes," a euphemism for underwear, figure in the state quandary debated by the House of Lords concerning replacing the king with his son, George, Jr., the Prince of Wales, or feigning national stability by concealing the king's exotic behaviors. Bennett manages to satirize eighteenth-century medical experimentation without losing sympathy for George, who regains control of his body, mind, and government in time to circumvent young George from dethroning him. (Baldick 1990; Bennett 1993; Boyle 1983; Corliss 1995; Crichton 1990; Cuddon 1984;

Esquivel 1992; Fowler 1989; Gay 1932; Gray 1992; McArthur 1992; Rabelais 1955; "Royal Treatment: Bennett's 'King George'" 1995; Salinger 1951; Shakespeare 1974; Swift 1958)

See also Boyle, T. Coraghessan; fabliau; *Gargantua and Pantagruel;* Gay, John; *Gulliver's Travels;* limerick; "The Miller's Tale"; Rabelais, François; satire; Swift, Jonathan; *A Tale of a Tub.*

SENECA

Recognized primarily as a moralist and philosopher, Lucius Annaeus Seneca the Elder lived a remarkable life and composed a lengthy list of memorable aphorisms. A native of Corduba (Cordova), Spain, he was born in 4 B.C. to Helvia, a strong-willed role model to her son, and Marcus Aurelius Seneca, a rhetorician and historian—a wealthy, success-oriented Equestrian family. Not wholly to his family's liking, Seneca moved to Rome with his aunt, studied under top-rank philosophers, became a vegetarian, developed a belief system based on the transmigration of the soul, and, despite bouts of asthma, traveled to his uncle's prefecture in Egypt to immerse himself in the lore of the Nile. Destined to climb the traditional political ladder, Seneca specialized in rhetoric and law, became a first-rate ethicist and playwright, and, despite the onset of consumption, rose from senator to quaestor.

The rapidity of Seneca's success challenged the intemperate emperor Caligula, who wanted him executed. Others in Seneca's family found their careers influenced by Rome's corrupt powermongers: Seneca's older brother, Marcus Annaeus Novatus, conducted the trial of St. Paul, whom Seneca befriended. Lucius Annaeus Mela, the younger of the brothers, suffered the suicide of his son Lucan, the witty court poet who died as a result of the failed plot to assassinate the crazed emperor Nero. Palace scandal sullied Seneca himself, whom Caligula exiled to Corsica in A.D. 41 on the Empress Messalina's unsubstantiated charges of seducing Julia Livilla, Caligula's sister. Before Seneca's banishment, his first wife died; he married Pompeia Paulina, mother of his only son, who died in childhood. Seneca, toughened by the loss of the best years of his early manhood, sent a powerful emotional essay, *Consolation* (ca. A.D. 41) to his mother, to whom he entrusted his remaining child, his daughter Novatilla.

Life on a barren isle produced two worthy qualities that forged a stronger man—the strengthening of stoicism and the emergence of satire in his writings. In the empty hours, Seneca turned to philosophy and relearned the truths of his school years from the point of view of bitter, undeserved personal experience. He wrote of the "barbarous land which rugged rocks surround,/Whose horrent cliffs with idle wastes are crowned." The island was too poor a soil and clime to produce autumn fruit, olives, spring buds, and herbs. Lacking bread and the sacred hearth of Rome, Corsica was suited only for "exile and the exile's grave."

Reprieved when Agrippina married the emperor Claudius in A.D. 49 and freed the popular stoic as a means of ingratiating herself with the citizenry, Seneca accepted the honor of tutoring the empress's son Nero. The power and influence that the writer gained from his insider's knowledge of palace intrigue fattened his coffers, but made him wary and poker-faced in difficult times. In A.D. 54, when Agrippina's successful poisoning of Claudius thrust 16-year-old Nero into power, Seneca lampooned the practice of conferring godhood on deceased emperors in his *Apocolocyntosis Divi Claudii [The Pumpkinification of the Divine Claudius]* (ca. A.D. 55), a jolly Menippean satire blending verse and prose at Claudius's expense. Set in the underworld, the work, opening on "the proceedings in heaven October 13 last," depicts Claudius—limping badly from polio—arriving among the spirits. Hercules, the one-man reception committee, tries to get straight answers from the stuttering Claudius and supports his admission to the god room. Augustus, unsettled by the imperial penchant for killings, objects. Hercules must try harder.

The parody, laced with undignified invective and scurrilous parody, envisions a dismal funeral train leading to the depths of hell. Mumbling to himself, Claudius accepts a just penalty: he must endure everlasting frustration in an endless dicing exercise, a game the emperor loved:

> For when he rattled with the box,
>   and thought he now had got 'em,
> The little cubes would vanish thru
>   the perforated bottom.
> Then he would pick 'em up again,
>   and once more set a-trying;
> The dice but served him the same trick:
>   away they went a-flying.
> So still he tries, and still he fails;
>   still searching long he lingers;
> And every time the tricksy things
>   go slipping thru' his fingers.

The pernicious jest at Claudius's expense leads to greater indignities: Caligula assigns Claudius to the post of law clerk, a hearty joke on the emperor, who flouted the law. Not up to Petronius's standards of wicked satire, Seneca's pumpkin-making suggests a petty whetting of the ax to strike at a dead man.

To provide stability for his charge and assure a smooth transfer of power, Seneca joined Sextus Afranius Burrus, head of the palace guard, in monitoring the reckless young emperor. Nero's mother eluded their plans and maneuvered her son to evil. After she turned on Nero and connived to put Claudius's son Britannicus on the throne, the emperor weakened the bolts on her boat and caused her to capsize on a jaunt from her spa at Baiae; hired killers finished the job. In Nero's defense, Seneca composed a defense, "Essay on Clemency" (ca. A.D. 55) and dispatched it to the senate. This letter suggests that both Burrus and Seneca may have played a part in Agrippina's assassination.

The latter stage of Seneca's role in the Roman power struggle brought him down after Poppaea, Nero's second wife, supplanted the gentle Octavia and corrupted the emperor, who became a capricious, murderous megalomaniac. Wisely withdrawing to Nomentum, his rural estate, in A.D. 62, when he could not forestall the emperor's second marriage, Seneca pled poor health and fatigue. He and his wife Paulina enjoyed three years of comfort, but he could not shield himself and his family from the debacle following Piso's conspiracy to murder the crazed emperor. Along with Lucan, Seneca and Paulina were forced to open their veins and received no opportunity to compose wills or bid farewell to family. Seneca, pitifully maimed in both frail ankles, knees, and wrists, dictated a final essay on ethics, swallowed poison, and slid underwater to drown in the bath. Under orders from Nero, the house staff saved Paulina from bleeding to death, but the remaining months of her life were absorbed in grief and memories of her husband.

One of Rome's most multitalented people, Seneca, like a host of collared intellectuals, compromised his brilliance by maintaining a close association with the corrupt seat of rule. Countering the political maneuverings that brought him down were his lifelong devotion to humanism and upright behavior, a product of his devotion to stoicism and his drive to end slavery and vicious pagan spectacles, the mark of imperial Rome's devaluation of life. A master of the crisp, memorable Latin sentence, he produced a wide range of works: a weighty 20 volumes of letters, 12 dialogues on ethics, 7 books on natural law, 3 works on mercy, and 9 stentorian dramas meant for the reading stage rather than performance. Among his most frequently cited lines are these favorites:

- There is no great genius without some touch of madness.
- What fools are mortals.
- The best ideas are common property.
- I was shipwrecked before I boarded.
- Do not ask for something you will regret.
- We are all sinners.

A major figure in the development of the aphorism and the essay, Seneca was admired by Romans Tacitus, Quintilian, and Juvenal, who declared, "If the people had a free vote, there is no doubt that they would choose Seneca over Nero." For centuries, schoolchildren translated and memorized Seneca's major essays. His stoic epistles and essays influenced early Christian philosophers—Jerome, Lactantius, Augustine, and Tertullian—some of whom revered the moralist as a prefiguration of Christianity. His dramas and essays influenced Geoffrey Chaucer, the Spanish tragedians, William Shakespeare, John Webster, Michel Montaigne, Denis Diderot, Father Abelard, and Roger Bacon. (*Classical and Medieval Literature Criticism* 1991; Feder 1986; Godolphin 1949; Hadas 1952, 1954; Hammond and Scullard 1992; Hornstein 1973; Howatson 1989; Mantinband 1956; Radice 1973; Seneca 1877, 1986a, 1986b)

See also didacticism; epigram; invective; Lucan; parody; satire.

SERMONES

The first published work of 35-year-old Quintus Horatius Flaccus, a volume of ten *Sermones [Satires]* (35 B.C.), or conversation pieces, received strong critical approval from Rome's literati for its reflection of the light, fluid Lucilian style developed in the thirty books of his mentor a century before. A balance of intertwined ruminations from a man who had read Greek classics in Rome and had studied philosophy in Athens, the books range over universal social topics in varied styles: dialogue, imaginary interview, epigram, memoir, rhetorical essay, taunts, outrageous jest, and sermonette. In Book 1, Horace moves directly to the heart of his appreciation of a settled life. Giving no quarter to the insatiable citified malcontent to whom plenty is never enough, he chides the greedy-gut who never ceases chasing new thrills that quickly pale into yesterday's fads. To Horace, good manners derive from the stoic philosophy: life demands that he accept his share of worldly pleasures, then gracefully withdraw from the table without grousing over the unfairness of his seat or the manner of his death.

Reading almost like a journal or scrapbook, Books 2 and 3 offer a clearer picture of Horace's wartime experience and youthful studies, both of which made him a ready swordsman and a writer more willing to defend himself than to attack an adversary with slashing blade or nitpicking. Yet he claims to remain true to the satirist's work of lambasting human weaknesses. In the fourth book, Horace expands on "the best of all fathers," who provided him day-to-day commentary on good and bad behavior by pointing out live examples. In his own words, the poet exults: "sic me formabat puerum dictis [thus he formed me from boyhood with his words]." From these frank, energetic conversations (with Horace playing both the speaker and the devil's advocate), the poet claims to have learned candor in his own dealings and to accept the critic's rebuttal with equanimity.

In proof of his embrace of every moment's possibilities, Horace fills Book 5 with a detailed sketch of a jouncing, rain-soaked journey to Brindisi with a friend, Heliodorus, the rhetorician. So pleased is Horace with his good-natured traveling companion that he claims friendship is a prime delight. An imaginary discussion of humble origins with Horace's patron Maecenas continues in the sixth satire with a disclaimer that prestige does not make the individual. In Horace's estimation, people who jump to conclusions about pedigrees enslave themselves to title, lineage, and endless kowtowing. Proud to be a freedman's son, the poet adds that, given the choice of parentage, he would select the same man to rear him. Concluding his literary rambles with praise to Lucilius, Horace acknowledges that mentorship and sycophancy are not synonymous. Without copying Lucilius's genius or slavishly challenging his fame, the poet seeks an individualized niche—neither the randy love lyrics or marriage hymns of his immediate predecessor, Catullus, nor the epic grandeur of Virgil or Varius. Secure in his satiric hexameters, Horace is very much at home with himself and his ambitions.

Horace's second collection of *Sermones* (30 B.C.) grows even more bold and self-assured, opening with a sharp set piece between himself and his lawyer Trebatius, who states the jurist's notion of the satirist's credo: He who chooses satire for his daily fare must be prepared to get what he dishes out, thrust for thrust, lawsuit for lawsuit. Horace replies with his classic touch that the proper statement of satire results in acknowledgment of truth rather than a scurrilous wrangle among disgruntled parties. After all, if Horace trounces a cad, the victim must recognize the truth of the accusation. Only bad satire ends in a court battle. A direct outgrowth of his appreciation for professionalism, one of his most famous epigrams from this segment of the *Sermones* encourages people to anticipate life with a hearty appetite brought on by hard work. His contrasting picture of the world-weary dilettante proclaims that overindulgence ruins the palate for quality food obtainable fresh from the country—oysters, trout, fowl, berries, apples, grapes, eggs, forest mushrooms, honey, shellfish, wine, oil, salt, pepper, venison, pork, and piquant sauce. Likewise, a gobbler's approach to sex ruins the lover's conquest by allowing his genitals to drive a body better controlled by the brain. Horace's adherence to the Golden Mean derives from his classic education and a firsthand study of Epicureanism and stoicism. His motto is "Nothing in excess," and he further advises:

> Live so that you tempt not the sea relentless,
> Neither press too close on the shore forbidding;
> Flee extremes, and choose thou the mean all-golden,
>   Treasure all priceless.

He concludes with an image of the wise captain who remains courageous in difficult times and wisely trims his sails "when a gale too prosp'rous/Swells out the canvas."

One of the most unusual stylistic touches in Horace's flow of hexameters occurs in Book 6, the beast fable known today as "The City Mouse and the Country Mouse." Often retold in children's storybooks and performed in cartoons, the brief narrative begins in typical "once upon a time" style with the departure of a frugal *mus rusticus* on a visit to the *mus urbanus,* his old friend. Surrounded with humble pease, oats, grape seed, and bacon, the rural mouse cuts to the heart of his fears: Has the city mouse weighed a full belly against the constant terrors that may lop days from his life? Laughing off the question, the city mouse initiates his bumpkin buddy into the proprieties of tucking in a napkin and reclining at the Roman table in anticipation of a full board, complete with many courses and a personal slave to taste each salver. Before the city mouse can relax with a citified first course, raucous hounds chase the two diners from the room. The country mouse waves a glad farewell and returns to the woods in good spirits to a simple hearth where he can eat in peace. (Feder 1986; Godolphin 1949; Horace 1888, 1892, 1899, 1902, 1909, 1959; Kilpatrick 1981; Monagan 1985; Moskovit 1983; Rudd 1982; Shackleton 1982)

See also beast lore; epigram; Juvenal; Martial; satire.

SHAKESPEARE, WILLIAM

The actor, theatrical producer, and playwright whose bravura canon constitutes the height of the English Renaissance, Shakespeare lived the pattern of the zeitgeist—a coming-of-age for drama that ideally suited the poet by offering him numerous opportunities to satisfy his genius. In Ben Jonson's words, "He was not of an age but for all time." Born April 23, 1564, in Stratford-on-Avon, Shakespeare was the third son of gentlewoman Mary Arden and glover, tanner, and magistrate John Shakespeare. The playwright studied at a Latin grammar school but may have ended formal education at age thirteen, when his father suffered financial difficulties. There remains little historical data from youth, but he was obviously well read and well versed in England's literature and lore, for example, the yearly St. George's Day pageant in Stratford, forest plants, and common nostrums. Because of the setbacks in his family's fortunes, Shakespeare was unable to attend a university and at age 18 married Anne Hathaway, who was eight years his senior and the daughter of a moneyed farming family of nearby Shottery. Following the birth of their daughter Susanna and twins, Judith and Hamnet, in 1584, Shakespeare left his wife and children at his father's house and sought to earn a living in London as an actor, then considered a shady, haphazard calling.

Amid a thriving theatrical atmosphere, Shakespeare—a popular, talented stage professional despite a late start—joined the Lord Chamberlain's Men around 1587. His career was briefly circumvented by an outbreak of plague, which killed up to a thousand Londoners a week and closed theaters from 1593 to 1595 with the constable's warning on the doors, "Lord have mercy on us." During this grim hiatus, the playwright wrote poetry and produced his long narrative verse, *Venus and Adonis* (1593) and *The Rape of Lucrece* (1594), which were skillful and appealing enough to inspire a public sneer from the envious university wit Robert Greene and to be bound in numerous Elizabethan anthologies. Undeterred by writers who boasted better lineage, extensive travel, and more ponderous university degrees, Shakespeare continued to make news. In 1592, under the patronage of the Earl of Southampton, Shakespeare initiated a lengthy sonnet sequence dedicated to an unnamed lady—possibly Emilia Lanier, cast-off mistress of Lord Chamberlain Hunsdon. The finished work, published in 1609, is rich in the evocative verse style that colored the 37 plays of his canon.

Under the aegis of Elizabeth I and her Scottish successor, James I, Shakespeare produced two plays per year for his own acting company, beginning with *Henry VI, Part 1* (ca. 1589), a sellout in its first performance. In roles that he designed to suit the talents of his actors, Shakespeare featured some of the stars of the era: tragedian Richard Burbage, comics Will Kempe and Robert Armin, and John Heminges. Shakespeare enjoyed the challenge of show business, in part because he knew what playgoers liked to see, hear, and experience during a performance: suspense, love stories, ghosts, murder, faraway settings, and the lives of royalty. If his experiments in tragedy, comedy, history, and romance were not welcomed by critics, he could take pride in pleasing audiences at London's major theaters, at court on the opening of the theater season, and at his capital venture, the Globe playhouse, neatly fitted with jutting center stage, trapdoor, and a multipurpose gallery suitable for musicians or love scenes, orations or an ornate gesture to the crowd below. The first English actor to own a share in a theater, Shakespeare, along with his partners, built across the Thames River in 1598, in part to avoid censorship by London's mayor and by dour Puritans, who disapproved of frivolity and of the living arrangements that placed young male actors alongside lecherous adult men of questionable repute.

Shakespeare's company charged a penny for the pit and extra for padded seats in the balcony. Above the ridicule of snippy critics and outright theft of his works by unscrupulous publishers, money brought him some peace of mind and allowed him to raise his father to honor in Stratford by appending a gentleman's coat-of-arms to the family name. In his fifties, Shakespeare retired to a large parcel of land in his hometown and built New Place, a sizable residence with a walled garden, and also purchased a house near Blackfriars in London. He continued writing, although his ties with London were never as close as they were during the height of his career, and London itself had lost its zest for drama as Puritanism strengthened its hold on the middle class. During the production of his last play, *Henry VIII* (ca. 1612), which the playwright embellished with a royal procession and cannon fire, sparks ignited the Globe's thatched roof. In a few hours, the theater burned to the ground. The investors rebuilt, but Shakespeare created no new dramas for the company.

A few years after inscribing a will leaving most of his property to his daughter Susanna, Shakespeare died of fever on April 23, 1616, and was buried in the chancel of Stratford's Holy Trinity Church. His tombstone contains a famous curse on any who disturb his bones. His works won the greatest of posthumous honors—publication in collections and a scholarly interest that elevated his works to the status of classics and made them available to ever more readers, collectors, and acting companies. Knowledgeable contemporaries valued the impressive *First Folio*, which was published in 1623; those who came after had wider choices, including the *Second Folio* (1632) and an edition by Alexander Pope, the literary lion of the Augustan Age.

Shakespeare's wide-ranging plots and settings reflect the Renaissance interest in universal matters and in human concerns, including love, treachery, family, loyalty, success, and failure. His use of rhetorical devices indicates his command of poesy:

- Marc Antony's diatribe and wit in *Julius Caesar* (ca. 1599)

- satire on pedantry and euphuism in the court comedy *Love's Labours Lost* (ca. 1593)

- Petruchio's ribald puns in *The Taming of the Shrew* (ca. 1589)

- the caricature of the wily servant in *A Comedy of Errors* (ca. 1580s)

- Mercutio's alternation of witty merriment and black humor in *Romeo and Juliet* (ca. 1593)

- parody and camp humor in the play-within-a-play or court masque in *A Midsummer Night's Dream* (ca. 1593)

- comic repartee between the wives and Falstaff in *The Merry Wives of Windsor* (ca. 1597)

- comic relief by Falstaff and his comrades in the tavern scenes in *Henry IV Parts 1 & 2* (ca. 1596–1597)

- low comedy involving Dogberry and his watch in *Much Ado about Nothing* (ca. 1598) and among Trinculo, Stephano, and Caliban in *The Tempest* (ca. 1610)

- the title character's anti-female diatribes in *Hamlet* (ca. 1699)

- Thersites's Juvenalian satire in *Troilus and Cressida* (ca. 1602)

- Jaques's portrayal of Shakespeare's anti-satirist mode and Touchstone's travesty of Jaques's ennui in *As You Like It* (ca. 1599)

- epigram and sarcasm in *The Merchant of Venice* (ca. 1596)

- Launce's malapropisms in *Two Gentlemen of Verona* (ca. 1613)

- Aufidius's diatribe against the title character in *Coriolanus* (ca. 1605)

Shakespeare's addition of incidental satire to nearly all his plays proves that he did not overlook the human capacity for folly and stupidity. Still fresh and viable on stage or in print, Shakespeare's works continue to delight, tease, and puzzle the scholar and the student of human nature. Memorable characters such as Sir John Falstaff, Shylock, Puck, Richard III, Iago, Hamlet, Lady Macbeth, Miranda, Dogberry, Mark Antony, Caliban, Cordelia, Antony, and Ariel stretch the imagination with their lifelike yearnings, complexity, and frailties. The human ambiguities of their behaviors and private thoughts have inspired generations to examine and discuss them as though they were real people. (Bentley 1961; Bermel 1982; Boorstin 1992; Boyce 1990; Campbell 1943; Chute 1949, 1951; Gassner and Quinn 1969; Lanier 1978; Miller 1989; Muir and Schoenbaum 1971; Sandler 1986; Shakespeare 1957a, 1957b, 1957c, 1958, 1959, 1963, 1966, 1967a, 1967b, 1974a, 1974b, 1980; White 1955)

See also black humor; caricature; comic relief; diatribe; epigram; Falstaff, Sir John; incidental satire; parody; Pope, Alexander; pun; sarcasm; wit.

SHAW, GEORGE BERNARD

A long-lived, vigorously pugnacious, and much acclaimed native of Dublin, George Bernard Shaw—dubbed "the Great Eccentric," the most significant dramatist since Shakespeare, "the Man of the Century," or simply G. B. S.—dominated the critical and theatrical scene at the end of the nineteenth century and well into the twentieth. The author of numerous witty comedies, including *The Philanderer* (1905), *Pygmalion* (1912), and *Androcles and the Lion* (1912), he also composed little-known satiric treasures such as *Back to Methuselah* (1921), a rigorous five-plays-in-one extension of the Garden of Eden myth, to which he appended one of his ponderous Shavian prefaces. He utilized a ready arsenal of wit, logic, analysis, enlightenment, anticlimax, and repartee to entertain, beguile, and enlighten audiences on the subject of the creative instinct. One line from Act I—"You see things; and say 'Why?' But I dream things that never were; and I say 'Why not?'"—is frequently cited by idealists who don't recognize the source as Satan, the glib-tongued traducer of Eve.

Born on July 26, 1856, the only son and last of three children to failed grain merchant George Carr and singer Lucinda Elizabeth Gurley Shaw, a genteelly poor Protestant family, Shaw suffered the silences and disagreements common to unhappily mated parents. He fared poorly in all but composition at the Wesleyan Connexional School; he endured tutoring from his uncle, the Reverend George Carroll; but he filled in his cultural gaps by reading, and he learned music from his mother, a skilled operatic coach. At age 15, after his alcoholic father deserted the family, Shaw operated a cash register and tried selling real estate, but soon gave up office work and abandoned Ireland. In 1876, he resettled in London with his mother and sister Lucy; while his mother entered the teaching profession, he, like Karl Marx, pored over books in the British Museum reading rooms. To earn a minimum income, Shaw clerked for the fledgling telephone company, collected coins for delivering impromptu public lectures in Hyde Park, and began a journalistic career for the *London Star, Pall Mall Gazette,* and *World* under the witty pseudonym *Corno di Bassetto* (literally "horn of the little bass"). An assertive commentator, reformer, and essayist, he gained a reputation for devastating opponents with strong, clearly stated opinions on war, women, education, propriety, persecution of minorities, abstinence from meat and alcohol, the flaccid state of the theater, vivisection, vaccination, and the peculiarities of English spelling. After establishing himself as a public lecturer and as art, music, and drama critic for the *Saturday Review,* he wrote novels, but, to the detriment of his first five titles, he also involved himself in Marxism beginning in 1882. From 1884 to 1911, he composed and edited tracts for the atheistic Fabian Society. As speaker, tractarian, and polemicist, he found his métier in salient essays on literature, economics, and politics; he braved new territories and set new standards of taste while retaining a genial respect for the best of his forebears.

Tall, red-haired, and abstemious, he engaged such intellectuals as actress Ellen Terry and writer Mrs. Patrick Campbell in flirtations and correspondence. Shy of intimacy with women, he established a celibate marriage with Charlotte Frances Payne-Townshend in 1898, an Irish heiress whose care improved his tenuous health and whose money allowed him to settle in Hertfordshire and to perfect drama as his most effective medium. His command of oratorical mode supported a vigorous blend of criticism and humor that held his audience spellbound. His satire *Arms and the Man* (1894) debunked the glories and pretensions of militarism. His best-received comedy, *Man and Superman* (1905), featured a known figure, Don Juan, in a search for edification through pleasure. Ten years later, he composed *Androcles and the Lion,* a blend of comedy, dialectic, irony, and whimsy mixed with beast fable and scenes of anti-Christian persecution during the Roman Empire.

Brash and judgmental over a seventy-year career, Shaw wrote voluminously in the twentieth century, covering such varied issues as women's rights and Hitler and fascism. He is remembered for keen aphorisms:

- If you do not say a thing in an irritating way, you may just as well not say it at all.

- My method is to take the utmost trouble to find the right thing to say, and then to say it with the utmost levity.

- The worst sin toward our fellow creatures is not to hate them, but to be indifferent to them: that's the essence of inhumanity.

- If parents would only realize how they bore their children!

- One man that has a mind and knows it can always beat ten men who haven't and don't.

Somewhat pompous and usually annoying or unflattering to a group, person, or ideology, he once wrote:

> I have to educate England. Several Continental nations require a little educating, but America most of all. And I shall die before I have educated America properly, but I am making a beginning.

Shaw's popularity took a giant leap forward in 1913 when he produced his most famous play, *Pygmalion,* depicting idiosyncratic miscommunication in male-female relations and touting the importance of speech to social acceptability. In 1925, two years after his successful *Saint Joan,* he received the Nobel Prize for literature, which he donated to the Anglo-Swedish Literary Foundation. Smug and vainglorious from his sudden spurt of fame, he made a world tour in 1933 and received the adulation of adoring audiences, even in America, which he claimed to abhor. The first filming of *Pygmalion* earned him an Academy Award in 1938. He died from hip injuries suffered in a fall on November 2, 1950. Four years later, *Pygmalion* was reworked as *My Fair Lady,* a musical stage romance that earned five Oscars and three Oscar nominations after its filming in 1964. (Bermel 1982; Brockett 1968; Gassner and Quinn 1969; Grigson 1963; Hill 1978; Holroyd 1989; Hornstein 1973; Johnson 1968; Kunitz 1942; Magill 1958; Negley and Patrick 1952; Shaw 1952a, 1952b, 1967, 1988)

See also *Back to Methuselah;* beast lore; irony; *Man and Superman; Pygmalion;* repartee; satire; whimsy; wit.

 # SIMON, NEIL

A 1995 Kennedy Center honoree who once worked in Warner Brothers' mailroom, Neil Marvin Simon has received both kudos and clops from critics who charge him with nonstop but predictable comedy and revile him for reaping bales of money off his talent by turning stage comedy into made-for-Hollywood rehashes. The most successful comedy writer in history and the only living playwright for whom a theater is named, Simon began in radio and television, launched a brilliant drama career, and continues producing for the Broadway stage and Hollywood the plays that local playhouses and dinner theaters clamber to add to their bills of fare.

A shy, self-effacing genius, Simon has led the charmed life of boy wonder on Broadway, on radio and television, and in Hollywood. Born July 4, 1927, the son of Mamie and Irving Simon, a Bronx clothing salesman, Neil Simon is urban to the core. His motifs of congested traffic, random crime, tattered marriages, and sibling rivalry derive from his own life and career, which, like those of Woody Allen, remain irrevocably embedded in New York City. After serving as a military journalist for the army air corps, Simon completed a year at New York University in 1946 while putting up mail at Warner Brothers. For 12 years, he flourished in radio and in television's golden age of comedy, writing for Phil Silvers, Tallulah Bankhead, Sid Caesar, Garry Moore, Jackie Gleason, and Red Buttons. The industry wore him down, driving him to emulate Charlie Chaplin and become his own man.

Simon's tentative beginning with collaborator Danny Simon, his brother, netted SRO audiences for *Come Blow Your Horn* (1960), which he adapted for Paramount in 1963 as a Frank Sinatra vehicle. Simon's next four winners—*Barefoot in the Park* (1962), *The Odd Couple* (1965), *Sweet Charity* (1966), and *Star-Spangled Girl* (1966)—also thrived as cinema. *The Odd Couple*, perhaps Simon's best-loved comedy, survived longest as a television series depicting mismated male roommates, one a slob, the other a glaring, self-martyring priss. As the steady string of Simon-style hits churned on, stage critics grew tired of the pat mechanical quality that guarantees laughs but leaves room for meatier themes. Cinema buffs grew peevish at movie scenes like the ins and outs of the two-dimensional *Plaza Suite* (1968). Nonetheless, Simon's hits continued, with *Promises, Promises* (1968), *The Last of the Red-Hot Lovers* (1969), *The Out of Towners* (1970), *The Sunshine Boys* (1972), *California Suite* (1976), and *Chapter Two* (1977), and he received seemingly endless Tony and Oscar nominations. Simon altered his formula by taking a more rigorous autobiographical turn with *Brighton Beach Memoirs* (1982) and his antimilitary satire, *Biloxi Blues* (1984), also amiably filmed in 1988 starring Matthew Broderick as the late-adolescent Simon.

Equally at home with domestic comedy, comedy of manners, irony, incongruity, repartee, and satire, Simon's wit turns on the gamut of human predicaments—ridiculous mixups, career dilemmas, family squabbles, and the pervasive malaise that coats big-city life like mud on chromium wire spokes. *Chapter Two*, one of the plays he wrote as a vehicle for his second wife, actress Marsha Mason, focuses on George Schneider, a recently divorced writer—and ego mirror image of Neil Simon—who fears intimacy with a potential second mate. To brother Leo's advice that he wait before committing himself to a new relationship, George giggles that he's crazy about Jennie. Leo remarks sarcastically, "Okay, okay. But what is she—Cinderella? She's leaving at twelve o'clock?

American playwright Neil Simon in 1967

Wait! You'd wait six weeks for a dentist appointment, and that's with pain in your mouth."

The play, like much of the Simon canon, is talky and slick, a combination sure to irritate critics. Accused of rendering too many scenes into smart comebacks, puns, wisecracks, and shtick, *Chapter Two* suffered the late-Simon syndrome of yes-but applause. Too funny, too snide, not painful enough, the movie took its mud balls and earned Marsha Mason an Oscar nomination. Like *Barefoot in the Park,* which in 1967 won Mildred Natwick an Oscar nomination, and *The Sunshine Boys* eight years later, which won George Burns an Oscar and Neil Simon and Walter Matthau obligatory nominations, *Chapter Two* extends Simon's reputation for one-liners. The stingers brim with wit, as in Ethel Banks's remark in *Barefoot,* "Make him feel important. If you do that, you'll have a happy and wonderful marriage—like two out of every ten couples." The weakness for Simon is the intervening fabric, which often saps his comedy of life by its weight and length. (Anderson 1971; *Contemporary Authors* 1994; Johnson 1983; Katz 1982; "Kennedy Center Honors 5" 1995; McGovern 1979; Monaco 1991; Simon 1978, 1979, 1986)

See also comedy; incongruity; irony; pun; repartee; sarcasm; satire.

SLAPSTICK

An energetic, rowdy comic performance, often as a portion of another style of drama (farce, travesty, or parody), slapstick derives its name from the paired slats joined at one end and spring-loaded to cause a rapid closure and maximum noise on impact, a wordless sound-and-sight gag. When applied to a mock victim in a pantomime, puppet show, or stage farce, the combination of the whap of the slapstick and the receiver's exaggerated facial expression, lurch, or sprawl suggests mock punishment, assault, persecution, or other violence. A stock weapon of Arlecchino in low comedy of the *commedia dell'arte,* slapstick also serves as the genre or classification of humor that derives from the patch-decked Harlequin who plays a stereotypical role of fool and knockabout and concocts ludicrous, transparent ruses to expose the duplicity or pomposity of a villain or adversary.

Slapstick is indigenous to the set pieces of comic fare—outraged fathers versus the witless seducers of daughters, inept governors battling bearers of ill tidings, masters subduing trickster slaves, and greedy-guts misers fending off imagined threats to their hoards. During the English Renaissance, William Shakespeare's class-based slapstick enlivened the lord's abuse or debasement of the disobedient servant in *The Comedy of Errors* (ca. 1580s), the military control of Dogberry and his band of enlistees in *Much Ado about Nothing* (ca. 1598), and the bumbling courtship of Sir John Falstaff in *The Merry Wives of Windsor* (ca. 1597). The broad-based drollery accompanying the most obvious kind of satire sinks to clownish pie-in-the-face stunts, pranks, shoving, mugging, and pratfalls, all stock elements of professional clowns, mummers, and the television skits of comics Lucille Ball, Red Skelton, Milton Berle, Goldie Hawn, and Carol Burnett. (Abrams 1971; Barnet, Berman, and Burto 1960; Cuddon 1984; Gassner and Quinn 1969; Gray 1992; Henry 1995; Holman and Harmon 1992)

See also comedy; *commedia dell'arte;* farce; trickster.

SLAUGHTERHOUSE-FIVE

In an interview comparing the apocalyptic novel *Slaughterhouse-Five* (1966) with the biblical account of the destruction of Sodom and Gomorrah, novelist Kurt Vonnegut claims to love Lot's wife because she heeds her humanistic instinct to look back at the doomed city and to empathize with suffering. The psychogenic conflict that caused Vonnegut to write *Slaughterhouse-Five* derives from his wartime experience, a cataclysmic Dresden firebombing that never acquired much public outcry or even media coverage. As though disgorging a repugnant but vital message lodged in his gullet, Vonnegut told the tale in painfully accurate autobiographical detail, then lapsed into depression, vowing never to look back or to vent his anguish at the terrible act of war that burned a lovely German city and its residents.

Making his usual departure from accepted literary convention, Vonnegut opens his historic satire with a mouthful of title and author:

> *Slaughterhouse-Five or The Children's Crusade: A Duty-Dance with Death,* by Kurt Vonnegut, Jr., a fourth-generation German-American now living in easy circumstances on Cape Cod [and smoking too much] who, as an American infantry scout *hors de combat*, witnessed the fire-bombing of Dresden, Germany, "The Florence of the Elbe," a long time ago, and survived to tell the tale. This is a novel somewhat in the telegraphic schizophrenic manner of tales of the planet Tralfamadore, where the flying saucers come from peace.

So warned, the reader enters the world of Billy Pilgrim and, like a moth trapped in a cyclotron, loops back in time to Billy's childhood in Ilium, New York, then forward to college, infantry service during World War II, capture and lodging in a meat locker, survival of a firebombing, return to home and family, and escape to Tralfamadore and the heavenly Montana Wildhack, his extraterrestrial mistress and mother of their love child. Told in first person from the point of view of a naive, self-effacing optometrist, the story strips death of its terror and life of its longitudinal parade of minutes, hours, and days. Thus, in one novel, Vonnegut manages to exorcise the living nightmare of war trauma and to embrace Everyman's night thoughts.

Born in 1922, the same year as the author, Billy Pilgrim is the weak, insecure son of an overbearing barber who callously tosses his son into the YMCA pool to teach him to swim. Overpowered by his father's notion of manhood and nibbled to distraction by his oversheltering mother, he enters optometry school, finds a wealthy girl and a future father-in-law who sets him up in his own office. Shortly after his father is killed in a hunting accident, Billy leaves training at a South Carolina military base and travels lightyears from safety to Luxembourg, where he wanders away from his unit during the Battle of the Bulge. Vonnegut's repeated satire of manhood rituals takes in the macho ribbing Billy endures for serving as chaplain's assistant and playing a portable harmonium with two stops, "vox humana and vox celeste," the extremes of human to heavenly.

The singular quality that sets Billy apart from his buddies is his ability to time-trip to the past or future and to contemplate what is about to happen or relive what has already occurred. After capture and transport in sealed boxcars to a German camp imprisoning New Zealanders, Englishmen, Dutchmen, Belgians, Frenchmen, Canadians, South Africans, and Americans, Billy is marched through the city and relieves his humiliation by looking above the heads of residents toward the rococo decorations that ice Dresden like a wedding cake. He grows fond of Edgar Derby, a warm-hearted middle-aged soldier who stands by him after he snaps from the emotional strain of wearing a fur-trimmed coat and silver boots. Derby sticks by Billy while he recovers in a prisoner infirmary bed and cowers from the "Golgotha sounds" of men digging holes. To Vonnegut, the surreal pilgrimage that Billy undergoes is an ongoing character-building exercise that relieves him of the need to prove his worthiness to family, wife, military, or captors. A counterpoint thrusts on Billy the knowledge of what will happen next: in 30 days, German rescue units will shoot Edgar after falsely charging him with looting a teapot from the smoking heaps that once constituted Dresden.

Vonnegut gets satiric mileage out of Billy's return to civilian life aboard a slow freighter called the *Lucretia A. Mott* and from his retreat to the rehab center at a VA hospital in Lake Placid. Unable to face fiancée Valencia Merble or his cooing mother, Billy withdraws into a mental funk. Friendship with fellow veteran Eliot Rosewater introduces Billy to the release of science fiction written by Kilgore Trout, who serves as a prophet in Billy's elongated wilderness. Ironically, among the "Four-eyed Bastards" who comprise Billy's optometric colleagues, visitor Trout is the only one who needs no corrective lenses to help him see human foibles. Flights out of the galaxy take Billy beyond the whine of his food-obsessed wife, officious daughter Barbara, and troubled son Robert, who distinguishes himself during the Vietnam War. On Barbara's wedding day, Billy is kidnapped by aliens and flown by spaceship to a geodesic dome on Tralfamadore. In a zoolike cell fitted with amenities from the United States, he mates with his movie fantasy, Montana Wildhack, while Tralfamadorans observe his behavior as though he were a gerbil in a wire cage.

The uneven rhythm of Billy's earthly life and the serene incarceration among aliens demonstrates Vonnegut's ridicule of a harried Casper Milquetoast who has no more power over his time in the cell than he does over the other chaotic events of his life: from his own experience of being tossed from a plane crash on a snowy Vermont mountainside to the death of Valencia from carbon monoxide poisoning in a freak car accident in her swank Cadillac. Barbara deludes herself into believing that house arrest will keep her father safe at home, where he can no longer embarrass the family by appearing on a radio talk show to tell of his intergalactic travel. Relieved of the fear of death, Billy relives his murder at the hands of stalker Paul Lazzaro, a deranged car thief and fellow POW whose paranoia centers on Billy. While addressing an assembly at a Chicago ball park, Billy tells of time travel as Lazzaro squeezes out the lethal bullet.

Vonnegut's intense details of the firebombing—the smoking corpses like little logs, the sky overcast with black smoke, and the alien landscape—link his plot with a singular image, the sight of the Children's Crusade, a procession of children believing they were marching to reclaim the Holy Land but who were in fact destined for slavery. Vonnegut's bitter comparison views Billy Pilgrim as an innocent marching toward a devastating waste of life and culture, a quirk of war that reduces Dresden without good cause. As an antiphonal response to the litany of flamethrowers and strafings, Vonnegut chants "So it goes," his acceptance of inhumanity, his benediction to the procession of human lives who have encountered or ever will encounter extremes of violence and mayhem. A literal restatement of the translation of Amen—"so be it"—the phrase "so it goes" is the knowing cadence of soldiers marching into the Dresden meat locker and nodding sagely at the vicissitudes of war. Above their heads, the birds, who, like Kilgore Trout, see more than the earthlings below, shake their heads and question "Poo-tee-weet?"

Like Jonathan Swift and Lemuel Gulliver, Vonnegut covers his personal tragedy with the mask of Billy Pilgrim, the wanderer in an alien land. In Chapter 10, Vonnegut lets slip the Everyman face to particularize the experience that haunts his life during the writing of *Slaughterhouse-Five*. A cumbersome layer of recent losses—Robert Kennedy, Martin Luther King, body counts from Vietnam—obscures the seedbed of the author's discontent, the Dresden fire. During a flight to Dresden with a war buddy, Vonnegut contemplated how it would feel to drop bombs on the winking lights below and what the new human beings on the planet would undergo in their brief sojourn. His mind, never stable for long in one era, returns to the war and to his part in mining corpses and observing the arbitrary execution of Derby. The absurd meeting of Billy and the calling bird that ends the novel resituates the antihero in nature, where he is no more culpable and no more valuable than any other living being. In Vonnegut's abrupt closure, the Tralfamadoran interest in Darwin becomes all the more relevant: the alien view of humanity born in a cell compares with the bird's-eye view of soldiers departing from war, in that all life accepts the crapshoot of fortune, however foul or sweet, and lives out a span, whether brief or long, with as much dignity as vulnerability will allow. (Broer 1988; Goldsmith 1972; Klinkowitz 1982; Merrill 1989; Morse 1991; Vonnegut 1963)

See also black humor; caricature; *Cat's Cradle*; Gulliver, Lemuel; parody; satire; Swift, Jonathan; Vonnegut, Kurt.

THE SPECTATOR

An eighteenth-century forerunner of the modern newspaper, *The Spectator*, an English broadside journal appearing in London Monday through Saturday, published witty, satiric, and thought-provoking essays for 555 issues, from March 1, 1711, through December 6, 1712. Authored by Joseph Addison and Richard Steele, the periodical featured works by Ambrose Philips, Eustace Budgell, John Hughes, and Alexander Pope, perhaps the most prestigious essayist of his day. To mask the identity of contributors to the Spectator Club, the publishers concocted fictional personae: Sir Roger de Coverley, the rural baronet; Sir Andrew Freeport, entrepreneur; Mr. Spectator, the citified gent; and Sir Will Honeycomb, quidnunc and purveyor of scandals.

Modeled itself on *The Tatler*, Addison and Steele's *Spectator*, a joint project begun two months after the first journal's demise, espoused a purpose: "to enliven morality with wit, and to temper wit with morality." The paper provided coffeehouse readers and salon-goers with tittle-tattle and moral essays charmingly enmeshed with satire aimed at the self-conscious foppery and normal foibles of any society. The main item of the day, usually a thoughtful essay, formed the paper's only focus. An example from No. 112, Monday, July 9, 1711, comments on Sir Roger's interest in religion:

> As Sir Roger is Landlord to the whole congregation; he keeps them in very good order, and will suffer nobody to sleep in it besides himself; for if by chance he has been surprised into a short nap at sermon, upon recovering out of it he stands up and looks about him, and if he sees anybody else nodding, either wakes them himself, or sends his servant to them.

In addition to this gently satiric commentary on sleeping in church and self-righteousness, readers got the usual features: help wanted ads, lost and stolen items, sale goods, and amusing filler. The two-man staff developed a complementary style: Addison, the reserved, somewhat prim observer, offset the roisterous good humor of Steele, a convivial partaker of fun and frivolity. Of the two, Dr. Samuel Johnson, master critic and arbiter of Augustan Era taste, preferred Addison for his polish and control.

An astonishing growth of readership boosted circulation of *The Spectator* from 3,000 to 20,000, a tremendous feat given the small population of Londoners who would have the money, interest, and reading skill to enjoy so particularized a paper. The controlled, urbane wit and anti-Whig politics of *The Spectator* found its audience in the growing middle classes, who thrived during the reign of Queen Anne and profited from the mildly admonishing tone of the pamphleteer. *The Spectator* targeted the hidden agendas of manipulators, tricksters, and disloyal companions who exuded the courtesies of the day yet harbored malicious or destructive intent. Concerning the application of wit, Joseph Addison wrote in No. 47:

> This art of wit is well enough, when confined to one day in a twelvemonth; but there is an ingenious tribe of men sprung up for late years, who are for making "April fools" every day in the year.

Addison deduces that the resulting laughter from pranks reveals "secret elation and pride of heart" by causing the prankster to feel superior to the dupe or fool. A particular case in point is Addison's personal grudge against coxcombs—jokers he compares to Sir John Falstaff—who disturb plays and club meetings with exhibitionism and foolery.

Another personal dislike of Addison is the purveyor of false wit, which he discusses in No. 62. The true wit, he maintains, assembles ideas into like patterns. The false wit, on the other hand:

> chiefly consists in the resemblance and congruity sometimes of single letters, as in anagrams, chronograms, lipograms, and acrostics; sometimes of syllables, as in echoes and doggerel rhymes; sometimes of words, as in puns and quibbles; and sometimes of whole sentences or poems, cast into the figures of eggs, axes, or altars: nay, some carry the notion of wit so far as to ascribe it even to external mimicry; and to look upon a man as an ingenious person, than can resemble the tone, posture, or face of another.

Driven to carry the matter over several pages of discourse, Addison takes issue with Dryden's definition of wit as "a propriety of words and thoughts adapted to the subject." This assault on lighter forms of wit suggests that Addison was less open than his partner and other coffeehouse cronies to general contributions of fun and good nature.

Addison saves laughter and satire to No. 249, when he notes that laughter "slackens and unbraces the mind, weakens the faculties, and causes a kind of remissness and dissolution in all the powers of the soul," but he admits that, from his own experience, the loss of control is worth the effort to dispel gloom, depression, and heavy spirits. The satirist, he notes, possesses a "qualification of little ungenerous tempers." People given to comedy and burlesque, the two branches of ridicule, are seriously imperfect beings who target "everything that is solemn and serious, decent and praiseworthy in human life." Addison's case in point is Samuel Butler's *Hudibras* (1663), a bit of doggerel that could have been turned into a more pleasing, useful verse. In contrast, Addison recommends John Milton's *L'Allegro* (1645), a celebratory verse that takes a more sensible attitude toward mirth.

In like style, Richard Steele uses No. 65 of *The Spectator* to criticize George Etherege's *Man of Mode* (1676), a Restoration comedy long out of fashion with eighteenth-century playgoers, who preferred sentimental comedies to the raucous, bawdy farce of the post-Puritan era. Steele concludes that "this whole celebrated piece is a perfect contradiction to good manners, good sense, and common honesty." By this point, English tastes had embraced the rationality of the Augustan Age. Steele supports the era's choice of intellectualism over sensuality. In Etherege's comedy, Steele can find "more frequent occasion to move sorrow and indignation than mirth and laughter." He summarizes his generation's castigation of "utmost corruption and degeneracy" in the heady days that followed the collapse of Oliver Cromwell's commonwealth and the return of Charles II to England's throne.

Clearly, given the range and depth of topics, extent of references to other spokespersons of the age, and literary interests of the writers, *The Spectator* served a purpose in informing the educated, well-read, observant reader of the inequities of politics, entertainment, and human relationships. In addition to these weightier matters, lighter studies of public conduct, such as an essay on men of fashion and the well-loved "The Coquette's Heart," provoked knowing smiles. The demise of the journal spurred numerous imitators, including Samuel Johnson's *Rambler* (1750–1752) and *Idler* (1758–1760), Richard Steele's *Guardian* (1713) and *Town Talk* (1715–1716), and Addison's reprise of *The Spectator* (1714). Audiences in the United States supported a similar venture in Washington Irving's *Salmagundi; or, the Whim-Whams and Opinions of Launcelot Longstaff, Esq. and Others* (1807–1808). (Addison 1973; Baugh 1948; Inglis and Spear 1952; Sheedy 1972; Steele 1973)

See also Addison, Joseph; burlesque; "The Coquette's Heart"; doggerel; Etherege, George; Falstaff, Sir John; farce; Irving, Washington; Pope, Alexander; pun; Restoration drama; satire; Steele, Sir Richard; *The Tatler*; wit.

STEELE, SIR RICHARD

A merry, clever amuser of urbane Londoners, Richard Steele, born in Dublin on March 12, 1672, and orphaned in youth, came to fruition as a master satirist of the Augustan era with his contributions to *The Tatler* (1709–1711) and *The Spectator* (1711–1712). His essays added jolly observations of manners, morals, and lapses among citified burghers who often screened their painfully plain backgrounds with effusive displays of gentility born of social climbing. An author of sentimental comedies—*The Funeral, or Grief à-la-Mode* (1701), a spoof on undertakers; *The Lying Lover* (1703); and *The Tender Husband* (1705)—Steele played a greater role in the evolution of eighteenth-century satire as a candid, good-natured essayist and journalist. Reared by Henry Gascoigne, his uncle, Steele was educated at Charterhouse School and formed a life-long bond with Joseph Addison. From Oxford, Steele rounded out his education with military experience and achieved the rank of captain in the Coldstream Guards before giving up the sword—and his reputation as a rake and duelist—and turning to the pen.

Steele's first published works—a poem, "The Procession" (1965), and a religious monograph, *The Christian Hero* (1701)—display little of the scintillating mirth that followed his early prose and string of moderately successful plays. Reformed from immature high spirits, he worked at editing *The London Gazette* in 1707. At age 37, settled in St. James with his second wife, Prue, he muffled himself in the persona of Isaac Bickerstaff and composed his first satiric essay for *The Tatler*, then, negligent of mounting debt, continued his witty observations in *The Spectator*, a best-selling satiric journal that he produced with Addison. The two, frequenters of Don Saltero's Coffeehouse in Chelsea, drew material and drama criticism from Oliver Goldsmith, Laurence Sterne, and Dr. Samuel Johnson; from a similar haunting of Dick's Coffeehouse on Fleet Street, Will's Coffeehouse in Covent Garden, and the Thatched House Tavern in St. James, the collaborators kept their thumbs to the pulse of London.

After the success of *The Spectator*, Steele began taking politics more seriously and turned to political commentary with *The Englishman*, a less spirited journal devoted to the Whig perspective. The next stage of his evolving interest in government was a run for parliament in 1713 representing Stockbridge. The August election produced a short-lived tenure of seven months, after which Tory enemies drove him from office on the basis of a Whig monograph, *The Crisis*, a libelous anti-Tory diatribe attributed to Steele. A shift to the left during the first months of the reign of George I settled Steele in a more suitable situation as manager of Drury Lane Theatre. Within a year, he returned to parliament and received a knighthood. Representing Boroughbridge, Steele remained comfortably mated to politics for five years before another shift removed him from, then recalled him to office. For a brief time in 1720, he published a new essay series, *The Theatre*.

At the end of his career, Steele's major work, *The Conscious Lovers* (1722), a sentimental comedy with a predictable, weepy plot reuniting daughter with father, achieved fame that temporarily eclipsed the satires of his middle years. Yet his puckishness still permeates the epilogue, in which he, unlike more intrusive authors, refuses to speak.

And yet I'm sav'd a world of pains that way.
I now can look, I now can move at ease,
Nor need I torture these poor limbs to please,
Nor with the hand or foot attempt surprise
Nor wrest my features, nor fatigue my eyes.

The play preceded Steele's rapid decline. Out of pocket and out of sorts, he lapsed into literary silence and public withdrawal in 1724 and suffered a stroke two years later, leaving unfinished *The School of Action* and *The Gentleman*, two farces that showcased Steele's penchant for wit. Spending his last five years bedfast at the Ty-Gwyn (Whale House), a farm cottage in Llangunnor, Carmarthen, Wales, left him by his wife, he died September 1, 1729, and was buried in the village churchyard, where a stone tablet over the font memorializes his career. (Bloom and Bloom 1980; Eagle and Stephens 1992; Gassner and Quinn 1969; Ketcham 1985; Steele 1952, 1973; Winston 1994)

See also Addison, Joseph; comedy; farce; Pope, Alexander; satire; *The Spectator*; *The Tatler*, wit.

SWIFT, JONATHAN

English tractarian and satirist, Jonathan Swift was the wonder of the eighteenth-century wits—friend of Alexander Pope, noted Anglican prelate, champion of the poor in an age of English philistinism and materialism at the expense of the Irish, and one of Western literature's most versatile, accomplished, and controversial writers. At the far end of negative criticism, Kenneth Rexroth has typified the paradoxical Swift as "a psychotic who hated all men, especially women, who was impotent, paranoid, and fixed in a clinging and cloying anal eroticism." On the positive side, lovers of satire hail Swift as the chief of English satirists, a rival of Juvenal and Martial, the Roman masters. Influenced by the anti-utopianism of Thomas Hobbes's *Leviathan* (1651), Swift's satire spotlights human shortcomings and sins, which he attempted to lessen by means of acrimonious humor and ridicule.

An Anglo native of Dublin and the grandson of the Reverend Thomas Swift, the conservative vicar of Goodrich, Herefordshire, and of an English parson in Leicestershire on his mother's side, Swift was born the second child and first son on November 30, 1667. His father, Jonathan Swift, Sr., a country lawyer and steward of King's Inns, died in the spring before Swift's birth; his mother, Abigail Erick Swift, abandoned Swift in childhood. When he was a year old, his wet nurse kidnapped him and took him to England, but returned him to the family when he was three years old. One of his father's four brothers, Godwin, reared Swift and grudgingly paid his tuition to the prestigious Kilkenny Grammar School and Trinity College, where Swift made no discernible effort at excellence, but obained a B.A. in 1688. Insecure, insolvent, and uncertain of direction, he earned an M.A. from Oxford four years later.

Between stages of his college education, Swift accepted a post at Moor Park, Surrey, as secretary to his mother's kinsman, Sir William Temple, who served as his mentor. The pay was reasonable—£20 annually and a place at the servants' table. With raw edges refined by self-directed reading, Swift was ready to put his gift for wit, satire, and contempt for human folly to the test in his first compositions, *The Battle of the Books* (1704) and *A Tale of a Tub* (1704), both published anonymously. His ease with poetry and his penchant for scatology were immediately discernible in the graceful, unflinching satire "Description of a City Shower, in Imitation of Virgil's Georgics," published October 17, 1710, in No. 238 of *The Tatler*. The poem pillories the corruption of his age with a detailed study of the unrest that precedes a cleansing rain. The cascading waters sluice offal into the kennels that course London streets:

> And bear their trophies with them as they go:
> Filths of all hues and odor seem to tell
> What street they sailed from by their sight and smell . . .
> Sweeping from butcher's stalls, dung, guts, and blood,
> Drowned puppies, stinking sprates, all drenched in mud,
> Dead cats, and turnip tops, come tumbling down the flood.

The splenetic juxtapositions preview the harsher criticisms that excoriate behaviors, worship, education, and cant in his masterpiece, *Gulliver's Travels* (1727), a unique three-sided view of humanity.

In 1694, recovering from a rebuff by the woman he loved, Swift entered the Anglican priesthood in Ireland, but departed ecclesiastical service in despair the following year after a brief post as chaplain of Dublin Castle and a dismal stint as parson of Kilroot, Antrim, near Belfast. The perpetual wrangle against church affairs prevented Swift from advancing to meatier posts. His return to Temple's service in England put him in close company with a massive library and with the wits of the eighteenth century, notably Joseph Addison, Richard Steele, and Alexander Pope. As literary sparring partner with the established church, Swift joined Addison, Steele, John Gay, and other of the coffeehouse wits in publishing biting essays in *The Tatler*, a forerunner of the modern magazine.

When Temple died in 1699, Swift obtained employment in Dublin as secretary to the Earl of Berkely. Before the death of Queen Anne, the political climate reshaped popular religious and contemporary philosophy. In 1710, a switch in political loyalties destroyed old friendships after Swift chose church over party and threw his support to the Tories. He formed loose associations with William Congreve and Thomas Parnell and, under the pseudonym of Bickerstaff, began needling a mountebank, John Partridge, who claimed to tell the future. Swift dispatched Partridge with a humorous obituary, which Partridge vigorously disclaimed. Swift turned to the serious job of editing the Tory *Examiner*. The reward was less than the English bishopric he had hoped for. In 1713, he was installed as dean of St. Patrick's Cathedral in Dublin, a disappointing post that brought him a small stipend.

Swift's private life blossomed from his admiration for Esther "Stella" Johnson, daughter of William Temple's housekeeper. Because of the earnest tone and candid execution of memoirs and prayers at the time of Stella's illness and death, some believe she may have been Swift's wife or mistress. He proclaims on January 28, 1728, in "On the Death of Mrs. Johnson" that she was attractive, affable, raven-haired, and companionable. His admiration for her "gifts of the mind" causes him to regret her feeble health and penury. Before her demise, he composed formal prayers that demonstrate along with his sincere concern for Stella a deep faith in God. Paralleling the Christian virtues, he pleads:

> We beseech thee also, O Lord, of thy infinite goodness to remember the good actions of this thy servant; that the naked she hath cloathed, the hungry she hath fed, the sick and the fatherless whom she hath relieved, may be reckoned according to thy gracious promise, as if they had been done unto thee.

The warmth of his affection and the sturdy Christian faith that bolstered his belief in a merciful deity contrast the other Swift, the one who fought in political arenas with a journalistic fervor that endangered his friendships and position in society.

An advocate for Irish freedom, Swift began donating a large portion of his income to poor parishioners and publishing tracts protesting England's disgraceful treatment of the neighboring isle, where the Church and absentee landlords held sway over a burdened populace. Among his most famous shorter satires are *The Drapier Letters* (1729) and *A Modest Proposal for Preventing the Children of Poor People of Ireland from Being a Burden to Their Parents* (1729), the latter a severely ironic attack on the ruling class's insensitivity to the poor. In 1726, as an outgrowth of his writings for the Scriblerus Club, he published under his own name his classic dystopian fantasy, *Gulliver's Travels*, a lethal jab at orthodoxy and a vision of the petty, gross, and vapidly idealized visions of world order. The final two of four books imply that innate faults prevent the improvement of the human race, which falls short of the standards of the Houynhnms, a fictional nation of horses.

Swift's final years brought pain, loneliness, and mental disintegration. He maintained correspondence with several women, including his long-standing love, Stella, and the mysterious and tumultuous Esther "Vanessa" Vanhomrigh, who relieved the intensity of his literary battles against the entrenched pillars of society with personal attacks of jealousy and spite. Both women predeceased Swift—Vanessa in 1723 and Stella in 1728, leaving him lonely for conversation and female companionship. Late in his seventies, deafness, dizzy spells, nausea, and melancholia (conjectured by medical historians to be either Ménière's disease or syphilis) destroyed his capacity to enjoy life and to craft the ironies that so enriched his prose, letters, journals, and verse. For five years, his cousin, Martha Whiteway, attended him following paralysis and aphasia from a stroke. On his deathbed, he managed to whisper a request that God "have a watchful care of me on this my last journey." (Thomas, p. 76) His death in Dublin on October 19, 1745, ended a distressing decline. Swift was buried alongside Stella in Dublin's St. Patrick's churchyard. He had prepared his epitaph, which bears the Roman didactic pessimism: Abi, viator, et imitare, si poteris strenuum pro virili libertatis vindicem [Go, journeyman, and imitate, if you can, a strong vindication of human liberty]. (Drabble 1985; Harrison 1967; Hornstein 1973; Johnson 1968; Magill 1958; Manguel and Guadalupi 1987; Pollard 1970; Rexroth 1969; Sheedy 1972; Swift 1958, 1976, 1989; Thomas 1943; Woods 1947)

See also Addison, Joseph; Gay, John; *Gulliver's Travels*; irony; Pope, Alexander; satire; scatology; Steele, Sir Richard; *A Tale of a Tub*; *The Tatler*; wit.

SYMPOSIUM

Written in Plato's standard dialogue form, this satire, set at Agathon's home in Athens in 416 B.C., depicts the state of social and moral behavior during the lamentable decline of Athens' Golden Age. A parody of a group of notables at a banquet, the work skillfully lampoons the style and personal reputation of each speaker. Related from second-hand information by Plato and Apollodorus, the story details the give-and-take of 12 male dinner guests at an all-night party. Among them are Phaedrus the mythographer, Pausanias the sophist, the playwright Aristophanes, the honorable Alcibiades, Dr. Eryximachus, and Socrates. The latter, returning from the local bathhouse, receives an impromptu invitation from Aristodemus to dine at the poet Agathon's house. There, Agathon offers him the choice seat at the host's left hand.

Platonic style requires the basics of informal debate. The men dismiss the flute player, a signal of serious intent, and adopt a single topic—love. They rotate turns at defining love. Phaedrus leads off with a simplistic definition based on Achilles's love for his army mate, Patroclus, in the *Iliad*; Pausanias follows with a differentiation between earthly and heavenly love. Plato ribs

Aristophanes, who, unable to stop a bout of hiccups, must leave the table without contributing his thoughts. The doctor suggests simple palliatives:

> Hold your breath a long time and see if the hiccup will stop; if it won't, gargle water. But if it still goes strong, pick up something to tickle your nose with, and sneeze; do this once or twice, and stop it will, even if it is very strong.

In place of Aristophanes, the doctor takes his turn and insists that love is a mighty power. Aristophanes returns, cured of hiccups, and espouses a romantic notion about a time when the earth was populated by three sexes: male, female, and a hermaphroditic monster. He surmises that every person has an ideal love object capable of completing a matched pair, whether male-female or male-male, and of establishing a lasting relationship.

Plato imposes greater control over the extent of the topics by having the host propose that the speakers limit their contributions to godly love. To his rather sophomoric insistence that love can overcome the worst human vices, the other guests applaud. When Agathon seats himself, the turn passes to Socrates, who delivers a paean to love that claims that it should be honored for its ability to link the human soul with God. At this climactic point in Socrates's speech, Alcibiades, the dissolute Athenian politician whom Socrates had rescued in battle 15 years earlier, crashes the dinner. Drunk and quarrelsome, he wanders toward the table and plunks down next to Agathon. Surprised to find himself alongside Socrates, the tippler shouts:

> What the deuce is this? Socrates here? You lay there again in wait for me, as you are always turning up all of a sudden where I never thought to see you! And now what have you come for? And again, why did you lie there, not by Aristophanes or some other funny man or would-be funny man, but you managed to get beside the handsomest of the company!

In mock consternation at Socrates's bold come-hither look, Alcibiades urges all to drink up and join him in inebriation.

An adjunct to Plato's focus, the physician bids Alcibiades to speak on the subject of love. The intruder twitters on about Socrates's flirtations and muses that the philosopher should be pleased to have Alcibiades as a lover. The drunken palaver continues in the same vein, concluding that Socrates always spurns advances from other men, no matter how worthy their intentions. Socrates, growing testy, suspects that Alcibiades is merely acting drunk and using the social scene as a method of publicly degrading him. The philosopher outwits Alcibiades by inviting Agathon to take the next couch. The ruse works, leaving Alcibiades to grouse, "where Socrates is, there is no one else [who] can get a share of the beauties!" (Plato, p. 116)

Plato signs off his serious topic by devising a rowdy end to his *Symposium*. A second party of merrymakers enters; some of the original guests depart. The high tone of the earlier conversation gives way to wine-bibbing, uproar, and snores. The only sober men—Socrates, Agathon, and Aristophanes—share a bowl of wine and retreat to a private discussion of comedy and tragedy, with Socrates insisting that skill in tragedy is the same as skill in comedy. The trio enjoys its intimate exchange until the cock crows at dawn. When his friends nod off, Socrates makes them comfy and slips away, sluices off the reek of the night's debauchery, and returns to his daily tasks. (Feder 1986; Flaceliere 1962; Hadas 1954; Hammond 1992; Hornstein 1973; Howatson 1989; Plato 1956; Radice 1973; Snodgrass 1988; Warner 1958)

See also Aristophanes; comedy; farce; parody.

A TALE OF A TUB

Composed in 1704 by Jonathan Swift, an Anglican dean in Dublin and England's most enduring satirist, *A Tale of a Tub,* a cumbersome, convoluted allegory, spoofs the evolution of Christian sects. The derivation of the title, as Swift explains in the preface, is a bit of sea lore: sailors toss a tub overboard as a diversionary measure against a belligerent whale. The exemplum that forms the thesis depicts a father leaving a coat to each of his three sons, Peter, Martin, and Jack. The garments come with a single stricture: the heirs are to make no alterations in the original design. In the sepulchral tones of a deathbed speech, the father warns:

> You must be very exact, to avoid the Penalties I have appointed for every Transgression or Neglect, upon which your future Fortunes will entirely depend. I have also commanded in my Will, that you should live together in one House like Brethren and Friends, for then you will be sure to thrive, and not otherwise.

Upon the father's death, the sons—satiric caricatures of Saint Peter, father of Roman Catholicism; Martin Luther, the founder of Anglicanism; and Jack, a nickname for John Calvin, leader of Christian dissent—separate and seek adventures. Over the next seven years they "encountred a reasonable Quantity of gyants and slew certain Dragons," Swift's comic recounting of early Church history.

To multiple satirical purpose, Swift expends one sentence on what happens after the trio fall in love with the Duchess d'Argent, Madame de Grands Titres, and the Countess d'Orgueil, allegorical figures representing greed, ambition, and pride. Because these grand ladies spurn their suitors, the brothers lapse into obnoxious habits:

> They Writ, and Raillyed, and Rhymed, and Sung, and Said, and said Nothing; They Drank, and Fought, and Whor'd, and Slept, and Swore, and took Snuff: They went to new plays on the first Night, haunted the *Chocolate*-Houses, beat the Watch, lay on Bulks, and got Claps; They bilkt Hackney-Coachmen, ran in Debt with Shop-Keepers, and lay with their Wives: They kil'd Bayliffs, kick'd Fidlers down Stairs, eat at *Locket's,* loytered at Will's: they talk'd of the Drawing-Room and never came there, Dined with Lords they never saw; Whisper'd

a Dutchess, and spoke never a Word; exposed the Scrawls of their Laundress for Billets-doux of Quality; came ever just from Court and were never seen in it; attended the Levee *sub dio;* Got a list of Peers by heart in one Company, and with great Familiarity retailed them in another.

Swift's *tour de force* summation of the era's duplicity and social ills in one tumbling hyperbole presages social decline and the fall of religion from its original purpose. As the narrator's sentence implies, the heirs deviate from their father's instructions and turn a unified church and God's generous gifts into a burlesque of religious gewgaws and gimcrackery, squabbles, and arrogance as the church distances itself from the father's dictum.

Swift's satire ventures dangerously near invective. Dumping a heavy load of shame on Catholics, he decries popery, bishops' costumes, and the concepts of confession, purgatory, Latin mass, transubstantiation, and excommunication. He pictures the Vatican as avoiding fallibility by "telling huge palpable *Lies* upon all Occasions; and swearing, not only to the Truth, but cursing the whole Company to Hell, if they pretended to make the least Scruple of believing Him." Martin viciously attacks the overdecorated Catholic clergy; in yanking off the shoulder knots and embroidery, he damages the cloth but leaves its tatters unstitched, a satiric jab at the Anglican failure to heal the wounds inflicted by Catholics. Jack, the spirit of dissent, redresses church faults by attacking religion with zeal. The narrator notes,

> I have deduced a *Histori-theo-physi-ological* Account of *Zeal*, shewing how it first proceeded from a *Notion* into a *Word*, and from then in a hot Summer, ripened into a *tangible Substance.*

Dismayed by his brothers' excesses, Jack rends his coat and tosses it into the kennel. The three-way brouhaha over religious decorum ignites Jack's short temper and reduces Martin to a monstrous sulk. The three temperaments are Swift's estimation of the faults of the triad: pride, indolence, and fanaticism.

Following his pattern of inserting digressions in segments of the narrative, Swift introduces comments on wind, a scatological bit of foolery that questions the use of language as a means of subterfuge and evasion. Jesting with classicists for citing defective texts, he adds to a digression on madness a flawed segment, "There is in Mankind a certain .... And this I take to be a clear Solution of the Matter." Upon returning to the scurrilous tale of the brothers, Swift focuses on Jack, who studies the will to the point of fanaticism, a satiric comment on fundamentalism and its obsession with inerrant interpretation of the Bible. Of Jack's skill with biblical text, the narrator notes:

> He had a Way of working it into any Shape he pleased; so that it served him for a Night-cap when he went to Bed, and for an Umbrello in rainy Weather. He would lap a Piece of it about a sore Toe, or when he had Fits, burn two Inches under his Nose; or if any Thing lay heavy on his Stomach, scrape off, and swallow as much of the Powder as would lie on a silver Penny, they were all infallible Remedies.

The narrator ridicules Jack's bizarre habits of falling on his knees in prayer in the gutter, serving as prayerful hangman, braying, persecuting artists, and fulminating in sermons blended from "a *Soporiferous Medicine* to be convey'd in at the *Ears;* It was a Compound of *Sulphur* and *Balm of Gilead*, with a little *Pilgrim's Salve*." After describing devious connivings and plottings, the narrator abandons his subject and concludes with a suitable parody of himself—a digression on writers who base whole dissertations on nothing. (Drabble 1985; Harrison 1967; Hornstein 1973; Magill 1958; Manguel and Guadalupi 1987; Pollard 1970; Sheedy 1972; Swift 1958; Woods 1947)

See also allegory; burlesque; parody; satire; Swift, Jonathan; wit.

TARTUFFE

Molière's classic serio-comedy, *Tartuffe,* performed in 1664 for Louis XIV, was deemed worthy of court audiences, but the archbishop banned it from public theaters because of its impious study of a pseudo-religious scoundrel whose speeches sounded too near Jesuit logic for comfort. Molière wrote a second version in 1667 and a third two years later before meeting the standards set by the church. A dark comedy pillorying the false, insidious piety common in France and even more deadly in England's Puritan-run Commonwealth, *Tartuffe,* like other farces of Molière, is a character play that centers on a single twisted type, the sanctimonious pharisee. To its credit, the play has remained in vogue, a popularity that indicates that religious fraud was not limited to Molière's generation alone.

The satiric plot reveals the foolishness of Orgon, a middle-class Parisian who embraces the phony preacher Tartuffe and plots to wed him to his daughter Mariane. In counterpoint to her father's grand scheme, Mariane declares that she will commit suicide rather than give up love of Valère and submit to the unctuous religious fake. In Molière's dramatic pattern, he places sensible commentary in the speeches of a low-class servant to remind the audience that not all wisdom belongs to the learned. Dorine, the observant housemaid, summarizes the obvious—that Tartuffe's loving behaviors are especially warm toward women and that he eats enough for six. She urges the family to bide their time and give Tartuffe an opportunity to trip up and expose himself.

In Act III, the appearance of the main character proves what the family fears. Tartuffe conceals his carnal appetites by demanding that Dorine take his handkerchief and cover her exposed bosom. He implies that he has prayed for Elmire, Orgon's wife, and restored her to health. While Orgon's son Damis hides to eavesdrop, Tartuffe drops his sanctimony and ogles Elmire openly. With a winning mix of piety and humanity, Tartuffe admits to Elmire:

Ah, pious though I be, I'm still a man.
And when one glimpses your celestial beauties,
The heart is captured, and it cannot argue. . . .
If you consent to bring me consolation,
To condescend to my unworthiness,
I'll vow to you, O lovely miracle,

Immeasurable worship and devotion.
And in my hands your honor runs no risk,
Nor need it fear any disgrace or scandal.

Elmire and Damis have proof of Tartuffe's hypocrisy, but so intent is Orgon on believing in the irreligious knave that he silences his son and will hear nothing of Tartuffe's scandalous behavior.

Molière brings down his naif with a painful thump. At the end of Act IV, Orgon realizes that he has fallen for a shyster's ploy and that he has confessed to aiding Argas, an exile. In a revealing change of character, Tartuffe, who has gained title to Orgon's estate and can blackmail him with the crime of abetting, warns:

You are in a bad position to insult me,
For I have means to break and punish imposture,
To avenge offended heaven, and make repent
Those who dare say that I must leave the house!

Elmire is outraged that her husband has signed away their worldly goods. Orgon hurries upstairs to recover the strongbox that incriminates him. At this point, the comic element gives place to potential catastrophe for a man who is too late wise to trickery.

A confrontation between the fraud and his mark hastens Molière's denouement. In Act V, Monsieur Loyal, a deceitful process server, brings the dreaded news that Tartuffe does own Orgon's home and demands that the family vacate. In a fit of anguish, Orgon mutters to himself a venomous hatred for Tartuffe:

How happily I'd give this very moment
My last remaining hundred golden louis
For the pleasure of landing on that ugly snout
The most enormous punch in history!

Before Tartuffe can steal Orgon's property and turn him over to the king as an outlaw, the king's officer, a *deus ex machina* on a par with those in Greek and Roman comedy, intervenes and promises:

Our present King is enemy of fraud,
His eyes can penetrate his subjects' hearts;
The art of charlatans cannot delude him.
And his great spirit, wise in the ways of men,
Watches his kingdom with discerning eyes.
No one can take him easily by surprise.

An obvious sop to Louis XIV, the concluding disentanglement reveals that Tartuffe is an alias for a known rogue with a criminal record long enough to fill 20 volumes. With the eviction notice rendered worthless, the king's pardon rescues Orgon's family from ruin. (Baugh 1948; Bermel 1982; Brockett 1968; Burdick 1974; Gassner and Quinn 1969; Guicharnaud 1967; Molière 1965; Roberts 1962)

See also *Le Bourgeois gentilhomme*; caricature; comedy; *commedia dell'arte*; farce; incongruity; Molière; *Les Précieuses ridicules*; satire; wit.

THE TATLER

Begun with the union of broadside and essay, *The Tatler*, Augustan England's triweekly news sheet issued from April 12, 1709, through January 2, 1711, showcased the talents of originator Richard Steele, Oxford-educated military captain turned Whig politician. Trumpeted with an avowed aim to "recommend truth, innocence, honor, virtue, as the chief ornaments of life," the periodical published contributions from Joseph Addison and other coffeehouse wits, who often assembled at Dick's Coffeehouse on Fleet Street and Don Saltero's on Cheyne Walk. Before folding as a result of political disagreements, the paper appeared under the *nom de plume* of Isaac Bickerstaff, whom Steele spooled out into a family consisting of Isaac's sister, Jenny Distaff, and her husband, Tranquillus. The choice of Bickerstaff proceeds from a London insider joke: it repeated the name of a fictional poseur whom Jonathan Swift devised to lampoon a quack prognosticator named Partridge. In his rival almanac, Swift penned an obituary for Partridge, still very much alive. Bickerstaff replied that, based on his calculations of the heavens, the real Partridge was dead; the claimant had to be an imposter.

Steele offered *The Tatler* free of charge on its initial appearance and a penny a page thereafter. On Tuesday, April 12, 1709, above an epigraph from Juvenal, Rome's sharp-tongued satirist, proclaiming any human activity the focus of this journal, the Prospectus addresses Londoners:

> I shall, from time to time, report and consider all matters of what kind soever that shall occur to me, and publish such my advices and reflections every Tuesday, Thursday, and Saturday in the week, for the convenience of the post.

With a snide gesture to female readers, Steele claims to have named the paper in their honor. Obviously satirizing himself, he neglects to add that he is the tatler who originated the concept. He maintains a jocular tone in rejecting dull international proclamations in favor of the latest gossip from White's Chocolate House and St. James's Coffeehouse in St. James's district, Will's Coffeehouse on Bow Street in Covent Garden, and the Grecian, and anything of interest from Steele's apartment. Steele promises to use his prophetic powers to discern the topics that readers will want to hear about, insofar as he does not "offend our superiors."

The personal responses that *The Tatler* manifests often spring from events occurring in the small area of downtown London. In No. 219, issued September 1, 1710, Steele, annoyed with the familiarity and audacity of a pushy self-proclaimed wit, describes the value of pleasant public behavior: "An easy manner of conversation is the most desirable quality a man can have." He describes how people violate a normal exchange of conversation by dominating the conversation or ridiculing others. Steele rejects any escape for the troublemaker:

> It is no excuse for being mischievous, that a man is mischievous without malice: nor will it be thought an atonement that the ill was done not to injure the party concerned, but to divert the indifferent.

He closes his argument against cruel jest with a comparison to *Don Quixote*, which "utterly destroyed the spirit of gallantry in the Spanish nation" just as blatant ridicule injures the ease of an English coffeehouse gathering.

Later issues moved from the subject of good company to stronger condemnation of poor breeding: dueling, gambling, and tasteless or uncivilized behavior. On the subject of a favorite, Lady Elizabeth Hastings, whom Steele called Aspasia, he complimented an unusual female quality: "Though her mien carries much more invitation than command, to behold her is an immediate check to loose behavior, and to love her is a liberal education." Addison, less outspoken than his colleague but smoother at rounding out a thought, graced No. 147 with a famous epigram that champions the whole idea of a journal: "Reading is to the mind what exercise is to the body." (Addison 1973; Baugh 1948; Inglis and Spear 1952; *Selections from The Tatler and The Spectator* 1970; Steele 1973)

See also epigram; Juvenal; pun; satire; *The Spectator*; Steele, Sir Richard; Swift, Jonathan; wit.

TERENCE

The smoother, more urbane of Rome's chief stage funsters, Terence, whose career flourished during the early Roman Empire (240–84 B.C.), has little in common with Plautus, with whom he is usually mentioned. Born a slave in Carthage (currently Tunis), north Africa, around 195 B.C., a half-century after Plautus's birth, Publius Terentius Afer ("the African") was most likely Negroid or of mixed Libyan-Phoenician parentage. He traveled with a post–Punic War coffle of captives to Rome, where an auctioneer posted him for sale. Luck put Terence into the hands of Publius Terentius Lucanus, a senator who made the boy his namesake and heir and reared him to exquisite taste and manners. Terence's character and sensitivity brought him into the Scipionic Circle with Scipio Aemilianus and Gaius Laelius, a consul.

On a scholarly sojourn in Greece, Terence studied plays from Menander's collection of 108 comedies, which Terence translated into Latin. This in-depth study of Greek new comedy inspired Terence's canon, of which six comedies remain. A neophyte playwright, he began with *Andria (The Girl from Andros)* (167 B.C.), which he read to magistrates who disdained his poor attire. Upon completion of the masterly text, he received a round of applause and an invitation to join the elite Romans at table. His next four works increased his fame and acceptance: *Hecyra (The Mother-in-law)* (165 B.C.), *Heautontimorumenos (The Self-Torturer)* (163 B.C.), *Eunuchus (The Eunuch)* (161 B.C.), and *Phormio* (161 B.C.). His most successful work, *Adelphi (The Brothers)* (160 B.C.) he composed during his final months in Rome. Upon his return to Greece, he made more translations of Menander's plays and, while arranging passage home in 159 B.C., died of unknown cause. Variations of his death indicate that he drowned in a shipwreck off the island of Leucas. A less credible report claims that he died of grief after his manuscripts were lost at sea.

Roman playwright Terence, circa 195–159 B.C.

A world away from the crude, bawdy humor and peasant dance-hall rhythms of Plautine comedy, Terence's plays appealed to the cultivated theatergoer, the equivalent of today's angels of the theater and holders of season tickets. Subtly blending verisimilitude into characterization, his casts strayed from the stereotypical *miles gloriosus* (boastful soldier), the mincing ingenue, skulking slaves, meddlers, grifters, and beetle-browed parents to a more benign, good-natured cast. By removing the standard narrative prologue and adding a philosophical introduction, Terence forced viewers to work harder at the plot, which he spiced with suspense and rapid changes of fortune. Adept at foreshadowing and dramatic irony, he avoided Plautus's wholesale copying of comedic scenes and blended his own dialogue from fresh inspiration. The naysayers who demanded Plautine conventions met stiff rejoinders from Terence, who refused to budge from his aim to rejuvenate Roman comedy with cerebral plots and realistic characterization, both aimed to please the intelligentsia. An unusual mix of commentators have praised Terence over the years, including the orator Cicero, Julius Caesar, poets Horace and Quintilian, biblical scholars St. Jerome and St. Augustine, and Hroswitha, a medieval nun. Still in vogue during northern Europe's romance with the stage, Terence's canon influenced Francis Beaumont and John Fletcher's *The Scornful Lady* (1610), William Wycherley's *The Country Wife* (1675), Richard Steele's *The Tender Husband* (1705), and works by David Garrick, Molière, Denis Diderot, Henry Fielding, and Thornton Wilder. (Feder 1986; Gassner and Quinn 1969; Godolphin 1949; Hadas 1954; Hammond and Scullard 1992; Hornstein 1973; Howatson 1989; Mantinband 1956; Plautus 1900; Radice 1973; Terence 1910, 1974)

See also *Adelphi*; comedy; irony; Plautus; satire.

THACKERAY, WILLIAM MAKEPEACE

The author of one of the Victorian era's most vivid satirical novels, William Makepeace Thackeray applies the vigorous caricature, epigram, irony, and rambling, discursive moralizing typical of the era. At times arch and at others sympathetic, he knows when to absent himself from emotion-charged scenes, like a well-mannered gentleman excusing himself from a contretemps that he has no right to overhear. His characters, particularly the singular Becky Sharp, perpetrate original wickedness and find themselves trapped by the silken webs they lay for their victims. Among the genteel speeches common to Mayfair society, Thackeray embeds the foibles, mannerisms, tics, and idiosyncrasies that doom and damn. The fates are inexorable, but the rewards uncommonly sweet.

Like Saki, George Orwell, and Rudyard Kipling, Thackeray was a nonresident Englishman native to the empire. His father, Richmond Thackeray, followed the family pattern of civil service and was a government worker for the East India Company in Calcutta on July 18, 1811, when Thackeray was born. Ann Becher Thackeray, his mother, who was in her mid-twenties when she was left a widow in 1816, remarried in two years to Major Henry Carmichael-Smyth and lived at Larkbeare in Devonshire. Thackeray boarded at a preparatory school at Chiswick and at Charterhouse School (which he dubbed "Slaughterhouse"), where he was known for writing parodies and ducking tedious games, which he never enjoyed.

In 1829, Thackeray entered law school at Trinity College, Cambridge, but was obliged to leave the next year, presumably because he didn't apply himself to his studies. Instead, he began a magazine called the *Snob,* a subject that haunted his writings. A brief stint traveling in Weimar and Paris and a period of art study preceded the loss of his annual stipend of £500 through gambling, bank failure, and the purchase of the *National Standard,* a failing newspaper. The resulting penury forced Thackeray into self-employment. During this period, he married Isabella Shawe, whose mental breakdown after the death of Jane, her second daughter, and the birth of her third, Harriet Marian, forced Thackeray to place Isabella in a private facility for the insane. Harriet and Anne—later Lady Anne Ritchie, who became a novelist and her father's biographer in the decade following his death—moved to Paris to live with their paternal grandmother. Although Thackeray was perceived to be a grief-stricken widower, his wife outlived him.

Thackeray realized that he could never earn enough from art to support himself and turned instead to journalism during a three-year stint at the *Constitutional* in Paris. Under the pseudonyms of Titmarsh and Fitz-Boodle, he began cranking out parodies of Edward Bulwer-Lytton and Benjamin Disraeli and satires on sentimental fiction for *Fraser's Magazine,* beginning with *Catherine* (1840) and *The History of Samuel Titmarsh and the Great Hoggarty Diamond* (1841). His first success was *The Luck of Barry Lyndon* (1844), a burlesque of the picaresque casanova. An insider's joke, *The Snobs of England, By One of Themselves* (1847), contains amusing detail and a hint of Thackeray's skill at satire. Published in 20 installments for *Punch,* a comic weekly London journal, *Vanity Fair, a Novel without a Hero* (1848), a study of middle-class envy of the corrupt aristocracy, was Thackeray's most enduring fiction and the impetus to his rising fortunes.

It is fortunate for the English novel that Thackeray received neither the appointment to postmaster that he sought in 1848 nor the secretaryship at the English Embassy in Washington, D.C. As his biographer and contemporary, Anthony Trollope, assures us, "There never was a man less fit for the Queen's coat." Already a polished writer, Thackeray achieved greater following for subsequent fiction: *Pendennis* (1850), *Henry Esmond* (1852), *The Newcomes* (1855), *The Virginians* (1859), and *Denis Duval* (published posthumously in 1864). In addition to composing novels, Thackeray lectured in the United States on British humorists and the four Georges, published collected essays and travel sketches, ran unsuccessfully for parliament, and edited the *Cornhill Magazine,* a quality journal that he started in 1859 and that featured the best Victorian writers: Alfred Tennyson, Harriet Beecher Stowe, Elizabeth Gaskell, Anthony Trollope, John Ruskin, Bulwer-Lytton, Elizabeth Barrett Browning, and Matthew Arnold.

English novelist William Makepeace Thackeray, 1811–1863

Loneliness, lack of exercise, and back spasms diminished Thackeray's enjoyment of life. He remained actively involved in his daughters' lives and adopted a third girl, Amy Crowe, in 1853. After his sudden death in London on December 24, 1863, Thackeray was buried in Kensal Green and honored with a portrait bust in Westminster Abbey. He had attained a strong reputation for realistic, panoramic fiction second only to Charles Dickens, whose sentimental, often mawkish crusading on behalf of the lowest levels of society paralleled Thackeray's more detached, satiric interest in the upper echelons. His caricatures of colonials, Semites, social climbers, hangers-on, and servants survive as vivid portraits of each satiric microcosm, a puppet milieu he manipulated without the social conscience manifest in Dickens but with the empathy of a fellow sinner. (Baugh 1948; Drabble 1985; Eagle and Stephens 1992; Fowler 1989; Hornstein 1973; Lovett and Hughes 1932; Thackeray 1985; Trollope 1902)

See also burlesque; caricature; didacticism; epigram; irony; parody; picaresque; satire; *Vanity Fair*.

THEATER OF THE ABSURD

In post–World War II dramatic philosophy, theater of the absurd names the comic literary attitude reflecting human beings attempting to deal with nothingness: the angst-ridden malaise that afflicts humanity after the collapse of tradition and values. In the absurdist cosmos, there are no givens, no justice. Doubts about God, patriotism, sanity, and self supplant the philosophies that had assured humankind of purpose, worth, and direction. Absurdism is a formalized point of view as old as classical mime and heavily influenced by literary movements:

- the "God is dead" theory of Friedrich Nietzche's *Also sprach Zarathustra* (1884), a prelude to the sense of abandonment in twentieth-century literature and philosophy

- existentialism in Franz Kafka's *The Trial* (1925) and *The Metamorphosis* (1915), Jean-Paul Sartre's *Nausea* (1938) and *No Exit* (1944), and Simone de Beauvoir's *The Blood of Others* (1948)

- antirealism or stream of consciousness of James Joyce's *Ulysses* (1922) and *Finnegan's Wake* (1939) and Virginia Woolf's *To the Lighthouse* (1927)

- the philosophical novel or novel of ideas, for example, John Barth's *End of the Road* (1958)

- the internalized reality of expressionism displayed in August Strindberg's *The Dream Play* (1907) and *The Ghost Sonata* (1907), William Faulkner's *As I Lay Dying* (1930), Virginia Woolf's *Orlando* (1928), and the verse of Gerard Manley Hopkins and Edith Sitwell

- dadaism, a nihilism that frees the artist from literary conventions, as demonstrated in the verse of T. S. Eliot and Ezra Pound

- the unconscious illogic of surrealism, as demonstrated by the verse of Paul Eluard and the novels of William Burroughs

Absurdist thought permeates the plays of Alfred Jarry, Jean Genet, Georg Büchner, Friedrich Dürrenmatt, Vaclav Havel, Arthur Adamov, Ann Jellicoe, Samuel Beckett, Eugène Ionesco, Edward Albee, Bertolt Brecht, Harold Pinter, and Jean Anouilh. The potential for an endless musing over absence of meaning eddies into the black humor of Albert Camus's *The Myth of Sisyphus* (1942), in which the author leaves the title character in jeopardy yet unaware of his misery:

> Each atom of that stone, each mineral flake of that night-filled mountain, in itself forms a world. The struggle itself toward the heights is enough to fill a man's heart. One must imagine Sisyphus happy.

Likewise, Joseph Heller's *Catch-22* (1961), Kurt Vonnegut's *Cat's Cradle* (1963) and *Slaughterhouse-Five* (1969), and Margaret Atwood's *The Handmaid's Tale* (1985) share a brooding, quizzical tone that fails to make sense of reality.

Theater of the absurd deconstructs the conventions of time, place, action, and willing suspension of disbelief that Aristotle established in the fifth century B.C. Since the opening sally of Ionesco's *The Bald Soprano* (1948), absurdism has subjected the playgoer to avant-garde drama that experiments freely with an incongruity, comic anonymity, and cosmic irony that bears a resemblance to comic-strip quips:

> Mrs. Smith: There, it's nine o'clock. We've drunk the soup, and eaten the fish and chips, and the English salad. The children have drunk English water. We've eaten well this evening. That's because we live in the suburbs of London and because our name is Smith.

Absurdism consists of a chaos or disharmony of antiheroic characterization, contradictions, unconventional stage design, coincidence, distortion, miscues, paranoia, brutality, and violence. In a hearty bit of foolery, Slawomir Mrozek's *Tango* (1965) lampoons conventional drama in Stomil's rhetorical question concerning the courage required in dancing the tango:

> Do you realize that in those days there were hardly any fallen women? That the only recognized style of painting was naturalism? That the theater was utterly bourgeois? Stifling. Insufferable.

Taking similar liberties with grammatical convention, Edward Albee's *Tiny Alice* (1965) pits lawyer against cardinal in a discussion of the use of the first-person singular and the editorial we. The lawyer qualifies his use of "we" as reserved for intimates, equals, or superiors. To the cardinal's insistence that he cease commenting on priestly venality, the lawyer retorts, "We have come down off our plural . . . when the stakes are high enough . . . and the hand, the kissed hand palsies out . . . for the LOOT!!" The cardinal's complaints about "unseemly talk" echo the playwright's use of unseemly dialogue to jolt the audience into a clearer understanding of religious subservience to the wealthy.

Theater of the absurd, a post–World War II philosophy, proposes that there are no givens and that God, patriotism, and justice are dead. Absurdist playwright Eugène Ionesco incorporated the philosophy into *Rhinoceros,* staged on Broadway in 1960. John, left (Zero Mostel), roars as Berrenger (Eli Wallach) looks on.

In absurdist literature, an excess of satire, energized farce, grotesquerie, dilemma, and improbable caricature dramatizes the unpredictability of human destiny; life stands at the mercy of random fate; for example, the numerous accidents that destroy parts of Claire's body in Dürrenmatt's *The Visit* (1956) convince her that she is impervious to death. By communicating the trauma and sterility of everyday life, the theater echoes the human questions that hammer away with interminable whys and either frivolous or incomprehensible replies or a silence as palpable and dismaying as the conclusion to Edward Albee's one-act *The Zoo Story*, in which Peter howls "OH MY GOD!" from offstage as Jerry, dying of a stab wound, whispers the echo, "Oh . . . my . . . God."

In response to a reality that lacks pattern, consequence, and predictability, theater of the absurd moves out of the mainstream by abandoning plot and motive. In place of a story, absurdism relies on fantasy, slapstick humor, satiric allegory, and illusion, often combining shadow pictures, slides, random sounds, feats of magic, and fragrances as stimuli to artistic expression. The resulting melange orders snatches of dialogue and events out of context to produce a nightmarish situation or impression of inadequacy, despair, or perplexity. Dream states and schizophrenic selves compete for control, as in Marsha Norman's darkly comic *Getting Out* (1977), in which conflicted points of view accompany Arlene from an asylum to a jangled, uncaring world that is certain to destroy her. Absurdist scenarios are highly charged with images that enhance the illusory state of free-floating discontent, menace, or unease. In a cheerful blend of realism with fantasy, Charlie meets the spirit of his deceased father in Hugh Leonard's *Da* (1973), a supernatural settling of old scores that produces wry, postfuneral humor. In similar fashion, David Mamet sets a deceptively humorous tone at the beginning of *American Buffalo* (1977) with a forward-thrust musical couplet that serves as the play's epigraph: "Mine eyes have seen the glory of the coming of the Lord./He is peeling down the alley in a black and yellow Ford." By the end of the highly repetitious, nonsensical dialogue, Mamet establishes no glory, but plenty of word-laden, inarticulate nothingness that passes for dialogue and human reconciliation.

Absurdism remarks on the alienation of characters from each other, from social institutions, and from the earth itself. Fragmented communication mimics a pass-the-time exchange that heightens the spaces between individuals whose broken links sputter like electric cables downed by a storm. Thus, for example, Berenger's comment in Eugène Ionesco's *Rhinoceros* (1960):

> I'm concious of my body all the time, as if it were made of lead, or as if I were carrying another man around on my back. I can't seem to get used to myself. I don't even know if I am me. Then as soon as I take a drink, the lead slips away and I recognize myself, I become me again.

The isolated speaker, intuitively cringing like a fly under the shadow of the swatter, suspects the imminence of doom and turns to a stopgap reliance on alcohol for consolation.

Most significant to the acceptance of theater of the absurd is the classic suspended state of Estragon and Vladimir in Samuel Beckett's two-character play *Waiting for Godot* (1953), a worldwide dramatic presence. A parody of reason, the play's hovering, gloom-ridden mood sounds a warning that all is not well with humankind and that expecting help from a metaphysical source is a fruitless wait:

Estragon:	What do we do now?
Vladimir:	I don't know.
Estragon:	Let's go.
Vladimir:	We can't.
Estragon:	Why not?
Vladimir:	We're waiting for Godot.

Like a wisp of spider web, the chattery nothingness of the characters' banal, staccato exchanges covers the chasm that separates their souls. Directionless, anxious, and eager to end the self-imposed paralysis of inaction, they keep up their conversation, the daily fragments that bring nervous laughter from the audience. (Abrams 1971; Albee 1959, 1965; Anderson 1971; Baldick 1990; Beckson and Ganz 1989; Brockett 1968; Camus 1991; Cuddon 1976; Drabble 1985; Dürrenmatt 1981; Gassner 1969; Gray 1992; Henry 1995; Holman 1980; Ionesco 1958, 1981; Leonard 1973; McArthur 1992; Mrozek 1981)

See also allegory; Beckett, Samuel; black humor; Brecht, Bertolt; caricature; *Catch-22;* Dürrenmatt, Friedrich; farce; *The Handmaid's Tale;* Heller, Joseph; incongruity; irony; Leonard, Hugh; Norman, Marsha; satire; slapstick; *Slaughterhouse-Five;* Vonnegut, Kurt.

 # TRICKSTER

A form of picaro or rascal, the trickster is endemic in literature, both oral and written, and blends the paradoxical qualities of the clever deceiver and the fool, mutually exclusive qualities that protect native comics from committing potentially sacrilegious, lethal, or catastrophic behaviors. In a melange of guises, the trickster is the focus of stories from virtually all cultures: Maori, Chinese, Semites, Greek, Japanese, Italian, French, Scandinavian, Inuit, and Balinese, to name several. In Native American lore, the trickster bears the face of the scolding jay, grinning fox, scampering raccoon, clever frog, insouciant rabbit, or Old Man Coyote, a perennial favorite. His tribal designations are vivid, down to the names and form by which he is known and the obscene, scatological nature of his stories:

- The Abenaki know him as Azeban, a raccoon.

- Named Sitconski, Inktonmi, Inktumni, or Inktomi by the Assiniboine, the traditional trickster lives during the time of the great flood. In a stereotypical comic scene, he falls victim to curiosity by getting his head stuck in a skull, a bit of black humor replicated in African lore by the equally curious monkey.

- To the Arapaho, the trickster is Iktomi the spider.

- The Blackfoot version of Old Man is Na-Pe, a frolicsome anthropomorphic deity who has more in common with the Greek Zeus than with the somber Judeo-Christian Yahweh.

- The Catawba call the trickster One Tail Clear of Hair, the opossum.

- The Cherokee maintain the sneaky nature of the trickster in the antics of the booger, a ceremonial clown who blends comic antics with a knowledge of the spirit world and the power of healing.

- For the Chippewa, Nanabozho or Wenabozho the hare aided the tribe by overcoming natural disaster.

- Alaskan Eskimos perceive the trickster as inua, a spirit capable of taking on many guises. To propitiate his power, crafters inscribe his likeness on harpoons, tools, kayaks, and ceremonial masks.

- Inuit lore names Amaguq the wolf as a prime deceiver.

- The Kiowa made a hero of their trickster Saynday, the teacher who led humanity to the bois d'arc for bow wood and created stone weapons and arrowheads. The stories utilize a recurrent phenomenon: they blend positive and negative character traits in Saynday, the paradoxical foolish wiseman.

- The Micmac of Nova Scotia revere Glooskap the frog, the wizard at handicrafts who taught humankind weaving, tanning, fishing and hunting, and beadwork.

- The spider trickster of the Oglala Sioux deviates even further from the warm-blooded animal to the insidious crawler and web-maker.

- The Penobscot of Maine named their trickster Gluscabi.

- The Lakota pictured the trickster as a hare. Their relatives, the Brulé Sioux, and the Shoshone recall stories of Old Man Coyote, a term derived from the Nahuatl word *coyotl*. In plains lore, Old Man carries mythic significance: he taught natives the elements of animism and the power of the Great Spirit. The Crow lengthened the trickster name to the Old Man Who Did Everything.

- The Nootka tell tales of two tricksters, Chulyen the crow and Guguyni the raven.

- For the Passamaquoddy, their trickster, the turtle Mikchich, evolved as Glooskap's sly uncle.

- The Ponca Ishtinike combines the power of the form-changer with the inventiveness of the comic trickster. He is capable of both silly and mercenary actions.

- Among the Pueblo, the trickster wears his most revealing costume—the patterned skeleton of the Koshare clown society, a wandering band of irreverent funmakers who mock priestly ceremonies and serve as a psychological buffer between the worshipper and an overly serious ceremony linked with food, rain, and tribal survival.

- The Tlingit trickster, a raven, interacts with fish, petrels, and deer, as well as human beings, while participating in the fine points of earth's creation.

- Among the Winnebago, the trickster's adventures are fraught with danger, comic losses of his penis, a slide in excrement, lethal flatus, human cannibalism, and constant plotting by bear, wolf, elk, mink, even the small-framed chipmunk. One cycle splits his nature into twins named Flesh and Stump.

An oral cornucopia predating Christopher Columbus and the coming of European domination to the Americas, the trickster lore of campfire tellings has in the last century moved more prominently into written stories, verse, children's books, and drama. As a result of renewed interest in mythology and multiculturalism, these stories have provided an energetic, rejuvenating force in Native American writing.

Anthropologists Paul Radin and Franz Boas studied the trickster motif during the early nineteenth century. They determined that the trickster blends a variety of native intelligence, instinct, and survival mechanisms with outright dishonesty, thievery, gluttony, bull-headedness, and viciousness. According to Radin, these animal lore cycles satirize human attempts to flout and elude tribal mores and taboos, for example, engaging in sexual activity before joining a war party or defiling the sacred war bundle. Usually male in whatever guise the rascal appears, the trickster teases and cajoles, amuses and circumvents the creator by deceiving human beings or, like Prometheus the fire-bringer, divulging heaven's secrets and defying death. In one humorous Winnebago story, the chief raises his standard, which is nothing more than his blanket atop an erect penis. In the most satisfying stories, the trickster grows so self-confident that he outdoes himself by losing his tail in a tight squeeze or trapping his head in a log. Overall, these satires serve as a primeval safety valve for human beings who are not permitted to question custom or law in any other way.

In European peasant lore, the trickster resides in Pulchinello of the *commedia dell'arte* and the male antagonist of the Punch-and-Judy puppet shows. On English pageant wagons, he was Satan, the provocative tempter in the devil suit. Migrated to the Caribbean and the Americas, the trickster becomes the leering, mugging demon of Mardi Gras, the pre-Lenten carnival that exhausts the Christian's urge for naughtiness before the serious fasting and self-examination of Lent. An unusual term in European literary criticism, the trickster nonetheless survives in multiple examples:

- The Greek Prometheus ("Forethought") and Epimetheus ("Afterthought"), an elemental doppelganger, who mold all creation, ending with humankind, the least equipped to thrive in a dangerous world.

Because Epimetheus deprives humans of fangs, wings, claws, or carapaced shell, Prometheus must become the savior and steal fire, the secret power that sets God over lesser creatures. In a contrasting myth, Epimetheus brings his own gift, Pandora, the Eve figure who spills multiple evils on earth but manages to rescue Hope, the personified figure who redeems humanity from utter despair.

- Hermes, the amoral roustabout in the Homeric *Hymns* and in Odysseus's trickery in Homer's *Odyssey* (eighth century B.C.). Recurring as the Greek messenger described in Hesiod's *Works and Days* and *Theogony* (seventh century B.C.), Hermes is a demonic god whose trickery and thievery are an outgrowth of magical power, betokened by the Caduceus, his snake-ringed staff.

- The conniving fox in Aesop's fables (sixth century B.C.), who retreats from admitting his foolishness by declaring anything he can't reach "sour grapes."

- Syrus, the manipulative slave who worms his way into manumission in Terence's *Adelphi* (160 B.C.).

- Phaedrus's fables, which reprise the tricksters from Aesop's fables and add more recent lore (first century A.D.).

- Krishna lore from the *Bhagavata Purana* (tenth century), which depicts the adventurer as gluttonous and childishly out of control.

- The medieval trickster Reynard the Fox (twelfth–thirteenth centuries).

- Jacob and Wilhelm Grimm's "Rumplestiltskin" (1815), the deformed, malevolent dwarf who plots child-stealing and dies from an outburst of temper that causes him to stamp his foot so hard that he sinks into the earth.

- François Rabelais's giant baby in his picaresque classic, *Gargantua and Pantagruel* (1553).

- Christopher Marlowe's Mephistopheles, the evildoer of the Faust legend (1592).

- Frontier yarns about Davy Crockett, the backwoods hayseed who outfoxes river pirates, bears, and common brigands before entering Congress in 1829, from whence came another blend of trickster lore published in Nashville from 1835 to 1841.

- An anonymous cycle of Appalachian Jack tales.

- Joel Chandler Harris's Br'er Rabbit, star of the most famous Uncle Remus tales (1881).

- The conniving wife in Isaac Singer's *Gimpel the Fool* (1957).

A given among the world's satiric mime shows, folly literature, peasant dramas, and television sitcoms, the trickster remains a symbol of anarchy, the recompense to a wicked, disobedient population that either cannot or will not obey godly injunctions. An antidote to barbarity, trickster stories maintain the shifting balance of good over evil, evil over good. Serving the external mind with entertainment, the trickster's distorted motives and unseemly behaviors strike to the inner landscapes of conscience, the war-swept plain that Freud described as the pitting of "I will" against "you mustn't." An overlay of hilarity and preposterous illogic redeems these episodic scrapes and gags from dull didacticism; at heart, however, trickster cycles are anything but trivial. As a repository of folk wisdom, the trickster tale is an archetypal oral guide to probity and religiosity, a pattern of redemptive schemata that rewards good intentions. (Beatty 1952; Bemister 1973; Brown 1947; Cuevas 1991; Dorson 1959; Feldman 1965; Fraser 1968; Lame Deer and Erdoes 1972; Leeming 1990; Lummis 1992; Marriott and Rachlin 1975; Patterson and Snodgrass 1994; Phaedrus 1992; Radin 1972; Rosenberg 1992; Turner 1974)

See also Adelphi; comedy; *commedia dell'arte*; didacticism; folly literature; *Gargantua and Pantagruel;* Harris, Joel Chandler; picaresque; Rabelais, François; Reynard the Fox; satire; Terence.

TWAIN, MARK

America's best-loved humorist, local-color aphorist, and satirist, Mark Twain was the author of two influential satires: *The Adventures of Huckleberry Finn* (1884), the most revered picaresque odyssey in U.S. literature, and *A Connecticut Yankee in King Arthur's Court* (1886), a dystopian fantasy that places a late nineteenth-century tinker in sixth-century Camelot. Twain, the pseudonym of Samuel Langhorne Clemens, was born in Florida, a backwoods Missouri community, on November 30, 1835, the sixth child and third son of storekeeper, justice of the peace, and judge John Marshall Clemens and Jane Lampton Clemens, a sweet-tempered Virginia aristocrat who taught her family to revere all living things. A talented mimic who absorbed the diversity and humor of many parts of the country, Twain grew up on the banks of the Mississippi River, the escape route he hoped would carry him far from his rural beginnings. In his dreams of glory as a riverboat pilot described in the autobiographical *Life on the Mississippi* (1883), he laughs at his childhood reveries:

> I went meekly aboard a few of the boats that lay packed together like sardines at the long St. Louis wharf, and very humbly inquired for the pilots, but got only a cold shoulder and short words from mates and clerks. I had to make the best of this sort of treatment for the time being, but I had comforting daydreams of a future when I should be a great and honored pilot, with plenty of money, and could kill some of these mates and clerks and pay for them.

In 1839, Twain moved to Hannibal and enjoyed idyllic country life; his father's death forced Twain to leave school at age eighteen and adopt the printer's trade, which he practiced journeyman-style in New York, Philadelphia, St. Louis,

Cincinnati, and Keokuk, Iowa. In daily contact with manuscripts and type for the Hannibal *Journal,* his older brother Orion's newspaper, from 1853 to 1854 Twain wrote under various pen names, including Epaminondas Adrastus Perkins, Josh, and Thomas Jefferson Snodgrass. After learning the complicated river maps and current charts to obtain his river pilot's license in 1859, he navigated the Mississippi River only four years aboard several vessels before river travel ceased in late April 1861.

The war, which destroyed Twain's childhood dream of piloting a sternwheeler, might have ended his life as well. After enlisting in the Confederate irregulars of Marion County, Missouri, Twain reconsidered his role in the military; two weeks later, he deserted. With his brother Orion, the newly appointed secretary to the governor of Nevada, he journeyed 19 days by stage to Carson City, mined quartz and prospected for silver, and in 1862 wrote for the Virginia City *Territorial Enterprise.* Published under his well-known pseudonym, Twain's first serious short story, "The Celebrated Jumping Frog of Calaveras County" (1867), launched a career enhanced by friendships with humorist Artemus Ward and local-colorist Bret Harte. Twain branched out to comedy, essays, young adult literature, autobiography, satire, lectures, history, and anecdotes. To this considerable list of genres he added travelogs on his visit to Panama, Nicaragua, the Azores, Gibraltar, Europe, Russia, Turkey, the Holy Land, and Hawaii, where he interviewed and observed in 1866 on assignment for the Sacramento *Union.*

On February 2, 1870, after a three-year courtship by letter, Twain wed Olivia "Livy" Langdon, the refined, citified daughter of a wealthy coal merchant of Elmira, New York, and settled in Buffalo, where he edited his father-in-law's paper, the Buffalo *Express,* and watched over Livy. Despite frail health that stemmed from tuberculosis of the spine, Livy gave birth to son Langdon and survived typhoid fever. The loss of Langdon to diphtheria preceded the births of Susy in 1872, Clara in 1874, and Jean in 1880. From New York, Twain moved his family into a self-styled gaudy, gingerbready riverboat mansion in Hartford, Connecticut, where he wrote *Roughing It* (1872), *The Adventures of Tom Sawyer* (1876), *The Prince and the Pauper* (1882), and *Life on the Mississippi* (1883). He reached the height of his fame with *The Adventures of Huckleberry Finn,* a classic work in the young adult canon, and followed two years later with *A Connecticut Yankee in King Arthur's Court.* A chaotic masterwork, the satiric historical novel reflects the author's belief in freedom and human rights, both endangered abstracts in medieval England and the antebellum South.

Although Twain never struck it rich from his publications, he profited from his genial frontier wit and charm and became a popular after-dinner speaker. His later years brought world-famous visitors George Washington Cable, Helen Keller, Rudyard Kipling, and Harriet Beecher Stowe to hear his store of anecdotes and jokes. Dressed in white linen suit, his face framed in silvery locks, he looked the picture of Old South contentment and thrilled English fans when he journeyed to Oxford to receive an honorary doctorate. In reality, lawsuits, poor financial planning, and, in 1885, ill-advised investments in the Paige compositor and Kaolatype machine depleted him, forcing him onto the lecture circuit to meet expenses. The deaths of daughter Susy in 1895 from meningitis and wife Olivia in 1904 and the severe epileptic seizures that killed daughter Jean in 1909 saddened and embittered him.

Some of Twain's most pointed satire, irony, and allegory attest to his unhappiness, in particular, "The Man Who Corrupted Hadleyburg" (1898), an allegory on hypocrisy and greed; *The Mysterious Stranger* (1916), a posthumous morality novella; and the caustic treatise on religion, "Letters from the Earth" (published posthumously in 1963) in which he boldly concludes:

> Man is a marvelous curiosity. . . . He thinks he is the Creator's pet. He believes the Creator is proud of him; he even believes the Creator loves him; has a passion for him; sits up nights to admire him; yes, and watch over him and keep him out of trouble. He prays to Him, and thinks He listens. Isn't it a quaint idea? Fills his prayers with crude and bald and florid flatteries of Him, and thinks He sits and purrs over these extravagancies and enjoys them. He prays . . . although no prayer of his has ever been answered.

To clarify some public misconceptions about his life and blatantly atheistic philosophy, Twain, who claimed to use "a pen warmed up in hell," began an autobiography in 1906, which he dictated to a stenographer. He left it unfinished at his death from heart disease at Stormfield in Redding, Connecticut, on April 21, 1910. Both Florida and Hannibal, Missouri, honor him with museums. On a knoll near Hannibal, a statue of Twain rises above the inscription: "His religion was humanity, and the whole world mourned for him when he died."

Twain remains Americans' best-loved teller of tales and most frequently cited satirist. His skill with humor, local color, and anecdote eased the disdainful message of his damning stories, which denote a streak of doubt that foolish humanity is worth saving. Collections of his satiric aphorisms display shrewd observations and canny evaluation of weakness and sin, often his own:

- When angry, count four; when very angry, swear.
- Everyone is a moon, and has a dark side which he never shows to anybody.
- I believe that our Heavenly Father invented man because he was disappointed in the monkey.
- Always do right. This will gratify some people, and astonish the rest.
- Nothing so needs reforming as other people's habits.
- Put all your eggs in the one basket and—WATCH THAT BASKET.
- When I was younger I could remember anything, whether it happened or not; but I am getting old, and soon I shall remember only the latter.
- If you pick up a starving dog and make him prosperous, he will not bite you. This is the principal difference between a dog and a man.

A controlled prose artist, Twain often spoke his satire to adoring audiences who packed lecture halls to hear his rambling commentary. A vehicle for Hal Holbrook and other imitators, one-man shows in the style of Twain continue to blend witty frontier humor with his decidedly dark view of the human condition. (Bloom 1986; Emerson 1985; Kaplan 1966; Rasmussen 1995; Shalit 1987; Thomas and Thomas 1943; Twain 1962a, 1962b, 1963, 1990, 1991)

See also The Adventures of Huckleberry Finn; allegory; *A Connecticut Yankee in King Arthur's Court;* epigram; irony; Morgan, Hank; picaresque; satire.

 VANITY FAIR

The product of England's voguish addiction to serial fiction, *Vanity Fair, a Novel without a Hero* appeared in monthly issues of *Punch*, a London humor magazine, from January 1847 until July 1848. William Makepeace Thackeray, a career journalist, lecturer, and essayist, experimented as peripatetic omniscient voice by traversing the novel like a ghost down marble halls, halting to discourse, gossip, and intrigue his readers and to emphasize the didactic commentary he imposes on his fiction. At the conclusion of its 20-issue run, the novel had achieved prominence in English fiction for its popular appeal and for its wit, suspense, caricature, and verisimilitude. Moving counter to the rhythms and aims of Charles Dickens's bathos and altruism, Thackeray's novel capitalizes on a droll re-creation of the Napoleonic era and the cultural clash between the social-climbing bourgeois and the effete upper class.

In the first chapters, Rebecca "Becky" Sharp—one of literature's most self-possessed rapscallions and the prototype for Margaret Mitchell's Scarlett O'Hara—lives the unenviable life of a charity case at Miss Pinkerton's academy. To earn her keep, she teaches French. Amid condescension from her betters, Becky accepts true love and charity from Amelia Sedley as a means of rising in society. A fictional version of Thackeray's wife Isabella and the model for *Gone with the Wind's* angelic Melanie Wilkes, Amelia possesses none of Becky's verve or talent for music and mimicry. Her naiveté supplies Becky with an inroad to the gentry, whom she hopes to infiltrate through marriage.

Flashing her green eyes, Becky blushes in vain at Amelia's dimwitted brother Jos, the pursy, overweight collector of the jungly Indian district of Boggley Wollah and a model of the parasitic nobility. Becky loses her first quarry and, like Samuel Richardson's Pamela Andrews, parries the lustful proposal of her ludicrous employer, Sir Pitt Crawley, a repulsive aristocratic ignoramus who takes advantage of her plight:

> "I'm an old man, but a good'n. I'm good for twenty years. I'll make you happy,
> zee if I don't. You shall do what you like; spend what you like; and 'av it all
> your own way. I'll make you a zettlement. I'll do everything reglar. Look year!"
> and the old man fell down on his knees and leered at her like a satyr.

Trapped by her own guile, Becky rejects his tempting offer because she has settled for Pitt's brother, Colonel Rawdon Crawley, whose aunt disowns him for marrying beneath his station. With instinctive survival skills, Becky wards off bill collectors and spends as she chooses. Thackeray notes, "'I'll make your fortune,' she said; and Delilah patted Samson's cheek."

Through the puppeteer's adroit pull on the strings, the characters reverse positions. After the Sedleys lose their fortune and faithless friends, George Osborne, Amelia's undeserving intended, refuses a mulatto heiress and proceeds with his marriage plans. His open rebellion against a tyrannical father triggers a disinheritance because of the Osbornes' distaste for the Sedleys' genteel poverty. By clever manipulation of rumors, Becky appears to rise in society and to profit by open flirtation with aristocrats. The couples live in the bustle of Paris until George's death at the Battle of Waterloo. William Dobbin, the faithful friend, hovers in the antechamber of Amelia's plight and supplies her and her infant son anonymously when her savings ebb.

Thackeray imbues his satiric protagonist with verve and persistence. Unfazed by public scandal, Becky prods Rawdon to succeed, entices his brother, the odious Sir Pitt, to unchaperoned evenings while her husband is away, and becomes the favorite of Lord Steyne, her patron and lover. At dinners and balls, Becky raises her charming voice to a thrilled audience, who press around her in awe:

> The Royal Personage declared, with an oath, that she was perfection, and engaged her again and again in conversation. Little Becky's soul swelled with pride and delight at these honours; she saw fortune, fame, fashion before her. Lord Steyne was her slave; followed her everywhere, and scarcely spoke to any one in the room beside, and paid her the most marked compliments and attention.

As her carriage rolls away from the admiring throng, Rawdon disconsolately lights his cigar and wonders how she has managed to rise so far above him.

To the author, the subservience of the husband forms the kernel of his satire. Indeed, Rawdon, the would-be heir of Queen's Crawley, becomes little more than Becky's factotum and seems unaware that his messmates have long shredded his wife's reputation for tartish behavior. Although he is a better parent to little Rawdon, he professes no more virtue than Becky. In a melodramatic scene *in flagrante delicto,* he hypocritically tosses out Steyne, his wife's seducer; chastises his wife; rummages through her locked cabinets and drawers; and begs his brother for money. Becky's sister-in-law, Jane Crawley, recoils from contagion:

> But righteous obedience has its limits, and I declare that I will not bear that— that woman again under my roof: if she enters it, I and my children will leave it. She is not worthy to sit down with Christian people.

With the aid of Steyne, Rawdon replaces the deceased governor of Coventry Island at £3,000 annually, settles a yearly stipend of £300 on his estranged wife, and dies of yellow fever far from home.

Thackeray exerts no effort to redeem either Becky's mercenary qualities or Amelia's spinelessness. As expected, the two widows face uncertainty in starkly contrasting methods. Garbed in black, Becky rouges more heavily, develops a taste for cognac, gambles while dodging creditors, and, beneath a contrived mask of conventionality, continues to stalk men throughout Europe:

> from Boulogne to Dieppe, from Dieppe to Caen, from Caen to Tours—trying with all her might to be respectable, and alas! always found out some day or other, and pecked out of the cage by the real daws.

Continuing the slide from hotel to houseguest to boardinghouse, she sinks to competition with "fly-blown beauties who frequented her landlady's *salons.*"

With the control of a master, Thackeray plays out the inevitable. Becky's comeuppance occurs at a banquet in Rome, where she encounters Lord Steyne, her nemesis, and the high-tempered Lady Belladonna. Reconnoitering the situation, Becky tries to shuck her escort while catching the lord's eye. Steyne looks as aghast as Macbeth gazing on Banquo's ghost. A secondhand message urges her to leave Rome to avoid the wrath of the offended lord. Thackeray, with the relish of a Hollywood gossip columnist, appends the demise of

> the Most Honourable George Gustavus, Marquis of Steyne, Earl of Gaunt and of Gaunt Castle, in the Peerage of Ireland, Viscount Hellborough, Baron Pitchly and Grillsby, a Knight of the Most Noble Order of the Garter, of the Golden Fleece of Spain, of the Russian Order of Saint Nicholas of the First Class, of the Turkish Order of the Crescent, First Lord of the Powder Closet and Groom of the Back Stairs, Colonel of the Gaunt or Regent's Own Regiment of Militia, a Trustee of the British Museum, an Elder Brother of the Trinity House, a Governor of the White Friars, and D. C. L.

Steyne dies of a seizure and receives an outpouring of honor. His body lies in Naples, his heart contained in a silver urn (perhaps a satiric jab at a similar interment for the heart of Percy Bysshe Shelley, who drowned off Leghorn, Italy). Mr. Wagg proclaims him a statesman and an ornament of England and defends Lady Belladonna, who apparently cleaned out his assets from the secretaire before her precipitous departure. When challenged by Dobbin as an unsuitable guest for Amelia's family, Becky presents a speech worthy of Blanche Dubois's "I have always depended upon the kindness of strangers." Draped in false piety, Becky claims to be "insulted because I am alone."

Thackeray compounds the expected end of the mother with the contrasting rise of the son, who achieves Becky's original goal without guile or plotting. He comes to think of his Aunt Jane as a parent, but dutifully writes to "that one" who abandoned him. In lieu of any other heir, Sir Pitt leaves Little Rawdon Queen's Crawley. In contrast to Becky's disinterest in motherhood, Amelia, a sacrificing martyr, is forced to hand young George into the care of his paternal grandfather. Through the intervention of the faithful Dobbin, Grandfather Osborne relents, accepts Amelia, and names young George his heir. Exploitive to the end, Becky usurps the title of Lady Crawley. Amelia, the angelic heroine, marries Dobbin; Becky continues to make money and prestige her life's goal.

Thackeray's satire, which extends from 1813 to 1830, parallels the situation in Jane Austen's *Pride and Prejudice* (1813): English gentry jostling for the best financial deal in marriage. The open worship of money and its attendant social position is the focal sin of *Vanity Fair,* Thackeray's fictional market-based cosmos, which he adapted from John Bunyan's allegorical *Pilgrim's Progress.* The introduction states that Thackeray intends to manage a performance to illustrate

> a great quantity of eating and drinking, making love and jilting, laughing and the contrary, smoking, cheating, fighting, dancing, and fiddling: there are bullies pushing about, bucks ogling the women, knaves picking pockets, policemen on the look-out, quacks . . . bawling in front of their booths, and yokels looking up at the tinselled dancers and poor old rouged tumblers, while the light-fingered folk are operating upon their pockets behind. Yes, this is Vanity Fair: not a moral place certainly; nor a merry one, though very noisy.

True to his promise, Thackeray confers life on his "Becky puppet" and his "Amelia doll" and orchestrates a cast of entertaining caricatures—Lord Tapeworm, Madame de Burst, Mrs. Hook Eagles, Dr. Swishtail, Sir Noodle, the Rev. Mr. Muff, Madame Strumpff, Gräfinn Fanny de Butterbrod, and the Earl of Bagwig. In deference to delicate sensibilities, the omniscient voice declares:

> Those who like may peep down under waves that are pretty transparent, and see it writhing and twirling, diabolically hideous and slimy, flapping amongst bones, or curling round corpses; but above the water-line, I ask, has not everything been proper, agreeable, and decorous, and has any the most squeamish immoralist in Vanity Fair a right to cry fie?

The author ends his vanity of vanities with a paternal code—an urbane quibble over the difference between true happiness and illusion. He signs off patronizingly, "Come children, let us shut up the box and the puppets, for our play is played out." (Baugh 1948; Drabble 1985; Eagle and Stephens 1992; Fowler 1989; Hornstein 1973; Lovett and Hughesl 1932; Thackeray 1985; Trollope 1902)

See also allegory; Austen, Jane; bathos; burlesque; caricature; didacticism; epigram; irony; parody; picaresque; *Pride and Prejudice;* Richardson, Samuel; satire; Thackeray, William Makepeace.

VARRO

A noted student of geography, rhetoric, science, law, and ancient history and a contemporary of Julius Caesar, Marcus Terentius Varro, born in 116 B.C., earned the nickname Reatinus for his hometown of Reate, Sabinus. Under the guidance of philologist Lucius Aelius Stilo and philosopher Antiochus of Ascalon, Varro prepared himself for a life of study. A supporter of Pompey's party, Varro served in Spain and Dalmatia during the civil war, received a corona for helping to clear the sea of pirates, and accepted posts as tribune, aedile, and judge. After Caesar overcame Pompey, Varro received a pardon for taking part in armed rebellion and was granted the tenuous position as Rome's archivist in charge of Greek and Roman literature, a plum job if he could have served under any other taskmaster. After Caesar's assassination, unsettled times brought Varro to Mark Antony's list of intended victims in 43 B.C., a terrifying close call that Varro escaped with Octavian's help, but not without forfeiture of land and many original volumes from his personal collection. One of his memorable satiric epigrams summarizes his joy in sacrificing books for life: "He who escapes in time lives to fight another day."

Sick, like most Romans, of war, political turmoil, and bloody purges, Varro and his wife retired from public involvement. He spent his energies helping to shape Suetonius's career and composed over 600 encyclopedic volumes on subjects ranging from music to dramatic criticism, medicine, anecdotes, and architecture. Of his vast store of scholarly notes and commentary, these survive: *De re rustica [On Agriculture]* in its entirety, which influenced Virgil's study of country life, and a quarter of *De lingua Latina [Of Latin]*, a study of grammar and etymology dedicated to the orator Cicero. In addition, there remain fragments of *Antiquitates rerum humanarum et divinarum [Human and Godly Antiquities]*, *De gente populi Romani [Of the Roman people]*, *Disciplinae [Studies]*, *Imagines [Portraits]*, a critical essay on Plautus and a list of his published plays, and snippets of Menippean satire presented in dialogue form. Looking back to a less pretentious era, Varro directed his satires against the vulgar posturing of late Republican Rome and sagely observed, "Not all who own harps are harpers." He is said to have died the scholar's death—holding his stylus. Treasured in his day by Cicero, Pliny the Elder, Virgil, and Quintilian, Varro found favor with St. Augustine, who applied Varro's study of city planning to *The City of God*. (Feder 1986; Godolphin 1949; Hadas 1954; Hammond 1992; Hornstein 1973; Howatson 1989; Mantinband 1956; Radice 1973)

See also epigram; Plautus; satire.

VOLTAIRE, FRANÇOIS

The pen name of Jean François-Marie Arouet, impish satirist, tractarian, aphorist, correspondent, poet, historian, conversationalist, and dramatist, Voltaire is best known as the author of *Candide* (1759), a witty, philosophical satire on human foibles and a retreat into a personalized, otherworldly utopia. A flamboyant egalitarian given to extravagant loves and hates, compassion and obsession, Voltaire lived his revolutionary themes by championing the Age of Enlightenment and battling ignorance, sophistry, and tyranny. He focused his energies on "écraser l'infâme [crushing infamy]," a target encompassing intolerance, superstition, and elitism. He used the proceeds of his bestselling epic, *L'Henriade* (1724), to underwrite altruistic projects, including a country school and hospital. For his outspoken opinions, privileged circles, particularly royalty, often responded to him with scurrilous accusations and vituperation.

Born in Poitou, France, on November 21, 1694, Voltaire was weak from infancy, but he grew into a precocious, vigorous intellect. His father, a wealthy lawyer and local magistrate, cultivated court connections and expected his son to profit from royal connections by pursuing the legal profession. By age 11, Voltaire, already known as an irrepressible child prodigy, recited his rhymes at the salon of Ninon de l'Enclos. Studies in law and classical literature with prelates at the Jesuit Collège Louis-le-Grand de Clermont from 1704 to 1711, as well as the influence of a deist godfather and Epicurean friends, led Voltaire to reject the concepts of the soul and religion, which he labeled destructive, and to carouse through Paris bistros with fellow libertines. A volatile, self-directed genius, he rebelled against his father's choice of a profession and began his career as the brilliant skeptic philosopher under the name Voltaire.

Because he understood the importance of patronage, Voltaire cultivated the best of the aristocracy and composed history, novels, pamphlets, tales, polemics, encyclopedia articles, essays, paeans to individual freedom, and spiteful satiric verse; the latter earned him enemies and frequent exiles from Paris. During his rises in fortune, he lived well and loved boldly; when his patrons fell from favor, he dodged lawsuits and duels and retreated to the country estates of friends. In 1717 and again in 1726, he was imprisoned in the Bastille for publishing libelous verses. In his cell he composed *Oedipe* (1718), the first of eight historic and often exotic tragedies in the classic mode—*Brutus* (1730), *Zaïre* (1732), *Alzire* (1736), *Mahomet* (1742), *Mérope* (1743), *Sémiramis* (1748), *L'Orphelin de la Chine [The Orphan from China]* (1755), *Tancrède* (1760), and *Irène* (1778)—and his epic *L'Henriade,* a somewhat tedious classical tribute to Henry IV. Voltaire's 50 plays ranged from farce to comedy and satire and inspired the *drame bourgeois,* a weepy middle-class drama typified by his *Nanine* (1749). He spent 20 of his most productive years in Holland, Switzerland, Germany, and England, where he met some of the world's greatest writers, including Alexander Pope, Jonathan Swift, William Congreve, and John Gay. Critics often credit these friendships and Voltaire's study of the works of William Shakespeare, Isaac Newton, Francis Bacon, and John Locke with rounding out Voltaire's education.

In 1733, Voltaire completed his *Lettres philosophiques sur les Anglais,* a shockingly anti-French treatise that caused book burnings and political repercussions and forced him into hiding, although he continued corresponding with his many friends. Among his most quotable lines are these epigrams, many of which derive from his letters:

- Virtue debases itself in justifying itself.

- Love truth, but pardon error.

- The secret of being a bore is to tell everything.

- He who is merely just is severe.

- There are truths which are not for all men, nor for all times.

- History is no more than the portrayal of crimes and misfortunes.

- I am very fond of truth, but not at all of martyrdom.

- Liberty of thought is the life of the soul.

- I disapprove of what you say, but I will defend to the death your right to say it.

A champion of tolerance and human rights, Voltaire settled in Lorraine at the home of Emilie, the Marquise du Châtelat, his long-time love and intellectual equal. Far from controversy and the grasp of power, he produced two of his best didactic and imaginative works—*Essai sur les moeurs [Essay on Manners]* (1754) and *Zadig* (1747), a satiric romance—and was elected to the Royal Academy and appointed royal historiographer for Louis XV in 1746. After Emilie died in childbirth in 1749, Voltaire retreated to the court of his friend, Frederick the Great of Prussia, at Potsdam and, as an ornament of enlightenment, worked amicably and profitably toward Plato's concept of the enlightened ruler until personal differences with his host over the condemnation of Voltaire's friend Koenig provoked a permanent schism four years later, for which Frederick detained Voltaire in a Frankfurt prison.

In 1760, Voltaire feared a bad reception in Paris and moved to Les Délices, his country home near Lausanne, Switzerland, where he built his own theater and cultivated a miniature village complete with pasture, arbors, grain, dairies, a quarry, tannery, tile works, and factories producing lace, watches, hosiery, and leather goods. His self-deprecating remark characterizes the change from scapegrace to worker:

> Quand on est jeune, il faut aimer comme un fou; quand on est vieux, travailler comme un diable. [When one is young, one must love like a fool; when one is old, he must work like the devil.]

Conservative Calvinists forced him over the French border to Château de Cirey, home of his niece and mistress, Madame Denis, in Ferney near Lake Geneva. Daily sport with his adopted daughter, Mlle. Varicourt, nicknamed "Belle et Bonne" ("Beautiful and Good") lightened his cares. A wealthy world celebrity, he welcomed numerous guests to his estate, supported victims of injustice and the rights of the underprivileged, submitted articles for Denis Diderot's *Encyclopédie*, pilloried formal religion and pompous prelates, and rained barbed pamphlets on the French. In three days following the Lisbon earthquake of 1755, he wrote *Candide, ou l'Optimisme*, his imaginative, anticlerical masterpiece of absurdity, parody, didacticism, and satire. The City Council of Geneva, still controlled by humorless Calvinists, inadvertently promoted the work by banning it.

When his self-imposed exile ended, Voltaire, already mortally ill from fatigue and failing health and resigned to die in peace, returned to Paris in 1778 to witness the staging of *Irène*, his final tragedy. The public cheered him; the French academy presented him a medal; dignitaries pressed to gain his influence. After he died within months of his triumph on May 30, 1778, Europe mourned his loss, but vindictive clerics conspired to shove his remains into a common trench reserved for apostates and scoffers at orthodoxy. Voltaire's supporters managed to spirit his body away and held a dignified interment at the Scellières in Champagne. Eleven years later, during the French Revolution, mourners buried his ashes in the Panthéon alongside French heroes. (Andrews 1981; Ayer 1986; Gassner and Quinn 1969; Gay 1988; Mason 1981; Richter and Ricardo 1980; Voltaire 1961, 1965)

VONNEGUT, KURT

A highly energized, unconventional, cartoonesque satirist, Kurt Vonnegut occupies his own space in the loosely defined gray area that bridges impressionistic fantasy literature with the futuristic branch of science fiction. In a humorous, self-deprecating jab at his meteoric rise to fame, Vonnegut noted to an interviewer for *Science Fiction* magazine that the magazine's golden era encouraged such "inexcusable trash" that inventors produced the electric typewriter at the same time that he achieved name recognition with the U.S. public. Primarily a humanist, Vonnegut excels as the literate iconoclast clawing away at mechanized society to get at the malaise and technological menace that plagues humankind. The post–Vietnam War era buoyed his ego by proclaiming him a cult figure and glorying in *Cat's Cradle* (1963), Vonnegut's first novel with staying power and one of the first U.S. war protest novels to succeed in both the United States and Russia.

Born November 11, 1922, in Indianapolis, Vonnegut, the son of Edith Lieber and Kurt Vonnegut, Sr., an architect, attended Shortridge High School and edited the school paper, the *Echo*. In 1945, after surviving a German POW camp, he returned home with a Purple Heart and recurring memories of Dresden's destruction. He married and fathered three children, later doubling his family by adopting the three children of his sister after her death. Vonnegut completed a degree in biochemistry from Cornell and an M.A. in anthropology from the Carnegie Institute of Technology and the University of Chicago. His unusual melange of experience and education prepared him for the police desk of the Chicago City News Bureau. For three years, he was publicist at General Electric headquarters in Schenectady. In 1950, Vonnegut had had enough of business and turned to writing, with submissions to *McCall's, Ladies' Home Journal, Playboy, Cosmopolitan,* and *Saturday Evening Post* and with his first novel, *Player Piano* (1952). Adept at essays, screenwriting, short fiction, and stage plays, he caught the public unawares with his boldly antiwar novel, *Slaughterhouse-Five* (1966), a bizarre blend of reality and fantasy that was filmed by Universal Studios in 1972. Later titles—*Breakfast of Champions* (1973), *Wampeters, Foma, and Grandfalloons* (1974), and *Deadeye Dick* (1982)—offer Vonnegut's fans greater innovation and frequent departures from his penchant for apocalyptic endings.

Critics have hashed and rehashed the idiosyncratic blend of tragicomedy, Gatling-gun sentences, coinages, neologisms, digressions, and black humor that suggest more than the usual amount of rebellion and panache in an underground author. A lover of parody and social satire, Vonnegut delights in the deceptively simple paragraph, the grabber chapter heading, and nonsensical slapstick. In Vonnegut's case, art and writing are more than self-expression: they assuage a ragged spirit dragged down by past failures and by the postwar trauma that followed the firebombing of Dresden, which he witnessed on February 13, 1945. He discovered that teaching was conducive to healing and taught at Hopefield School in Sandwich, Massachusetts; the University of Iowa Writers Workshop; and Harvard University. Kudos from the Guggenheim Foundation, the National Institute of Arts and Letters, and Hobart and William Smith colleges, along with an Emmy for the television version of his touching story "D.P.," have combined with the support of wife Jill Krementz and the adulation of writers Graham Greene and Michael Crichton to elevate Vonnegut to a status in keeping with his unusual talents. (Broer 1988; Goldsmith 1972; Klinkowitz 1982; Merrill 1989; Morse 1991; Vonnegut 1966, 1990)

See also black humor; *Cat's Cradle*; parody; political satire; satire; slapstick; *Slaughterhouse-Five*.

WAITING FOR GODOT

Babylon in Paris, *En Attendant Godot*—which Samuel Beckett translated into English in 1954—is considered the quintessential absurdist drama, a blend of black humor, word games, stage comedy, and existential philosophy that denies comfort and hope to the modern audience. Critics have marveled that the final lines in the second act leave audiences in their seats and talking excitedly with other playgoers as if determined to thrash out the drama's ambiguities.

Subtitled a "tragicomedy in two acts," the play opens at sundown near a tree on a country road in an unidentifiable setting. Estragon "Gogo," a confused, lethargic wanderer, is yanking on his ill-fitting boot when Vladimir "Didi," his comforter and companion of 50 years, appears. Wearing baggy, Chaplinesque pants and bowler hats like a pair of Laurel and Hardys, the two wait for Godot and pass the time in meaningless satiric repartee, a common element in theater of the absurd.

Beckett contrasts the two amiable travelers with two new arrivals, a tyrannic master and cowed servant. The newcomers enter with a clatter: Pozzo, a self-important, land-proud man, holds Lucky by a rope leash and drives him with monosyllabic commands and a whip. Lucky, the dray who must carry bag, stool, coat, and basket, leads the way. Pozzo shows Lucky no compassion or courtesy: ignoring the servant's hunger, Pozzo eats chicken from the basket and tosses the bone to Estragon. Vladimir examines Lucky's collar and locates an infected sore. The uncomplaining Lucky does his master's bidding but is unaware that he goes to market to be sold. He weeps at the news. Estragon comforts him; Lucky kicks him in the shins. The spontaneous violence and brutality is typical of absurdist drama, which offers no explanation for random cruel behaviors or capricious fits of compassion.

The playwright salts the dialogue with a brand of nonsense typical of clown lingo and absurdism. Before Pozzo leaves, he has Lucky entertain Estragon and Vladimir with a brief dance entitled "the Scapegoat's Agony," which gives way to a rambling doggerel monologue:

> Given the existence as uttered forth in the pubic works of Puncher and Wattman of a person God quaquaquaqua with white beard quaquaaquaqua outside time without extension who from the heights of divine apathia divine athambia

divine aphasia loves us dearly with some exceptions for reasons unknown but time will tell and suffers like the divine Miranda. . . .

Lucky's caricature of the quacking god in Lucky's outburst depicts the incommunicative deity who, like the maiden Miranda in William Shakespeare's *The Tempest*, has no experience with men other than her father. Critics also interpret the lengthy tirade as an indictment of stream-of-consciousness literature that orates at length and creates a greater muddle than it intends to settle.

Beckett returns to Gogo and Didi, the original pair, after master and beast of burden journey on. Godot's goatherd appears with a note for Mr. Albert that Monsieur Godot will not come until the next day. Beckett's comment that Godot does nothing and that the boy's brother is sick expresses the playwright's loss of faith in a caring god and his dismay that human suffering has no meaning. Vladimir sends a reply that he received the message. With no warning or apparent motivation, Estragon considers committing suicide. The two journeymen decide to leave, but they remain on the hill.

Act II, a continuation of Beckett's spare, austere circular drama, opens on the same nonsensical conversation and the same tree, which has sprouted leaves. In their relationship of victim and rescuer, the childlike Estragon loses hope; Vladimir, Beckett's parental figure, rummages in the turnips to locate a radish for his fretful companion, helps him put on his boots, and croons a lullaby. They imitate Pozzo and Lucky by hurling epithets at each other:

Vladimir:	Moron!
Estragon:	Vermin!
Vladimir:	Abortion!
Estragon:	Morpion!
Vladimir:	Sewer-Rat!
Estragon:	Curate!
Vladimir:	Cretin!

Eventually, they run dry of suitably withering retorts. Estragon cries out for God's pity. Vladimir suspects that Godot has arrived and quarrels with Estragon.

The next meeting of pairs reveals a vast change in the master-slave relationship. When Pozzo and Lucky return, Lucky is mute; the master is blind and stumbles along after his slave. Dismayed by the long wait, Estragon declares, "We were beginning to weaken. Now we're sure to see the evening out." The climax of the play occurs when Vladimir compels Estragon to assist Pozzo, a representative of "all humanity." The four collapse in a heap. Estragon, bereft of his rescuer, entreats, "Don't leave me! They'll kill me!" The quartet's ineffectual dealing with events suggests that no single individual—neither victim nor rescuer, master nor slave—is capable of uplifting another. Only the soulless, wordless tree stands tall.

In the first optimistic moments of the play, Estragon and Vladimir seem attuned to another's misery; by the play's end, pessimism reigns. At Pozzo's urging, Estragon kicks Lucky, but he stops because kicking hurts his foot. Vladimir asks Lucky to entertain them. Pozzo departs in anger, leaving the

Waiting for Godot, first produced in Paris in 1952 and translated from the French by Irish playwright Samuel Beckett, is a standard absurdist play. Earle Hyman, right, as Vladimir, and Manton Moreland as Estragon performed in the two-act play in 1957.

journeymen to contemplate his summation of human existence: "They give birth astride of a grave, the light gleams an instant, then it's night once more." The play concludes with Vladimir continuing to ponder life and purpose. The shepherd's brother brings a second message and leaves with the same reply he carried the previous day. When the moon rises, Estragon proposes that they hang themselves, but they have no suitable rope. As the scene ends, the two, wracked by despair and ennui, remain motionless. Beckett's obvious challenge to the audience is to consider the mutual nature of life and death. Whatever the point of view, the playwright insists, it is human nature to ponder a supreme being, humanity, suffering, and the frail possibility of salvation. (Abbott 1973; Anderson 1971; Beckett 1954; Ben-Zvi 1986; Esslin 1965; Gassner and Quinn 1969)

See also Beckett, Samuel; black humor; caricature; repartee; theater of the absurd.

 # WHIMSY

A unique blend of imaginative, bizarre, surreal, or eccentric elements with unusual settings or stylistic techniques, whimsy often occurs without warning, producing capricious, fantastic, or unexpected connections, surprise events, or unexpected meetings of characters—for example, the unusual encounters in Lewis Carroll's *Alice in Wonderland* (1865) and L. Frank Baum's *The Wizard of Oz* (1900), two classic children's odysseys. An unbridled flight of imagination occurring when the mind breaks free of the conventional ties of time and place, whimsy occupies a slender niche of satiric fiction and gives wings to the great fantasists by lightening the load of natural law and slipping the bonds of gravity, sanity, and logic. Lodged in the nether realm of the supernatural are the great works of whimsical satire:

- Aristophanes's *The Birds* (414 B.C.), the Greek dystopic comedy that inspired Rome's Plautus and Terence

- William Shakespeare's *A Midsummer Night's Dream* (ca. 1593), a blend of human loves and fairy lore

- Jonathan Swift's dystopic *Gulliver's Travels* (1727)

- playful limericks by Victorian master Edward Lear

- Karel Capek's dystopic robot drama, *R. U. R.* (1920)

- the out-of-bounds fiction of fantasy spinners Kurt Vonnegut and Ray Bradbury

- Richard Adams's mythic beast fable *Watership Down* (1972)

A satisfying unleashing of deliberate illogic on those readers willing to suspend disbelief, whimsy—a negation of verisimilitude—often suits the purpose and approach of the satirist or the creator of incidental satire.

One of young adult literature's most successful sustained fantasies, Norton Juster's *The Phantom Tollbooth* (1961) carries an unwary Milo from his humdrum school-to-home cycle to a more inviting form of education in Dictionopolis, which he traverses in an electric car accompanied by a loyal watchdog, Tock. After amazing encounters with Princess Rhyme, Princess Reason, Kakofonous A. Dischord, Dodecahedron, and Mathemagician, Milo, like John Bunyan's pilgrim, flees the gorgons and demons of lack-logic and returns safely. A blue envelope communicates a positive message:

> We trust that everything has been satisfactory, and hope you understand why we had to come and collect [the Phantom Tollbooth]. You see, there are so many other boys and girls waiting to use it, too. It's true that there are many lands you've still to visit . . . but we're quite sure that if you really want to, you'll find a way to reach them all by yourself.

Perhaps more didactic than most fantasy, the whimsical jaunt was intended as a learning experience. Signed only with a smear, the note leaves Milo with a confidence in the value of learning and logic that he had failed to develop through ordinary schooling.

In a humorous example of adult whimsy taken from French drama, the "man from the sky" scene in Edmond Rostand's *Cyrano de Bergerac* (1897) spoofs half-baked notions of interplanetary travel by explaining how the title character arrived on the moon:

> After taking a dip in the sea, I lay on the beach at the hour when the moon was exerting the pull that causes the tides, and I was lifted into the air—headfirst, of course, since it was my hair that held the most moisture. I was rising straight up, slowly and effortlessly, like an angel, when suddenly I felt a shock! Then . . .

A transparent artifice intended to ward off interruption of the marriage of Christian and Roxane, the fantasy abruptly ends with De Guiche, the talespinner's sole audience, anticipating the next episode. Cyrano, his purpose achieved, drops his comic voice and announces straightfaced, "The quarter of an hour has passed, so I won't keep you any longer. The wedding is over." Chagrined at the gulling he takes from the famed swordsman, De Guiche displays his poor sportsmanship by immediately commandeering the groom for battlefield duty, a deliberate contrast with the airy nonsense spun by Cyrano.

Whimsy surfaces in unlikely sources, often as a result of an experimental or uncharacteristic deviation from the author's usual style and tone. Robert Frost, noted for down-to-earth poetry, catches unawares an audience inured to "Mending Wall," "Stopping by Woods on a Snowy Evening," "Out, Out—," and "The Death of the Hired Man" with his quick-witted jest at the expense of a hesitant suitor in "The Telephone." Like the surrealist painting a fanciful communication device, the poet depicts the old-fashioned telephone as a flower. In playful conversation, the speaker remarks on answering the phone after a long walk. Far from home, the speaker had driven away a bee and leaned against the blossom for the message, but now hesitates to repeat it. The unidentified respondent, cagey and unforthcoming, demands a replay of the words. The speaker replies that the word sounded like a name or like the word "Come."

The poem, dancing tantalizingly beyond the reader's grasp, concludes with a telepathic message—the respondent admits thinking the word, but not saying it. In the final line, Frost shifts the speaker's tactics: no longer hesitant, the speaker chooses to confront the respondent face to face.

A favorite twentieth-century model of fancy and imagination is the introduction to the mock-heroic escapades of Bilbo Baggins, the unwilling burglar in J. R. R. Tolkien's *The Hobbit* (1937). Normally cozy in his subterranean den, Bilbo enjoys the sybarite's pleasures of his made-to-fit hobbit-hole:

> It had a perfectly round door like a porthole, painted green, with a shiny yellow brass nob in the exact middle. The door opened on to a tube-shaped hall like a tunnel: a very comfortable tunnel without smoke, with panelled walls, and floor tiled and carpeted . . . The best rooms were all on the lefthand side (going in), for these were the only ones to have windows, deep-set round windows looking over his garden and meadows.

The setting, similar to the backdrops of beast fable, both acknowledges and denies Bilbo's humanity by satirizing his reliance on creature comforts, especially food. After Tolkien trots the hesitant hero over a landscape populated with fierce spiders, elves, dwarves, trolls, a wizard, and a crack squadron of eagles, the story zigzags to a near post mortem as "Messrs. Grubb, Grubb, and Burrowes" prepare to auction "the effects of the late Bilbo Baggins Esquire" in a presumptuous land grab that Bilbo narrowly circumvents. Tolkien's fanciful creature demonstrates a blend of human and imaginative traits—a satiric return of the wanderer to the real world of rapacious relatives.

Unlike Tolkien, fantasist Ray Bradbury has composed some of the twentieth century's most earthbound flights of imagination. In the frequently excerpted fifth chapter of *Dandelion Wine* (1957), the author recalls the genial exchange between Doug Spaulding and Mr. Sanderson, the shoe store owner who must be persuaded to hire Doug so the boy can purchase the magical pair of sneakers that inflame his imagination. The deal made, Doug departs in his "Royal Crown Cream-Sponge Para Litefoot Tennis Shoes: Like Menthol on Your Feet," leaving the adult muttering:

> "Antelopes . . . Gazelles." He bent to pick up the boy's abandoned winter shoes, heavy with forgotten rains and long-melted snows. Moving out of the blazing sun, walking softly, lightly, slowly, he headed back toward civilization.

The warmth of Bradbury's boyish remembrance of excessive emotion and exaggerated hopes and dreams turns an uncritical eye on the object of his satire—bloated advertising that conjures up images of speed, weightlessness, and freedom from constraint. Like Doug, the bedazzled reader accepts the lure of inflated ad copy by reliving the universal delight in a new pair of tennis shoes.

An unassuming figure in midwestern satiric jest is Jean Shepherd, author of numerous essays, magazine articles, and collections on his boyhood home, Hohman, Indiana. The country itself is epic in its wretchedness:

> A sandy, rolling country, cooled, nay, frozen to rigidity in the Winter by howling gales that got their start near the Arctic Circle, picked up force over the

frozen wastes of Lake Michigan, and petered out in downtown Hohman, after freezing ears, cracking blocks, and stunting the Summer hopes in many a breast.

The steel mills of his hometown provide work at the cost of clean air. Even precipitation pays the price of industry in rusty mounds of orange-tinted snow. Shepherd's boyhood recollections of the rust belt predate mordant diatribes against land despoiled by industry.

Whimsy need not reflect simplicity, greatness, or gaiety alone. In the opening scene of Maya Angelou's *I Know Why the Caged Bird Sings,* her first in a series of five autobiographies, a fancy-rich moment of a different sort brightens the flight of Marguerite. Escaping the children's section of the Colored Methodist Episcopal Church, the child holds up two fingers, the signal for a toilet emergency. Because no one acknowledges her need, the child trips over feet and flees down the aisle as the congregation sings "Were you there when they crucified my Lord?" Stumbling, inarticulate, Maya experiences

> a green persimmon, or it could have been a lemon, [that] caught me between the legs and squeezed. I tasted the sour on my tongue and felt it in the back of my mouth. Then before I reached the door, the sting was burning down my legs and into my Sunday socks.

The fanciful introduction to the autobiographical character prepares the reader for a *tour de force* account of Angelou's growing-up years in Stamps, Arkansas, where she lives temporarily with her brother Bailey, maternal grandmother, and uncle. The lemon taste that accompanies the slip of the bladder prefigures the sour experience of St. Louis, where the central character resides with a finger-snapping, hug-dancing mother and her live-in lover, who rapes Maya and threatens to murder Bailey. Angelou's deft touch of whimsy exaggerates the free association of childhood, where mental leaps from reality to image are a normal part of coping and a major source of satire. (Abrams 1971; Angelou 1970; Baldick 1990; Bradbury 1959; Cuddon 1984; Frost 1962; Gray 1992; Holman and Harmon 1992; Juster 1961; Rostand 1972; Shepherd 1972; Tolkien 1966)

See also *Alice in Wonderland;* Aristophanes; Carroll, Lewis; Gulliver; *Gulliver's Travels;* Shakespeare, William; Swift, Jonathan; wit.

THE WIFE OF BATH

One of the enduring female personae from satiric literature, Alice, the Wife of Bath, relieves the tedium of the Canterbury pilgrims with her fulsome, earthy good humor. Perhaps too jolly and too loud because of her hearing loss, she dresses in bold red and tops her hair with a massive headdress. The effusive talk and banter that springs from her lips and the gap-toothed smile indicate a generous woman who expects from life a suitable reward of worldly pleasure, which she has had in her previous five husbands, even Jankyn, whom she battered for abusing her. Less noble than Dorigen, certainly wiser than

Chaunticleer's mincing Dame Partlet, the Wife of Bath embodies the spirit of bibulous evenings shared by the travelers and of the raucous, often ribald fun of their tales and jests.

In her lengthy prologue, she allows digression and example to outweigh narrative. Chaucer's balanced satire suits the infraction: Alice is both merry and obnoxious, yet memorable among the pilgrims, who range from seedy monk and pardoner to self-important guildsman, gentle nun, courteous franklin, and jovial Harry Bailly, the hostler of the Tabard Inn. The vigor of Alice's telling leads the story cycle from weighty, lugubrious exempla to Alice's pseudo-scientific study of men and procreation. With no regard to taste or discretion, she asserts:

> Tell me also, to what end
> Were the organs of generation made,
> And a person so perfectly designed:
> Trust to it, they were not made for nothing.
> Interpret whoever will, and say it up and down
> That they were made for the elimination
> Of urine, and both our little things
> Were there to tell a female from a male,
> And for no other cause—do you say no?

In extensive debate with herself, she carries on her one-sided dialectic about the value of an active sex life until she suspects that her audience grows weary. Wise, perhaps from other occasions when she overextended her portion of the conversation, she returns to her story but is soon revisiting the same argument for procreation.

Chaucer's rich irony adorns Alice's prologue and overstatement of her innocence of bigamy. Likewise, the story of what women want from matrimony suits the teller, a self-proclaimed expert on marriage. After an appropriate buildup of the utopian Arthurian kingdom, she turns to the serious subject of rape with a familiar kiss-and-transform conclusion. The knight who ravishes a lone maiden raises such a stir that he merits capital punishment. At the queen's insistence, Arthur allows "a twelvemonth and a day" for the knight to learn the answer to an age-old question. The span of months seems appropriate to Alice's lengthy prologue, which is long on debate and short on action. Under the guise of the knight's contemplation of his quest, Alice continues debating her favorite topic—the ins and outs of an amiable domestic arrangement.

Chaucer's satiric jest derives from Alice's implication that husbands do not always treasure a worthy spouse. Applying magic to her story, Alice devises an old woman who presents the knight the answer to save his head. From the wrinkled hag—perhaps a decline of beauty and skin tone that Alice begins to see in her own face—the knight carries back to court an answer that is Alice's philosophy in brief:

> A woman wants the self-same sovereignty
> Over her husband as over her lover
> And master him; he must not be above her.

The immediate concurrence from women at court fills the knight with joy until the crone interrupts with a reminder that his victory comes at a price.

Alice seems to know more about women than the simplistic answer given the court. Herself a veteran flirt, she is aware of the fleeting period of youth that women can claim and use to advantage. To free her main character of the loss of bargaining points, Alice assigns blistering lines to her female character:

> "Just now," she said, "you spoke of gentle birth,
> Such as descends from ancient wealth and worth.
> If that's the claim you make for gentlemen
> Such arrogance is hardly worth a hen."

With a glimmer of literary elegance, Alice pursues the moral with examples from Dante, Valerian, Boethius, Juvenal, and Cicero. Gleefully, she puts into the knight's mouth the words she would hear from her own mates—that she may have control of the relationship. The story ends with the magic kiss of fairy tales—the crone the knight must marry becomes a beautiful young woman—leaving the reader to wonder if Alice perhaps indulges in Snow White reveries as she contemplates a sixth trip to the altar. (Chaucer 1966a, 1966b, 1969, 1992, 1993a, 1993b; Chute 1946; Gardner 1977; Robinson 1957; Scott 1974)

See also allegory; *Canterbury Tales*; Chaucer, Geoffrey; Chaunticleer; irony; "The Miller's Tale"; satire.

WILDE, OSCAR

One of England's noted aesthetes and facile aphorists, Dubliner Oscar Wilde excelled at verse, critical essay, autobiography, novel, macabre tales, and entertaining, satiric drama. A controversial figure in a grimly moralistic age that abhorred fops, dandies, and gays, Wilde was forced to conceal his homosexuality through bizarre ruses and died in ignominy. His libertinism was the stuff of legend, which swamped his literary and humanitarian reputation in the early twentieth century, but his incisive, sybaritic epigrams recurred in print and public declamation, often by speakers who misunderstood the source and Wildean nature of their origin. Favorites ridiculing Victorian hypocrisy include these:

- I can resist everything except temptation.

- If one tells the truth, one is sure, sooner or later, to be found out.

- The first duty in life is to be as artificial as possible. What the second duty is no one has as yet discovered.

- Wickedness is a myth invented by good people to account for the curious attractiveness of others.

- Science is the record of dead religions.

- Work is the curse of the drinking classes.

Irish playwright and novelist Oscar Wilde

- A cynic is a man who knows the price of everything and the value of nothing.

- Life is far too important a thing ever to talk seriously about it.

- To love oneself is the beginning of a lifelong romance.

- A man cannot be too careful in the choice of his enemies.

Because of his popularity as a keen observer of social behaviors, Wilde redeemed himself in part for rejecting superficiality and moral compromise. In a more tolerant era, his work has appeared throughout Europe and America and on the kabuki stage. By believers in art for art's sake, he is regarded as a champion of individualism and artistic freedom. The son of poet Jane Francisca "Speranza" Elgee and Sir William Robert Wills Wilde, a distinguished ear and eye surgeon and oculist to Queen Victoria, Oscar Fingal O'Flahertie Wills Wilde was born October 15, 1856. He set himself apart from boyish rough-and-tumble by collecting peacock feathers and blue china, carrying lilies, and wearing a sunflower as a boutonniere. His brilliance at the Portora Royal School, Enniskillen, preceded scholarly awards in classical literature earned at Dublin's Trinity College and Magdalen College, Oxford, where he extolled the works of the Pre-Raphaelites, John Ruskin, Matthew Arnold, and Walter Pater and won the Newdigate poetry prize for his poem "Ravenna." Often ridiculed for dramatic shoulder-length curls, effete mannerisms, black silk hose, and velveteen suits, Wilde openly courted attention, earning a reputation for exhibitionism.

Wilde settled in London in 1879 and published minor essays and poems for the popular press. His wit and eccentric charm adorn his contributions to the *Pall Mall Gazette, Irish Monthly, Kottobos, Pan, Catholic Mirror, Month*, and *Woman's World*, which he edited from 1887 to 1889. In the early 1880s, proclaiming himself professor of aesthetics, he toured and lectured on interior design in the United States, where his play *Vera* (1882) introduced his cleverness as a comic playwright who parodied stage conventions by laying them bare before the audience. During this period, *Punch* caricatured him as Jellaby Postlethwaite, and Gilbert and Sullivan lampooned him with *Patience* (1881), a satiric stage farce depicting Wilde as Bunthorne, the "fleshly poet." Although his gothic melodrama, *The Picture of Dorian Gray* (1891), brought fame after it was serialized in *Lippincott's Magazine,* he became a public figure with *Lady Windermere's Fan* (1892), a complex comedy about parental sacrifice and the vehicle of some of his cleverest one-liners. He achieved stardom with *The Importance of Being Earnest* (1895), a witty farce that presaged the style of Somerset Maugham, George Bernard Shaw, and Noel Coward in its well-paced dialogue and satiric jabs at England's stuffiness and shallow, conventional morals. Lesser works—*An Ideal Husband* (1895) and *A Woman of No Importance* (1893)—reprised the light social comedy of the Restoration era. Because of the salacious nature of his last melodrama, *Salomé* (1893), the play, starring Sarah Bernhardt, was rejected by London's Lord Chamberlain and opened in Paris to a more worldly, shockproof audience.

In his late twenties, Wilde's career as London's wittiest satirist began to upend and slide to the depths of shame and recrimination. His enemies declared that his 1884 marriage to Constance Lloyd, a wealthy heiress, was a cover for blatant homosexuality. For a brief time, he carried off the sham relationship and, while living in Chelsea, published *The Happy Prince and Other Tales* (1888) for his sons, Cyril and Vyvyan. A public scandal arose after the Marquis of Queensberry publicly reviled the poet for his relationship with his son, Lord Alfred Douglas, by leaving a card at Wilde's club labeling him a sodomite. A sensational trial created a stir over his overt imagery, which barristers read aloud to the jury. The failed lawsuit for libel against Queensberry collapsed after Wilde revealed on the witness stand the existence of a letter to Douglas that verified illegal sexual activities, which Queensberry claimed corrupted his innocent son. To Wilde's humiliation, the letter had circulated among blackmailers, friends, and a business associate who was producing Wilde's plays. Wilde refused to flee the country and, while drinking with his lover at the Cadogan Hotel, was arrested for sexual perversion. The court sentenced him to two years at hard labor in Wandsworth Prison and disallowed visits with his sons, who passed into the guardianship of their mother's cousin, Adrian Hope. After two months in the prison infirmary, Wilde, in manacles and prison dress, was transferred on public roads to Reading Gaol, where his main task was shredding rope into oakum for ship caulking.

Although personal correspondence remained in the prison safe, Major Nelson, the prison governor, ameliorated Wilde's isolation by allowing him to continue writing, but Nelson issued prison notepaper one sheet at a time, which was collected before another was dispensed. Wilde used his persuasive skill in a letter to the *Daily Chronicle* protesting floggings of the insane, indecent sanitation, repulsive rations of gruel and suet, persistent diarrhea, punishment on the treadmill, and imprisonment of children. Of their incarceration, he says:

> Their cheerfulness under terrible circumstances, their sympathy for each other, their humility, their gentleness, their pleasant smiles of greeting when they meet each other, their complete acquiescence in their punishments, are all quite wonderful, and I myself learnt many sound lessons from them.

In 1896, he composed a remorseful letter regretting that acts of "Love that dares not tell its name" had harmed his wife and children; the letter expressed concern for the upkeep of his mother's grave and a horror of dying in a cell "in silence and misery." On April 1, 1897, Wilde observed in a letter to Robert Ross, inscribed to "my dear Robbie":

> On the other side of the prison wall there are some poor black soot-besmirched trees that are just breaking out into buds of an almost shrill green. I know quite well what they are going through. They are finding expression.

That same spring, he urged his wife to divorce him and rejected a stipend from her as a humiliation. Before his release, his mother and wife died. On May 19, the warden released Wilde and, against regulations, handed him his prison manuscript.

Overcome with self-abasement for falling into the hands of Lord Douglas, a shallow young manipulator, and declaring himself an antinomian, Wilde believed himself an unwelcome ghost "grey with long imprisonment and crooked with pain." His last years in self-imposed exile in Italy, Sicily, and France cost him friends, copyrights of his works, and a fortune in art and rare books. He immortalized his imprisonment the following year in *The Ballad of Reading Gaol* (1898), a sincere plea for justice that he signed with his prison number, C.3.3, and he continued to petition for humane prison reform through letters to the *Daily Chronicle*. Several unsuccessful works appeared in print under the pseudonym Sebastian Melmoth, the title of a novel by his great-uncle, Charles Maturin. Wilde's final weeks were filled with desperation. He depended on Robert Ross to conduct his affairs, which included demands for payment from abusers of copyrighted material. In October 1900, he underwent an operation to ease the pain in his ear and survived several weeks in a morphine-clouded daze. After his death from cerebral meningitis on November 30, 1900, in a Paris hotel, he was buried nearby, then relocated in 1909 to Père Lachaise cemetery to an ornate art deco vault that lured streams of mourners and the curious.

The posthumous publication of *De Profundis* (1905), a stirringly painful 80-page, handwritten confessional and accusation of Lord Douglas for distracting Wilde from his career, expressed the writer's despair at a life of pretense, hedonism, and debauchery during the time Wilde was writing *An Ideal Husband*. Summing up the squalid dehumanization of prison life, Wilde turned his skillful satire into poignant self-negation:

> Everything about my tragedy has been hideous, mean, repellent, lacking in style; our very dress makes us grotesque. We are the zanies of sorrow. We are clowns whose hearts are broken. We are specially design to appeal to the sense of humour.

He insisted that the print copy be typed by a lady typist who was to be fed through a latticed door until she could emulate the Vatican cardinal electing a pope and proclaim, "Habet Mundus Epistolam! [The world has a letter!]." Melodramatically, he subtitled the work "Epistola: in Carcere et Vinculis [Letter: in Prison and Chains"]. The manuscript remained sealed in the British Museum until 1913 when Douglas's suit against a Wilde autobiographer required a public reading, which opened the document to printing in the *Times* and a hurried publication in New York. (Bermel 1982; Brockett 1968; Gassner and Quinn 1969; Grigson 1963; Hart-Davis 1962; Hornstein 1973; Magill 1958; McArthur 1992; Miller 1989; Wilde 1923, 1954, 1965, 1995a, 1995b, 1995c)

See also caricature; Coward, Noel; epigram; farce; Gilbert, Sir William Schwenck; kabuki; lampoon; parody; satire; Shaw, George Bernard.

 # WIT

The marriage of invention to word play, wit represents the mind at its most flexible and imaginative, a form of divergent thinking that flees the cliché in favor of a thought or word assembly that opens a new path to insight. An explosive connection similar to the gestalt "Aha!" experience, wit derives from the Anglo-Saxon for know. It exercises mental facility and ingenuity by testing the quickness and agility of thinking processes. A jack-in-the-box feature of wit is the surprise factor, a springing of the punchline or a pause for the audience to savor a clever alliance of words or images. Whether couched in repartee, chiseled epigram, or skillful mot juste, wit, like spice in cooking, enlivens the mental taste buds and whets the appetite.

During the Restoration era, John Dryden, England's first literary critic and one of its first-rate verse satirists, applied his well-disciplined prose to the definition of wit. He concluded:

> Wit writing is no other than the faculty of imagination in the writer, which, like a nimble spaniel, beats over and ranges through the field of memory, till it springs the quarry it hunted after. Wit written is that which is well defined, the happy result of thought, or product of imagination.

He concludes that wit is a "propriety of thoughts and words" that require elegant application to a subject.

In a lighter vein, wit is also essential to love poetry, perhaps because amorous outpourings appeal too intimately to the people involved and thus shut out the reader. Without generous saltings of skillful, clever wording, the lover's plaint could easily subside into a snivel. In Percy Bysshe Shelley's "Love's Philosophy" (1819), the speaker turns to advantage the clichéd conventions of love ballads, formal complaints, and sentimental occasional verse by reciting nature's minglings, clutchings, and "kissings" by moonlight, fountain, and ocean tide. Buoyed by nature's vast number of meetings, he carries the second stanza into an intense display of the lover's logic:

> See the mountains kiss high Heaven
> And the waves clasp one another;
> No sister-flower would be forgiven
> If it disdained its brother,
> And the sunlight clasps the earth
> And the moonbeams kiss the sea:
> What is all this sweet work worth
> If thou kiss not me?

The poet, unable to reconcile this achingly unfair disparity, lapses into a snit that these exchanges are worthless if the human niche of creation lacks the fervid union granted to insensate beings. Because Shelley lifts his satiric verse from the personal to the universal, he pleads his case before a wider tribunal.

With similar understanding of the universality of love, Mary Coleridge's "Gibberish" plays with paradox by assigning avian qualities to flowers and floral qualities to birds. She achieves her aim—a humorous view of the lover who wings away on the updraft of love:

> Many a flower have I seen blossom,
> Many a bird for me will sing.

Never heard I so sweet a singer,
Never saw I so fair a thing.

She is a bird, a bird that blossoms,
She is a flower, a flower that sings;
And I a flower when I behold her,
And when I hear her, I have wings.

Blending precise rhyme scheme—abcb, abcb—with repetition of "never," "blossom," "flower," "her," "she," and "sing" and with a unifying alliteration, the poet controls the likely illusion of brainless choplogic, one of the symptoms of the speaker's infatuation. Thus, the reader forgives the lover the image of a flower sprouting wings instead of leaves and petals. (Barnet, Berman, and Burto 1960; Coleridge 1988; Cuddon 1984; Gassner and Quinn 1969; Gray 1992; Holman and Harmon 1992; McArthur 1992; Shelley 1948; Wilson 1965)

See also Dryden, John; epigram; irony; repartee; satire.

WYCHERLEY, WILLIAM

Joining William Congreve and George Etherege in the triad of Restoration comedy masters, William Wycherley was an ornament to the late seventeenth-century stage and a facile writer of some of England's bawdiest satire. Born May 28, 1641, at Clive, near Shrewsbury, Shropshire, he was the son of Bethia Shrimpton and Daniel Wycherley, an accountant to the royal treasury and later manager of the estate of the Marquis of Winchester. Dispatched to London in 1656 after ten years of his father's tutoring, Wycherley defied family authority by receiving Catholic instruction and defeated his family's grand plans by dawdling in the salon of the Duchesse de Montausier. Returned to England in disgrace for comporting himself like a French courtier, he was forced to rejoin the Anglican church and enroll at Queen's College, Oxford; for less than a year, he half-heartedly studied law at the Inner Temple in 1659. A frequenter of Will's Coffeehouse in Covent Garden, he allied himself with the local wits, studied theater, and produced a collection of verse, *Hero and Leander in Burlesque* (1669).

A famed wordsmith of the Restoration era, Wycherley charmed London with his first rather lame comedy of manners, *Love in a Wood, or St. James's Park* (1671), a limp duplication of Thomas Sedley's *Mulberry Garden*. The play earned Wycherley the love of King Charles II's mistress, Barbara Villiers Palmer, the Duchess of Cleveland, a benefactress who established him as commissioner of Lord Buckingham's infantry regiment in 1672. Following a stint with the British navy and action at sea during the third Dutch war, Wycherley served a week as captain of the Duke of Buckingham's guard. Upon his resignation, he completed his second comedy, *The Gentleman Dancing Master* (1672). The clever farce won acclaim for intrigue and satire on pretense. His masterpiece, *The Country Wife* (1675), modeled on Molière's *École des femmes* (1662), contrasts rural and city manners and morals. *The Country Wife* is a salacious lampoon of the roué who implies that he is impotent so that he can more easily size up likely victims of his lechery. Although devoid of scorn or pessimism, the plot outraged refined reviewers, who considered the subject matter taboo for public presentation. Later critics have placed the work among the best of dramatic farces.

The times quickly brought Wycherley down from the heights. He published his most disillusioned play, *The Plain Dealer* (1676), based on Molière's *Le Misanthrope* and Racine's *Les Plaideurs* (1668). Although praised by the parsimonious critic John Dryden as "one of the most bold, most general, and most useful satires which has ever been presented on the English theater," Wycherley's darkly comic vision offers a substantial hint that England was tiring of the era's puerile raciness and hypocrisy. His physical downfall followed illness from an unspecified fever in 1678, a year's recuperation in Montpellier, France, at the king's expense, and an ill-fated secret marriage to the wealthy Laetitia Isabella, Countess of Drogheda, in 1679. The match brought Wycherley daily torment from his jealous, suspicious spouse and temporary wealth upon her death three years later, which provoked a spate of legal battles that ate up his inheritance. Because King Charles II disapproved of the union, he withdrew an offer to make Wycherley a tutor of the prince, the Duke of Richmond, at the handsome salary of £1,500. A seven-year incarceration in debtor's prison rallied Wycherley's supporters, including James II, who held a benefit show of *The Plain Dealer* at Whitehall in 1685 to requite creditors and bail the playwright out of Fleet Prison. For three years preceding England's civil war, he enjoyed a state pension of £200; the next year, he profited from his father's estate, but, because of an entail on the property, found himself land rich and cash poor.

After the publication of his verse collection *Miscellany Poems* (1704), Wycherley allied himself with an unusual mentor, 16-year-old Alexander Pope, who severely overedited the poet's work and ridiculed Wycherley in *An Essay on Criticism* (1711). Wycherley's final years were marred by diffidence, poor health, and advancing senility and memory loss. In the last two weeks of his life, he married Elizabeth Jackson to prevent his nephew from inheriting his property, which passed to Elizabeth's subsequent husband, Thomas Shrimpton, Wycherley's cousin. The disruption of Wycherley's peaceful retirement appears to have weakened his frail body. Before his death on January 1, 1716, he renewed his Catholic vows and received extreme unction. He was buried in St. Paul's Church. (Baugh 1948; Brockett 1968; Burdick 1974; Gassner and Quinn 1969; Kunitz and Haycraft 1952; McMillin 1973; Person 1988; Roberts 1962; Wilson 1965; Wycherley 1953)

See also Behn, Aphra; caricature; comedy; Congreve, William; *The Country Wife*; Dryden, John; Etherege, George; farce; Pope, Alexander; repartee; satire.

YOSSARIAN

A captain in the 256th Air Force Squadron in Joseph Heller's satiric novel *Catch-22* (1961), John Yossarian is a paradox: he gains stature as he loses it—by exerting sense and fleeing the senseless death machine that forces battle-weary squadrons to fly greater numbers of bomb runs. At the height of the squad's combat performance, Yossarian moves aggressively against the city of Ferrara, tends a dying man, and becomes a decorated war hero. In private, he successfully counters a whimsical cast of fools and foils—an obsessive roommate tearing down the stove valve, a screaming airman battling nightmares, a chaplain too soul-starved to comfort the bereaved, a pilot too immature to realize the dangers of each mission, and a family that requests a visit with a dying son, whom Yossarian portrays. Simultaneously, he copes with lifelong paranoia; he confides that the anti-Assyrians can't outflank a combination of "Tarzan, Mandrake, Flash Gordon . . . Bill Shakespeare . . . Cain, Ulysses, the Flying Dutchman . . . Lot . . . Deirdre of the Sorrows, Sweeney in the nightingales among trees."

Blessed with confidence in the early months of battle service, Yossarian is sure of victory. As the stakes rise, the zany scapegrace channels every force into a cosmic scuffle with death. He fights the outward war against the Axis powers and the toughest battle, the inward prolife muddle, which could turn Yossarian into as real a corpse as Mudd, the dead man in his tent. The increasing frequency of adrenalin-charged scenes drives him to a summary act of desperation, which he nearly commits when he has his hands around McWatt's throat and forces him to pull the plane out of a dive. In contrast to the death-dealing bombardier, a deranged Milo Minderbinder serves as a foil for hovering death by providing the men "abundant sources of fresh veal, beef, duck, baby lamb chops, mushroom caps, broccoli, South African rock lobster tails, shrimp, hams, puddings, grapes, ice cream, strawberries, and artichokes." In contrast to his largesse, Milo chooses profit over patriotism and cashes in on wartime profiteering by bombing and strafing the camp, a hellishly comic scene that carries the novel to its peak of insanity and pushes Yossarian into decisive action. Ambivalent toward the dilemmas posed by wartime law, Yossarian chooses to go AWOL in Rome, the "Eternal City" for which the chapter is named. Like the epic hero traversing the underworld, he tries to salvage friends, but the inhabitants have fallen victim to the madness of Catch-22. He attempts to reason with Aarfy, who has raped a hotel maid and thrown her out a window; repulsed, Yossarian reaches the breaking point after military police overlook the crime and arrest him for leaving the base without a pass. From this point to the end, Yossarian wrestles with guilt and ambivalence that stalk him as certainly as the ubiquitous knife-wielding whore, who pops up like a cartoon figure.

Suspenseful to the end, Heller's dark satire pits the stalwart against the seamy by dumping into a single pot the full range of wartime behaviors. The closer Yossarian comes to discharge from the air force, the worse his quandary. In league with his real enemies, Colonels Cathcart and Korn, Yossarian earns the nickname of "Yo-Yo" because he agrees to conceal his rebellion against increased bomb runs if they will free him from war and send him home a hero. During the private conference with Yossarian, Korn sums up the captain's strengths:

> I really do admire you a bit. You're an intelligent person of great moral character who has taken a very courageous stand. I'm an intelligent person with no moral character at all, so I'm in an ideal position to appreciate it.

Maneuvering Yossarian with outright blackmail—court-martial or compliance—Korn demands that Yossarian like them, be their pal. His principles having taken more definite form, Yossarian debates their offer, but can't buy it. The intensity of mental struggle turns satire to drama as Yossarian weighs his alternatives.

In a melange of fact-turned-falsehood, Yossarian witnesses a Mad Hatter's Tea Party of nonsense. A crazed whore blames him for Nately's death and stabs him in the thigh with a steak knife. The night after Yossarian undergoes surgery, an unidentified voice claims, "We've got your pal, buddy." The next day, Major Danby clarifies Yossarian's tenuous position: if he follows through on his deal with Cathcart and Korn, he returns home a hero; if not, the affidavits prove that an innocent girl stabbed him because he took part in black-marketeering and declare that he refused to follow orders during the strike on Ferrara. Because his comrades can be maneuvered into false testimony for the good of the country, Yossarian has no choice. As Danby sums up the situation, a court-martial would repudiate the good record of the entire squadron. Despite his innocence, the loner who refuses to march with the majority jeopardizes the country's well-being. In a crystal moment of self-analysis, Yossarian comments on the MPs, Scheisskopfs, Peckems, Korns, and Cathcarts who perpetually violate his ideals. Unwilling to let go of his principles, Yossarian recoils from "people cashing in on every decent impulse and every human tragedy." As though jolted into a choice, the antihero embraces life, leaps out of range of German flak and stalker, and heads for Sweden. On his departure, he wins the reader's godspeed by accepting the dangers that come with his glad leap at life. (*Contemporary Authors* 1994; *Discovering Authors* 1993; Heller 1961; Merrill 1987; Nagel 1984; Potts 1982)

See also black humor; *Catch-22*; Heller, Joseph; satire.

Joseph Heller's satirical 1961 novel, *Catch-22*, made into a movie in 1970, finds bombardier John Yossarian (Alan Arkin) up a tree and naked. Heller's black humor traps Yossarian in the circular logic of an insanity plea denied because it is a sane reaction to the insanity of war.

YOU CAN'T TAKE IT WITH YOU

A Pulitzer Prize-winning play for 1936, Moss Hart and George S. Kaufman's *You Can't Take It with You* earned a place among the early twentieth century's best-loved satiric comedies. After it opened for a lengthy run, moved to Britain and, over time, into numerous anthologies and community revivals, critics determined that its draw, like Mary Chase's *Harvey* (1944) and the Shirley Temple phenomenon, is its ability to relieve the weight of whatever concerns plague its enthusiastic audiences. The eccentric Sycamore family, a fictional enclave living contentedly near Columbia University, creates a spiritually up-lifting vision of life on a shoestring among family members and visitors whom they welcome to a menage that includes a printing press that cranks out leftist propaganda, a fireworks lab in the basement, ballet lessons from a Russian emigré, and a cook who concocts menus from whatever happens to be in the refrigerator. The satire on smug upper management elaborates on a time-honored theme: that working-class people make less money but have more fun.

The play opens on an unlikely middle-class living room where the oddball Sycamores juxtapose a xylophone, typewriter, skull-shaped candy dish, and snake collection. To the detriment of daughter Alice's plans to marry Tony Kirby, the boss's son, the family plunges ahead with an unpredictable blend of hob-bies and interests: Grandpa Vanderhof attends speeches at Columbia, Penny paints a discus thrower, Essie invents candies called Love Dreams, her hus-band prints leftist pamphlets, and Mr. De Pinna, a visitor who never went home, assists in building skyrockets. A clever bit of repartee engages Grandpa and Mr. Henderson, an IRS agent, in a dust-up over paying income taxes:

Grandpa:	What's the Government give me?
Henderson:	Why, the Government gives you everything. It protects you.
Grandpa:	What from?
Henderson:	Well—invasion. Foreigners that might come over here and take everything you've got.

Because Grandpa declines U.S. intervention in his affairs, the argument goes nowhere; Mr. Henderson departs yelling threats to jail Grandpa if he doesn't pay his portion according to the law. The scene melds smoothly into an evening visit from Tony, who has never met the Sycamores. The family applies a live-and-let-live philosophy to Alice's love life, but Alice recognizes that Tony's staid, conservative background clashes with the chaos at the Sycamore home:

> Listen, you're of a different world . . . a whole different kind of people. Oh I don't mean money or socially. . . . That's too silly. But your family and mine . . . it just wouldn't work, Tony.

To prove Alice wrong, Tony maneuvers his family into visiting the Sycamores and deliberately confuses the dates so the Kirbys will arrive on the wrong evening.

The playwrights' benevolent satire lampoons the disorganized family. A comic meeting between the Sycamores and Mr. Kirby, a caricature of the Wall

Street mogul, coalesces into a mixed-up affair of Campbell's soup, canned corn, and pickled pigs' feet from the A&P for the hurried menu; an impromptu wrestling match; and a game of Forget-Me-Not. The nonstop social faux pas so disgust the Kirbys that they depart with noses uplifted. Before they can get away, the house is surrounded by federal agents and the Sycamores and their guests are arrested for subversive activities. An unforeseen explosion in the downstairs fireworks lab caps the night with typical Sycamore hoopla. After the families depart in the paddy wagon and spend a night in jail, Grandpa smirks, "I'll bet you Bar Harbor is going to seem pretty dull to the Kirbys this summer." The judge reduces the charge to manufacturing fireworks without a permit. Alice packs to leave for the Adirondacks, causing her parents to blame themselves for opposing Alice's engagement to a rich man's son. Grandpa, the savant of the family, soothes them with a witty comeback: "Suppose she goes to the Adirondacks? She'll be back. You can take just so much Adirondacks, and then you come home."

The falling action juxtaposes more bizarre elements as Kolenkhov, the supercilious ballet master, escorts to dinner the Grand Duchess Olga Katrina, part of the fallen Romanov monarchy. Her offbeat remarks emphasize the newcomers' embracing of U.S. beliefs in hard work and ambition and their simultaneous snobbery about minimum-wage jobs:

> My uncle, the Grand Duke Sergei—he is an elevator man at Macy's. A very nice man. Then there is my cousin, Prince Alexis. He will not speak to the rest of us because he works at Hattie Carnegie. He is in ladies' underwear.

Against the rhythms of Russian guests and preparations for dinner, Mr. Kirby arrives to argue with his wayward son. Grandpa intercedes with a hearty wish that Tony not fritter away his youth and enthusiasm on stocks and bonds and become embittered like his father. To Grandpa, success by Wall Street's standards amounts to living death: the "same kind of mail every morning, same kind of deals, same kind of meetings, same dinners at night, same indigestion." Mr. Kirby, defending his turf, bristles at the implied putdown of his profession.

The final untangling of values that Grandpa oversees assists Mr. Kirby in recognizing the source of his delicate stomach—a life's work in the financial maw, churning and stewing over money, suppression of urges to play the saxophone and run away to join the circus, and never allowing himself to relax. Hart and Kaufman's satire results in the typical ending for a comedy of manners: Alice and Tony find happiness, Mr. Kirby allows a little liberalism to creep into his Wall Street lifestyle, Grandpa satisfies the IRS, and the family returns to its off-kilter conversations, meals, hobbies, and guests. The 1938 film version, directed by Frank Capra, earned two Oscars and four nominations and starred a sparkling cast—Jean Arthur, Lionel Barrymore, James Stewart, Edward Arnold, Spring Byington, and Eddie Anderson—and featured the music of Dmitri Tiomkin. (Bermel 1982; Ehrlich and Carruth 1982; Hart and Kaufman 1961; Katz 1982; Kunitz 1942; Magnusson 1990)

See also Algonquin Club; caricature; Hart, Moss; *Harvey;* Kaufman, George S.; repartee; satire; whimsy.

CHRONOLOGY OF SATIRICAL LITERATURE

18th century B.C.	*Batrachomyomachia (The Battle of the Frogs and Mice)*
7th century B.C.	Archilochus's verse
6th century B.C.	Aesop's fables
423 B.C.	Aristophanes, *Clouds*
416 B.C.	Plato, *Symposium*
414 B.C.	Aristophanes, *The Birds*
411 B.C.	Aristophanes, *Lysistrata*
405 B.C.	Aristophanes, *The Frogs*
349-344 B.C.	Demosthenes, *Philippics*
Early 4th century B.C.	Plato, *Symposium*
Ca. 316 B.C.	Menander, *Dyskolos*
200 B.C.	*Panchatantra*
200 B.C.	Plautus, *Stichus*
191 B.C.	Plautus, *Pseudolus*
Ca. 180s B.C.	Plautus, *Captivi* and *Amphytrion*
Ca. 186 B.C.	Plautus, *Menaechmi*
2d century B.C.	Lucillus, *Sermones (Satires)*
167 B.C.	Terence, *Andria (The Girl from Andros)*
165 B.C.	Terence, *Hecyra (The Mother-in-law)*
163 B.C.	Terence, *Heautontimorumenos (The Self-Torturer)*
161 B.C.	Terence, *Eunuchus (The Eunuch)*
161 B.C.	Terence, *Phormio*
160 B.C.	Terence, *Adelphi (The Brothers)*
1st century B.C.	Juvenal, epigrams
1st century B.C.	Varro, epigrams
60 B.C.	Catullus, verse
35 B.C.	Horace, *Sermones (Book 1)*
30 B.C.	Horace, *Sermones (Book 2)*
Ca. A.D. 48	Phaedrus, *Fables*
Ca. A.D. 55	Seneca, *Apocolocyntosis (The Pumpkinification)*
A.D. 60	Petronius Arbiter, *The Satyricon*
Ca. A.D. 63	Persius, *Satirae*
A.D. 80	Martial, *Liber Spectaculorum (A Book of Spectacles)*

Ca. A.D. 85	Martial, *Epigrammata (Epigrams)*
110-127 A.D.	Juvenal, *Satirae*
Ca. 160 A.D.	Apuleius, *The Golden Ass*
2d century A.D.	Aulus Gellius, *Noctes Atticae (Attic Nights)*
12th–13th century	*Le Roman de Renard*
13th century	*Carmina Burana*
1280	*Roman de la Rose (Romance of the Rose)*
14th century	William Langland, *The Vision of William Concerning Piers the Plowman*
1387	Geoffrey Chaucer, *Canterbury Tales*
Ca. 1450	*Noah; The Second Shepherd, Play of the Wakefield Cycle*
1481	Poggio Bracciolini, *Facetiae (Fables of Poge the Florentine)*
1494	Sebastian Brant, *Das Narrenschiff (Ship of Fools)*
1509	Desiderius Erasmus, *Encomium Moriae (The Praise of Folly)*
1514	Desiderius Erasmus (attributed), *Julius exclusus (Julius Shut Out [of Heaven])*
1518	Niccolò Machiavelli, *Mandragola*
1526	*A Hundred Merry Tales*
1535	*Merry Tales and Quick Answers*
1545	John Heywood, *The Foure P's*
Ca. 1550	John Skelton, "The Tunning of Elinour Rumming"
1551	Hans Sachs, *Kasper Conjures Up the Devil*
1553	François Rabelais, *Gargantua and Pantagruel*
1554	*La Vida de Lazarillo de tormes y de sus fortunas y adversidades*
1566	Thomas Drant, *Medicinable Morall*
1567	John Skelton, *Merie Tales Newly Imprinted & Made by Maister Skelton Poet Laureate*
Ca. 1580s	William Shakespeare, *A Comedy of Errors*
1591	Edmund Spenser, *Muiopotmos*
1593	Jean Leroy, *États généraux*
1594	Thomas Nashe, *The Unfortunate Traveller, Or the life of Jacke Wilton*
Ca. 1597	William Shakespeare, *The Merry Wives of Windsor*
1598	Ben Jonson, *Every Man in His Humour*
Ca. 1598	William Shakespeare, *Much Ado about Nothing*
1599	Ben Jonson, *Every Man out of His Humour*
1606	Ben Jonson, *Volpone*
1607	Francis Beaumont, *The Knight of the Burning Pestle*
1610	Ben Jonson, *The Alchemist*
1615	Miguel de Cervantes, *Don Quixote*
1621	Robert Burton, *Anatomy of Melancholy*
1622	Alessandro Tassoni, *La Secchia Rapita (The Rape of the Bucket)*
1655	Molière, *L'Étourdi ou les contretemps (The Scatterbrain, or The Blunders)*
1656	Molière, *Le Dépit amoureux (The Amorous Quarrel)*
1658	Molière, *Le Docteur amoureux (The Lovelorn Doctor)*
1659	Molière, *Les Précieuses ridicules (The Ridiculous Bluestockings)*

1661	Molière, *L'École des maris (The School for Husbands)*
1662	Molière, *L'École des femmes (The School for Wives)*
1662	Molière, *Les Fâcheux (The Impertinents)*
1662	Samuel Butler, *Hudibras*
1664	George Etherege, *Comical Revenge, or Love in a Tub*
1664	Molière, *Tartuffe, ou l'hypocrite (Tartuffe, or The Hypocrite)*
1665	Molière, *Don Juan, L'Amour médecin (Love's the Best Doctor)*
1665	Molière, *Don Juan, ou Le Festin de pierre (Don Juan, or The Feast of the Stone)*
1666	Molière, *Le Misanthrope*
1666	Molière, *Le Médecin malgré lui (The Doctor in Spite of Himself)*
1668	George Etherege, *She Would If She Could*
1668	Molière, *Amphitryon; Georges Dandin, ou le mari confondu (George Dandin, or The Confused Husband)*
1669	Molière, *Monsieur de Pourceaugnac*
1670	Molière, *Le Bourgeois gentilhomme (The Bourgeois Gentleman)*
1670	Molière, *Les Amants magnifiques (The Magnificent Lovers)*
1671	George Villiers, *The Rehearsal*
1672	Molière, *Femmes savantes (The Learned Ladies)*
1672	William Wycherley, *The Gentleman Dancing Master*
1672	Molière, *Les Fourberies de Scapin (The Cheats of Scapin)*
1673	John Dryden, *Marriage à la Mode*
1673	Molière, *Le Malade imaginaire (The Hypochondriac)*
1675	William Wycherley, *The Country Wife*
1676	George Etherege, *Man of Mode, or, Sir Fopling Flutter*
1677	Aphra Behn, *The Rover, or The Banish'd Cavaliers*
1678	John Dryden, *All for Love, or the World Well Lost*
1681	John Dryden, *Absalom and Achitophel*
1682	Alexander Radcliffe, *The Ramble: News from Hell*
1682	Aphra Behn, *The City Heiress*
1682	John Dryden, *MacFlecknoe, or a Satyr upon the True-Blew-Protestant Poet, T. S.*
1682	John Dryden, *The Medall: A Satyre Against Sedition*
1683	Nicolas Boileau, *Le Lutrin (The Lectern)*
1687	John Dryden, *The Hind and the Panther*
1694	Jean de La Fontaine, *Fables*
1695	William Congreve, *Love for Love*
1696	Colley Cibber, *Love's Last Shift*
1699	Samuel Garth, *The Dispensary*
1700	John Dryden, *Fables Ancient and Modern*
1700	William Congreve, *The Way of the World*
1704	Jonathan Swift, *A Tale of a Tub*
1704	Jonathan Swift, *The Battle of the Books*
1705	John Phillips, *The Splendid Shilling: An Imitation of Milton*
1705	Bernard de Mandeville, *Fable of the Bees*
1709	Jonathan Swift, *Baucis and Philemon*
1710	Jonathan Swift, "Description of a City Shower"

1711	Alexander Pope, *Essay on Criticism*
1711	John Gay, *The Present State of Wit*
1712	Joseph Addison, "The Coquette's Heart"
1714	Alexander Pope, *The Rape of the Lock*
1715	John Gay, *The What D'ye Call It*
1716	John Gay, *Trivia; or, The Art of Walking the Streets of London*
1717	John Gay, *John Arbuthnot and Alexander Pope, Three Hours after Marriage*
1722	Daniel Defoe, *The Fortunes and Misfortunes of the Famous Moll Flanders*
1722	Richard Steele, *The Conscious Lovers*
1723	Benjamin Franklin, "Dogood Papers"
1724	Jonathan Swift, *The Drapier Letters*
1726	Jonathan Swift, *Gulliver's Travels*
1727	Alexander Pope, "Martinus Scriblerus" and *Peri Bathous, or the Art of Sinking in Poetry*
1727	John Gay, *Fables*
1728	Alexander Pope, *The Dunciad*
1728	John Gay, *The Beggar's Opera*
1729	Alexander Pope, *Dunciad Variorum*
1729	John Gay, *Polly*
1729	Jonathan Swift, *A Modest Proposal*
1730	Benjamin Franklin, "Busy-Body Papers"
1730	Henry Fielding, *Tom Thumb*
1733–1758	Benjamin Franklin, *Poor Richard's Almanack*
1734	Alexander Pope, *Essay on Man*
1735	Alexander Pope, "An Epistle from Mr. Pope, to Dr. Arbuthnot"
1737	Alexander Pope, *Imitations of Horace*
1740	Samuel Richardson, *Pamela*
1741	Henry Fielding, *Shamela*
1741	Samuel Richardson, *Pamela in Her Exalted Condition*
1742	Henry Fielding, *Joseph Andrews*
1742	*Narukami*
1743	Henry Fielding, *Jonathan Wild*
1747	Voltaire, *Zadig*
1747	Benjamin Franklin, "Speech of Polly Baker"
1748	Thomas Gray, "Ode on the Death of a Favourite Cat, Drowned in a Tub of Gold Fishes"
1748	Tobias Smollett, *The Adventures of Roderick Random*
1749	Henry Fielding, *Tom Jones*
1751	Tobias Smollett, *The Adventures of Peregrine Pickle*
1753	Alain-René LeSage, *Gil Blas*
1753	Tobias Smollett, *Ferdinand, Count Fathom*
1755	Samuel Johnson, *Dictionary of the English Language*
1759	Voltaire, *Candide*
1773	Benjamin Franklin, "Rules by Which a Great Empire May Be Reduced to a Small One" and "Edict by the King of Prussia"
1773	Oliver Goldsmith, *She Stoops To Conquer*

1774	Pierre Beaumarchais, *Le Barbier de Séville (The Barber of Seville)*
1775	Richard Sheridan, *The Rivals*
1777	Richard Sheridan, *The School for Scandal*
1778	Pierre Beaumarchais, *Mémoires du Sieur Beaumarchais par lui-même (Beaumarchais, Autobiographical Memoirs)*
1779	Richard Sheridan, *The Critic*
1780	Johann Goethe, *Reinhart Fuchs*
1784	Pierre Beaumarchais, *La Folle journée, ou le mariage de Figaro (The Foolish Day's Work, or The Marriage of Figaro)*
1786	Robert Burns, "Epistle to J. Lapraik"
1796	Pierre Beaumarchais, *La Mère coupable (The Guilty Mother)*
1807–1808	Washington Irving, *Salmagundi*
1809	Washington Irving, *A History of New York, from the Beginning of the World to the End of the Dutch Dynasty*
1811	Jane Austen, *Sense and Sensibility*
1813	Jane Austen, *Pride and Prejudice*
1871	John Hookham Frere, *Whistlecraft*
1818	Lord Byron, *Beppo: A Venetian Story*
1818	Thomas Love Peacock, *Nightmare Abbey*
1818	Washington Irving, *The Sketch Book of Geoffrey Crayon, Gent.*
1822	Washington Irving, *Bracebridge Hall, or the Humourists: A Medley*
1824	Lord Byron, *Don Juan*
1824	Washington Irving, *Tales of a Traveler*
1829	Sir Walter Scott, *Memoirs of Vidoq*
1836	Nikolai Gogol, *The Inspector General*
1842	Robert Browning, "Soliloquy of the Spanish Cloister"
1844	William Makepeace Thackeray, *The Luck of Barry Lyndon*
1846	Edward Lear, *The Book of Nonsense*
1848	William Makepeace Thackeray, *Vanity Fair*
1848–1908	Joel Chandler Harris, Uncle Remus stories
1850	Ivan Turgenev, *A Month in the Country*
1852	William Makepeace Thackeray, *Memoirs of Barry Lyndon*
1863	Charles Godfrey Leland, *Ye Book of Copperheads*
1865	Lewis Carroll, *Alice in Wonderland*
1867	Mark Twain, "The Celebrated Jumping Frog of Calaveras County"
1872	Lewis Carroll, *Through the Looking-Glass and What Alice Found There*
1875	Gilbert and Sullivan, *Trial by Jury*
1878	Gilbert and Sullivan, *H.M.S. Pinafore*
1879	Gilbert and Sullivan, *The Pirates of Penzance*
1879	Kawatake Mokuami, *Ningen Ganji Kane Yo No Naka*
1880	Joel Chandler Harris, *Uncle Remus: His Songs and His Sayings*
1882	Oscar Wilde, *Vera*
1883	Joel Chandler Harris, *Nights with Uncle Remus*
1884	Mark Twain, *The Adventures of Huckleberry Finn*

1885	Gilbert and Sullivan, *The Mikado, or the Town of Titipu*
1886	Mark Twain, *A Connecticut Yankee in King Arthur's Court*
1888	Gilbert and Sullivan, *Yeomen of the Guard*
1892	Brandon Thomas, *Charley's Aunt*
1894	George Bernard Shaw, *Arms and the Man*
1895	Oscar Wilde, *The Importance of Being Earnest*
1902	Saki, *Not So Stories*
1903	George Bernard Shaw, *Man and Superman*
1903	Samuel Butler, *The Way of All Flesh*
1904	Saki, *Reginald*
1910	Joel Chandler Harris, *Uncle Remus and the Little Boy*
1910	Max Beerbohm, "Ballade Tragique à Double Refrain"
1910	Saki, *Reginald in Russia*
1910	*The Zen Substitute*
1911	Max Beerbohm, *Zuleika Dobson*
1912	George Bernard Shaw, *Androcles and the Lion*
1912	Rudyard Kipling, "Rikki Tikki Tavi" and *Just So Stories*
1912	Saki, *The Chronicles of Clovis*
1912	George Bernard Shaw, *Pygmalion*
1914	George Jean Nathan and H. L. Mencken, *The Smart Set: A Magazine of Cleverness*
1914	Saki, *Beasts and Super-Beasts*
1914–1933	George Nathan and H. L. Mencken, *American Mercury*
1916	H. L. Mencken, *A Book of Burlesques*
1917	H. L. Mencken, *A Book of Prefaces*
1919	Saki, *The Toys of Peace*
1920	Ring Lardner, *The Young Immigrants*
1920	Saki, "The Open Window"
1920	Karel Capek, *R. U. R.*
1920	Sinclair Lewis, *Main Street*
1921	George Bernard Shaw, *Back to Methuselah*
1922	Sinclair Lewis, *Babbitt*
1924	Saki, *The Square Egg*
1925	Noel Coward, *Hay Fever*
1925	Sinclair Lewis, *Arrowsmith*
1926	Dorothy Parker, *Enough Rope*
1927	Anita Loos, *But Gentlemen Marry Brunettes*
1927	Sinclair Lewis, *Elmer Gantry*
1928	Aldous Huxley, *Point Counter Point*
1928	Bertolt Brecht and Kurt Weill, *The Threepenny Opera*
1928	Dorothy Parker, *Sunset Gun*
1928	Virginia Woolf, *Orlando*
1929	*Nemuru Ga Rakuda Monogatari*
1929	Sinclair Lewis, *Dodsworth*
1930	Moss Hart and George S. Kaufman, *Once in a Lifetime*
1930	Noel Coward, *Private Lives*
1931	Dorothy Parker, *Death and Taxes*
1932	Moss Hart, *Face the Music*
1934	Moss Hart, *Merrily We Roll Along*
1935	Sinclair Lewis, *It Can't Happen Here*

1936	Dorothy Parker, *Not So Deep as a Well*
1936	George S. Kaufman and Moss Hart, *You Can't Take It with You*
1937	Moss Hart, *I'd Rather Be Right*
1939	Aldous Huxley, *Brave New World*
1939	André Breton, *Anthologie de l'humour noir*
1939	Howard Lindsay and Russell Crouse, *Life with Father*
1939	Moss Hart and George S. Kaufman, *The Man Who Came to Dinner*
1940	James Thurber, *Fables for Our Time*
1940	Moss Hart, *George Washington Slept Here*
1941	Noel Coward, *Blithe Spirit*
1943	H. L. Mencken, *Heathen Days, 1890–1936*
1944	Bertolt Brecht, *The Private Life of the Master Race*
1944	Mary Chase, *Harvey*
1944	Jean-Paul Sartre, *No Exit*
1945	Bertolt Brecht, *The Caucasian Chalk Circle*
1945	Colette, *Gigi*
1945	George Orwell, *Animal Farm*
1947	George S. Kaufman, *The Senator Was Indiscreet*
1948	Eugène Ionesco, *La Cantatrice chauve (The Bald Soprano)*
1948	Shirley Jackson, "The Lottery"
1948	Thomas Heggen and Joshua Logan, *Mr. Roberts*
1948	Wyndham Lewis and Charles Lee, *The Stuffed Owl: An Anthology of Bad Verse*
1949	Jean Genet, *Journal du voleur (Diary of a Thief)*
1950	T. S. Eliot, *The Cocktail Party*
1951	Richard Rodgers and Oscar Hammerstein, *The King and I*
1952	Bernard Malamud, *The Natural*
1952	Samuel Beckett, *En attendant Godot (Waiting for Godot)*
1953	Ray Bradbury, *Fahrenheit 451*
1954	Evelyn Waugh, *The Man Who Liked Dickens*
1954	Roald Dahl, "Lamb to the Slaughter"
1955	Gore Vidal, *A Visit to a Small Planet*
1955	Tennessee Williams, *Cat on a Hot Tin Roof*
1956	Friedrich Dürrenmatt, *Der Besuch der alten Dame (The Visit)*
1956	Harry Golden, "The Vertical Negro"
1956	Ira Levin and Mac Hyman, *No Time for Sergeants*
1957	Isaac Singer, *Gimpel the Fool*
1957	Ted Geisel, *How the Grinch Stole Christmas*
1958	Harold Pinter, *The Birthday Party*
1960	Eugène Ionesco, *Rhinoceros*
1960	Norton Juster, *The Phantom Tollbooth*
1961	Joseph Heller, *Catch-22*
1962	Edward Albee, *Who's Afraid of Virginia Woolf?*
1963	Billy Wilder and I. A. L. Diamond, *Irma la Douce*
1963	Burt Shevelove, Larry Gelbart, and Stephen Sondheim, *A Funny Thing Happened on the Way to the Forum*
1963	Kurt Vonnegut, *Cat's Cradle*

1963	William and Tania Rose, *It's a Mad Mad Mad Mad World*
1965	Edward Albee, *Tiny Alice*
1965	Harold Pinter, *The Homecoming*
1965	Neil Simon, *The Odd Couple*
1965	Slawomir Mrozek, *Tango*
1965	Thomas Berger, *Little Big Man*
1966	Kurt Vonnegut, *Slaughterhouse-Five*
1968	Charles Portis, *True Grit*
1968	Hugh Leonard, *The Au Pair Man*
1968	James Goldman, *The Lion in Winter*
1968	Neil Simon, *Plaza Suite*
1968	Richard Hooker, *MASH*
1969	Jean Giraudoux, *The Madwoman of Chaillot*
1969	Joe Orton, *What the Butler Saw*
1969	Neil Simon, *Sweet Charity*
1970	Mart Crowley, *The Boys in the Band*
1970	Tom Wolfe, *Mau-Mauing the Flak Catchers*
1971	John Gardner, *Grendel*
1972	Neil Simon, *The Last of the Red Hot Lovers*
1973	Hugh Leonard, *Da*
1973	Kurt Vonnegut, *Breakfast of Champions*
1974	Kurt Vonnegut, *Wampeters, Foma, and Grandfalloons*
1975	Florence King, *Southern Ladies and Gentlemen*
1976	Florence King, *WASP, Where Is Thy Sting*
1977	David Mamet, *American Buffalo*
1977	Marsha Norman, *Getting Out*
1977	Neil Simon, *Chapter Two*
1978	Florence King, *He: An Irreverent Look at the American Male*
1979	Beth Henley, *Crimes of the Heart*
1979	Harvey Fierstein, *Torch Song Trilogy*
1982	Kurt Vonnegut, *Deadeye Dick*
1982	Florence King, *When Sisterhood Was in Flower*
1985	Florence King, *Confessions of a Failed Southern Lady*
1982	Marsha Norman, *'night Mother*
1982	Neil Simon, *Brighton Beach Memoirs*
1982	T. Coraghessan Boyle, *Water Music*
1984	Neil Simon, *Biloxi Blues*
1985	Joseph Heller, *God Knows*
1986	Margaret Atwood, *The Handmaid's Tale*
1987	Alfred Uhry, *Driving Miss Daisy*
1987	Larry Larson, Levi Lee, and Rebecca Wackler, *Tent Meeting*
1987	Terry McMillan, *Mama*
1988	Anne Fine, *Alias Madame Doubtfire*
1989	Florence King, *Reflections in a Jaundiced Eye*
1989	Jon Scieszka, *The True Story of the Three Little Pigs!*
1989	T. Coraghessan Boyle, *If the River Was Whiskey*
1990	Kazuo Ishiguro, *Remains of the Day*
1990	T. Coraghessan Boyle, *East Is East*

1991	Calder Willingham, *Rambling Rose*
1991	Florence King, *Lump It or Leave It*
1991	Molly Ivins, *Molly Ivins Can't Say Those Things, Can She?*
1992	Jon Scieszka, *The Stinky Cheese Man and Other Fairly Stupid Tales*
1992	Terry McMillan, *Waiting to Exhale*
1992	Florence King, *With Charity for None*
1992	Laura Esquivel, *Like Water for Chocolate*
1993	Alan Bennett, *The Madness of George III*
1993	Margaret Atwood, *The Robber Bride*
1993	T. Coraghessan Boyle, *The Road to Wellville*
1995	Florence King, *The Florence King Reader*
1995	Winston Groom, *Forrest Gump*

PRIMARY SOURCES

Achebe, Chinua. 1959. *Things Fall Apart*. New York: Fawcett Crest.

Adams, Richard. 1972. *Watership Down*. New York: Avon.

Addison, Joseph. 1952. *Cato*. In *Eighteenth-Century Plays*. New York: Modern Library.

———. 1973. *The Spectator*. In *Restoration and Eighteenth-Century Comedy*. New York: Norton.

Aesop's Fables. 1986. Ed. George Fyler Townsend. Los Angeles: Troubador.

Albee, Edward. 1959. *The Zoo Story*. In *The American Dream and The Zoo Story*. New York: Signet.

———. 1965. *Tiny Alice*. New York: Pocket.

Allende, Isabel. 1987. *Of Love and Shadows*. New York: Bantam.

Angelou, Maya. 1970. *I Know Why the Caged Bird Sings*. New York: Bantam.

Aristophanes. 1952. *The Frogs* in *Classics in Translation*. Madison: University of Wisconsin Press.

———. 1955. *Five Comedies of Aristophanes*. Garden City, NY: Doubleday Anchor.

———. 1962. *The Birds*. In *Four Comedies*. New York: Harcourt Brace Jovanovich.

———. 1993. *The Birds*. London: David Brown.

Atwood, Margaret. 1992. *Surfacing; Life before Men; The Handmaid's Tale*. New York: Quality Paperback Club.

———. 1993. *The Robber Bride*. New York: Doubleday.

Austen, Jane. 1961. *Pride and Prejudice*. New York: New American Library.

Bailey, Pearl. 1973. *Pearl's Kitchen*. New York: HarBrace.

Baum, L. Frank. 1983. *The Annotated Wizard of Oz*. New York: Schocken.

Beaumarchais, Pierre-Augustin de. 1964. *The Barber of Seville; The Marriage of Figaro*. New York: Penguin.

Beckett, Samuel. 1954. *Waiting for Godot*. New York: Grove.

Beerbohm, Max. 1967. "Ballade Tragique à Double Refrain." In *Western Literature: Themes and Writers*. New York: McGraw-Hill.

Behn, Aphra. 1915. *The Works of Aphra Behn*. London: William Heinemann.

Benchley, Robert. 1940. *Chips Off the Old Benchley*. New York: Harper & Brothers.

Bennett, Alan. 1993. *The Madness of George III*. New York: Faber & Faber.

Bierce, Ambrose. 1991. *The Devil's Dictionary*. New York: Laurel.

Boileau, Nicolas. 1965. "L'Art Poetique." In *A Survey of French Literature*. New York: Harcourt Brace Jovanovich.

Böll, Heinrich. 1991. "My Melancholy Face." In *World Masterpieces*. Englewood Cliffs, NJ: Prentice-Hall.

Boyle, T. Coraghessan. 1983. *Water Music*. New York: Viking.

———. 1985. *Greasy Lake*. New York: Viking.

———. 1989. *If the River Was Whiskey*. New York: Viking.

———. 1990. *East Is East*. New York: Viking.

———. 1993. *The Road to Wellville*. New York: Viking.

Bradbury, Ray. 1953. *Fahrenheit 451*. New York: Ballantine.

———. 1959. *Dandelion Wine*. New York: Bantam.

Brecht, Bertolt. 1967. *The Good Woman of Setzuan*. In *Plays for the Theatre*. San Francisco, CA: Rinehart.

———. 1981. *The Caucasian Chalk Circle*. In *Nine Plays of the Modern Theater*. New York: Grove.

Brontë, Charlotte. 1981. *Jane Eyre*. New York: Bantam.

Browning, Robert. 1949. "Soliloquy of the Spanish Cloister." In *Victorian and Later English Poets*. New York: American Book Company.

Buchwald, Art. 1987. *I Think I Don't Remember*. New York: Putnam.

Bunyan, John. 1986. *Pilgrim's Progress and the Holy War*. Chicago: Pilgrim.

Burns, Robert. 1948. "Epistle to J. Lapraik." In *Anthology of Romanticism*. New York: Ronald.

Butler, Samuel. 1960. *The Way of All Flesh*. New York: New American Library.

Byron, George. 1959. *Don Juan*. In *Major British Writers*. New York: Harcourt, Brace & World.

Camus, Albert. 1991. "The Myth of Sisyphus." In *World Masterpieces*. Englewood Cliffs, NJ: Prentice-Hall.

Carmina Burana: Die Gedichte des Codex Buranus Lateinisch und Deutsch. 1974. Zurich: Artemis Verlag.

Carroll, Lewis. 1960. *Alice in Wonderland; "Jabberwocky"; Through the Looking Glass*. In *The Annotated Alice*. New York: Bramhall House.

———. 1994. *The Hunting of the Snark*. Leicester, UK: Windward.

Catullus. *Catullus*. Cambridge, MA: Harvard University Press.

Cervantes Saavedra, Miguel de. 1957. *Don Quixote*. New York: Mentor.

Chase, Mary. 1958. *Harvey*. In *Best American Plays*. New York: Crown.

Chaucer, Geoffrey. 1957. *The Works of Geoffrey Chaucer*. Boston: Houghton Mifflin.

———. 1966a. *Chaucer's Canterbury Tales: The Prologue*. Lincoln, NE: Cliffs Notes.

———. 1966b. *Chaucer's Canterbury Tales: The Wife of Bath*. Lincoln, NE: Cliffs Notes.

———. 1969. *Selected Canterbury Tales*. New York: Holt, Rinehart and Winston.

———. 1992. *The Canterbury Tales*. London: Cresset.

———. 1993. *The Wife of Bath's Tale*. (audiocassette) Prince Frederick, MD: Recorded Books.

Chekhov, Anton. 1958. "A Slander." In *Adventures in Appreciation*. New York: Harcourt Brace Jovanovich.

Churchill, Winston. 1967. "Harrow." In *Western Literature: Themes and Writers*. New York: McGraw-Hill.

Coleridge, Mary, "Gibberish." On *My Spirits Sang All Day*. CD. Hayes, Middlesex: EMI Records.

Colette. 1945. *Gigi*. Navarre: Ferenczi.

———. 1949. *Journey for Myself*. Indianapolis: Bobbs Merrill.

———. 1962. *Gigi*. In *XXe Siècle: Les Grands Auteurs Français*. Paris: Bordas.

Congreve, William. 1953. *The Way of the World*. In *Restoration Plays*. New York: Modern Library.

Cosby, Bill. 1986. *Fatherhood*. Garden City, NY: Dolphin.

————. 1991. *Childhood*. New York: Putnam's.

Coward, Noel. 1965. *Three Plays*. New York: Grove Weidenfeld.

Crichton, Michael. 1990. *Jurassic Park*. New York: Ballantine.

Crimmins, Cathy, and Tom Maeder. 1995. *Newt Gingrich's Bedtime Stories for Orphans*. Beverly Hills, CA: Dove.

Dahl, Roald. 1995. *Lamb to the Slaughter and Other Stories*. New York: Penguin.

Delany, Sarah L., and A. Elizabeth Delany with Amy Hill Hearth. 1994. *Having Our Say: The Delany Sisters' First 100 Years*. New York: Dell.

Dickens, Charles. 1960. *A Tale of Two Cities*. New York: New American Library.

————. 1986. *Hard Times; Oliver Twist; A Tale of Two Cities*. In *The Annotated Dickens*. New York: Clarkson N. Potter.

Dinesen, Isak. 1958. *Babette's Feast and Other Anecdotes of Destiny*. New York: Vintage.

Dryden, John. 1953. *All for Love*. In *Restoration Plays*. New York: Modern Library.

————. 1959. *All for Love*. In *Six Restoration Plays*. Boston: Riverson.

————. 1973. *Preface to An Evening's Love*. In *Restoration and Eighteenth-Century Comedy*. New York: Norton.

Dürrenmatt, Friedrich. 1981. *The Visit*. In *Nine Plays of the Modern Theater*. New York: Grove.

Eco, Umberto. 1983. *The Name of the Rose*. New York: Harcourt Brace Jovanovich.

Eliot, George. 1960. *Silas Marner*. New York: Signet.

Eliot, T. S. 1950. *The Cocktail Party*. New York: Samuel French.

Erasmus, Desiderius. 1941. *The Praise of Folly*. Princeton, NJ: Princeton University Press.

————. 1954. "Praise of Folly." In *The Renaissance in England; Non-dramatic Prose and Verse of the Sixteenth Century*. Boston: D. C. Heath.

Esquivel, Laura. 1992. *Like Water for Chocolate*. New York: Anchor.

Etherege, Sir George. 1953. *The Man of Mode*. In *Restoration Plays*. New York: Modern Library.

Faludi, Susan, and Molly Ivins. 1992. *Women on the Verge!* Audiocassette. Boulder, CO: Sounds True Recordings.

Faulkner, William. 1967. *The Portable Faulkner*. New York: Penguin.

————. 1977. *Collected Stories*. New York: Vintage.

Feinberg, Leonard. 1967. *Introduction to Satire*. Ames: Iowa State University Press.

Fierstein, Harvey. 1979. *Torch Song Trilogy*. New York: Gay Presses of New York.

Fine, Anne. 1990. *Alias Madame Doubtfire*. New York: Bantam.

Fleischer, Leonore. 1985. *Agnes of God*. New York: New American Library.

Forster, E. M. 1984. *E. M. Forster*. New York: Harcourt Brace.

Franklin, Benjamin. 1982. *The Autobiography and Other Writings*. New York: Bantam.

———. 1987. "Moral Perfection." In *The United States in Literature*. Glenview, IL: Scott, Foresman.

Frost, Robert. 1962. *Robert Frost's Poems*. New York: Washington Square.

Gardner, John. 1971. *Grendel*. New York: Ballantine.

———. 1984. *The Art of Fiction: Notes on Craft for Young Writers*. New York: Knopf.

Garner, James Finn. 1994. *Politically Correct Bedtime Stories*. New York: Macmillan.

———. 1995. *Once Upon a More Enlightened Time*. New York: Macmillan.

Gay, John. 1932. *Trivia*. In *A Collection of English Poems, 1660–1800*. New York: Harper & Row.

———. 1952. *The Beggar's Opera*. In *Eighteenth-Century Plays*. New York: Modern Library.

Gilbert, William Schwenck. *The Complete Plays of Gilbert and Sullivan*. 1962. New York: Modern Library.

———. 1967. *H.M.S. Pinafore*. In *Nineteenth-Century British Drama*. Glenview, IL: Scott, Foresman.

———. 1992. *The Mikado*. New York: Dover.

Golden, Harry. 1958. *Only in America*. New York: World Publishing.

———. 1972. *The Golden Book of Jewish Humor*. New York: Putnam's.

Goldman, James. 1968. *The Lion in Winter*. New York: Dell.

"Goliardic Verse." 1994. In *The Medieval Reader*. New York: HarperCollins.

Gray, Thomas. 1932. "Ode on the Death of a Favourite Cat, Drown in a Tub of Gold Fishes." In *A Collection of English Poems, 1660–1800*. New York: Harper & Row.

Gregory, Dick. 1964. *Nigger*. New York: E. P. Dutton.

Hamilton, Virginia. 1985. *The People Could Fly*. New York: Knopf.

Hampton, Christopher. 1985. *Les Liaisons Dangereuses, A Dramatization of the Novel by Choderlos de Laclos*. London: Faber and Faber.

Hansberry, Lorraine. 1988. *A Raisin in the Sun*. New York: Penguin.

Harris, Joel Chandler. 1952. *Uncle Remus Stories*. In *The Literature of the South*. Chicago: Scott, Foresman.

Hart, Moss, and George S. Kaufman. 1961. *You Can't Take It with You*. In *Three Comedies of American Family Life*. New York: Washington Square.

Heathorn, R. J. 1958. "Learn with BOOK." In *Adventures in Appreciation*. New York: Harcourt Brace Jovanovich.

Heggen, Thomas, and Joshua Logan. 1951. *Mr. Roberts*. In *Six Modern American Plays*. New York: Modern Library.

Heller, Joseph. 1961. *Catch-22*. New York: Dell.

Henley, Beth. 1981. *Crimes of the Heart*. New York: Viking.

Hesiod. 1973. *Works and Days*. Ann Arbor: University of Michigan Press.

Hinojosa, Rolando. 1990. *Becky and Her Friends*. Houston, TX: Arte Publico.

Hooker, Richard. 1969. *MASH*. New York: Pocket.

Hopkins, Gerard Manley. 1970. *The Poems of Gerard Manley Hopkins*. New York: Oxford University Press.

Horace. 1888. *The Satires and Epistles*. Boston: Ginn.

———. 1891. *The Works of Horace*. New York: Harper.

———. 1892. *The Works of Horace*. New York: Hinds, Noble & Eldredge.

———. 1899. *Selections from Horace*. Philadelphia: Eldredge.

———. 1902. *The Odes, Epodes, and Carmen Saeculare*. New York: American Book Company.

———. 1909. *The Satires*. New York: American Book Company.

———. 1959. *Satires and Epistles*. Chicago: Phoenix.

Houston, James D. 1973. "Gasoline." In *Gasoline: The Automotive Adventures of Charlie Bates*. Santa Barbara, CA: Capra.

Huxley, Aldous. 1946. *Brave New World*. New York: Bantam.

Ionesco, Eugène. 1958. *Four Plays*. New York: Grove.

———. 1981. *The Rhinoceros*. In *Nine Plays of the Modern Theater*. New York: Grove.

Irving, Washington. 1855. *Wolfert's Roost and Others*. New York: Putnam.

———.1978. "Rip Van Winkle." In *Focus on Literature: America*. Boston: Houghton Mifflin.

———. 1983. *Bracebridge Hall; Tales of a Traveller; The Alhambra*. New York: Library of America.

———. 1987. "The Devil and Tom Walker." In *The United States in Literature*. Glenview, IL: Scott, Foresman.

Ishiguro, Kazuo. 1990. *Remains of the Day*. New York: Random House, 1990.

Ivins, Molly. 1991. *Molly Ivins Can't Say Those Things, Can She?* New York: Random House.

———. 1995. "Commentary: Behold the Powell Bubble." Lincoln, NE, *Star*, September 27.

Izumo, Takeda, et al. 1971. *Chushingura*. New York: Columbia University Press.

Jackson, Shirley. 1982. *The Lottery and Other Stories*. New York: Farrar, Straus & Giroux.

Jhabvala, Ruth Prawer. 1975. *Heat and Dust*. New York: Touchstone.

Johnson, Samuel. 1952. *Dictionary in Adventures in English Literature*. New York: Harcourt, Brace & World.

Juster, Norton. 1961. *The Phantom Tollbooth*. New York: Random House.

Juvenal. 1890. *The Satires of Juvenal*. New York: American Book Company.

———. 1892. *The Satires of Juvenal*. Boston: Allyn and Bacon.

———. 1992. *The Satires*. New York: Oxford University Press.

Keyes, Daniel. 1967. *Flowers for Algernon*. New York: Bantam.

King, Florence. 1975. *Southern Ladies and Gentlemen*. New York: St. Martin's.

———. 1989. *Reflections in a Jaundiced Eye*. New York: St. Martin's.

———. 1990. *Lump It or Leave It*. New York: St. Martin's.

———. 1995. *The Florence King Reader*. New York: St. Martin's.

Kipling, Rudyard. 1974. *Just So Stories*. New York: Signet.

La Fontaine, Jean. 1965. "Le Loup et l'Agneau." In *A Survey of French Literature*. New York: Harcourt Brace Jovanovich.

Landon, Margaret. 1944. *Anna and the King of Siam*. New York: Pocket.

Larson, Larry, Levi Lee, and Rebecca Wackler. 1987. *Tent Meeting*. New York: Dramatists Play Service.

Lawrence, Jerome, and Robert E. Lee. 1960. *Inherit the Wind*. New York: Bantam.

———. 1971. *The Night Thoreau Spent in Jail*. New York: Bantam.

Lederer, William J., and Eugene Burdick. 1958. *The Ugly American*. New York: Fawcett Crest.

Lem, Stanislaw. 1991. "The First Sally (A) OR Trurl's Electronic Bard." In *World Masterpieces*. Englewood Cliffs, NJ: Prentice-Hall, 1991.

The Lenny Bruce Performance Film. 1982. Stamford, CT: Vestron Video.

Leonard, Hugh. 1973. *Da*. New York: Atheneum.

Levin, Ira, and Mac Hyman. 1958. *No Time for Sergeants*. In *Best American Plays*. New York: Crown.

Lewis, Sinclair. 1980. *Babbitt*. New York: New American Library.

Lindsay, Howard, and Russel Crouse. 1961. *Life with Father*. In *Three Comedies of American Family Life*. New York: Washington Square.

Lowell, James Russell. 1992. *The Complete Writings of James Russell Lowell*. Temecula, CA: Reprint Service.

Malamud, Bernard. 1952. *The Natural*. New York: Avon.

Martial. 1981. *The Twelve Books of Epigrams*. Darby, PA: Darby.

McMillan, Terry. 1987. *Mama*. New York: Washington Square.

———. 1989. *Disappearing Acts*. New York: Viking.

———. 1992. *Waiting to Exhale*. New York: Viking.

Mencken, H. L. 1983. *The Vintage Mencken*. New York: Vintage.

———. 1991. *The Impossible H. L. Mencken*. New York: Anchor.

Mitchell, Margaret. 1936. *Gone with the Wind*. New York: Warner.

Molière. 1965. *Le Bourgeois gentilhomme*. In *A Survey of French Literature*. New York: Harcourt Brace Jovanovich.

Morrison, Toni. 1988. *Beloved*. New York: Penguin.

Mrozek, Slawomir. 1981. *The Tango*. In *Nine Plays of the Modern Theater*. New York: Grove.

Norman, Marsha. 1983. *'night Mother*. New York: Hill and Wang.

"Numskull and the Rabbit." 1991. In *Literature: World Masterpieces*. Englewood Cliffs, NJ: Prentice-Hall.

"Old Man Coyote and Buffalo Power." 1975. In *Plains Indian Mythology*. New York: Meridian.

Orwell, George. 1946. *Animal Farm*. New York: Signet.

———. 1958. "Shooting an Elephant." In *Adventures in English Literature*. New York: Harcourt, Brace & World.

————. 1962. *Burmese Days*. New York: Harcourt Brave Jovanovich.

————. 1983. *1984*. New York: New American Library.

Parker, Dorothy. 1976. *The Portable Dorothy Parker*. New York: Penguin.

————. 1994. *The Poetry and Short Stories of Dorothy Parker*. New York: Modern Library.

Pepys, Samuel. 1926. *The Diary of Samuel Pepys*. New York: Harper & Row.

Petronius. 1925. *The Cena Trimalchionis of Petronius*. Oxford: Clarendon.

————. *Satyricon*. New York: Book Collectors.

Phaedrus. 1992. *The Fables of Phaedrus*. Austin: University of Texas Press.

Philips, John. 1932. "The Splendid Shilling." In *A Collection of English Poems, 1660–1800*. New York: Harper & Row.

Piercy, Marge. 1995. "The Grey Flannel Sexual Harassment Suit." *The Longings of Women*. New York: Fawcett Columbine.

Plato. 1956. *Great Dialogues of Plato*. New York: Mentor Classics.

Plautus. 1900. *Captivi*. Boston: Allyn and Bacon.

Pope, Alexander. 1932. "An Epistle from Mr. Pope, to Dr. Arbuthnot." In *A Collection of English Poems, 1660–1800*. New York: Harper & Row.

————. 1965. *Alexander Pope: Selected Poetry and Prose*. New York: Holt, Rinehart and Winston.

Portis, Charles. 1968. *True Grit*. New York: New American Library.

Rabelais, François. 1955. *Gargantua and Pantagruel*. New York: Viking Penguin.

Radcliffe, James. 1915. *The Ramble: News from Hell*. In *The Works of Aphra Behn*. London: William Heinemann.

"Renard the Fox: Bourgeois Contempt for the Nobility." 1994. In *The Medieval Reader*. New York: HarperCollins.

Robinson, Edwin Arlington. 1976. "Mr. Flood's Party." In *Understanding Poetry*. New York: Holt, Rinehart and Winston.

Rodgers, Richard, and Oscar Hammerstein II. 1958. *The King and I*. In *Adventures in Appreciation*. New York: Harcourt, Brace & World.

Rostand, Edmond. 1972. *Cyrano de Bergerac*. New York: New American Library.

Saki. 1958a. "The Open Window." In *Short Story Masterpieces*. New York: Dell.

————. 1958b. *The Short Stories of Saki*. New York: Modern Library.

————. 1967. "The Storyteller." In *Western Literature: Themes and Writers*. New York: McGraw-Hill.

Salinger, J. D. 1951. *The Catcher in the Rye*. New York: Bantam.

Scieszka, Jon. 1989. *The True Story of Three Little Pigs*. New York: Viking.

Scieszka, Jon, and Lane Smith. 1992. *The Stinky Cheese Man and Other Fairly Stupid Tales*. New York: Viking.

Selections from the Tatler and the Spectator. 1970. New York: Harcourt Brace.

Seneca. 1877. *Moral Essays*. New York: American Book Company.

————. 1986a. *Selected Moral Epistles*. Decatur, GA.: Scholars.

————. 1986b. *Seventeen Letters*. Oak Park, IL: Bolchazy-Carducci.

Shakespeare, William. 1957a. *King Lear*. New York: Washington Square.

————. 1957b. *The Merchant of Venice*. New York: Washington Square.

————. 1957c. *Othello*. New York: Washington Square.

————. 1958. *A Midsummer Night's Dream*. New York: Washington Square.

————. 1959. *Romeo and Juliet*. New York: Washington Square.

————. 1963. *The Taming of the Shrew*. New York: Washington Square.

————. 1967. *Hamlet; Juliet Caesar; The Tempest*. Complete Study Edition. Lincoln, NE: Cliffs Notes.

————. 1974. *Antony and Cleopatra; Henry IV, Part 2; The Merry Wives of Windsor*. In *The Riverside Shakespeare*. Boston: Houghton Mifflin.

————. 1980. *Much Ado about Nothing*. New York: Bantam.

Shaw, George Bernard. 1950. *Man and Superman*. New York: Viking.

————. 1952a. *Bernard Shaw's Saint Joan; Major Barbara; Androcles and the Lion*. New York: Modern Library.

————. 1952b. *Pygmalion*. In *Adventures in English Literature*. New York: Harcourt, Brace & World.

————. 1967. *Androcles and the Lion*. In *Western Literature: Themes and Writers*. New York: McGraw-Hill.

————. 1988. *Back to Methuselah*. New York: Penguin.

Shelley, Percy Bysshe. 1948. "Love's Philosophy," "Ode to the West Wind." In *Anthology of Romanticism*. New York: Ronald.

Shepherd, Jean. 1972. *In God We Trust: All Others Pay Cash*. Garden City, NY: Doubleday.

Sheridan, Richard. 1967. *The School for Scandal*. In *Plays for the Theatre*. San Francisco, CA: Rinehart.

Shevelove, Burt, and Larry Gelbart. 1991. *A Funny Thing Happened on the Way to the Forum*. New York: Applause Theatre.

Simon, Neil. 1978. *Chapter Two.* New York: Random House.

———. 1979. *The Collected Plays of Neil Simon.* New York: Random House.

———. 1986. *The Comedy of Neil Simon.* New York: New American Library.

Skelton, John. 1954. "The Tunning of Elinour Rumming." In *The Renaissance in England; Non-Dramatic Prose and Verse of the Sixteenth Century.* Boston: D. C. Heath.

Sophocles. 1958. *The Oedipus Plays of Sophocles.* New York: New American Library.

Steele, Richard. 1952. *The Conscious Lovers.* In *Eighteenth-Century Plays.* New York: Modern Library.

———. 1973. *The Tatler and the Spectator.* In *Restoration and Eighteenth-Century Comedy.* New York: Norton.

Steinbeck, John. 1962. *Travels with Charley.* New York: Bantam.

Swift, Jonathan. 1958. *Gulliver's Travels and Other Writings.* New York: Modern Library.

———. 1976. "A City Shower." In *Understanding Poetry.* New York: Holt, Rinehart and Winston.

Tan, Amy. 1992. *The Kitchen God's Wife.* New York: Ivy.

———. 1995. *The Hundred Secret Senses.* New York: Putnam's Sons.

Tennyson, Alfred. 1958. *Idylls of the King.* In *Adventures in Appreciation.* New York: Harcourt, Brace & World.

Terence. 1910. *The Comedies of Terence.* New York: Oxford University Press.

———. 1974. *The Complete Comedies of Terence.* New Brunswick, NJ: Rutgers University Press.

Thackeray, William Makepeace. 1967. "The Influence of the Aristocracy on Snobs." In *Western Literature: Themes and Writers.* New York: McGraw-Hill.

———. 1985. *Vanity Fair.* New York: Penguin.

Tolkien, J. R. R. 1966. *The Hobbit.* New York: Ballantine.

Tsao Hsueh-Chin. 1958. *The Dream of the Red Chamber.* New York: Doubleday.

Twain, Mark. 1962a. *The Adventures of Huckleberry Finn.* New York: Airmont.

———. 1962b. *The Adventures of Tom Sawyer.* New York: Airmont.

———. 1962c. *Letters from the Earth.* New York: Harper and Row.

———. 1963. *A Connecticut Yankee in King Arthur's Court.* New York: New American Library.

———. 1990. *Life on the Mississippi.* New York: Oxford University Press.

———. 1991. *A Pen Warmed Up in Hell: Mark Twain in Protest.* San Bernardino, CA: Borgo.

———. 1995. "The Celebrated Jumping Frog of Calaveras County." Audiocassette and guide. Prince Frederick, MD: Recorded Books.

Uhry, Alfred. 1990. *Driving Miss Daisy.* New York: Dramatists Play Service.

van Druten, John. 1961. *I Remember Mama.* In *Three Comedies of American Family Life.* New York: Washington Square.

Villon, François. 1967. "No, I Am Not as Others Are." In *Western Literature: Themes and Writers.* New York: Harcourt Brace Jovanovich.

Voltaire, François. 1961. *Candide, Zadig, and Selected Stories.* New York: New American Library.

———. *Candide, ou L'Optimisme.* In *A Survey of French Literature.* New York: Harcourt Brace Jovanovich.

Vonnegut, Kurt. 1966. *Slaughterhouse Five.* New York: Dell.

———. 1990. *Cat's Cradle.* New York: Henry Holt.

Walker, Alice. 1982. *The Color Purple.* New York: Pocket.

Waugh, Evelyn. 1958. *The Man Who Liked Dickens.* In *Adventures in Appreciation.* New York: Harcourt, Brace & World.

West, Jessamyn. 1969. *Except for Me and Thee.* New York: Avon.

Wilde, Oscar. 1923. *The Complete Works of Oscar Wilde.* Volume 11. Garden City, NY: Doubleday.

———. 1954. *Plays.* Middlesex, UK: Penguin.

———. 1965. *De Profundis.* New York: Philosophical Library.

———. 1995a. "The Canterville Ghost." Audiocassette. New York: Recorded Books.

———. 1995b. *The Complete Oscar Wilde.* New York: Crescent.

Wilder, Thornton. 1958. *The Matchmaker.* In *Best American Plays.* New York: Crown.

Wolfe, Tom. 1970. *Radical Chic and Mau-Mauing the Flak Catchers.* London: Cardinal.

Woolf, Virginia. 1928. *Orlando.* New York: Harcourt Brace.

Wright, Richard. 1966. *Black Boy.* New York: HarperPerennial.

Wycherley, William. 1953. *The Country Wife.* In *Restoration Plays.* New York: Modern Library.

Zindel, Paul. 1972. *The Effect of Gamma Rays on Man-in-the-Moon Marigolds.* New York: Bantam.

BIBLIOGRAPHY

Abbott, H. Porter. 1973. *The Fiction of Samuel Beckett: Form and Affect.* Berkeley: University of Southern California Press.

Abbott, Walter M., et al. 1969. *The Bible Reader: An Interfaith Interpretation.* New York: Bruce.

Abrams, M. H. 1971. *A Glossary of Literary Terms.* New York: Holt, Rinehart and Winston.

Alok, Roi. 1981. *Orwell and the Politics of Despair: A Critical Study of the Writings of George Orwell.* New York: Cambridge University Press.

Amadeus. 1984. Video. United States: Saul Zaentz.

Anderson, Michael, et al. 1971. *Crowell's Handbook of Contemporary Drama.* New York: Thomas Y. Crowell.

Andrews, Wayne. 1981. *Voltaire.* New York: New Directions.

Auden, W. H., and Louis Kronenberger, comps. 1966. *The Viking Book of Aphorisms.* New York: Dorset.

Authors in the News. 1976. Volume 1. Detroit: Gale Research.

Ayer, A. J. 1986. *Voltaire.* New York: Random House.

Baldick, Chris. 1990. *The Concise Oxford Dictionary of Literary Terms.* New York: Oxford University Press.

Barnet, Sylvan, Morton Berman, and William Burto. 1960. *A Dictionary of Literary Terms.* Boston: Little, Brown.

Baugh, Albert C., ed. 1948. *A Literary History of England.* New York: Appleton-Century-Crofts.

Beatty, Richmond Croom, et al., eds. 1952. *The Literature of the South.* Chicago: Scott, Foresman.

Beckson, Karl, and Arthur Ganz. 1989. *Literary Terms: A Dictionary.* New York: Noonday.

Bemister, Margaret. 1973. *Thirty Indian Legends of Canada*. Vancouver: Douglas & McIntyre.

Bentley, Gerald E. 1961. *Shakespeare: A Biographical Handbook*. New Haven, CT: Yale University Press.

Benton, Mike. 1989. *The Comic Book in America: An Illustrated History*. Dallas, TX: Taylor.

Ben-Zvi, Linda. 1986. *Samuel Beckett*. Boston: Twayne.

Bergman, David, ed. 1993. *Camp Grounds: Style and Homosexuality*. Amherst: University of Massachusetts Press.

Bermel, Albert. 1982. *Farce: A History from Aristophanes to Woody Allen*. New York: Simon and Schuster.

Biblia Sacra: Vulgatae Editionis. 1957. Rome: Editiones Paulinae.

Bishop, Morris. 1965. *A Survey of French Literature: Volume One: The Middle Ages to 1800*. New York: Harcourt Brace.

Bloom, Edward, and Lillian Bloom. 1980. *Addison and Steele: The Critical Heritage*. London: Routledge.

Bloom, Harold. 1986a. *Cervantes*. New York: Chelsea House.

———. 1986b. *Mark Twain*. New York: Chelsea House.

Bontemps, Arna, ed. 1974. *American Negro Poetry*. New York: Hill and Wang.

Boorstin, Daniel J. 1922. *The Creators: A History of Heroes of the Imagination*. New York: Vintage.

Bowden, Mary. 1981. *Washington Irving*. Boston: Twayne.

Bowder, Diana, ed. 1980. *Who's Who in the Roman World*. New York: Washington Square Press.

Boyce, Charles. 1990. *Shakespeare A to Z*. New York: Facts on File.

Branagh, Kenneth. 1993. *Much Ado about Nothing*. New York: Norton.

Brockett, Oscar G. 1968. *History of the Theatre*. Boston: Allyn & Bacon.

Broer, Lawrence. 1988. *Sanity Plea: Schizophrenia in the Novels of Kurt Vonnegut*. Ann Arbor: University of Michigan.

Brown, Edward James. 1976. *Brave New World, 1984, and We*. Ann Arbor, MI: Ardis.

Brown, Norman O. 1947. *Hermes the Thief: The Evolution of a Myth*. New York: Vintage.

Buck, Claire, ed. 1992. *The Bloomsbury Guide to Women's Literature*. New York: Prentice-Hall.

Budd, Louis J. 1983. *Critical Essays on Mark Twain*. Boston: G. K. Hall.

Buitehuis, Peter, and Ira B. Nadel, eds. 1988. *George Orwell: A Reassessment.* New York: St. Martin's.

Burdick, Jacques. 1974. *Theater.* New York: Newsweek.

Byron, William. 1988. *Cervantes: A Biography.* New York: Paragon House.

Calder, Jenni. 1987. *Animal Farm and Nineteen Eighty-Four.* New York: Taylor and Francis.

Campbell, Oscar James. 1943. *Shakespeare's Satire.* New York: Oxford University Press.

Cavendish, Marshall. 1970. *Man, Myth and Magic.* New York: Marshall Cavendish.

Cawley, A. C., ed. 1959. *Everyman and Medieval Miracle Plays.* New York: E. P. Dutton.

Chapman, Abraham, ed. 1968. *Black Voices.* New York: New American Library.

Chapman, R. W. 1948. *Jane Austen: Facts and Problems.* London: Oxford University Press.

Chute, Marchette. 1946. *Geoffrey Chaucer of England.* New York: E. P. Dutton.

———. 1949. *Shakespeare of London.* New York: E. P. Dutton.

———. 1951. *An Introduction to Shakespeare.* New York: E. P. Dutton.

Clark, Ronald W. 1983. *Benjamin Franklin.* New York: Random House.

Classical and Medieval Literature Criticism. 1991. Detroit: Gale Research.

Connelly, Mark. 1986. *The Diminished Self: Orwell and the Loss of Freedom.* Pittsburgh, PA: Duquesne.

Contemporary Authors. 1994. (CD-ROM). Detroit: Gale Research.

Contemporary Authors New Revision Series. 1989. Volume 33. Detroit: Gale Research.

Contemporary Literary Criticism. 1987. Volume 44. Detroit: Gale Research.

Cowart, David. 1983. *Arches and Light: The Fiction of John Gardner.* Carbondale: Southern Illinois University Press.

Cowie, Alexander. 1951. *The Rise of the American Novel.* New York: American Book Company.

Cowler, Rosemary, ed. 1969. *Twentieth Century Interpretations of Pamela.* Englewood Cliffs, NJ: Prentice-Hall.

Crick, Bernard. 1980. *George Orwell: A Life.* Boston: Little, Brown.

Cross, Milton. 1947. *Complete Stories of the Great Operas.* Garden City, NY: Doubleday.

Cuddon, J. A. 1984. *A Dictionary of Literary Terms.* New York: Penguin.

Cuevas, Lou. 1991. *Apache Legends.* Happy Camp, CA: Naturegraph.

Davidson, Cathy N., and Linda Wagner-Martin. 1995. *The Oxford Companion to Women's Writing.* New York: Oxford University Press.

Davison, Peter. 1971. *Songs of the British Music Hall.* New York: Oak Publications.

Dictionary of Literary Biography. 1978. Volume 2. Detroit: Gale Research.

Discovering Authors. 1993. (CD-ROM) Detroit: Gale Research.

Dolby, William. 1976. *A History of Chinese Drama.* London: Paul Elek.

Dorson, Richard M. 1959. *American Folklore.* Chicago: University of Chicago Press.

Drabble, Margaret, ed. 1985. *The Oxford Companion to English Literature.* New York: Oxford University Press.

Duran, Manual. 1974. *Cervantes.* Boston: G. K. Hall.

Eagle, Dorothy, and Meic Stephens, eds. 1992. *The Oxford Illustrated Literary Guide to Great Britain and Ireland.* New York: Oxford University Press.

Ehrlich, Eugene. 1985. *Amo, Amas, Amat and More: How to Use Latin to Your Own Advantage and to the Astonishment of Others.* New York: Harper & Row.

Ehrlich, Eugene, and Gorton Carruth. 1982. *The Oxford Illustrated Literary Guide to the United States.* New York: Oxford University Press.

Ekstrom, Reynolds R. 1995. *The New Concise Catholic Dictionary.* Mystic, CT: Twenty-Third Publications.

Emerson, Everett. 1985. *The Authentic Mark Twain: A Literary Biography of Samuel L. Clemens.* Philadelphia: University of Pennsylvania Press.

Encarta. 1994. (CD-ROM) Redmond, WA: Microsoft.

Esslin, Martin. 1965. *Samuel Beckett: A Collection of Critical Essays.* Englewood Cliffs, NJ: Prentice-Hall.

Farley, Christopher John. 1996. "Reborn To Be Wild." *Time,* January 22.

Feder, Lillian. 1986. *The Meridian Handbook of Classical Literature.* New York: New American Library.

Feinberg, Leonard. 1967. *Introduction to Satire.* Ames: Iowa State University Press.

Feldman, Susan, ed. 1965. *The Story-Telling Stone.* New York: Laurel.

Ferrell, Keith. 1988. *George Orwell: The Political Pen.* New York: M. Evans.

Flaceliere, Robert. 1962. *A Literary History of Greece.* New York: Mentor.

Fowler, Alastair. 1989. *A History of English Literature.* Cambridge, MA: Harvard University Press.

Foxx, Redd, and Norma Miller. 1977. *The Redd Foxx Encyclopedia of Black Humor.* Pasadena, CA: W. Ritchie.

Fraser, Frances. 1968. *The Bear Who Stole the Chinook.* Vancouver: Douglas & McIntyre.

Frewin, Leslie. 1986. *The Late Mrs. Dorothy Parker.* New York: Macmillan.

Friedrich, Otto. 1965. *Ring Lardner.* Minneapolis: University of Minnesota Press.

Gardner, Averil. 1987. *George Orwell.* Boston: G. K. Hall.

Gardner, John. *The Life and Times of Chaucer.* 1977. New York: Knopf, 1977.

————. 1984. *The Art of Fiction: Notes on Craft for Young Writers.* New York: Knopf.

Gassner, John, and Edward Quinn, eds. 19969. *The Reader's Encyclopedia of World Drama.* New York: Thomas Y. Crowell.

Gay, Peter. 1988. *Voltaire's Politics: The Poet as Realist.* New Haven, CT: Yale University Press.

Gentz, William H., gen. ed. 1973. *The Dictionary of Bible and Religion.* Nashville, Tenn.: Abingdon.

Gilman, Stephen. 1989. *The Novel According to Cervantes.* Berkeley: University of California Press.

Godolphin, Francis R. B., ed. 1949. *The Latin Poets.* New York: Modern Library.

Goldsmith, David H. 1972. *Kurt Vonnegut: Fantasist of Fire and Ice.* Bowling Green, OH: Bowling Green University.

Gray, Martin. 1992. *A Dictionary of Literary Terms.* Essex: Longman.

Grigson, Geoffrey. 1963. *The Concise Encyclopedia of Modern World Literature.* New York: Hawthorn.

Guicharnaud, Jacques. 1967. Introduction. In *Seventeenth-Century French Drama.* New York: Modern Library.

Hadas, Moses. 1952. *A History of Latin Literature.* New York: Columbia University Press.

————. 1954. *Ancilla to Classical Reading.* New York: Columbia University Press.

Halliwell, Leslie. 1995. *Halliwell's Film Guide.* New York: Harper Perennnial.

Halperin, John. 1984. *The Life of Jane Austen.* Baltimore: Johns Hopkins University Press.

Hammond, N. G. L., and H. H. Scullard, eds. 1992. *The Oxford Classical Dictionary.* Oxford: Clarendon.

Hardy, Phil, and Dave Laing. 1987. *The Encyclopedia of Rock.* New York: Macdonald.

Harris, Brice, ed. 1953. *Restoration Plays*. New York: Modern Library.

Harris, Leon A. 1964. *The Fine Art of Political Wit*. New York: E. P. Dutton.

Harrison, G. B., et al., eds. 1867. *Major British Writers*. New York: Harcourt Brace Jovanovich.

Hart, James D. 1983. *The Oxford Companion to American Literature*. New York: Oxford University Press.

Hart-Davis, Rupert, ed. 1962. *The Collected Letters of Oscar Wilde*. New York: Harcourt Brace.

Hartnell, Phyllis, ed. 1983. *The Oxford Companion to the Theater*. New York: Oxford University Press.

Heller, Joseph, and Speed Vogel. 1986. *No Laughing Matter*. New York: Putnam's.

Henry, Laurie. 1995. *The Fiction Dictionary*. Cincinnati, OH: Story.

Highet, Gilbert. 1962. *The Anatomy of Satire*. Princeton, NJ: Princeton University Press.

Hill, Eldon C. 1978. *George Bernard Shaw*. Boston: G. K. Hall.

Hitchcock, H. Wiley, and Stanley Sadie, eds. 1980. *The New Grove Dictionary of American Music*. New York: Macmillan.

Hoffman, A. J. 1988. *Twain's Heroes, Twain's Worlds*. Philadelphia: University of Pennsylvania Press.

Holman, C. Hugh, and William Harmon. 1992. *A Handbook to Literature*. New York: Macmillan.

Holroyd, Michael. 1989. *Bernard Shaw*. New York: Random House.

Hornstein, Lillian Herlands, ed. 1973. *The Reader's Companion to World Literature*. New York: New American Library.

Howatson, M. C., ed. 1989. *The Oxford Companion to Classical Literature*. New York: Oxford University Press.

Hughes, Glenn. 1938. *The Story of the Theatre*. New York: Samuel French.

Humor on Wry. 1991. Audiocassette. Audio Partners.

Hynes, Samuel, ed. 1974. *Twentieth-Century Interpretations of 1984: A Collection of Critical Essays*. Englewood Cliffs, NJ: Prentice-Hall.

Ingersoll, Earl G., ed. 1991. *Margaret Atwood: Conversations*. Princeton, NJ: Ontario Review.

Inglis, Rewey Belle, and Josephine Spear. 1952. *Adventures in English Literature*. New York: Harcourt, Brace & World.

Jenson, Ejner, J., ed. 1984. *The Future of Nineteen Eighty-Four*. Ann Arbor: University of Michigan Press.

Johnson, J. W., ed. 1968. *Utopian Literature: A Selection.* New York: Modern Library.

Johnson, Kevin Orlin. 1994. *Expression of the Catholic Faith.* New York: Ballantine.

Johnson, Robert K. 1983. *Neil Simon.* Boston: Twayne.

Kaplan, Justin. 1966. *Mister Clemens and Mark Twain: A Biography.* New York: Simon and Schuster.

Kaplan, Justin, gen. ed. 1992. *Familiar Quotations.* Boston: Little, Brown.

Katz, Ephraim. 1982. *The Film Encyclopedia.* New York: Perigee.

Keates, Jonathan, and Angelo Hornak. 1994. *Canterbury Cathedral.* London: Scala.

Keats, John. 1970. *You Might As Well Live.* New York: Simon & Schuster.

Kernan, Alvin. 1959. *The Cankered Muse: Satire of the English Renaissance.* New Haven, CT: Yale University Press.

Kesterson, David B., ed. 1979. *Critics on Mark Twain.* Baltimore: University of Miami Press.

Ketcham, Michael G. 1985. *Transparent Designs: Reading, Performance, and Form in the Spectator Papers.* Athens: University of Georgia Press.

Klinkowitz, Jerome. 1982. *Kurt Vonnegut.* New York: Routledge Chapman and Hall.

Knight, R. C. 1981. *Corneille. Horace.* Wolfeboro, NH: Longwood.

Kunitz, Stanley J., and Howard Haycrraft, eds. 1952. *British Authors before 1800: A Biographical Dictionary.* New York: H. W. Wilson.

Kunitz, Stanley. 1942. *Twentieth Century Authors.* New York: H. W. Wilson.

Lanier, Emilia. 1978. *The Poems of Shakespeare's Dark Lady.* New York: Clarkson N. Potter.

Leeming, David Adams. 1990. *The World of Myth.* New York: Oxford University Press.

Lehrer, Tom. 1981. *Too Many Songs by Tom Lehrer with Not Enough Drawings by Ronald Searle.* New York: Pantheon.

Leiter, Samuel L. 1979. *Kabuki Encyclopedia: An English-Language Adaptation of Kabuki Jiten.* Westport, CT: Greenwood.

Lesley, Cole. 1976. *Remembered Laughter: The Life of Noel Coward.* New York: Knopf.

Lewis, Dominic B. 1969. *Doctor Rabelais.* New York: Greenwood.

Loban, Walter, Dorothy Holmstrom, and Luella B. Cook, eds. 1958. *Adventures in Appreciation.* New York: Harcourt, Brace & World.

Lord, Louis E. 1963. *Aristophanes: His Plays and His Influence.* New York: Cooper Square.

Lovett, Robert Morss, and Helen Sard Hughes. 1932. *The History of the Novel in England.* Boston: Houghton Mifflin.

Lummis, Charles F. 1992. *Pueblo Indian Folk-Stories.* Lincoln: University of Nebraska Press.

McArthur, Tom, ed. 1992. *The Oxford Companion to the English Language.* New York: Oxford University Press.

McCombs, Judith, ed. 1988. *Critical Essays on Margaret Atwood.* Boston: G. K. Hall.

McGovern, Edythe M. 1979. *Neil Simon: A Critical Study.* New York: Ungar.

Mack, Maynard, gen. ed. 1962. *The Continental Edition of Old Masterpieces.* New York: Norton.

MacKendrick, Paul, and Herbert M. Howe, eds. 1952. *Classics in Translation.* Madison: University of Wisconsin Press, 1952.

McMillin, Scott, ed. 1973. *Restoration and Eighteenth-Century Comedy.* New York: Norton.

Maggio, Rosalie, comp. 1992. *The Beacon Book of Quotations by Women.* Boston: Beacon.

Magill, Frank N., ed. 1958. *Cyclopedia of World Authors.* New York: Harper & Brothers.

Magnusson, Magnus, gen. ed. 1990. *Cambridge Biographical Dictionary.* New York: Cambridge University Press.

Major Twentieth-Century Writers. 1990. Detroit: Gale Research.

Manguel, Alberto, and Gianni Guadalupi. 1987. *The Dictionary of Imaginary Places.* New York: Harcourt Brace Jovanovich.

Mantinband, James H. 1956. *Dictionary of Latin Literature.* New York: Philosophical Library.

Marriott, Alice, and Carol K. Rachlin. 1975. *Plains Indian Mythology.* New York: Meridian.

Mason, Haydn. 1981. *Voltaire: A Biography.* Baltimore: Johns Hopkins University Press.

Mays, James L., gen. ed. 1988. *Harper's Bible Commentary.* San Francisco: Harper & Row.

Meade, Marion. 1987. *What Fresh Hell Is This?* New York: Penguin.

Merrill, Robert. 1987. *Joseph Heller.* Boston: Twayne.

———. 1989. *Critical Essays on Kurt Vonnegut.* Boston: G. K. Hall.

Miller, Luree. 1989. *Literary Villages of London.* Washington, D.C.: Starrhill.

Monaco, James, ed. 1991. *The Encyclopedia of Film.* New York: Perigee.

Monagan, John S. 1985. *Horace: Priest of the Poor.* Washington, D.C.: Georgetown University Press.

Morace, Robert A., and Kathryn Van Spanckeren. 1982. *John Gardner: Critical Perspectives.* Carbondale: Southern Illinois University Press.

Morse, Donald E. 1991. *Kurt Vonnegut.* Mercer Island, WA: Starmont House.

Moskovit, Leonard, trans. 1983. *Horace: Twelve Odes.* Boston: Rowan Tree.

Muir, Kenneth, and Samuel Schoenbaum. 1971. *A New Companion to Shakespearean Studies.* Cambridge, MA: Harvard University Press.

Muir, Percy. 1954. *English Children's Books: 1600 to 1900.* London: Batsford.

Nabokov, Vladimir. 1984. *Lectures on Don Quixote.* San Diego, CA: Harbrace.

Nagel, James. 1984. *Critical Essays on Joseph Heller.* Boston: Twayne.

Negley, Glenn, and J. Max Patrick. 1952. *The Quest for Utopia.* New York: Henry Schumann.

Nicoll, Allardyce. 1937. *The Development of the Theatre.* New York: Harcourt Brace.

Oldsey, Bernard, and Joseph Browne, eds. 1986. *Critical Essays on George Orwell.* Boston: G. K. Hall.

O'Neill, Judith, ed. 1970. *Critics on Jane Austen: Readings in Literary Criticism.* Coral Gables, FL: University of Miami Press.

Padgett, Ron, ed. 1987. *The Teachers and Writers Handbook of Poetic Forms.* New York: Teachers & Writers Collaborative.

Panati, Charles. 1991. *Panati's Parade of Fads, Follies, and Manias: The Origins of Our Most Cherished Obsessions.* New York: HarperPerennial.

Patterson, Lotsee, and Mary Ellen Snodgrass. 1994. *Indian Terms.* Englewood, CO: Libraries Unlimited.

Perkins, Dorothy. 1991. *Encyclopedia of Japan.* New York: Facts on File.

Perkins, George, et al., eds. 1991. *Benét's Reader's Encyclopedia of American Literature.* New York: HarperCollins.

Person, James E., Jr., ed. 1988. *Literature Criticism from 1400 to 1800.* Detroit: Gale Research.

Philip, Alex J., and W. Laurence Gadd. 1928. *A Dickens Dictionary.* Leipzig: G. Hedeler.

Pollard, Arthur. 1970. *Satire.* London: Methuen.

Potts, Stephen W. 1982. *From Here to Absurdity: The Moral Battlefields of Joseph Heller.* San Bernardino, CA: Borgo.

Predmore, Richard L. 1990. *The World of Don Quixote*. Ann Arbor, MI: Books on Demand.

Putnam, Samuel. 1993. *François Rabelais, Man of the Renaissance: A Spiritual Biography*. Salem, NH: Ayer.

Quintana, Ricardo, intro. 1958. *Gulliver's Travels and Other Writings*. New York: Modern Library.

Radice, Betty. 1973. *Who's Who in the Ancient World*. New York: Penguin.

Radin, Paul. 1972. *The Trickster: A Study in American Indian Mythology*. New York: Schocken.

Rasmussen, R. Kent. 1995. *Mark Twain A to Z: The Essential Reference to His Life and Writings*. New York: Facts on File.

Rawson, Hugh, and Margaret Miner, comps. 1986. *The New International Dictionary of Quotations*. New York: Mentor.

Reilly, Patrick. 1989. *George Orwell: The Age's Adversary*. New York: St. Martin's.

Richter, Peyton, and Ilona Ricardo. 1980. *Voltaire*. Boston: G. K. Hall.

Riley, E. C. 1986. *Don Quixote*. Winchester, MA: Unwin Hyman.

Roberts, Vera Mowry. 1962. *On Stage: A History of Theatre*. New York: Harper & Row.

Robinson, F. N., ed. 1957. *The Works of Geoffrey Chaucer*. Boston: Houghton Mifflin.

Rollins, Hyder E., and Herschel Baker, eds. 1954. *The Renaissance in England; Non-dramatic Prose and Verse of the Sixteenth Century*. Boston: D. C. Heath.

Rosenberg, Donna. 1992. *World Mythology*. Lincolnwood, IL: Passport.

Rothe, Anna, ed. 1949. *Current Biography: Who's News and Why*. New York: H. W. Wilson.

Rudd, Niall. 1982. *The Satires of Horace and Persius*. Berkeley: University of California Press.

Russell, P. E. 1985. *Cervantes*. New York: Oxford University Press.

Sandler, Robert, ed. 1986. *Northrop Frye on Shakespeare*. New Haven, CT: Yale University Press.

Scott, A. F. 1974. *Who's Who in Chaucer*. New York: Hawthorn.

Screech, M. A. 1980. *Rabelais*. Ithaca, NY: Cornell University Press.

Seldes, George, comp. 1967. *The Great Quotations*. New York: Kangaroo.

Shackleton, Bailey. 1982. *A Profile of Horace*. Cambridge, MA: Harvard University Press.

Shalit, Gene, ed. 1987. *Laughing Matters: A Celebration of American Humor.* Garden City, NY: Doubleday.

Sheedy, John J. 1972. *English Essayists and Utopians: Bacon, More, Addison, Steele.* New York: Holt Rinehart.

Simmen, René. 1972. *The World of Puppets.* New York: Thomas Y. Crowell.

Snodgrass, Mary Ellen. 1987. *The Great American English Handbook.* Jacksonville, IL: Perma-Bound.

———. 1988a. *Greek Classics.* Lincoln, NE: Cliffs Notes.

———. 1988b. *Roman Classics.* Lincoln, NE: Cliffs Notes.

———. 1991. *Characters from Young Adult Literature.* Englewood, CO: Libraries Unlimited.

———. 1995. *Encyclopedia of Utopian Literature.* Santa Barbara, CA: ABC-Clio.

Something about the Author. 1984. Volume 36. Detroit: Gale Research.

Sontag, Susan. 1966. "Notes on Camp." In *Against Interpretation.* New York: Farrar, Straus & Giroux.

Sorkin, Adam J., ed. 1993. *Conversation with Joseph Heller.* Jackson: University Press of Mississippi.

Spatz, Lois. 1978. *Aristophanes.* Boston: Twayne.

Stansky, Peter, ed. 1984. *On Nineteen Eighty-Four.* New York: W. H. Freeman.

Stephens, James, Edwin L. Beck, and Royall H. Snow, eds. 1949. *Victorian and Later English Poets.* New York: American Book Company.

Stern, Jane, and Michael Stern. 1992. *Encyclopedia of Pop Culture.* New York: HarperPerennial.

Sutherland, James, ed. 1975. *The Oxford Book of Literary Anecdotes.* New York: Touchstone.

This Fabulous Century: 60 Years of American Life. 1969. Volume 3. New York: Time-Life.

Thomas, Henry, and Dana Lee Thomas. 1943. *Living Biographies of Famous Novelists.* Garden City, NY: Blue Ribbon.

Tripp, Edward. 1970. *The Meridian Handbook of Classical Mythology.* New York: New American Library.

Trollope, Anthony. 1902. *Thackeray.* New York: Harper & Brothers.

Turner, Frederick, ed. 1974. *The Portable North American Indian Reader.* New York: Penguin.

Van Doren, Mark, ed. 1936. *An Anthology of World Poetry.* New York: Harcourt Brace.

Van Spanckeren, Kathryn, and Jan G. Castro, eds. 1988. *Margaret Atwood: Vision and Forms.* Carbondale: Southern Illinois University Press.

Walker, John, ed. 1994. *Halliwell's Film Guide.* New York: HarperPerennial.

Warner, Rex. 1958. *The Greek Philosophers.* New York: New American Library.

White, Frederic R. 1955. *Famous Utopias of the Renaissance.* New York: Hendricks House.

White, Ray Lewis. 1968. *Gore Vidal.* Boston: Twayne.

Wilson, Charles Reagan, and William Ferris, eds. 1989. *Encyclopedia of Southern Culture.* Chapel Hill: University of North Carolina Press.

Wilson, John Harold. 1965. *A Preface to Restoration Drama.* Boston: Houghton Mifflin.

Wilson, Sharon Rose. 1993. *Margaret Atwood's Fairy Tale Sexual Politics.* Oxford: University Press of Mississippi.

Winston, Calhoun. 1994. *Captain Steele: The Early Career of Richard Steele.* Ann Arbor, MI: Books on Demand.

Woods, George B., et al., eds. 1947. *The Literature of England.* Chicago: Scott, Foresman.

Wu, Shih-chiang. 1961. *On the "Red Chamber Dream."* Oxford: Clarendon.

Zimbardo, Rose. 1965. *William Wycherley: A Link in the Development of English Satire.* New Haven, CT: Yale University Press.

Articles and Monographs

Babuscio, Jack. 1993. "Camp and the Gay Sensibility." In *Camp Grounds: Style and Homosexuality.* Amherst: University of Massachusetts Press.

Bickerdyke, Percy. 1995. "Stars of Yesterday: Noel Coward." *This England,* winter, pp. 52–53.

Blair, M. Elizabeth. 1993. "Commercialization of the Rap Music Youth Subculture." *Journal of Popular Culture,* Winter, pp. 21–34.

Broun, Heywood Hale. 1989. "The Algonquin-Nights at the Round Table." *Architectural Digest,* November, pp. 184–194.

———. 1991. "Wit's End." *Vogue,* December, pp. 167–173.

Chambers, Veronica. 1995. "Review of *Waiting to Exhale.*" *New York Times,* August 16, C1.

Corliss, Richard. 1995. "Bard of Embarrassment." *Time,* February 27, pp. 65–66.

Davidson, Cathy N. 1986. "A Feminist 1984." *Ms.* February, pp. 24–26.

Dreifus, Claudia. 1992. "Margaret Atwood." *Progressive*, March, pp. 30–33.

Fein, Esther B. 1992. "Fiction Verite: Characters Ring True." *New York Times*, July 1, B1, B5.

Groer, Annie. 1995. "King Accuses Colleague of Plagiarism." *Charlotte Observer*, August 20, 6C.

Hainer, Cathy. 1995. "Jane Austen's Hollywood Star Rising." *USA Today*, September 6, D1.

Hammer, Stephanie Barbé. 1990. "The World as It Will Be? Female Satire and the Technology of Power in *The Handmaid's Tale*." *Modern Language Studies*, Spring, pp. 39–49.

Hargrove, Nancy D. 1984. "The Tragicomic Vision of Beth Henley's Drama." *Southern Quarterly*, Summer, pp. 54–70.

"Kennedy Center Honors 5." 1995. *USA Today*, September 6, D1.

Krohn, Franklin B., and Frances L. Suazo. 1995. "Contemporary Urban Music: Controversial Messages in Hip-Hop and Rap Lyrics." *A Review of General Semantics*, Summer, 139–155.

Laughlin, Karen L. 1986. "Criminality, Desire, and Community; A Feminist Approach to Beth Henley's *Crimes of the Heart*." In *Women and Performance*. New York: New York University/Tisch School of the Arts, pp. 35–51.

"Margaret Atwood: Interview." 1983. Audiocassette. Englewood Cliffs, NJ: Prentice-Hall.

Long, Scott. 1989. "Useful Laughter: Camp and Seriousness." *Southwest Review*, Winter, pp. 58–70.

Malia, Peter. 1983. "Washington Irving." *American History Illustrated*, May, pp. 17–25.

Miller, Ward S. 1967. "The Comic-Tragic Vision of Jonathan Swift." *Christianity Today*.

Norment, Lynn. 1995. "Whitney Houston, Angela Bassett Share Joys and Pains in *Waiting to Exhale*," *Ebony*, December, pp. 24–26, 28–29.

Rickelman, Melinda. 1992. "Women Who Rap." *Crisis*, March, pp. 7–9.

Roman, David. 1992. "It's My Party and I'll Die If I Want to: Gay Men, AIDS, and the Circulation of Camp in U.S. Theatre." *Theatre Journal*, October, pp. 305–327.

"Royal Treatment: Bennett's 'King George.'" 1995. *Commonweal*, March 10, pp. 15–16.

Schroeder, Patricia R. 1989. "Locked behind the Proscenium: Feminist Strategies in *Getting Out* and *My Sister in This House*." *Modern Drama*, March, pp. 104–114.

Schickel, Richard. 1995. "Kissing Cousins." *Time*, December 18, pp. 72–74.

Smith, Wendy. 1992. "Terry McMillan." *Publishers Weekly*, May 11, pp. 50–51.

Spencer, Jenny S. 1987. "Norman's *'night Mother:* Psychodrama of Female Identity." *Modern Drama*, September, pp. 364–375.

Spencer, Jon Michael. 1992. "Rhapsody in Black: Utopian Aspirations." *Theology Today*, January, pp. 444–452.

Steinberg, Sybil. 1992. "Disappearing Acts." *Publishers Weekly*, June 16, p. 56.

Talese, Nan A. 1993. *Book Group Companion to Margaret Atwood's The Robber Bride*. New York: Doubleday.

"The Uses of History." 1993. *New York Times Book Review*, April 25, p. 28.

Waters, Harry F., and George Hackett. 1983. "The Real Hawkeye Pierce." *Newsweek*, February 28, p. 50.

ILLUSTRATION CREDITS

177   Corbis-Bettmann.

188   The Pierpont Morgan Library 85498/Art Resource, New York.

199   Corbis-Bettmann.

204   Photofest.

207   Bettmann Archive.

219   UPI/Corbis-Bettmann.

224   Corbis-Bettmann.

242   Corbis-Bettmann.

247   Photofest.

249   UPI/Corbis-Bettmann.

252   Corbis-Bettmann.

263   Columbia Pictures. Photofest.

283   Corbis-Bettmann.

289   Okumura Masanubu, 1691–1768, Japanese, Edo period, *Perspective View of the Interior of the Nakamura Theatre.* Gift of Mr. and Mrs. J. H. Wade. Cleveland Museum of Art 1916.1154.

292   Corbis-Bettmann.

317   AP/Wide World Photos.

324   UPI/Corbis-Bettmann.

330   Pierpont Morgan Library 45444/Art Resource, New York.

349   UPI/Corbis-Bettmann.

365   *MAD Magazine* is a trademark of E.C. Publications, Inc. ©1995. All rights reserved. Used with permission.

369   Engraving by J. Faber, from a painting by J. B. Van Loo. Corbis-Bettmann.

378   Photofest.

396   Drawing by Susanna Highmore Dunscombe. Pierpont Morgan Library MA-1024-5/Art Resource, New York.

409   Pierre Mariette. Bibliotheque Nationale, Paris. Giraudon/Art Resource, New York.

414   Photofest.

431   UPI/Corbis-Bettmann.

451   Corbis-Bettmann.

ILLUSTRATION CREDITS

INDEX

Note: Page numbers in **boldface** denote major entry headings.